Essays: Moral, Political, and Literary, Volume 1

David Hume, Thomas Hill Green, Thomas Hodge Grose

Nabu Public Domain Reprints:

You are holding a reproduction of an original work published before 1923 that is in the public domain in the United States of America, and possibly other countries. You may freely copy and distribute this work as no entity (individual or corporate) has a copyright on the body of the work. This book may contain prior copyright references, and library stamps (as most of these works were scanned from library copies). These have been scanned and retained as part of the historical artifact.

This book may have occasional imperfections such as missing or blurred pages, poor pictures, errant marks, etc. that were either part of the original artifact, or were introduced by the scanning process. We believe this work is culturally important, and despite the imperfections, have elected to bring it back into print as part of our continuing commitment to the preservation of printed works worldwide. We appreciate your understanding of the imperfections in the preservation process, and hope you enjoy this valuable book.

ESSAYS

MORAL, POLITICAL, AND LITERARY

BY DAVID HUME

EDITED, WITH PRELIMINARY DISSERTATIONS AND NOTES, BY

T. H. GREEN   AND   T. H. GROSE

LATE FELLOW AND TUTOR OF BALLIOL COLLEGE, OXFORD   FELLOW AND TUTOR OF QUEEN'S COLLEGE, OXFORD

IN TWO VOLUMES

Vol. I.

NEW IMPRESSION

LONGMANS, GREEN, AND CO.
39 PATERNOSTER ROW, LONDON
NEW YORK AND BOMBAY
1898

BIBLIOGRAPHICAL NOTE
First printed January 1875.
Reprinted September 1882; January 1889;
July 1898.

ADVERTISEMENT.

Most of the principles, and reasonings, contained in this volume, were published in a work in three volumes, called *A Treatise of Human Nature:* A work which the Author had projected before he left College, and which he wrote and published not long after. But not finding it successful, he was sensible of his error in going to the press too early, and he cast the whole anew in the following pieces, where some negligences in his former reasoning and more in the expression, are, he hopes, corrected. Yet several writers, who have honoured the Author's Philosophy with answers, have taken care to direct all their batteries against the juvenile work, which the Author never acknowledged, and have affected to triumph in any advantages, which, they imagined, they had obtained over it: A practice very contrary to all rules of candour and fair-dealing, and a strong instance of those polemical artifices, which a bigotted zeal thinks itself authorised to employ. Henceforth, the Author desires, that the following Pieces may alone be regarded as containing his philosophical sentiments and principles.[1]

[1] [For the history of this Advertisement, which was first published in the second volume of the posthumous Edition of 1777, see Vol. III. p. 38.—Ed.]

CONTENTS

OF

THE FIRST VOLUME.

	PAGE
MY OWN LIFE	1
LETTER FROM ADAM SMITH, LL.D., TO WILLIAM STRAHAN, ESQ.	9
HISTORY OF THE EDITIONS	15
LIST OF EDITIONS	85

PART I.

ESSAY		PAGE
I.	Of the Delicacy of Taste and Passion	91
II.	Of the Liberty of the Press	94
III.	That Politics may be reduced to a Science	98
IV.	Of the First Principles of Government	109
V.	Of the Origin of Government	113
VI.	On the Independency of Parliament	117
VII.	Whether the British Government inclines more to Absolute Monarchy, or to a Republic	122
VIII.	Of Parties in General	127
IX.	Of the Parties of Great Britain	133
X.	Of Superstition and Enthusiasm	144
XI.	Of the Dignity or Meanness of Human Nature	150
XII.	Of Civil Liberty	156
XIII.	Of Eloquence	163
XIV.	Of the Rise and Progress of the Arts and Sciences	174
XV.	The Epicurean	197
XVI.	The Stoic	203
XVII.	The Platonist	210
XVIII.	The Sceptic	213
XIX.	Of Polygamy and Divorces	231
XX.	Of Simplicity and Refinement in Writing	240
XXI.	Of National Characters	244
XXII.	Of Tragedy	258
XXIII.	Of the Standard of Taste	266

PART II.

ESSAY		PAGE
I.	Of Commerce.	287
II.	Of Refinement in the Arts.	299
III.	Of Money	309
IV.	Of Interest.	320
V.	Of the Balance of Trade	330
VI.	Of the Jealousy of Trade	345
VII.	Of the Balance of Power	348
VIII.	Of Taxes	356
IX.	Of Public Credit.	360
X.	Of Some Remarkable Customs.	374
XI.	Of the Populousness of Ancient Nations	381
XII.	Of the Original Contract	443
XIII.	Of Passive Obedience	460
XIV.	Of the Coalition of Parties	464
XV.	Of the Protestant Succession.	470
XVI.	Idea of a Perfect Commonwealth	480

MY OWN LIFE.[1]

It is difficult for a man to speak long of himself without vanity; therefore, I shall be short. It may be thought an instance of vanity that I pretend at all to write my life; but this Narrative shall contain little more than the History of my Writings; as, indeed, almost all my life has been spent in literary pursuits and occupations. The first success of most of my writings was not such as to be an object of vanity.

I was born the 26th of April 1711, old style, at Edinburgh. I was of a good family, both by father and mother: my father's family is a branch of the Earl of Home's, or Hume's; and my ancestors had been proprietors of the estate, which my brother possesses, for several generations. My mother was daughter of Sir David Falconer, President of the College of Justice: the title of Lord Halkerton came by succession to her brother.

My family, however, was not rich, and being myself a younger brother, my patrimony, according to the mode of my country, was of course very slender. My father, who passed for a man of parts, died when I was an infant, leaving me, with an elder brother and a sister, under the care of our mother, a woman of singular merit, who, though young and handsome, devoted herself entirely to the rearing and educating of her children. I passed through the ordinary course of education with success, and was seized very early with a passion for literature, which has been the ruling passion of my life, and the great source of my enjoyments. My studious

---

[1] [For the circumstances attending the publication of this autobiography, see p. 80.—Ed.]

disposition, my sobriety, and my industry, gave my family a notion that the law was a proper profession for me; but I found an unsurmountable aversion to every thing but the pursuits of philosophy and general learning; and while they fancied I was poring upon Voet and Vinnius, Cicero and Virgil were the authors which I was secretly devouring.

My very slender fortune, however, being unsuitable to this plan of life, and my health being a little broken by my ardent application, I was tempted, or rather forced, to make a very feeble trial for entering into a more active scene of life. In 1734, I went to Bristol, with some recommendations to eminent merchants, but in a few months found that scene totally unsuitable to me. I went over to France, with a view of prosecuting my studies in a country retreat; and I there laid that plan of life, which I have steadily and successfully pursued. I resolved to make a very rigid frugality supply my deficiency of fortune, to maintain unimpaired my independency, and to regard every object as contemptible, except the improvement of my talents in literature.

During my retreat in France, first at Reims, but chiefly at La Fleche, in Anjou, I composed my *Treatise of Human Nature*. After passing three years very agreeably in that country, I came over to London in 1737. In the end of 1738,[1] I published my Treatise, and immediately went down to my mother and my brother, who lived at his country house, and was employing himself very judiciously and successfully in the improvement of his fortune.

Never literary attempt was more unfortunate than my Treatise of Human Nature. It fell *dead-born from the press*, without reaching such distinction, as even to excite a murmur among the zealots. But being naturally of a cheerful and sanguine temper, I very soon recovered the blow, and prosecuted with great ardour my studies in the country. In 1742[2] I printed at Edinburgh the first part of my Essays: the work was favourably received, and soon made me entirely forget my former disappointment. I continued with my mother and brother in the country, and in that time recovered the knowledge of the Greek language, which I had too much neglected in my early youth.

In 1745, I received a letter from the Marquis of Annandale, inviting me to come and live with him in England; I found

[1] [Vols. i. and ii., in 1739. Vol. iii. in 1740.—ED.]   [2] [Vol. i. in 1741.—ED.]

also, that the friends and family of that young nobleman were desirous of putting him under my care and direction, for the state of his mind and health required it. I lived with him a twelvemonth. My appointments during that time made a considerable accession to my small fortune. I then received an invitation from General St. Clair to attend him as a secretary to his expedition, which was at first meant against Canada, but ended in an incursion on the coast of France. Next year, to wit, 1747, I received an invitation from the General to attend him in the same station in his military embassy to the courts of Vienna and Turin. I then wore the uniform of an officer, and was introduced at these courts as aide-de-camp to the general, along with Sir Harry Erskine and Captain Grant, now General Grant. These two years were almost the only interruptions which my studies have received during the course of my life: I passed them agreeably and in good company; and my appointments, with my frugality, had made me reach a fortune, which I called independent, though most of my friends were inclined to smile when I said so; in short, I was now master of near a thousand pounds.

I had always entertained a notion, that my want of success in publishing the Treatise of Human Nature, had proceeded more from the manner than the matter, and that I had been guilty of a very usual indiscretion, in going to the press too early. I, therefore, cast the first part of that work anew in the Enquiry concerning Human Understanding, which was published while I was at Turin.[1] But this piece was at first little more successful than the Treatise of Human Nature. On my return from Italy, I had the mortification to find all England in a ferment, on account of Dr. Middleton's Free Enquiry, while my performance was entirely overlooked and neglected. A new edition, which had been published at London, of my Essays, moral and political, met not with a much better reception.[2]

Such is the force of natural temper, that these disappointments made little or no impression on me. I went down in 1749, and lived two years with my brother at his country house, for my mother was now dead. I there composed the second part of my Essays, which I called Political Discourses, and also my Enquiry concerning the Principles of Morals,

[1] [In April, before starting for Turin.—Ed.]   [2] [In November.—Ed.]

which is another part of my treatise that I cast anew. Meanwhile, my bookseller, A. Millar, informed me, that my former publications (all but the unfortunate Treatise) were beginning to be the subject of conversation; that the sale of them was gradually increasing, and that new editions were demanded. Answers by Reverends, and Right Reverends, came out two or three in a year; and I found, by Dr. Warburton's railing, that the books were beginning to be esteemed in good company. However, I had fixed a resolution, which I inflexibly maintained, never to reply to anybody; and not being very irascible in my temper, I have easily kept myself clear of all literary squabbles. These symptoms of a rising reputation gave me encouragement, as I was ever more disposed to see the favourable than unfavourable side of things; a turn of mind which it is more happy to possess, than to be born to an estate of ten thousand a year.

In 1751, I removed from the country to the town, the true scene for a man of letters. In 1752, were published at Edinburgh, where I then lived, my Political Discourses, the only work of mine that was successful on the first publication. It was well received abroad and at home. In the same year[1] was published at London, my Enquiry concerning the Principles of Morals; which, in my own opinion (who ought not to judge on that subject), is of all my writings, historical, philosophical, or literary, incomparably the best. It came unnoticed and unobserved into the world.

In 1752, the Faculty of Advocates chose me their Librarian, an office from which I received little or no emolument, but which gave me the command of a large library. I then formed the plan of writing the History of England; but being frightened with the notion of continuing a narrative through a period of 1700 years, I commenced with the accession of the House of Stuart, an epoch when, I thought, the misrepresentations of faction began chiefly to take place. I was, I own, sanguine in my expectations of the success of this work. I thought that I was the only historian, that had at once neglected present power, interest, and authority, and the cry of popular prejudices; and as the subject was suited to every capacity, I expected proportional applause. But miserable was my disappointment: I was assailed by one cry of reproach, disapprobation, and even detestation; English, Scotch,

---

[1] [In 1751.—Ed.]

and Irish, Whig and Tory, churchman and sectary, freethinker and religionist, patriot and courtier, united in their rage against the man, who had presumed to shed a generous tear for the fate of Charles I. and the Earl of Strafford; and after the first ebullitions of their fury were over, what was still more mortifying, the book seemed to sink into oblivion. Mr. Millar told me, that in a twelvemonth he sold only forty-five copies of it. I scarcely, indeed, heard of one man in the three kingdoms, considerable for rank or letters, that could endure the book. I must only except the primate of England, Dr. Herring, and the primate of Ireland, Dr. Stone, which seem two odd exceptions. These dignified prelates separately sent me messages not to be discouraged.

I was, however, I confess, discouraged; and had not the war been at that time breaking out between France and England, I had certainly retired to some provincial town of the former kingdom, have changed my name, and never more have returned to my native country. But as this scheme was not now practicable, and the subsequent volume was considerably advanced, I resolved to pick up courage and to persevere.

In this interval,[1] I published at London my Natural History of Religion, along with some other small pieces: its public entry was rather obscure, except only that Dr. Hurd wrote a pamphlet against it, with all the illiberal petulance, arrogance, and scurrility which distinguish the Warburtonian school. This pamphlet gave me some consolation for the otherwise indifferent reception of my performance.[2]

In 1756, two years after the fall of the first volume, was published the second volume of my History, containing the period from the death of Charles I. till the Revolution. This performance happened to give less displeasure to the Whigs, and was better received. It not only rose itself, but helped to buoy up its unfortunate brother.

But though I had been taught by experience, that the Whig party were in possession of bestowing all places, both in the state and in literature, I was so little inclined to yield to their senseless clamour, that in about a hundred alterations, which farther study, reading, or reflection engaged me to make in the reigns of the first two Stuarts, I have made all of them invariably to the Tory side. It is ridiculous to

[1] In 1757.   [2] [See p. 62.—ED.]

consider the English constitution before that period as a regular plan of liberty.

In 1759, I published my History of the House of Tudor. The clamour against this performance was almost equal to that against the History of the two first Stuarts. The reign of Elizabeth was particularly obnoxious. But I was now callous against the impressions of public folly, and continued very peaceably and contentedly in my retreat at Edinburgh, to finish, in two volumes, the more early part of the English History, which I gave to the public in 1761, with tolerable, and but tolerable success.

But, notwithstanding this variety of winds and seasons, to which my writings had been exposed, they had still been making such advances, that the copy-money given me by the booksellers, much exceeded any thing formerly known in England; I was become not only independent, but opulent. I retired to my native country of Scotland, determined never more to set my foot out of it; and retaining the satisfaction of never having preferred a request to one great man, or even making advances of friendship to any of them. As I was now turned of fifty, I thought of passing all the rest of my life in this philosophical manner, when I received, in 1763, an invitation from the Earl of Hertford, with whom I was not in the least acquainted, to attend him on his embassy to Paris, with a near prospect of being appointed secretary to the embassy; and, in the meanwhile, of performing the functions of that office. This offer, however inviting, I at first declined, both because I was reluctant to begin connexions with the great, and because I was afraid that the civilities and gay company of Paris, would prove disagreeable to a person of my age and humour: but on his lordship's repeating the invitation, I accepted of it. I have every reason, both of pleasure and interest, to think myself happy in my connexions with that nobleman, as well as afterwards with his brother, General Conway.

Those who have not seen the strange effects of modes, will never imagine the reception I met with at Paris, from men and women of all ranks and stations. The more I resiled from their excessive civilities, the more I was loaded with them. There is, however, a real satisfaction in living at Paris, from the great number of sensible, knowing, and polite company with which that city abounds above all places in the universe. I thought once of settling there for life.

I was appointed secretary to the embassy; and in summer 1765, Lord Hertford left me, being appointed Lord Lieutenant of Ireland. I was *chargé d'affaires* till the arrival of the Duke of Richmond, towards the end of the year. In the beginning of 1766, I left Paris, and next summer went to Edinburgh, with the same view as formerly, of burying myself in a philosophical retreat. I returned to that place, not richer, but with much more money, and a much larger income, by means of Lord Hertford's friendship, than I left it; and I was desirous of trying what superfluity could produce, as I had formerly made an experiment of a competency. But in 1767, I received from Mr. Conway an invitation to be Under-secretary; and this invitation, both the character of the person, and my connexions with Lord Hertford, prevented me from declining. I returned to Edinburgh in 1769, very opulent (for I possessed a revenue of 1,000*l.* a year), healthy, and though somewhat stricken in years, with the prospect of enjoying long my ease, and of seeing the increase of my reputation.

In spring 1775, I was struck with a disorder in my bowels, which at first gave me no alarm, but has since, as I apprehend it, become mortal and incurable. I now reckon upon a speedy dissolution. I have suffered very little pain from my disorder; and what is more strange, have, notwithstanding the great decline of my person, never suffered a moment's abatement of my spirits; insomuch, that were I to name the period of my life, which I should most choose to pass over again, I might be tempted to point to this latter period. I possess the same ardour as ever in study, and the same gaiety in company. I consider, besides, that a man of sixty-five, by dying, cuts off only a few years of infirmities; and though I see many symptoms of my literary reputation's breaking out at last with additional lustre, I knew that I could have but few years to enjoy it. It is difficult to be more detached from life than I am at present.

To conclude historically with my own character. I am, or rather was (for that is the style I must now use in speaking of myself, which emboldens me the more to speak my sentiments); I was, I say, a man of mild dispositions, of command of temper, of an open, social, and cheerful humour, capable of attachment, but little susceptible of enmity, and of great moderation in all my passions. Even my love of literary fame, my ruling passion, never soured my temper, notwithstanding my frequent disappointments. My company was not unacceptable to the young and careless, as well as to the studious and literary; and as I took a particular pleasure in the company of modest women, I had no reason to be displeased with the reception I met with from them. In a word, though most men anywise eminent, have found reason to complain of calumny, I never was touched, or even attacked by her baleful tooth: and though, I wantonly exposed myself to the rage of both civil and religious factions, they seemed to be disarmed in my behalf of their wonted fury. My friends never had occasion to vindicate any one circumstance of my character and conduct: not but that the zealots, we may well suppose, would have been glad to invent and propagate any story to my disadvantage, but they could never find any which they thought would wear the face of probability. I cannot say there is no vanity in making this funeral oration of myself, but I hope it is not a misplaced one; and this is a matter of fact which is easily cleared and ascertained.

APRIL 18, 1776.

LETTER FROM ADAM SMITH, LL.D.,

TO

WILLIAM STRAHAN, ESQ.[1]

Kirkaldy, Fifeshire, Nov. 9, 1776.

DEAR SIR,—It is with a real, though a very melancholy pleasure, that I sit down to give you some account of the behaviour of our late excellent friend, Mr. Hume, during his last illness.

Though, in his own judgment, his disease was mortal and incurable, yet he allowed himself to be prevailed upon, by the entreaty of his friends, to try what might be the effects of a long journey. A few days before he set out, he wrote that account of his own life, which, together with his other papers, he has left to your care. My account, therefore, shall begin where his ends.

He set out for London towards the end of April, and at Morpeth met with Mr. John Home and myself, who had both come down from London on purpose to see him, expecting to have found him at Edinburgh. Mr. Home returned with him, and attended him during the whole of his stay in England, with that care and attention which might be expected from a temper so perfectly friendly and affectionate. As I had written to my mother that she might expect me in Scotland, I was under the necessity of continuing my journey. His disease seemed to yield to exercise and change of air, and when he arrived in London, he was apparently in much better health than when he left Edinburgh. He was advised

[1] [For the circumstances attending the publication of this letter, see p. 80.—ED.]

to go to Bath to drink the waters, which appeared for some time to have so good an effect upon him, that even he himself began to entertain, what he was not apt to do, a better opinion of his own health. His symptoms, however, soon returned with their usual violence, and from that moment he gave up all thoughts of recovery, but submitted with the utmost cheerfulness, and the most perfect complacency and resignation. Upon his return to Edinburgh, though he found himself much weaker, yet his cheerfulness never abated, and he continued to divert himself, as usual, with correcting his own works for a new edition, with reading books of amusement, with the conversation of his friends; and, sometimes in the evening, with a party at his favourite game of whist. His cheerfulness was so great, his conversation and amusements run so much in their usual strain, that, notwithstanding all bad symptoms, many people could not believe he was dying. 'I shall tell your friend, Colonel Edmondstone,' said Doctor Dundas to him one day, 'that I left you much better, and in a fair way of recovery.' 'Doctor,' said he, 'as I believe you would not chuse to tell any thing but the truth, you had better tell him, that I am dying as fast as my enemies, if I have any, could wish, and as easily and cheerfully as my best friends could desire.' Colonel Edmondstone soon afterwards came to see him, and take leave of him; and on his way home, he could not forbear writing him a letter bidding him once more an eternal adieu, and applying to him, as to a dying man, the beautiful French verses in which the Abbé Chaulieu, in expectation of his own death, laments his approaching separation from his friend, the Marquis de la Fare. Mr. Hume's magnanimity and firmness were such, that his most affectionate friends knew, that they hazarded nothing in talking or writing to him as to a dying man, and that so far from being hurt by this frankness, he was rather pleased and flattered by it. I happened to come into his room while he was reading this letter, which he had just received, and which he immediately showed me. I told him, that though I was sensible how very much he was weakened, and that appearances were in many respects very bad, yet his cheerfulness was still so great, the spirit of life seemed still to be so very strong in him, that I could not help entertaining some faint hopes. He answered, 'Your hopes are groundless. An habitual diarrhœa of more than a year's standing, would be a very bad disease at any age: at my age it is a mortal one. When I lie down in the evening, I feel myself weaker than when I rose in the morning; and when I rise in the morning, weaker than when I lay down in the evening. I am sensible, besides, that some of my vital parts are affected, so that I must soon die.' 'Well,' said I, 'if it must be so, you have at least the satisfaction of leaving all your friends, your brother's family in particular, in great prosperity.' He said that he felt that satisfaction so sensibly, that when he was reading, a few days before, Lucian's Dialogues of the Dead, among all the excuses which are alleged to Charon for not entering readily into his boat, he could not find one that fitted him; he had no house to finish, he had no daughter to provide for, he had no enemies upon whom he wished to revenge himself. 'I could not well imagine,' said he, 'what excuse I could make to Charon in order to obtain a little delay. I have done every thing of consequence which I ever meant to do; and I could at no time expect to leave my relations and friends in a better situation than that in which I am now likely to leave them; I, therefore, have all reason to die contented.' He then diverted himself with inventing several jocular excuses, which he supposed he might make to Charon, and with imagining the very surly answers which it might suit the character of Charon to return to them. 'Upon further consideration,' said he, 'I thought I might say to him, Good Charon, I have been correcting my works for a new edition. Allow me a little time, that I may see how the Public receives the alterations.' But Charon would answer, 'When you have seen the effect of these, you will be for making other alterations. There will be no end of such excuses; so, honest friend, please step into the boat.' But I might still urge, 'Have a little patience, good Charon; I have been endeavouring to open the eyes of the Public. If I live a few years longer, I may have the satisfaction of seeing the downfall of some of the prevailing systems of superstition.' But Charon would then lose all temper and decency. 'You loitering rogue, that will not happen these many hundred years. Do you fancy I will grant you a lease for so long a term? Get into the boat this instant, you lazy loitering rogue.'

But, though Mr. Hume always talked of his approaching

dissolution with great cheerfulness, he never affected to make any parade of his magnanimity. He never mentioned the subject but when the conversation naturally lead to it, and never dwelt longer upon it than the course of the conversation happened to require: it was a subject indeed which occurred pretty frequently, in consequence of the inquiries which his friends, who came to see him, naturally made concerning the state of his health. The conversation which I mentioned above, and which passed on Thursday the 8th of August, was the last, except one, that I ever had with him. He had now become so very weak, that the company of his most intimate friends fatigued him; for his cheerfulness was still so great, his complaisance and social disposition were still so entire, that when any friend was with him, he could not help talking more, and with greater exertion, than suited the weakness of his body. At his own desire, therefore, I agreed to leave Edinburgh, where I was staying partly upon his account, and returned to my mother's house here, at Kirkaldy, upon condition that he would send for me whenever he wished to see me; the physician who saw him most frequently, Dr. Black, undertaking, in the mean time, to write me occasionally an account of the state of his health.

On the 22d of August, the Doctor wrote me the following letter:

'Since my last, Mr. Hume has passed his time pretty easily, but is much weaker. He sits up, goes down stairs once a day, and amuses himself with reading, but seldom sees anybody. He finds that even the conversation of his most intimate friends fatigues and oppresses him; and it is happy that he does not need it, for he is quite free from anxiety, impatience, or low spirits, and passes his time very well with the assistance of amusing books.'

I received the day after a letter from Mr. Hume himself, of which the following is an extract.

'Edinburgh, 23d August, 1776.

'MY DEAREST FRIEND,—I am obliged to make use of my nephew's hand in writing to you, as I do not rise to-day.

* * * * * * * *

'I go very fast to decline, and last night had a small fever, which I hoped might put a quicker period to this tedious illness, but unluckily it has, in a great measure, gone off. I cannot submit to your coming over here on my account, as it is possible for me to see you so small a part of the day, but Doctor Black can better inform you concerning the degree of strength which may from time to time remain with me. Adieu,' etc.

Three days after I received the following letter from Doctor Black.

'Edinburgh, Monday, 26th August, 1776.

'DEAR SIR,—Yesterday, about four o'clock afternoon, Mr. Hume expired. The near approach of his death became evident in the night between Thursday and Friday, when his disease became excessive, and soon weakened him so much, that he could no longer rise out of his bed. He continued to the last perfectly sensible, and free from much pain or feelings of distress. He never dropped the smallest expression of impatience; but when he had occasion to speak to the people about him, always did it with affection and tenderness. I thought it improper to write to bring you over, especially as I heard that he had dictated a letter to you desiring you not to come. When he became very weak, it cost him an effort to speak, and he died in such a happy composure of mind, that nothing could exceed it.'

Thus died our most excellent, and never to be forgotten friend; concerning whose philosophical opinions men will, no doubt, judge variously, every one approving, or condemning them, according as they happen to coincide or disagree with his own; but concerning whose character and conduct there can scarce be a difference of opinion. His temper, indeed, seemed to be more happily balanced, if I may be allowed such an expression, than that perhaps of any other man I have ever known. Even in the lowest state of his fortune, his great and necessary frugality never hindered him from exercising, upon proper occasions, acts both of charity and generosity. It was a frugality, founded, not upon avarice, but upon the love of independency. The extreme gentleness of his nature never weakened either the firmness of his mind or the steadiness of his resolutions. His constant pleasantry was the genuine effusion of good-nature and good-humour, tempered with delicacy and modesty, and without even the slightest tincture of malignity, so frequently the disagreeable source of what is called wit in other men. It never was the meaning of his raillery to mortify; and therefore, far from offending, it seldom failed to please and delight, even those who were the objects of it. To his friends, who were frequently the objects of it, there was not perhaps any one of all his great and amiable qualities, which contributed more to endear his conversation. And that gaiety of temper, so agreeable in society, but which is so often accompanied with frivolous and superficial qualities, was in him certainly attended with the most severe application, the most extensive learning, the greatest depth of thought, and a capacity in every respect the most comprehensive. Upon the whole, I have always considered him, both in his lifetime and since his death, as approaching as nearly to the idea of a perfectly wise and virtuous man, as perhaps the nature of human frailty will permit.

I ever am, dear Sir,

Most affectionately your's,

ADAM SMITH.

HISTORY OF THE EDITIONS.

HUME has told us in his autobiography, that very early in life he was seized with a passion for literature: an expression which, strong as it is, does not err on the side of exaggeration. From the time of leaving school, he seems to have been absorbed in literary pursuits and ambitions. He was incessantly engaged in working at questions suggested by the writings of Locke and Berkeley. He came to believe that he had discovered new truths; and he dreamed of a general recognition of his genius. Mingling with these ambitious aspirations, there was a set purpose to curb an irritable, excited temper, and to realize the calm elevation of the philosopher.

In the hope of achieving these results, he declined to train himself for the law or for business. His income, though small, was sufficient for the time; and he expected that his writings would bring wealth as well as fame.

The following letter[1] to his friend Michael Ramsay, written shortly after his seventeenth birthday, is the earliest record which we possess, and it gives a picture, equally graphic and astonishing, of his boyhood.

'July 4, 1727.

'Dr M.—I received all the books you writ of, and your Milton among the rest. When I saw it, I perceived there was a difference betwixt preaching and practising: you accuse me of niceness, and yet practise it most egregiously yourself. What was the necessity of sending your Milton, which I knew you were so fond of? Why, I lent your's and can't get it. But would you not, in the same manner, have

[1] Life and Correspondence of David Hume. By John Hill Burton, Esq., Advocate. Vol. i., p. 12.

lent your own? Yes. Then, why this ceremony and good breeding? I write all this to show you how easily any action may be brought to bear the countenance of a fault. You may justify yourself very well, by saying it was kindness; and I am satisfied with it, and thank you for it. So, in the same manner, I may justify myself from your reproofs. You say that I would not send in my papers, because they were not polished nor brought to any form: which you say is nicety. But was it not reasonable? Would you have me send in my loose incorrect thoughts? Were such worth the transcribing? All the progress that I made is but drawing the outlines, on loose bits of paper: here a hint of a passion; there a phenomenon in the mind accounted for: in another the alteration of these accounts; sometimes a remark upon an author I have been reading; and none of them worth to any body, and I believe scarce to myself. The only design I had of mentioning any of them at all, was to see what you would have said of your own, whether they were of the same kind, and if you would send any; and I have got my end, for you have given a most satisfactory reason for not communicating them, by promising they shall be told *vivá voce*—a much better way indeed, and in which I promise myself much satisfaction; for the free conversation of a friend is what I would prefer to any entertainment. Just now I am entirely confined to myself and library for diversion since we parted.

―――― ea sola voluptus,
Solamenque mali—

And indeed to me they are not a small one: for I take no more of them than I please; for I hate task-reading, and I diversify them at pleasure—sometimes a philosopher, sometimes a poet—which change is not unpleasant nor disserviceable neither; for what will more surely engrave upon my mind a Tusculan disputation of Cicero's De Ægritudine Lenienda, than an eclogue or georgick of Virgil's? The philosopher's wise man and the poet's husbandman agree in peace of mind, in a liberty and independency on fortune, and contempt of riches, power, and glory. Every thing is placid and quiet in both: nothing perturbed or disordered.

At secura quies, et nescia fallere vita——
Speluncæ, vivique laci; at frigida Tempe,
Mugitusque boum, mollesque sub arbore somni
Non absint.

'These lines will, in my opinion, come nothing short of the instruction of the finest sentence in Cicero: and is more to me, as Virgil's life is more the subject of my ambition, being what I can apprehend to be more within my power. For the perfectly wise man, that outbraves fortune, is surely greater than the husbandman who slips by her; and, indeed, this pastoral and saturnian happiness I have in a great measure come at just now. I live like a king, pretty much by myself, neither full of action nor perturbation,—*molles somnos*. This state, however, I can foresee is not to be relied on. My peace of mind is not sufficiently confirmed by philosophy to withstand the blows of fortune. This greatness and elevation of soul is to be found only in study and contemplation—this can alone teach us to look down on human accidents. You must allow [me] to talk thus, like a philosopher: 'tis a subject I think much on, and could talk all day long of. But I know I must not trouble you. Wherefore I wisely practise my rules, which prescribe to check our appetite; and, for a mortification, shall descend from these superior regions to low and ordinary life; and so far as to tell you, that John has bought a horse: he thinks it neither cheap nor dear. It cost six guineas, but will be sold cheaper against winter, which he is not resolved on as yet. It has no fault, but bogles a little. It is tolerably well favoured, and paces naturally. Mamma bids me tell you, that Sir John Home is not going to town; but he saw Eccles in the country, who says he will do nothing in that affair, for he is only taking off old adjudications, so it is needless to let him see the papers. He desires you would trouble yourself to inquire about the Earle's affairs, and advise us what to do in this affair.

'If it were not breaking the formal rule of connexions I have prescribed myself in this letter—and it did not seem unnatural to raise myself from so low affairs as horses and papers, to so high and elevate things as books and study—I would tell you that I read some of Longinus already, and that I am mightily delighted with him. I think he does really answer the character of being the great sublime he describes. He delivers his precepts with such force, as if he were enchanted with the subject; and is himself an author that may be cited for an example to his own rules, by any one who shall be so adventurous as to write upon his subject.'

Thus he was occupied for four years: devouring books, cross-examining the English metaphysicians, and jotting down his desultory doubts and criticisms. So he describes himself in a letter of a later date:

'' Tis not long ago that I burned an old manuscript book, wrote before I was twenty, which contained, page after page, the gradual progress of my thoughts on that head. It began with an anxious search after arguments, to confirm the common opinion; doubts stole in, dissipated, returned; were again dissipated, returned again; and it was a perpetual struggle of a restless imagination against inclination, perhaps against reason.'[1]

At last his health was a little broken. He appears to have suffered from torpidity of liver, caused by sedentary occupations and poor food. In a letter[2] to a physician, never despatched, but found by Mr. Burton among the papers in the possession of the Royal Society of Edinburgh, Hume describes minutely his manner of life, his hopes and his fears. The letter appears to have been written in 1734, when he was twenty-three years of age: and, with the exception of the medical details, it is here printed in full.

'SIR,—Not being acquainted with this handwriting, you will probably look to the bottom to find the subscription, and not finding any, will certainly wonder at this strange method of addressing you. I must here in the beginning beg you to excuse it, and, to persuade you to read what follows with some attention, must tell you, that this gives you an opportunity to do a very good-natured action, which I believe is the most powerful argument I can use. I need not tell you, that I am your countryman, a Scotsman; for without any such tie, I dare rely upon your humanity even to a perfect stranger, such as I am. The favour I beg of you is your advice, and the reason why I address myself in particular to you, need not be told,—as one must be a skilful physician, a man of letters, of wit, of good sense, and of great humanity, to give me a satisfying answer. I wish fame had pointed out to me more persons, in whom these qualities are united, in order to have kept me some time in suspense. This I say in the sincerity of my heart, and without any intention of

[1] March 10, 1751. Life. Vol. i., p. 332. The immediate reference is to the argument of Cleanthes, in the 'Dialogues Concerning Natural Religion.'
[2] Life. Vol. i., p. 30.

making a compliment; for though it may seem necessary, that, in the beginning of so unusual a letter, I should say some fine things, to bespeak your good opinion, and remove any prejudices you may conceive at it, yet such an endeavour to be witty, would ill suit with the present condition of my mind; which, I must confess, is not without anxiety concerning the judgment you will form of me. Trusting, however, to your candour and generosity, I shall, without further preface, proceed to open up to you the present condition of my health, and to do that the more effectually, shall give you a kind of history of my life, after which you will easily learn why I keep my name a secret.

'You must know then that, from my earliest infancy, I found always a strong inclination to books and letters. As our college education in Scotland, extending little further than the languages, ends commonly when we are about fourteen or fifteen years of age, I was after that left to my own choice in my reading, and found it incline me almost equally to books of reasoning and philosophy, and to poetry and the polite authors. Every one who is acquainted either with the philosophers or critics, knows that there is nothing yet established in either of these two sciences, and that they contain little more than endless disputes, even in the most fundamental articles. Upon examination of these, I found a certain boldness of temper growing in me, which was not inclined to submit to any authority in these subjects, but led me to seek out some new medium, by which truth might be established. After much study and reflection on this, at last, when I was about eighteen years of age, there seemed to be opened up to me a new scene of thought, which transported me beyond measure, and made me, with an ardour natural to young men, throw up every other pleasure or business to apply entirely to it. The law, which was the business I designed to follow, appeared nauseous to me, and I could think of no other way of pushing my fortune in the world, but that of a scholar and philosopher. I was infinitely happy in this course of life for some months; till at last, about the beginning of September, 1729, all my ardour seemed in a moment to be extinguished, and I could no longer raise my mind to that pitch, which formerly gave me such excessive pleasure. I felt no uneasiness or want of spirits, when I laid aside my book; and therefore never imagined there was any bodily distemper in the case, but that my coldness proceeded from a laziness of temper, which must be overcome by redoubling my application. In this condition I remained for nine months, very uneasy to myself, as you may well imagine, but without growing any worse, which was a miracle. There was another particular, which contributed, more than any thing, to waste my spirits and bring on me this distemper, which was, that having read many books of morality, such as Cicero, Seneca, and Plutarch, and being smit with their beautiful representations of virtue and philosophy, I undertook the improvement of my temper and will, along with my reason and understanding. I was continually fortifying myself with reflections against death, and poverty, and shame, and pain, and all the other calamities of life. These no doubt are exceeding useful, when joined with an active life, because the occasion being presented along with the reflection, works it into the soul, and makes it take a deep impression; but in solitude they serve to little other purpose, than to waste the spirits, the force of the mind meeting with no resistance, but wasting itself in the air, like our arm when it misses its aim. This, however, I did not learn but by experience, and till I had already ruined my health, though I was not sensible of it. * * *

'Though I was sorry to find myself engaged with so tedious a distemper, yet the knowledge of it set me very much at ease, by satisfying me that my former coldness proceeded not from any defect of temper or genius, but from a disease to which any one may be subject. I now began to take some indulgence to myself; studied moderately, and only when I found my spirits at their highest pitch, leaving off before I was weary, and trifling away the rest of my time in the best manner I could. In this way, I lived with satisfaction enough; and on my return to town next winter found my spirits very much recruited, so that, though they sank under me in the higher flights of genius, yet I was able to make considerable progress in my former designs. I was very regular in my diet and way of life from the beginning, and all that winter made it a constant rule to ride twice or thrice a-week, and walk every day. For these reasons I expected, when I returned to the country, and could renew my exercise with less interruption, that I would perfectly recover. But in this I was much mistaken. * * *

'Thus I have given you a full account of the condition of my body; and without staying to ask pardon, as I ought to do, for so tedious a story, shall explain to you how my mind stood all this time, which on every occasion, especially in this distemper, have a very near connexion together. Having now time and leisure to cool my inflamed imagination, I began to consider seriously how I should proceed in my philosophical inquiries. I found that the moral philosophy transmitted to us by antiquity laboured under the same inconvenience that has been found in their natural philosophy, of being entirely hypothetical, and depending more upon invention than experience: every one consulted his fancy in erecting schemes of virtue and of happiness, without regarding human nature, upon which every moral conclusion must depend. This, therefore, I resolved to make my principal study, and the source from which I would derive every truth in criticism as well as morality. I believe it is a certain fact, that most of the philosophers who have gone before us, have been overthrown by the greatness of their genius, and that little more is required to make a man succeed in this study, than to throw off all prejudices either for his own opinions or for those of others. At least this is all I have to depend on for the truth of my reasonings, which I have multiplied to such a degree, that within these three years, I find I have scribbled many a quire of paper, in which there is nothing contained but my own inventions. This, with the reading most of the celebrated books in Latin, French, and English, and acquiring the Italian, you may think a sufficient business for one in perfect health, and so it would had it been done to any purpose; but my disease was a cruel encumbrance on me. I found that I was not able to follow out any train of thought, by one continued stretch of view, but by repeated interruptions, and by refreshing my eye from time to time upon other objects. Yet with this inconvenience I have collected the rude materials for many volumes; but in reducing these to words, when one must bring the idea he comprehended in gross, nearer to him, so as to contemplate its minutest parts, and keep it steadily in his eye, so as to copy these parts in order,—this I found impracticable for me, nor were my spirits equal to so severe an employment. Here lay my greatest calamity. I had no hopes of delivering my opinions with such elegance and neatness, as to draw to me the attention of the world, and I would rather live and die in obscurity than produce them maimed and imperfect.

'Such a miserable disappointment I scarce ever remember to have heard of. The small distance betwixt me and perfect health makes me the more uneasy in my present situation. It is a weakness rather than a lowness of spirits which troubles me, and there seems to be as great a difference betwixt my distemper and common vapours, as betwixt vapours and madness. I have noticed in the writings of the French mystics, and in those of our fanatics here, that when they give a history of the situation of their souls, they mention a coldness and desertion of the spirit, which frequently returns; and some of them, at the beginning, have been tormented with it many years. As this kind of devotion depends entirely on the force of passion, and consequently of the animal spirits, I have often thought that their case and mine were pretty parallel, and that their rapturous admirations might discompose the fabric of the nerves and brain, as much as profound reflections, and that warmth or enthusiasm which is inseparable from them.

'However this may be, I have not come out of the cloud so well as they commonly tell us they have done, or rather began to despair of ever recovering. To keep myself from being melancholy on so dismal a prospect, my only security was in peevish reflections on the vanity of the world and of all human glory; which, however just sentiments they may be esteemed, I have found can never be sincere, except in those who are possessed of them. Being sensible that all my philosophy would never make me contented in my present situation, I began to rouse up myself; and being encouraged by instances of recovery from worse degrees of this distemper, as well as by the assurances of my physicians, I began to think of something more effectual than I had hitherto tried. I found, that as there are two things very bad for this distemper, study and idleness, so there are two things very good, business and diversion; and that my whole time was spent betwixt the bad, with little or no share of the good. For this reason I resolved to seek out a more active life, and though I could not quit my pretensions in learning but with my last breath, to lay them aside for some time, in order the more effectually to resume them. Upon examination, I found my choice confined to two kinds of life, that of a travelling governor, and that of a merchant. The first, besides that it is in some respects an idle life, was, I found, unfit for me; and that because from a sedentary and retired way of living, from a bashful temper, and from a narrow fortune, I had been little accustomed to general companies, and had not confidence and knowledge enough of the world to push my fortune, or to be serviceable in that way. I therefore fixed my choice upon a merchant; and having got recommendation to a considerable trader in Bristol, I am just now hastening thither, with a resolution to forget myself, and every thing that is past, to engage myself, as far as is possible, in that course of life, and to toss about the world, from the one pole to the other, till I leave this distemper behind me.'

In consequence of this indisposition, his friends induced him to enter a merchant's office at Bristol; but after a brief trial he returned to his favourite pursuits, and crossing to France, and settling 'first at Reims, but chiefly at La Flèche in Anjou,' he occupied three years in collecting the passages in his manuscripts which dealt with the philosophies of Locke and Berkeley, and in preparing them for the press. Towards the close of 1737 he left France, and came to London, to negotiate for the publication of two volumes of a 'Treatise of Human Nature.' The following letters to Henry Home, afterwards Lord Kames, deserve to be quoted:—

'London, December 2, 1737.

'DEAR SIR,—I am sorry I am not able to satisfy your curiosity by giving you some general notion of the plan upon which I proceed. But my opinions are so new, and even some terms that I am obliged to make use of, that I could not propose, by any abridgment, to give my system an air of likelihood, or so much as make it intelligible. It is a thing I have in vain attempted already, at a gentleman's request in this place, who thought it would help him to comprehend and judge of my notions, if he saw them all at once before him. I have had a greater desire of communicating to you the plan of the whole, that I believe it will not appear in public before the beginning of next winter. For, besides that it would be difficult to have it printed before the rising of the parliament, I must confess I am not ill pleased with a little delay, that it may appear with as few imperfections as possible. I have been here near three months, always within a week of agreeing with my printers; and you may imagine I did not forget the work itself during that time, where I began to feel some passages weaker for the style and diction than I could have wished. The nearness and greatness of the event roused up my attention, and made me more difficult to please, than when I was alone in perfect tranquillity in France. But here I must tell you one of my foibles. I have a great inclination to go down to Scotland this spring to see my friends; and have your advice concerning my philosophical discoveries; but cannot overcome a certain shame-facedness I have to appear among you at my years, without having yet a settlement, or so much as attempted any. How happens it that we philosophers cannot as heartily despise the world as it despises us? I think in my conscience the contempt were as well founded on our side as on the other. * * *

'Your thoughts and mine agree with respect to Dr. Butler, and I would be glad to be introduced to him. I am at present castrating my work, that is, cutting off its nobler parts; that is, endeavouring it shall give as little offence as possible, before which, I could not pretend to put it into the Doctor's hands. This is a piece of cowardice, for which I blame myself, though I believe none of my friends will blame me. But I was resolved not to be an enthusiast in philosophy, while I was blaming other enthusiasms.'[1]

Again, on March 4, 1738, he writes :—

'I shall not trouble you with any formal compliments or thanks, which would be but an ill return for the kindness you have done me in writing in my behalf, to one you are so little acquainted with as Dr. Butler; and, I am afraid, stretching the truth in favour of a friend. I have called upon the Doctor, with a design of delivering him your letter, but find he is at present in the country. I am a little anxious to have the Doctor's opinion. My own I dare not trust to; both because it concerns myself, and because it is so variable, that I know not how to fix it. Sometimes it elevates me above the clouds; at other times, it depresses me with doubts and fears; so that, whatever be my success, I cannot be entirely disappointed. Somebody has told me that you might perhaps be in London this spring. I should esteem this a very lucky event; and notwithstanding all the pleasures of

[1] Life. Vol. i., p. 62.

the town, I would certainly engage you to pass some philosophical evenings with me, and either correct my judgment, where you differ from me, or confirm it where we agree. I believe I have some need of the one, as well as the other; and though the propensity to diffidence be an error on the better side, yet 'tis an error, and dangerous as well as disagreeable.'[1]

On September 26, 1738, he sold the copyright of the two volumes for 50*l*. to John Noone, of Cheapside, and they appeared in January 1739, with the following advertisement:—

'ADVERTISEMENT.

'MY design in the present Work is sufficiently explained in the Introduction. The reader must only observe, that all the subjects I have there planned out to myself are not treated in these two volumes. The subjects of the Understanding and Passions make a complete chain of reasoning by themselves; and I was willing to take advantage of this natural division, in order to try the taste of the Public. If I have the good fortune to meet with success, I shall proceed to the examination of Morals, Politics, and Criticism, which will complete this Treatise of Human Nature. The approbation of the Public I consider as the greatest reward of my labours; but am determined to regard its judgment, whatever it be, as my best instruction.'

On February 13, he wrote to H. Home:—

'SIR,—I thought to have wrote this from a place nearer you than London, but have been detained here by contrary winds, which have kept all Berwick ships from sailing. 'Tis now a fortnight since my book was published; and, besides many other considerations, I thought it would contribute very much to my tranquillity, and might spare me many mortifications, to be in the country while the success of the work was doubtful. I am afraid 'twill remain so very long. Those who are accustomed to reflect on such abstract subjects, are commonly full of prejudices; and those who are unprejudiced are unacquainted with metaphysical reasonings. My principles are also so remote from all the vulgar sentiments on the subject, that were they to take place, they would produce almost a total alteration in philosophy; and you know, revolutions of this kind are not easily brought about. I am

[1] Life. Vol. i., p. 64.

young enough to see what will become of the matter; but am apprehensive lest the chief reward I shall have for some time will be the pleasure of studying on such important subjects, and the approbation of a few judges. Among the rest, you may believe I aspire to your approbation; .and next to that, to your free censure and criticism. I shall present you with a copy as soon as I come to Scotland; and hope your curiosity, as well as friendship, will make you take the pains of perusing it.

'If you know anybody that is a judge, you would do me a sensible pleasure in engaging him to a serious perusal of the book. 'Tis so rare to meet with one that will take pains on a book, that does not come recommended by some great name or authority, that I must confess I am as fond of meeting with such a one as if I were sure of his approbation. I am, however, so doubtful in that particular, that I have endeavoured all I could to conceal my name; though I believe I have not been so cautious in this respect as I ought to have been.

'I have sent the Bishop of Bristol a copy, but could not wait on him with your letter after he had arrived at that dignity. At least I thought it would be to no purpose after I began the printing. You'll excuse the frailty of an author in writing so long a letter about nothing but his own performances. Authors have this privilege in common with lovers; and founded on the same reason, that they are both besotted with a blind fondness of their object. I have been upon my guard against this frailty; but perhaps this has rather turned to my prejudice. The reflection on our caution is apt to give us a more implicit confidence afterwards, when we come to form a judgment.'[1]

About the same time, he wrote to Michael Ramsay.

'As to myself, no alteration has happened to my fortune: nor have I taken the least step towards it. I hope things will be riper next winter; and I would not aim at any thing till I could judge of my success in my grand undertaking, and see upon what footing I shall stand in the world. I am afraid, however, that I shall not have any great success of a sudden. Such performances make their way very heavily at first, when they are not recommended by any great name or authority.'[2]

[1] Life Vol. i., p. 105.   [2] Life. Vol. i., p. 107.

The next letter is dated June 1, and is addressed to H. Home.

'DEAR SIR,—You see I am better than my word, having sent you two papers instead of one. I have hints for two or three more, which I shall execute at my leisure. I am not much in the humour of such compositions at present, having received news from London of the success of my Philosophy, which is but indifferent, if I may judge by the sale of the book, and if I may believe my bookseller. I am now out of humour with myself; but doubt not, in a little time, to be only out of humour with the world, like other unsuccessful authors. After all, I am sensible of my folly in entertaining any discontent, much more despair, upon this account, since I could not expect any better from such abstract reasoning; nor, indeed, did I promise myself much better. My fondness for what I imagined new discoveries, made me overlook all common rules of prudence; and, having enjoyed the usual satisfaction of projectors, 'tis but just I should meet with their disappointments. However, as 'tis observed with such sort of people, one project generally succeeds another, I doubt not but in a day or two I shall be as easy as ever, in hopes that truth will prevail at last over the indifference and opposition of the world.

'You see I might at present subscribe myself your most *humble* servant with great propriety: but, notwithstanding, shall presume to call myself your most affectionate friend as well as humble servant.'[1]

Nevertherless, he would not abandon hope, and busied himself with preparing a third volume for the press. This he submitted to Francis Hutcheson, then Professor of Moral Philosophy in the University of Glasgow. On receiving Hutcheson's comments, he replied as follows:—

'Ninewells, 17th Sept., 1739.

'SIR,—I am much obliged to you for your reflections on my papers. I have perused them with care, and find they will be of use to me. You have mistaken my meaning in some passages, which, upon examination, I have found to proceed from some ambiguity or defect in my expression.

'What affected me most in your remarks, is your observing that there wants a certain warmth in the cause of virtue,

[1] Life. Vol. i., p. 108.

which you think all good men would relish, and could not displease amidst abstract inquiries. I must own this has not happened by chance, but is the effect of a reasoning either good or bad. There are different ways of examining the mind, as well as the body. One may consider it either as an anatomist or as a painter: either to discover its most secret springs and principles, or to describe the grace and beauty of its actions. I imagine it impossible to conjoin these two views. Where you pull off the skin, and display all the minute parts, there appears something trivial, even in the noblest attitudes and most vigorous actions; nor can you ever render the object graceful or engaging, but by clothing the parts again with skin and flesh, and presenting only their bare outside. An anatomist, however, can give very good advice to a painter or statuary. And, in like manner, I am persuaded that a metaphysician may be very helpful to a moralist, though I cannot easily conceive these two characters united in the same work. Any warm sentiment of morals, I am afraid, would have the air of declamation amidst abstract reasonings, and would be esteemed contrary to good taste. And though I am much more ambitious of being esteemed a friend to virtue than a writer of taste, yet I must always carry the latter in my eye, otherwise I must despair of ever being serviceable to virtue. I hope these reasons will satisfy you; though at the same time I intend to make a new trial, if it be possible to make the moralist and metaphysician agree a little better.

'I cannot agree to your sense of *natural.* 'Tis founded on final causes, which is a consideration that appears to me pretty uncertain and unphilosophical. For, pray, what is the end of man? Is he created for happiness, or for virtue? for this life, or for the next? for himself, or for his Maker? Your definition of *natural* depends upon solving these questions, which are endless, and quite wide of my purpose. I have never called justice unnatural, but only artificial. "*Atque ipsa utilitas, justi prope mater et æqui,*" says one of the best moralists of antiquity. Grotius and Puffendorf, to be consistent, must assert the same.

'Whether natural abilities be virtue, is a dispute of words. I think I follow the common use of language; *virtus* signified chiefly courage among the Romans. I was just now reading this character of Alexander VI. in Guicciardin. "In Alessandro sesto fu solertia et sagacità singulare: consiglio eccellente, efficacia a persuadere maravigliosa, et a tutte le faccende gravi, sollicitudine, et destrezza incredibile. Ma erano queste virtù avanzate di grande intervallo da vitii." Were benevolence the only virtue, no characters could be mixed, but would depend entirely on their degrees of benevolence. Upon the whole, I desire to take my catalogue of virtues from "Cicero's Offices," not from "The Whole Duty of Man." I had indeed the former book in my eye in all my reasonings.

'I have many other reflections to communicate to you; but it would be troublesome. I shall therefore conclude with telling you, that I intend to follow your advice in altering most of those passages you have remarked as defective in point of prudence; though, I must own, I think you a little too delicate. Except a man be in orders, or be immediately concerned in the instruction of youth, I do not think his character depends upon his philosophical speculations, as the world is now modelled; and a little liberty seems requisite to bring into the public notice a book that is calculated for few readers. I hope you will allow me the freedom of consulting you when I am in any difficulty, and believe me, &c.

'P.S.—I cannot forbear recommending another thing to your consideration. Actions are not virtuous nor vicious, but only so far as they are proofs of certain qualities or durable principles in the mind. This is a point I should have established more expressly than I have done. Now, I desire you to consider if there be any quality that is virtuous, without having a tendency either to the public good or to the good of the person who possesses it. If there be none without these tendencies, we may conclude that their merit is derived from sympathy. I desire you would only consider the *tendencies* of qualities, not their actual operations, which depend on chance. *Brutus* riveted the chains of *Rome* faster by his opposition; but the natural tendency of his noble dispositions — his public spirit and magnanimity — was to establish her liberty.

'You are a great admirer of *Cicero* as well as I am. Please to review the fourth book *De Finibus Bonorum et Malorum*: where you find him prove against the *Stoics*, that if there be no other goods but virtue, 'tis impossible there can be any virtue, because the mind would then want all motives to begin its actions upon; and 'tis on the goodness or badness of the motives that the virtue of the action depends. This proves, that to every virtuous action there must be a motive or impelling passion distinct from the virtue, and that virtue can never be the sole motive to any action. You do not assent to this: though I think there is no proposition more certain or important. I must own my proofs were not distinct enough and must be altered. You see with what reluctance I part with you, though I believe it is time I should ask your pardon for so much trouble.'[1]

When this volume was ready, Hume changed his publisher. Although, as Mr. Burton observes, 50*l*. was a fair sum 'for an edition of a new metaphysical work, by an unknown and young author, born and brought up in a remote part of the empire,' and although Noone reported that the book did not sell, Hume was suspicious, and, looking back upon it as a bad bargain, availed himself of Hutcheson's good offices to obtain an introduction to Thomas Longman. Upon this subject he wrote to Hutcheson,—

'16th March, 1740.

'DEAR SIR,—I must trouble you to write that letter you was so kind as to offer to Longman the bookseller. I concluded somewhat of a hasty bargain with my bookseller, from indolence and an aversion to bargaining: as also because I was told that few or no booksellers would engage for one edition with a new author. I was also determined to keep my name a secret for some time, though I find I have failed in that point. I sold one edition of these two volumes for fifty guineas, and also engaged myself heedlessly in a clause, which may prove troublesome, viz. that upon printing a second edition I shall take all the copies remaining upon hand at the bookseller's price at the time. 'Tis in order to have some check upon my bookseller, that I would willingly engage with another: and I doubt not but your recommendation would be very serviceable to me, even though you be not personally acquainted with him.

'I wait with some impatience for a second edition, principally on account of alterations I intend to make in my performance. This is an advantage that we authors possess since the invention of printing, and renders the *nonum prematur in annum* not so necessary to us as to the ancients.

[1] Life. Vol. i., p. 112.

Without it I should have been guilty of a very great temerity, to publish at my years so many novelties in so delicate a part of philosophy; and at any rate, I am afraid that I must plead as my excuse that very circumstance of youth which may be urged against me. I assure you, that without running any of the heights of scepticism, I am apt in a cool hour to suspect, in general, that most of my reasonings will be more useful by furnishing hints and exciting people's curiosity, than as containing any principles that will augment the stock of knowledge, that must pass to future ages. I wish I could discover more fully the particulars wherein I have failed. I admire so much the candour I have observed in Mr. Locke, yourself, and a very few more, that I would be extremely ambitious of imitating it, by frankly confessing my errors. If I do not imitate it, it must proceed neither from my being free from errors nor want of inclination, but from my real unaffected ignorance. I shall consider more carefully all the particulars you mention to me: though with regard to *abstract ideas*, 'tis with difficulty I can entertain a doubt on that head, notwithstanding your authority. Our conversation together has furnished me a hint, with which I shall augment the second edition. 'Tis this—the word *simple idea* is an abstract term, comprehending different individuals that are similar. Yet the point of their similarity, from the very nature of such ideas, is not distinct nor separable from the rest. Is not this a proof, among many others, that there may be a similarity without any possible separation even in thought?

'I must consult you in a point of prudence. I have concluded a reasoning with these two sentences: "When you pronounce any action or character to be vicious, you mean nothing but that, from the particular constitution of your nature, you have a feeling or sentiment of blame from the contemplation of it. Vice and virtue, therefore, may be compared to sounds, colours, heat, and cold, which, according to modern philosophy, are not qualities in objects, but perceptions in the mind. And this discovery in morals, like that other in physics, is to be regarded as a mighty advancement of the speculative sciences, though like that too it has little or no influence on practice."[1]

[1] 'See this passage in the "Treatise of Human Nature," Book iii. Part i. sect. 1. where it appears with no other variation than the substitution of the word

'Is not this laid a little too strong? I desire your opinion of it, though I cannot entirely promise to conform myself to it. I wish from my heart I could avoid concluding, that since morality, according to your opinion, as well as mine, is determined merely by sentiment, it regards only human nature and human life. This has been often urged against you, and the consequences are very momentous. If you make any alterations in your performances, I can assure you, there are many who desire you would more fully consider this point, if you think that the truth lies on the popular side. Otherwise common prudence, your character, and situation, forbid you [to] touch upon it. If morality were determined by reason, that is the same to all rational beings; but nothing but experience can assure us that the sentiments are the same. What experience have we with regard to superior beings? How can we ascribe to them any sentiments at all? They have implanted those sentiments in us for the conduct of life like our bodily sensations, which they possess not themselves. I expect no answer to these difficulties in the compass of a letter. 'Tis enough if you have patience to read so long a letter as this.'[1]

Mr. Longman published the volume; on what terms, is not known.

The following advertisement was prefixed to it:—

'I think it proper to inform the public, that tho' this be a third volume of the "Treatise of Human Nature," yet 'tis in some measure independent of the other two, and requires not that the reader shou'd enter into all the abstract reasonings contain'd in them. I am hopeful it may be understood by ordinary readers, with as little attention as is usually given to any books of reasoning. It must only be observ'd, that I continue to make use of the terms, *impressions* and *ideas*, in the same sense as formerly; and that by impressions I mean our stronger perceptions, such as our sensations, affections and sentiments; and by ideas the fainter perceptions, or the copies of these in the memory and imagination.'

In the letter to Hutcheson last quoted, it will be noticed that Hume still anticipated a second edition. But although

"considerable," for mighty. It thus appears that whatever remarks Hutcheson made on the passage, they were not such as to induce the author materially to alter it.'—Mr. BURTON.

[1] Life. Vol. i., p. 117

HISTORY OF THE EDITIONS.

his hopes were not quenched, a tone of disappointment can be detected in the third volume. In 1739, he had spoken favourably of the attention paid to Philosophy in England. 'Reckoning from Thales to Socrates, the space of time is nearly equal to that betwixt my Lord Bacon and some late philosophers in England, (Mr. Locke, my Lord Shaftsbury, Dr. Mandeville, Mr. Hutchinson, Dr. Butler, &c.), who have begun to put the science of man on a new footing, and have engaged the attention, and excited the curiosity of the public. So true it is, that however other nations may rival us in poetry, and excel us in some other agreeable arts, the improvements in reason and philosophy can only be owing to a land of toleration and of liberty.'[1] 'We now proceed to explain the nature of *personal identity*, which has become so great a question in philosophy, especially of late years, in England, where all the abstruser sciences are studied with a peculiar ardour and application.'[2] But in the third volume he wrote: 'Without this advantage, I never should have ventured upon a third volume of such abstruse philosophy, in an age wherein the greatest part of men seem agreed to convert reading into an amusement and to reject every thing that requires any considerable degree of attention to be comprehended.'[3] And, further, it may be observed that the Advertisement attempts to dissociate this volume from the preceding ones, and to secure for it a wider audience.

Before long his hopes were finally dashed to the ground. As he says in his autobiography, 'Never literary attempt was more unfortunate than my "Treatise of Human Nature." It fell *dead-born from the press*, without reaching such distinction as even to excite a murmur among the zealots.' The last statement admits of a trifling correction. In a letter[4] to Hutcheson dated March 4, 1740, he says:—

'My bookseller has sent to Mr. Smith[5] a copy of my book, which I hope he has received, as well as your letter. I have not yet heard what he has done with the abstract; perhaps you have. I have got it printed in London, but not in *The Works of the Learned*, there having been an article with regard to my book, somewhat abusive, printed in that work, before I sent up the abstract.'[6]

[1] Vol. i., p. 308.
[2] Vol. i., p. 539.
[3] Vol. ii., p. 234.
[4] Life. Vol. i., p. 116.
[5] Mr. Burton believes that this was Adam Smith.
[6] MS. R.S.E. Of this abstract the Editor has discovered no trace.

The review in question, one of the longest in this magazine, consists of two notices in the numbers for November and December, 1739, occupying in all 51 pages. The object of the reviewer is not to discuss the argument of the book, but to give a synopsis of its contents, and, as far as possible, to leave the author to speak for himself in lengthy quotations, which, however, are accompanied by an ironical comment. At the outset the reviewer remarks upon the most prominent blemish in style. 'This work abounds throughout with *Egotisms*. The Author could scarcely use that Form of Speech more frequently, if he had written his own Memoirs.'

He is delighted, as might be expected, with the passage in which mistaken reasoning is explained by the blunders of the animal spirits in rummaging among the cells of the brain. The melancholy confessions of the Conclusion of the Fourth Part of Book I. receive a fair share of compassion: and the article ends with the following paragraphs:

'I will take Leave of our Author while he is in this chearful Mood, in this agreeable Situation; for, by looking forward, I perceive him extremely ready to relapse into profound Meditations on incomprehensible Subjects, and so into Scepticism, Chagrin, and all that gloomy frightful Train of Ideas from whence he is but this Moment emerged. Whether I shall wait upon him any more, and venture with him into those immense Depths of Philosophy which he launches into in his second Volume, I am not yet determined. Perhaps I have already and sufficiently answered the End of this Article, which is to make the Treatise it refers to more generally known than I think it has been; to bring it, as far as I am able, into the Observation of the Learned, who are the proper Judges of its Contents, who will give a Sanction to its Doctrines, where they are true and useful, and who have Authority to correct the Mistakes where they are of a different Nature; and lastly, to hint to the ingenious Writer, whoever he is, some Particulars in his Performance, that may require a very serious Reconsideration. It bears indeed incontestable Marks of a great Capacity, of a soaring Genius, but young, and not yet thoroughly practised. The Subject is vast and noble as any that can exercise the Understanding; but it requires a very mature Judgment to handle it as becomes its Dignity and Importance; the utmost Prudence, Tenderness and Delicacy, are requisite to this desirable Issue. Time and Use may ripen these Qualities in our Author; and we shall probably have Reason to consider this, compared with his later Productions, in the same Light as we view the *Juvenile* Works of *Milton*, or the first Manner of a *Raphael*, to other celebrated Painters.'

Two passages in the article may be quoted, as illustrating the repute in which Locke and Berkeley were held at the time.

'A man, who has never had the Pleasure of reading Mr. *Locke's* incomparable Essay, will peruse our Author with much less Disgust, than those can who have been used to the irresistible Reasoning and wonderful Perspicuity of that admirable Writer.' ....

'It is above twenty Years since I looked over that Piece of Dr. *Berkeley's*, which contains this most precious discovery,[1] and, if I remember right, that Gentleman himself boasts of some mighty Advantages that would accrue from it to the Commonwealth of Learning. The Acquisition of Science was to become exceeding easy, and several Difficulties, that were used grievously to perplex Mathematicians and Metaphysicians, were to sink before it: In short, it was to do such Feats in behalf of Knowledge, as no Principle beside was able to perform. But notwithstanding all these Benefits that were to accompany it, I do not find it has met with any favourable Reception among the Literati; or that many Persons of Ability and Penetration are become Disciples: Its Fortune may now perhaps be more prosperous under the Auspices of its new Patron, who, we see, undertakes to raise it above all Opposition.'

The intention to return to the subject was never fulfilled by the reviewer: neither the second nor the third volume is mentioned in the History of the Works of the Learned. With the exception of this criticism the Treatise was unnoticed, and Hume believed that the labour of his life had been thrown away. This was the severest blow that Hume ever experienced, and its history supplies the clue to the development of his character.

Henceforth, by a natural revulsion of sentiment, he regarded the Treatise with aversion. This feeling was strengthened by a growing dislike to the many faults of style which disfigure it. The abundant Scotticisms[2] became more and

[1] Berkeley's doctrine of Abstract General Ideas.
[2] 'I told him that David Hume had made a short collection of Scotticisms. "I wonder (said Johnson) that *he* should find them."'—Boswell. The collection of Scotticisms is printed in Vol. iv.

more repugnant to a writer, who ardently desired to be mistaken for an Englishman in grammar and diction. The constant repetition of such egotisms as 'I think' and 'I am convinc'd' disgusted a critic, who fastidiously weighed every phrase of his Essays as they passed through successive editions. The fragmentary nature of the argument: the lack of literary finish: the traces of a recluse, who had mixed little in society: the dogmatic tone of the argument: the dry, *a priori* mode of reasoning: the close adherence to the lines marked out by Locke and Berkeley, owing to which the Treatise can hardly stand alone: a certain want of coherence between the various trains of thought: all these were further considerations which tended to inflame a bitter sense of mortification. Few men of letters have been at heart so vain and greedy of fame as was Hume. In all other respects he learned to school his temper; but his appetite for applause was insatiable, and even his publisher had on occasion to rebuke the philosopher.

Of his feelings at the time we possess no record; but the following letter, written long afterwards, exhibits his maturer judgment.

'I believe the Philosophical Essays contain every thing of consequence relating to the understanding, which you would meet with in the Treatise; and I give you my advice against reading the latter. By shortening and simplifying the questions, I really render them much more complete. *Addo dum minuo.* The philosophical principles are the same in both; but I was carried away by the heat of youth and invention to publish too precipitately.—So vast an undertaking, planned before I was one-and-twenty, and composed before twenty-five, must necessarily be very defective. I have repented my haste a hundred, and a hundred times.'[1]

Another letter may be quoted; to whom written, and when, is not known: Mr. Burton conjectures, at an advanced period of life.

'That you may see I would no way scruple of owning my mistakes in argument, I shall acknowledge (what is infinitely more material) a very great mistake in conduct, viz. my publishing at all the "Treatise of Human Nature," a book which pretended to innovate in all the sublimest paths of philosophy, and which I composed before I was five-and-twenty; above

[1] Letter to Gilbert Elliot of Minto, 1751. Life. Vol. i., p. 337.

HISTORY OF THE EDITIONS.

all, the positive air which prevails in that book, and which may be imputed to the ardour of youth, so much displeases me, that I have not patience to review it. But what success the same doctrines, better illustrated and expressed, may meet with, *adhuc sub judice lis est.* The arguments have been laid before the world, and by some philosophical minds have been attended to. I am willing to be instructed by the public; though human life is so short, that I despair of ever seeing the decision. I wish I had always confined myself to the more easy parts of erudition; but you will excuse me from submitting to a proverbial decision, let it even be in Greek.'[1]

From these extracts it appears that the Treatise was written between one-and-twenty and five-and-twenty. In the Advertisement to the posthumous edition of his Essays, he published the statement, that it was projected before he left college, and written and published 'not long after.' There is some difficulty in these dates. Hume entered the University of Edinburgh in 1723, when he was nearly twelve years of age. There is no direct evidence as to the time when he 'left college.' Mr. Burton says, 'We find him speaking of having received the usual college education of Scotland, which terminates when the student is fourteen or fifteen years old.'[2] In a letter already quoted (p. 19) Hume has spoken as if this had been his own case. If so, he left college, at latest, early in 1727, and as the Treatise was published in 1739, the interval was not a short one. It appears probable that Hume confounded the date of leaving college with the year in which, as the same letter informs us, he first discovered a 'new medium, by which truth might be established.' This happened in 1729, when he was eighteen; the next eight years were occupied in elaborating the discovery, and the work was definitely finished in 1736, before he 'was five-and-twenty,' and a year before he quitted La Flèche.

It was in the Advertisement from which this statement has been quoted, that Hume expressed his desire, that the Treatise might no longer be regarded as expressing his sentiments. It runs as follows:

'Most of the principles, and reasonings, contained in this volume, were published in a work in three volumes, called *A Treatise of Human Nature*: A work which the Author

[1] Life. Vol. i., p. 98. [2] Life. Vol. i., p. 10.

had projected before he left College, and which he wrote and published not long after. But not finding it successful, he was sensible of his error in going to the press too early, and he cast the whole anew in the following pieces, where some negligences in his former reasoning and more in the expression, are, he hopes, corrected. Yet several writers, who have honoured the Author's Philosophy with answers, have taken care to direct all their batteries against that juvenile work, which the Author never acknowledged, and have affected to triumph in any advantages, which, they imagined, they had obtained over it: A practice very contrary to all rules of candour and fair-dealing, and a strong instance of those polemical artifices, which a bigotted zeal thinks itself authorised to employ. Henceforth, the Author desires, that the following Pieces may alone be regarded as containing his philosophical sentiments and principles.'

This Advertisement was first printed by way of preface to the posthumous and authoritative edition of 1777. One blunder has already been examined. Another occurs in the assertion, that the whole had been cast anew in the Inquiries. Without going into details, we may mention that Vol. i., Part II., Of the Ideas of Space and Time, was indeed re-written, but the monograph never appeared; and that Part IV. of the same volume, in many respects the most interesting portion of the Treatise, was never resumed.

In the Life of Hume Mr. Burton appears, if not to have made a mistake about this Advertisement, at least to have written what is calculated to mislead. Speaking of the publication of the Inquiry concerning the Human Understanding in 1748, he says: 'He now desired that the "Treatise of Human Nature" should be treated as a work blotted out of literature, and that the "Inquiry" should be substituted in its place. In the subsequent editions of the latter work, he complained that this had not been complied with; that the world still looked at those forbidden volumes of which he had dictated the suppression.'[1] The only reference to the Treatise in Hume's writings is that in the Advertisement to the posthumous edition, which has just been quoted.

But we quite agree with Mr. Burton, that it is impossible 'to detach this book from general literature.' In deference to Hume's wishes, an author should always remind his

[1] Life. Vol. i., p. 273.

audience, if they require the warning, that the Treatise does not represent Hume's later sentiments; and to those who are interested in the biographies of philosophers, this episode is interesting. But it would be ridiculous to consign such a book to oblivion out of respect to its author's change of feeling. By so doing, we should wilfully ignore some of the acutest speculations of one of our acutest thinkers; and those, too, on points which are not discussed in any of his subsequent writings. We should miss the instructive lesson which is gained by observing how closely the course of his speculations was determined for him by Locke and Berkeley. We should lose the key to much philosophy, both Scotch and German.

It would not appear requisite to say much on this head, but that men of mark, like Professor Fowler and Mr. Hunt, appear to pride themselves on ignorance of the Treatise. The former says ('Inductive Logic,' p. 24): 'In quoting or referring to Hume, I have employed only his *Essays*. Many writers persist in making references to his *Treatise of Human Nature*, a work which he himself repudiated, as containing an immature expression of his opinions. In the *Advertisement* to his Essays, he desires that "the following pieces may alone be regarded as containing the author's sentiments and principles."' Mr. Hunt is more violent ('Contemporary Review,' May 1869; p. 79): 'Hume's first publication was the "Treatise of Human Nature." As this work was afterwards disowned by its author, we need not do more than mention it. Its place was supplied by the "Essays," in which the chief questions were treated with more accuracy and clearness, while many of the more intricate and ingenious but less important reasonings were omitted.' After this one is prepared to learn that Professor Fowler never quotes the Æneid as Virgil's, and that Mr. Hunt never quotes it at all.[1]

It might, perhaps, have been expected that Hume's residence in France would have exercised a perceptible influence upon the reasonings of the Treatise. Yet it is not too much to say, that, with a few unimportant exceptions, there is no trace of it. The writer was little acquainted with, and is

[1] From Mr. Hunt's estimate of the relative merits of the Treatise and the Essays, we presume to differ *in toto*. Professor Fowler's readers receive no hint that the advertisement was the posthumous utterance of a splenetic invalid.

little interested in, any foreign school of philosophy. His knowledge of Spinoza was derived from Bayle's dictionary. Twice he gives a direct reference to 'Malbranch.' He refers in one paragraph to the Port Royal Logic, whence, too, he borrows the instance of the chiliagon. There is no trace of a direct knowledge of Des Cartes. The only French writer, besides, whom he quotes for other than ornamental purposes, is Malezieu, and this reference, no doubt, owes its origin to Hume's residence at La Flèche. At least, the 'Eléments de Géométrie de M. le duc de Bourgoyne' does not seem to have been generally known in England; and at the present day no copy of it is to be found in the British Museum, or in Bodley's Library. In short, the Treatise from beginning to end is the work of a solitary Scotchman, who has devoted himself to the critical study of Locke and Berkeley. That he lived for three years in France, was an accident which has left no trace either in the tone or in the matter of his book.

In style, however, so far as the structure of sentences is concerned, no doubt he was already influenced by the literature of France.[1] The style of the Treatise is indeed immature, but it reveals the tendencies which were ripened by incessant labour, until Hume became the one master of philosophic English.

Whatever disappointment had fallen to Hume's share, so active and sanguine a mind could not lie quiet. In 1741 he published anonymously a volume of 'Essays, Moral and Political;' which ran into a 'Second Edition, Corrected,' in the following year, when also a second volume was added.

Unlike the ill-starred Treatise this venture was successful. Hume himself says in his Autobiography: 'In 1742 I printed at Edinburgh the first part of my Essays: the work was favourably received, and soon made me entirely forget my former disappointment.' And in a letter to Henry Home, dated June 13, 1742, he adds:[2] 'The *Essays* are all sold in London, as I am informed by two letters from English gentlemen of my acquaintance. There is a demand for

---

[1] 'The conversation now turned upon Mr. David Hume's style. Johnson: "Why, sir, his style is not English; the structure of his sentences is French. Now the French structure and the English structure may, in the nature of things, be equally good. But if you allow that the English language is established, he is wrong. My name might originally have been Nicholson, as well as Johnson, but were you to call me Nicholson, you would call me very absurdly."—Boswell.

[2] Life. Vol. i., p. 143.

them; and, as one of them tells me, Innys, the great bookseller in Paul's Churchyard, wonders there is not a new edition, for that he cannot find copies for his customers. I am also told that Dr. Butler has everywhere recommended them; so that I hope they will have some success. They may prove like dung with marl, and bring forward the rest of my Philosophy, which is of a more durable, though of a harder and more stubborn nature. You see I can talk to you in your own style.' It appears that Hume was recovering from his disappointment, and was gratified to have won the ear of Bp. Butler, whose judgment on the 'Treatise' he had been so anxious to obtain.

But how were these Essays to bring forward the rest of his Philosophy? Like the Treatise, they were published anonymously: in the Advertisement he assumed the character of an author who is making his first appearance. There is no evidence to decide this question: but the conjecture is almost certain, that he had already determined to abandon the Treatise, and to reproduce portions of it in a more popular form.

The Preface to the original volume of Essays, runs as follows:—

'Most of these ESSAYS were wrote with a View of being published as WEEKLY-PAPERS, and were intended to comprehend the Designs both of the SPECTATORS & CRAFTSMEN. But having dropt that Undertaking, partly from LAZINESS, partly from WANT of LEISURE, and being willing to make Trial of my Talents for Writing, before I ventur'd upon any more serious Compositions, I was induced to communicate these Trifles to the Judgment of the Public. Like most new Authors, I must confess, I feel some Anxiety concerning the Success of my Work: But one Thing makes me more secure; That the READER may condemn my Abilities, but must approve of my Moderation and Impartiality in my Method of handling POLITICAL SUBJECTS: And as long as my Moral Character is in Safety, I can, with less Anxiety, abandon my Learning and Capacity to the most severe Censure and Examination. Public Spirit, methinks, shou'd engage us to love the Public, and to bear an equal Affection to all our Country-Men; not to hate one Half of them, under Pretext of loving the Whole. This PARTY-RAGE I have endeavour'd to repress, as far as possible; and I hope this Design will be acceptable to the moderate of both Parties; at the same Time, that, perhaps, it may displease the Bigots of both.

'The READER must not look for any Connexion among these Essays, but must consider each of them as a Work apart. This is an Indulgence that is given to all ESSAY-WRITERS, and is an equal Ease both to WRITER and Reader, by freeing them from any tiresome stretch of Attention or Application.'

The volume contains 15 Essays:—

1. Of the Delicacy of Taste and Reason.
2. Of the Liberty of the Press.
3. Of Impudence and Modesty.
4. That Politics may be reduc'd to a Science.
5. Of the first Principles of Government.
6. Of Love and Marriage.
7. Of the Study of History.
8. Of the Independency of Parliament.
9. Whether the British Government inclines more to Absolute Monarchy or to a Republic.
10. Of Parties in general.
11. Of the Parties of Gt. Britain.
12. Of Superstition and Enthusiasm.
13. Of Avarice.
14. Of the Dignity of Human Nature.
15. Of Liberty and Despotism.

The corrections in the second edition are few and unimportant, chiefly concerning unguarded statements on points of Roman History. The Second Volume, which is not referred to in the title-page of either edition of the First, contains 12 Essays:—

1. Of Essay Writing.
2. Of Eloquence.
3. Of Moral Prejudices.
4. Of the Middle Station of Life.
5. Of the Rise and Progress of Arts and Sciences.
6. The Epicurean.
7. The Stoic.
8. The Platonist.
9. The Sceptic.
10. Of Polygamy and Divorces.
11. Of Simplicity and Refinement.
12. A Character of Sir Robert Walpole.

The first Essay in the second volume, Of Essay Writing, (which will be found at the end of vol. iv.), was certainly written, when the author designed, as he says in the Advertisement, to publish his Essays in a series of weekly papers, to which it would have served as an introduction. Lamenting that the Learned and the Conversible Worlds have been estranged of late, he proposes to act as an Ambassador between them, and to reside at the Court of the latter, where it will be his mission to communicate the latest news of the Learned World. He begins therefore by paying his respects to the fair sex, who constitute the Sovereignty of the Kingdom, and invites them to imitate the example of Parisian Society by assuming the high functions of criticism and frowning down those barbarous eccentricities which disfigure English Literature. As he says elsewhere: 'The elegance and propriety of style have been very much neglected among us. We have no dictionary of our language, and scarcely a tolerable grammar. The first polite prose we have, was writ by a man who is still alive.'[1] In this Essay he expresses himself confident, that if the Ladies only threw off a false shame, they might do much to ameliorate this state of things, there being only one branch of literature in which their judgment is to be distrusted, *i.e.* books of gallantry and devotion, 'which they commonly affect as high flown as possible.' It was no doubt with the design of conciliating his fair critics, that Hume included several papers on lighter subjects, such as Love and Marriage, Impudence and Modesty, &c., which can hardly have been much to their writer's taste, and which mingle strangely with a series of discussions on the British Constitution. Nor were they successful; that the challenge was taken up by a coterie of ladies, who condemned his efforts, appears from a letter to William Mure of Caldwell.

'With my humble compliments to the ladies, and tell them, I should endeavour to satisfy them, if they would name the subject of the essay they desire. For my part, I know not a better subject than themselves; if it were not, that being accused of being unintelligible in some of my writings, I should be extremely in danger of falling into that fault, when I should treat of a subject so little to be understood as women. I would, therefore, rather have them assign me the

---

[1] Essay xii. . . . . . Dean Swift.

deiform fund of the soul, the passive unions of nothing with nothing, or any other of those mystical points, which I would endeavour to clear up, and render perspicuous to the meanest readers.'[1]

With this Essay six others may be classed, apparently designed to attract the attention of ladies, and marked by the mannerisms of what was then a fashionable literature. The paper 'Of Moral Prejudices' contains the character of an imaginary Eugenius, and a narrative of French gallantry, which a purer taste rejected. That on the 'Middle Station of Life' cannot have cost much pains, and abounds in expressions of personal opinion. These three were never reprinted. The next to go were those on 'Impudence,' on 'Love and Marriage,' and on the 'Study of History,' lingering, however, to the Edition of 1764: that they survived so long, is, perhaps, surprising. Lastly, the 'Essay on Avarice' was dropt in the Edition of 1770.

The 'Political Essays' are the most valuable part of these two volumes. It is probable that portions of them existed in manuscript, before the publication of the Treatise, and that in printing them Hume was redeeming his conditional promise, made in the Advertisement to the first volume of the 'Treatise,' to 'proceed to the examination of Morals, Politics, and Criticism.' Of Morals he had treated in the volume of 1740; the Essays of 1741-2 handle political, and, to some extent, critical questions.

The Political Essays do not attempt to found a system: they are entirely special in their character, dealing with the topics of the day. It is true that Hume enriches them with brief discussions of political principles, and with a copious fund of historical illustration. But these episodes were conventional, suiting the fashion of an age which delighted in references to the statesmanship of Athens and Rome, and to the fortunes of Venice and Poland. What is peculiar to the author, will be found in his treatment of the debated questions of the Freedom of the Press, the Independency of Parliament, and the nature of Parties. In this choice of subjects he followed the 'Craftsman'; and the best illustration of these papers is to be found in the numbers of that journal. They frequently read like a running criticism upon the arguments of the 'Craftsman,' and even particular phrases and Latin quotations are borrowed thence. But their passionless

[1] Life. Vol. i., p. 159.

moderation contrasts strongly with the savage invectives of 'Mist's Journal' and the 'Craftsman,' and must have recommended itself to Dr. Butler quite apart from the penetrating insight which divides so sharply the contemporaneous questions of politics.

Of this group of Essays perhaps the best remembered is the Character of Sir Robert Walpole. Of this Hume said in the Advertisement:

'The character of SIR ROBERT WALPOLE was drawn some months ago, when that Great MAN was in the Zenith of his Power. I must confess, that, at present, when he seems to be upon the Decline, I am inclin'd to think more favourably of him, and to suspect, that the Antipathy, which every true born *Briton* naturally bears to Ministers of State, inspir'd me with some Prejudice against him. The impartial READER, if any such there be; or Posterity, if such a Trifle can reach them, will be best able to correct any Mistakes in this Particular.'

In the edition of 1748, this Essay was degraded to the rank of a foot-note, and appended to the paper headed 'That Politics may be reduced to a Science.' The Advertisement having disappeared, it was prefaced as follows: 'What our author's opinion was of the famous minister here pointed at, may be learned from that essay, printed in the former editions,'—it only so occurs in Edition C—'under the title of A Character of Sir ROBERT WALPOLE. It was as follows.' The Essay will be found in vol. iv. 'The author is pleased to find, that after animosities are laid, and calumny has ceased, the whole nation almost have returned to the same moderate sentiments with regard to this great man, if they are not rather become more favourable to him, by a very natural transition, from one extreme to another. The author would not oppose those humane sentiments towards the dead; though he cannot forbear observing that the not paying more of our public debts was, as hinted in this character, a great, and the only great error in that long administration.' In 1770, the whole was omitted.

After these may be placed a group of Essays, on which the author had expended more than ordinary care, ornamenting them with florid imagery, and polishing the sentences with such precision, that the subsequent editions made scarcely an alteration in their language. Of these he says in the Advertisement: ''Tis proper to inform the READER, that, in those Essays, intitled, the Epicurean, Stoic, &c., a certain Character is personated; and therefore, no Offence ought to be taken at any Sentiments contain'd in them.' Offence is not likely to be taken; but the question has been mooted, whether any one of them gives evidence of a bias in the author's mind. Mr. Burton decides in favour of 'The Stoic': 'The reader expects to find an attempt to draw his own picture in "The Sceptic," but it is not to be found there The sceptic of the essays is not a man analyzing the principles of knowledge, to find wherein they consist, but one who is dissatisfied with rules of morality, and who, examining the current codes one after another, tosses them aside as unsatisfactory. It is into "The Stoic" that the writer has thrown most of his heart and sympathy; and it is in that sketch that, though probably without intention, some of the features of his own character are portrayed. There are passages which have considerable unison of tone with those autobiographical documents already quoted, in which he describes himself as having laboured to subdue the rebellious passions, to reduce the mind to a regulated system, to drive from it the influence of petty impressions,—to hold one great object of life in view, and to sacrifice before that object whatever stood in the way of his firmly settled purpose.'[1] It is true that there are sentences in 'The Stoic' which justify this statement. It is also true that the opening paragraphs of 'The Sceptic' do not represent Hume's habitual state of mind. On reviewing the Treatise and the Inquiries, a remarkable difference will be found between his treatment of metaphysical and of moral questions. In discussing the former, he is uniformly sceptical; in discussing the latter, he assumes an opposite attitude, and becomes dogmatic in his enunciations. He not merely dissents from those who deny the reality of moral distinctions; he brands them with the character of disingenuous disputants. The same impatience breaks out when he considers the fashionable belief which resolved all the virtues into modes of self-love. So far, then, as 'The Sceptic' tosses aside the current codes as unsatisfactory, without substituting a better system, it is written in character, and the author is not chargeable with its sentiments. It may be added that a strong tendency to materialistic explanations pervades these portions, whereas in

[1] Life. Vol. i., p. 142.

'The Treatise' Hume only resorts to that hypothesis when he is driven to extremities. But after allowance has been made for these points of divergence from his usual methods, it cannot fail to be remarked, that whereas in the companion Essays Hume adopted a high-flown style which is unique in his writings, in 'The Sceptic' he returns to that sober and quiet English, which was not more in accordance with the immediate occasion, than with his habitual tone of thought. The practical maxims for the rule of life agree as closely with his biography as the scattered sentences in 'The Stoic.' The pungent criticism of Pope's argument expressed briefly what he wrote at large in his Inquiry concerning the Principles of Morals; and lastly, whereas 'The Stoic,' 'The Platonist,' and 'The Epicurean' are dismissed without comment, a note is added to 'The Sceptic' for the express purpose of setting out the whole truth, in which the preceding paragraphs are only corrected because they are incomplete.

For three years Hume continued to reside in Edinburgh, and made an attempt to succeed Dr. Pringle in the chair of Ethics and Pneumatic Philosophy. Then, in 1745, he accepted an engagement to act as tutor to the Marquis of Annandale, an irritable invalid, 'who was,' according to an expression used by Sir James Johnstone, when writing to Hume, 'charmed with something contained in his Essays.' The narrative of the disputes and intrigues which finally drove Hume away in April '46, will be found in Mr. Burton's 'Life of Hume.' In the same year he went as secretary with General St. Clair on an expedition which sailed from Plymouth September 14, to attack Port L'Orient, and was appointed Judge Advocate of all the forces under command. On their return, he passed a few months at Ninewells, and then, in February, 1748, accepted an invitation from General St. Clair again to accompany him as secretary on a diplomatic mission to the court of Turin, which lasted till the end of the year.

But during the quiet time which preceded his engagements with General St. Clair, Hume had not been idle. From expressions dropt in his correspondence it appears that as early as 1746 he had formed the project of writing history. For the present these plans were allowed to stand over. But during the year 1748 two works appeared, of which he thus speaks in a letter to H. Home, February 9:

'I leave here two works going on: a new edition of my Essays, all of which you have seen, except one, "Of the Protestant Succession," where I treat that subject as coolly and indifferently as I would the dispute between Cæsar and Pompey. The conclusion shows me a Whig, but a very sceptical one. Some people would frighten me with the consequences that may attend this candour, considering my present station; but I own I cannot apprehend any thing.

'The other work is the "Philosophical Essays," which you dissuaded me from printing. I won't justify the prudence of this step, any other way than by expressing my indifference about all the consequences that may follow.'[1]

It will be convenient to consider the new edition first, which is advertised in the 'Gentleman's Magazine' for November, 1748, about the date of Hume's return from Turin. This reprint was the first of his publications that bore the Author's name. According to the autobiography the sale was indifferent. Few changes had been made. As has already been said, the character of Sir R. Walpole was now given as a foot-note; and three papers, Of Essay Writing, Of Moral Prejudices, and Of the Middle Station of Life were omitted. In their place three new Essays were inserted.

Those on Original Contract and on Passive Obedience pursue the same vein of political inquiry which had been so successfully worked in the first edition. They are distinguished by the same tone of impartial criticism, and apply the same principles: but this judicial attitude causes less surprise where the controversy is one that had ceased to rage, and that occupied but a secondary place in public debate.

The Essay 'Of the Protestant Succession,' which was spoken of in the last extract from his correspondence, was not printed. It was held over until the publication of his Political Discourses in 1752, where it appeared incongruously enough. The result disappointed his fears. In a letter to Dr. Clephane, dated February 4, 1752, he says:

'About a fortnight before, I had published a Discourse of the Protestant Succession, wherein I had very liberally abused both Whigs and Tories; yet I enjoyed the favour of both parties.'[2]

The third Essay, which was now printed for the first time, 'Of National Characters,' is of some interest, because it

[1] Life. Vol. i., p. 239. [2] Life. Vol. i., p. 372.

directly enters upon a topic which is rarely mentioned in Hume's philosophical writings, although they frequently suggest it. In it he examined the influence of physical conditions on the temper and genius of men: but although he was always delighted to point out the extravagant variations in moral customs and religious observances which exist among neighbouring races, he distinctly asserted on this occasion that 'physical causes have no discernible operation on the human mind:' and that 'if we run over the globe, or revolve the annals of history, we shall discern everywhere signs of a sympathy or contagion of manners, none of the influence of air and climate:' and the only exceptions to this statement are the jealous love of southern climates and the propensity of northern races to drinking.

In the April of the same year, before starting for Turin, he had published 'Philosophical Essays concerning Human Understanding by the Author of The Essays Moral and Political,'—a new edition of which appeared, as we have seen, with the author's name in the following November. There is no preface or advertisement to these Essays. It is a rare book, not to be found in the British Museum, the Bodleian, or the Advocates' Library. This then was the first instalment of his design to recast the unfortunate Treatise piece by piece. Of this he says in his Autobiography:

'I had always entertained a notion, that my want of success in publishing the Treatise of Human Nature, had proceeded more from the manner than the matter, and that I had been guilty of a very usual indiscretion, in going to the press too early. I, therefore, cast the first part of that work anew in the Enquiry concerning Human Understanding, which was published while I was at Turin.'—Here his memory failed him.—'But this piece was at first little more successful than the Treatise of Human Nature. On my return from Italy, I had the mortification to find all England in a ferment, on account of Dr. Middleton's Free Enquiry, while my performance was entirely overlooked and neglected.'

The rarity of the book confirms these statements; but there are circumstances which indicate that, although the work was neglected at first, it began to sell before long, assisted, perhaps, by the revelation of the author's name in November. In a letter dated April 18, 1750, Hume says: 'You'll scarcely believe what I am going to tell you; but it is literally true. Millar had printed off, some months ago, a new edition of certain philosophical essays, but he tells me very gravely that he has delayed publishing because of the earthquakes.'¹ In his Autobiography, he says further: 'Meanwhile, my bookseller, A. Millar, informed me that my former publications (all but the unfortunate Treatise) were beginning to be the subject of conversation; that the sale of them was gradually increasing, and that new editions were demanded. Answers by Reverends and Right Reverends, came out two or three in a year; and I found, by Dr. Warburton's railing, that the books were beginning to be esteemed in good company.' A specimen of 'Dr. Warburton's railing' is given by Bishop Hurd: 'In a letter of September 28, of that year (1749), to a friend at Cambridge, he says, "I am tempted to have a stroke at Hume in parting. He is the author of a little book called *Philosophical Essays*: In one part of which he argues against the being of a GOD, and in another (very needlessly, you will say) against the possibility of miracles. He has crowned the liberty of the press. And yet he has a considerable post under the government. I have a great mind to do justice on his arguments against miracles, which I think might be done in few words. But does he deserve this notice? Is he known amongst you? Pray, answer me these questions. For if his own weight keeps him down, I should be sorry to contribute to his advancement to any place, but the pillory." No encouraging answer, I suppose, was returned to this letter; and so the author of the Essays escaped for this time.'²

A 'few words' from the 'arguments against miracles' appear among Warburton's Unfinished Papers, p. 311.

The Essay on Miracles has a history of its own. In a letter to Principal Campbell, dated February 7, 1762, Hume gives an account of the circumstances which first led him to that train of thought.

'It may perhaps amuse you to learn the first hint, which suggested to me that argument which you have so strenuously attacked. I was walking in the cloisters of the Jesuits' College of La Flèche, a town in which I passed two years of my youth, and engaged in a conversation with a Jesuit of some parts and learning, who was relating to me, and urging some nonsensical miracle performed lately in their convent, when I was tempted to dispute against him; and as my head

---

¹ Life, vol. i. p. 300. ² Hurd's *Life of Warburton*.

was full of the topics of my Treatise of Human Nature, which I was at that time composing, this argument immediately occurred to me, and I thought it very much gravelled my companion; but at last he observed to me, that it was impossible for that argument to have any solidity, because it operated equally against the Gospel as the Catholic miracles;—which observation I thought proper to admit as a sufficient answer. I believe you will allow, that the freedom at least of this reasoning makes it somewhat extraordinary to have been the produce of a convent of Jesuits, though perhaps you may think the sophistry of it savours plainly of the place of its birth.'[1]

Again in the letter to H. Home of December 2, 1737, from which an extract has already been given,[2] he says further:

'Having a franked letter, I was resolved to make use of it; and accordingly enclose some "*Reasonings concerning Miracles*," which I once thought of publishing with the rest, but which I am afraid will give too much offence, even as the world is disposed at present. There is something in the turn of thought, and a good deal in the turn of expression, which will not perhaps appear so proper, for want of knowing the context: but the force of the argument you'll be judge of, as it stands. Tell me your thoughts of it. Is not the style too diffuse? though, as that was a popular argument, I have spread it out much more than the other parts of the work. I beg of you to show it to nobody, except to Mr. Hamilton, if he pleases; and let me know at your leisure that you have received it, read it, and burnt it.'[3]

The second edition of the Philosophical Essays, which had been delayed by the earthquakes, appeared in 1751, and bore the author's name on the title-page. Few changes were made. Section xi. now received the heading Of a Particular Providence and of a Future State, having previously been called Of the Practical Consequences of Natural Religion.

These two editions contain the unguarded statement, 'upon the whole, then, it appears, that no testimony for any kind of miracle *can ever amount* to a probability, much less to a proof.' For the words in italics he subsequently wrote, 'has ever amounted.'

In the December of the same year he published an En-

[1] Life, vol. i. p. 57. [2] Ibid. p. 18. [3] Ibid. p. 63.

quiry concerning the Principles of Morals: 'which in my own opinion (who ought not to judge on that subject) is of all my writings, historical, philosophical, or literary, incomparably the best. It came unnoticed and unobserved into the world.'

The Dialogue which is contained in this volume, was a very favourite piece with its author. In a letter to Gilbert Elliot (February 10, 1751), he says:

'About six week ago, I gave our friend, Jack Stuart, the trouble of delivering you a letter, and some papers enclosed, which I was desirous to submit to your criticism and examination. I say not this by way of compliment and ceremonial, but seriously and in good earnest: it is pretty usual for people to be pleased with their own performance, especially in the heat of composition; but I have scarcely wrote any thing more whimsical, or whose merit I am more diffident of.'[1]

Elliot's reply may be quoted as an additional illustration of the difference in Hume's handling of ethical questions.

'I have read over your Dialogue, with all the application I am master of. Though I have never looked into any thing of your writing, which did not either entertain or instruct me; yet, I must freely own to you, that I have received from this last piece an additional satisfaction, and what indeed I have a thousand times wished for in some of your other performances. In the first part of this work, you have given full scope to the native bent of your genius. The ancients and moderns, how opposite soever in other respects, equally combine in favour of the most unbounded scepticism. Principles, customs, and manners, the most contradictory, all seemingly lead to the same end; and agreeably to your laudable practice, the poor reader is left in the most disconsolate state of doubt and uncertainty. When I had got thus far, what do you think were my sentiments? I will not be so candid as to tell you; but how agreeable was my surprise, when I found you had led me into this maze, with no other view, than to point out to me more clearly the direct road. Why can't you always write in this manner? Indulge yourself as much as you will in starting difficulties, and perplexing received opinions: but let us be convinced at length, that you have not less ability to establish true principles, than subtlety to detect false ones. This unphilosophical, or,

[1] Life, vol. i. p 321.

if you will, this lazy disposition of mine, you are at liberty to treat as you think proper; yet I am no enemy to free enquiry, and I would gladly flatter myself, no slave to prejudice or authority. ' I admit also that there is no writing or talking of any subject that is of importance enough to become the object of reasoning, without having recourse to some degree of subtlety or refinement. The only question is, where to stop,—how far we can go, and why no farther. To this question I should be extremely happy to receive a satisfactory answer. I can't tell if I shall rightly express what I have just now in my mind: but I often imagine to myself, that I perceive within me a certain instinctive feeling, which shoves away at once all subtle refinements, and tells me with authority, that these air-built notions are inconsistent with life and experience, and, by consequence, cannot be true or solid. From this I am led to think, that the speculative principles of our nature ought to go hand in hand with the practical ones; and, for my own part, when the former are so far pushed, as to leave the latter quite out of sight, I am always apt to suspect that we have transgressed our limits. If it should be asked—how far will these practical principles go ? I can only answer, that the former difficulty will recur, unless it be found that there is something in the intellectual part of our nature, resembling the moral sentiment in the moral part of our nature, which determines this, as it were, instinctively. Very possibly I have wrote nonsense. However, this notion first occurred to me at London, in conversation with a man of some depth of thinking; and talking of it since to your friend H. Home, he seems to entertain some notions nearly of the same kind, and to have pushed them much farther.

'This is but an idle digression, so I return to the Dialogue.

'With regard to the composition in general, I have nothing to observe, as it appears to me to be conducted with the greatest propriety, and the artifice in the beginning occasions, I think, a very agreeable surprise. I don't know, if, in the account of the modern manners, you [had] an eye to Bruyere's introduction to his translation of Theophrastes. If you had not, as he has a thought handled pretty much in that manner, perhaps looking into it might furnish some farther hints to embellish that part of your work.'[1]

[1] Life, vol. i. p. 323.

Hume replies:

'Your notion of correcting subtlety of sentiment, is certainly very just with regard to morals, which depend upon sentiment; and in politics and natural philosophy, whatever conclusion is contrary to certain matters of fact, must certainly be wrong, and there must some error lie somewhere in the argument, whether we be able to show it or not. But in metaphysics or theology, I cannot see how either of these plain and obvious standards of truth can have place. Nothing there can correct bad reasoning but good reasoning, and sophistry must be opposed by syllogisms. About seventy or eighty years ago, I observe, a principle like that which you advance prevailed very much in France among some philosophers and *beaux esprits*. The occasion of it was this: The famous Mons. Nicole of the Port Royal, in his *Perpétuité de la Foi*, pushed the Protestants very hard upon the impossibility of the people's reaching a conviction of their religion by the way of private judgment; which required so many disquisitions, reasonings, researches, eruditions, impartiality, and penetration, as not one in a hundred even among men of education, is capable of. Mons. Claude and the Protestants answered him, not by solving his difficulties (which seems impossible), but by retorting them (which is very easy). They showed that to reach the way of authority which the Catholics insist on, as long a train of acute reasoning, and as great erudition, was requisite, as would be sufficient for a Protestant. We must first prove all the truths of natural religion, the foundation of morals, the divine authority of the Scripture, the deference which it commands to the church, the tradition of the church, &c. The comparison of these controversial writings begot an idea in some, that it was neither by reasoning nor authority we learn our religion, but by sentiment: and certainly this were a very convenient way, and what a philosopher would be very well pleased to comply with, if he could distinguish sentiment from education. But to all appearance the sentiment of Stockholm, Geneva, Rome ancient and modern, Athens and Memphis, have the same characters; and no sensible man can implicitly assent to any of them, but from the general principle, that as the truth in these subjects is beyond human capacity, and that as for one's own ease he must adopt some tenets, there is most satisfaction and convenience in holding to the Catholicism we have been first taught. Now this I have nothing to say against. I have only to observe, that such a conduct is founded on the most universal and determined scepticism, joined to a little indolence; for more curiosity and research gives a direct opposite turn from the same principles.'[1]

During the same period Hume composed the 'Dialogues concerning Natural Religion,' of which Mr. Burton says:

'The manuscript of this work is full of emendations and corrections; and while the sentiments appear to be substantially the same as when they were first set down, the alterations in the method of announcing them are a register of the improvements in their author's style, for a period apparently of twenty-seven years. Here at least he could not plead the excuse of youth and indiscretion. The work, penned in the full vigour of his faculties, comes to us with the sanction of his mature years, and his approval when he was within sight of the grave. Whatever sentiments, therefore, in this work, may be justly found to excite censure, carry with them a reproach from which their author's name cannot escape.'[2]

Hume's friends prevailed on him not to publish the Dialogues, fearing that the odium under which he laboured, would be fanned to a flame, and the prospects of the author materially injured. In a letter to Elliot, dated March 12, 1763, he complains: 'Is it not hard and tyrannical in you, more hard and tyrannical than any act of the Stuarts, not to allow me to publish my Dialogues? Pray, do you not think that a proper dedication may atone for what is exceptionable in them? I am become of my friend Corbyn Morrice's mind, who says, that he writes all his books for the sake of the dedications.'[3] Such caution was unnecessary, when Hume settled down to pass the remainder of his days in ease and comfort at Edinburgh, enjoying an abundant income, and surrounded by a society of affectionate friends, familiar with his tenets and not likely to be estranged by any new publication of them. Yet the Dialogues remained in manuscript. The history of their posthumous publication will be found at p. 77.

These four years must have been the busiest period of Hume's lifetime. Not content with preparing the new edition of the Essay on the Human Understanding, and writing

[1] Life, vol. i. p. 325. [2] Ibid. p. 328. [3] Ibid. vol. ii. p. 146.

the companion treatise on Moral Philosophy, and with completing the Dialogues, he was all the while, as his correspondence shows, actively employed upon the Political Discourses, which were published in February 1752: 'the only work of mine that was successful on the first publication.' A reprint appeared before the close of the year.

After remarking on the value and fame of these essays, Mr. Burton proceeds to say:

'The "Political Discourses" introduced Hume to the literature of the continent. The works of Quesnay, Rivière, Mirabeau, Raynal, and Turgot, had not yet appeared, but the public mind of France had been opened for novel doctrines by the bold appeal of Vauban, and by the curious and original enquiries of Montesquieu. The Discourses appear to have been first translated by Eléazer Mauvillon, a native of Provence, and private secretary to Frederic Augustus, King of Poland, who published his translation in 1753. Another, and better known translation, by the Abbé Le Blanc, was published in 1754.'[1]

Perhaps, however, the Essay which is best known at the present day, is that on the Populousness of Ancient Nations: no inadequate monument of the author's reading and judgment. The first mention of it in his correspondence occurs in the letter to Dr. Clephane, April 18, 1750:

'You would perhaps ask, how I employ my time in this leisure and solitude, and what are my occupations? Pray, do you expect I should convey to you an encyclopedia, in the compass of a letter? The last thing I took my hand from was a very learned, elaborate discourse, concerning the populousness of antiquity; not altogether in opposition to *Vossius* and *Montesquieu*, who exaggerate that affair infinitely: but, starting some doubts, and scruples, and difficulties, sufficient to make us suspend our judgment on that head. Amongst other topics, it fell in my way to consider the greatness of ancient *Rome*; and in looking over the discourse, I find the following period. "If we may judge by the younger Pliny's account of his house, and by the plans of ancient buildings in Dr. Mead's collection, the men of quality had very spacious palaces, and their buildings were like the Chinese houses, where each apartment is separate from the rest, and rises no higher than a single story." Pray, on

[1] Life, vol. i. p. 365.

what authority are those plans founded? If I remember right, I was told they were discovered on the walls of the baths, and other subterraneous buildings. Is this the proper method of citing them? If you have occasion to communicate this to Dr. Mead, I beg that my sincere respects may be joined.'[1]

On February 18, 1751, he enquires again:

'When I take a second perusal of your letter, I find you resemble the Papists, who deal much in penitence, but neglect extremely *les bonnes œuvres*. I asked you a question with regard to the plans of ancient buildings in Dr. Mead's collection. Pray, are they authentic enough to be cited in a discourse of erudition and reasoning? have they never been published in any collection? and what are the proper terms in which I ought to cite them? I know you are a great proficient in the *virtu*, and consequently can resolve my doubts. This word I suppose you pretend to speak with an (e), which I own is an improvement: but admitting your orthography, you must naturally have a desire of doing a good-natured action, and instructing the ignorant.'[2]

In the Essay Bartoli's name appears, not Dr. Mead's.

On February 19, 1751, he writes to Elliot:

'I have amused myself lately with an essay or dissertation on the populousness of antiquity, which led me into many disquisitions concerning both the public and domestic life of the ancients. Having read over almost all the classics both Greek and Latin, since I formed that plan, I have extracted what served most to my purpose. But I have not a Strabo, and know not where to get one in this neighbourhood. He is an author I never read. I know your library—I mean the Advocates'—is scrupulous of lending classics; but perhaps that difficulty may be got over. I should be much obliged to you, if you could procure me the loan of a copy, either in the original language or even in a good translation.'[3]

Later on he returns Strabo, whom he has 'found very judicious and useful.'

The Essay was accompanied by the following note:

'An eminent clergyman in *Edinburgh*, having wrote, some years ago, a discourse on the same question with this, of the populousness of antient nations, was pleas'd lately to communicate it to the author. It maintain'd the opposite side

[1] Life, vol. i. p. 297. [2] Ibid. p. 316. [3] Ibid. p. 326.

of the argument, to what is here insisted on, and contained much erudition and good reasoning. The author acknowledges to have borrow'd, with some variations, from that discourse, two computations, that with regard to the number of inhabitants in *Belgium*, and that with regard to those in *Epirus*. If this learned gentleman be prevail'd on to publish his dissertation, it will serve to give great light into the present question, the most curious and important of all questions of erudition.'

Dr. Wallace accepted the invitation, and published his discourse the year following anonymously: 'A dissertation on the numbers of mankind in antient and modern times; with an appendix containing observations on the same subject, and remarks on Mr. Hume's discourse on the populousness of antient nations.' Hence in the editions from 1756 to 1768 another note was substituted for the preceding:

'An ingenious writer has honoured this discourse with an answer, full of politeness, erudition, and good sense. So learned a refutation would have made the author suspect, that his reasonings were entirely overthrown, had he not used the precaution, from the beginning, to keep himself on the sceptical side; and having taken this advantage of the ground, he was enabled, tho' with much inferior forces, to preserve himself from a total defeat. That Reverend gentleman will always find, where his antagonist is so entrenched, that it will be difficult to force him. VARRO, in such a situation, could defend himself against HANNIBAL, PHARNACES against CÆSAR. The author, however, very willingly acknowledges, that his antagonist has detected many mistakes both in his authorities and reasonings; and it was owing entirely to that gentleman's indulgence, that many more errors were not remarked. In this edition, advantage has been taken of his learned animadversions, and the Essay has been rendered less imperfect than formerly.'

Nevertheless, the corrections introduced at Dr. Wallace's suggestion are very few, and the vast majority of the 'animadversions' were passed over in silence. A misquotation from Livy was omitted:[1] a paragraph was inserted quoting Justin[2]; a new note was given to strengthen the argument about Thebes:[3] and a trifling correction was introduced in a

[1] Page 386. [2] Page 425. [3] Page 422.

reference to Diodorus.¹ Perhaps this list exhausts the alterations which were due to Dr. Wallace.²

The circumstances under which the paper, Of the Protestant Succession, was inserted in this volume, have already been detailed.³

In 1752 Hume was appointed Keeper of the Advocates' Library. This position, giving him 'the command of a large library,' finally determined him to gratify his long cherished design of writing history, and from this time he almost abandoned philosophy. The first volume of the History of Great Britain, containing the reigns of James I. and Charles I., appeared in the autumn of 1754. Previously, however, he had collected the varied labours of thirteen years in a uniform edition, in four volumes; the first three being published in 1753, and the fourth in 1754. In a letter to Adam Smith, September 24, 1752, he says:

'I am just now diverted for a moment, by correcting my "Essays Moral and Political," for a new edition. If any thing occur to you to be inserted or retrenched, I shall be obliged to you for the hint. In case you should not have the last edition by you, I shall send you a copy of it. In that edition I was engaged to act contrary to my judgment, in retaining the sixth and seventh Essays, which I had resolved to throw out, as too frivolous for the rest, and not very agreeable neither, even in that trifling manner: but Millar, my bookseller, made such protestations against it, and told me how much he had heard them praised by the best judges, that the bowels of a parent melted, and I preserved them alive.'⁴

For the second time Hume relented; no change was made in the list of contents, but the numerous notes added in this edition, abounding in references to Greek and Latin literature, show how well he used the Advocates' Library.

About this period Hume began a translation of Plutarch's Lives, but soon laid it aside. He declined an invitation from Millar to edit a newspaper in London. In 1756 the second volume of the History brought down the narrative to the Revolution.

---

¹ Page 424.
² He also objected, that he could not find the passage referred to in Isocrates' Panegyric (note 6, p. 390), but no notice was taken of the objection.
³ Vol. i. p. 449.
⁴ Life, vol. i. p. 375.

In 1755 Hume wrote to Millar:

'I give you a great many thanks for thinking of me in your project of a weekly paper. I approve very much of the design, as you explain it to me; and there is nobody I would more willingly engage with. But, as I have another work in hand, which requires great labour and care to finish, I cannot think of entering on a new undertaking, till I have brought this to a conclusion. Your scheme would require me immediately to remove to London; and I live here, at present, in great tranquillity, with all my books around me; and I cannot think of changing while I have so great a work in hand as the finishing of my History.

'There are four short Dissertations, which I have kept some years by me, in order to polish them as much as possible. One of them is that which Allan Ramsay mentioned to you. Another, of the Passions; a third, of Tragedy; a fourth, some Considerations previous to Geometry and Natural Philosophy. The whole, I think, would make a volume, a fourth less than my Inquiry, as nearly as I can calculate; but it would be proper to print it in a larger type, in order to bring it to the same size and price. I would have it published about the new year; and I offer you the property for fifty guineas, payable at the publication. You may judge, by my being so moderate in my demands, that I do not propose to make any words about the bargain. It would be more convenient for me to print here, especially one of the Dissertations, where there is a good deal of literature; but, as the manuscript is distinct and accurate, it would not be impossible for me to correct it, though printed at London. I leave it to your choice; though I believe that it might be as cheaply and conveniently and safely executed here. However, the matter is pretty near indifferent to me.'[1]

The volume was not completed until early in 1757, when it appeared with the following title 'Four Dissertations. 1. The Natural History of Religion. 2. Of the Passions. 3. Of Tragedy. 4. Of the Standard of Taste. By David Hume, Esq.'

From this list of contents 'the Considerations previous to Geometry and Natural Philosophy' will be missed: they were never published. There can be no doubt that they embodied Part II. Book I. of the Treatise. Why they were withdrawn, we can only conjecture: perhaps the author

[1] Life, vol. i. p. 421.

despaired of the subject being popular. The dissertation on the Passions is a series of extracts verbatim from the second volume of the Treatise. The Natural History of Religion is no doubt the Dissertation, 'where there is a good deal of literature,—which Allan Ramsay mentioned to you.' The periphrasis under which Hume alludes to it, was probably due to his presentiment that its arguments would be offensive to many readers.

Dr. Warburton saw a copy of the book, before it was published, and wrote to Millar, asking for its suppression.[1]

'February 7, 1757.

'SIR,—I supposed you would be glad to know what sort of book it is which you are about to publish with Hume's name and yours to it. The design of the first essay is the very same with all Lord Bolingbroke's, to establish *naturalism*, a species of atheism, instead of religion; and he employs one of Bolingbroke's capital arguments for it. All the difference is, it is without Bolingbroke's abusive language.

'All the good his mutilation and fitting it up for the public has done, is only to add to its other follies that of contradiction. He is establishing atheism; and in one single line of a long essay professes to believe Christianity. All this I shall show in a very few words on a proper occasion.

'In the mean time, if you think you have not money enough, and can satisfy your conscience, you will do well to publish it; for there is no doubt of the sale among a people so feverish, that to-day they burn with superstition, and to-morrow freeze with atheism. But the day of the publication and the *fast day* will be an admirable contrast to one another.

'I dare say you knew nothing of the contents; but the caution of poor Mr. K. was admirable on a like occasion with this very man, Hume. He wrote to Mr. K. to offer him a copy, that had nothing to do with religion, as he said. Mr. K. replied, that might be; but as he had given great offence, and he (Mr. K.) was himself no judge of these matters, he desired to be excused.

'You have often told me of this man's moral virtues. He may have many, for aught I know; but let me observe to you, there are vices of the *mind* as well as of the *body*; and I think a wickeder mind, and more obstinately bent on public mischief, I never knew. W. W.'

Of this book Hume says in his Autobiography:

[1] Warburton's Unpublished Papers, p. 309.

'In this interval, I published at London my Natural History of Religion, along with some other small pieces: its public entry was rather obscure, except only that Dr. Hurd wrote a pamphlet against it, with all the illiberal petulance, arrogance, and scurrility, which distinguish the Warburtonian school. This pamphlet gave me some consolation for the otherwise indifferent reception of my performance.'

The pamphlet in question, which was anonymous and dedicated to Warburton, was the joint product of Warburton and Hurd. The latter tells the narrative of their pious fraud with great simplicity:

'This book came out early in 1757, and falling into the hands of Dr. Warburton, provoked him, by its uncommon licentiousness, to enter on the margin, as he went along, such remarks as occurred to him; and when that was too narrow to contain them all, he put down the rest on loose scraps of paper, which he stuck between the leaves. In this state the book was shown to me (as I chanced at that time to be in London with the author) merely as matter of curiosity, and to give me an idea of the contents, how mischievous and extravagant they were. He had then written remarks on about two-thirds of the volume: And I liked them so well, that I advised him, by all means, to carry them on through the remaining parts of it, and then to fit them up, in what way he thought best, for public use, which I told him they very well deserved. He put by this proposal slightly; but, when I pressed him again on this head, some time after, in a letter from Cambridge, he wrote me the following answer: "As to Hume, I had laid it aside ever since you were here. I will now, however, finish my skeleton. It will be hardly that. If then you think anything can be made of it, and will give yourself the trouble, we may perhaps between us do a little good, which I dare say, we shall both think will be worth a little pains. If I have any force in the first rude beating out the mass, you are best able to give it the elegance of form and splendour of polish. This will answer my purpose, to labour together in a joint work to do a little good. I will tell you fairly, it is no more the thing it should be, than the Dantzick iron at the forge is the gilt and painted ware at Birmingham. It will make no more than a pamphlet; but you shall take your own time, and make it your summer's amusement, if you will. I propose it bear something like this title—'Remarks on Mr. Hume's late Essay, called, *The Natural History of Religion*, by a Gentleman of Cambridge, in a Letter to the Rev. Dr. Warburton.'—I propose the address should be with the dryness and reserve of a stranger, who likes the method of the Letters on Bolingbroke's philosophy, and follows it here, against the same sort of writer, inculcating the same impiety, Naturalism, and employing the same kind of arguments. The address will remove it from me; the author, a Gentleman of Cambridge, from you; and the secrecy of printing, from us both." I saw by this letter, he was not disposed to take much trouble about the thing. Accordingly his papers were soon after sent down to me at Cambridge, pretty much in the state I had seen them in at London, so far as they then went, only with additional entries in the latter part of the book. However, in this careless detached form, I thought his observations too good to be lost. And the hint of the *Address* suggested the means of preserving them, without any injury to his reputation, and indeed without much labour to myself. Having, therefore, transcribed the Remarks, with little alteration, I only wrote a short introduction and conclusion, merely to colour the proposed fiction, and in this form, sent them to the press. When Dr. Warburton saw the pamphlet, he said, I should have done much more, and worked up his hasty remarks in my own way. He doubted, also, whether the contrivance, as I had managed it, would not be seen through. But in this he was mistaken; for the disguise, as thin as it was, answered its purpose in keeping the real author out of sight. Mr. Hume in particular (understanding, I suppose, from his bookseller, who was also mine, that the manuscript came from me) was the first to fall into the trap. He was much hurt, and no wonder, by so lively an attack upon him, and could not help confessing it in what he calls his *own Life*; in which he has thought fit to honour me with greater marks of his resentment, than any other of the writers against him: nay the spiteful man goes so far as to upbraid me with being a *follower* (indeed, a closer, in this instance, than he apprehended) *of the Warburtonian school*. This idle story would not have been worth the telling, but for the reason already given, That I could not, in justice to the author, take the merit of so fine a work to myself. And yet in disclaiming it, the reader sees, I make but an awkward figure, as being obliged to open the secret of our little stratagem, in which the grace of it mainly consists.'[1]

The 'thin disguise' was more than suspected by Hume. who wrote to Millar, September 3, 1757.

'Apropos to anger; I am positively assured, that Dr. Warburton wrote that letter to himself, which you sent me; and indeed the style discovers him sufficiently. I should answer him; but he attacks so small a corner of my building, that I can abandon it without drawing great consequences after it. If he would come into the field and dispute concerning the principal topics of my philosophy, I should probably accept the challenge: at present nothing could tempt me to take the pen in hand but anger, of which I feel myself incapable, even upon this provocation. . . . .

'I should not be displeased that you read to Dr. Warburton, the paragraph in the first page of my letter, with regard to himself. The hopes of getting an answer, might probably engage him to give us something farther of the same kind; which, at least, saves you the expense of advertising. I see the doctor likes a literary squabble.'[2]

At the time when the Dissertations were printing, Hume was in ecstasies over the merit of 'Douglas,' and wrote a Dedication to Home. But before the volume appeared, he withdrew it for fear of injuring Home's prospects in the Kirk. Shortly afterwards Home resigned his living, and Hume directed that the Dedication should be restored. It is found in some copies, and not in others. Hume's correspondence contains the following passages on the subject:

To Adam Smith.

'The dedication to John Home, you have probably seen; for I find it has been inserted in some of the weekly papers, both here and in London. Some of my friends thought it was indiscreet in me to make myself responsible to the public, for the productions of another. But the author had lain under such singular and unaccountable obstructions in his road to fame, that I thought it incumbent on his well-wishers to go as much out of the common road to assist him. I believe the composition of the dedication will be esteemed very prudent, and not inelegant.'[3]

[1] Hurd's *Life of Warburton*. [2] *Life*, vol. ii. p. 35. [3] Ibid. p. 17.

To Andrew Millar.

'The dedication of my Dissertations to Mr. Hume was shown to some of his friends here, men of very good sense, who were seized with an apprehension that it would hurt that party in the church, with which he had always been connected, and would involve him, and them of consequence, in the suspicion of infidelity. Neither he nor I were in the least affected with their panic; but to satisfy them, we agreed to stand by the arbitration of one person, of great rank and of known prudence; and I promised them to write to you to suspend the publication for one post, in case you should have resolved to publish it presently. Next post you shall be sure to hear from me; and if we be obliged to suppress it, you'll be pleased to place the charges of print and paper to my account.'[1]

To William Mure.

'Pray, whether do you pity or blame me most, with regard to this dedication of my Dissertations to my friend, the poet? I am sure I never executed any thing which was either more elegant in the composition, or more generous in the intention; yet such an alarm seized some fools here, (men of very good sense, but fools in that particular,) that they assailed both him and me with the utmost violence; and engaged us to change our intention. I wrote to Millar to suppress that dedication; two posts after, I retracted that order. Can any thing be more unlucky than that, in the interval of these four days, he should have opened his sale, and disposed of eight hundred copies, without that dedication, whence, I imagined, my friend would reap some advantage, and myself so much honour? I have not been so heartily vexed at any accident of a long time. However, I have insisted that the dedication shall still be published.'[2]

The Preface, which was not reprinted, runs thus:

To the Reverend Mr. Hume, Author of 'Douglas,' a Tragedy.

'MY DEAR SIR,—It was the practice of the antients to address their compositions only to friends and equals, and to render their dedications monuments of regard and affection,

---

[1] Life, vol. ii. p. 18.   [2] Ibid. p. 21.

not of servility and flattery. In those days of ingenuous and candid liberty, a dedication did honour to the person to whom it was addressed, without degrading the author. If any partiality appeared towards the patron, it was at least the partiality of friendship and affection.

'Another instance of true liberty, of which antient times can alone afford us an example, is the liberty of thought, which engaged men of letters, however different in their abstract opinions, to maintain a mutual friendship and regard; and never to quarrel about principles, while they agreed in inclinations and manners. Science was often the subject of disputation, never of animosity. *Cicero*, an academic, addressed his philosophical treatises, sometimes to *Brutus*, a stoic; sometimes to *Atticus*, an epicurean.

'I have been seized with a strong desire of renewing these laudable practices of antiquity, by addressing the following dissertations to you, my good friend: For such I will ever call and esteem you, notwithstanding the opposition, which prevails between us, with regard to many of our speculative tenets. These differences of opinion I have only found to enliven our conversation; while our common passion for science and letters served as a cement to our friendship. I still admired your genius, even when I imagined, that you lay under the influence of prejudice; and you sometimes told me, that you excused my errors, on account of the candor and sincerity, which, you thought, accompanied them.

'But to tell truth, it is less my admiration of your fine genius, which has engaged me to make this address to you, than my esteem of your character and my affection to your person. That generosity of mind which ever accompanies you; that cordiality of friendship, that spirited honour and integrity, have long interested me strongly in your behalf, and have made me desirous, that a monument of our mutual amity should be publicly erected, and, if possible, be preserved to posterity.

'I own too, that I have the ambition to be the first who shall in public express his admiration of your noble tragedy of Douglas; one of the most interesting and pathetic pieces, that was ever exhibited on any theatre. Should I give it the preference to the *Merope* of *Maffei*, and to that of *Voltaire*, which it resembles in its subject; should I affirm, that it contained more fire and spirit than the former, more tenderness and simplicity than the latter; I might be accused of partiality: And how could I entirely acquit myself, after the professions of friendship, which I have made you? But the unfeigned tears which flowed from every eye, in the numerous representations which were made of it on this theatre; the unparalleled command, which you appeared to have over every affection of the human breast: These are incontestible proofs, that you possess the true theatric genius of *Shakespear* and *Otway*, refined from the unhappy barbarism of the one, and licentiousness of the other.

My enemies, you know, and, I own, even sometimes my friends, have reproached me with the love of paradoxes and singular opinions; and I expect to be exposed to the same imputation, on account of the character which I have here given of your DOUGLAS. I shall be told, no doubt, that I had artfully chosen the only time, when this high esteem of that piece could be regarded as a paradox, to wit, before its publication; and that not being able to contradict in this particular the sentiments of the public, I have, at least, resolved to go before them. But I shall be amply compensated for all these pleasantries, if you accept this testimony of my regard, and believe me to be, with the greatest sincerity,

'Dear Sir,
'Your most affectionate Friend,
and humble Servant,
'DAVID HUME.

'EDINBURGH: 3 *January*, 1757.'

The history of this volume is not yet concluded. It is now proved that Hume originally intended to include in it Essays on Suicide and on the Immortality of the Soul, and that they were already in print, when he yielded to his dislike to stirring a nest of hornets, and sent orders for them to be expunged.

He was extremely anxious that no copy containing these Essays should remain in existence: what then was his annoyance on finding that Wilkes was possessed of one? He writes to Millar, April 23, 1764:

'I never see Mr. Wilkes here but at chapel, where he is a most regular, and devout, and edifying, and pious attendant; I take him to be entirely regenerate. He told me last Sunday, that you had given him a copy of my Dissertations, with the two which I had suppressed; and that he, foreseeing danger, from the sale of his library, had wrote to you to find out that copy, and to tear out the two obnoxious dissertations. Pray how stands that fact? It was imprudent in you to intrust him with that copy: it was very prudent in him to use that precaution. Yet I do not naturally suspect you of imprudence, nor him of prudence. I must hear a little farther before I pronounce.'[1]

Millar replied:

'I take Mr. Wilkes to be the same man he was,—acting a part. He has forgot the story of the *two* dissertations. The fact is, upon importunity, I lent to him the only copy I preserved, and for years never could recollect he had it, till his books came to be sold; upon this I went immediately to the gentleman that directed the sale, told him the fact, and reclaimed the two dissertations which were my property. Mr. Coates, who was the person, immediately delivered me the volume; and so soon as I got home, I tore them out and burnt them, that I might not lend them to any for the future. Two days after, Mr. Coates sent me a note for the volume, as Mr. Wilkes had desired it should be sent to him at Paris; I returned the volume, but told him the two dissertations, I had torn out of the volume and burnt, being my property. This is the truth of the matter, and nothing but the truth. It was certainly imprudent for me to lend them to him.'[2]

It was no secret, however, that some Essays had been suppressed. The volume itself preserves the traces of mutilation, and Dr. Warburton, in his letter to Millar, alluded to it. So too Dr. Horne, in his letter to Adam Smith, dated 1777, enquired, 'when the great work of *benevolence* and *charity*, of *wisdom* and *virtue*, shall be crowned by the publication of a treatise designed to prove the SOUL'S MORTALITY, and another to justify and recommend SELF-MURDER; for which, without doubt, the present and every future age will bless the name of the *gentle* and *amiable* author.' From the 'Gentleman's Magazine' for July 1777, it appears that rumour had magnified the number and the wickedness of the Essays: the reviewer speaks of 'the tracts in defence of suicide, adultery, &c., whose publication, if we are rightly informed, authority has hitherto prevented.' A correspondent

[1] Life, vol. ii. p. 202.   [2] Ibid.

326) instances suicide and adultery
praiseworthy according to Hume's
to say: 'If report says true, and
Essay on Suicide has been published,
public authority. A great legacy was
seller to publish it again, and, on his
others; and when the more generous
refused to give birth to such a na-
tched into Holland, to return hither,
pestilential influence over the fellow-
citizens of the *good*, the *humane*, the
story of the legacy is evidently due
facts' with the Dialogues concerning
the publication of which Hume had
which had not yet appeared. The
facts' had once been published, and
public authority, is no doubt an error,
with great circumstantiality in the
Gentleman's Magazine' for August 1784: p. 607. 'These Essays, it is well known, were printed and advertised by Mr. Millar, with some others by Mr. Hume, near thirty years ago; but before the day of publication, being intimidated by threats of a prosecution, the bookseller called in some copies that he had dispersed, cancelled the two Essays, and (with difficulty) prevailed on Mr. Hume to substitute some others less obnoxious.' This story does not appear to be consistent with Hume's mention of the suppression in his letter to Millar; and nothing in 'the Life of Hume' renders it probable.

In 1784 a book was published with the following title-page: 'Essays on Suicide and the Immortality of the Soul, ascribed to the late David Hume, Esq. Never before published. With REMARKS, intended as an Antidote to the Poison contained in these Performances, by the Editor; To which is added, Two letters on Suicide, from Rosseau's Eloisa. London: Printed for M. Smith; and sold by the Booksellers in Piccadilly, Fleet Street, and Paternoster Row. 1783. Price 3*s*. 6*d*. sewed.'

The Editor's Preface runs as follows:

'These two Essays on *Suicide* and the *Immortality of the Soul*, though not published in any edition of his works, are generally attributed to the late ingenious Mr. Hume.

'The well-known contempt of this eminent philosopher for

the common convictions of mankind, raised an apprehension of the contents from the very title of these pieces. But the celebrity of the author's name, renders them, notwithstanding, in some degree objects of great curiosity.

'Owing to this circumstance, a few copies have been clandestinely circulated, at a large price, for some time, but without any comment. The very mystery attending this mode of selling them, made them more an object of request than they would otherwise have been.

'The present publication comes abroad under no such restraint, and possesses very superior advantages. The *Notes* annexed are intended to expose the sophistry contained in the original Essays, and may show how little we have to fear from the adversaries of these great truths, from the pitiful figure which even Mr. Hume makes in thus violently exhausting his last strength in an abortive attempt to traduce or discredit them.

'The two very masterly Letters from the Eloisa of Rosseau on the subject of *Suicide*, have been much celebrated, and we hope will be considered as materially increasing the value of this curious collection.

'The admirers of *Mr. Hume* will be pleased with seeing the remains of a favourite author rescued in this manner from that oblivion, to which the prejudices of his countrymen had, in all appearance, consigned them; and even the religious part of mankind have some reason of triumph, from the striking instance here given of truth's superiority to error, even when error has all the advantage of an elegant genius, and a great literary reputation to recommend it.'

The third paragraph probably alludes to copies of the original proof-sheets; but the statement of the title-page, that the Essays had not previously been printed, is untrue. They had been published in 1777, without the printer's name. A copy in the British Museum has for title-page: 'Two Essays. London. M.DCC.LXVII. Price Five Shillings.' There is no preface, note, or comment. The Essays are word for word the same with those of 1784. It is possible that this is the Edition, printed in Holland, to which the writer in the 'Gentleman's Magazine' referred: but, if so, he had not seen the book, for he only knows the subject of one of the Essays.

These 'tracts,' as they appear in these two editions, had

generally been accepted as genuine, partly on the evidence of style, and partly because of the silence of Hume's friends, who were challenged to disavow them. But no direct evidence was known to exist, until the Advocates' Library became possessed of a bound copy of proof-sheets of the original volume; corrected, it appears, by Hume, and containing one of the Essays in question. The book has the following note:

'This book contains a piece of Mr. D. Hume's, of which there is, I believe, but another copy existing. Having printed the volume as it here stands, Mr. Hume was advised by a friend, to suppress the Dissertation upon Suicide; which he accordingly did. A copy, however, had somehow got into the hands of Mr. Muirhead, a man of letters, who had made a very valuable collection of books. Mr. Hume, after the death of Mr. Muirhead, employed me to beg that copy from his nephew, who very politely delivered it up. Upon this Mr. Hume gave me leave to keep the present copy, which he had lent me: I promising not to show it to any body.

'A. R.'

These are believed to be the initials of Allan Ramsay. There is no title-page; but at the beginning there is written, perhaps in Hume's handwriting: 'Five Dissertations, to wit, The Natural History of Religion. Of the Passions. Of Tragedy. Of Suicide. Of the Immortality of the Soul.' In this copy the Essay on Suicide has been cut out; but the companion Essay remains in its entirety. Allan Ramsay's note informs us, that it was the former of these which Hume's friend called in question:—and his phrase confirms the belief that the writers in the 'Gentleman's Magazine' blundered in stating that the book was published and suppressed by public authority; but he leaves it doubtful whether the copy, when Hume gave it him, contained both Essays, or not; and when and by whom the Dissertation on Suicide was cut out. However this may be, as the Essay on the Immortality of the Soul in this copy is identical with that which was published under the same title, first in 1777, and then again in 1783, there can be no reasonable doubt that the Essay on Suicide, which was printed with it on both occasions, is also genuine.

As has been said, the 'Four Dissertations' is a volume, which shows signs of mutilation: and, in brief, its history seems to have been this. (i.) The Dissertations on Geometry, on the Natural History of Religion, on Tragedy, and on the Passions were in manuscript in 1755. (ii.) The first of these never went to the press. (iii.) Between 1755 and 1757 Hume wrote the two Essays on Suicide and on the Immortality of the Soul. (iv.) The five remaining Dissertations were then printed in the above order, the first three occupying 200 pages, and ending with the fourth sheet of signature K. The Essay on Suicide began on K 5; and was followed by the Essay on the Immortality of the Soul. (v.) First, the Essay on Suicide was cut out; leaving the next Essay to begin in Allan Ramsay's copy at L 4. Afterwards, this was also destroyed, and, to make a volume of decent size, a new Dissertation, On the Standard of Taste, was written, and printed on a new signature, L; so that K 4 to 6 appear as mutilated strips of leaves. The ten missing sheets in Ramsay's copy would exactly accommodate the Essay on Suicide.

In 1758 the Four Dissertations were combined with the rest of Hume's literary works, and published in a quarto edition of one volume, with the title-page, 'Essays and Treatises on several Subjects, by David Hume, Esq.; a new edition:' and with the following Advertisement: 'Some Alterations are made on the Titles of the Treatises, contained in the following Volume. What in former Editions was called *Essays Moral and Political*, is here entitled *Essays, Moral, Political and Literary*, Part I. The *Political Discourses* form the second Part. What in former Editions was called, *Philosophical Essays concerning Human Understanding* is here entitled *An Enquiry concerning Human Understanding*. The *Four Dissertations* lately published are dispersed thro' different Parts of this Volume.' None of the contents of the previous editions were omitted, with the exception of the Dedication to John Home; but after the book had been printed and paged, two new Essays were bound up with it, arriving too late to be inserted in the list of contents. These are the papers on the Jealousy of Trade and on the Coalition of Parties. This was the first edition that added an Index, 'which cost him more trouble than he was aware of when he began it.'[1]

From this time the editions assume a settled shape, and

---

[1] Life, vol. ii. p. 36.

may be enumerated briefly. In 1760 they were published in four volumes, duodecimo: in 1764, in two volumes, octavo; when the three Essays on Impudence and Modesty, on Love and Marriage, and on the Study of History, whose fate had long been trembling on the balance, were omitted; and Section VI. Part I. of the Enquiry concerning the Principles of Morals was degraded to the Appendix, where it appeared with the heading, Of some Verbal Disputes. In 1768, there was a quarto edition of two volumes, with a portrait of the Author by Donaldson. In 1770, the edition consisted of four volumes, octavo; the Essay on Avarice was omitted; and the whole of the contents had been carefully revised, so that this ranks with the edition of 1754 as containing more important changes than any of the intermediate ones. Finally, in 1777 appeared the posthumous and authoritative edition, in which there were few changes of expression: on the other hand, a new Essay, on the Origin of Government, and the famous Advertisement, which has been quoted at page 37, were added: and what had hitherto been Section II. Part I. of the Enquiry concerning the Principles of Morals was transferred to the Appendix with the title, Of Self Love.

It has already been observed that Hume bestowed extraordinary pains upon preparing the various editions of his Essays for the press, and a few of the changes have been noted. It may be interesting to review briefly the variations of sentiment which come to the surface. In politics, for instance, as he grew older, he became a confirmed opponent of the Whigs, and the successive editions of his History were marked by an effort to be rid of 'the plaguy prejudices of Whiggism,'[1] which shows itself particularly in the narrative of the seventeenth century. The Essays were from time to time modified in the same direction. In Editions A to P the second Essay, 'Of the Liberty of the Press,' contained a long discussion of the question, 'Whether the unlimited exercise of this liberty be advantageous or prejudicial to the public;' and decided strongly in the former sense: Edition Q, in 1770, dropt the discussion. This, however, is the strongest instance: most of the other omissions or corrections, so far as concerned English politics, were due to the fact, that the public had ceased to discuss such points as Instructions, and

[1] Life, vol. ii. p. 144.

that impartial observation on the history and conduct of the Court and Country Parties was obsolete.

The study of English History appears to have occasioned but few alterations in statements of fact: the clearest being on the first page of 'The Balance of Trade,'[1] where Editions N and O vary with the progress of his 'History.' The course of contemporary politics relieved him of the fear that Europe would be swallowed up by enormous monarchies;[2] and in 1770 he omitted passages which boasted of England as the bulwark against French aggression.[3] As regards the Roman Catholic religion, and indeed religion generally, he softened or withdrew offensive expressions, though the general tenor of his sentiments remained unchanged, and in 1770 he added a paragraph on the doctrine of the Intention of the Priest, characterizing it as positive, arrogant, and dogmatical.[4] There is a marked change in his opinion of Lord Bolingbroke, who, up to 1748, was instanced as 'a cultivated genius for oratory:' the citation was changed in the next edition, when also praise of his oratory was modified in another passage.[5] At the same time he omitted an invective against Dr. Swift, as an author, 'who has more humour than knowledge, more taste than judgment, and more spleen, prejudice, and passion than any of these qualities:' however to the last he was called the first Englishman to write polite prose.[6] Rapin had a sudden downfall in his good graces. In the edition of 1752 he is styled 'the most judicious of historians;' Edition K in 1754—the year in which the first volume of the History of the Stuarts was published—censures his 'usual malignity and partiality.'[7]

The general development of style may easily be seen, by comparing either the Treatise or the Essays which only appeared in Edition A with the language of the text, as he finally left it. A few words and phrases deserve special notice. For some years he invariably wrote Britain, not Great Britain. 'Something of the Misanthrope'[8] was struck out in 1770. From 1742 to 1748 he wrote, 'to the Œstrum or Verve of the poets:'[9] from 1754 to 1768 it is their 'Œstrum or native enthusiasm:' in 1770 the barbarous

---

[1] Vol. iii. p. 331.
[2] Vol. iii. p. 355.
[3] Vol. iii. pp. 353, 476.
[4] In a note to the Enquiry Concerning the Principles of Morals, sec. iii.
[5] Vol. iii. pp. 170, 173.
[6] Vol. iii. pp. 332, 159.
[7] Vol. iii. p. 473.
[8] Vol. iii. p. 151.
[9] Vol. iii. p. 197.

word disappeared. In 1748 he replaced 'Gaieté de Cœur' by 'gaiety of heart.'[1] Up to 1754 he apologized for speaking of the absurd naivety of Sancho Panza, 'a word which I have borrow'd from the *French*, and which is wanted in our language:'[2] in 1758 the apology was thought unnecessary. Lastly, we may notice that in 1770 he dropt the obsolete phrase, 'the stated clubs at the inns.'[3]

On reviewing the history of Hume's literary and philosophical works, we are at once struck by the suddenness with which his labours in philosophy came to an end. The Treatise on Human Nature was written when he was five-and-twenty: that is, in the beginning of 1736; it was published in 1739–40, and after that date he wrote little that was new. The Essay on Miracles was already drafted in manuscript. The Enquiries are for the most part popular reproductions. Even a large portion of the Essays appears to have been written before 1739. The only additions which philosophy received from Hume, are to be found in the Natural History of Religion and the Dialogues concerning Natural Religion: the latter were written before 1751, and the former 'he had kept some years by him' in 1755. To be brief: Hume's contributions to metaphysics were written by 1736, when he was five-and-twenty: his contribution to the philosophy of religion, by 1750, when he was thirty-nine: and after this date he added nothing.

Various theories have been invented to account for this. It has been suggested that the negative character of Hume's speculation reacted upon their author, chilling the earnest spirit of enquiry which had composed the Treatise, and reconciling him to lazy acquiescence. It is said that indifference of this sort explains the candour and impartiality with which Hume treated the political disputes of his day. The same supposition has been adduced to explain the habitual irony with which he wrote on religious topics. Mr. Hunt, following the late Professor Maurice, adopts language to a similar effect.

'The title generally applied to Hume is that of Sceptic, and this both in philosophy and religion. He follows experience till he finds there is something beyond experience. Then he either acknowledges that we must fall back upon natural instincts, and trust to reason, such as it is, or he

[1] Vol. iii. p. 230. [2] Vol. iii. p. 240. [3] Vol. iii. p. 320.

gives way to despair, and with an easy indifference flings the problem aside as insoluble, bidding us be content with our ignorance, for all is an enigma, a riddle, and a mystery. These two states of mind are clearly distinguishable in Hume. They are both called Scepticism, yet they are so different that the one leads to inquiry, the other to indolence. The one was a quality of his own keen intellect, the other was learned in France.'[1] Had this evil scepticism been attributed to the effect of French literature, the charge would have been more difficult to prove or disprove: worded as it is, it throws a burden of proof upon Mr. Hunt. He has already promised that he will not refer to the Treatise; his allusion, therefore, is to the Enquiry concerning the Human Understanding, which was published eleven years after Hume's return from France. Neither the Treatise nor the Essays which followed are characterised by indolent scepticism; the malady, therefore, was latent for these eleven years.

A more commonplace explanation may be suggested. Hume had brought his criticism of the philosophy of experience to a point, where, as he saw clearly, negation had done its work, and either he must leave the subject, or else attempt a reconstruction. For the latter Hume certainly lacked the disposition, and probably the ability: few philosophers have been at once critical and constructive. He turned to the philosophy of religion, a subject which throughout his life exercised a strong fascination upon him; but his friends would not suffer him to publish his maturest questionings. Meanwhile an early taste for politics and history was growing upon him. His discussion of political questions gained the praise of Bishop Butler: the Political Discourses ran into a second edition within the year. Yet he retained a firm belief in the value of his metaphysical speculations: he was willing to explain points here and there in letters to personal friends, and he was determined that at least some portion of his discoveries should win the ear of the public. It must also be borne in mind that he was by no means rich; that from early life he had looked to his pen to win a competency: and that on various occasions he showed a Scotch tenacity in the pursuit of money. On reviewing the Treatise, he must have seen that the general result gave him a vantage-ground from which he could ply the weapons of

[1] Contemporary Review, May, 1869; p. 80.

scepticism and irony in a novel and popular fashion; but that if he maintained the earnest spirit of his youth, he must be content to remain unread. He selected for 'recasting' precisely those portions which lent themselves to this manner, and which were likely to excite public attention. To this day, although his fame is established, few students of philosophy turn to the Treatise.

The candour of the political Essays is also capable of explanation from his life and character. Naturally of a sensitive, irritable disposition, the ideal which he set before himself, was all that was dignified and judicial.

The following narrative of the circumstances attending the posthumous publication of the Dialogues concerning Natural Religion is borrowed from Mr. Burton:—

'He appointed Smith his literary executor, in the following terms: "To my friend Dr. Adam Smith, late Professor of Moral Philosophy in Glasgow, I leave all my manuscripts without exception, desiring him to publish my 'Dialogues on Natural Religion,' which are comprehended in this present bequest; but to publish no other papers which he suspects not to have been written within these five years, but to destroy them all at his leisure. And I even leave him full power over all my papers, except the Dialogues above mentioned; and though I can trust to that intimate and sincere friendship, which has ever subsisted between us, for his faithful execution of this part of my will, yet, as a small recompense of his pains in correcting and publishing this work, I leave him two hundred pounds, to be paid immediately after the publication of it."[1] . . . .

'Previous to his journey to Bath, Hume appears to have informed Smith of the desire expressed in his will, that he should undertake the publication of the "Dialogues on Natural Religion." The intimation was probably verbal, as it does not form part of any letter among Hume's papers. Elliot was opposed to the publication of this work. Blair pleaded strongly for its suppression; and Smith, who had made up his mind that he would not edit the work, seems to have desired that the testamentary injunction laid on him might be revoked. Hume, however, before his death, took effectual steps to guard against its suppression.

'Thus, after having good-naturedly abstained, for nearly

[1] Life, vol. ii. p. 489.

thirty years, from the publication of a work, which might give pain and umbrage to his dearest friends; at the close of life, and when the lapse of time since it was written might have been supposed to render him indifferent to its fate,—because there appeared some danger of its final suppression, he took decided and well-pondered steps to avert from it this fate. Such was the character of the man!

Hume to Adam Smith.

"London, May 3, 1776

'"My dear Friend,—I send you enclosed an ostensible letter, conformably to your desire. I think, however, your scruples groundless. Was Mallet any wise hurt by his publication of Lord Bolingbroke? He received an office afterwards from the present king and Lord Bute, the most prudish men in the world; and he always justified himself by his sacred regard to the will of a dead friend. At the same time, I own that your scruples have a specious appearance. But my opinion is, that if upon my death you determine never to publish these papers, you should leave them sealed up with my brother and family, with some inscription that you reserve to yourself the power of reclaiming them whenever you think proper. If I live a few years longer, I shall publish them myself. I consider an observation of Rochefoucault, that a wind, though it extinguishes a candle, blows up a fire"[1]. . . . .

'The "ostensible lettter" which was to serve as Smith's justification, if he should decline to follow the injunctions of the will, is as follows:—

'"London, May 3, 1776.

'"My dear Sir,—After reflecting more maturely on that article of my will by which I left you the disposal of all my papers, with a request that you should publish my 'Dialogues concerning Natural Religion,' I have become sensible that, both on account of the nature of the work, and of your situation, it may be improper to hurry on that publication. I therefore take the present opportunity of qualifying that friendly request. I am content to leave it entirely to your discretion, at what time you will publish that piece, or whether you will publish it at all.

'"You will find among my papers a very inoffensive piece,

[1] Life, vol. ii. p. 491.

called 'my own Life,' which I composed a few days before I left Edinburgh; when I thought, as did all my friends, that my life was despaired of. There can be no objection, that the small piece should be sent to Messrs. Strahan and Cadell, and the proprietors of my other works, to be prefixed to any future edition of them."

'Smith did not absolutely refuse to edit the "Dialogues," but Hume saw pretty clearly that it was a task that would not be performed by him. That he was correct in this supposition, appears by a letter from Smith to Strahan after Hume's death, where he says:

'" I once had persuaded him to leave it entirely to my discretion either to publish them at what time I thought proper, or not to publish them at all. Had he continued of this mind, the manuscript should have been most carefully preserved, and upon my decease restored to his family; but it never should have been published in my lifetime. When you have read it, you will perhaps think it not unreasonable to consult some prudent friend about what you ought to do."

'By a codicil to his will, dated 7th August, he thus altered the arrangement referred to in these letters. "In my later will and disposition, I made some destinations with regard to my manuscripts: All these I now retract, and leave my manuscripts to the care of Mr. William Strahan of London, member of Parliament, trusting to the friendship that has long subsisted between us, for his careful and faithful execution of my intentions. I desire that my 'Dialogues concerning Natural Religion' may be printed and published, any time within two years after my death." . . .

'There is then a new paragraph appended as follows:

'" I do ordain that if my 'Dialogues,' from whatever cause, be not published within two years and a half after my death, as also the account of my life, the property shall return to my nephew, David, whose duty in publishing them, as the last request of his uncle, must be approved of by all the world."

'Both Hume and Smith seem to have thought that Strahan would undertake the publication as a mere matter of business. But this book, like the little hunchback in the "Arabian Nights," was a commodity which every one seemed anxious to transfer to his neighbour. Strahan declined to undertake the task, and the "Dialogues" did not appear until 1779, when they were published by their author's nephew.'[1]

The title-page consists simply of the words 'Dialogues concerning Natural Religion, by David Hume, Esq.,' and bears no publisher's name.

The book is noticed in 'The Gentleman's Magazine,' October, 1779. Although, perhaps, the most finished of its author's productions, it has not excited general attention; there seems to be a deep-seated reluctance to discuss such fundamental questions.

The larger toleration, which characterises the present age, makes it, perhaps, difficult to understand why Adam Smith was so reluctant to put the book through the press for his friend. Unhappily, it is too certain, that, if he desired peace, he was prudent in declining to do so. A storm of obloquy burst upon him for his share in publishing Hume's autobiography and for the letter which accompanied it. The autobiography in question, dated April 18, 1776—Hume died August 25—appeared in 1777, as 'The Life of David Hume, Esq. Written by himself. Price 1s. 6d. London: Printed for W. Strahan; and T. Cadell in the Strand.' The Preface runs as follows:—'Mr. Hume, a few months before his death, wrote the following short account of his own Life; and, in a codicil to his will, desired that it might be prefixed to the next edition of his Works. That edition cannot be published for a considerable time.[2] The Editor,[3] in the mean while, in order to serve the purchasers of the former editions; and, at the same time, to gratify the impatience of the public curiosity; has thought proper to publish it separately, without altering even the title or superscription, which was written in Mr. Hume's own hand on the cover of the manuscript.'

The Autobiography and Letter are printed at the beginning of this volume. Adam Smith was promptly taken to task. In the same year was written 'A Letter to Adam Smith, LL.D. on the Life, Death, and Philosophy of his friend David Hume, Esq. By One of the People called Christians.

> Ibant obscuri, sola sub nocte, per umbram,
> Perque domos Ditis vacuas, et inania regna.'

In the Advertisement the author declines to give his name,

---

[1] Life, vol. ii. pp. 491-495.
[2] Nevertheless it appeared in the same year.
[3] Adam Smith.

which can have no bearing on the argument; and, as his book costs only a shilling, deprecates the anger of those readers who will disagree with him; while he entreats the friends of Religion, in so critical a time, to speak well of it. But for a desire to be anonymous, he would have prefixed his portrait, with an effort to wear as happy an expression as Hume himself. The letter begins: 'Sir,—You have been lately employed in embalming a philosopher; his *body*, I believe I must say; for concerning the other part of him, neither you nor he seem to have entertained an idea, sleeping or waking. Else, it surely might have claimed a little of your care and attention; and one would think, the belief of the soul's existence and immortality could do no harm, if it did no good, in a *Theory of Moral Sentiments*. But every gentleman understands his own business best.' After asserting that his own good humour and literary tastes are such as to make him an impartial judge, he proceeds to state his point; that since the social qualities of David, however amiable, by no means prevented him from being guilty of the atrocious wickedness of diffusing atheism through the land, it was a scandal for Doctor Smith to pronounce him one who approached as nearly to the idea of a perfectly wise and virtuous man, as perhaps the nature of human frailty will permit. The letter, which is devoid of argument, repeats this point from time to time with a variety of scurrilous jests and coarse comparisons. It places Hume in the same category with John the Painter, who may have played whist well, in spite of an odd fancy of firing all the dockyards in the kingdom. Returning to the charge, it says that only on atheistical principles is it right in our last hours to read Lucian, to play at whist, to droll upon Charon and his boat, to die as foolish and insensible, as much like our brother philosophers, the calves of the field, and the asses of the desert, as we can, for the life of us. Still further to illustrate so shocking a death-bed, the 'drollery' is paraphrased as follows: 'LORD, I have only one reason why I should wish to live. Suffer me so to do, I most humbly beseech Thee, yet a little while, till mine eyes shall behold the success of my undertaking to overthrow, by my metaphysics, the faith which thy SON descended from heaven to plant, and to root out the knowledge and the love of thee from the earth.'

After reprobating the inhumanity of an author who could

impugn the comfortable doctrines of the Christian Faith, Bishop Horne insinuates that Hume was by no means so insensible to attack as his Life pretends, asking if there was not an author—meaning Beattie; he has already assured Dr. Smith that his own name does not begin with B.—whose name could not be mentioned to Hume, or else he would 'fly out into a transport of passion and swearing'?

Waxing hot with indignation at Smith's approval of Hume's manner of death, the Bishop tells him that he who can behold with complacency such a mischievous life, so evil a death, may smile over Babylon in ruins, esteem the earthquake which destroyed Lisbon an agreeable occurrence, and congratulate the hardened Pharaoh on his overthrow in the Red Sea. Drollery in such circumstances is neither more nor less than

> Moody Madness, laughing wild,
> Amid severest woe.

Would we know the baneful and pestilential influences of false philosophy on the human heart, we need only contemplate them in this most deplorable instance of Mr. Hume.

That this 'drolling upon Charon and his boat' gave dire offence, appears also from a sermon of John Wesley's:[1]

'Did that right honourable wretch, compared to whom Sir R—— was a saint, know the heart of man,—he that so earnestly advised his own son, "never to speak the truth, to lie or dissemble as often as he speaks, to wear a mask continually?" that earnestly counselled him, "not to debauch *single women*," (because some inconveniences might follow), "but always married women?" Would one imagine this grovelling animal ever had a wife or a married daughter of his own? O rare Lord C——! Did ever man so well deserve, though he was a Peer of the realm, to die by the side of Newgate? Or did ever book so well deserve to be burned by the common hangman, as his Letters? Did Mr. David Hume, lower, if possible, than either of the former, know the heart of man? No more than a worm or a beetle does. After "playing so idly with the darts of death," do you now find it a laughing matter? What think you now of Charon? Has he ferried you over Styx? At length he has taught you to know a little of your own heart! At length you know, it is a fearful thing to fall into the hands of the living God!'

---

[1] No. 123. Preached at Halifax, April 21, 1790. On the Deceitfulness of the Human Heart.

One or two passages may be cited from Boswell in further illustration of the bitter feeling with which Hume's death was expected. 'When we were alone, I introduced the subject of death, and endeavoured to maintain that the fear of it might be got over. I told him that David Hume said to me, he was no more uneasy to think he should *not* be after his life, than that he *had not been* before he began to exist. *Johnson*: "Sir, if he really thinks so, his perceptions are disturbed; he is mad: if he does not think so, he lies. He may tell you, he holds his finger in the flame of a candle, without feeling pain; would you believe him? When he dies, he at least gives up all he has." *Boswell*: "Foote, Sir, told me, that when he was very ill he was not afraid to die?" *Johnson*: "It is not true, Sir. Hold a pistol to Foote's breast, or to Hume's breast, and threaten to kill them, and you'll see how they behave."' . . . Letter from Boswell to Johnson: 'Without doubt you have read what is called "The *Life* of David Hume," written by himself, with the letter from Dr. Adam Smith subjoined to it. Is not this an age of daring effrontery? My friend Mr. Anderson, Professor of Natural Philosophy at Glasgow, at whose house you and I supped, and to whose care Mr. Windham, of Norfolk, was intrusted at that University, paid me a visit lately; and after we had talked with indignation and contempt of the poisonous productions with which this age is infested, he said there was now an excellent opportunity for Dr. Johnson to step forth. I agreed with him that you might knock Hume's and Smith's heads together, and make vain and ostentatious infidelity exceedingly ridiculous. Would it not be worth your while to crush such noxious weeds in the moral garden?' . . . 'I mentioned to Dr. Johnson, that David Hume's persisting in his infidelity, when he was dying, shocked me much. *Johnson*: "Why should it shock you, Sir? Hume owned he had never read the New Testament with attention. Here then was a man who had been at no pains to inquire into the truth of religion, and had continually turned his mind the other way. It was not to be expected that the prospect of death would alter his way of thinking, unless God should send an angel to set him right." I said, I had reason to believe that the thought of annihilation gave Hume no pain. *Johnson*: "It was not so, Sir. He had a vanity in being thought easy. It is more probable that he should assume an appearance of ease, than so very improbable a thing should be, as a man not afraid of going (as, in spite of his delusive theory, he cannot be sure but he may go) into an unknown state, and not being uneasy at leaving all he knew. And you are to consider, that upon his own principle of annihilation he had no motive to speak the truth."'

According to the author of the 'Supplement to the Life of David Hume' (1777), it was thought necessary that his grave should be watched by two men for eight nights, and the droppings of grease from their lanterns were long visible on the tomb.

In this Edition the text of the Treatise of Human Nature has been followed in all its curiosities of spelling and punctuation. In the Essays the posthumous edition of 1777 has been reprinted; the variations of earlier editions are given in the notes, which in all cases adopt the latest text. The Essays, which did not survive, will be found at the end of Vol. IV. Many thanks are due to Mr. Burton, both for personal kindness, and for permission to make free use of his 'Life of Hume.'

T. H. GROSE.

QUEEN'S COLLEGE: *Feb. 2, 1874.*

LIST OF EDITIONS.

Essays Moral and Political.—
    Tros Rutulusve *fuat, nullo discrimine habebo.*—VIRG.:
Edinburgh: Printed by R. FLEMING and A. ALISON, for A. KINCAID, Bookseller, and sold at his shop above the Cross. MDCCXLI. One vol. octavo. 2s. 6d. Gent. Mag., March 1742. Brit. Mus. and Bodl. Edition A.
  The Second Edition, Corrected. MDCCXLII. Brit. Mus. Edition B.

Essays Moral and Political.—Volume II. MDCCXLII. Brit. Mus. Edition C.

Essays Moral and Political.—By David HUME, Esq. The Third Edition, Corrected with Additions. London: Printed for A. MILLAR, over against Catharine Street, in the Strand, and A. KINCAID in Edinburgh. MDCCXLVIII. One vol. octavo. 3s. Gent. Mag., Nov. 1748. Bodl. Edition D.

Philosophical Essays concerning Human Understanding.—By the Author of the Essays Moral and Political. London: A. MILLAR. MDCCXLVIII. One vol. octavo. 3s. Gent. Mag., April 1748. (The only copy the Editor has seen is in Mr. Burton's possession.) Edition E.

Ditto. The Second Edition, with Additions and Corrections. By Mr. HUME, Author of the Essays Moral and Political. London: Printed for M. COOPER, at the Globe in Paternoster Row. MDCCLI. Bodl. Edition F.

An Enquiry concerning the Principles of Morals.—By DAVID HUME, Esq. London: A. MILLAR. 1751. One vol. octavo. 3s. Bodl. Edition G.

Political Discourses.—By DAVID HUME, Esq. Edinburgh: Printed by R. FLEMING, for A. KINCAID and A. DONALDSON. MDCCLII. One vol. octavo. Gent. Mag. Feb. 1742. Bodl. Edition H.

Ditto. The Second Edition. Bodl. Edition I.

Essays and Treatises on Several Subjects.—By DAVID HUME, Esq.; in Four Volumes. London: A. MILLAR. Edinburgh: A. KINCAID and A. DONALDSON. MDCCLIII-IV. Octavo. Edition K.

Four Dissertations. I. *The Natural History of Religion.* II. *Of the Passions.* III. *Of Tragedy.* IV. *Of the Standard of Taste.*—By DAVID HUME, Esq. London: A. MILLAR. MDCCLVII. One vol. octavo. 3s. Gent. Mag., Feb. 1757. Bodl. Edition L.

First Proof of the Above. No Title-page: but in (?) Hume's handwriting—*Five Dissertations, to wit, The Natural History of Religion: Of the Passions: Of Tragedy: Of Suicide: Of the Immortality of the Soul.* In the Advocates' Library, Edinburgh.

Essays and Treatises on Several Subjects.—By DAVID HUME, Esq. A New Edition. London: A. MILLAR. Edinburgh: A. KINCAID and A. DONALDSON. MDCCLVIII. Brit. Mus. Edition M.

Ditto, MDCCLX. Four vols. duodecimo. Brit. Mus. Edition N.

Ditto, MDCCLXIV. Two vols. octavo. Brit. Mus. Edition O.

Ditto. London: Printed for A. MILLAR, A. KINCAID, J. BELL, and A. DONALDSON, in Edinburgh. And sold by T. CADELL, in the Strand. MDCCLXVIII. Two vols. quarto. Brit. Mus. Edition P.

Ditto. Printed for T. CADELL, (Successor to Mr. MILLAR), in the Strand; and A. KINCAID and A. DONALDSON, at Edinburgh. MDCCLXX. Four vols. octavo. Brit. Mus. Edition Q.

Ditto, Printed for T. CADELL, in the Strand; and W. DONALDSON and W. CREECH, at Edinburgh. MDCCLXXVII. 2 vols. octavo. Brit. Mus. and Bodl. Edition R.

Two Essays.—London. MDCCLXVII. Price Five Shillings. (On Suicide and the Immortality of the Soul.)

Dialogues concerning Natural Religion.—By DAVID HUME, Esq. 1779.

This list exhausts the Editions: all have been collated by the present Editor.

ESSAYS

AND

TREATISES

ON

SEVERAL SUBJECTS.

In TWO VOLUMES.

By DAVID HUME, Esq;

VOL. I.

CONTAINING

ESSAYS, MORAL, POLITICAL, and LITERARY.

A NEW EDITION.

LONDON:

Printed for T. CADELL, in the Strand: and
A. DONALDSON, and W. CREECH, at Edinburgh.
MDCCLXXVII.

ESSAYS,

MORAL, POLITICAL,

AND

LITERARY.

PART I.*

* Published in 1742. [This Note was added in Ed. M, 1758].

ESSAYS.

PART I.

Essay I.—*Of the Delicacy of Taste and Passion.*

SOME People are subject to a certain *delicacy* of *passion*, which makes them extremely sensible to all the accidents of life, and gives them a lively joy upon every prosperous event, as well as a piercing grief, when they meet with misfortunes and adversity. Favours and good offices easily engage their friendship; while the smallest injury provokes their resentment. Any honour or mark of distinction elevates them above measure; but they are as sensibly touched with contempt. People of this character have, no doubt, more lively enjoyments, as well as more pungent sorrows, than men of cool and sedate tempers: But, I believe, when every thing is balanced, there is no one, who would not rather be of the latter character, were he entirely master of his own disposition. Good or ill fortune is very little at our disposal: And when a person, that has this sensibility of temper, meets with any misfortune, his sorrow or resentment takes entire possession of him, and deprives him of all relish in the common occurrences of life; the right enjoyment of which forms the chief part of our happiness. Great pleasures are much less frequent than great pains; so that a sensible temper must meet with fewer trials in the former way than in the latter. Not to mention, that men of such lively passions are apt to be transported beyond all bounds of prudence and discretion, and to take false steps in the conduct of life, which are often irretrievable.

There is a *delicacy of taste* observable in some men, which very much resembles this *delicacy* of *passion*, and produces the same sensibility to beauty and deformity of every kind, as that does to prosperity and adversity, obligations and injuries. When you present a poem or a picture to a man possessed of this talent, the delicacy of his feeling makes him be sensibly touched with every part of it; nor are the masterly strokes perceived with more exquisite relish and satisfaction, than the negligences or absurdities with disgust and uneasiness. A polite and judicious conversation affords him the highest entertainment; rudeness or impertinence is as great a punishment to him. In short, delicacy of taste has the same effect as delicacy of passion: It enlarges the sphere both of our happiness and misery, and makes us sensible to pains as well as pleasures, which escape the rest of mankind.

I believe, however, every one will agree with me, that, notwithstanding this resemblance, delicacy of taste is as much to be desired and cultivated as delicacy of passion is to be lamented, and to be remedied, if possible. The good or ill accidents of life are very little at our disposal; but we are pretty much masters what books we shall read, what diversions we shall partake of, and what company we shall keep. Philosophers have endeavoured to render happiness entirely independent of every thing external. That degree of perfection is impossible to be *attained*: But every wise man will endeavour to place his happiness on such objects chiefly as depend upon himself: and *that* is not to be *attained* so much by any other means as by this delicacy of sentiment. When a man is possessed of that talent, he is more happy by what pleases his taste, than by what gratifies his appetites, and receives more enjoyment from a poem or a piece of reasoning than the most expensive luxury can afford.[1]

Whatever connexion there may be originally between these two species of delicacy, I am persuaded, that nothing is so proper to cure us of this delicacy of passion, as the cultivating of that higher and more refined taste, which

[1] [How far delicacy of taste, and that of passion, are connected together in the original frame of the mind, it is hard to determine. To me there appears a very considerable connexion between them. For we may observe that women, who have more delicate passions than men, have also a more delicate taste of the ornaments of life, of dress, equipage, and the ordinary decencies of behaviour. Any excellency in these hits their taste much sooner than ours; and when you please their taste, you soon engage their affections.—Editions A to Q; the latter omits the last sentence.]

enables us to judge of the characters of men, of compositions of genius, and of the productions of the nobler arts. A greater or less relish for those obvious beauties, which strike the senses, depends entirely upon the greater or less sensibility of the temper: But with regard to the sciences and liberal arts, a fine taste is, in some measure, the same with strong sense, or at least depends so much upon it, that they are inseparable. In order to judge aright of a composition of genius, there are so many views to be taken in, so many circumstances to be compared, and such a knowledge of human nature requisite, that no man, who is not possessed of the soundest judgment, will ever make a tolerable critic in such performances. And this is a new reason for cultivating a relish in the liberal arts. Our judgment will strengthen by this exercise: We shall form juster notions of life: Many things, which please or afflict others, will appear to us too frivolous to engage our attention: And we shall lose by degrees that sensibility and delicacy of passion, which is so incommodious.

But perhaps I have gone too far in saying, that a cultivated taste for the polite arts extinguishes the passions, and renders us indifferent to those objects, which are so fondly pursued by the rest of mankind. On farther reflection, I find, that it rather improves our sensibility for all the tender and agreeable passions; at the same time that it renders the mind incapable of the rougher and more boisterous emotions.

Ingenuas didicisse fideliter artes,
Emollit mores, nec sinit esse feros.

For this, I think there may be assigned two very natural reasons. In the *first* place, nothing is so improving to the temper as the study of the beauties, either of poetry, eloquence, music, or painting. They give a certain elegance of sentiment to which the rest of mankind are strangers. The emotions which they excite are soft and tender. They draw off the mind from the hurry of business and interest; cherish reflection; dispose to tranquillity; and produce an agreeable melancholy, which, of all dispositions of the mind, is the best suited to love and friendship.

In the *second* place, a delicacy of taste is favourable to love and friendship, by confining our choice to few people, and making us indifferent to the company and conversation of the greater part of men. You will seldom find, that mere men of the world, whatever strong sense they may be endowed with, are very nice in distinguishing characters, or in marking those insensible differences and gradations, which make one man preferable to another. Any one, that has competent sense, is sufficient for their entertainment: They talk to him, of their pleasure and affairs, with the same frankness that they would to another; and finding many, who are fit to supply his place, they never feel any vacancy or want in his absence. But to make use of the allusion of a celebrated French[1] author, the judgment may be compared to a clock or watch, where the most ordinary machine is sufficient to tell the hours; but the most elaborate alone can point out the minutes and seconds, and distinguish the smallest differences of time. One that has well digested his knowledge both of books and men, has little enjoyment but in the company of a few select companions. He feels too sensibly, how much all the rest of mankind fall short of the notions which he has entertained. And, his affections being thus confined within a narrow circle, no wonder he carries them further, than if they were more general and undistinguished. The gaiety and frolic of a bottle companion improves with him into a solid friendship: And the ardours of a youthful appetite become an elegant passion.

Essay II.—*Of the Liberty of the Press.*

NOTHING is more apt to surprize a foreigner, than the extreme liberty, which we enjoy in this country, of communicating whatever we please to the public, and of openly censuring every measure, entered into by the king or his ministers. If the administration resolve upon war, it is affirmed, that, either wilfully or ignorantly, they mistake the interests of the nation, and that peace, in the present situation of affairs, is infinitely preferable. If the passion of the ministers lie towards peace, our political writers breathe nothing but war and devastation, and represent the pacific conduct of the government as mean and pusillanimous. As this liberty is not indulged in any other government, either republican or monarchical; in HOLLAND and VENICE,

[1] *Mons.* FONTENELLE, *Pluralité des Mondes.* Soir. 6.

more than in FRANCE or SPAIN; it may very naturally give occasion to a question, *How it happens that* GREAT BRITAIN *alone enjoys this peculiar privilege?*[1]

The reason, why the laws indulge us in such a liberty seems to be derived from our mixed form of government, which is neither wholly monarchical, nor wholly republican. It will be found, if I mistake not, a true observation in politics, that the two extremes in government, liberty and slavery, commonly approach nearest to each other; and that, as you depart from the extremes, and mix a little of monarchy with liberty, the government becomes always the more free; and on the other hand, when you mix a little of liberty with monarchy, the yoke becomes always the more grievous and intolerable.[2] In a government, such as that of FRANCE, which is absolute, and where law, custom, and religion concur, all of them, to make people fully satisfied with their condition, the monarch cannot entertain any *jealousy* against his subjects, and therefore is apt to indulge them in great *liberties* both of speech and action. In a government altogether republican, such as that of HOLLAND, where there is no magistrate so eminent as to give *jealousy* to the state, there is no danger in intrusting the magistrates with large discretionary powers; and though many advantages result from such powers, in preserving peace and order, yet they lay a considerable restraint on men's actions, and make every private citizen pay a great respect to the government. Thus it seems evident, that the two extremes of absolute monarchy and of a republic, approach near to each other in some material circumstances. In the *first*, the magistrate has no jealousy of the people: in the *second*, the people have none of the magistrate: Which want of jealousy begets a mutual confidence and trust in both cases, and produces a species of liberty in monarchies, and of arbitrary power in republics.

To justify the other part of the foregoing observation, that, in every government, the means are most wide of each other, and that the mixtures of monarchy and liberty render the yoke more easy or more grievous; I must take notice of a remark in TACITUS with regard to the ROMANS under the

---

[1] [And whether the unlimited exercise of this liberty be advantageous or prejudicial to the public?—Editions A to P.]

[2] [I shall endeavour to explain myself.—Editions D to P.]

emperors, that they neither could bear total slavery nor total liberty, *Nec totam servitutem, nec totam libertatem pati possunt.* This remark a celebrated poet has translated and applied to the ENGLISH, in his lively description of queen ELIZABETH's policy and government,

> *Et fit aimer son joug a l'Anglois indompté,*
> *Qui ne peut ni servir, ni vivre en liberté.*
>
> HENRIADE, *liv.* 1.

According to these remarks, we are to consider the ROMAN government under the emperors as a mixture of despotism and liberty, where the despotism prevailed; and the ENGLISH government as a mixture of the same kind, where the liberty predominates. The consequences are conformable to the foregoing observation; and such as may be expected from those mixed forms of government, which beget a mutual watchfulness and jealousy. The ROMAN emperors were, many of them, the most frightful tyrants that ever disgraced human nature; and it is evident, that their cruelty was chiefly excited by their *jealousy*, and by their observing that all the great men of ROME bore with impatience the dominion of a family, which, but a little before, was no wise superior to their own. On the other hand, as the republican part of the government prevails in ENGLAND, though with a great mixture of monarchy, it is obliged, for its own preservation, to maintain a watchful *jealousy* over the magistrates, to remove all discretionary powers, and to secure every one's life and fortune by general and inflexible laws. No action must be deemed a crime but what the law has plainly determined to be such: No crime must be imputed to a man but from a legal proof before his judges; and even these judges must be his fellow-subjects, who are obliged, by their own interest, to have a watchful eye over the encroachments and violence of the ministers. From these causes it proceeds, that there is as much liberty, and, even, perhaps, licentiousness in GREAT BRITAIN, as there were formerly slavery and tyranny in ROME.

These principles account for the great liberty of the press in these kingdoms, beyond what is indulged in any other government. [1] It is apprehended, that arbitrary power would steal in upon us, were we not careful to prevent its progress,

---

[1] ['Tis sufficiently known.—Editions A to P.]

and were there not an easy method of conveying the alarm from one end of the kingdom to the other. The spirit of the people must frequently be rouzed, in order to curb the ambition of the court; and the dread of rouzing this spirit must be employed to prevent that ambition. Nothing so effectual to this purpose as the liberty of the press, by which all the learning, wit, and genius of the nation may be employed on the side of freedom, and every one be animated to its defence. As long, therefore, as the republican part of our government can maintain itself against the monarchical, it will naturally be careful to keep the press open, as of importance to its own preservation.

[1] It must however be allowed, that the unbounded liberty

---

[1] [Edition Q omits the concluding sentence. Editions A to P have in place of it the following:—

Since therefore that liberty is so essential to the support of our mixed government; this sufficiently decides the second question, *Whether such a liberty be advantageous or prejudicial*; there being nothing of greater importance in every state than the preservation of the ancient government, especially if it be a free one. But I would fain go a step farther, and assert, that this liberty is attended with so few inconveniencies, that it may be claimed as the common right of mankind, and ought to be indulged them almost in every government: except the ecclesiastical, to which indeed it would prove fatal. We need not dread from this liberty any such ill consequences as followed from the harangues of the popular demagogues of ATHENS and tribunes of ROME. A man reads a book or pamphlet alone and coolly. There is none present from whom he can catch the passion by contagion. He is not hurried away by the force and energy of action. And should he be wrought up to ever so seditious a humour, there is no violent resolution presented to him, by which he can immediately vent his passion. The liberty of the press, therefore, however abused, can scarce ever excite popular tumults or rebellion. And as to those murmurs or secret discontents it may occasion, 'tis better they should get vent in words, that they may come to the knowledge of the magistrate before it be too late, in order to his providing a remedy against them. Mankind, it is true, have always a greater propension to believe what is said to the disadvantage of their governors, than the contrary; but this inclination is inseparable from them, whether they have liberty or not. A whisper may fly as quick, and be as pernicious as a pamphlet. Nay, it will be more pernicious, where men are not accustomed to think freely, or distinguish between truth and falshood.

It has also been found, as the experience of mankind increases, that the *people* are no such dangerous monster as they have been represented, and that it is in every respect better to guide them, like rational creatures, than to lead or drive them, like brute beasts. Before the United Provinces set the example, toleration was deemed incompatible with good government; and it was thought impossible, that a number of religious sects could live together in harmony and peace, and have all of them an equal affection to their common country, and to each other. ENGLAND has set a like example of civil liberty; and though this liberty seems to occasion some small ferment at present, it has not as yet produced any pernicious effects; and it is to be hoped, that men, being every day more accustomed to the free discussion of public affairs, will improve in the judgment of them, and be with greater difficulty seduced by every idle rumour and popular clamour.

It is a very comfortable reflection to the lovers of liberty, that this peculiar privilege of BRITAIN is of a kind that cannot easily be wrested from us, but

of the press, though it be difficult, perhaps impossible, to propose a suitable remedy for it, is one of the evils, attending those mixt forms of government.

ESSAY III.—*That Politics may be reduced to a Science.*

IT is a question with several, whether there be any essential difference between one form of government and another? and, whether every form may not become good or bad, according as it is well or ill administered?[1] Were it once admitted, that all governments are alike, and that the only difference consists in the character and conduct of the governors, most political disputes would be at an end, and all *Zeal* for one constitution above another, must be esteemed mere bigotry and folly. But, though a friend to moderation, I cannot forbear condemning this sentiment, and should be sorry to think, that human affairs admit of no greater stability, than what they receive from the casual humours and characters of particular men.

It is true; those who maintain, that the goodness of all government consists in the goodness of the administration, may cite some particular instances in history, where the very same government, in different hands, has varied suddenly into the two opposite extremes of good and bad. Compare the FRENCH government under HENRY III. and under HENRY IV. Oppression, levity, artifice on the part of the rulers; faction, sedition, treachery, rebellion, disloyalty on the part of the subjects: These compose the character of the former miserable æra. But when the patriot and heroic prince, who succeeded, was once firmly seated on the throne, the government, the people, every

must last as long as our government remains, in any degree, free and independent. It is seldom, that liberty of any kind is lost all at once. Slavery has so frightful an aspect to men accustomed to freedom, that it must steal upon them by degrees, and must disguise itself in a thousand shapes, in order to be received. But, if the liberty of the press ever be lost, it must be lost at once. The general laws against sedition and libelling are at present as strong as they possibly can be made. Nothing can impose a farther restraint, but either the clapping an IMPRIMATUR upon the press, or the giving to the court very large discretionary powers to punish whatever displeases them. But these concessions would be such a bare-faced violation of liberty, that they will probably be the last efforts of a despotic government. We may conclude, that the liberty of *Britain* is gone for ever when these attempts shall succeed.]

[1] *For forms of government let fools contest,*
Whate'er is best administer'd is best.
ESSAY ON MAN, Book 3.

thing seemed to be totally changed; and all from the difference of the temper and conduct of these two sovereigns.[1] Instances of this kind may be multiplied, almost without number, from ancient as well as modern history, foreign as well as domestic.

But here it may be proper to make a distinction. All absolute governments[2] must very much depend on the administration; and this is one of the great inconveniences attending that form of government. But a republican and free government would be an obvious absurdity, if the particular checks and controuls, provided by the constitution, had really no influence, and made it not the interest, even of bad men, to act for the public good. Such is the intention of these forms of government, and such is their real effect, where they are wisely constituted: As on the other hand, they are the source of all disorder, and of the blackest crimes, where either skill or honesty has been wanting in their original frame and institution.

So great is the force of laws, and of particular forms of government, and so little dependence have they on the humours and tempers of men, that consequences almost as general and certain may sometimes be deduced from them, as any which the mathematical sciences afford us.

The constitution of the ROMAN republic gave the whole legislative power to the people, without allowing a negative voice either to the nobility or consuls. This unbounded power they possessed in a collective, not in a representative body. The consequences were: When the people, by success and conquest, had become very numerous, and had spread themselves to a great distance from the capital, the city-tribes, though the most contemptible, carried almost every vote: They were, therefore, most cajoled by every one that affected popularity: They were supported in idleness by the general distribution of corn, and by particular bribes, which they received from almost every candidate: By this means, they became every day more licentious, and the

---

[1] [Editions A to P insert the following:—An equal difference of a contrary kind, may be found on comparing the reigns of ELIZABETH and JAMES, at least with regard to foreign affairs.
They omit the words 'foreign as well as domestic' in the next sentence.]

[2] [Editions A to Q insert: And such, in a great measure, was that of ENGLAND, till the middle of the last century, notwithstanding the numerous panegyrics on ancient ENGLISH liberty. Editions A and B stop at the word *century*.]

CAMPUS MARTIUS was a perpetual scene of tumult and sedition: Armed slaves were introduced among these rascally citizens; so that the whole government fell into anarchy, and the greatest happiness, which the ROMANS could look for, was the despotic power of the CÆSARS. Such are the effects of democracy without a representative.

A Nobility may possess the whole, or any part of the legislative power of a state, in two different ways. Either every nobleman shares the power as part of the whole body, or the whole body enjoys the power as composed of parts, which have each a distinct power and authority. The VENETIAN aristocracy is an instance of the first kind of government: The POLISH of the second. In the VENETIAN government the whole body of nobility possesses the whole power, and no nobleman has any authority which he receives not from the whole. In the POLISH government every nobleman, by means of his fiefs, has a distinct hereditary authority over his vassals, and the whole body has no authority but what it receives from the concurrence of its parts. The different operations and tendencies of these two species of government might be made apparent even *à priori*. A VENETIAN nobility is preferable to a POLISH, let the humours and education of men be ever so much varied. A nobility, who possess their power in common, will preserve peace and order, both among themselves, and their subjects; and no member can have authority enough to controul the laws for a moment. The nobles will preserve their authority over the people, but without any grievous tyranny, or any breach of private property; because such a tyrannical government promotes not the interests of the whole body, however it may that of some individuals. There will be a distinction of rank between the nobility and people, but this will be the only distinction in the state. The whole nobility will form one body, and the whole people another, without any of those private feuds and animosities, which spread ruin and desolation every where. It is easy to see the disadvantages of a POLISH nobility in every one of these particulars.

It is possible so to constitute a free government, as that a single person, call him doge, prince, or king, shall possess a large share of power, and shall form a proper balance or counterpoise to the other parts of the legislature. This chief magistrate may be either *elective* or *hereditary*; and though the former institution may, to a superficial view, appear the most advantageous; yet a more accurate inspection will discover in it greater inconveniencies than in the latter, and such as are founded on causes and principles eternal and immutable. The filling of the throne, in such a government, is a point of too great and too general interest, not to divide the whole people into factions: Whence a civil war, the greatest of ills, may be apprehended, almost with certainty, upon every vacancy. The prince elected must be either a *Foreigner* or a *Native*: The former will be ignorant of the people whom he is to govern; suspicious of his new subjects, and suspected by them; giving his confidence entirely to strangers, who will have no other care but of enriching themselves in the quickest manner, while their master's favour and authority are able to support them. A native will carry into the throne all his private animosities and friendships, and will never be viewed in his elevation, without exciting the sentiment of envy in those, who formerly considered him as their equal. Not to mention that a crown is too high a reward ever to be given to merit alone, and will always induce the candidates to employ force, or money, or intrigue, to procure the votes of the electors: So that such an election will give no better chance for superior merit in the prince, than if the state had trusted to birth alone for determining their sovereign.

It may therefore be pronounced as an universal axiom in politics, *That an hereditary prince, a nobility without vassals, and a people voting by their representatives, form the best* MONARCHY, ARISTOCRACY, *and* DEMOCRACY. But in order to prove more fully, that politics admit of general truths, which are invariable by the humour or education either of subject or sovereign, it may not be amiss to observe some other principles of this science, which may seem to deserve that character.

It may easily be observed, that, though free governments have been commonly the most happy for those who partake of their freedom; yet are they the most ruinous and oppressive to their provinces: And this observation may, I believe, be fixed as a maxim of the kind we are here speaking of. When a monarch extends his dominions by conquest, he soon learns to consider his old and his new subjects as on the same footing; because, in reality, all his subjects are to him the same, except the few friends and favourites, with whom he is personally acquainted. He does not, therefore, make any distinction between them in his *general* laws; and, at the same time, is careful to prevent all *particular* acts of oppression on the one as well as on the other. But a free state necessarily makes a great distinction, and must always do so, till men learn to love their neighbours as well as themselves. The conquerors, in such a government, are all legislators, and will be sure to contrive matters, by restrictions on trade, and by taxes, so as to draw some private, as well as public, advantage from their conquests. Provincial governors have also a better chance, in a republic, to escape with their plunder, by means of bribery or intrigue; and their fellow-citizens, who find their own state to be enriched by the spoils of the subject provinces, will be more inclined to tolerate such abuses. Not to mention, that it is a necessary precaution in a free state to change the governors frequently; which obliges these temporary tyrants to be more expeditious and rapacious, that they may accumulate sufficient wealth before they give place to their successors. What cruel tyrants were the ROMANS over the world during the time of their commonwealth! It is true, they had laws to prevent oppression in their provincial magistrates; but CICERO informs us, that the ROMANS could not better consult the interests of the provinces than by repealing these very laws. For, in that case, says he, our magistrates, having entire impunity, would plunder no more than would satisfy their own rapaciousness; whereas, at present, they must also satisfy that of their judges, and of all the great men in ROME, of whose protection they stand in need. Who can read of the cruelties and oppressions of VERRES without horror and astonishment? And who is not touched with indignation to hear, that, after CICERO had exhausted on that abandoned criminal all the thunders of his eloquence, and had prevailed so far as to get him condemned to the utmost extent of the laws; yet that cruel tyrant lived peaceably to old age, in opulence and ease, and, thirty years afterwards, was put into the proscription by MARK ANTHONY, on account of his exorbitant wealth, where he fell with CICERO himself, and all the most virtuous men of ROME? After the dissolution of the commonwealth, the ROMAN yoke became easier upon the provinces, as TACITUS informs us[1]; and it may be observed, that many of the worst emperors, DOMITIAN,[2] for instance, were careful to prevent all oppression on the provinces. In [3] TIBERIUS's time, GAUL was esteemed richer than ITALY itself: Nor, do I find, during the whole time of the ROMAN monarchy, that the empire became less rich or populous in any of its provinces; though indeed its valour and military discipline were always upon the decline. [4] The oppression and tyranny of the CARTHAGINIANS over their subject states in AFRICA went so far, as we learn from POLYBIUS,[5] that, not content with exacting the half of all the produce of the land, which of itself was a very high rent, they also loaded them with many other taxes. If we pass from ancient to modern times, we shall still find the observation to hold. The provinces of absolute monarchies are always better treated than those of free states. Compare the *Païs conquis* of FRANCE with IRELAND, and you will be convinced of this truth; though this latter kingdom, being, in a good measure, peopled from ENGLAND, possesses so many rights and privileges as should naturally make it challenge better treatment than that of a conquered province. CORSICA is also an obvious instance to the same purpose.

There is an observation in MACHIAVEL, with regard to the conquests of ALEXANDER the Great, which I think, may be regarded as one of those eternal political truths, which no time nor accidents can vary. It may seem strange, says that politician, that such sudden conquests, as those of ALEXANDER, should be possessed so peaceably by his successors, and that the PERSIANS, during all the confusions and civil wars among the GREEKS, never made the smallest effort towards the recovery of their former independent government. To satisfy us concerning the cause of this remarkable event, we may consider, that a monarch may govern his subjects in two different ways. He may either follow the maxims of the eastern princes, and stretch his authority so far as to leave no distinction of rank among his subjects, but

---

[1] Ann. lib. 1. cap. 2.
[2] SUET. in vita DOMIT. c. 8.
[3] *Egregium resumendæ libertati tempus, si ipsi florentes, quam inops* ITALIA, *quam imbellis urbana plebs, nihil validum in exercitibus, nisi quod externum cogitarent.* TACIT. Ann. lib. 3. 40. [Ed. A reads *Vespasian's*, and gives no reference.]
[4] [This sentence and the notes 1 and 2 were added in Edition K.]
[5] Lib. 1. cap. 72.

what proceeds immediately from himself: no advantages of birth; no hereditary honours and possessions; and, in a word, no credit among the people, except from his commission alone. Or a monarch may exert his power after a milder manner, like other EUROPEAN princes; and leave other sources of honour, beside his smile and favour: Birth, titles, possessions, valour, integrity, knowledge, or great and fortunate atchievements. In the former species of government, after a conquest, it is impossible ever to shake off the yoke; since no one possesses, among the people, so much personal credit and authority as to begin such an enterprize: Whereas, in the latter, the least misfortune, or discord among the victors, will encourage the vanquished to take arms, who have leaders ready to prompt and conduct them in every undertaking.[1]

[1] I have taken it for granted, according to the supposition of MACHIAVEL, that the ancient PERSIANS had no nobility; though there is reason to suspect, that the FLORENTINE secretary, who seems to have been better acquainted with the ROMAN than the GREEK authors, was mistaken in this particular. The more ancient PERSIANS, whose manners are described by XENOPHON, were a free people, and had nobility. Their ὁμότιμοι were preserved even after the extending of their conquests and the consequent change of their government. ARRIAN mentions them in DARIUS's time, De exped. ALEX, lib. ii. 11. Historians also speak often of the persons in command as men of family. TYGRANES, who was general of the MEDES under XERXES, was of the race of ACHMÆNES, HEROD. lib. vii. cap. 62. ARTACHÆAS, who directed the cutting of the canal about mount ATHOS, was of the same family. Id. cap. 117. MEGABYZUS was one of the seven eminent PERSIANS who conspired against the MAGI. His son, ZOPYRUS, was in the highest command under DARIUS, and delivered BABYLON to him. His grandson, MEGABYZUS, commanded the army, defeated at MARATHON. His great-grandson, ZOPYRUS, was also eminent, and was banished PERSIA. HEROD. lib. iii. 160. THUC. lib. i. 109. ROSACES, who commanded an army in EGYPT under ARTAXERXES, was also descended from one of the seven conspirators, DIOD. SIC. lib. xvi. 47. AGESILAUS, in XENOPHON, Hist. GRÆC. lib. iv. 1, being desirous of making a marriage betwixt king COTYS his ally, and the daughter of SPITHRIDATES, a PERSIAN of rank, who had deserted to him, first asks COTYS what family SPITHRIDATES is of. One of the most considerable in PERSIA, says COTYS. ARIÆUS, when offered the sovereignty by CLEARCHUS and the ten thousand GREEKS, refused it as of too low a rank, and said, that so many eminent PERSIANS would never endure his rule. Id. de exped. lib. ii. Some of the families descended from the seven PERSIANS abovementioned remained during all ALEXANDER's successors; and MITHRIDATES, in ANTIOCHUS's time, is said by POLYBIUS to be descended from one of them, lib. v. cap. 43. ARTABAZUS was esteemed, as ARRIAN says, ἐν τοῖς πρώτοις Περσῶν. lib. iii. 23. And when ALEXANDER married in one day 80 of his captains to PERSIAN women, his intention plainly was to ally the MACEDONIANS with the most eminent PERSIAN families. Id. lib. vii. 4. DIODORUS SICULUS says they were of the most noble birth in PERSIA, lib. xvii. 107. The government of PERSIA was despotic, and conducted in many respects, after the eastern manner, but was not carried so far as to extirpate all nobility, and confound all ranks and orders. It left men who were still great, by themselves and their family, independent of their office and commission. And the reason why the MACEDONIANS kept so easily dominion over them was owing to other

Such is the reasoning of MACHIAVEL, which seems solid and conclusive; though I wish he had not mixed falsehood with truth, in asserting, that monarchies, governed according to eastern policy, though more easily kept when once subdued, yet are the most difficult to subdue; since they cannot contain any powerful subject, whose discontent and faction may facilitate the enterprizes of an army. For besides, that such a tyrannical government enervates the courage of men, and renders them indifferent towards the fortunes of their sovereign; besides this, I say, we find by experience, that even the temporary and delegated authority of the generals and magistrates; being always, in such governments, as absolute within its sphere, as that of the prince himself; is able, with barbarians, accustomed to a blind submission, to produce the most dangerous and fatal revolutions. So that, in every respect, a gentle government is preferable, and gives the greatest security to the sovereign as well as to the subject.

Legislators, therefore, ought not to trust the future government of a state entirely to chance, but ought to provide a system of laws to regulate the administration of public affairs to the latest posterity. Effects will always correspond to causes; and wise regulations in any commonwealth are the most valuable legacy that can be left to future ages. In the smallest court or office, the stated forms and methods, by which business must be conducted, are found to be a considerable check on the natural depravity of mankind. Why should not the case be the same in public affairs? Can we ascribe the stability and wisdom of the VENETIAN government, through so many ages, to any thing but the form of government? And is it not easy to point out those defects in the original constitution, which produced the tumultuous governments of ATHENS and ROME, and ended at last in the ruin of these two famous republics? And so little dependance has this affair on the humours and education of particular men, that one part of the same republic may be wisely conducted, and another weakly, by the very same men, merely on account of the difference of the forms and institutions, by which these parts are regulated. Historians inform us that this was actually the case with GENOA. For while the state

causes easy to be found in the historians; though it must be owned that MACHIAVEL'S reasoning is, in itself, just, however doubtful its application to the present case. [This note was added in Edition K.]

was always full of sedition, and tumult, and disorder, the bank of St. GEORGE, which had become a considerable part of the people, was conducted, for several ages, with the utmost integrity and wisdom.[1]

[2]The ages of greatest public spirit are not always most eminent for private virtue. Good laws may beget order and moderation in the government, where the manners and customs have instilled little humanity or justice into the tempers of men. The most illustrious period of the ROMAN history, considered in a political view, is that between the beginning of the first and end of the last PUNIC war; the due balance between the nobility and people being then fixed by the contests of the tribunes, and not being yet lost by the extent of conquests. Yet at this very time, the horrid practice of poisoning was so common, that, during part of a season, a *Prætor* punished capitally for this crime above three thousand[3] persons in a part of ITALY; and found informations of this nature still multiplying upon him. There is a similar, or rather a worse instance,[4] in the more early times of the commonwealth. So depraved in private life were that people, whom in their histories we so much admire. I doubt not but they were really more virtuous during the time of the *Triumvirates*; when they were tearing their common country to pieces, and spreading slaughter and desolation over the face of the earth, merely for the choice of tyrants.[5]

Here, then, is a sufficient inducement to maintain, with the utmost ZEAL, in every free state, those forms and institutions, by which liberty is secured, the public good consulted, and the avarice or ambition of particular men restrained and punished. Nothing does more honour to human nature, than to see it susceptible of so noble a passion; as nothing can be a greater indication of meanness of heart in any man, than to see him destitute of it. A man who loves only him-

---

[1] *Essempio veramente raro, & da Filosofi intante loro imaginate & vedute Republiche mai non trovato, vedere dentro ad un medesimo cerchio, fra medesimi cittadini, la liberta & la tirannide, la vita civile & la corotta, la giustitia & la licenza; perche quello ordine solo mantiere quella citta piena di costumi antichi & venerabili. E s'egli auvenisse (che col tempo in ogni modo auverrà) que SAN GIORGIO tutta quel la città occupasse, sarrebbe quella una Republica piu dalla VENETIANA memorabile.* Della Hist. Florentinè, lib. 8.

[2] [This paragraph was added in Edition D.]

[3] T. LIVII, lib. 40. cap. 43.

[4] *Id.* lib. 8. cap. 18.

[5] *L'Aigle contre L'Aigle,* ROMAINS *contre* ROMAINS,
Combatans seulement pour le choix de tyrans.
CORNEILLE.

self, without regard to friendship and desert, merits the severest blame; and a man, who is only susceptible of friendship, without public spirit, or a regard to the community, is deficient in the most material part of virtue.

But this is a subject which needs not be longer insisted on at present. There are enow of zealots on both sides who kindle up the passions of their partizans, and under pretence of public good, pursue the interests and ends of their particular faction. For my part, I shall always be more fond of promoting moderation than zeal; though perhaps the surest way of producing moderation in every party is to increase our zeal for the public. Let us therefore try, if it be possible, from the foregoing doctrine, to draw a lesson of moderation with regard to the parties, into which our country is at present[1] divided; at the same time, that we allow not this moderation to abate the industry and passion, with which every individual is bound to pursue the good of his country.

Those who either attack or defend a minister in such a government as ours, where the utmost liberty is allowed, always carry matters to an extreme, and exaggerate his merit or demerit with regard to the public. His enemies are sure to charge him with the greatest enormities, both in domestic and foreign management; and there is no meanness or crime, of which, in their account, he is not capable. Unnecessary wars, scandalous treaties, profusion of public treasure, oppressive taxes, every kind of mal-administration is ascribed to him. To aggravate the charge, his pernicious conduct, it is said, will extend its baleful influence even to posterity, by undermining the best constitution in the world, and disordering that wise system of laws, institutions, and customs, by which our ancestors, during so many centuries, have been so happily governed. He is not only a wicked minister in himself, but has removed every security provided against wicked ministers for the future.

On the other hand, the partizans of the minister make his panegyric run as high as the accusation against him, and celebrate his wise, steady, and moderate conduct in every part of his administration. The honour and interest of the nation supported abroad, public credit maintained at home, persecution restrained, faction subdued; the merit of all these blessings is ascribed solely to the minister. At the

[1] [Editions D to N give the date 1742.]

same time, he crowns all his other merits by a religious care of the best constitution in the world, which he has preserved in all its parts, and has transmitted entire, to be the happiness and security of the latest posterity.

When this accusation and panegyric are received by the partizans of each party, no wonder they beget an extraordinary ferment on both sides, and fill the nation with violent animosities. But I would fain persuade these party-zealots, that there is a flat contradiction both in the accusation and panegyric, and that it were impossible for either of them to run so high, were it not for this contradiction. If our constitution be really *that noble fabric, the pride of* BRITAIN, *the envy of our neighbours, raised by the labour of so many centuries, repaired at the expence of so many millions, and cemented by such a profusion of blood* [1]; I say, if our constitution does in any degree deserve these [2]eulogies, it would never have suffered a wicked and weak minister to govern triumphantly for a course of twenty years, when opposed by the greatest geniuses in the nation, who exercised the utmost liberty of tongue and pen, in parliament, and in their frequent appeals to the people. But, if the minister be wicked and weak, to the degree so strenuously insisted on, the constitution must be faulty in its original principles, and he cannot consistently be charged with undermining the best form of government in the world. A constitution is only so far good, as it provides a remedy against mal-administration; and if the BRITISH, when in its greatest vigour, and repaired by two such remarkable events, as the *Revolution* and *Accession*, by which our ancient royal family was sacrificed to it; if our constitution, I say, with so great advantages, does not, in fact, provide any such remedy, we are rather beholden to any minister who undermines it, and affords us an opportunity of erecting a better in its place.

I would employ the same topics to moderate the zeal of those who defend the minister. *Is our constitution so excellent?* Then a change of ministry can be no such dreadful event; since it is essential to such a constitution, in every ministry, both to preserve itself from violation, and to prevent all enormities in the administration. *Is our constitution very bad?* Then so extraordinary a jealousy and ap-

---

[1] *Dissertation on parties*, Letter 10.
[2] [Elogiums: Editions A to D. The word is frequently so written in the Treatise.]

prehension, on account of changes, is ill placed; and a man should no more be anxious in this case, than a husband, who had married a woman from the stews, should be watchful to prevent her infidelity. Public affairs, in such a government, must necessarily go to confusion, by whatever hands they are conducted; and the zeal of *patriots* is in that case much less requisite than the patience and submission of *philosophers*. The virtue and good intentions of CATO and BRUTUS are highly laudable; but, to what purpose did their zeal serve? Only to hasten the fatal period of the ROMAN government, and render its convulsions and dying agonies more violent and painful.

I would not be understood to mean, that public affairs deserve no care and attention at all. Would men be moderate and consistent, their claims might be admitted; at least might be examined. The *country-party* might still assert, that our constitution, though excellent, will admit of mal-administration to a certain degree; and therefore, if the minister be bad, it is proper to oppose him with a *suitable* degree of zeal. And, on the other hand, the *court-party* may be allowed, upon the supposition that the minister were good, to defend, and with *some* zeal too, his administration. I would only persuade men not to contend, as if they were fighting *pro aris & focis*, and change a good constitution into a bad one, by the violence of their factions.[1]

I have not here considered any thing that is personal in the present controversy. In the best civil constitution, where every man is constrained by the most rigid laws, it is easy to discover either the good or bad intentions of a minister, and to judge, whether his personal character deserve love or hatred. But such questions are of little importance to the public, and lay those, who employ their pens upon them, under a just suspicion either of malevolence or of flattery.

ESSAY IV.—*Of the First Principles of Government.*

NOTHING appears more surprizing to those, who consider human affairs with a philosophical eye, than the easiness with which the many are governed by the few; and the

---

[1] [Editions D to P give in a note the well-known Character of Sir Robert Walpole. It will be found in the concluding section of Vol. IV.—ED.]

implicit submission, with which men resign their own sentiments and passions to those of their rulers. When we enquire by what means this wonder is effected, we shall find, that, as FORCE is always on the side of the governed, the governors have nothing to support them but opinion. It is therefore, on opinion only that government is founded; and this maxim extends to the most despotic and most military governments, as well as to the most free and most popular. The soldan of EGYPT, or the emperor of ROME, might drive his harmless subjects, like brute beasts, against their sentiments and inclination: But he must, at least, have led his *mamalukes*, or *prætorian bands*, like men, by their opinion.

Opinion is of two kinds, to wit, opinion of INTEREST, and opinion of RIGHT. By opinion of interest, I chiefly understand the sense of the general advantage which is reaped from government; together with the persuasion, that the particular government, which is established, is equally advantageous with any other that could easily be settled. When this opinion prevails among the generality of a state, or among those who have the force in their hands, it gives great security to any government.

Right is of two kinds, right to POWER and right to PROPERTY. What prevalence opinion of the first kind has over mankind, may easily be understood, by observing the attachment which all nations have to their ancient government, and even to those names, which have had the sanction of antiquity. Antiquity always begets the opinion of right; and whatever disadvantageous sentiments we may entertain of mankind, they are always found to be prodigal both of blood and treasure in the maintenance of public justice.[1] There is, indeed, no particular, in which, at first sight, there may appear a greater contradiction in the frame of the human mind than the present. When men act in a faction, they are apt, without shame or remorse, to neglect all the ties of honour and morality, in order to serve their party; and yet, when a faction is formed upon a point of right or principle, there is no occasion, where men discover a greater

---

[1] [Editions A to P insert as follows:—This passion we may denominate enthusiasm, or we may give it what appellation we please; but a politician, who should overlook its influence on human affairs, would prove himself but of a very limited understanding.

Editions A and B omit the remainder of the paragraph.]

obstinacy, and a more determined sense of justice and equity. The same social disposition of mankind is the cause of these contradictory appearances.

It is sufficiently understood, that the opinion of right to property is of moment in all matters of government. A noted author[1] has made property the foundation of all government; and most of our political writers seem inclined to follow him in that particular. This is carrying the matter too far; but still it must be owned, that the opinion of right to property has a great influence in this subject.

Upon these three opinions, therefore, of public *interest*, of *right to power*, and of *right to property*, are all governments founded, and all authority of the few over the many. There are indeed other principles, which add force to these, and determine, limit, or alter their operation; such as *self-interest, fear*, and *affection*: But still we may assert, that these other principles can have no influence alone, but suppose the antecedent influence of those opinions above-mentioned. They are, therefore, to be esteemed the secondary, not the original principles of government.

For, *first*, as to *self-interest*, by which I mean the expectation of particular rewards, distinct from the general protection which we receive from government, it is evident that the magistrate's authority must be antecedently established, at least be hoped for, in order to produce this expectation. The prospect of reward may augment his authority with regard to some particular persons; but can never give birth to it, with regard to the public. Men naturally look for the greatest favours from their friends and acquaintance; and therefore, the hopes of any considerable number of the state would never center in any particular set of men, if these men had no other title to magistracy, and had no separate influence over the opinions of mankind. The same observation may be extended to the other two principles of *fear* and *affection*. No man would have any reason to *fear* the fury of a tyrant, if he had no authority over any but from fear; since, as a single man, his bodily force can reach but a small way, and all the farther power he possesses must be founded either on our own opinion, or on the presumed opinion of others. And though *affection* to wisdom and virtue in a *sovereign* extends very far, and has great in-

[1] [Harrington: see p. 122.—Ed.]

fluence; yet he must antecedently be supposed invested with a public character, otherwise the public esteem will serve him in no stead, nor will his virtue have any influence beyond a narrow sphere.

A government may endure for several ages, though the balance of power, and the balance of property do not coincide. This chiefly happens, where any rank or order of the state has acquired a large share in the property; but from the original constitution of the government, has no share in the power. Under what pretence would any individual of that order assume authority in public affairs? As men are commonly much attached to their ancient government, it is not to be expected, that the public would ever favour such usurpations. But where the original constitution allows any share of power, though small, to an order of men, who possess a large share of the property, it is easy for them gradually to stretch their authority, and bring the balance of power to coincide with that of property. This has been the case with the house of commons in ENGLAND.

Most writers, that have treated of the BRITISH government, have supposed, that, as the lower house represents all the commons of GREAT BRITAIN, its weight in the scale is proportioned to the property and power of all whom it represents. But this principle must not be received as absolutely true. For though the people are apt to attach themselves more to the house of commons, than to any other member of the constitution; that house being chosen by them as their representatives, and as the public guardians of their liberty; yet are there instances where the house, even when in opposition to the crown, has not been followed by the people; as we may particularly observe of the *tory* house of commons in the reign of king WILLIAM. Were the members obliged to receive instructions from their constituents, like the DUTCH deputies, this would entirely alter the case; and if such immense power and riches, as those of all the commons of GREAT BRITAIN, were brought into the scale, it is not easy to conceive, that the crown could either influence that multitude of people, or withstand that overbalance of property. It is true, the crown has great influence over the collective body in the elections of members; but were this influence, which at present is only exerted once in seven years, to be employed in bringing over the people to every vote, it would soon be wasted; and no skill, popularity, or revenue, could support it. I must, therefore, be of opinion, that an alteration in this particular would introduce a total alteration in our government, and would soon reduce it to a pure republic; and, perhaps, to a republic of no inconvenient form. For though the people, collected in a body like the ROMAN tribes, be quite unfit for government, yet when dispersed in small bodies, they are more susceptible both of reason and order; the force of popular currents and tides is, in a great measure, broken; and the public interest may be pursued with some method and constancy. But it is needless to reason any farther concerning a form of government, which is never likely to have place in GREAT BRITAIN, and which seems not to be the aim of any party amongst us. Let us cherish and improve our ancient government as much as possible, without encouraging a passion for such dangerous novelties.[1]

ESSAY V.[2]—*Of the Origin of Government.*

MAN, born in a family, is compelled to maintain society, from necessity, from natural inclination, and from habit. The same creature, in his farther progress, is engaged to establish political society, in order to administer justice; without which there can be no peace among them, nor safety, nor mutual intercourse. We are, therefore, to look upon all the vast apparatus of our government, as having ultimately

---

[1] [Editions A to N add the following paragraph:—I shall conclude this subject with observing, that the present political controversy, with regard to instructions, is a very frivolous one, and can never be brought to any decision, as it is managed by both parties. The country-party pretend not, that a member is absolutely bound to follow instructions, as an ambassador or general is confined by his orders, and that his vote is not to be received in the house, but so far as it is conformable to them. The court-party again, pretend not, that the sentiments of the people ought to have no weight with every member; much less that he ought to despise the sentiments of those he represents, and with whom he is more particularly connected. And if their sentiments be of weight, why ought they not to express these sentiments? The question, then, is only concerning the degrees of weight, which ought to be plac'd on instructions. But such is the nature of language, that it is impossible for it to express distinctly these different degrees; and if men will carry on a controversy on this head, it may well happen, that they differ in their language, and yet agree in their sentiments; or differ in their sentiments, and yet agree in their language. Besides, how is it possible to find these degrees, considering the variety of affairs which come before the house, and the variety of places which members represent? Ought the instructions of TOTNESS to have the same weight as those of LONDON? or instructions, with regard to the *Convention*, which respected foreign politics, to have the same weight as those with regard to the *excise*, which respected only our domestic affairs?]

[2] [This Essay was added in the last Edition.]

no other object or purpose but <u>the distribution of justice</u>, or, in other words, the support of the twelve judges. Kings and parliaments, fleets and armies, officers of the court and revenue, ambassadors, ministers, and privy-counsellors, are all subordinate in their end to this part of administration. Even the clergy, as their duty leads them to inculcate morality, may justly be thought, so far as regards this world, to have no other useful object of their institution.

All men are sensible of the necessity of justice to maintain peace and order; and all men are sensible of the necessity of peace and order for the maintenance of society. Yet, notwithstanding this strong and obvious necessity, such is the frailty or perverseness of our nature! it is impossible to keep men, faithfully and unerringly, in the paths of justice. Some extraordinary circumstances may happen, in which a man finds his interests to be more promoted by fraud or rapine, than hurt by the breach which his injustice makes in the social union. But much more frequently, he is seduced from his great and important, but distant interests, by the allurement of present, though often very frivolous temptations. <u>This great weakness</u> is incurable in human nature.

Men must, therefore, endeavour to palliate what they cannot cure. They must institute some persons, under the appellation of magistrates, whose peculiar office it is, to point out the decrees of equity, to punish transgressors, to correct fraud and violence, and to oblige men, however reluctant, to consult their own real and permanent interests. In a word, OBEDIENCE is a new duty which must be invented to support that of JUSTICE; and the tyes of equity must be corroborated by those of allegiance.

But still, viewing matters in an abstract light, it may be thought, that nothing is gained by this alliance, and that the factitious duty of obedience, from its very nature, lays as feeble a hold of the human mind, as the primitive and natural duty of justice. Peculiar interests and present temptations may overcome the one as well as the other. They are equally exposed to the same inconvenience. And the man, who is inclined to be a bad neighbour, must be led by the same motives, well or ill understood, to be a bad citizen and subject. Not to mention, that the magistrate himself may often be negligent, or partial, or unjust in his administration.

Experience, however, proves, that there is a great difference between the cases. Order in society, we find, is much better maintained by means of government; and our duty to the magistrate is more strictly guarded by the principles of human nature, than our duty to our fellow-citizens. The love of dominion is so strong in the breast of man, that many, not only submit to, but court all the dangers, and fatigues, and cares of government; and men, once raised to that station, though often led astray by private passions, find, in ordinary cases, a visible interest in the impartial administration of justice. The persons, who first attain this distinction by the consent, tacit or express, of the people, must be endowed with superior personal qualities of valour, force, integrity, or prudence, which command respect and confidence: and after government is established, a regard to birth, rank, and station has a mighty influence over men, and enforces the decrees of the magistrate. The prince or leader exclaims against every disorder, which disturbs his society. He summons all his partizans and all men of probity to aid him in correcting and redressing it: and he is readily followed by all indifferent persons in the execution of his office. He soon acquires the power of rewarding these services; and in the progress of society, he establishes subordinate ministers and often a military force, who find an immediate and a visible interest, in supporting his authority. Habit soon consolidates what other principles of human nature had imperfectly founded; and men, once accustomed to obedience, never think of departing from that path, in which they and their ancestors have constantly trod, and to which they are confined by so many urgent and visible motives.

But though this progress of human affairs may appear certain and inevitable, and though the support which allegiance brings to justice, be founded on obvious principles of human nature, it cannot be expected that men should beforehand be able to discover them, or foresee their operation. Government commences more casually and more imperfectly. It is probable, that the first ascendant of one man over multitudes begun during a state of war; where the superiority of courage and of genius discovers itself most visibly, where unanimity and concert are most requisite, and where the pernicious effects of disorder are most sensibly felt. The long continuance of that state, an incident common among savage tribes, enured the people to submission; and if the chieftain possessed as much equity as prudence and valour, he became, even during peace, the arbiter of all differences, and could gradually, by a mixture of force and consent, establish his authority. The benefit sensibly felt from his influence, made it be cherished by the people, at least by the peaceable and well disposed among them; and if his son enjoyed the same good qualities, government advanced the sooner to maturity and perfection; but was still in a feeble state, till the farther progress of improvement procured the magistrate a revenue, and enabled him to bestow rewards on the several instruments of his administration, and to inflict punishments on the refractory and disobedient. Before that period, each exertion of his influence must have been particular, and founded on the peculiar circumstances of the case. After it, submission was no longer a matter of choice in the bulk of the community, but was rigorously exacted by the authority of the supreme magistrate.

In all governments, there is a perpetual intestine struggle, open or secret, between AUTHORITY and LIBERTY; and neither of them can ever absolutely prevail in the contest. A great sacrifice of liberty must necessarily be made in every government; yet even the authority, which confines liberty, can never, and perhaps ought never, in any constitution, to become quite entire and uncontroulable. The sultan is master of the life and fortune of any individual; but will not be permitted to impose new taxes on his subjects: a French monarch can impose taxes at pleasure; but would find it dangerous to attempt the lives and fortunes of individuals. Religion also, in most countries, is commonly found to be a very intractable principle; and other principles or prejudices frequently resist all the authority of the civil magistrate; whose power, being founded on opinion, can never subvert other opinions, equally rooted with that of his title to dominion. The government, which, in common appellation, receives the appellation of free, is that which admits of a partition of power among several members, whose united authority is no less, or is commonly greater than that of any monarch; but who, in the usual course of administration, must act by general and equal laws, that are previously known to all the members and to all their subjects. In this sense, it must be owned, that liberty is the perfection of civil society; but still authority must be acknowledged essential to its very existence: and in those contests, which so often take place between the one and the other, the latter may, on that account, challenge the preference. Unless perhaps one may say (and it may be said with some reason) that a circumstance, which is essential to the existence of civil society, must always support itself, and needs be guarded with less jealousy, than one that contributes only to its perfection, which the indolence of men is so apt to neglect, or their ignorance to overlook.

ESSAY VI.—*On the Independency of Parliament.*[1]

POLITICAL writers have established it as a maxim, that, in contriving any system of government, and fixing the several checks and controuls of the constitution, every man ought to

---

[1] [In Editions A to N this Essay is introduced by the following examination of the spirit of parties.

I have frequently observed, in comparing the conduct of the *court* and *country* parties, that the former are commonly less assuming and dogmatical in conversation, more apt to make concessions; and tho' not, perhaps, more susceptible of conviction, yet more able to bear contradiction than the latter; who are apt to fly out upon any opposition, and to regard one as a mercenary designing fellow, if he argues with any coolness and impartiality, or makes any concessions to their adversaries. This is a fact, which, I believe, every one may have observed, who has been much in companies where political questions have been discussed; tho', were one to ask the reason of this difference, every party would be apt to assign a different reason. Gentlemen in the *Opposition* will ascribe it to the very nature of their party, which, being founded on public spirit, and a zeal for the constitution, cannot easily endure such doctrines, as are of pernicious consequence to liberty. The courtiers, on the other hand, will be apt to put us in mind of the clown mentioned by lord SHAFTSBURY. "A clown," says that excellent author,[1] "once took a fancy to hear the *Latin* disputes of doctors at an university. He was asked what pleasure he could take in viewing such combatants, when he could never know so much, as which of the parties had the better. *For that matter,* replied the clown, *I a'n't such a fool neither, but I can see who's the first that puts t'other into a passion.* Nature herself dictated this lesson to the clown, that he who had the better of the argument would be easy and well-humoured: But he who was unable to support his cause by reason would naturally lose his temper and grow violent."

To which of these reasons shall we adhere? To neither of them, in my opinion; unless we have a mind to enlist ourselves and become zealots in either party. I believe I can assign the reason of this different conduct of the two parties, without offending either. The country party are plainly most popular at present, and perhaps have been so in most administrations: So that, being accustomed to prevail in company, they cannot endure to hear their opinions controverted, but are as confident on the public favour, as if they were supported in all their sentiments by the most infallible demonstration. The courtiers, on the other hand, are commonly so run down by popular talkers, that if you speak to them with any moderation, or make them the smallest concessions, they think themselves extremely beholden to you, and are apt to return the favour by a like moderation and facility on their part. To be furious and passionate, they know, would only gain them

[1] Miscellaneous Reflections, 107.

be supposed a *knave*, and to have no other end, in all his actions, than private interest. By this interest we must govern him, and, by means of it, make him, notwithstanding his insatiable avarice and ambition, co-operate to public good. Without this, say they, we shall in vain boast of the advantages of any constitution, and shall find, in the end, that we have no security for our liberties or possessions, except the good-will of our rulers; that is, we shall have no security at all.

It is, therefore, a just *political* maxim, *that every man must be supposed a knave*: Though at the same time, it appears somewhat strange, that a maxim should be true in *politics*,

---

the character of *shameless mercenaries*; not that of *zealous patriots*, which is the character that such a warm behaviour is apt to acquire to the other party.

In all controversies, we find, without regarding the truth or falshood on either side, that those who defend the established and popular opinions, are always the most dogmatical and imperious in their stile: while their adversaries affect almost extraordinary gentleness and moderation, in order to soften, as much as possible, any prejudices that may lye against them. Consider the behaviour of our *free-thinkers* of all denominations, whether they be such as decry all revelation, or only oppose the exorbitant power of the clergy; *Collins, Tindal, Foster, Hoadley*. Compare their moderation and good manners with the furious zeal and scurrility of their adversaries, and you will be convinced of the truth of my observation. A like difference may be observed in the conduct of those French writers, who maintained the controversy with regard to ancient and modern learning. *Boileau*, Monsieur and Madame *Dacier*, l'Abbé de *Bos*, who defended the party of the ancients, mixed their reasonings with satire and invective; while Fontenelle, la Motte, Charpentier, and even Perrault, never transgressed the bounds of moderation and good breeding; though provoked by the most injurious treatment of their adversaries.

[I must, however, observe, that this Remark with regard to the seeming Moderation of the *Court* Party, is entirely confin'd to Conversation, and to Gentlemen, who have been engag'd by Interest or Inclination in that Party. For as to the Court-Writers, being commonly hir'd Scriblers, they are altogether as scurrilous as the Mercenaries of the other Party; nor has the *Gazetter* any Advantage, in this Respect, above *Common Sense*. A man of Education will, in any Party, discover himself to be such, by his Good-breeding and Decency; as a Scoundrel will always betray the opposite Qualities. *The false Accusers accus'd*, &c. is very scurrilous, tho' that Side of the Question, being least popular, shou'd be defended with most Moderation. When L — d B — e, L — d M — t, Mr. L — n take the Pen in Hand, tho' they write with Warmth, they presume not upon their Popularity so far as to transgress the Bounds of Decency.[1]]

I am led into this train of reflection, by considering some papers wrote upon that grand topic of *court influence and parliamentary dependence*, where, in my humble opinion, the country party, besides vehemence and satyre, shew too rigid an inflexibility, and too great a jealousy of making concessions to their adversaries. Their reasonings lose their force by being carried too far; and the popularity of their opinions has seduced them to neglect in some measure their justness and solidity. The following reason will, I hope, serve to justify me in this opinion.]

---

[1] [This paragraph is only found in Editions A and B.]

which is false in *fact*. But to satisfy us on this head, we may consider, that men are generally more honest in their private than in their public capacity, and will go greater lengths to serve a party, than when their own private interest is alone concerned. Honour is a great check upon mankind: But where a considerable body of men act together, this check is, in a great measure, removed; since a man is sure to be approved of by his own party, for what promotes the common interest; and he soon learns to despise the clamours of adversaries. To which we may add, that every court or senate is determined by the greater number of voices; so that, if self-interest influences only the majority, (as it will always do[1]) the whole senate follows the allurements of this separate interest, and acts as if it contained not one member, who had any regard to public interest and liberty.

When there offers, therefore, to our censure and examination, any plan of government, real or imaginary, where the power is distributed among several courts, and several orders of men, we should always consider the separate interest of each court, and each order; and, if we find that, by the skilful division of power, this interest must necessarily, in its operation, concur with public, we may pronounce that government to be wise and happy. If, on the contrary, separate interest be not checked, and be not directed to the public, we ought to look for nothing but faction, disorder, and tyranny from such a government. In this opinion I am justified by experience, as well as by the authority of all philosophers and politicians, both antient and modern.

How much, therefore, would it have surprised such a genius as CICERO, or TACITUS, to have been told, that, in a future age, there should arise a very regular system of *mixed* government, where the authority was so distributed, that one rank, whenever it pleased, might swallow up all the rest, and engross the whole power of the constitution. Such a government, they would say, will not be a mixed government. For so great is the natural ambition of men, that they are never satisfied with power; and if one order of men, by pursuing its own interest, can usurp upon every other order, it will certainly do so, and render itself, as far as possible, absolute and uncontroulable.

But, in this opinion, experience shews they would have

[1] [In the present depraved state of mankind. Editions A to D.]

been mistaken. For this is actually the case with the BRITISH constitution. The share of power, allotted by our constitution to the house of commons, is so great, that it absolutely commands all the other parts of the government. The king's legislative power is plainly no proper check to it. For though the king has a negative in framing laws; yet this, in fact, is esteemed of so little moment, that whatever is voted by the two houses, is always sure to pass into a law, and the royal assent is little better than a form. The principal weight of the crown lies in the executive power. But besides that the executive power in every government is altogether subordinate to the legislative; besides this, I say, the exercise of this power requires an immense expence; and the commons have assumed to themselves the sole right of granting money. How easy, therefore, would it be for that house to wrest from the crown all these powers, one after another; by making every grant conditional, and choosing their time so well, that their refusal of supply should only distress the government, without giving foreign powers any advantage over us? Did the house of commons depend in the same manner on the king, and had none of the members any property but from his gift, would not he command all their resolutions, and be from that moment absolute? As to the house of lords, they are a very powerful support to the Crown, so long as they are, in their turn, supported by it; but both experience and reason shew, that they have no force or authority sufficient to maintain themselves alone, without such support.

How, therefore, shall we solve this paradox? And by what means is this member of our constitution confined within the proper limits; since, from our very constitution, it must necessarily have as much power as it demands, and can only be confined by itself? How is this consistent with our experience of human nature? I answer, that the interest of the body is here restrained by that of the individuals, and that the house of commons stretches not its power, because such an usurpation would be contrary to the interest of the majority of its members. The crown has so many offices at its disposal, that, when assisted by the honest and disinterested part of the house, it will always command the resolutions of the whole so far, at least, as to preserve the antient constitution from danger. We may, therefore, give to this influence what name we please; we may call it by the invidious appellations of *corruption* and *dependence*; but some degree and some kind of it are inseparable from the very nature of the constitution, and necessary to the preservation of our mixed government.

Instead then of asserting[1] absolutely, that the dependence of parliament, in every degree, is an infringement of BRITISH liberty, the country-party should have made some concessions to their adversaries, and have only examined what was the proper degree of this dependence, beyond which it became dangerous to liberty. But such a moderation is not to be expected in party-men of any kind. After a concession of this nature, all declamation must be abandoned; and a calm enquiry into the proper degree of court-influence and parliamentary dependence would have been expected by the readers. And though the advantage, in such a controversy, might possibly remain to the *country-party*; yet the victory would not be so compleat as they wish for, nor would a true patriot have given an entire loose to his zeal, for fear of running matters into a contrary extreme, by diminishing too[2] far the influence of the crown. It was, therefore, thought best to deny, that this extreme could ever be dangerous to the constitution, or that the crown could ever have too little influence over members of parliament.

All questions concerning the proper medium between extremes are difficult to be decided; both because it is not easy to find *words* proper to fix this medium, and because the good and ill, in such cases, run so gradually into each other, as even to render our *sentiments* doubtful and uncertain. But there is a peculiar difficulty in the present case, which would embarrass the most knowing and most impartial examiner. The power of the crown is always lodged in a single person, either king or minister; and as this person may have either a greater or less degree of ambition, capacity, courage, popularity, or fortune, the power, which is too great in one hand,

---

[1] See *Dissertation on Parties*, throughout.

[2] By that *influence of the crown*, which I would justify, I mean only, that arising from the offices and honours which are at the disposal of the crown. As to private *bribery*, it may be considered in the same light as the practice of employing spies, which is scarce justifiable in a good minister, and is infamous in a bad one: But to be a spy, or to be corrupted, is always infamous under all ministers, and is to be regarded as a shameless prostitution. POLYBIUS justly esteems the pecuniary influence of the senate and censors to be one of the regular and constitutional weights, which preserved the balance of the ROMAN government, Lib. 6, cap. 15. [The reference to Polybius was added in Edition K.]

may become too little in another. In pure republics, where the authority is distributed among several assemblies or senates, the checks and controuls are more regular in their operation; because the members of such numerous assemblies may be presumed to be always nearly equal in capacity and virtue; and it is only their number, riches, or authority, which enter into consideration. But a limited monarchy admits not of any such stability; nor is it possible to assign to the crown such a determinate degree of power, as will, in every hand, form a proper counterbalance to the other parts of the constitution. This is an unavoidable disadvantage, among the many advantages, attending that species of government.

ESSAY VII.—*Whether the British Government inclines more to Absolute Monarchy, or to a Republic.*

IT affords a violent prejudice against almost every science, that no prudent man, however sure of his principles, dares prophesy concerning any event, or foretel the remote consequences of things. A physician will not venture to pronounce concerning the condition of his patient a fortnight or month after: And still less dares a politician foretel the situation of public affairs a few years hence. HARRINGTON thought himself so sure of his general principle, *that the balance of power depends on that of property*, that he ventured to pronounce it impossible ever to re-establish monarchy in ENGLAND: But his book was scarcely published when the king was restored; and we see, that monarchy has ever since subsisted upon the same footing as before. Notwithstanding this unlucky example, I will venture to examine an important question, to wit, *Whether the* BRITISH *government inclines more to absolute monarchy, or to a republic; and in which of these two species of government it will most probably terminate?* As there seems not to be any great danger of a sudden revolution either way, I shall at least escape the shame attending my temerity, if I should be found to have been mistaken.

Those who assert, that the balance of our government inclines towards absolute monarchy, may support their opinion by the following reasons. That property has a great influence on power cannot possibly be denied; but yet the general maxim, *that the balance of one depends on the balance of the other*, must be received with several limitations. It is evident, that much less property in a single hand will be able to counterbalance a greater property in several; not only because it is difficult to make many persons combine in the same views and measures; but because property, when united, causes much greater dependence, than the same property, when dispersed. A hundred persons, of 1000*l.* a year a-piece, can consume all their income, and no body shall ever be the better for them, except their servants and tradesmen, who justly regard their profits as the product of their own labour. But a man possessed of 100,000*l.* a year, if he has either any generosity or any cunning, may create a great dependence by obligations, and still a greater by expectations. Hence we may observe, that, in all free governments, any subject exorbitantly rich has always created jealousy, even though his riches bore no proportion to those of the state. CRASSUS's fortune, if I remember well, amounted[1] only to[2] about two millions and a half of our money; yet we find, that, though his genius was nothing extraordinary, he was able, by means of his riches alone, to counterbalance, during his lifetime, the power of POMPEY as well as that of CÆSAR, who afterwards became master of the world. The wealth of the MEDICI made them masters of FLORENCE; though, it is probable, it was not considerable, compared to the united property of that opulent republic.

These considerations are apt to make one entertain a magnificent idea of the BRITISH spirit and love of liberty; since we could maintain our free government, during so many centuries, against our sovereigns, who, besides the power and dignity and majesty of the crown, have always been possessed of much more property than any subject has ever enjoyed in any commonwealth. But it may be said, that this spirit, however great, will never be able to support itself against that immense property, which is now lodged in the king, and which is still encreasing. Upon a moderate computation, there are near three millions a year at the disposal of the crown. The civil list amounts to near a million; the collection of all taxes to another; and the employments in the

---

[1] [Editions A and B: to Three Thousand Talents a Year, about 400,000*l.* Sterling.—Editions D to Q: only to about sixteen hundred thousand pounds in our money.]

[2] [Editions D to Q add: As interest in Rome was higher than with us, this might yield above 100,000*l.* a year.]

army and navy, together with ecclesiastical preferments, to above a third million: An enormous sum, and what may fairly be computed to be more than a thirtieth part of the whole income and labour of the kingdom. When we add to this great property, the encreasing luxury of the nation, our proneness to corruption, together with the great power and prerogatives of the crown, and the command of military force, there is no one but must despair of being able, without extraordinary efforts, to support our free government much longer under these disadvantages.

On the other hand, those who maintain, that the byass of the BRITISH government leans towards a republic, may support their opinion by specious arguments. It may be said, that, though this immense property in the crown, be joined to the dignity of first magistrate, and to many other legal powers and prerogatives, which should naturally give it greater influence; yet it really becomes less dangerous to liberty upon that very account. Were ENGLAND a republic, and were any private man possessed of a revenue, a third, or even a tenth part as large as that of the crown, he would very justly excite jealousy; because he would infallibly have great authority, in the government: And such an irregular authority, not avowed by the laws, is always more dangerous than a much greater authority, derived from them. A man, possessed of usurped power, can set no bounds to his pretensions:[1] His partizans have liberty to hope for every thing in his favour: His enemies provoke his ambition, with his fears, by the violence of their opposition: And the government being thrown into a ferment, every corrupted humour in the state naturally gathers to him. On the contrary, a legal authority, though great, has always some bounds, which terminate both the hopes and pretensions of the person possessed of it: The laws must have provided a remedy against its excesses: Such an eminent magistrate has much to fear, and little to hope from his usurpations: And as his legal authority is quietly submitted to, he has small temptation and small opportunity of extending it farther. Besides, it happens, with regard to ambitious aims and projects, what may be observed with regard to sects of philosophy and reli-

---

[1] [Editions A to N have the note: On ne monte jamais si haut que quand on ne scait pas ou on va, said Cromwell to the President de Bellievre.—De Retz's Memoirs.]

gion. A new sect excites such a ferment, and is both opposed and defended with such vehemence, that it always spreads faster, and multiplies its partizans with greater rapidity, than any old established opinion, recommended by the sanction of the laws and of antiquity. Such is the nature of novelty, that, where any thing pleases, it becomes doubly agreeable, if new; but if it displeases, it is doubly displeasing, upon that very account. And, in most cases, the violence of enemies is favourable to ambitious projects, as well as the zeal of partizans.

It may farther be said, that, though men be much governed by interest; yet even interest itself, and all human affairs, are entirely governed by *opinion*. Now, there has been a sudden and sensible change in the opinions of men within these last fifty years, by the progress of learning and of liberty. Most people, in this island, have divested themselves of all superstitious reverence to names and authority: The clergy have[1] much lost their credit: Their pretensions and doctrines have been ridiculed; and even religion can scarcely support itself in the world. The mere name of *king* commands little respect; and to talk of a king as GOD's viceregent on earth, or to give him any of those magnificent titles, which formerly dazzled mankind, would but excite laughter in every one. Though the crown, by means of its large revenue, may maintain its authority in times of tranquillity, upon private interest and influence; yet, as the least shock or convulsion must break all these interests to pieces, the royal power, being no longer supported by the settled principles and opinions of men, will immediately dissolve. Had men been in the same disposition at the *revolution*, as they are at present, monarchy would have run a great risque of being entirely lost in this island.

Durst I venture to deliver my own sentiments amidst these opposite arguments, I would assert, that, unless there happen some extraordinary convulsion, the power of the crown, by means of its large revenue, is rather upon the encrease; though, at the same time I own, that its progress seems very slow, and almost insensible. The tide has run long, and with some rapidity, to the side of popular government, and is just beginning to turn towards monarchy.

It is well known, that every government must come to a

[1] [Editions A to D read: have entirely lost.]

period, and that death is unavoidable to the political as well as to the animal body. But, as one kind of death may be preferable to another, it may be enquired, whether it be more desirable for the BRITISH constitution to terminate in a popular government, or in absolute monarchy? Here I would frankly declare, that, though liberty be preferable to slavery, in almost every case; yet I should rather wish to see an absolute monarch than a republic in this island. For, let us consider, what kind of republic we have reason to expect. The question is not concerning any fine imaginary republic, of which a man may form a plan in his closet. There is no doubt, but a popular government may be imagined more perfect than absolute monarchy, or even than our present constitution. But what reason have we to expect that any such government will ever be established in GREAT BRITAIN, upon the dissolution of our monarchy? If any single person acquire power enough to take our constitution to pieces, and put it up a-new, he is really an absolute monarch; and we have already had an instance of this kind, sufficient to convince us, that such a person will never resign his power, or establish any free government. Matters, therefore, must be trusted to their natural progress and operation; and the house of commons, according to its present constitution, must be the only legislature in such a popular government. The inconveniencies attending such a situation of affairs, present themselves by thousands. If the house of commons, in such a case, ever dissolve itself, which is not to be expected, we may look for a civil war every election. If it continue itself, we shall suffer all the tyranny of a faction, subdivided into new factions. And as such a violent government cannot long subsist, we shall, at last, after many convulsions, and civil wars, find repose in absolute monarchy, which it would have been happier for us to have established peaceably from the beginning. Absolute monarchy, therefore, is the easiest death, the true *Euthanasia* of the BRITISH constitution.

Thus, if we have reason to be more jealous of monarchy, because the danger is more imminent from that quarter; we have also reason to be more jealous of popular government, because that danger is more terrible. This may teach us a lesson of moderation in all our political controversies.

Essay VIII.—*Of Parties in General.*

OF all men, that distinguish themselves by memorable atchievements, the first place of honour seems due to LEGISLATORS and founders of states, who transmit a system of laws and institutions to secure the peace, happiness, and liberty of future generations. The influence of useful inventions in the arts and sciences may, perhaps, extend farther than that of wise laws, whose effects are limited both in time and place; but the benefit arising from the former, is not so sensible as that which results from the latter. Speculative sciences do, indeed, improve the mind; but this advantage reaches only to a few persons, who have leisure to apply themselves to them. And as to practical arts, which encrease the commodities and enjoyments of life, it is well known, that men's happiness consists not so much in an abundance of these, as in the peace and security with which they possess them; and those blessings can only be derived from good government. Not to mention, that general virtue and good morals in a state, which are so requisite to happiness, can never arise from the most refined precepts of philosophy, or even the severest injunctions of religion; but must proceed entirely from the virtuous education of youth, the effect of wise laws and institutions. I must, therefore, presume to differ from Lord BACON in this particular, and must regard antiquity as somewhat unjust in its distribution of honours, when it made gods of all the inventors of useful arts, such as CERES, BACCHUS, ÆSCULAPIUS; and dignify legislators, such as ROMULUS and THESEUS, only with the appellation of demigods and heroes.

As much as legislators and founders of states ought to be honoured and respected among men, as much ought the founders of sects and factions to be detested and hated; because the influence of faction is directly contrary to that of laws. Factions subvert government, render laws impotent, and beget the fiercest animosities among men of the same nation, who ought to give mutual assistance and protection to each other. And what should render the founders of parties more odious is, the difficulty of extirpating these weeds, when once they have taken root in any state. They naturally propagate themselves for many centuries, and seldom end but by the total dissolution of that government, in which they are sown. They are, besides, plants which grow most plentifully in the richest soil; and though absolute governments be not wholly free from them, it must be confessed, that they rise more easily, and propagate themselves faster in free governments, where they always infect the legislature itself, which alone could be able, by the steady application of rewards and punishments, to eradicate them.

Factions may be divided into PERSONAL and REAL; that is, into factions, founded on personal friendship or animosity among such as compose the contending parties, and into those founded on some real difference of sentiment or interest. The reason of this distinction is obvious; though I must acknowledge, that parties are seldom found pure and unmixed, either of the one kind or the other. It is not often seen, that a government divides into factions, where there is no difference in the views of the constituent members, either real or apparent, trivial or material: And in those factions, which are founded on the most real and most material difference, there is always observed a great deal of personal animosity or affection. But notwithstanding this mixture, a party may be denominated either personal or real, according to that principle which is predominant, and is found to have the greatest influence.

Personal factions arise most easily in small republics. Every domestic quarrel, there, becomes an affair of state. Love, vanity, emulation, any passion, as well as ambition and resentment, begets public division. The NERI and BIANCHI of FLORENCE, the FREGOSI and ADORNI of GENOA, the COLONESI and ORSINI of modern ROME, were parties of this kind.

Men have such a propensity to divide into personal factions, that the smallest appearance of real difference will produce them. What can be imagined more trivial than the difference between one colour of livery and another in horse races? Yet this difference begat two most inveterate factions in the GREEK empire, the PRASINI and VENETI, who never suspended their animosities, till they ruined that unhappy government.

[1] We find in the ROMAN history a remarkable dissension between two tribes, the POLLIA and PAPIRIA, which continued for the space of near three hundred years, and discovered

---

[1] [This paragraph was added in Edition B.]

itself in their suffrages at every election of magistrates.[1] This faction was the more remarkable, as it could continue for so long a tract of time; even though it did not spread itself, nor draw any of the other tribes into a share of the quarrel. If mankind had not a strong propensity to such divisions, the indifference of the rest of the community must have suppressed this foolish animosity, that had not any aliment of new benefits and injuries, of general sympathy and antipathy, which never fail to take place, when the whole state is rent into two equal factions.

Nothing is more usual than to see parties, which have begun upon a real difference, continue even after that difference is lost. When men are once inlisted on opposite sides, they contract an affection to the persons with whom they are united, and an animosity against their antagonists: And these passions they often transmit to their posterity. The real difference between GUELF and GHIBBELLINE was long lost in Italy, before these factions were extinguished. The GUELFS adhered to the pope, the GHIBBELLINES to the emperor; yet the family of SFORZA, who were in alliance with the emperor, though they were GUELFS, being expelled MILAN by the king[2] of FRANCE, assisted by JACOMO TRIVULZIO and the GHIBBELLINES, the pope concurred with the latter, and they formed leagues with the pope against the emperor.

The civil wars which arose some few years ago in MOROCCO, between the *blacks* and *whites*, merely on account of their complexion, are founded on a pleasant difference. We laugh at them; but I believe, were things rightly examined, we afford much more occasion of ridicule to the MOORS. For, what are all the wars of religion, which have prevailed in this polite and knowing part of the world? They are certainly more absurd than the MOORISH civil wars.

---

[1] As this fact has not been much observed by antiquaries or politicians, I shall deliver it in the words of the ROMAN historian. *Populus* TUSCULANUS *cum conjugibus ac liberis* ROMAM *venit: Ea multitudo, veste mutata, et specie reorum tribus circuit, genibus se omnium advolvens. Plus itaque misericordia ad poenae veniam impetrandam, quam causa ad crimen purgandum valuit. Tribus omnes praeter* POLLIAM, *antiquarunt legem.* POLLIAE *sententia fuit, puberes verberatos necari, liberos conjugesque sub corona lege belli venire: Memoriamque ejus irae* TUSCULANIS *in poenae tam atrocis auctores mansisse ad patris aetatem constat; nec quemquam fere ex* POLLIA *tribu candidatum* PAPIRIAM *ferre solitam,* T. LIVII, lib. 8. 37. The CASTELANI and NICOLLOTI are two mobbish factions in VENICE, who frequently box together, and then lay aside their quarrels presently. [The last sentence was added in Edition D.]

[2] LEWIS XII.

The difference of complexion is a sensible and a real difference: But the controversy about an article of faith, which is utterly absurd and unintelligible, is not a difference in sentiment, but in a few phrases and expressions, which one party accepts of, without understanding them; and the other refuses in the same manner.[1]

Real factions may be divided into those from *interest*, from *principle*, and from *affection*. Of all factions, the first are the most reasonable, and the most excusable. When two orders of men, such as the nobles and people, have a distinct authority in a government, not very accurately balanced and modelled, they naturally follow a distinct interest; nor can we reasonably expect a different conduct, considering that degree of selfishness implanted in human nature. It requires great skill in a legislator to prevent such parties; and many philosophers are of opinion, that this secret, like the *grand elixir*, or *perpetual motion*, may amuse men in theory, but can never possibly be reduced to practice. In despotic governments, indeed, factions often do not appear; but they are not the less real; or rather, they are more real and more pernicious, upon that very account. The distinct orders of men, nobles and people, soldiers and merchants, have all a distinct interest; but the more powerful oppresses the weaker with impunity, and without resistance; which begets a seeming tranquillity in such governments.[2]

There has been an attempt in ENGLAND to divide the *landed* and *trading* part of the nation; but without success. The interests of these two bodies are not really distinct, and never will be so, till our public debts encrease to such a degree, as to become altogether oppressive and intolerable.

Parties from *principle*, especially abstract speculative principle, are known only to modern times, and are, perhaps, the most extraordinary and unaccountable *phænomenon*, that has yet appeared in human affairs. Where different principles beget a contrariety of conduct, which is the case with all different political principles, the matter may be more

---

[1] [Editions A to P add the following: Besides, I do not find that the *whites* in MOROCCO ever imposed on the *blacks* any necessity of altering their complexion, or threatened them with inquisitions and penal laws in case of obstinacy: nor have the *blacks* been more unreasonable in this particular. But is a man's opinion, where he is able to form a real opinion, more at his disposal than his complexion? And can one be induced by force or fear to do more than paint and disguise in the one case as well as in the other?]

[2] [See *Considerations sur le Grandeur et sur la Decadence de Romains*. Edition K.]

easily explained. A man, who esteems the true right of government to lie in one man, or one family, cannot easily agree with his fellow-citizen, who thinks that another man or family is possessed of this right. Each naturally wishes that right may take place, according to his own notions of it. But where the difference of principle is attended with no contrariety of action, but every one may follow his own way, without interfering with his neighbour, as happens in all religious controversies: what madness, what fury can beget such unhappy and such fatal divisions?

Two men travelling on the highway, the one east, the other west, can easily pass each other, if the way be broad enough: But two men, reasoning upon opposite principles of religion, cannot so easily pass, without shocking; though one should think, that the way were also, in that case, sufficiently broad, and that each might proceed, without interruption, in his own course. But such is the nature of the human mind, that it always lays hold on every mind that approaches it; and as it is wonderfully fortified by an unanimity of sentiments, so is it shocked and disturbed by any contrariety. Hence the eagerness, which most people discover in a dispute; and hence their impatience of opposition, even in the most speculative and indifferent opinions.

This principle, however frivolous it may appear, seems to have been the origin of all religious wars and divisions. But as this principle is universal in human nature, its effects would not have been confined to one age, and to one sect of religion, did it not there concur with other more accidental causes, which raise it to such a height, as to produce the greatest misery and devastation. Most religions of the ancient world arose in the unknown ages of government, when men were as yet barbarous and uninstructed, and the prince, as well as the peasant, was disposed to receive, with implicit faith, every pious tale of fiction, which was offered him. The magistrate embraced the religion of the people, and entering cordially into the care of sacred matters, naturally acquired an authority in them, and united the ecclesiastical with the civil power. But the *Christian* religion arising, while principles directly opposite to it were firmly established in the polite part of the world who despised the nation that first broached this novelty; no wonder, that, in such circumstances, it was but little countenanced by the civil magistrate, and that the priesthood was allowed to engross all the authority in the new sect. So bad a use did they make of this power, even in those early times, that the primitive persecutions may, perhaps, *in part*,[1] be ascribed to the violence instilled by them into their followers. And the same principles of priestly government continuing, after Christianity became the established religion, they have engendered a spirit of persecution, which has ever since been the poison of human society, and the source of the most inveterate factions in every government. Such divisions, therefore, on the part of the people, may justly be esteemed factions of *principle*; but, on the part of the priests, who are the prime movers, they are really factions of *interest*.

There is another cause (beside the authority of the priests, and the separation of the ecclesiastical and civil powers) which has contributed to render CHRISTENDOM the scene of religious wars and divisions. Religions, that arise in ages totally ignorant and barbarous, consist mostly of traditional tales and fictions, which may be different in every sect, without being contrary to each other; and even when they are contrary, every one adheres to the tradition of his own sect, without much reasoning or disputation. But as philosophy was widely spread over the world, at the time when Christianity arose, the teachers of the new sect were obliged to form a system of speculative opinions; to divide, with some accuracy, their articles of faith; and to explain, comment,

---

[1] I say, *in part*; For it is a vulgar error to imagine, that the ancients were as great friends to toleration as the ENGLISH or DUTCH are at present. The laws against external superstition, amongst the ROMANS, were as ancient [as the time of the twelve tables]; and the JEWS as well as CHRISTIANS were sometimes punished by them; though, in general, these laws were not rigorously executed. Immediately after the conquest of GAUL, they forbad all but the natives to be initiated into the religion of the DRUIDS; and this was a kind of persecution. In about a century after this conquest, [the emperor, CLAUDIUS,] quite abolished that superstition by penal laws; which would have been a very grievous persecution, if the imitation of the ROMAN manners had not, before-hand, weaned the GAULS from their ancient prejudices. SUETONIUS *in vita* CLAUDII. [PLINY ascribes the abolition of the Druidical superstitions to TIBERIUS, probably because that emperor had taken some steps towards restraining them (lib. xxx. cap. i.)] This is an instance of the usual caution and moderation of the ROMANS in such cases; and very different from their violent and sanguinary method of treating the *Christians*. Hence we may entertain a suspicion, that those furious persecutions of *Christianity* were in some measure owing to the imprudent zeal and bigotry of the first propagators of that sect; and Ecclesiastical history affords us many reasons to confirm this suspicion. [This note is not in A. B and D read: 'were very ancient,' 'they quite,' and omit the reference to PLINY.]

confute, and defend with all the subtilty of argument and science. Hence naturally arose keenness in dispute, when the Christian religion came to be split into new divisions and heresies: And this keenness assisted the priests in their policy, of begetting a mutual hatred and antipathy among their deluded followers. Sects of philosophy, in the ancient world, were more zealous than parties of religion; but in modern times, parties of religion are more furious and enraged than the most cruel factions that ever arose from interest and ambition.

I have mentioned parties from *affection* as a kind of *real* parties, beside those from *interest* and *principle*. By parties from affection, I understand those which are founded on the different attachments of men towards particular families and persons, whom they desire to rule over them. These factions are often very violent; though, I must own, it may seem unaccountable, that men should attach themselves so strongly to persons, with whom they are no wise acquainted, whom perhaps they never saw, and from whom they never received, nor can ever hope for any favour. Yet this we often find to be the case, and even with men, who, on other occasions, discover no great generosity of spirit, nor are found to be easily transported by friendship beyond their own interest. We are apt to think the relation between us and our sovereign very close and intimate. The splendour of majesty and power bestows an importance on the fortunes even of a single person. And when a man's good-nature does not give him this imaginary interest, his ill-nature will, from spite and opposition to persons whose sentiments are different from his own.

Essay IX.—*Of the Parties of Great Britain.*

WERE the British Government proposed as a subject of speculation, one would immediately perceive in it a source of division and party, which it would be almost impossible for it, under any administration, to avoid. The just balance between the republican and monarchical part of our constitution is really, in itself, so extremely delicate and uncertain, that, when joined to men's passions and prejudices, it is impossible but different opinions must arise concerning it, even among persons of the best understanding. Those of mild tempers, who love peace and order, and detest sedition and civil wars, will always entertain more favourable sentiments of monarchy, than men of bold and generous spirits, who are passionate lovers of liberty, and think no evil comparable to subjection and slavery. And though all reasonable men agree in general to preserve our mixed government; yet, when they come to particulars, some will incline to trust greater powers to the crown, to bestow on it more influence, and to guard against its encroachments with less caution, than others who are terrified at the most distant approaches of tyranny and despotic power. Thus are there parties of PRINCIPLE involved in the very nature of our constitution, which may properly enough be denominated those of COURT and COUNTRY.[1] The strength and violence of each of these parties will much depend upon the particular administration. An administration may be so bad, as to throw a great majority into the opposition; as a good administration will reconcile to the court many of the most passionate lovers of liberty. But however the nation may fluctuate between them, the parties themselves will always subsist, so long as we are governed by a limited monarchy.

But, besides this difference of *Principle*, those parties are very much fomented by a difference of INTEREST, without which they could scarcely ever be dangerous or violent. The crown will naturally bestow all trust and power upon those, whose principles, real or pretended, are most favourable to monarchical government; and this temptation will naturally engage them to go greater lengths than their principles would otherwise carry them. Their antagonists, who were disappointed in their ambitious aims, throw themselves into the party whose sentiments incline them to be most jealous of royal power, and naturally carry those sentiments to a greater height than sound politics will justify. Thus *Court* and *Country*, which are the genuine offspring of the BRITISH

---

[1] [Editions A to P add the following note: These words have become of general use, and therefore I shall employ them, without intending to express by them an universal blame of the one party, or approbation of the other. The court-party may, no doubt, on some occasions consult best the interest of the country, and the country-party oppose it. In like manner, the ROMAN parties were denominated *Optimates* and *Populares*; and CICERO, like a true party man, defines the *Optimates* to be such as, in all public conduct, regulated themselves by the sentiments of the best and worthiest of the ROMANS: *Pro Sextio, cap.* 45. The term of *Country-party* may afford a favourable definition or etymology of the same kind: But it would be folly to draw any argument from that head, and I have regard to it in employing these terms.]

government, are a kind of mixed parties, and are influenced both by principle and by interest. The heads of the factions are commonly most governed by the latter motive; the inferior members of them by the former.[1]

As to ecclesiastical parties; we may observe, that, in all ages of the world, priests have been enemies to liberty;[2] and it is certain, that this steady conduct of theirs must have been founded on fixed reasons of interest and ambition. Liberty of thinking, and of expressing our thoughts, is always fatal to priestly power, and to those pious frauds, on which it is commonly founded; and, by an infallible connexion, which prevails among all kinds of liberty, this privilege can never be enjoyed, at least has never yet been enjoyed, but in a free government. Hence it must happen, in such a constitution as that of GREAT BRITAIN, that the established clergy, while things are in their natural situation, will always be of the *Court*-party; as, on the contrary, dissenters of all kinds will be of the *Country*-party; since they can never hope for that toleration, which they stand in need of, but by means of our free government. All princes, that have aimed at despotic power, have known of what importance it was to gain the established clergy: As the clergy, on their part, have shewn a great facility on entering into the views of such princes.[3] GUSTAVUS VAZA was, perhaps, the only ambitious monarch, that ever depressed the church, at the same time that he discouraged liberty. But the exorbitant power of the bishops in SWEDEN, who, at that time, overtopped the crown itself, together with their attachment to a foreign family, was the reason of his embracing such an unusual system of politics.

[1] [Editions A to P add the following: I must be understood to mean this of persons who have motives for taking party on any side. For, to tell the truth, the greatest part are commonly men who associate themselves they know not why; from example, from passion, from idleness. But still it is requisite, that there be some source of division, either in principle or interest; otherwise such persons would not find parties, to which they could associate themselves.]

[2] [Editions B to P add the note: This proposition is true, notwithstanding, that in the early times of the ENGLISH government, the clergy were the great and principal opposers of the crown: But, at that time, their possessions were so immensely great, that they composed a considerable part of the proprietors of ENGLAND, and in many contests were direct rivals of the crown.]

[3] Judæi sibi ipsi reges imposuere; qui mobilitate vulgi expulsi, resumpta per arma dominatione; fugas civium, urbium eversiones, fratrum, conjugum, parentum neces, aliaque solita regibus ausi, superstitionem fovebant; quia honor sacerdotii firmamentum potentiæ assumebatur. TACIT. *hist. lib.* v. 8. [This note was added in Edition K.]

This observation, concerning the propensity of priests to the government of a single person, is not true with regard to one sect only. The *Presbyterian* and *Calvinistic* clergy in HOLLAND were professed friends to the family of ORANGE; as the *Arminians*, who were esteemed heretics, were of the LOUVESTEIN faction, and zealous for liberty. But if a prince have the choice of both, it is easy to see, that he will prefer the episcopal to the presbyterian form of government, both because of the greater affinity between monarchy and episcopacy, and because of the facility, which he will find, in such a government, of ruling the clergy, by means of their ecclesiastical superiors.[1]

If we consider the first rise of parties in ENGLAND, during the great rebellion, we shall observe, that it was conformable to this general theory, and that the species of government gave birth to them, by a regular and infallible operation. The ENGLISH constitution, before that period, had lain in a kind of confusion; yet so, as that the subjects possessed many noble privileges, which, though not exactly bounded and secured by law, were universally deemed, from long possession, to belong to them as their birth-right. An ambitious, or rather a misguided, prince arose, who deemed all these privileges to be concessions of his predecessors, revokeable at pleasure; and, in prosecution of this principle, he openly acted in violation of liberty, during the course of several years. Necessity, at last, constrained him to call a parliament: The spirit of liberty arose and spread itself: The prince, being without any support, was obliged to grant every thing required of him: And his enemies, jealous and implacable, set no bounds to their pretensions. Here then began those contests, in which it was no wonder, that men of that age were divided into different parties; since, even at this day, the impartial are at a loss to decide concerning the justice of the quarrel. The pretensions of the parliament, if yielded to, broke the balance of the constitution, by rendering the government almost entirely republican. If not yielded to, the nation was, perhaps, still in danger of absolute power, from the settled principles and inveterate habits of the king, which had plainly appeared in every concession that he had been constrained to make to his people. In this

---

[1] Populi imperium juxta libertatem: paucorum dominatio regiæ libidini proprior est. TACIT. *Ann. lib.* vi. 41. [This note was added in Edition K.]

question, so delicate and uncertain, men naturally fell to the side which was most conformable to their usual principles; and the more passionate favourers of monarchy declared for the king, as the zealous friends of liberty sided with the parliament. The hopes of success being nearly equal on both sides, *interest* had no general influence in this contest: So that ROUND-HEAD and CAVALIER were merely parties of principles; neither of which disowned either monarchy or liberty; but the former party inclined most to the republican part of our government, the latter to the monarchical. In this respect, they may be considered as court and country-party, enflamed into a civil war, by an unhappy concurrence of circumstances, and by the turbulent spirit of the age. The commonwealth's men, and the partizans of absolute power, lay concealed in both parties, and formed but an inconsiderable part of them.

The clergy had concurred with the king's arbitrary designs; and, in return, were allowed to persecute their adversaries, whom they called heretics and schismatics. The established clergy were episcopal; the non-conformists presbyterian: So that all things concurred to throw the former, without reserve, into the king's party; and the latter into that of the parliament.[1]

Every one knows the event of this quarrel; fatal to the king first, to the parliament afterwards. After many confusions and revolutions, the royal family was at last restored, and the ancient government re-established. CHARLES II. was not made wiser by the example of his father; but prosecuted the same measures, though at first, with more secrecy and caution. New parties arose, under the appellation of *Whig* and *Tory*, which have continued ever since to confound and distract our government. To determine the nature of these

---

[1] [For this paragraph Editions A to P substitute the following: 'The clergy had concurred[2] with the king's arbitrary designs, according to their usual maxims in such cases: And, in return, were allowed to persecute their adversaries, whom they called heretics and schismatics. The established clergy were episcopal; the non-conformists presbyterian: So that all things concurred to throw the former, without reserve, into the king's party; and the latter into that of the parliament. The *Cavaliers* being the court-party, and the *Round-heads* the country-party, the union was infallible between the former and the established prelacy, and between the latter and presbyterian non-conformists. This union is so natural, according to the general principles of politics, that it requires some very extraordinary situation of affairs to break it.]

[2] [In a shameless manner: A to K.]

parties is, perhaps, one of the most difficult problems, that can be met with, and is a proof that history may contain questions, as uncertain as any to be found in the most abstract sciences. We have seen the conduct of the two parties, during the course of seventy years, in a vast variety of circumstances, possessed of power, and deprived of it, during peace, and during war: Persons, who profess themselves of one side or other, we meet with every hour, in company, in our pleasures, in our serious occupations: We ourselves are constrained, in a manner, to take party; and living in a country of the highest liberty, every one may openly declare all his sentiments and opinions; Yet are we at a loss to tell the nature, pretensions, and principles of the different factions.[1]

When we compare the parties of WHIG and TORY with those of ROUND-HEAD and CAVALIER, the most obvious difference, that appears between them, consists in the principles of *passive obedience*, and *indefeasible right*, which were but little heard of among the CAVALIERS, but became the universal doctrine, and were esteemed the true characteristic of a TORY. Were these principles pushed into their most obvious consequences, they imply a formal renunciation of all our liberties, and an avowal of absolute monarchy; since nothing can be a greater absurdity than a limited power, which must not be resisted, even when it exceeds its limitations. But as the most rational principles are often but a weak counterpoise to passion; it is no wonder that these absurd principles[2] were found too weak for that effect. The TORIES, as men, were enemies to oppression; and also as ENGLISHMEN, they were enemies to arbitrary power. Their zeal for liberty, was, perhaps, less fervent than that of their antagonists; but was sufficient to make them forget all their general principles, when they saw themselves openly threatened with a subversion of the ancient government. From these sentiments arose the *revolution*; an event of mighty consequence, and the firmest foundation of BRITISH liberty. The conduct of the TORIES, during that event, and after it, will afford us a true insight into the nature of that party.

In the *first* place, they appear to have had the genuine sentiments of BRITONS in their affection for liberty, and in

[1] [Editions A to P add: The question is, perhaps, in itself, somewhat difficult; but has been rendered more so, by the prejudice and violence of party.]

[2] [Editions A to P add: *sufficient*, according to a celebrated author, (Dissertation on Parties, Letter 2d.) *to shock the common sense of a* HOTTENTOT *or* SAMOIEDE.]

their determined resolution not to sacrifice it to any abstract principle whatsoever, or to any imaginary rights of princes. This part of their character might justly have been doubted of before the *revolution*, from the obvious tendency of their avowed principles, and from their[1] compliances with a court, which seemed to make little secret of its arbitrary designs. The *revolution* shewed them to have been, in this respect, nothing, but a genuine *court-party*, such as might be expected in a BRITISH government: That is, *Lovers of liberty, but greater lovers of monarchy*. It must, however, be confessed, that they carried their monarchical principles farther, even in practice, but more so in theory, than was, in any degree, consistent with a limited government.

Secondly, Neither their principles nor affections concurred, entirely or heartily, with the settlement made at the *revolution*, or with that which has since taken place. This part of their character may seem opposite to the former; since any other settlement, in those circumstances of the nation, must probably have been dangerous, if not fatal to liberty. But the heart of man is made to reconcile contradictions: and this contradiction is not greater than that between *passive obedience*, and the *resistance* employed at the *revolution*. A TORY, therefore, since the *revolution*, may be defined in a few words, to be *a lover of monarchy, though without abandoning liberty; and a partizan of the family of* STUART. As a WHIG may be defined to be *a lover of liberty though without renouncing monarchy; and a friend to the settlement in the* PROTESTANT *line*.[2]

These different views, with regard to the settlement of the crown, were accidental, but natural additions to the principles

---

[1] [Editions A to K read: *almost unbounded* compliances. M to Q: *great* compliances.]

[2] [Editions A to P add the following note: The author[1] above cited has asserted, that the REAL distinction betwixt WHIG and TORY was lost at the *revolution*, and that ever since they have continued to be mere *personal* parties, like the GUELFS and GIBBELINES, after the emperors had lost all authority in ITALY. Such an opinion, were it received, would turn our whole history into an ænigma; [and is, indeed, so contrary to the strongest Evidence, that a Man must have a great Opinion of his own Eloquence to attempt the proving of it.—A and B.]

I shall first mention, as a proof of a real distinction between these parties, what every one may have observed or heard concerning the conduct and conversation of all his friends and acquaintance on both sides. Have not the TORIES always borne an avowed affection to the family of STUART, and have not their adversaries always opposed with vigour the succession of that family?

The TORY principles are confessedly

---

[1] [Celebrated writer: A, B, and D.]

of the *court* and *country* parties, which are the genuine divisions in the BRITISH government. A passionate lover of monarchy is apt to be displeased at any change of the succession; as savouring too much of a commonwealth: A passionate lover of liberty is apt to think that every part of the government ought to be subordinate to the interests of liberty.

Some, who will not venture to assert, that the *real* difference between WHIG and TORY was lost at the *revolution*, seem inclined to think, that the difference is now abolished, and that affairs are so far returned to their natural state, that there are at present no other parties among us but *court* and *country*; that is, men, who, by interest or principle, are attached either to monarchy or liberty. The TORIES have been so long obliged to talk in the republican stile, that they seem to have made converts of themselves by their hypocrisy, and to have embraced the sentiments, as well as language of their adversaries. There are, however, very considerable remains of that party in ENGLAND, with all their old prejudices; and a proof that *court* and *country* are not our only parties, is, that almost all the dissenters side with the court, and the lower clergy, at least, of the church of ENGLAND, with the opposition. This may convince us, that some biass still hangs upon our constitution, some extrinsic weight,

the most favourable to monarchy. Yet the Tories have almost always opposed the court those fifty years; nor were they cordial friends to King WILLIAM, even when employed by him. Their quarrel, therefore, cannot be supposed to have lain with the throne, but with the person who sat on it.

They concurred heartily with the court during the four last years of Queen ANNE. But is any one at a loss to find the reason?

[1] The succession of the crown in the BRITISH government is a point of too great consequence to be absolutely indifferent to persons who concern themselves, in any degree, about the fortune of the public; much less can it be supposed that the TORY party, who never valued themselves upon moderation, could maintain a *stoical* indifference in a point of such importance. Were they, therefore, zealous for the house of HANOVER? Or was there any thing that kept an opposite zeal from openly appearing, if it did not openly appear, but prudence, and a sense of decency?

'Tis monstrous to see an established episcopal clergy in declared opposition to the court, and a non-conformist presbyterian clergy in conjunction with it. What could have produced such an unnatural conduct in both? Nothing, but that the former espoused monarchical principles too high for the present settlement, which is founded on principles of liberty: And the latter, being afraid of the prevalence of those high principles, adhered to that party from whom they had reason to expect liberty and toleration.

The different conduct of the two parties, with regard to foreign politics, is also a proof to the same purpose. HOLLAND has always been most favoured by one, and FRANCE by the other. In short, the proofs of this kind seem so palpable and evident, that 'tis almost needless to collect them.]

---

[1] [This paragraph is not in A and B.]

which turns it from its natural course, and causes a confusion in our parties.[1]

[So the Essay concludes in Editions Q and R. In place of the last paragraph, the preceding Editions read as follows:]

'Tis however remarkable, that tho' the principles of WHIG and TORY were both of them of a compound nature; yet the ingredients, which predominated in both, were not correspondent to each other. A TORY loved monarchy, and bore an affection to the family of STUART; but the latter affection was the predominant inclination of the party. A WHIG loved liberty, and was a friend to the settlement in the PROTESTANT line; but the love of liberty was professedly his predominant inclination. The TORIES have frequently acted as republicans, where either policy or revenge has engaged them to that conduct; and there was no one of that party, who, upon the supposition, that he was to be disappointed in his views with regard to the succession, would not have desired to impose the strictest limitations on the crown, and to bring our form of government as near republican as possible, in order to depress the family, which, according to his apprehension, succeeded without any just title. The WHIGS, 'tis true, have also taken steps dangerous to liberty, under colour of securing the succession and settlement of the crown, according to their views: But as the body of the party had no passion for that succession, otherwise than as the means of securing liberty, they have been betrayed into these steps by ignorance, or frailty, or the interests of their leaders. The succession of the crown was, therefore, the chief point with the TORIES; the security of our liberties with the WHIGS.[2] Nor is this seeming irregularity at all difficult to be accounted for, by our present theory. *Court* and *country* parties are the true parents of TORY and WHIG. But 'tis almost impossible, that the attachment of the *court* party to monarchy should not degenerate into an attachment to the monarch; there being so close a connexion between them, and the latter being so much the more natural object. How easily does the worship of the divinity degenerate into a

---

[1] Some of the opinions delivered in these Essays, with regard to the public transactions in the last century, the Author, on more accurate examination, found reason to retract in his *History of Great Britain*. And as he would not enslave himself to the systems of either party, neither would he fetter his judgment by his own preconceived opinions and principles; nor is he ashamed to acknowledge his mistakes. These mistakes were indeed, at that time, almost universal in this kingdom.

[2] [The remainder of this paragraph is not in A and B.]

worship of the idol? The connexion is not so great between liberty, the divinity of the old *country* party or WHIGS, and any monarch or royal family; nor is it so reasonable to suppose, that in that party, the worship can be so easily transferred from the one to the other. Tho' even that would be no great miracle.

'Tis difficult to penetrate into the thoughts and sentiments of any particular man; but 'tis almost impossible to distinguish those of a whole party, where it often happens, that no two persons agree precisely in the same maxims of conduct. Yet I will venture to affirm, that it was not so much PRINCIPLE, or an opinion of indefeasible right, which attached the TORIES to the ancient royal family, as AFFECTION, or a certain love and esteem for their persons. The same cause divided ENGLAND formerly between the houses of YORK and LANCASTER, and SCOTLAND between the families of BRUCE and BALIOL; in an age, when political disputes were but little in fashion, and when political *principles* must of course have had but little influence on mankind. The doctrine of passive obedience is so absurd in itself, and so opposite to our liberties, that it seems to have been chiefly left to pulpit-declaimers, and to their deluded followers among the vulgar. Men of better sense were guided by *affection*; and as to the leaders of this party, 'tis probable, that *interest* was their chief motive, and that they acted more contrary to their private sentiments, than the leaders of the opposite party. ¹ Tho' 'tis almost impossible to maintain with zeal the right of any person or family, without acquiring a good-will to them, and changing the *principle* into *affection*; yet this is less natural to people of an elevated station and liberal education, who have had full opportunity of observing the weakness, folly, and arrogance of monarchs, and have found them to be nothing superior, if not rather inferior to the rest of mankind. The *interest*, therefore, of being heads of a party does often, with such people, supply the place both of *principle* and *affection*.

Some, who will not venture to assert, that the *real* difference between WHIG and TORY was lost at the *revolution*, seem inclined to think, that the difference is now abolished, and that affairs are so far returned to their natural state, that there are at present no other parties amongst us but

---

¹ [The remainder of this paragraph is not in A and B.]

court and *country*; that is, men, who by interest or principle, are attached either to monarchy or to liberty. It must, indeed, be confest, that the TORY party seem, of late, to have decayed much in their numbers; still more in their zeal; and I may venture to say, still more in their credit and authority. There are few men of knowledge or learning, at least, few philosophers, since Mr. LOCKE has wrote, who would not be ashamed to be thought of that party; and in almost all companies the name of OLD WHIG is mentioned as an uncontestable appellation of honour and dignity. Accordingly, the enemies of the ministry, as a reproach, call the courtiers the true TORIES; and as an honour, denominate the gentlemen in the *opposition* the true WHIGS.[1] The TORIES have been so long obliged to talk in the republican stile, that they seem to have made converts of themselves by their hypocrisy, and to have embraced the sentiments, as well as language of their adversaries. There are, however, very considerable remains of that party in ENGLAND, with all their old prejudices; and a proof that *court* and *country* are not our only parties, is, that almost all the dissenters side with the court, and the lower clergy, at least, of the church of ENGLAND, with the opposition. This may convince us, that some biass still hangs upon our constitution, some intrinsic weight, which turns it from its natural course, and causes a confusion in our parties.[2]

I shall conclude this subject with observing that we never had any TORIES in SCOTLAND, according to the proper signification of the word, and that the division of parties in this country was really into WHIGS and JACOBITES. A JACOBITE seems to be a TORY, who has no regard to the constitution, but is either a zealous partizan of absolute monarchy, or at least willing to sacrifice our liberties to the obtaining the succession in that family to which he is attached. The reason of the difference between ENGLAND and SCOTLAND, I take to be this: Political and religious divisions in the latter country, have been, since the *revolution*, regularly correspondent to each other. The PRESBYTERIANS were all WHIGS without exception: Those who favoured *episcopacy*, of the opposite party. And as the clergy of the latter sect were turned out of the churches at the *revolution*, they had no motive for

[1] [The last two sentences were omitted in P. A. and B read *no man*, omitting 'at least — wrote.']

[2] [This sentence does not occur in A.]

making any compliances with the government in their oaths, or their forms of prayers, but openly avowed the highest principles of their party; which is the cause why their followers have been more violent than their brethren of the TORY party in ENGLAND.[1]

ESSAY X.—*Of Superstition and Enthusiasm.*

THAT *the corruption of the best things produces the worst*, is grown into a maxim, and is commonly proved, among other instances, by the pernicious effects of *superstition* and *enthusiasm*, the corruptions of true religion.

These two species of false religion, though both pernicious, are yet of a very different, and even of a contrary nature. The mind of man is subject to certain unaccountable terrors and apprehensions, proceeding either from the unhappy situation of private or public affairs, from ill health, from a gloomy and melancholy disposition, or from the concurrence of all these circumstances. In such a state of mind, infinite unknown evils are dreaded from unknown agents; and where real objects of terror are wanting, the soul, active to its own prejudice, and fostering its predominant inclination, finds imaginary ones, to whose power and malevolence it sets no limits. As these enemies are entirely

---

[1] Some of the opinions, delivered in these Essays, with regard to the public transactions in the last century, the Author, on more accurate examination, found reason to retract in his *History of* GREAT BRITAIN. And as he would not enslave himself to the systems of either party, neither would he fetter his judgment by his own preconceived opinions and principles; nor is he ashamed to acknowledge his mistakes.[1]

[1] [This note does not occur in any edition prior to M. A and B add the following paragraph to the text:—As violent Things have not commonly so long a Duration as moderate, we actually find, that the *Jacobite* Party is almost entirely vanish'd from among us, and that the Distinction of *Court* and *Country*, which is but creeping in at LONDON, is the only one that is ever mention'd in this *kingdom*. Beside the Violence and Openness of the JACOBITE party, another Reason has, perhaps, contributed to produce so sudden and so visible an Alteration in this part of BRITAIN. There are only two Ranks of Men among us; Gentlemen, who have some Fortune and Education, and the meanest slaving Poor; without any considerable Number of that middling Rank of Men, which abounds more in ENGLAND, both in Cities and in the Country, than in any other Part of the World. The slaving Poor are incapable of any Principles: Gentlemen may be converted to true Principles, by Time and Experience. The middling Rank of Men have Curiosity and Knowledge enough to form Principles, but not enough to form true ones, or correct any Prejudices that they may have imbib'd: And 'tis among the middling Rank, that TORY Principles do at present prevail most in ENGLAND.]

invisible and unknown, the methods taken to appease them are equally unaccountable, and consist in ceremonies, observances, mortifications, sacrifices, presents, or in any practice, however absurd or frivolous, which either folly or knavery recommends to a blind and terrified credulity. Weakness, fear, melancholy, together with ignorance, are, therefore, the true sources of SUPERSTITION.

But the mind of man is also subject to an unaccountable elevation and presumption, arising from prosperous success, from luxuriant health, from strong spirits, or from a bold and confident disposition. In such a state of mind, the imagination swells with great, but confused conceptions, to which no sublunary beauties or enjoyments can correspond. Every thing mortal and perishable vanishes as unworthy of attention. And a full range is given to the fancy in the invisible regions or world of spirits, where the soul is at liberty to indulge itself in every imagination, which may best suit its present taste and disposition. Hence arise raptures, transports, and surprising flights of fancy; and confidence and presumption still encreasing, these raptures, being altogether unaccountable, and seeming quite beyond the reach of our ordinary faculties, are attributed to the immediate inspiration of that Divine Being, who is the object of devotion. In a little time, the inspired person comes to regard himself as a distinguished favourite of the Divinity; and when this frenzy once takes place, which is the summit of enthusiasm, every whimsy is consecrated: Human reason, and even morality are rejected as fallacious guides: And the fanatic madman delivers himself over, blindly, and without reserve, to the supposed illapses of the spirit, and to inspiration from above. Hope, pride, presumption, a warm imagination, together with ignorance, are, therefore, the true sources of ENTHUSIASM.

These two species of false religion might afford occasion to many speculations; but I shall confine myself, at present, to a few reflections concerning their different influence on government and society.

[1] My first reflection is, *That superstition is favourable to*

---

[1] [In Editions A and B, this and the three next paragraphs were written as follows: My first Reflection is, that Religions, which partake of Enthusiasm are, on their first Rise, much more furious and violent than those which partake of Superstition; but in a little Time become much more gentle and moderate. The Violence of this Species of Religion, when excited by Novelty, and animated

priestly power, and enthusiasm not less or rather more contrary to it, than sound reason and philosophy. As superstition is founded on fear, sorrow, and a depression of spirits, it represents the man to himself in such despicable colours, that

by Opposition, appears from numberless Instances; of the *Anabaptists* in *Germany*, the *Camisars* in *France*, the *Levellers* and other Fanaticks in *England*, and the *Covenanters* in *Scotland*. As Enthusiasm is founded on strong Spirits and a presumptuous Boldness of Character, it naturally begets the most extreme Resolutions; especially after it rises to that Height as to inspire the deluded Fanaticks with the Opinion of Divine Illuminations, and with a Contempt of the common Rules of Reason, Morality and Prudence.

'Tis thus Enthusiasm produces the most cruel Desolation in human Society: But its Fury is like that of Thunder and Tempest, which exhaust themselves in a little Time, and leave the Air more calm and serene than before. The Reason of this will appear evidently, by comparing Enthusiasm to Superstition, the other Species of false Religion; and tracing the natural Consequences of each. As Superstition is founded on Fear, Sorrow, and a Depression of Spirits, it represents the Person to himself in such despicable Colours, that he appears unworthy, in his own Eyes, of approaching the Divine Presence, and naturally has Recourse to any other Person, whose Sanctity of Life, or, perhaps, Impudence and Cunning, have made him be supposed to be more favoured by the Divinity. To him they entrust their Devotions: To his Care they recommend their Prayers, Petitions, and Sacrifices: And, by his Means, hope to render their Addresses acceptable to their incensed Deity. Hence the Origin of PRIESTS,[1] who may justly be regarded as one of the grossest Inventions of a timorous and abject Superstition, which, ever diffident of itself, dares not offer up its own Devotions, but ignorantly thinks to recommend itself to the Divinity, by the Mediation of his supposed Friends and Servants. As Superstition is a considerable Ingredient of almost all Religions, even the most fanatical; there being nothing but Philosophy able to conquer entirely these unaccountable Terrors; hence it proceeds, that in almost every Sect of Religion there are Priests to be found: But the stronger Mixture there is of Superstition, the higher is the Authority of the Priesthood. Modern Judaism and Popery, especially the latter, being the most barbarous and absurd Superstitions that have yet been known in the World, are the most enslav'd by their Priests. As the Church of ENGLAND may justly be said to retain a strong Mixture of Popish Superstition, it partakes also, in its original Constitution, of a Propensity to Priestly Power and Dominion; particularly in the Respect it exacts to the Priest. And though, according to the Sentiments of that Church, the Prayers of the Priest must be accompanied with those of the Laity; yet is he the mouth of the Congregation, his Person is sacred, and without his Presence few would think their public Devotions, or the Sacraments, and other Rites, acceptable to the Divinity.

On the other Hand, it may be observed, That all Enthusiasts have been free from the Yoke of Ecclesiastics, and have exprest a great Independence in their Devotion; with a contempt of Forms, Tradition and Authorities. The *Quakers* are the most egregious, tho', at the same Time, the most innocent, Enthusiasts that have been yet known; and are, perhaps, the only Sect, that have never admitted Priests among them. The *Independents*, of all the ENGLISH Sectaries, approach nearest to the QUAKERS in Fanaticism, and in their Freedom from Priestly Bondage. The *Presbyterians* follow after, at an equal Distance in both these Particulars.

---

[1] [By *Priests* I understand only the Pretenders to Power and Dominion, and to a superior Sanctity of Character, distinct from Virtue and good Morals. These are very different from *Clergymen*, who are set apart ([2] by the Laws) to the care of sacred Matters, and the conducting our public Devotions with greater Decency and Order. There is no Rank of Men more to be respected than the latter.]

[2] [Added in Edition B.]

he appears unworthy, in his own eyes, of approaching the divine presence, and naturally has recourse to any other person, whose sanctity of life, or, perhaps, impudence and cunning, have made him be supposed more favoured by the Divinity. To him the superstitious entrust their devotions: To his care they recommend their prayers, petitions, and sacrifices: And by his means, they hope to render their addresses acceptable to their incensed Deity. Hence the origin of PRIESTS,[1] who may justly be regarded[2] as an invention of a timorous and abject superstition, which, ever diffident of itself, dares not offer up its own devotions, but ignorantly thinks to recommend itself to the Divinity, by the mediation of his supposed friends and servants. As superstition is a considerable ingredient in almost all religions, even the most fanatical; there being nothing but philosophy able entirely to conquer these unaccountable terrors; hence it proceeds, that in almost every sect of religion there are priests to be found: But the stronger mix-

In short, this Observation is founded on the most certain Experience; and will also appear to be founded on Reason, if we consider, that as Enthusiasm arises from a presumptuous Pride and Confidence, it thinks itself sufficiently qualified to *approach* the Divinity without any human Mediator. Its rapturous Devotions are so fervent, that it even imagines itself *actually* to *approach* him by the Way of Contemplation and inward Converse; which makes it neglect all those outward Ceremonies and Observances, to which the Assistance of the Priests appears so requisite in the Eyes of their superstitious Votaries. The Fanatick consecrates himself, and bestows on his own Person a sacred Character, much superior to what Forms and ceremonious Institutions can confer on any other.

'Tis therefore an infallible Rule, That Superstition is favourable to Priestly Power, and Enthusiasm as much, or rather more, contrary to it than sound Reason and Philosophy. The Consequences are evident. When the first Fire of Enthusiasm is spent, Men naturally, in such fanatical Sects, sink into the greatest Remissness and Coolness in Sacred Matters; there being no Body of Men amongst them, endow'd with sufficient Authority, whose Interest is concerned, to support the religious Spirit.

Superstition, on the contrary, steals in gradually and insensibly; renders Men tame and submissive; is acceptable to the Magistrate, and seems inoffensive to the People: Till at last the Priest, having firmly establish'd his Authority, becomes the Tyrant and Disturber of human Society, by his endless Contentions, Persecutions, and religious Wars. How smoothly did the *Romish* Church advance in their Acquisition of Power? But into what dismal Convulsions did they throw all EUROPE, in order to maintain it? On the other Hand, our Sectaries, who were formerly such dangerous Bigots, are now become our greatest Free-thinkers; and the *Quakers* are, perhaps, the only regular Body of *Deists* in the Universe, except the *Literati* or Disciples of *Confucius* in *China*.]

[1] [The following note is appended in Editions D to N: By *Priests*, I here mean only the pretenders to power and dominion, and to a superior sanctity of character, distinct from virtue and good morals. These are very different from *clergymen*, who are set apart *by the laws*, to the care of sacred matters, and to the conducting our public devotions with greater decency and order. There is no rank of men more to be respected than the latter.]

[2] [As one of the grossest inventions. D to N.]

ture there is of superstition, the higher is the authority of the priesthood.[1]

On the other hand, it may be observed, that all enthusiasts have been free from the yoke of ecclesiastics, and have expressed great independence in their devotion; with a contempt of forms, ceremonies, and traditions. The *quakers* are the most egregious, though, at the same time, the most innocent enthusiasts that have yet been known; and are, perhaps, the only sect, that have never admitted priests amongst them. The *independents*, of all the ENGLISH sectaries, approach nearest to the *quakers* in fanaticism, and in their freedom from priestly bondage. The *presbyterians* follow after, at an equal distance in both particulars. In short this observation is founded in experience; and will also appear to be founded in reason, if we consider, that, as enthusiasm arises from a presumptuous pride and confidence, it thinks itself sufficiently qualified to *approach* the Divinity, without any human mediator. Its rapturous devotions are so fervent, that it even imagines itself *actually* to *approach* him by the way of contemplation and inward converse; which makes it neglect all those outward ceremonies and observances, to which the assistance of the priests appears so requisite in the eyes of their superstitious votaries. The fanatic consecrates himself, and bestows on his own person a sacred character, much superior to what forms and ceremonious institutions can confer on any other.

My *second* reflection with regard to these species of false religion is, *that religions, which partake of enthusiasm are, on their first rise, more furious and violent than those which partake of superstition; but in a little time become more gentle and moderate.* The violence of this species of religion, when excited by novelty, and animated by opposition, appears from numberless instances; of the *anabaptists* in GERMANY, the *camisars* in FRANCE, the *levellers* and other fanatics in ENG-

---

[1] [Here D to P add: Modern Judaism and popery, (especially the latter) being the most unphilosophical and absurd superstitions which have yet been known in the world, are the most enslaved by their priests. As the church of ENGLAND may justly be said to retain some mixture of Popish superstition, it partakes also, in its original constitution, of a propensity to priestly power and dominion; particularly in the respect it exacts to the sacerdotal character. And though, according to the sentiments of that Church, the prayers of the priest must be accompanied with those of the laity; yet is he the mouth of the congregation, his person is sacred, and without his presence few would think their public devotions, or the sacraments, and other rites, acceptable to the divinity.]

LAND, and the *covenanters* in SCOTLAND. Enthusiasm being founded on strong spirits, and a presumptuous boldness of character, it naturally begets the most extreme resolutions; especially after it rises to that height as to inspire the deluded fanatic with the opinion of divine illuminations, and with a contempt for the common rules of reason, morality, and prudence.

It is thus enthusiasm produces the most cruel disorders in human society; but its fury is like that of thunder and tempest, which exhaust themselves in a little time, and leave the air more calm and pure than before. When the first fire of enthusiasm is spent, men naturally, in all fanatical sects, sink into the greatest remissness and coolness in sacred matters; there being no body of men among them, endowed with sufficient authority, whose interest is concerned to support the religious spirit: No rites, no ceremonies, no holy observances, which may enter into the common train of life, and preserve the sacred principles from oblivion. Superstition, on the contrary, steals in gradually and insensibly; renders men tame and submissive; is acceptable to the magistrate, and seems inoffensive to the people: Till at last the priest, having firmly established his authority, becomes the tyrant and disturber of human society, by his endless contentions, persecutions, and religious wars. How smoothly did the ROMISH church advance in her acquisition of power? But into what dismal convulsions did she throw all EUROPE, in order to maintain it? On the other hand, our sectaries, who were formerly such dangerous bigots, are now become very free reasoners; and the *quakers* seem to approach nearly the only regular body of *deists* in the universe, the *literati*, or the disciples of CONFUCIUS in CHINA.[1]

My *third* observation on this head is, *that superstition is an enemy to civil liberty, and enthusiasm a friend to it.* As superstition groans under the dominion of priests, and enthusiasm is destructive of all ecclesiastical power, this sufficiently accounts for the present observation. Not to mention, that enthusiasm, being the infirmity of bold and ambitious tempers, is naturally accompanied with a spirit of liberty; as superstition, on the contrary, renders men tame

[1] The CHINESE Literati have no priests or ecclesiastical establishment. This note is not in D and K, which read in the text: and the quakers seem to approach nearly the only regular body of deists in the universe, the *literati*, or the disciples of *Confucius* in *China*.¹

and abject, and fits them for slavery. We learn from ENGLISH history, that, during the civil wars, the *independents* and *deists*, though the most opposite in their religious principles; yet were united in their political ones, and were alike passionate for a commonwealth. And since the origin of *whig* and *tory*, the leaders of the *whigs* have either been *deists* or profest *latitudinarians* in their principles; that is, friends to toleration, and indifferent to any particular sect of *christians*: While the sectaries, who have all a strong tincture of enthusiasm, have always, without exception, concurred with that party, in defence of civil liberty. The resemblance in their superstitions long united the high-church *tories*, and the *Roman catholics*, in support of prerogative and kingly power; though experience of the tolerating spirit of the *whigs* seems of late to have reconciled the *catholics* to that party.

The *molinists* and *jansenists* in FRANCE have a thousand unintelligible disputes, which are not worthy the reflection of a man of sense: But what principally distinguishes these two sects, and alone merits attention, is the different spirit of their religion. The *molinists* conducted by the *jesuits*, are great friends to superstition, rigid observers of external forms and ceremonies, and devoted to the authority of the priests, and to tradition. The *jansenists* are enthusiasts, and zealous promoters of the passionate devotion, and of the inward life; little influenced by authority; and, in a word, but half catholics. The consequences are exactly conformable to the foregoing reasoning. The *jesuits* are the tyrants of the people, and the slaves of the court: And the *jansenists* preserve alive the small sparks of the love of liberty, which are to be found in the FRENCH nation.

ESSAY XI.—*Of the Dignity or Meanness of Human Nature.*[1]

THERE are certain sects, which secretly form themselves in the learned world, as well as factions in the political; and though sometimes they come not to an open rupture, they give a different turn to the ways of thinking of those who have taken part on either side. The most remarkable of this kind are the sects, founded on the different sentiments with

---

[1] [All the Editions from A to P are headed: Of the Dignity of Human Nature.]

regard to the *dignity of human nature*; which is a point that seems to have divided philosophers and poets, as well as divines, from the beginning of the world to this day. Some exalt our species to the skies, and represent man as a kind of human demigod, who derives his origin from heaven, and retains evident marks of his lineage and descent. Others insist upon the blind sides of human nature, and can discover nothing, except vanity, in which man surpasses the other animals, whom he affects so much to despise. If an author possess the talent of rhetoric and declamation, he commonly takes part with the former: If his turn lie towards irony and ridicule, he naturally throws himself into the other extreme.

I am far from thinking, that all those, who have depreciated our species, have been enemies to virtue, and have exposed the frailties of their fellow creatures with any bad intention. On the contrary, I am sensible that a delicate sense of morals, especially when attended with a splenetic temper,[1] is apt to give a man a disgust of the world, and to make him consider the common course of human affairs with too much indignation. I must, however, be of opinion, that the sentiments of those, who are inclined to think favourably of mankind, are more advantageous to virtue, than the contrary principles, which give us a mean opinion of our nature. When a man is prepossessed with a high notion of his rank and character in the creation, he will naturally endeavour to act up to it, and will scorn to do a base or vicious action, which might sink him below that figure which he makes in his own imagination. Accordingly we find, that all our polite and fashionable moralists insist upon this topic, and endeavour to represent vice as unworthy of man, as well as odious in itself.[2]

We find few disputes, that are not founded on some ambiguity in the expression; and I am persuaded, that the present dispute, concerning the dignity or meanness of human nature, is not more exempt from it than any other. It may, therefore, be worth while to consider, what is real, and what is only verbal, in this controversy.

---

[1] [Editions A to P read: especially when attended with somewhat of the *Misanthrope.*]

[2] [Editions A to P add the following: Women are generally much more flattered in their youth than men; which may proceed from this reason, among others, that their chief point of honour is considered as much more difficult than ours, and requires to be supported by all that decent pride, which can be instilled into them.]

That there is a natural difference between merit and demerit, virtue and vice, wisdom and folly, no reasonable man will deny: Yet is it evident, that in affixing the term, which denotes either our approbation or blame, we are commonly more influenced by comparison than by any fixed unalterable standard in the nature of things. In like manner, quantity, and extension, and bulk, are by every one acknowledged to be real things: But when we call any animal *great* or *little*, we always form a secret comparison between that animal and others of the same species; and it is that comparison which regulates our judgment concerning its greatness. A dog and a horse may be of the very same size, while the one is admired for the greatness of its bulk, and the other for the smallness. When I am present, therefore, at any dispute, I always consider with myself, whether it be a question of comparison or not that is the subject of the controversy; and if it be, whether the disputants compare the same objects together, or talk of things that are widely different.[1]

In forming our notions of human nature, we are apt to make a comparison between men and animals, the only creatures endowed with thought that fall under our senses. Certainly this comparison is favourable to mankind. On the one hand, we see a creature, whose thoughts are not limited by any narrow bounds, either of place or time; who carries his researches into the most distant regions of this globe, and beyond this globe, to the planets and heavenly bodies; looks backward to consider the first origin, at least, the history of human race; casts his eye forward to see the influence of his actions upon posterity, and the judgments which will be formed of his character a thousand years hence; a creature, who traces causes and effects to a great length and intricacy; extracts general principles from particular appearances; improves upon his discoveries; corrects his mistakes; and makes his very errors profitable. On the other hand, we are presented with a creature the very reverse of this; limited in its observations and reasonings to a few sensible objects which surround it; without curiosity, without foresight; blindly conducted by instinct, and attaining, in a short time,

---

[1] [Editions A to P add: As the latter is commonly the case, I have long since learnt to neglect such disputes as manifest abuses of leisure, the most valuable present that could be made to mortals.]

its utmost perfection, beyond which it is never able to advance a single step. What a wide difference is there between these creatures! And how exalted a notion must we entertain of the former, in comparison of the latter!

There are two means commonly employed to destroy this conclusion: *First*, By making an unfair representation of the case, and insisting only upon the weaknesses of human nature. And *secondly*, By forming a new and secret comparison between man and beings of the most perfect wisdom. Among the other excellencies of man, this is one, that he can form an idea of perfections much beyond what he has experience of in himself; and is not limited in his conception of wisdom and virtue. He can easily exalt his notions and conceive a degree of knowledge, which, when compared to his own, will make the latter appear very contemptible, and will cause the difference between that and the sagacity of animals, in a manner, to disappear and vanish. Now this being a point, in which all the world is agreed, that human understanding falls infinitely short of perfect wisdom; it is proper we should know when this comparison takes place, that we may not dispute where there is no real difference in our sentiments. Man falls much more short of perfect wisdom, and even of his own ideas of perfect wisdom, than animals do of man; yet the latter difference is so considerable, that nothing but a comparison with the former can make it appear of little moment.

It is also usual to *compare* one man with another; and finding very few whom we can call *wise* or *virtuous*, we are apt to entertain a contemptible notion of our species in general. That we may be sensible of the fallacy of this way of reasoning, we may observe, that the honourable appellations of wise and virtuous, are not annexed to any particular degree of those qualities of *wisdom* and *virtue*; but arise altogether from the comparison we make between one man and another. When we find a man, who arrives at such a pitch of wisdom as is very uncommon, we pronounce him a wise man: So that to say, there are few wise men in the world, is really to say nothing; since it is only by their scarcity, that they merit that appellation. Were the lowest of our species as wise as TULLY, or lord BACON, we should still have reason to say, that there are few wise men. For in that case we should exalt our notions of wisdom, and should not pay a singular honour to any one, who was not singularly distinguished by his talents. In like manner, I have heard it observed by thoughtless people, that there are few women possessed of beauty, in comparison of those who want it; not considering, that we bestow the epithet of *beautiful* only on such as possess a degree of beauty, that is common to them with a few. The same degree of beauty in a woman is called deformity, which is treated as real beauty in one of our sex.

As it is usual, in forming a notion of our species, to *compare* it with the other species above or below it, or to compare the individuals of the species among themselves; so we often compare together the different motives or actuating principles of human nature, in order to regulate our judgment concerning it. And, indeed, this is the only kind of comparison, which is worth our attention, or decides any thing in the present question. Were our selfish and vicious principles so much predominant above our social and virtuous, as is asserted by some philosophers, we ought undoubtedly to entertain a contemptible notion of human nature.

[1] There is much of a dispute of words in all this controversy. When a man denies the sincerity of all public spirit or affection to a country and community, I am at a loss what to think of him. Perhaps he never felt this in so clear and distinct a manner as to remove all his doubts concerning its force and reality. But when he proceeds afterwards to reject all private friendship, if no interest or self-love intermix itself; I am then confident that he abuses terms, and confounds the ideas of things; since it is impossible for any one to be so selfish, or rather so stupid, as to make no difference between one man and another, and give no preference to qualities, which engage his approbation and esteem. Is he also, say I, as insensible to anger as he pretends to be to friendship? And does injury and wrong no more affect him than kindness or benefits? Impossible: He does not know himself: He has forgotten the movements of his heart; or rather he makes

---

[1] [This paragraph does not occur in Editions A to D, which read instead of it: I may, perhaps, treat more fully of this Subject in some future Essay. In the mean Time, I shall observe, what has been prov'd beyond Question by several great Moralists of the present Age, that the social Passions are by far the most powerful of any, and that even all the other Passions receive from them their chief Force and Influence. Whoever desires to see this Question treated at large, with the greatest Force of Argument and Eloquence, may consult my Lord SHAFTSBURY's Enquiry concerning Virtue.]

use of a different language from the rest of his countrymen, and calls not things by their proper names. What say you of natural affection? (I subjoin) Is that also a species of self-love? Yes: All is self-love. *Your* children are loved only because they are yours: *Your* friend for a like reason: And *your* country engages you only so far as it has a connexion with *yourself*: Were the idea of self removed, nothing would affect you: You would be altogether unactive and insensible: Or, if you ever gave yourself any movement, it would only be from vanity, and a desire of fame and reputation to this same self. I am willing, reply I, to receive your interpretation of human actions, provided you admit the facts. That species of self-love, which displays itself in kindness to others, you must allow to have great influence over human actions, and even greater, on many occasions, than that which remains in its original shape and form. For how few are there, who, having a family, children, and relations, do not spend more on the maintenance and education of these than on their own pleasures? This, indeed, you justly observe, may proceed from their self-love, since the prosperity of their family and friends is one, or the chief of their pleasures, as well as their chief honour. Be you also one of these men, and you are sure of every one's good opinion and good will; or not to shock your ears with these expressions, the self-love of every one, and mine among the rest, will then incline us to serve you, and speak well of you.

In my opinion, there are two things which have led astray those philosophers, that have insisted so much on the selfishness of man. In the *first* place, they found, that every act of virtue or friendship was attended with a secret pleasure; whence they concluded, that friendship and virtue could not be disinterested. But the fallacy of this is obvious. The virtuous sentiment or passion produces the pleasure, and does not arise from it. I feel a pleasure in doing good to my friend, because I love him; but do not love him for the sake of that pleasure.

In the *second* place, it has always been found, that the virtuous are far from being indifferent to praise; and therefore they have been represented as a set of vain-glorious men, who had nothing in view but the applauses of others. But this also is a fallacy. It is very unjust in the world, when they find any tincture of vanity in a laudable action, to depreciate it upon that account, or ascribe it entirely to that motive. The case is not the same with vanity, as with other passions. Where avarice or revenge enters into any seemingly virtuous action, it is difficult for us to determine how far it enters, and it is natural to suppose it the sole actuating principle. But vanity is so closely allied to virtue, and to love the fame of laudable actions approaches so near the love of laudable actions for their own sake, that these passions are more capable of mixture, than any other kinds of affection; and it is almost impossible to have the latter without some degree of the former. Accordingly, we find, that this passion for glory is always warped and varied according to the particular taste or disposition of the mind on which it falls. NERO had the same vanity in driving a chariot, that TRAJAN had in governing the empire with justice and ability. To love the glory of virtuous deeds is a sure proof of the love of virtue.

ESSAY XII.—*Of Civil Liberty.*[1]

THOSE who employ their pens on political subjects, free from party-rage, and party-prejudices, cultivate a science, which, of all others, contributes most to public utility, and even to the private satisfaction of those who addict themselves to the study of it. I am apt, however, to entertain a suspicion, that the world is still too young to fix many general truths in politics, which will remain true to the latest posterity. We have not as yet had experience of three thousand years; so that not only the art of reasoning is still imperfect in this science, as in all others, but we even want sufficient materials upon which we can reason. It is not fully known, what degree of refinement, either in virtue or vice, human nature is susceptible of; nor what may be expected of mankind from any great revolution in their education, customs, or principles. MACHIAVEL was certainly a great genius; but having confined his study to the furious and tyrannical governments of ancient times, or to the little disorderly principalities of ITALY, his reasonings especially upon monarchical government, have been found extremely defective; and there scarcely is any maxim in his *prince*, which subsequent experience has not entirely refuted. *A weak prince*, says he, *is incapable of receiving good counsel;*

[1] [Editions A to K have the title: Of Liberty and Despotism.]

for if he consult with several, he will not be able to choose among their different counsels. If he abandon himself to one, that minister may, perhaps, have capacity; but he will not long be a minister: He will be sure to dispossess his master, and place himself and his family upon the throne. I mention this, among many instances of the errors of that politician, proceeding, in a great measure, from his having lived in too early an age of the world, to be a good judge of political truth. Almost all the princes of EUROPE are at present governed by their ministers; and have been so for near two centuries; and yet no such event has ever happened, or can possibly happen. SEJANUS might project dethroning the CÆSARS; but FLEURY, though ever so vicious, could not, while in his senses, entertain the least hopes of dispossessing the BOURBONS.

Trade was never esteemed an affair of state till the last century; and there scarcely is any ancient writer on politics, who has made mention of it.[1] Even the ITALIANS have kept a profound silence with regard to it, though it has now engaged the chief attention, as well of ministers of state, as of speculative reasoners. The great opulence, grandeur, and military atchievements of the two maritime powers seem first to have instructed mankind in the importance of an extensive commerce.

Having, therefore, intended in this essay to make a full comparison of civil liberty and absolute government, and to show[2] the great advantages of the former above the latter; I began to entertain a suspicion, that no man in this age was sufficiently qualified for such an undertaking; and that whatever any one should advance on that head would, in all probability, be refuted by further experience, and be rejected by posterity. Such mighty revolutions have happened in human affairs, and so many events have arisen contrary to the expectation of the ancients, that they are sufficient to beget the suspicion of still further changes.

It has been observed by the ancients, that all the arts and sciences arose among free nations; and, that the PERSIANS and EGYPTIANS, notwithstanding their ease, opulence, and luxury, made but faint efforts towards a relish in those finer

---

[1] XENOPHON mentions it; but with a doubt if it be of any advantage to a state. Εἰ δὲ καὶ ἐμπορία ὠφελεῖ τι πόλιν, &c. XEN. HIERO. 9. 9. PLATO totally excludes it from his imaginary republic De legibus, lib. iv. [This note was added in Ed. K.]

[2] [Editions A to D read: the Advantages and Disadvantages of each.]

pleasures, which were carried to such perfection by the GREEKS, amidst continual wars, attended with poverty, and the greatest simplicity of life and manners. It had also been observed, that, when the GREEKS lost their liberty, though they increased mightily in riches, by means of the conquests of ALEXANDER; yet the arts, from that moment, declined among them, and have never since been able to raise their head in that climate. Learning was transplanted to ROME, the only free nation at that time in the universe; and having met with so favourable a soil, it made prodigious shoots for above a century; till the decay of liberty produced also the decay of letters, and spread a total barbarism over the world. From these two experiments, of which each was double in its kind, and shewed the fall of learning in absolute governments, as well as its rise in popular ones, LONGINUS thought himself sufficiently justified, in asserting, that the arts and sciences could never flourish, but in a free government: And in this opinion, he has been followed by several eminent writers[1] in our own country, who either confined their view merely to ancient facts, or entertained too great a partiality in favour of that form of government, established amongst us.

But what would these writers have said, to the instances of modern ROME and of FLORENCE? Of which the former carried to perfection all the finer arts of sculpture, painting, and music, as well as poetry, though it groaned under tyranny, and under the tyranny of priests: While the latter made its chief progress in the arts and sciences, after it began to lose its liberty by the usurpation of the family of MEDICI. ARIOSTO, TASSO, GALILEO, more than RAPHAEL, and MICHAEL ANGELO, were not born in republics. And though the LOMBARD school was famous as well as the ROMAN, yet the VENETIANS have had the smallest share in its honours, and seem rather inferior to the other ITALIANS, in their genius for the arts and sciences. RUBENS established his school at ANTWERP, not at AMSTERDAM: DRESDEN, not HAMBURGH, is the centre of politeness in GERMANY.

But the most eminent instance of the flourishing of learning in absolute governments, is that of FRANCE, which scarcely ever enjoyed any established liberty, and yet has

---

[1] Mr. ADDISON and Lord SHAFTESBURY.

carried the arts and sciences as near perfection as any other nation. The ENGLISH are, perhaps, greater philosophers;[1] the ITALIANS better painters and musicians; the ROMANS were greater orators: But the FRENCH are the only people, except the GREEKS, who have been at once philosophers, poets, orators, historians, painters, architects, sculptors, and musicians. With regard to the stage, they have excelled even the GREEKS,[2] who far excelled the ENGLISH. And, in common life, they have, in a great measure, perfected that art, the most useful and agreeable of any, *l'Art de Vivre*, the art of society and conversation.

If we consider the state of the sciences and polite arts in our own country, HORACE's observation, with regard to the ROMANS, may, in a great measure, be applied to the BRITISH.

*———Sed in longum tamen ævum
Manserunt, hodieque manent vestigia ruris.*

The elegance and propriety of style have been very much neglected among us. We have no dictionary of our language, and scarcely a tolerable grammar. The first polite prose we have, was writ by a man who is still alive.[3] As to SPRAT, LOCKE, and even TEMPLE, they knew too little of the rules of art to be esteemed elegant writers. The prose of BACON, HARRINGTON, and MILTON, is altogether stiff and pedantic; though their sense be excellent. Men, in this country, have been so much occupied in the great disputes of *Religion*, *Politics*, and *Philosophy*, that they had no relish for the seemingly minute observations of grammar and criticism. And though this turn of thinking must have considerably improved our sense and our talent of reasoning; it must be confessed, that, even in those sciences above-mentioned, we have not any standard book which we can transmit to posterity: And the utmost we have to boast of, are a few essays towards a more just philosophy; which, indeed, promise well, but have not, as yet, reached any degree of perfection.

It has become an established opinion, that commerce can never flourish but in a free government; and this opinion seems to be founded on a longer and larger experience than the foregoing, with regard to the arts and sciences. If we

---

[1] [N.B. This was published in 1742. So Edition P.]
[2] [Who—English; added in Edition K.]
[3] Dr. SWIFT.

trace commerce in its progress through TYRE, ATHENS, SYRACUSE, CARTHAGE, VENICE, FLORENCE, GENOA, ANTWERP, HOLLAND, ENGLAND, &c. we shall always find it to have fixed its seat in free governments. The three greatest towns in Europe, are LONDON, AMSTERDAM, and HAMBURGH; all free cities, and protestant cities; that is, enjoying a double liberty. It must, however, be observed, that the great jealousy entertained of late, with regard to the commerce of FRANCE, seems to prove, that this maxim is no more certain and infallible than the foregoing, and that the subjects of an absolute prince may become our rivals in commerce, as well as in learning.

Durst I deliver my opinion in an affair of so much uncertainty, I would assert, that, notwithstanding the efforts of the FRENCH, there is something hurtful to commerce inherent in the very nature of absolute government, and inseparable from it: Though the reason I should assign for this opinion, is somewhat different from that which is commonly insisted on. Private property seems to me almost as secure in a civilized EUROPEAN monarchy, as in a republic; nor is danger much apprehended in such a government, from the violence of the sovereign; more than we commonly dread harm from thunder, or earthquakes, or any accident the most unusual and extraordinary. Avarice, the spur of industry, is so obstinate a passion, and works its way through so many real dangers and difficulties, that it is not likely to be scared by an imaginary danger, which is so small, that it scarcely admits of calculation. Commerce, therefore, in my opinion, is apt to decay in absolute governments, not because it is there less *secure*, but because it is less *honourable*. A subordination of ranks is absolutely necessary to the support of monarchy. Birth, titles, and place, must be honoured above industry and riches. And while these notions prevail, all the considerable traders will be tempted to throw up their commerce, in order to purchase some of those employments, to which privileges and honours are annexed.

Since I am upon this head, of the alterations which time has produced, or may produce in politics, I must observe, that all kinds of government, free and absolute, seem to have undergone, in modern times, a great change for the better, with regard both to foreign and domestic management. The *balance of power* is a secret in politics, fully known only to the present age; and I must add, that the internal POLICE of states has also received great improvements within the last century. We are informed by SALLUST, that CATILINE's army was much augmented by the accession of the highwaymen about ROME; though I believe, that all of that profession, who are at present dispersed over EUROPE, would not amount to a regiment. In CICERO's pleadings for MILO, I find this argument, among others, made use of to prove, that his client had not assassinated CLODIUS. Had MILO, said he, intended to have killed CLODIUS, he had not attacked him in the day-time, and at such a distance from the city: He had way-laid him at night, near the suburbs, where it might have been pretended, that he was killed by robbers; and the frequency of the accident would have favoured the deceit. This is a surprizing proof of the loose police of ROME, and of the number and force of these robbers; since CLODIUS[1] was at that time attended by thirty slaves, who were completely armed, and sufficiently accustomed to blood and danger in the frequent tumults excited by that seditious tribune.[2]

But though all kinds of government be improved in modern times, yet monarchical government seems to have made the greatest advances towards perfection. It may now be affirmed of civilized monarchies, what was formerly said in praise of republics alone, *that they are a government of Laws, not of Men.* They are found susceptible of order, method, and constancy, to a surprizing degree. Property is there secure; industry encouraged; the arts flourish; and the prince lives secure among his subjects, like a father among his children. [3]There are perhaps, and have been for two centuries, nearly two hundred absolute princes, great and small, in EUROPE; and allowing twenty years to each reign, we may suppose, that there have been in the whole two thousand monarchs or tyrants, as the GREEKS would have called them: Yet of these there has not been one, not even PHILIP II. of SPAIN, so bad as TIBERIUS, CALIGULA, NERO, or DOMITIAN, who were four in twelve amongst the ROMAN emperors. It must, however, be confessed, that, though monarchical governments have approached nearer to popular

---

[1] *Vide Asc. Ped. in Orat. pro Milone.*

[2] [Edition A added: and, by the *Roman* Laws, answerable, upon their own Lives, for the Life of their Master.]

[3] [This sentence was added in Edition K.]

ones, in gentleness and stability; they are still inferior. Our modern education and customs instil more humanity and moderation than the ancient; but have not as yet been able to overcome entirely the disadvantages of that form of government.

But here I must beg leave to advance a conjecture, which seems probable, but which posterity alone can fully judge of. I am apt to think, that, in monarchical governments there is a source of improvement, and in popular governments a source of degeneracy, which in time will bring these species of civil polity still nearer an equality. The greatest abuses, which arise in FRANCE, the most perfect model of pure monarchy, proceed not from the number or weight of the taxes, beyond what are to be met with in free countries; but from the expensive, unequal, arbitrary, and intricate method of levying them, by which the industry of the poor, especially of the peasants and farmers, is, in a great measure, discouraged, and agriculture rendered a beggarly and slavish employment. But to whose advantage do these abuses tend? If to that of the nobility, they might be esteemed inherent in that form of government; since the nobility are the true supports of monarchy; and it is natural their interest should be more consulted, in such a constitution, than that of the people. But the nobility are, in reality, the chief losers by this oppression; since it ruins their estates, and beggars their tenants. The only gainers by it are the *Finançiers*,[1] a race of men rather odious to the nobility and the whole kingdom. If a prince or minister, therefore, should arise, endowed with sufficient discernment to know his own and the public interest, and with sufficient force of mind to break through the ancient customs, we might expect to see these abuses remedied; in which case, the difference between that absolute government and our free one, would not appear so considerable as at present.

The source of degeneracy, which may be remarked in free governments, consists in the practice of contracting debt, and mortgaging the public revenues, by which taxes may, in time, become altogether intolerable, and all the property of the state be brought into the hands of the public. This

---

[1] [The cedilla is not found in B, or in some Editions of the Political Discourses, where the word occurs.]

practice is of modern date. The ATHENIANS,[1] though governed by a republic, paid near two hundred *per Cent.* for those sums of money, which any emergence made it necessary for them to borrow; as we learn from XENOPHON.[2] Among the moderns, the DUTCH first introduced the practice of borrowing great sums at low interest, and have well nigh ruined themselves by it. Absolute princes have also contracted debt; but as an absolute prince may make a bankruptcy when he pleases, his people can never be oppressed by his debts. In popular governments, the people, and chiefly those who have the highest offices, being commonly the public creditors, it is difficult for the state to make use of this remedy, which, however it may sometimes be necessary, is always cruel and barbarous. This, therefore, seems to be an inconvenience, which nearly threatens all free governments; especially our own, at the present juncture of affairs. And what a strong motive is this, to encrease our frugality of public money; lest for want of it, we be reduced, by the multiplicity of taxes, or what is worse, by our public impotence and inability for defence, to curse our very liberty, and wish ourselves in the same state of servitude with all the nations that surround us?

ESSAY XIII.—*Of Eloquence.*

THOSE, who consider the periods and revolutions of human kind, as represented in history, are entertained with a spectacle full of pleasure and variety, and see, with surprize, the manners, customs, and opinions of the same species susceptible of such prodigious changes in different periods of time. It may, however, be observed, that, in *civil* history, there is found a much greater uniformity than in the history of learn-

---

[1] [The *Athenians*, though a Republic, paid Twenty *per Cent.* for Money, as we learn from Xenophon.—Edition A: and no note.

The *Athenians*, though govern'd by a Republic, paid Twenty *per Cent.* for those sums of Money, which any emergent Occasion made it necessary for them to borrow; as we learn from Xenophon.—Edition B: and no note.

The Athenians, though governed by a republic, paid near two hundred *per Cent.* for those sums of money, which any emergent occasion made it necessary for them to borrow; as we learn from Xenophon.—Editions D to Q: and note.]

[2] Κτῆσιν δὲ ἀπ' οὐδενὸς ἂν οὕτω καλὴν κτήσαιντο, ὥσπερ ἀφ' οὗ ἂν προτελέσωσιν εἰς τὴν ἀφορμήν—οἱ δέ γε πλεῖστοι Ἀθηναίων πλείονα λήψονται κατ' ἐνιαυτόν ἢ ὅσα ἂν εἰσενέγκωσιν· οἱ γὰρ μνᾶν προτελέσαντες, ἐγγὺς δυοῖν μναῖν πρόσοδον ἕξουσι—ὃ δοκεῖ τῶν ἀνθρωπίνων ἀσφαλέστατόν τε καὶ πολυχρονιώτατον εἶναι. ΞΕΝ. ΠΟΡΟΙ. III. 9. 10.

ing and science, and that the wars, negociations, and politics of one age resemble more those of another, than the taste, wit, and speculative principles. Interest and ambition, honour and shame, friendship and enmity, gratitude and revenge, are the prime movers in all public transactions; and these passions are of a very stubborn and intractable nature, in comparison of the sentiments and understanding, which are easily varied by education and example. The GOTHS were much more inferior to the ROMANS, in taste and science, than in courage and virtue.

But not to compare together nations so widely different;[1] it may be observed, that even this later period of human learning is, in many respects, of an opposite character to the ancient; and that, if we be superior in philosophy, we are still, notwithstanding all our refinements, much inferior in eloquence.

In ancient times, no work of genius was thought to require so great parts and capacity, as the speaking in public; and some eminent writers have pronounced the talents, even of a great poet or philosopher, to be of an inferior nature to those which are requisite for such an undertaking. GREECE and ROME produced, each of them, but one accomplished orator; and whatever praises the other celebrated speakers might merit, they were still esteemed much inferior to these great models of eloquence. It is observable, that the ancient critics could scarcely find two orators in any age, who deserved to be placed precisely in the same rank, and possessed the same degree of merit. CALVUS, CÆLIUS, CURIO, HORTENSIUS, CÆSAR rose one above another: But the greatest of that age was inferior to CICERO, the most eloquent speaker, that had ever appeared in ROME. Those of fine taste, however, pronounce this judgment of the ROMAN orator, as well as of the GRECIAN, that both of them surpassed in eloquence all that had ever appeared, but that they were far from reaching the perfection of their art, which was infinite, and not only exceeded human force to attain, but human imagination to conceive. CICERO declares himself dissatisfied with his own performances; nay, even with those of DEMO-

---

[1] [Editions C to Padd: that they may almost be esteemed of a different species.]

STHENES. *Ita sunt avidœ & capaces meœ aures*, says he, *& semper aliquid immensum, infinitumque desiderant.*[1]

Of all the polite and learned nations, ENGLAND alone possesses a popular government, or admits into the legislature such numerous assemblies as can be supposed to lie under the dominion of eloquence. But what has ENGLAND to boast of in this particular? In enumerating the great men, who have done honour to our country, we exult in our poets and philosophers; but what orators are ever mentioned? Or where are the monuments of their genius to be met with? There are found, indeed, in our histories, the names of several, who directed the resolutions of our parliament: But neither themselves nor others have taken the pains to preserve their speeches; and the authority, which they possessed, seems to have been owing to their experience, wisdom, or power, more than to their talents for oratory. At present, there are above half a dozen speakers in the two houses, who, in the judgment of the public, have reached very near the same pitch of eloquence; and no man pretends to give any one the preference above the rest. This seems to me a certain proof, that none of them have attained much beyond a mediocrity in their art, and that the species of eloquence, which they aspire to, gives no exercise to the sublimer faculties of the mind, but may be reached by ordinary talents and a slight application. A hundred cabinet-makers in LONDON can work a table or a chair equally well; but no one poet can write verses with such spirit and elegance as Mr. POPE.

We are told, that, when DEMOSTHENES was to plead, all ingenious men flocked to ATHENS from the most remote parts of GREECE, as to the most celebrated spectacle of the world.[2] At LONDON you may see men sauntering in the court of requests, while the most important debate is carrying on in the two houses; and many do not think themselves sufficiently compensated, for the losing of their dinners, by all the eloquence of our most celebrated speakers. When old

---

[1] [Editions C to P add: This single circumstance is sufficient to make us apprehend the wide difference between ancient and modern eloquence, and to let us see how much the latter is inferior to the former.]

[2] Ne illud quidem intelligunt, non modo ita memoriæ proditum esse, sed ita necesse fuisse, cum DEMOSTHENES dicturus esset, ut concursus, audiendi causa, ex tota GRECIA fierent. At cum isti ATTICI dicunt, non modo a corona (quod est ipsum miserabile) sed etiam ab advocatis relinquuntur.
CICERO de Claris Oratoribus, c. 84.

CIBBER is to act, the curiosity of several is more excited, than when our prime minister is to defend himself from a motion for his removal or impeachment.

Even a person, unacquainted with the noble remains of ancient orators, may judge, from a few strokes, that the stile or species of their eloquence was infinitely more sublime than that which modern orators aspire to. How absurd would it appear, in our temperate and calm speakers, to make use of an *Apostrophe*, like that noble one of DEMOSTHENES, so much celebrated by QUINTILIAN and LONGINUS, when justifying the unsuccessful battle of CHÆRONEA, he breaks out, *No, my Fellow-Citizens, No: You have not erred. I swear by the manes of those heroes, who fought for the same cause in the plains of* MARATHON *and* PLATÆA. Who could now endure such a bold and poetical figure, as that which CICERO employs, after describing in the most tragical terms the crucifixion of a ROMAN citizen. *Should I paint the horrors of this scene, not to* ROMAN *citizens, not to the allies of our state, not to those who have ever heard of the* ROMAN *Name, not even to men, but to brute-creatures; or, to go farther, should I lift up my voice in the most desolate solitude, to the rocks and mountains, yet should I surely see those rude and inanimate parts of nature moved with horror and indignation at the recital of so enormous an action.*[1] With what a blaze of eloquence must such a sentence be surrounded to give it grace, or cause it to make any impression on the hearers? And what noble art and sublime talents are requisite to arrive, by just degrees, at a sentiment so bold and excessive: To inflame the audience, so as to make them accompany the speaker in such violent passions, and such elevated conceptions: And to conceal, under a torrent of eloquence, the artifice, by which all this is effectuated! [2] Should this sentiment even appear to us excessive, as perhaps it justly may, it will at least serve to give an idea of the stile of ancient eloquence, where such swelling expressions were not rejected as wholly monstrous and gigantic.

Suitable to this vehemence of thought and expression,

---

[1] *The original is;* Quod si hæc non ad cives Romanos, non ad aliquos amicos nostræ civitatis, non ad eos qui populi Romani nomen audissent; denique, si non ad homines, verum ad bestias; aut etiam, ut longius progrediar, si in aliqua desertissima solitudine, ad saxa & ad scopulos hæc conqueri & deplorare vellem, tamen omnia muta atque inanima, tanta & tam indigna rerum atrocitate commoverentur Cic. in Ver. Act ii. Lib. v. c. 67.

[2] [This sentence was added in Edition P.]

was the vehemence of action, observed in the ancient orators. The *supplosio pedis*, or stamping with the foot, was one of the most usual and moderate gestures which they made use of;[1] though that is now esteemed too violent, either for the senate, bar, or pulpit, and is only admitted into the theatre, to accompany the most violent passions, which are there represented.

One is somewhat at a loss to what cause we may ascribe so sensible a decline of eloquence in later ages. The genius of mankind, at all times, is, perhaps, equal: The moderns have applied themselves, with great industry and success, to all the other arts and sciences: And a learned nation possesses a popular government; a circumstance which seems requisite for the full display of these noble talents: But notwithstanding all these advantages, our progress in eloquence is very inconsiderable, in comparison of the advances, which we have made in all other parts of learning.

Shall we assert, that the strains of ancient eloquence are unsuitable to our age, and ought not to be imitated by modern orators? Whatever reasons may be made use of to prove this, I am persuaded that they will be found, upon examination to be unsound and unsatisfactory.

First, It may be said, that, in ancient times, during the flourishing period of GREEK and ROMAN learning, the municipal laws, in every state, were but few and simple, and the decision of causes, was, in a great measure, left to the equity and common sense of the judges. The study of the laws was not then a laborious occupation, requiring the drudgery of a whole life to finish it, and incompatible with every other study or profession. The great statesmen and generals among the ROMANS were all lawyers; and CICERO, to shew the facility of acquiring this science, declares, that, in the midst of all his occupations, he would undertake, in a few days, to make himself a compleat civilian. Now, where a pleader addresses himself to the equity of his judges, he has much more room to display his eloquence, than where he must draw his arguments from strict laws, statutes, and precedents. In the former case, many circumstances must be

---

[1] Ubi dolor? Ubi ardor animi, qui etiam ex infantium ingeniis elicere voces & querelas solet? nulla perturbatio animi, nulla corporis: frons non percussa, non femur; pedis (*quod minimum est*) nulla supplosio. Itaque tantum abfuit ut inflammares nostros animos; somnum isto loco vix tenebamus.—CICERO de Claris Oratoribus, c. 80.

taken in; many personal considerations regarded; and even favour and inclination, which it belongs to the orator, by his art and eloquence, to conciliate, may be disguised under the appearance of equity. But how shall a modern lawyer have leisure to quit his toilsome occupations, in order to gather the flowers of PARNASSUS? Or what opportunity shall he have of displaying them, amidst the rigid and subtile arguments, objections, and replies, which he is obliged to make use of? The greatest genius, the greatest orator, who should pretend to plead before the *Chancellor*, after a month's study of the laws, would only labour to make himself ridiculous.

I am ready to own, that this circumstance, of the multiplicity and intricacy of laws, is a discouragement to eloquence in modern times: But I assert, that it will not entirely account for the decline of that noble art. It may banish oratory from WESTMINSTER-HALL, but not from either house of parliament. Among the ATHENIANS, the AREOPAGITES expressly forbad all allurements of eloquence; and some have pretended that in the GREEK orations, written in the *judiciary* form, there is not so bold and rhetorical a stile, as appears in the ROMAN. But to what a pitch did the ATHENIANS carry their eloquence in the *deliberative* kind, when affairs of state were canvassed, and the liberty, happiness, and honour of the republic were the subject of debate? Disputes of this nature elevate the genius above all others, and give the fullest scope to eloquence; and such disputes are very frequent in this nation.

Secondly, It may be pretended that the decline of eloquence is owing to the superior good sense of the moderns, who reject with disdain all those rhetorical tricks, employed to seduce the judges, and will admit of nothing but solid argument in any debate of deliberation. If a man be accused of murder, the fact must be proved by witnesses and evidence; and the laws will afterwards determine the punishment of the criminal. It would be ridiculous to describe, in strong colours, the horror and cruelty of the action: To introduce the relations of the dead; and, at a signal, make them throw themselves at the feet of the judges, imploring justice with tears and lamentations: And still more ridiculous would it be, to employ a picture representing the bloody deed, in order to move the judges by the display of so tragical a spectacle: Though we know, that this artifice was sometimes practised by the pleaders of old.[1] Now, banish the pathetic from public discourses, and you reduce the speakers merely to modern eloquence; that is, to good sense, delivered in proper expression.

Perhaps it may be acknowledged, that our modern customs, or our superior good sense, if you will, should make our orators more cautious and reserved than the ancient, in attempting to inflame the passions, or elevate the imagination of their audience: But, I see no reason, why it should make them despair absolutely of succeeding in that attempt. It should make them redouble their art, not abandon it entirely. The ancient orators seem also to have been on their guard against this jealousy of their audience; but they took a different way of eluding it.[2] They hurried away with such a torrent of sublime and pathetic, that they left their hearers no leisure to perceive the artifice, by which they were deceived. Nay, to consider the matter aright, they were not deceived by any artifice. The orator, by force of his own genius and eloquence, first inflamed himself with anger, indignation, pity, sorrow; and then communicated those impetuous movements to his audience.

Does any man pretend to have more good sense than JULIUS CÆSAR? yet that haughty conqueror, we know, was so subdued by the charms of CICERO's eloquence, that he was, in a manner, constrained to change his settled purpose and resolution, and to absolve a criminal, whom, before that orator pleaded, he was determined to condemn.

[3] Some objections, I own, notwithstanding his vast success, may lie against some passages of the ROMAN orator. He is too florid and rhetorical: His figures are too striking and palpable: The divisions of his discourse are drawn chiefly from the rules of the schools: And his wit disdains not the artifice even of a pun, rhyme, or jingle of words. The GRECIAN addressed himself to an audience much less refined than the ROMAN senate or judges. The lowest vulgar of ATHENS were his sovereigns, and the arbiters of his eloquence.[4] Yet is his manner more chaste and austere than

[1] QUINTIL. lib. vi. cap. 1.
[2] LONGINUS, cap. 15.
[3] [The paragraph was added in Edition K.]
[4] The orators formed the taste of the ATHENIAN people, not the people of the orators. GORGIAS LEONTINUS was very taking with them, till they became acquainted with a better manner. His figures of speech, says DIODORUS SICU-

that of the other. Could it be copied, its success would be infallible over a modern assembly. It is rapid harmony, exactly adjusted to the sense: It is vehement reasoning, without any appearance of art: It is disdain, anger, boldness, freedom, involved in a continued stream of argument: And of all human productions, the orations of DEMOSTHENES present to us the models, which approach the nearest to perfection.

Thirdly, It may be pretended, that the disorders of the ancient governments, and the enormous crimes, of which the citizens were often guilty, afforded much ampler matter for eloquence than can be met with among the moderns. Were there no VERRES or CATILINE, there would be no CICERO. But that this reason can have no great influence, is evident. It would be easy to find a PHILIP in modern times; but where shall we find a DEMOSTHENES?

What remains, then, but that we lay the blame on the want of genius, or of judgment in our speakers, who either found themselves incapable of reaching the heights of ancient eloquence, or rejected all such endeavours, as unsuitable to the spirit of modern assemblies? A few successful attempts of this nature might rouse the genius of the nation, excite the emulation of the youth, and accustom our ears to a more sublime and more pathetic elocution, than what we have been hitherto entertained with. There is certainly something accidental in the first rise and the progress of the arts in any nation. I doubt whether a very satisfactory reason can be given, why ancient ROME, though it received all its refinements from GREECE, could attain only to a relish for statuary, painting and architecture, without reaching the practice of these arts: While modern ROME has been excited, by a few remains found among the ruins of antiquity, and has produced artists of the greatest eminence and distinction. Had such a cultivated genius for oratory, as WALLER'S [1] for poetry, arisen, during the civil wars, when liberty began to be fully established, and popular assemblies to enter into all the most material points of government; I

LUS, his antithesis, his ισόκωλον, his ὁμοιοτέλευτον, which are now despised, had a great effect upon the audience. Lib. xii. page 106. *ex editione* RHOD. It is in vain therefore for modern orators to plead the taste of their hearers as an apology for their lame performances. It would be strange prejudice in favour of antiquity, not to allow a BRITISH parliament to be naturally superior in judgment and delicacy to an ATHENIAN mob.

[1] [As my Lord Bolingbroke.—C. and D.]

am persuaded so illustrious an example would have given a quite different turn to BRITISH eloquence, and made us reach the perfection of the ancient model. Our orators would then have done honour to their country, as well as our poets, geometers, and philosophers, and BRITISH CICEROS have appeared, as well as BRITISH [1] ARCHIMEDESES and VIRGILS.[2]

---

[1] [Platos and Virgils.—C. D. Plutarchs and Virgils.—K. to P.]

[2] [C to P proceed: I have confest that there is something accidental in the origin and progress of the arts in any nation; and yet I cannot forbear thinking, that if the other learned and polite nations of EUROPE had possest the same advantages of a popular government, they would probably have carried eloquence to a greater height than it has yet reached in BRITAIN. The FRENCH sermons, especially those of FLECHIER and BOSSUET, are much superior to the ENGLISH in this particular; and [1] in both these authors are found many strokes of the most sublime poetry. None but private causes, in that country, are ever debated before their parliaments or courts of judicature; but notwithstanding this disadvantage, there appears a spirit of eloquence in many of their lawyers, which, with proper cultivation and encouragement, might rise to the greatest height. The pleadings of PATRU are very elegant, and give us room to imagine what so fine a genius could have performed in questions concerning public liberty or slavery, peace or war, who exerts himself with such success in debates concerning the price of an old horse, or a gossiping story of a quarrel between an abbess and her nuns. For 'tis remarkable, that this polite writer, tho' esteemed by all the men of wit in his time, was never employed in the most considerable causes of their courts of judicature, but lived and died in poverty: From an ancient prejudice industriously propagated by the dunces in all countries, *That a man of genius is unfit for business.* The disorders produced by the factions against cardinal MAZARINE, made the parliament of PARIS enter into the discussion of public affairs, and during that short interval, there appeared many symptoms of the revival of ancient eloquence. The *avocat general* TALON, in an oration, invoked on his knees, the spirit of St. LOUIS to look down with compassion on his divided and unhappy people, and to inspire them, from above, with the love of concord and unanimity.[2] The members of the FRENCH academy have attempted to give us models of eloquence in their harangues at their admittance: But, having no subject to discourse upon, they have run altogether into a fulsome strain of panegyric and flattery, the most barren of all subjects. Their stile, however, is commonly, on these occasions, very elevated and sublime, and might reach the greatest heights, were it employed on a subject more favourable and engaging.

There are some circumstances, I confess, in the ENGLISH temper and genius, which are disadvantageous to the progress of eloquence, and render all attempts of that kind more dangerous and difficult among them than among any other nation. The ENGLISH are conspicuous for *good-sense*, which makes them very jealous of any attempts to deceive them by the flowers of rhetoric and elocution. They are also peculiarly *modest*; which makes them consider it as a piece of arrogance to offer any thing but reason to public assemblies, or attempt to guide them by passion or fancy. I may, perhaps, be allowed to add, that the people in general are not remarkable for delicacy of taste, or for sensibility to the charms of the muses. Their *musical parts*, to use the expression of a noble author, are but indifferent. Hence their comic poets, to move them, must have recourse to ob-

---

[1] [C and D: and in *Flechier* there are found many strokes of the most sublime poetry. His funeral sermon on the Marechal de Turenne is a good instance.]

[2] [De RETZ's Memoirs.]

It is seldom or never found, when a false taste in poetry or eloquence prevails among any people, that it has been preferred to a true, upon comparison and reflection. It commonly prevails merely from ignorance of the true, and from the want of perfect models, to lead men into a juster apprehension, and more refined relish of those productions of genius. When *these* appear, they soon unite all suffrages in their favour, and, by their natural and powerful charms, gain over, even the most prejudiced, to the love and admiration of them. The principles of every passion, and of every sentiment, is in every man; and when touched properly, they rise to life, and warm the heart, and convey that satisfaction, by which a work of genius is distinguished from the adulterate beauties of a capricious wit and fancy. And if this observation be true, with regard to all the liberal arts, it must be peculiarly so, with regard to eloquence; which, being merely calculated for the public, and for men of the world, cannot, with any pretence of reason, appeal from the people to more refined judges; but must submit to the public verdict, without reserve or limitation. Whoever, upon comparison, is deemed by a common audience the greatest orator, ought most certainly to be pronounced such, by men of science and erudition. And though an indifferent speaker may triumph for a long time, and be esteemed altogether perfect by the vulgar, who are satisfied with his accomplishments, and know not in what he is defective: Yet, whenever the true genius arises, *he* draws to him the attention of every one, and immediately appears superior to his rival.

Now to judge by this rule, ancient eloquence, that is, the sublime and passionate, is of a much juster taste than the modern, or the argumentative and rational; and, if pro-

scenity; their tragic poets to blood and slaughter: And hence their orators, being deprived of any such resource, have abandoned altogether the hopes of moving them, and have confined themselves to plain argument and reasoning.

These circumstances, joined to particular accidents, may, perhaps, have retarded the growth of eloquence in this kingdom; but will not be able to prevent its success, if ever it appear amongst us: And one may safely pronounce, that this is a field, in which the most flourishing laurels may yet be gathered, if any youth of accomplished genius, thoroughly acquainted with all the polite arts, and not ignorant of public business, should appear in parliament, and accustom our ears to an eloquence more commanding and pathetic. And to confirm me in this opinion, there occur two considerations, the one derived from ancient, the other from modern times.]

perly executed, will always have more command and authority over mankind. We are satisfied with our mediocrity, because we have had no experience of anything better: But the ancients had experience of both, and, upon comparison, gave the preference to that kind, of which they have left us such applauded models. For, if I mistake not, our modern eloquence is of the same stile or species with that which ancient critics denominated ATTIC eloquence, that is, calm, elegant, and subtile, which instructed the reason more than affected the passions, and never raised its tone above argument or common discourse. Such was the eloquence of LYSIAS among the ATHENIANS, and of CALVUS among the ROMANS. These were esteemed in their time; but when compared with DEMOSTHENES and CICERO, were eclipsed like a taper when set in the rays of a meridian sun. Those latter orators possessed the same elegance, and subtilty, and force of argument, with the former; but what rendered them chiefly admirable, was that pathetic and sublime, which, on proper occasions, they threw into their discourse, and by which they commanded the resolution of their audience.

Of this species of eloquence we have scarcely any instance in ENGLAND, at least in our public speakers. In our writers, we have had some instances, which have met with great applause, and might assure our ambitious youth of equal or superior glory in attempts for the revival of ancient eloquence. Lord BOLINGBROKE's productions, [1] with all their defects in argument, method and precision, contain a force and energy which our orators scarcely ever aim at; though it is evident, that such an elevated stile has much better grace in a speaker than in a writer, and is assured of more prompt and more astonishing success. It is there seconded by the graces of voice and action: The movements are mutually communicated between the orator and the audience: And the very aspect of a large assembly, attentive to the discourse of one man, must inspire him with a peculiar elevation, sufficient to give a propriety to the strongest figures and expressions. It is true, there is a great prejudice against *set speeches*; and a man cannot escape ridicule, who repeats a discourse as a school-boy does his lesson, and takes no notice of any thing that has been advanced in the course of the debate. But where is the necessity of falling

[1] ['with—precision';—this clause was added in Edition K.]

into this absurdity? A public speaker must know beforehand the question under debate. He may compose all the arguments, objections, and answers, such as he thinks will be most proper for his discourse.[1] If any thing new occur, he may supply it from his invention; nor will the difference be very apparent between his elaborate and his extemporary compositions. The mind naturally continues with the same *impetus* or *force*, which it has acquired by its motion; as a vessel, once impelled by the oars, carries on its course for some time, when the original impulse is suspended.

I shall conclude this subject with observing, that, even though our modern orators should not elevate their stile or aspire to a rivalship with the ancient; yet is there, in most of their speeches, a material defect, which they might correct, without departing from that composed air of argument and reasoning, to which they limit their ambition. Their great affectation of extemporary discourses has made them reject all order and method, which seems so requisite to argument, and without which it is scarcely possible to produce an entire conviction on the mind. It is not, that one would recommend many divisions in a public discourse, unless the subject very evidently offer them: But it is easy, without this formality, to observe a method, and make that method conspicuous to the hearers, who will be infinitely pleased to see the arguments rise naturally from one another, and will retain a more thorough persuasion, than can arise from the strongest reasons, which are thrown together in confusion.

Essay XIV.—*Of the Rise and Progress of the Arts and Sciences.*

Nothing requires greater nicety, in our enquiries concerning human affairs, than to distinguish exactly what is owing to *chance*, and what proceeds from *causes*; nor is there any subject, in which an author is more liable to deceive himself by false subtilties and refinements. To say, that any event is derived from chance, cuts short all farther enquiry concerning it, and leaves the writer in the same state of ignorance

---

[1] The first of the Athenians, who composed and wrote his speeches, was Pericles, a man of business and a man of sense, if ever there was one, Πρῶτος γραπτὸν λόγον ἐν δικαστηρίῳ εἶπε, τῶν πρὸ αὑτοῦ σχεδιαζόντων.—Suidas in Περικλῆς.

with the rest of mankind. But when the event is supposed to proceed from certain and stable causes, he may then display his ingenuity, in assigning these causes; and as a man of any subtilty can never be at a loss in this particular, he has thereby an opportunity of swelling his volumes, and discovering his profound knowledge, in observing what escapes the vulgar and ignorant.

The distinguishing between chance and causes must depend upon every particular man's sagacity, in considering every particular incident. But, if I were to assign any general rule to help us in applying this distinction, it would be the following, *What depends upon a few persons is, in a great measure, to be ascribed to chance, or secret and unknown causes: What arises from a great number, may often be accounted for by determinate and known causes.*

Two natural reasons may be assigned for this rule. *First,* If you suppose a dye to have any biass, however small, to a particular side, this biass, though, perhaps, it may not appear in a few throws, will certainly prevail in a great number, and will cast the balance entirely to that side. In like manner, when any *causes* beget a particular inclination or passion, at a certain time, and among a certain people; though many individuals may escape the contagion, and be ruled by passions peculiar to themselves; yet the multitude will certainly be seized by the common affection, and be governed by it in all their actions.

Secondly, Those principles of causes, which are fitted to operate on a multitude, are always of a grosser and more stubborn nature, less subject to accidents, and less influenced by whim and private fancy, than those which operate on a few only. The latter are commonly so delicate and refined, that the smallest incident in the health, education, or fortune of a particular person, is sufficient to divert their course, and retard their operation; nor is it possible to reduce them to any general maxims or observations. Their influence at one time will never assure us concerning their influence at another; even though all the general circumstances should be the same in both cases.

To judge by this rule, the domestic and the gradual revolutions of a state must be a more proper subject of reasoning and observation, than the foreign and the violent, which are commonly produced by single persons, and are more influenced by whim, folly, or caprice, than by general passions and interests. The depression of the lords, and rise of the commons in ENGLAND, after the statutes of alienation and the encrease of trade and industry, are more easily accounted for by general principles, than the depression of the SPANISH, and rise of the FRENCH monarchy, after the death of CHARLES QUINT. Had HARRY IV. Cardinal RICHLIEU, and LOUIS XIV. been SPANIARDS; and PHILIP II. III. and IV. and CHARLES II. been FRENCHMEN, the history of these two nations had been entirely reversed.

For the same reason, it is more easy to account for the rise and progress of commerce in any kingdom, than for that of learning; and a state, which should apply itself to the encouragement of the one, would be more assured of success, than one which should cultivate the other. Avarice, or the desire of gain, is an universal passion, which operates at all times, in all places, and upon all persons: But curiosity, or the love of knowledge, has a very limited influence, and requires youth, leisure, education, genius, and example, to make it govern any person. You will never want booksellers, while there are buyers of books: But there may frequently be readers where there are no authors. Multitudes of people, necessity and liberty, have begotten commerce in HOLLAND: But study and application have scarcely produced any eminent writers.

We may, therefore, conclude, that there is no subject, in which we must proceed with more caution, than in tracing the history of the arts and sciences; lest we assign causes which never existed, and reduce what is merely contingent to stable and universal principles. Those who cultivate the sciences in any state, are always few in number: The passion, which governs them, limited: Their taste and judgment delicate and easily perverted: And their application disturbed with the smallest accident. Chance, therefore, or secret and unknown causes, must have a great influence on the rise and progress of all the refined arts.

But there is a reason, which induces me not to ascribe the matter altogether to chance. Though the persons, who cultivate the sciences with such astonishing success, as to attract the admiration of posterity, be always few, in all nations and all ages; it is impossible but a share of the same spirit and genius must be antecedently diffused throughout the people among whom they arise, in order to produce, form, and cultivate, from their earliest infancy, the taste and judgment of those eminent writers. The mass cannot be altogether insipid, from which such refined spirits are extracted. *There is a God within us,* says OVID, *who breathes that divine fire, by which we are animated.*[1] Poets, in all ages, have advanced this claim to inspiration. There is not, however, any thing supernatural in the case. Their fire is not kindled from heaven. It only runs along the earth; is caught from one breast to another; and burns brightest, where the materials are best prepared, and most happily disposed. The question, therefore, concerning the rise and progress of the arts and sciences, is not altogether a question concerning the taste, genius, and spirit of a few, but concerning those of a whole people; and may, therefore, be accounted for, in some measure, by general causes and principles. I grant, that a man, who should enquire, why such a particular poet, as HOMER, for instance, existed, at such a place, in such a time, would throw himself headlong into chimæra, and could never treat of such a subject, without a multitude of false subtilties and refinements. He might as well pretend to give a reason, why such particular generals, as FABIUS and SCIPIO, lived in ROME at such a time, and why FABIUS came into the world before SCIPIO. For such incidents as these, no other reason can be given than that of HORACE:

> *Scit genius, natale comes, qui temperat astrum,*
> *Naturæ Deus humanæ, mortalis in unum——*
> *——Quodque caput, vultu mutabilis, albus & ater.*

But I am persuaded, that in many cases good reasons might be given, why such a nation is more polite and learned, at a particular time, than any of its neighbours. At least, this is so curious a subject, that it were a pity to abandon it entirely, before we have found whether it be susceptible of reasoning, and can be reduced to any general principles.[2]

My first observation on this head is, *That it is impossible for the arts and sciences to arise, at first, among any people unless that people enjoy the blessing of a free government.*

---

[1] Est Deus in nobis; agitante calescimus illo:
Impetus hic, sacræ semina mentis habet.
OVID, *Fast. lib.* vi. 5.

[2] [Editions C to P add: I shall therefore proceed to deliver a few observations on this subject, which I submit to the censure and examination of the learned.]

In the first ages of the world, when men are as yet barbarous and ignorant, they seek no farther security against mutual violence and injustice, than the choice of some rulers, few or many, in whom they place an implicit confidence, without providing any security, by laws or political institutions, against the violence and injustice of these rulers. If the authority be centered in a single person, and if the people, either by conquest, or by the ordinary course of propagation, encrease to a great multitude, the monarch, finding it impossible, in his own person, to execute every office of sovereignty, in every place, must delegate his authority to inferior magistrates, who preserve peace and order in their respective districts. As experience and education have not yet refined the judgments of men to any considerable degree, the prince, who is himself unrestrained, never dreams of restraining his ministers, but delegates his full authority to every one, whom he sets over any portion of the people. All general laws are attended with inconveniencies, when applied to particular cases; and it requires great penetration and experience, both to perceive that these inconveniencies are fewer than what result from full discretionary powers in every magistrate; and also to discern what general laws are, upon the whole, attended with fewest inconveniencies. This is a matter of so great difficulty, that men may have made some advances, even in the sublime arts of poetry and eloquence, where a rapidity of genius and imagination assist their progress, before they have arrived at any great refinement in their municipal laws, where frequent trials and diligent observation can alone direct their improvements. It is not, therefore, to be supposed, that a barbarous monarch, unrestrained and uninstructed, will ever become a legislator, or think of restraining his *Bashaws*, in every province, or even his *Cadis* in every village. We are told, that the late *Czar*, though actuated with a noble genius, and smit with the love and admiration of EUROPEAN arts; yet professed an esteem for the TURKISH policy in this particular, and approved of such summary decisions of causes, as are practised in that barbarous monarchy, where the judges are not restrained by any methods, forms, or laws. He did not perceive, how contrary such a practice would have been to all his other endeavours for refining his people. Arbitrary power, in all cases, is somewhat oppressive and debasing; but it is altogether ruinous and intolerable, when contracted into a small compass; and becomes still worse, when the person, who possesses it, knows that the time of his authority is limited and uncertain. *Habet subjectos tanquam suos; viles, ut alienos.*[1] He governs the subjects with full authority, as if they were his own; and with negligence or tyranny, as belonging to another. A people, governed after such a manner, are slaves in the full and proper sense of the word; and it is impossible they can ever aspire to any refinements or taste or reason. They dare not so much as pretend to enjoy the necessaries of life in plenty or security.

To expect, therefore, that the arts and sciences should take their first rise in a monarchy, is to expect a contradiction. Before these refinements have taken place, the monarch is ignorant and uninstructed; and not having knowledge sufficient to make him sensible of the necessity of balancing his government upon general laws, he delegates his full power to all inferior magistrates. This barbarous policy debases the people, and for ever prevents all improvements. Were it possible, that, before science were known in the world, a monarch could possess so much wisdom as to become a legislator, and govern his people by law, not by the arbitrary will of their fellow-subjects, it might be possible for that species of government to be the first nursery of arts and sciences. But that supposition seems scarcely to be consistent or rational.

It may happen, that a republic, in its infant state, may be supported by as few laws as a barbarous monarchy, and may entrust as unlimited an authority to its magistrates or judges. But, besides that the frequent elections by the people, are a considerable check upon authority; it is impossible, but, in time, the necessity of restraining the magistrates, in order to preserve liberty, must at last appear, and give rise to general laws and statutes. The ROMAN Consuls, for some time, decided all causes, without being confined by any positive statutes, till the people, bearing this yoke with impatience, created the *decemvirs*, who promulgated the *twelve tables*; a body of laws, which, though, perhaps, they were not equal in bulk to one ENGLISH act of parliament, were almost the only written rules, which regulated

---

[1] TACIT. hist. lib. i. 37.

property and punishment, for some ages, in that famous republic. They were, however, sufficient, together with the forms of a free government, to secure the lives and properties of the citizens, to exempt one man from the dominion of another; and to protect every one against the violence or tyranny of his fellow-citizens. In such a situation the sciences may raise their heads and flourish: But never can have being amidst such a scene of oppression and slavery, as always results from barbarous monarchies, where the people alone are restrained by the authority of the magistrates, and the magistrates are not restrained by any law or statute. An unlimited despotism of this nature, while it exists, effectually puts a stop to all improvements, and keeps men from attaining that knowledge, which is requisite to instruct them in the advantages, arising from a better police, and more moderate authority.

Here then are the advantages of free states. Though a republic should be barbarous, it necessarily, by an infallible operation, gives rise to LAW, even before mankind have made any considerable advances in the other sciences. From law arises security: From security curiosity: And from curiosity knowledge. The latter steps of this progress may be more accidental; but the former are altogether necessary. A republic without laws can never have any duration. On the contrary, in a monarchical government, law arises not necessarily from the forms of government. Monarchy, when absolute, contains even something repugnant to law. Great wisdom and reflection can alone reconcile them. But such a degree of wisdom can never be expected, before the greater refinements and improvements of human reason. These refinements require curiosity, security, and law. The *first* growth, therefore, of the arts and sciences can never be expected in despotic governments.[1]

There are other causes, which discourage the rise of the refined arts in despotic governments; though I take the want of laws, and the delegation of full powers to every petty magistrate, to be the principal. Eloquence certainly

[1] [Editions C to P add: According to the necessary progress of things, law must precede science. In republics law may precede science, and may arise from the very nature of the government. In monarchies it arises not from the nature of the government, and cannot precede science. An absolute prince, who is barbarous, renders all his ministers and magistrates as absolute as himself: And there needs no more to prevent, for ever, all industry, curiosity, and science.]

springs up more naturally in popular governments: Emulation too in every accomplishment must there be more animated and enlivened: And genius and capacity have a fuller scope and career. All these causes render free governments the only proper *nursery* for the arts and sciences.

The next observation, which I shall make on this head, is, *That nothing is more favourable to the rise of politeness and learning, than a number of neighbouring and independent states, connected together by commerce and policy.* The emulation, which naturally arises among those neighbouring states, is an obvious source of improvement: But what I would chiefly insist on is the stop, which such limited territories give both to *power* and to *authority*.

Extended governments, where a single person has great influence, soon become absolute; but small ones change naturally into commonwealths. A large government is accustomed by degrees to tyranny; because each act of violence is at first performed upon a part, which, being distant from the majority, is not taken notice of, nor excites any violent ferment. Besides, a large government, though the whole be discontented, may, by a little art, be kept in obedience; while each part, ignorant of the resolutions of the rest, is afraid to begin any commotion or insurrection. Not to mention, that there is a superstitious reverence for princes, which mankind naturally contract when they do not often see the sovereign, and when many of them become not acquainted with him so as to perceive his weaknesses. And as large states can afford a great expence, in order to support the pomp of majesty; this is a kind of fascination on men, and naturally contributes to the enslaving of them.

In a small government, any act of oppression is immediately known throughout the whole: The murmurs and discontents, proceeding from it, are easily communicated: And the indignation arises the higher, because the subjects are not apt to apprehend in such states, that the distance is very wide between themselves and their sovereign. 'No man,' said the prince of CONDE, 'is a hero to his *Valet de Chambre.*' It is certain that admiration and acquaintance are altogether incompatible towards any mortal creature.[1] Sleep and love con-

---

[1] [Editions C to K add the following: *Antigonus*, being complimented by his flatterers, as a deity, and as the son of that glorious planet, which illuminates the universe, *Upon that head,* says he, *you may consult the person that empties my close stool.*]

vinced even ALEXANDER himself that he was not a God: But I suppose that such as daily attended him could easily, from the numberless weaknesses to which he was subject, have given him many still more convincing proofs of his humanity.

But the divisions into small states are favourable to learning, by stopping the progress of *authority* as well as that of *power*. Reputation is often as great a fascination upon men as sovereignty, and is equally destructive to the freedom of thought and examination. But where a number of neighbouring states have a great intercourse of arts and commerce, their mutual jealousy keeps them from receiving too lightly the law from each other, in matters of taste and of reasoning, and makes them examine every work of art with the greatest care and accuracy. The contagion of popular opinion spreads not so easily from one place to another. It readily receives a check in some state or other, where it concurs not with the prevailing prejudices. And nothing but nature and reason,[1] or, at least, what bears them a strong resemblance, can force its way through all obstacles, and unite the most rival nations into an esteem and admiration of it.

GREECE was a cluster of little principalities, which soon became republics; and being united both by their near neighbourhood, and by the ties of the same language and interest, they entered into the closest intercourse of commerce and learning. There concurred a happy climate, a soil not unfertile, and a most harmonious and comprehensive language; so that every circumstance among that people seemed to favour the rise of the arts and sciences. Each city produced its several artists and philosophers, who refused to yield the preference to those of the neighbouring republics: Their contention and debates sharpened the wits of men: A variety of objects was presented to the judgment, while each challenged the preference to the rest: and the sciences, not being dwarfed by the restraint of authority, were enabled to make such considerable shoots, as are, even at this time, the objects of our admiration. After the ROMAN *christian*, or *catholic* church had spread itself over the civilized world, and had engrossed all the learning of the times; being really one large state within itself, and united under one head; this variety of sects immediately disappeared, and the PERIPATETIC philosophy was alone admitted into all the

[1] [Or — resemblance: omitted in C and D.]

schools, to the utter depravation of every kind of learning But mankind, having at length thrown off this yoke, affairs are now returned nearly to the same situation as before, and EUROPE is at present a copy at large, of what GREECE was formerly a pattern in miniature. We have seen the advantage of this situation in several instances. What checked the progress of the CARTESIAN philosophy, to which the FRENCH nation shewed such a strong propensity towards the end of the last century, but the opposition made to it by the other nations of EUROPE, who soon discovered the weak sides of that philosophy? The severest scrutiny, which NEWTON'S theory has undergone, proceeded not from his own countrymen, but from foreigners; and if it can overcome the obstacles, which it meets with at present in all parts of EUROPE, it will probably go down triumphant to the latest posterity. The ENGLISH are become sensible of the scandalous licentiousness of their stage, from the example of the FRENCH decency and morals. The FRENCH are convinced, that their theatre has become somewhat effeminate, by too much love and gallantry; and begin to approve of the more masculine taste of some neighbouring nations.

In CHINA, there seems to be a pretty considerable stock of politeness and science, which, in the course of so many centuries, might naturally be expected to ripen into something more perfect and finished, than what has yet arisen from them. But CHINA is one vast empire, speaking one language, governed by one law, and sympathizing in the same manners. The authority of any teacher, such as CONFUCIUS, was propagated easily from one corner of the empire to the other. None had courage to resist the torrent of popular opinion. And posterity was not bold enough to dispute what had been universally received by their ancestors. This seems to be one natural reason, why the sciences have made so slow a progress in that mighty empire.[1]

[1] If it be asked how we can reconcile to the foregoing principles the happiness, riches, and good police of the CHINESE, who have always been governed by a sole monarch, and can scarce form an idea of a free government; I would answer, that tho' the CHINESE government be a pure monarchy, it is not, properly speaking, absolute. This proceeds from a peculiarity of the situation of that country: They have no neighbours, except the TARTARS, from whom they were, in some measure secured, at least seemed to be secured, by their famous wall, and by the great superiority of their numbers. By this means, military discipline has always been much neglected amongst them; and their standing forces are mere militia, of the worst kind; and unfit to suppress any general insurrection in countries so extremely populous.

If we consider the face of the globe, EUROPE, of all the four parts of the world, is the most broken by seas, rivers, and mountains; and GREECE of all countries of EUROPE. Hence these regions were naturally divided into several distinct governments. And hence the sciences arose in GREECE; and EUROPE has been hitherto the most constant habitation of them.

I have sometimes been inclined to think, that interruptions in the periods of learning, were they not attended with such a destruction of ancient books, and the records of history, would be rather favourable to the arts and sciences, by breaking the progress of authority, and dethroning the tyrannical usurpers over human reason. In this particular, they have the same influence, as interruptions in political governments and societies. Consider the blind submission of the ancient philosophers to the several masters in each school, and you will be convinced, that little good could be expected from a hundred centuries of such a servile philosophy. Even the ECLECTICS, who arose about the age of AUGUSTUS, notwithstanding their professing to chuse freely what pleased them from every different sect, were yet, in the main, as slavish and dependent as any of their brethren since they sought for truth not in nature, but in the several schools; where they supposed she must necessarily be found, though not united in a body, yet dispersed in parts. Upon the revival of learning, those sects of STOICS and EPICUREANS, PLATONISTS and PYTHAGORICIANS, could never regain any credit or authority; and, at the same time, by the example of their fall, kept men from submitting, with such blind deference, to those new sects, which have attempted to gain an ascendant over them.

The *third* observation, which I shall form on this head, of the rise and progress of the arts and sciences, is, *That though the only proper* Nursery *of these noble plants be a free state; yet may they be transplanted into any government; and that a*

The sword, therefore, may properly be said to be always in the hands of the people, which is a sufficient restraint upon the monarch, and obliges him to lay his *mandarins* or governors of provinces under the restraint of general laws, in order to prevent those rebellions, which we learn from history to have been so frequent and dangerous in that government. Perhaps, a pure monarchy of this kind, were it fitted for a defence against foreign enemies, would be the best of all governments, as having both the tranquillity attending kingly power, and the moderation and liberty of popular assemblies.

republic is most favourable to the growth of the sciences, a civilized monarchy to that of the polite arts.

To balance a large state or society, whether monarchical or republican, on general laws, is a work of so great difficulty, that no human genius, however comprehensive, is able, by the mere dint of reason and reflection, to effect it. The judgments of many must unite in this work: Experience must guide their labour: Time must bring it to perfection: And the feeling of inconveniencies must correct the mistakes, which they inevitably fall into, in their first trials and experiments. Hence appears the impossibility, that this undertaking should be begun and carried on in any monarchy; since such a form of government, ere civilized, knows no other secret or policy, than that of entrusting unlimited powers to every governor or magistrate, and subdividing the people into so many classes and orders of slavery. From such a situation, no improvement can ever be expected in the sciences, in the liberal arts, in laws, and scarcely in the manual arts and manufactures. The same barbarism and ignorance, with which the government commences, is propagated to all posterity, and can never come to a period by the efforts or ingenuity of such unhappy slaves.

But though law, the source of all security and happiness, arises late in any government, and is the slow product of order and of liberty, it is not preserved with the same difficulty, with which it is produced; but when it has once taken root, is a hardy plant, which will scarcely ever perish through the ill culture of men, or the rigour of the seasons. The arts of luxury, and much more the liberal arts, which depend on a refined taste or sentiment, are easily lost; because they are always relished by a few only, whose leisure, fortune, and genius fit them for such amusements. But what is profitable to every mortal, and in common life, when once discovered, can scarcely fall into oblivion, but by the total subversion of society, and by such furious inundations of barbarous invaders, as obliterate all memory of former arts and civility. Imitation also is apt to transport these coarser and more useful arts from one climate to another, and make them precede the refined arts in their progress; though perhaps they sprang after them in their first rise and propagation. From these causes proceed civilized monarchies; where the arts of government, first invented in free states, are preserved to the mutual advantage and security of sovereign and subject.

However perfect, therefore, the monarchical form may appear to some politicians, it owes all its perfection to the republican; nor is it possible, that a pure despotism, established among a barbarous people, can ever, by its native force and energy, refine and polish itself. It must borrow its laws, and methods, and institutions, and consequently its stability and order, from free governments. These advantages are the sole growth of republics. The extensive despotism of a barbarous monarchy, by entering into the detail of the government, as well as into the principal points of administration, for ever prevents all such improvement.

In a civilized monarchy, the prince alone is unrestrained in the exercise of his authority, and possesses alone a power, which is not bounded by any thing but custom, example, and the sense of his own interest. Every minister or magistrate, however eminent, must submit to the general laws, which govern the whole society, and must exert the authority delegated to him after the manner, which is prescribed. The people depend on none but their sovereign, for the security of their property. He is so far removed from them, and is so much exempt from private jealousies or interests, that this dependence is scarcely felt. And thus a species of government arises, to which, in a high political rant, we may give the name of *Tyranny*, but which, by a just and prudent administration, may afford tolerable security to the people, and may answer most of the ends of political society.

But though in a civilized monarchy, as well as in a republic, the people have security for the enjoyment of their property; yet in both these forms of government, those who possess the supreme authority have the disposal of many honours and advantages, which excite the ambition and avarice of mankind. The only difference is, that, in a republic, the candidates for office must look downwards, to gain the suffrages of the people; in a monarchy, they must turn their attention upwards, to court the good graces and favour of the great. To be successful in the former way, it is necessary for a man to make himself *useful*, by his industry, capacity, or knowledge: To be prosperous in the latter way, it is requisite for him to render himself *agreeable*, by his wit, complaisance, or civility. A strong genius succeeds best in republics: A refined taste in monarchies. And consequently the sciences are the more natural growth of the one, and the polite arts of the other.

Not to mention, that monarchies, receiving their chief stability from a superstitious reverence to priests and princes, have commonly abridged the liberty of reasoning, with regard to religion, and politics, and consequently metaphysics and morals. All these form the most considerable branches of science. Mathematics and natural philosophy, which only remain, are not half so valuable.[1]

Among the arts of conversation, no one pleases more than mutual deference or civility, which leads us to resign our own inclinations to those of our companion, and to curb and conceal that presumption and arrogance, so natural to the human mind. A good-natured man, who is well educated, practises this civility to every mortal, without premeditation or interest. But in order to render that valuable quality general among any people, it seems necessary to assist the natural disposition by some general motive. Where power rises upwards from the people to the great, as in all republics, such refinements of civility are apt to be little practised; since the whole state is, by that means, brought near to a level, and every member of it is rendered, in a great measure, independent of another. The people have the advantage, by the authority of their suffrages: The great, by the superiority of their station. But in a civilized monarchy, there is a long train of dependence from the prince to the peasant, which is not great enough to render property precarious, or depress the minds of the people; but is sufficient to beget in every one an inclination to please his superiors, and to form himself upon those models, which are most acceptable to people of condition and education. Politeness of manners, therefore, arises most naturally in monarchies and courts; and where that flourishes, none of the liberal arts will be altogether neglected or despised.

The republics in EUROPE are at present noted for want of politeness. *The good-manners of a* SWISS *civilized in* HOLLAND[2],

---

[1] [Editions C to P: There is a very great connection among all the arts, which contribute to pleasure; and the same delicacy of taste, which enables us to make improvements in one, will not allow the others to remain altogether rude and barbarous.]

[2] C'est la politesse d'un Suisse En HOLLANDE civilisé.
ROUSSEAU.

is an expression for rusticity among the FRENCH. The ENGLISH, in some degree, fall under the same censure, notwithstanding their learning and genius. And if the VENETIANS be an exception to the rule, they owe it, perhaps, to their communication with the other ITALIANS, most of whose governments beget a dependence more than sufficient for civilizing their manners.

It is difficult to pronounce any judgment concerning the refinements of the ancient republics in this particular: But I am apt to suspect, that the arts of conversation were not brought so near to perfection among them as the arts of writing and composition. The scurrility of the ancient orators, in many instances, is quite shocking, and exceeds all belief. Vanity too is often not a little offensive in authors of those ages [1]; as well as the common licentiousness and immodesty of their stile, *Quicunque impudicus, adulter, ganeo, manu, ventre, pene, bona patria laceraverat,* says SALLUST in one of the gravest and most moral passages of his history. *Nam fuit ante Helenam Cunnus teterrima belli Causa,* is an expression of HORACE, in tracing the origin of moral good and evil. OVID and LUCRETIUS [2] are almost as licentious in their stile as Lord ROCHESTER; though the former were fine gentlemen and delicate writers, and the latter [3], from the corruptions of that court, in which he lived, seems to have thrown off all regard to shame and decency. JUVENAL inculcates modesty with great zeal; but sets a very bad example of it, if we consider the impudence of his expressions.

I shall also be bold to affirm, that among the ancients, there was not much delicacy of breeding, or that polite deference and respect, which civility obliges us either to express or counterfeit towards the persons with whom we converse. CICERO was certainly one of the finest gentlemen of his age;

---

[1] It is needless to cite CICERO or PLINY on this head: They are too much noted: But one is a little surprised to find ARRIAN, a very grave, judicious writer, interrupt the thread of his narration all of a sudden, to tell his readers that he himself is as eminent among the GREEKS for eloquence as ALEXANDER was for arms. Lib. i. 12.

[2] This poet (See lib. iv. 1175.) recommends a very extraordinary cure for love, and what one expects not to meet with in so elegant and philosophical a poem. It seems to have been the original of some of Dr. SWIFT's [1] images. The elegant CATULLUS and PHÆDRUS fall under the same censure.

[3] [Editions C and D read: was an abandon'd and shameless Profligate.]

---

[1] [C to P insert: beautiful and cleanly.]

yet I must confess I have frequently been shocked with the poor figure under which he represents his friend ATTICUS, in those dialogues, where he himself is introduced as a speaker. That learned and virtuous ROMAN, whose dignity, though he was only a private gentleman, was inferior to that of no one in ROME, is there shewn in rather a more pitiful light than PHILALETHES'S friend in our modern dialogues. He is a humble admirer of the orator, pays him frequent compliments, and receives his instructions, with all the deference which a scholar owes to his master[1]. Even CATO is treated in somewhat of a cavalier manner in the dialogues *de finibus*.[2]

[3] One of the most particular details of a real dialogue, which we meet with in antiquity, is related by POLYBIUS[4]; when PHILIP, king of MACEDON, a prince of wit and parts, met with TITUS FLAMININUS, one of the politest of the ROMANS, as we learn from PLUTARCH[5], accompanied with ambassadors from almost all the GREEK cities. The ÆTOLIAN ambassador very abruptly tells the king, that he talked like a fool or a madman (ληρεῖν). *That's evident*, says his majesty, *even to a blind man*; which was a raillery on the blindness of his excellency. Yet all this did not pass the usual bounds: For the conference was not disturbed; and FLAMININUS was very well diverted with these strokes of humour. At the end, when PHILIP craved a little time to consult with his friends, of whom he had none present, the ROMAN general, being desirous also to shew his wit, as the historian says, tells him, *that perhaps the reason, why he had none of his friends with him, was because he had murdered them all*; which was actually the case. This unprovoked piece of rusticity is not condemned by the historian; caused no

---

[1] ATT. Non mihi videtur ad beate vivendum satis esse virtutem. MAR. At hercule BRUTO meo videtur; cujus ego judicium, pace tua dixerim, longe antepono tuo. Tusc. Quæst. lib. v. 5.

[2] [Editions C to P add the following: And 'tis remarkable, that CICERO, being a great sceptic in matters of religion, and unwilling to determine any thing on that head among the different sects of philosophy, introduces his friends disputing concerning the being and nature of the gods, while he is only a hearer; because, forsooth, it would have been an impropriety for so great a genius as himself, had he spoke, not to have said something decisive on the subject, and have carried every thing before him, as he always does on other occasions. There is also a spirit of dialogue observed in the eloquent books *de Oratore*, and a tolerable equality maintained among the speakers: But then these speakers are the great men of the age preceding the author, and he recounts the conference as only from hearsay.]

[3] [This paragraph is not found in Editions C and D.]

[4] Lib. xvii. 4.

[5] In vita FLAMIN., c. 2.

farther resentment in PHILIP, than to excite a SARDONIAN smile, or what we call a grin; and hindered him not from renewing the conference next day. PLUTARCH[1] too mentions this raillery amongst the witty and agreeable sayings of FLAMININUS.[2]

[1] PLUT. in vita FLAMIN. c. 17.

[2] [Editions C to P insert: 'Tis but an indifferent compliment, which HORACE pays to his friend GROSPHUS, in the ode addressed to him. *No one, says he, is happy in every respect. And I may perhaps enjoy some advantages, which you are deprived of. You possess great riches: Your bellowing herds cover the SICILIAN plains: Your chariot is drawn by the finest horses: And you are arrayed in the richest purple. But the indulgent fates, with a small inheritance, have given* ME *a fine genius, and have endowed me with a contempt for the malignant judgments of the vulgar.*[1] PHÆDRUS says to his patron, EUTYCHUS, *If you intend to read my works, I shall be pleased: If not, I shall, at least, have the advantage of pleasing posterity.*[2] I am apt to think that a modern poet would not have been guilty of such an impropriety as that which may be observed in VIRGIL's address to AUGUSTUS, when, after a great deal of extravagant flattery, and after having deified the emperor, according to the custom of those times, he, at last, places this god on the same level with himself. *By your gracious nod,* says he, *render my undertaking prosperous; and taking pity,* together with me, *of the Swains ignorant of husbandry, bestow your favourable influence on this work.*[3] Had men, in that age, been accustomed to observe such niceties, a writer so delicate as VIRGIL would certainly have given a different turn to this sentence. The court of AUGUSTUS, however polite, had not yet, it seems, worn off the manners of the republic.

[1] ——— Nihil est ab omni
    Parte beatum.
Abstulit clarum cita mors ACHILLEM,
Longa TITHONUM minuit senectûs,
Et mihi forsan, tibi quod negarit,
    Porriget hora.
Te greges centum, Siculæque circum
Mugiunt vaccæ: tibi tollit, hinni-
Tum apta quadrigis equa: te bis Afro
    Murice tinctæ
Vestiunt lanæ: mihi parva rura, &
Spiritum Graiæ tenuem Camœnæ
Parca non mendax dedit & malignum
    Spernere vulgus.
    Lib. 2. Ode 16.

[2] Quem si leges, lætabor; sin autem minus,
Habebunt certe quo se oblectent posteri.
    Lib. 3. Prol. 31.

[3] Ignarosque viæ *mecum* miseratus agrestes
Ingredere, & votis jam nunc assuesce vocari.
    Georg. Lib. 1. 41.

One would not say to a prince or great man, 'When you and I were in such a place, we saw such a thing happen.' But, 'When you were in such a place, I attended you: And such a thing happened.'

Here I cannot forbear mentioning a piece of delicacy observed in FRANCE, which seems to me excessive and ridiculous. You must not say, 'That is a very fine dog, Madam.' But, 'Madam, that is a very fine dog.' They think it indecent that those words, *dog* and *madam*, should be coupled together in the sentence; though they have no reference to each other in the sense.

After all, I acknowledge, that this reasoning from single passages of ancient authors may seem fallacious; and that the foregoing arguments cannot have great force, but with those who are well acquainted with these writers, and know the truth of the general position. For instance, what absurdity would it be to assert, that VIRGIL understood not the force of the terms he employs, and could not chuse his epithets with propriety? Because in the following lines, addressed also to AUGUSTUS, he has failed in that particular, and has ascribed to the INDIANS a quality, which seems, in a manner, to turn his hero into ridicule.

——— Et te, maxime CÆSAR,
Qui nunc extremis ASIÆ jam victor in oris
Imbellem avertis ROMANIS arcibus Indum.
    Georg. Lib. 2. 171.]

Cardinal WOLSEY apologized for his famous piece of insolence, in saying, EGO ET REX MEUS, *I and my king*, by observing, that this expression was conformable to the *Latin* idiom, and that a ROMAN always named himself before the person to whom, or of whom he spake. Yet this seems to have been an instance of want of civility among that people. The ancients made it a rule, that the person of the greatest dignity should be mentioned first in the discourse; insomuch, that we find the spring of a quarrel and jealousy between the ROMANS and ÆTOLIANS, to have been a poet's naming the ÆTOLIANS before the ROMANS, in celebrating a victory gained by their united arms over the MACEDONIANS.[1] [2] Thus LIVIA disgusted TIBERIUS by placing her own name before his in an inscription.[3]

No advantages in this world are pure and unmixed. In like manner, as modern politeness, which is naturally so ornamental, runs often into affectation and foppery, disguise and insincerity; so the ancient simplicity, which is naturally so amiable and affecting, often degenerates into rusticity and abuse, scurrility and obscenity.

If the superiority in politeness should be allowed to modern times, the modern notions of *gallantry*, the natural produce of courts and monarchies, will probably be assigned as the causes of this refinement. No one denies this invention to be modern[4]: But some of the more zealous partizans of the ancients, have asserted it to be foppish and ridiculous, and a reproach, rather than a credit, to the present age.[5] It may here be proper to examine this question.

Nature has implanted in all living creatures an affection between the sexes, which, even in the fiercest and most rapacious animals, is not merely confined to the satisfaction of the bodily appetite, but begets a friendship and mutual sympathy, which runs through the whole tenor of their lives. Nay, even in those species, where nature limits the indulgence of this appetite to one season and to one object, and forms a kind of marriage or association between a single male and female, there is yet a visible complacency and benevolence,

---

[1] PLUT. in vita FLAMIN. c. 9.
[2] [This sentence and the paragraph next following were added in Edition K.]
[3] TACIT. Ann. lib. iii. cap. 64.
[4] In the *Self-Tormentor* of TERENCE, CLINIAS, whenever he comes to town, instead of waiting on his mistress, sends for her to come to him.
[5] Lord SHAFTESBURY, see his *Moralists*.

which extends farther, and mutually softens the affections of the sexes towards each other.[1] How much more must this have place in man, where the confinement of the appetite is not natural; but either is derived accidentally from some strong charm of love, or arises from reflections on duty and convenience? Nothing, therefore, can proceed less from affectation than the passion of gallantry. It is *natural* in the highest degree. Art and education, in the most elegant courts, make no more alteration on it, than on all the other laudable passions. They only turn the mind more towards it; they refine it; they polish it; and give it a proper grace and expression.

But gallantry is as *generous* as it is *natural*. To correct such gross vices, as lead us to commit real injury on others, is the part of morals, and the object of the most ordinary education. Where *that* is not attended to, in some degree, no human society can subsist. But in order to render conversation, and the intercourse of minds more easy and agreeable, good-manners have been invented, and have carried the matter somewhat farther. Wherever nature has given the mind a propensity to any vice, or to any passion disagreeable to others, refined breeding has taught men to throw the biass on the opposite side, and to preserve, in all their behaviour, the appearance of sentiments different from those to which they naturally incline. Thus, as we are commonly proud and selfish, and apt to assume the preference above others, a polite man learns to behave with deference towards his companions, and to yield the superiority to them in all the common incidents of society. In like manner, wherever a person's situation may naturally beget any disagreeable suspicion in him, it is the part of good-manners to prevent it, by a studied display of sentiments, directly contrary to those of which he is apt to be jealous. Thus, old men know their infirmities, and naturally dread contempt from the youth: Hence, well-educated youth redouble the instances of respect and deference to their elders. Strangers and foreigners are without protection: Hence, in all polite countries, they receive the

---

[1] [Editions C to P add the following quotation.

Tutti gli altri ánimai che sono in terra,
  O che vivon quieti & stanno in pace;
O se vengon a rissa, & si fan guerra,
  A la femina il maschio non la face.
L'orsa con l'orso al bosco sicura erra,
  La Leonessa appresso il Leon giace,
Con Lupo vive il Lupa sicura,
  Nè la Giuvenca ha del Torel paura.
      ARIOSTO, Canto 5.

highest civilities, and are entitled to the first place in every company. A man is lord in his own family, and his guests are, in a manner, subject to his authority: Hence, he is always the lowest person in the company; attentive to the wants of every one; and giving himself all the trouble, in order to please, which may not betray too visible an affectation, or impose too much constraint on his guests.[1] Gallantry is nothing but an instance of the same generous attention. As nature has given *man* the superiority above *woman*, by endowing him with greater strength both of mind and body; it is his part to alleviate that superiority, as much as possible, by the generosity of his behaviour, and by a studied deference and complaisance for all her inclinations and opinions. Barbarous nations display this superiority, by reducing their females to the most abject slavery; by confining them, by beating them, by selling them, by killing them. But the male sex, among a polite people, discover their authority in a more generous, though not a less evident manner; by civility, by respect, by complaisance, and, in a word, by gallantry. In good company, you need not ask, Who is the master of the feast? The man, who sits in the lowest place, and who is always industrious in helping every one, is certainly the person. We must either condemn all such instances of generosity, as foppish and affected, or admit of gallantry among the rest. The ancient MUSCOVITES wedded their wives with a whip, instead of a ring. The same people, in their own houses, took always the precedency above foreigners, even[2] foreign ambassadors. These two instances of their generosity and politeness are much of a piece.

Gallantry is not less compatible with *wisdom* and *prudence*, than with *nature* and *generosity*; and when under proper regulations, contributes more than any other invention, to the *entertainment* and *improvement* of the youth of both sexes.[3] Among every species of animals, nature has founded on the

---

[1] The frequent mention in ancient authors of that ill-bred custom of the master of the family's eating better bread or drinking better wine at table, than he afforded his guests, is but an indifferent mark of the civility of those ages. See JUVENAL, sat. 5. PLINII lib. xiv. cap. 13. Also PLINII *Epist. Lucian de mercede conductis, Saturnalia, &c.* There is scarcely any part of EUROPE at present so uncivilized as to admit of such a custom.

[2] See *Relation of three Embassies*, by the Earl of CARLISLE.

[3] [Editions C to P read: In all vegetables, 'tis observable, that the flower and the seed are always connected together; and in like manner, among every species, &c.]

love between the sexes their sweetest and best enjoyment. But the satisfaction of the bodily appetite is not alone sufficient to gratify the mind; and even among brute-creatures, we find, that their play and dalliance, and other expressions of fondness, form the greatest part of the entertainment. In rational beings, we must certainly admit the mind for a considerable share. Were we to rob the feast of all its garniture of reason, discourse, sympathy, friendship, and gaiety, what remains would scarcely be worth acceptance, in the judgment of the truly elegant and luxurious.

What better school for manners, than the company of virtuous women; where the mutual endeavour to please must insensibly polish the mind, where the example of the female softness and modesty must communicate itself to their admirers, and where the delicacy of that sex puts every one on his guard, lest he give offence by any breach of decency[1].

Among the ancients, the character of the fair-sex was considered as altogether domestic; nor were they regarded as part of the polite world or of good company. This, perhaps, is the true reason why the ancients have not left us one piece of pleasantry that is excellent, (unless one may except the Banquet of XENOPHON, and the Dialogues of LUCIAN) though many of their serious compositions are altogether inimitable. HORACE condemns the coarse railleries and cold jests of PLAUTUS: But, though the most easy, agreeable, and judicious writer in the world, is his own talent for ridicule very striking or refined? This, therefore, is one considerable improvement, which the polite arts have received from gallantry, and from courts, where it first arose.[2]

---

[1] [C to O add: I must confess, That my own particular choice rather leads me to prefer the company of a few select companions, with whom I can, calmly and peaceably, enjoy the feast of reason, and try the justness of every reflection, whether gay or serious, that may occur to me. But as such a delightful society is not every day to be met with, I must think, that mixt companies, without the fair-sex, are the most insipid entertainment in the world, and destitute of gaiety and politeness, as much as of sense and reason. Nothing can keep them from excessive dulness but hard drinking; a remedy worse than the disease.]

[2] [Editions C to P insert the following: The point of *honour*, or duelling, is a modern invention, as well as *gallantry*; and by some esteemed equally useful for the refining of manners: But how it has contributed to that effect, I am at a loss to determine. Conversation, among the greatest rustics, is not commonly invested with such rudeness as can give occasion to duels. even according to the most refined laws of this fantastic honour; and as to the other small indecencies, which are the most offensive, because the most frequent, they can never be cured by the practice of duelling. But these notions are not only *useless*: They are also *pernicious*. By separating the man of honour from the

But, to return from this digression, I shall advance it as a *fourth* observation on this subject, of the rise and progress of the arts and sciences, *That when the arts and sciences come to perfection in any state, from that moment they naturally, or rather necessarily decline, and seldom or never revive in that nation, where they formerly flourished.*

It must be confessed, that this maxim, though conformable to experience, may, at first sight, be esteemed contrary to reason. If the natural genius of mankind be the same in all ages, and in almost all countries, (as seems to be the truth) it must very much forward and cultivate this genius, to be possessed of patterns in every art, which may regulate the taste, and fix the objects of imitation. The models left us by the ancients gave birth to all the arts about 200 years ago, and have mightily advanced their progress in every country of EUROPE: Why had they not a like effect during the reign of TRAJAN and his successors; when they were much more entire, and were still admired and studied by the whole world? So late as the emperor JUSTINIAN, the POET, by way of distinction, was understood, among the GREEKS, to be HOMER; among the ROMANS, VIRGIL. Such admiration still remained for these divine geniuses; though no poet had appeared for many centuries, who could justly pretend to have imitated them.

A man's genius is always, in the beginning of life, as much unknown to himself as to others; and it is only after frequent trials, attended with success, that he dares think himself equal to those undertakings, in which those, who have succeeded, have fixed the admiration of mankind. If his own nation be already possessed of many models of eloquence, he

man of virtue, the greatest profligates have got something to value themselves upon, and have been able to keep themselves in countenance, tho' guilty of the most shameful and most dangerous vices. They are debauchees, spendthrifts, and never pay a farthing they owe: But they are men of honour; and therefore are to be received as gentlemen in all companies.

There are some of the parts of modern honour, which are the most essential parts of morality; such as fidelity, the observing promises, and telling truth. These points of honour Mr. ADDISON had in his eye when he made JUBA say,

Honour's a sacred tye, the law of kings,
The noble mind's distinguishing perfection,
That aids and strengthens virtue when it meets her,
And imitates her actions where she is not:
It ought not to be sported with.

These lines are very beautiful: But I am afraid, that Mr. ADDISON has here been guilty of that impropriety of sentiment, with which, on other occasions, he has so justly reproached our poets. The ancients certainly never had any notion of *honour* as distinct from *virtue*.]

naturally compares his own juvenile exercises with these; and being sensible of the great disproportion, is discouraged from any farther attempts, and never aims at a rivalship with those authors, whom he so much admires. A noble emulation is the source of every excellence. Admiration and modesty naturally extinguish this emulation. And no one is so liable to an excess of admiration and modesty, as a truly great genius.

Next to emulation, the greatest encourager of the noble arts is praise and glory. A writer is animated with new force, when he hears the applauses of the world for his former productions; and, being roused by such a motive, he often reaches a pitch of perfection, which is equally surprizing to himself and to his readers. But when the posts of honour are all occupied, his first attempts are but coldly received by the public; being compared to productions, which are both in themselves more excellent, and have already the advantage of an established reputation. Were MOLIERE and CORNEILLE to bring upon the stage at present their early productions, which were formerly so well received, it would discourage the young poets, to see the indifference and disdain of the public. The ignorance of the age alone could have given admission to the *Prince of* TYRE; but it is to that we owe *the Moor*: Had *Every man in his humour* been rejected, we had never seen VOLPONE.

Perhaps, it may not be for the advantage of any nation to have the arts imported from their neighbours in too great perfection. This extinguishes emulation, and sinks the ardour of the generous youth. So many models of ITALIAN painting brought into ENGLAND, instead of exciting our artists, is the cause of their small progress in that noble art. The same, perhaps, was the case of ROME, when it received the arts from GREECE. That multitude of polite productions in the FRENCH language, dispersed all over GERMANY and the NORTH, hinder these nations from cultivating their own language, and keep them still dependent on their neighbours for those elegant entertainments.

It is true, the ancients had left us models in every kind of writing, which are highly worthy of admiration. But besides that they were written in languages, known only to the learned; besides this, I say, the comparison is not so perfect or entire between modern wits, and those who lived in so remote an age. Had WALLER been born in ROME, during the reign of TIBERIUS, his first productions had been despised, when compared to the finished odes of HORACE. But in this island the superiority of the ROMAN poet diminished nothing from the fame of the ENGLISH. We esteemed ourselves sufficiently happy, that our climate and language could produce but a faint copy of so excellent an original.

In short, the arts and sciences, like some plants, require a fresh soil; and however rich the land may be, and however you may recruit it by art or care, it will never, when once exhausted, produce any thing that is perfect or finished in the kind.

ESSAY XV.—*The Epicurean*.[1]

IT is a great mortification to the vanity of man, that his utmost art and industry can never equal the meanest of nature's productions, either for beauty or value. Art is only the under-workman, and is employed to give a few strokes of embellishment to those pieces, which come from the hand of the master. Some of the drapery may be of his drawing; but he is not allowed to touch the principal figure. Art may make a suit of clothes: But nature must produce a man.

Even in those productions, commonly denominated works of art, we find that the noblest of the kind are beholden for their chief beauty to the force and happy influence of nature. To the[2] native enthusiasm of the poets, we owe whatever is admirable in their productions. The greatest genius, where nature at any time fails him, (for she is not equal) throws aside the lyre, and hopes not, from the rules of art, to reach that divine harmony, which must proceed from her inspiration alone. How poor are those songs, where a happy flow of fancy has not furnished materials for art to embellish and refine!

But of all the fruitless attempts of art, no one is so ridiculous, as that which the severe philosophers have undertaken,

[1] OR, *The man of elegance and pleasure*. The intention of this and the three following essays is not so much to explain accurately the sentiments of the ancient sects of philosophy, as to deliver the sentiments of sects. that naturally form themselves in the world, and entertain different ideas of human life and of happiness. I have given each of them the name of the philosophical sect, to which it bears the greatest affinity.

[2] [Editions C to D: To the *Oestrum* or *Verve*. K to P: To the *Oestrum* or native enthusiasm.]

the producing of an *artificial happiness*, and making us be pleased by rules of reason, and by reflection. Why did none of them claim the reward, which XERXES promised to him, who should invent a new pleasure? Unless, perhaps, they invented so many pleasures for their own use, that they despised riches, and stood in no need of any enjoyments, which the rewards of that monarch could procure them. I am apt, indeed, to think, that they were not willing to furnish the PERSIAN court with a new pleasure, by presenting it with so new and unusual an object of ridicule. Their speculations, when confined to theory, and gravely delivered in the schools of GREECE, might excite admiration in their ignorant pupils: But the attempting to reduce such principles to practice would soon have betrayed their absurdity.

You pretend to make me happy by reason, and by rules of art. You must, then, create me anew by rules of art. For on my original frame and structure does my happiness depend. But you want power to effect this; and skill too, I am afraid: Nor can I entertain a less opinion of nature's wisdom than of yours. And let her conduct the machine, which she has so wisely framed. I find, that I should only spoil it by my tampering.

To what purpose should I pretend to regulate, refine, or invigorate any of those springs or principles, which nature has implanted in me? Is this the road by which I must reach happiness? But happiness implies ease, contentment, repose, and pleasure; not watchfulness, care, and fatigue. The health of my body consists in the facility, with which all its operations are performed. The stomach digests the aliments: The heart circulates the blood: The brain separates and refines the spirits: And all this without my concerning myself in the matter. When by my will alone I can stop the blood, as it runs with impetuosity along its canals, then may I hope to change the course of my sentiments and passions. In vain should I strain my faculties, and endeavour to receive pleasure from an object, which is not fitted by nature to affect my organs with delight. I may give myself pain by my fruitless endeavours; but shall never reach any pleasure.

Away then with all those vain pretences of making ourselves happy within ourselves, of feasting on our own thoughts, of being satisfied with the consciousness of well-doing, and of despising all assistance and all supplies from external objects. This is the voice of PRIDE, not of NATURE. And it were well, if even this pride could support itself, and communicate a real *inward* pleasure, however melancholy or severe. But this impotent pride can do no more than regulate the *outside*; and with infinite pains and attention compose the language and countenance to a philosophical dignity, in order to deceive the ignorant vulgar. The heart, mean while, is empty of all enjoyment: And the mind, unsupported by its proper objects, sinks into the deepest sorrow and dejection. Miserable, but vain mortal! Thy mind be happy within itself! With what resources is it endowed to fill so immense a void, and supply the place of all thy bodily senses and faculties? Can thy head subsist without thy other members? In such a situation,

What foolish figure must it make!
Do nothing else but sleep *and* ake.

Into such a lethargy, or such a melancholy, must thy mind be plunged, when deprived of foreign occupations and enjoyments.

Keep me, therefore, no longer in this violent constraint. Confine me not within myself; but point out to me those objects and pleasures, which afford the chief enjoyment. But why do I apply to you, proud and ignorant sages, to shew me the road to happiness? Let me consult my own passions and inclinations. In them must I read the dictates of nature; not in your frivolous discourses.

But see, propitious to my wishes, the divine, the amiable PLEASURE,[1] the supreme love of GODS and men, advances towards me. At her approach, my heart beats with genial heat, and every sense and every faculty is dissolved in joy; while she pours around me all the embellishments of the spring, and all the treasures of the autumn. The melody of her voice charms my ears with the softest music, as she invites me to partake of those delicious fruits, which, with a smile that diffuses a glory on the heavens and the earth, she presents to me. The sportive CUPIDS, who attend her, or fan me with their odoriferous wings, or pour on my head the most fragrant oils, or offer me their sparkling nectar in

[1] *Dia Voluptas.* LUCRET.

golden goblets. O! for ever let me spread my limbs on this bed of roses, and thus, thus feel the delicious moments with soft and downy steps, glide along. But cruel chance! Whither do you fly so fast? Why do my ardent wishes, and that load of pleasures, under which you labour, rather hasten than retard your unrelenting pace? Suffer me to enjoy this soft repose, after all my fatigues in search of happiness. Suffer me to satiate myself with these delicacies, after the pains of so long and so foolish an abstinence.

But it will not do. The roses have lost their hue: The fruit its flavour: And that delicious wine, whose fumes, so late, intoxicated all my senses with such delight, now solicits in vain the sated palate. *Pleasure* smiles at my languor. She beckons her sister, *Virtue*, to come to her assistance. The gay, the frolic *Virtue* observes the call, and brings along the whole troop of my jovial friends. Welcome, thrice welcome, my ever dear companions, to these shady bowers, and to this luxurious repast. Your presence has restored to the rose its hue, and to the fruit its flavour. The vapours of this sprightly nectar now again play around my heart; while you partake of my delights, and discover in your cheerful looks, the pleasure which you receive from my happiness and satisfaction. The like do I receive from yours; and encouraged by your joyous presence, shall again renew the feast, with which, from too much enjoyment, my senses were well nigh sated; while the mind kept not pace with the body, nor afforded relief to her o'er-burthened partner.

In our cheerful discourses, better than in the formal reasonings of the schools, is true wisdom to be found. In our friendly endearments, better than in the hollow debates of statesmen and pretended patriots, does true virtue display itself. Forgetful of the past, secure of the future, let us here enjoy the present; and while we yet possess a being, let us fix some good, beyond the power of fate or fortune. To-morrow will bring its own pleasures along with it: Or should it disappoint our fond wishes, we shall at least enjoy the pleasure of reflecting on the pleasures of to-day.

Fear not, my friends, that the barbarous dissonance of BACCHUS, and of his revellers, should break in upon this entertainment, and confound us with their turbulent and clamorous pleasures. The sprightly muses wait around;

and with their charming symphony, sufficient to soften the wolves and tygers of the savage desert, inspire a soft joy into every bosom. Peace, harmony and concord reign in this retreat; nor is the silence ever broken but by the music of our songs, or the cheerful accents of our friendly voices.

But hark! the favourite of the muses, the gentle DAMON, strikes the lyre; and while he accompanies its harmonious notes with his more harmonious song, he inspires us with the same happy debauch of fancy, by which he is himself transported. 'Ye happy youth,' he sings, 'Ye favoured of heaven,[1] while the wanton spring pours upon you all her blooming honours, let not *glory* seduce you, with her delusive blaze, to pass in perils and dangers this delicious season, this prime of life. Wisdom points out to you the road to pleasure: Nature too beckons you to follow her in that smooth and flowery path. Will you shut your ears to their commanding voice? Will you harden your heart to their soft allurements? Oh, deluded mortals, thus to lose your youth, thus to throw away so invaluable a present, to trifle with so perishing a blessing. Contemplate well your recompence. Consider that glory, which so allures your proud hearts, and seduces you with your own praises. It is an echo, a dream, nay the shadow of a dream, dissipated by every wind, and lost by every contrary breath of the ignorant and ill-judging multitude. You fear not that even death itself shall ravish it from you. But behold! while you are yet alive, calumny bereaves you of it; ignorance neglects it; nature enjoys it not; fancy alone, renouncing every pleasure, receives this airy recompence, empty and unstable as herself.'

Thus the hours passed unperceived along, and lead in their wanton train all the pleasures of sense, and all the joys of harmony and friendship. Smiling *innocence* closes the procession; and while she presents herself to our ravished eyes, she embellishes the whole scene, and renders the view of these pleasures as transporting, after they have past us, as when, with laughing countenances, they were yet advancing toward us.

---

[1] An imitation of the SYREN's song in TASSO.
'O Giovinetti, mentre APRILE & MAGGIO V' ammantan di fiorité & verde spoglie,' &c.
Giuresalemme liberata, *Canto* 14.

But the sun has sunk below the horizon; and darkness, stealing silently upon us, has now buried all nature in an universal shade. 'Rejoice, my friends, continue your repast, or change it for soft repose. Though absent, your joy or your tranquillity shall still be mine.' *But whither do you go? Or what new pleasures call you from our society? Is there aught agreeable without your friends? And can aught please, in which we partake not?* 'Yes, my friends; the joy which I now seek, admits not of your participation. Here alone I wish your absence: And here alone can I find a sufficient compensation for the loss of your society.'

But I have not advanced far through the shades of the thick wood, which spreads a double night around me, ere, methinks, I perceive through the gloom, the charming CÆLIA, the mistress of my wishes, who wanders impatient through the grove, and preventing the appointed hour, silently chides my tardy steps. But the joy, which she receives from my presence, best pleads my excuse; and dissipating every anxious and every angry thought, leaves room for nought but mutual joy and rapture. With what words, my fair one, shall I express my tenderness or describe the emotions which now warm my transported bosom! Words are too faint to describe my love; and if, alas! you feel not the same flame within you, in vain shall I endeavour to convey to you a just conception of it. But your every word and every motion suffice to remove this doubt; and while they express your passion, serve also to enflame mine. How amiable this solitude, this silence, this darkness! No objects now importune the ravished soul. The thought, the sense, all full of nothing but our mutual happiness, wholly possess the mind, and convey a pleasure, which deluded mortals vainly seek for in every other enjoyment———

But why[1] does your bosom heave with these sighs, while tears bathe your glowing cheeks? Why distract your heart with such vain anxieties? Why so often ask me, *How long my love shall yet endure?* Alas, my CÆLIA! can I resolve this question? *Do I know how long my life shall yet endure?* But does this also disturb your tender breast? And is the image of our frail mortality for ever present with you, to throw a damp on your gayest hours, and poison even those joys which love inspires! Consider rather, that if life be

---

[1] [Edition C: after our tumultuous joys.]

frail, if youth be transitory, we should well employ the present moment, and lose no part of so perishable an existence. Yet a little moment and *these* shall be no more. We shall be, as if we had never been. Not a memory of us be left upon earth; and even the fabulous shades below will not afford us a habitation. Our fruitless anxieties, our vain projects, our uncertain speculations shall all be swallowed up and lost. Our present doubts, concerning the original cause of all things, must never, alas! be resolved. This alone we may be certain of, that, if any governing mind preside, he must be pleased to see us fulfil the ends of our being, and enjoy that pleasure, for which alone we were created. Let this reflection give ease to your anxious thoughts; but render not your joys too serious, by dwelling for ever upon it. It is sufficient, once, to be acquainted with this philosophy, in order to give an unbounded loose to love and jollity, and remove all the scruples of a vain superstition: But while youth and passion, my fair one, prompt our eager desires, we must find gayer subjects of discourse, to intermix with these amorous caresses.

Essay XVI.—*The Stoic.*[1]

THERE is this obvious and material difference in the conduct of nature, with regard to man and other animals, that, having endowed the former with a sublime celestial spirit, and having given him an affinity with superior beings, she allows not such noble faculties to lie lethargic or idle; but urges him, by necessity, to employ, on every emergence, his utmost *art* and *industry*. Brute-creatures have many of their necessities supplied by nature, being cloathed and armed by this beneficent parent of all things: And where their own *industry* is requisite on any occasion, nature, by implanting instincts, still supplies them with the *art*, and guides them to their good by her unerring precepts. But man, exposed naked and indigent to the rude elements, rises slowly from that helpless state, by the care and vigilance of his parents; and having attained his utmost growth and perfection, reaches only a capacity of subsisting, by his own care and vigilance. Every thing is sold to skill and labour; and where

---

[1] Or the man of action and virtue.

nature furnishes the materials, they are still rude and unfinished, till industry, ever active and intelligent, refines them from their brute state, and fits them for human use and convenience.

Acknowledge, therefore, O man, the beneficence of nature; for she has given thee that intelligence which supplies all thy necessities. But let not indolence, under the false appearance of gratitude, persuade thee to rest contented with her presents. Wouldest thou return to the raw herbage for thy food, to the open sky for thy covering, and to stones and clubs for thy defence against the ravenous animals of the desert? Then return also to thy savage manners, to thy timorous superstition, to thy brutal ignorance; and sink thyself below those animals, whose condition thou admirest, and wouldest so fondly imitate.

Thy kind parent, nature, having given thee art and intelligence, has filled the whole globe with materials to employ these talents: Hearken to her voice, which so plainly tells thee, that thou, thyself shouldest also be the object of thy industry, and that by art and attention alone thou canst acquire that ability, which will raise thee to thy proper station in the universe. Behold this artizan, who converts a rude and shapeless stone into a noble metal; and moulding that metal by his cunning hands, creates, as it were by magic, every weapon for his defence, and every utensil for his convenience. He has not this skill from nature: Use and practice have taught it him: And if thou wouldest emulate his success, thou must follow his laborious footsteps.

But while thou *ambitiously* aspirest to perfecting thy bodily powers and faculties, wouldest thou *meanly* neglect thy mind, and from a preposterous sloth, leave it still rude and uncultivated, as it came from the hands of nature? Far be such folly and negligence from every rational being. If nature has been frugal in her gifts and endowments, there is the more need of art to supply her defects. If she has been generous and liberal, know that she still expects industry and application on our part, and revenges herself in proportion to our negligent ingratitude. The richest genius, like the most fertile soil, when uncultivated, shoots up into the rankest weeds; and instead of vines and olives for the pleasure and use of man, produces, to its slothful owner, the most abundant crop of poisons.

The great end of all human industry, is the attainment of happiness. For this were arts invented, sciences cultivated, laws ordained, and societies modelled, by the most profound wisdom of patriots and legislators. Even the lonely savage, who lies exposed to the inclemency of the elements, and the fury of wild beasts, forgets not, for a moment, this grand object of his being. Ignorant as he is of every art of life, he still keeps in view the end of all those arts, and eagerly seeks for felicity amidst that darkness with which he is environed. But as much as the wildest savage is inferior to the polished citizen, who, under the protection of laws, enjoys every convenience which industry has invented; so much is this citizen himself inferior to the man of virtue, and the true philosopher, who governs his appetites, subdues his passions, and has learned, from reason, to set a just value on every pursuit and enjoyment. For is there an art and an apprenticeship necessary for every other attainment? And is there no art of life, no rule, no precepts to direct us in this principal concern? Can no particular pleasure be attained without skill; and can the whole be regulated without reflection or intelligence, by the blind guidance of appetite and instinct? Surely then no mistakes are ever committed in this affair; but every man, however dissolute and negligent, proceeds in the pursuit of happiness, with as unerring a motion, as that which the celestial bodies observe, when, conducted by the hand of the Almighty, they roll along the ethereal plains. But if mistakes be often, be inevitably committed, let us register these mistakes; let us consider their causes; let us weigh their importance; let us enquire for their remedies. When from this we have fixed all their rules of conduct, we are *philosophers:* When we have reduced these rules to practice, we are *sages.*

Like many subordinate artists, employed to form the several wheels and springs of a machine: Such are those who excel in all the particular arts of life. *He* is the master workman who puts those several parts together; moves them according to just harmony and proportion: and produces true felicity as the result of their conspiring order.

While thou hast such an alluring object in view, shall that

labour and attention, requisite to the attainment of thy end, ever seem burdensome and intolerable? Know, that this labour itself is the chief ingredient of the felicity to which thou aspirest, and that every enjoyment soon becomes insipid and distasteful, when not acquired by fatigue and industry. See the hardy hunters rise from their downy couches, shake off the slumbers which still weigh down their heavy eye-lids, and, ere *Aurora* has yet covered the heavens with her flaming mantle, hasten to the forest. They leave behind, in their own houses, and in the neighbouring plains, animals of every kind, whose flesh furnishes the most delicious fare, and which offer themselves to the fatal stroke. Laborious man disdains so easy a purchase. He seeks for a prey, which hides itself from his search, or flies from his pursuit, or defends itself from his violence. Having exerted in the chace every passion of the mind, and every member of the body, he then finds the charms of repose, and with joy compares its pleasures to those of his engaging labours.

And can vigorous industry give pleasure to the pursuit even of the most worthless prey, which frequently escapes our toils? And cannot the same industry render the cultivating of our mind, the moderating of our passions, the enlightening of our reason, an agreeable occupation; while we are every day sensible of our progress, and behold our inward features and countenance brightening incessantly with new charms? Begin by curing yourself of this lethargic indolence; the task is not difficult: You need but taste the sweets of honest labour. Proceed to learn the just value of every pursuit; long study is not requisite: Compare, though but for once, the mind to the body, virtue to fortune, and glory to pleasure. You will then perceive the advantages of industry: You will then be sensible what are the proper objects of your industry.

In vain do you seek repose from beds of roses: In vain do you hope for enjoyment from the most delicious wines and fruits. Your indolence itself becomes a fatigue: Your pleasure itself creates disgust. The mind, unexercised, finds every delight insipid and loathsome; and ere yet the body, full of noxious humours, feels the torment of its multiplied diseases, your nobler part is sensible of the invading poison, and seeks in vain to relieve its anxiety by new pleasures, which still augment the fatal malady.

I need not tell you, that, by this eager pursuit of pleasure, you more and more expose yourself to fortune and accidents, and rivet your affections on external objects, which chance may, in a moment, ravish from you. I shall suppose, that your indulgent stars favour you still with the enjoyment of your riches and possessions. I prove to you, that even in the midst of your luxurious pleasures, you are unhappy; and that by too much indulgence, you are incapable of enjoying what prosperous fortune still allows you to possess.

But surely the instability of fortune is a consideration not to be overlooked or neglected. Happiness cannot possibly exist, where there is no security; and security can have no place, where fortune has any dominion. Though that unstable deity should not exert her rage against you, the dread of it would still torment you; would disturb your slumbers, haunt your dreams, and throw a damp on the jollity of your most delicious banquets.

The temple of wisdom is seated on a rock, above the rage of the fighting elements, and inaccessible to all the malice of man. The rolling thunder breaks below; and those more terrible instruments of human fury reach not to so sublime a height. The sage, while he breathes that serene air, looks down with pleasure, mixed with compassion, on the errors of mistaken mortals, who blindly seek for the true path of life, and pursue riches, nobility, honour, or power, for genuine felicity. The greater part he beholds disappointed of their fond wishes: Some lament, that having once possessed the object of their desires, it is ravished from them by envious fortune: And all complain, that even their own vows, though granted, cannot give them happiness, or relieve the anxiety of their distracted minds.

But does the sage always preserve himself in this philosophical indifference, and rest contented with lamenting the miseries of mankind, without ever employing himself for their relief? Does he constantly indulge this severe wisdom, which, by pretending to elevate him above human accidents, does in reality harden his heart, and render him careless of the interests of mankind, and of society? No; he knows that in this sullen *Apathy*, neither true wisdom nor true happiness can be found. He feels too strongly the charm of the social affections ever to counteract so sweet, so natural, so virtuous a propensity. Even when, bathed in tears, he laments the miseries of human race, of his country, of his friends, and unable to give succour, can only relieve them by compassion; he yet rejoices in the generous disposition, and feels a satisfaction superior to that of the most indulged sense. So engaging are the sentiments of humanity, that they brighten up the very face of sorrow, and operate like the sun, which, shining on a dusky cloud or falling rain, paints on them the most glorious colours which are to be found in the whole circle of nature.

But it is not here alone, that the social virtues display their energy. With whatever ingredient you mix them, they are still predominant. As sorrow cannot overcome them, so neither can sensual pleasure obscure them. The joys of love, however tumultuous, banish not the tender sentiments of sympathy and affection. They even derive their chief influence from that generous passion; and when presented alone, afford nothing to the unhappy mind but lassitude and disgust. Behold this sprightly debauchee, who professes a contempt of all other pleasures but those of wine and jollity: Separate him from his companions, like a spark from a fire, where before it contributed to the general blaze: His alacrity suddenly extinguishes; and though surrounded with every other means of delight, he lothes the sumptuous banquet, and prefers even the most abstracted study and speculation, as more agreeable and entertaining.

But the social passions never afford such transporting pleasures, or make so glorious an appearance in the eyes both of GOD and man, as when, shaking off every earthly mixture, they associate themselves with the sentiments of virtue, and prompt us to laudable and worthy actions. As harmonious colours mutually give and receive a lustre by their friendly union; so do these ennobling sentiments of the human mind. See the triumph of nature in parental affection! What selfish passion; what sensual delight is a match for it! Whether a man exults in the prosperity and virtue of his offspring, or flies to their succour, through the most threatening and tremendous dangers?

Proceed still in purifying the generous passion, you will still the more admire its shining glories. What charms are there in the harmony of minds, and in a friendship founded on mutual esteem and gratitude! What satisfaction in relieving the distressed, in comforting the afflicted, in raising the fallen, and in stopping the career of cruel fortune, or of more cruel man, in their insults over the good and virtuous! But what supreme joy in the victories over vice as well as misery, when, by virtuous example or wise exhortation, our fellow-creatures are taught to govern their passions, reform their vices, and subdue their worst enemies, which inhabit within their own bosoms?

But these objects are still too limited for the human mind, which, being of celestial origin, swells with the divinest and most enlarged affections, and carrying its attention beyond kindred and acquaintance, extends its benevolent wishes to the most distant posterity. It views liberty and laws as the source of human happiness, and devotes itself, with the utmost alacrity, to their guardianship and protection. Toils, dangers, death itself carry their charms, when we brave them for the public good, and ennoble that being, which we generously sacrifice for the interests of our country. Happy the man, whom indulgent fortune allows to pay to virtue what he owes to nature, and to make a generous gift of what must otherwise be ravished from him by cruel necessity!

In the true sage and patriot are united whatever can distinguish human nature, or elevate mortal man to a resemblance with the divinity. The softest benevolence, the most undaunted resolution, the tenderest sentiments, the most sublime love of virtue, all these animate successively his transported bosom. What satisfaction, when he looks within, to find the most turbulent passions turned to just harmony and concord, and every jarring sound banished from this enchanting music! If the contemplation, even of inanimate beauty, is so delightful; if it ravishes the senses, even when the fair form is foreign to us: What must be the effects of moral beauty? And what influence must it have, when it embellishes our own mind, and is the result of our own reflection and industry?

But where is the reward of virtue? And what recompence has nature provided for such important sacrifices, as those of life and fortune, which we must often make to it? Oh, sons of earth! Are ye ignorant of the value of this celestial mistress? And do ye meanly enquire for her portion, when ye observe her genuine charms? But know, that nature has been indulgent to human weakness, and has not left this favourite child, naked and unendowed. She has provided virtue with the richest dowry; but being careful, lest the allurements of interest should engage such suitors, as were insensible of the native worth of so divine a beauty, she has wisely provided, that this dowry can have no charms but in the eyes of those who are already transported with the love of virtue. GLORY is the portion of virtue, the sweet reward of honourable toils, the triumphant crown, which covers the thoughtful head of the disinterested patriot, or the dusty brow of the victorious warrior. Elevated by so sublime a prize, the man of virtue looks down with contempt on all the allurements of pleasure, and all the menaces of danger. Death itself loses its terrors, when he considers, that its dominion extends only over a part of him, and that, in spite of death and time, the rage of the elements, and the endless vicissitudes of human affairs, he is assured of an immortal fame among all the sons of men.

There surely is a being who presides over the universe; and who, with infinite wisdom and power, has reduced the jarring elements into just order and proportion. Let speculative reasoners dispute, how far this beneficent being extends his care, and whether he prolongs our existence beyond the grave, in order to bestow on virtue its just reward, and render it fully triumphant. The man of morals, without deciding any thing on so dubious a subject, is satisfied with the portion, marked out to him by the supreme disposer of all things. Gratefully he accepts of that farther reward prepared for him; but if disappointed, he thinks not virtue an empty name; but justly esteeming it its own reward, he gratefully acknowledges the bounty of his creator, who, by calling him into existence, has thereby afforded him an opportunity of once acquiring so invaluable a possession.

ESSAY XVII.—*The Platonist.*[1]

To some philosophers it appears matter of surprize, that all mankind, possessing the same nature, and being endowed with the same faculties, should yet differ so widely in their pursuits and inclinations, and that one should utterly condemn what is fondly sought after by another. To some it appears matter of still more surprize, that a man should

---

[1] Or, the man of contemplation, and *philosophical* devotion.

differ so widely from himself at different times; and, after possession, reject with disdain what, before, was the object of all his vows and wishes. To me this feverish uncertainty and irresolution, in human conduct, seems altogether unavoidable; nor can a rational soul, made for the contemplation of the Supreme Being, and of his works, ever enjoy tranquillity or satisfaction, while detained in the ignoble pursuits of sensual pleasure or popular applause. The divinity is a boundless ocean of bliss and glory: Human minds are smaller streams, which, arising at first from this ocean, seek still, amid all their wanderings, to return to it, and to lose themselves in that immensity of perfection. When checked in this natural course, by vice or folly, they become furious and enraged; and, swelling to a torrent, do then spread horror and devastation on the neighbouring plains.

In vain, by pompous phrase and passionate expression, each recommends his own pursuit, and invites the credulous hearers to an imitation of his life and manners. The heart belies the countenance, and sensibly feels, even amid the highest success, the unsatisfactory nature of all those pleasures, which detain it from its true object. I examine the voluptuous man before enjoyment; I measure the vehemence of his desire, and the importance of his object; I find that all his happiness proceeds only from that hurry of thought, which takes him from himself, and turns his view from his guilt and misery. I consider him a moment after; he has now enjoyed the pleasure, which he fondly sought after: The sense of his guilt and misery returns upon him with double anguish: His mind tormented with fear and remorse; his body depressed with disgust and satiety.

But a more august, at least a more haughty personage, presents himself boldly to our censure; and assuming the title of a philosopher and a man of morals, offers to submit to the most rigid examination. He challenges, with a visible, though concealed impatience, our approbation and applause; and seems offended, that we should hesitate a moment before we break out into admiration of his virtue. Seeing this impatience, I hesitate still more: I begin to examine the motives of his seeming virtue: But behold! ere I can enter upon this enquiry, he flings himself from me; and addressing his discourse to that crowd of heedless auditors, fondly abuses them by his magnificent pretensions.

O philosopher! thy wisdom is vain, and thy virtue unprofitable. Thou seekest the ignorant applauses of men, not the solid reflections of thy own conscience, or the more solid approbation of that being, who, with one regard of his all-seeing eye, penetrates the universe. Thou surely art conscious of the hollowness of thy pretended probity, whilst calling thyself a citizen, a son, a friend, thou forgettest thy higher sovereign, thy true father, thy greatest benefactor. Where is the adoration due to infinite perfection, whence every thing good and valuable is derived? Where is the gratitude, owing to thy creator, who called thee forth from nothing, who placed thee in all these relations to thy fellow-creatures, and requiring thee to fulfil the duty of each relation, forbids thee to neglect what thou owest to himself, the most perfect being, to whom thou art connected by the closest tye?

But thou art thyself thy own idol: Thou worshippest thy *imaginary* perfections: Or rather, sensible of thy *real* imperfections, thou seekest only to deceive the world, and to please thy fancy, by multiplying thy ignorant admirers. Thus, not content with neglecting what is most excellent in the universe, thou desirest to substitute in his place what is most vile and contemptible.

Consider all the works of men's hands; all the inventions of human wit, in which thou affectest so nice a discernment: Thou wilt find, that the most perfect production still proceeds from the most perfect thought, and that it is MIND alone, which we admire, while we bestow our applause on the graces of a well-proportioned statue, or the symmetry of a noble pile. The statuary, the architect comes still in view, and makes us reflect on the beauty of his art and contrivance, which, from a heap of unformed matter, could extract such expressions and proportions. This superior beauty of thought and intelligence thou thyself acknowledgest, while thou invitest us to contemplate, in thy conduct, the harmony of affections, the dignity of sentiments, and all those graces of a mind, which chiefly merit our attention. But why stoppest thou short? Seest thou nothing farther that is valuable? Amid thy rapturous applauses of beauty and order, art thou still ignorant where is to be found the most consummate beauty? the most perfect order? Compare the works of art with those of nature. The one are but imitations of the other. The nearer art approaches to nature, the more perfect is it esteemed. But still, how wide are its nearest approaches, and what an immense interval may be observed between them? Art copies only the outside of nature, leaving the inward and more admirable springs and principles; as exceeding her imitation; as beyond her comprehension. Art copies only the minute productions of nature, despairing to reach that grandeur and magnificence, which are so astonishing in the masterly works of her original. Can we then be so blind as not to discover an intelligence and a design in the exquisite and most stupendous contrivance of the universe? Can we be so stupid as not to feel the warmest raptures of worship and adoration, upon the contemplation of that intelligent being, so infinitely good and wise?

The most perfect happiness, surely, must arise from the contemplation of the most perfect object. But what more perfect than beauty and virtue? And where is beauty to be found equal to that of the universe? Or virtue, which can be compared to the benevolence and justice of the Deity? If aught can diminish the pleasure of this contemplation, it must be either the narrowness of our faculties, which conceals from us the greatest part of these beauties and perfections; or the shortness of our lives, which allows not time sufficient to instruct us in them. But it is our comfort, that, if we employ worthily the faculties here assigned us, they will be enlarged in another state of existence, so as to render us more suitable worshippers of our maker: And that the task, which can never be finished in time, will be the business of an eternity.

Essay XVIII.—*The Sceptic.*

I HAVE long entertained a suspicion, with regard to the decisions of philosophers upon all subjects, and found in myself a greater inclination to dispute, than assent to their conclusions. There is one mistake, to which they seem liable, almost without exception; they confine too much their principles, and make no account of that vast variety, which nature has so much affected in all her operations. When a philosopher has once laid hold of a favourite principle, which perhaps accounts for many natural effects, he extends the same principle over the whole creation, and reduces to it every phænomenon, though by the most violent and absurd reasoning. Our own mind being narrow and contracted, we cannot extend our conception to the variety and extent of nature; but imagine, that she is as much bounded in her operations, as we are in our speculation.

But if ever this infirmity of philosophers is to be suspected on any occasion, it is in their reasonings concerning human life, and the methods of attaining happiness. In that case, they are led astray, not only by the narrowness of their understandings, but by that also of their passions. Almost every one has a predominant inclination, to which his other desires and affections submit, and which governs him, though, perhaps, with some intervals, through the whole course of his life. It is difficult for him to apprehend, that any thing, which appears totally indifferent to him, can ever give enjoyment to any person, or can possess charms, which altogether escape his observation. His own pursuits are always, in his account, the most engaging: The objects of his passion, the most valuable: And the road, which he pursues, the only one that leads to happiness.

But would these prejudiced reasoners reflect a moment, there are many obvious instances and arguments, sufficient to undeceive them, and make them enlarge their maxims and principles. Do they not see the vast variety of inclinations and pursuits among our species; where each man seems fully satisfied with his own course of life, and would esteem it the greatest unhappiness to be confined to that of his neighbour? Do they not feel in themselves, that what pleases at one time, displeases at another, by the change of inclination; and that it is not in their power, by their utmost efforts, to recall that taste or appetite, which formerly bestowed charms on what now appears indifferent or disagreeable? What is the meaning therefore of those general preferences of the town or country life, of a life of action or one of pleasure, of retirement or society; when besides the different inclinations of different men, every one's experience may convince him, that each of these kinds of life is agreeable in its turn, and that their variety or their judicious mixture chiefly contributes to the rendering all of them agreeable.

But shall this business be allowed to go altogether at adventures? And must a man consult only his humour and inclination, in order to determine his course of life, without employing his reason to inform him what road is preferable, and leads most surely to happiness! Is there no difference then between one man's conduct and another?

I answer, there is a great difference. One man, following his inclination, in chusing his course of life, may employ much surer means for succeeding than another, who is led by his inclination into the same course of life, and pursues the same object. *Are riches the chief object of your desires?* Acquire skill in your profession; be diligent in the exercise of it; enlarge the circle of your friends and acquaintance; avoid pleasure and expense; and never be generous, but with a view of gaining more than you could save by frugality. *Would you acquire the public esteem?* Guard equally against the extremes of arrogance and fawning. Let it appear that you set a value upon yourself, but without despising others. If you fall into either of the extremes, you either provoke men's pride by your insolence, or teach them to despise you by your timorous submission, and by the mean opinion which you seem to entertain of yourself.

These, you say, are the maxims of common prudence, and discretion; what every parent inculcates on his child, and what every man of sense pursues in the course of life, which he has chosen.—What is it then you desire more? Do you come to a philosopher as to a *cunning man*, to learn something by magic or witchcraft, beyond what can be known by common prudence and discretion?————Yes; we come to a philosopher to be instructed, how we shall chuse our ends, more than the means for attaining these ends: We want to know what desire we shall gratify, what passion we shall comply with, what appetite we shall indulge. As to the rest, we trust to common sense, and the general maxims of the world for our instruction.

I am sorry then, I have pretended to be a philosopher: For I find your questions very perplexing; and am in danger, if my answer be too rigid and severe, of passing for a pedant and scholastic: if it be too easy and free, of being taken for a preacher of vice and immorality. However, to satisfy you, I shall deliver my opinion upon the matter, and shall only desire you to esteem it of as little consequence as I do myself. By that means you will neither think it worthy of your ridicule nor your anger.

If we can depend upon any principle, which we learn from philosophy, this, I think, may be considered as certain and undoubted, that there is nothing, in itself, valuable or despicable, desirable or hateful, beautiful or deformed; but that these attributes arise from the particular constitution and fabric of human sentiment and affection. What seems the most delicious food to one animal, appears loathsome to another: What affects the feeling of one with delight, produces uneasiness in another. This is confessedly the case with regard to all the bodily senses: But if we examine the matter more accurately, we shall find, that the same observation holds even where the mind concurs with the body, and mingles its sentiment with the exterior appetite.

Desire this passionate lover to give you a character of his mistress: He will tell you, that he is at a loss for words to describe her charms, and will ask you very seriously if ever you were acquainted with a goddess or an angel? If you answer that you never were: He will then say, that it is impossible for you to form a conception of such divine beauties as those which his charmer possesses; so complete a shape; such well-proportioned features; so engaging an air; such sweetness of disposition; such gaiety of humour. You can infer nothing, however, from all this discourse, but that the poor man is in love; and that the general appetite between the sexes, which nature has infused into all animals, is in him determined to a particular object by some qualities, which give him pleasure. The same divine creature, not only to a different animal, but also to a different man, appears a mere mortal being, and is beheld with the utmost indifference.

Nature has given all animals a like prejudice in favour of their offspring. As soon as the helpless infant sees the light, though in every other eye it appears a despicable and a miserable creature, it is regarded by its fond parent with the utmost affection, and is preferred to every other object, however perfect and accomplished. The passion alone, arising from the original structure and formation of human nature, bestows a value on the most insignificant object.

We may push the same observation further, and may conclude, that, even when the mind operates alone, and feeling the sentiment of blame or approbation, pronounces one object deformed and odious, another beautiful and amiable; I say, that, even in this case, those qualities are not really in the objects, but belong entirely to the sentiment of that mind which blames or praises. I grant, that it will be more difficult to make this proposition evident, and as it were, palpable, to negligent thinkers; because nature is more uniform in the sentiments of the mind than in most feelings of the body, and produces a nearer resemblance in the inward than in the outward part of human kind. There is something approaching to principles in mental tastes; and critics can reason and dispute more plausibly than cooks or perfumers. We may observe, however, that this uniformity among human kind, hinders not, but that there is a considerable diversity in the sentiments of beauty and worth, and that education, custom, prejudice, caprice, and humour, frequently vary our taste of this kind. You will never convince a man, who is not accustomed to ITALIAN music, and has not an ear to follow its intricacies, that a SCOTCH tune is not preferable. You have not even any single argument, beyond your own taste, which you can employ in your behalf: And to your antagonist, his particular taste will always appear a more convincing argument to the contrary. If you be wise, each of you will allow, that the other may be in the right; and having many other instances of this diversity of taste, you will both confess, that beauty and worth are merely of a relative nature, and consist in an agreeable sentiment, produced by an object in a particular mind, according to the peculiar structure and constitution of that mind.

By this diversity of sentiment, observable in human kind, nature has, perhaps, intended to make us sensible of her authority, and let us see what surprizing changes she could produce on the passions and desires of mankind, merely by the change of their inward fabric, without any alteration on the objects. The vulgar may even be convinced by this argument: But men, accustomed to thinking, may draw a more convincing, at least a more general argument, from the very nature of the subject.

In the operation of reasoning, the mind does nothing but run over its objects, as they are supposed to stand in reality, without adding any thing to them, or diminishing any thing from them. If I examine the PTOLOMAIC and COPERNICAN systems, I endeavour only, by my enquiries, to know the real situation of the planets; that is, in other words, I endeavour to give them, in my conception, the same relations, that they bear towards each other in the heavens. To this operation of the mind, therefore, there seems to be always a real, though often an unknown standard, in the nature of things; nor is truth or falsehood variable by the various apprehensions of mankind. Though all human race should for ever conclude, that the sun moves, and the earth remains at rest, the sun stirs not an inch from his place for all these reasonings; and such conclusions are eternally false and erroneous.

But the case is not the same with the qualities of *beautiful and deformed, desirable and odious,* as with truth and falsehood. In the former case, the mind is not content with merely surveying its objects, as they stand in themselves: It also feels a sentiment of delight or uneasiness, approbation or blame, consequent to that survey; and this sentiment determines it to affix the epithet *beautiful or deformed, desirable or odious.* Now, it is evident, that this sentiment must depend upon the particular fabric or structure of the mind, which enables such particular forms to operate in such a particular manner, and produces a sympathy or conformity between the mind and its objects. Vary the structure of the mind or inward organs, the sentiment no longer follows, though the form remains the same. The sentiment being different from the object, and arising from its operations upon the organs of the mind, an alteration upon the latter must vary the effect, nor can the same object, presented to a mind totally different, produce the same sentiment.

This conclusion every one is apt to draw of himself, without much philosophy, where the sentiment is evidently distinguishable from the object. Who is not sensible, that power, and glory, and vengeance, are not desirable of themselves, but derive all their value from the structure of human passions, which begets a desire towards such particular pursuits? But with regard to beauty, either natural or moral, the case is commonly supposed to be different. The agreeable quality is thought to lie in the object, not in the sentiment; and that merely because the sentiment is not so turbulent and violent as to distinguish itself, in an evident manner, from the perception of the object.

But a little reflection suffices to distinguish them. A man may know exactly all the circles and ellipses of the COPERNICAN system, and all the irregular spirals of the PTOLOMAIC, without perceiving that the former is more beautiful than the latter. EUCLID has fully explained every quality of the circle, but has not, in any proposition, said a word of its beauty. The reason is evident. Beauty is not a quality of the circle. It lies not in any part of the line *whose* parts are all equally distant from a common center. It is only the effect, which that figure produces upon a mind, whose particular fabric or structure renders it susceptible of such sentiments. In vain would you look for it in the circle, or seek it, either by your senses, or by mathematical reasonings, in all the properties of that figure.

The mathematician, who took no other pleasure in reading VIRGIL, but that of examining ENEAS's voyage by the map, might perfectly understand the meaning of every Latin word, employed by that divine author; and consequently, might have a distinct idea of the whole narration. He would even have a more distinct idea of it, than they could attain who had not studied so exactly the geography of the poem. He knew, therefore, every thing in the poem: But he was ignorant of its beauty; because the beauty, properly speaking, lies not in the poem, but in the sentiment or taste of the reader. And where a man has no such delicacy of temper, as to make him feel this sentiment, he must be ignorant of the beauty, though possessed of the science and understanding of an angel.[1]

The inference upon the whole is, that it is not from the value or worth of the object, which any person pursues, that we can determine his enjoyment, but merely from the passion with which he pursues it, and the success which he meets with in his pursuit. Objects have absolutely no worth or value in themselves. They derive their worth merely from the passion. If that be strong, and steady, and successful, the person is happy. It cannot reasonably be doubted, but

---

[1] Were I not afraid of appearing too philosophical, I should remind my reader of that famous doctrine, supposed to be fully proved in modern times, 'That tastes and colours, and all other sensible qualities, lie not in the bodies, but merely in the senses.' The case is the same with beauty and deformity, virtue and vice. This doctrine, however, takes off no more from the reality of the latter qualities, than from that of the former; nor need it give any umbrage either to critics or moralists. Tho' colours were allowed to lie only in the eye, would dyers or painters ever be less regarded or esteemed? There is a sufficient uniformity in the senses and feelings of mankind, to make all these qualities the objects of art and reasoning, and to have the greatest influence on life and manners. And as 'tis certain, that the discovery above-mentioned in natural philosophy, makes no alteration on action and conduct; why should a like discovery in moral philosophy make any alteration?

a little miss, dressed in a new gown for a dancing-school ball, receives as compleat enjoyment as the greatest orator, who triumphs in the splendour of his eloquence, while he governs the passions and resolutions of a numerous assembly.

All the difference, therefore, between one man and another, with regard to life, consists either in the *passion*, or in the *enjoyment*: And these differences are sufficient to produce the wide extremes of happiness and misery.

To be happy, the *passion* must neither be too violent nor too remiss. In the first case, the mind is in a perpetual hurry and tumult; in the second, it sinks into a disagreeable indolence and lethargy.

To be happy, the passion must be benign and social; not rough or fierce. The affections of the latter kind are not near so agreeable to the feeling, as those of the former. Who will compare rancour and animosity, envy and revenge, to friendship, benignity, clemency, and gratitude?

To be happy, the passion must be chearful and gay, not gloomy and melancholy. A propensity to hope and joy is real riches: One to fear and sorrow, real poverty.

Some passions or inclinations, in the *enjoyment* of their object, are not so steady or constant as others, nor convey such durable pleasure and satisfaction. *Philosophical devotion*, for instance, like the enthusiasm of a poet, is the transitory effect of high spirits, great leisure, a fine genius, and a habit of study and contemplation: But notwithstanding all these circumstances, an abstract, invisible object, like that which *natural* religion alone presents to us, cannot long actuate the mind, or be of any moment in life. To render the passion of continuance, we must find some method of affecting the senses and imagination, and must embrace some *historical,* as well as *philosophical* account of the divinity. Popular superstitions and observances are even found to be of use in this particular.

Though the tempers of men be very different, yet we may safely pronounce in general, that a life of pleasure cannot support itself so long as one of business, but is much more subject to satiety and disgust. The amusements, which are the most durable, have all a mixture of application and attention in them; such as gaming and hunting. And in general, business and action fill up all the great vacancies in human life.

But where the temper is the best disposed for any *enjoyment*, the object is often wanting: And in this respect, the passions, which pursue external objects, contribute not so much to happiness, as those which rest in ourselves; since we are neither so certain of attaining such objects, nor so secure in possessing them. A passion for learning is preferable, with regard to happiness, to one for riches.

Some men are possessed of great strength of mind; and even when they pursue *external* objects, are not much affected by a disappointment, but renew their application and industry with the greatest chearfulness. Nothing contributes more to happiness than such a turn of mind.

According to this short and imperfect sketch of human life, the happiest disposition of mind is the *virtuous*; or, in other words, that which leads to action and employment, renders us sensible to the social passions, steels the heart against the assaults of fortune, reduces the affections to a just moderation, makes our own thoughts an entertainment to us, and inclines us rather to the pleasures of society and conversation, than to those of the senses. This, in the mean time, must be obvious to the most careless reasoner, that all dispositions of mind are not alike favourable to happiness, and that one passion or humour may be extremely desirable, while another is equally disagreeable. And indeed, all the difference between the conditions of life depends upon the mind; nor is there any one situation of affairs, in itself, preferable to another. Good and ill, both natural and moral, are entirely relative to human sentiment and affection. No man would ever be unhappy, could he alter his feelings. PROTEUS-like, he would elude all attacks, by the continual alterations of his shape and form.

But of this resource nature has, in a great measure, deprived us. The fabric and constitution of our mind no more depends on our choice, than that of our body. The generality of men have not even the smallest notion, that any alteration in this respect can ever be desirable. As a stream necessarily follows the several inclinations of the ground, on which it runs; so are the ignorant and thoughtless part of mankind actuated by their natural propensities. Such are effectually excluded from all pretensions to philosophy, and the *medicine of the mind*, so much boasted. But even upon the wise and thoughtful, nature has a prodigious influence; nor is it always in a man's power, by the utmost art and industry, to correct his temper, and attain that virtuous character, to which he aspires. The empire of philosophy extends over a few; and with regard to these too, her authority is very weak and limited. Men may well be sensible of the value of virtue, and may desire to attain it; but it is not always certain, that they will be successful in their wishes.

Whoever considers, without prejudice, the course of human actions, will find, that mankind are almost entirely guided by constitution and temper, and that general maxims have little influence, so far as they affect our taste or sentiment. If a man have a lively sense of honour and virtue, with moderate passions, his conduct will always be conformable to the rules of morality; or if he depart from them, his return will be easy and expeditious. On the other hand, where one is born of so perverse a frame of mind, of so callous and insensible a disposition, as to have no relish for virtue and humanity, no sympathy with his fellow-creatures, no desire of esteem and applause; such a one must be allowed entirely incurable, nor is there any remedy in philosophy. He reaps no satisfaction but from low and sensual objects, or from the indulgence of malignant passions: He feels no remorse to controul his vicious inclinations: He has not even that sense or taste, which is requisite to make him desire a better character: For my part, I know not how I should address myself to such a one, or by what arguments I should endeavour to reform him. Should I tell him of the inward satisfaction which results from laudable and humane actions, the delicate pleasure of disinterested love and friendship, the lasting enjoyments of a good name and an established character, he might still reply, that these were, perhaps, pleasures to such as were susceptible of them; but that, for his part, he finds himself of a quite different turn and disposition. I must repeat it; my philosophy affords no remedy in such a case, nor could I do anything but lament this person's unhappy condition. But then I ask, If any other philosophy can afford a remedy; or if it be possible, by any system, to render all mankind virtuous, however perverse may be their natural frame of mind? Experience will soon convince us of the contrary; and I will venture to affirm, that, perhaps, the chief benefit, which results from philosophy, arises in an indirect manner,[1] and proceeds more from its secret, insensible influence, than from its immediate application.

It is certain, that a serious attention to the sciences and liberal arts softens and humanizes the temper, and cherishes those fine emotions, in which true virtue and honour consists. It rarely, very rarely happens, that a man of taste and learning is not, at least, an honest man, whatever frailties may attend him. The bent of his mind to speculative studies must mortify in him the passions of interest and ambition, and must, at the same time, give him a greater sensibility of all the decencies and duties of life. He feels more fully a moral distinction in characters and manners; nor is his sense of this kind diminished, but, on the contrary, it is much encreased, by speculation.

Besides such insensible changes upon the temper and disposition, it is highly probable, that others may be produced by study and application. The prodigious effects of education may convince us, that the mind is not altogether stubborn and inflexible, but will admit of many alterations from its original make and structure. Let a man propose to himself the model of a character, which he approves: Let him be well acquainted with those particulars, in which his own character deviates from this model: Let him keep a constant watch over himself, and bend his mind, by a continual effort, from the vices, towards the virtues; and I doubt not but, in time, he will find, in his temper, an alteration for the better.

Habit is another powerful means of reforming the mind, and implanting in it good dispositions and inclinations. A man, who continues in a course of sobriety and temperance, will hate riot and disorder: If he engage in business or study, indolence will seem a punishment to him: If he constrain himself to practise beneficence and affability, he will soon abhor all instances of pride and violence. Where one is thoroughly convinced that the virtuous course of life is preferable; if he have but resolution enough, for some time, to impose a violence on himself; his reformation needs not be despaired of. The misfortune is, that this conviction and this resolution never can have place, unless a man be, beforehand, tolerably virtuous.

[1] [The remainder of this sentence does not occur in Editions C and D.]

Here then is the chief triumph of art and philosophy: It insensibly refines the temper, and it points out to us those dispositions which we should endeavour to attain, by a constant *bent* of mind, and by repeated *habit*. Beyond this I cannot acknowledge it to have great influence; and I must entertain doubts concerning all those exhortations and consolations, which are in such vogue among speculative reasoners.

We have already observed, that no objects are, in themselves, desirable or odious, valuable or despicable; but that objects acquire these qualities from the particular character and constitution of the mind, which surveys them. To diminish therefore, or augment any person's value for an object, to excite or moderate his passions, there are no direct arguments or reasons, which can be employed with any force or influence. The catching of flies, like DOMITIAN, if it give more pleasure, is preferable to the hunting of wild beasts, like WILLIAM RUFUS, or conquering of kingdoms, like ALEXANDER.

But though the value of every object can be determined only by the sentiment or passion of every individual, we may observe, that the passion, in pronouncing its verdict, considers not the object simply, as it is in itself, but surveys it with all the circumstances, which attend it. A man transported with joy, on account of his possessing a diamond, confines not his view to the glistering stone before him: He also considers its rarity, and thence chiefly arises his pleasure and exultation. Here therefore a philosopher may step in, and suggest particular views, and considerations, and circumstances, which otherwise would have escaped us; and, by that means, he may either moderate or excite any particular passion.

It may seem unreasonable absolutely to deny the authority of philosophy in this respect: But it must be confessed, that there lies this strong presumption against it, that, if these views be natural and obvious, they would have occurred of themselves, without the assistance of philosophy; if they be not natural, they never can have any influence on the affections. *These* are of a very delicate nature, and cannot be forced or constrained by the utmost art or industry. A consideration, which we seek for on purpose, which we enter into with difficulty, which we cannot retain without care and attention, will never produce those genuine and durable movements of passion, which are the result of nature, and the constitution of the mind. A man may as well pretend to cure himself of love, by viewing his mistress through the *artificial* medium of a microscope or prospect, and beholding there the coarseness of her skin, and monstrous disproportion of her features, as hope to excite or moderate any passion by the *artificial* arguments of a SENECA or an EPICTETUS. The remembrance of the natural aspect and situation of the object, will, in both cases, still recur upon him. The reflections of philosophy are too subtile and distant to take place in common life, or eradicate any affection. The air is too fine to breathe in, where it is above the winds and clouds of the atmosphere.

Another defect of those refined reflections, which philosophy suggests to us, is, that commonly they cannot diminish or extinguish our vicious passions, without diminishing or extinguishing such as are virtuous, and rendering the mind totally indifferent and unactive. They are, for the most part, general, and are applicable to all our affections. In vain do we hope to direct their influence only to one side. If by incessant study and meditation we have rendered them intimate and present to us, they will operate throughout, and spread an universal insensibility over the mind. When we destroy the nerves, we extinguish the sense of pleasure, together with that of pain, in the human body.

It will be easy, by one glance of the eye to find one or other of these defects in most of those philosophical reflections, so much celebrated both in ancient and modern times. *Let not the injuries or violence of men,* say the philosophers,[1] *ever discompose you by anger or hatred. Would you be angry at the ape for its malice, or the tyger for its ferocity?* This reflection leads us into a bad opinion of human nature, and must extinguish the social affections. It tends also to prevent all remorse for a man's own crimes; when he considers, that vice is as natural to mankind, as the particular instincts to brute-creatures.

All ills arise from the order of the universe, which is absolutely perfect. Would you wish to disturb so divine an order for the sake of your own particular interest? What if the ills I suffer arise from malice or oppression? But the vices and

[1] PLUT. *de ira cohibenda.*

imperfections of men are also comprehended in the order of the universe:

> *If plagues and earthquakes break not heav'n's design,*
> *Why then a* BORGIA *or a* CATILINE?

Let this be allowed; and my own vices will also be a part of the same order.

[1]To one who said, that none were happy, who were not above opinion, a SPARTAN replied, *then none are happy but knaves and robbers.*[2]

Man is born to be miserable; and is he surprised at any particular misfortune? And can he give way to sorrow and lamentation upon account of any disaster? Yes: He very reasonably laments, that he should be born to be miserable. Your consolation presents a hundred ills for one, of which you pretend to ease him.

You should always have before your eyes death, disease, poverty, blindness, exile, calumny, and infamy, as ills which are incident to human nature. If any one of these ills fall to your lot, you will bear it the better, when you have reckoned upon it. I answer, if we confine ourselves to a general and distant reflection on the ills of human life, *that* can have no effect to prepare us for them. If by close and intense meditation we render them present and intimate to us, *that* is the true secret for poisoning all our pleasures, and rendering us perpetually miserable.

Your sorrow is fruitless, and will not change the course of destiny. Very true: And for that very reason I am sorry.

Cicero's consolation for deafness is somewhat curious, *How many languages are there,* says he, *which you do not understand?* The PUNIC, SPANISH, GALLIC, ÆGYPTIAN, &c. *With regard to all these, you are as if you were deaf, yet you are indifferent about the matter. Is it then so great a misfortune to be deaf to one language more?*[3]

I like better the repartee of ANTIPATER the CYRENIAC, when some women were condoling with him for his blindness: *What!* says he, *Do you think there are no pleasures in the dark?*

Nothing can be more destructive, says FONTENELLE, *to ambition, and the passion for conquest, than the true system of*

---

[1] [This paragraph does not occur in Editions C and D.]
[2] PLUT. *Lacon. Apophtheg.*
[3] Tusc. *Quæst.* lib. v. 40.

astronomy. What a poor thing is even the whole globe in comparison of the infinite extent of nature? This consideration is evidently too distant ever to have any effect. Or, if it had any, would it not destroy patriotism as well as ambition? The same gallant author adds with some reason, that the bright eyes of the ladies are the only objects, which lose nothing of their lustre or value from the most extensive views of astronomy, but stand proof against every system. Would philosophers advise us to limit our affection to them?

[1] *Exile,* says PLUTARCH *to a friend in banishment, is no evil: Mathematicians tell us, that the whole earth is but a point, compared to the heavens. To change one's country then is little more than to remove from one street to another. Man is not a plant, rooted to a certain spot of earth: All soils and all climates are alike suited to him* [2]. These topics are admirable, could they fall only into the hands of banished persons. But what if they come also to the knowledge of those who are employed in public affairs, and destroy all their attachment to their native country? Or will they operate like the quack's medicine, which is equally good for a diabetes and a dropsy?

It is certain, were a superior being thrust into a human body, that the whole of life would to him appear so mean, contemptible, and puerile, that he never could be induced to take part in any thing, and would scarcely give attention to what passes around him. To engage him to such a condescension as to play even the part of a PHILIP with zeal and alacrity, would be much more difficult, than to constrain the same PHILIP, after having been a king and a conqueror during fifty years, to mend old shoes with proper care and attention; the occupation which LUCIAN assigns him in the infernal regions. Now all the same topics of disdain towards human affairs, which could operate on this supposed being, occur also to a philosopher; but being, in some measure, disproportioned to human capacity, and not being fortified by the experience of any thing better, they make not a full impression on him. He sees, but he feels not sufficiently their truth; and is always a sublime philosopher, when he needs not; that is, as long as nothing disturbs him, or rouzes his affections. While others play, he wonders at their keen-

[1] [The two following paragraphs do not occur in Editions C and D.]
[2] *De exilio.*

ness and ardour; but he no sooner puts in his own stake, than he is commonly transported with the same passions, that he had so much condemned, while he remained a simple spectator.

There are two considerations chiefly, to be met with in books of philosophy, from which any important effect is to be expected, and that because these considerations are drawn from common life, and occur upon the most superficial view of human affairs. When we reflect on the shortness and uncertainty of life, how despicable seem all our pursuits of happiness? And even, if we would extend our concern beyond our own life, how frivolous appear our most enlarged and most generous projects; when we consider the incessant changes and revolutions of human affairs, by which laws and learning, books and governments are hurried away by time, as by a rapid stream, and are lost in the immense ocean of matter? Such a reflection certainly tends to mortify all our passions: But does it not thereby counterwork the artifice of nature, who has happily deceived us into an opinion, that human life is of some importance? And may not such a reflection be employed with success by voluptuous reasoners, in order to lead us, from the paths of action and virtue, into the flowery fields of indolence and pleasure?

We are informed by THUCYDIDES, that, during the famous plague of ATHENS, when death seemed present to every one, a dissolute mirth and gaiety prevailed among the people, who exhorted one another to make the most of life as long as it endured. [1] The same observation is made by BOCCACE with regard to the plague of FLORENCE. A like principle makes soldiers, during war, be more addicted to riot and expence, than any other race of men. [2] Present pleasure is always of importance; and whatever diminishes the importance of all other objects must bestow on it an additional influence and value.

The *second* philosophical consideration, which may often have an influence on the affections, is derived from a comparison of our own condition with the condition of others. This comparison we are continually making, even in common

---

[1] [This sentence does not occur in Editions C and D.]

[2] [In place of this sentence Editions C and D read as follows: And 'tis observable, in this Kingdom, that long Peace, by producing Security, has much alter'd them in this Particular, and has quite remov'd our Officers from the generous Character of their Profession.]

life; but the misfortune is, that we are rather apt to compare our situation with that of our superiors, than with that of our inferiors. A philosopher corrects this natural infirmity, by turning his view to the other side, in order to render himself easy in the situation, to which fortune has confined him. There are few people, who are not susceptible of some consolation from this reflection, though, to a very good-natured man, the view of human miseries should rather produce sorrow than comfort, and add, to his lamentations for his own misfortunes, a deep compassion for those of others. Such is the imperfection, even of the best of these philosophical topics of consolation.[1]

I shall conclude this subject with observing, that, though virtue be undoubtedly the best choice, when it is attainable; yet such is the disorder and confusion of human affairs, that

---

[1] The Sceptic, perhaps, carries the matter too far, when he limits all philosophical topics and reflections to these two. There seem to be others, whose truth is undeniable, and whose natural tendency is to tranquillize and soften all the passions. Philosophy greedily seizes these, studies them, weighs them, commits them to the memory, and familiarizes them to the mind: And their influence on tempers, which are thoughtful, gentle, and moderate, may be considerable. But what is their influence, you will say, if the temper be antecedently disposed after the same manner as that to which they pretend to form it? They may, at least, fortify that temper, and furnish it with views, by which it may entertain and nourish itself. Here are a few examples of such philosophical reflections.

1. Is it not certain, that every condition has concealed ills? Then why envy any body?
2. Every one has known ills; and there is a compensation throughout. Why not be contented with the present?
3. Custom deadens the sense both of the good and the ill, and levels every thing.
4. Health and humour all. The rest of little consequence, except these be affected.
5. How many other good things have I? Then why be vexed for one ill?
6. How many are happy in the condition of which I complain? How many envy me?
7. Every good must be paid for: Fortune by labour, favour by flattery. Would I keep the price, yet have the commodity?
8. Expect not too great happiness in life. Human nature admits it not.
9. Propose not a happiness too complicated. But does that depend on me? Yes: The first choice does. Life is like a game: One may choose the game: And passion, by degrees, seizes the proper object.
10. Anticipate by your hopes and fancy future consolation, which time infallibly brings to every affliction.
11. I desire to be rich. Why? That I may possess many fine objects; houses, gardens, equipage, &c. How many fine objects does nature offer to every one without expence? If enjoyed, sufficient. If not: See the effect of custom or of temper, which would soon take off the relish of the riches.
12. I desire fame. Let this occur: If I act well, I shall have the esteem of all my acquaintance. And what is all the rest to me?

These reflections are so obvious, that it is a wonder they occur not to every man: So convincing, that it is a wonder they persuade not every man. But perhaps they do occur to and persuade most men; when they consider human life, by a general and calm survey: But where any real, affecting incident happens; when passion is awakened, fancy agitated, example draws, and counsel urges; the philosopher is lost in the man, and he seeks in vain for

no perfect or regular distribution of happiness and misery is ever, in this life, to be expected. Not only the goods of fortune, and the endowments of the body (both of which are important), not only these advantages, I say, are unequally divided between the virtuous and vicious, but even the mind itself partakes, in some degree, of this disorder, and the most worthy character, by the very constitution of the passions, enjoys not always the highest felicity.

It is observable, that, though every bodily pain proceeds from some disorder in the part or organ, yet the pain is not always proportioned to the disorder; but is greater or less, according to the greater or less sensibility of the part, upon which the noxious humours exert their influence. A *tooth-ach* produces more violent convulsions of pain than a *phthisis* or a *dropsy*. In like manner, with regard to the œconomy of the mind, we may observe, that all vice is indeed pernicious; yet the disturbance or pain is not measured out by nature with exact proportion to the degree of vice, nor is the man of highest virtue, even abstracting from external accidents, always the most happy. A gloomy and melancholy disposition is certainly, *to our sentiments*, a vice or imperfection; but as it may be accompanied with great sense of honour and great integrity, it may be found in very worthy characters; though it is sufficient alone to imbitter life, and render the person affected with it completely miserable. On the other hand, a selfish villain may possess a spring and alacrity of temper, a certain [1] *gaiety of heart*, which is indeed a good quality, but which is rewarded much beyond its merit, and when attended with good fortune, will compensate for the uneasiness and remorse arising from all the other vices.

I shall add, as an observation to the same purpose, that, if a man be liable to a vice or imperfection, it may often happen, that a good quality, which he possesses along with it,

---

that persuasion which before seemed so firm and unshaken. What remedy for this inconvenience? Assist yourself by a frequent perusal of the entertaining moralists: Have recourse to the learning of PLUTARCH, the imagination of LUCIAN, the eloquence of CICERO, the wit of SENECA, the gaiety of MONTAIGNE, the sublimity of SHAFTESBURY. Moral precepts, so couched, strike deep, and fortify the mind against the illusions of passion. But trust not altogether to external aid: By habit and study acquire that philosophical temper which both gives force to reflection, and by rendering a great part of your happiness independent, takes off the edge from all disorderly passions, and tranquillizes the mind. Despise not these helps; but confide not too much in them neither; unless nature has been favourable in the temper, with which she has endowed you.

[1] [Gaieté de Cœur: Edition C.]

will render him more miserable, than if he were completely vicious. A person of such imbecility of temper as to be easily broken by affliction, is more unhappy for being endowed with a generous and friendly disposition, which gives him a lively concern for others, and exposes him the more to fortune and accidents. A sense of shame, in an imperfect character, is certainly a virtue; but produces great uneasiness and remorse, from which the abandoned villain is entirely free. A very amorous complexion, with a heart incapable of friendship, is happier than the same excess in love, with a generosity of temper, which transports a man beyond himself, and renders him a total slave to the object of his passion.

In a word, human life is more governed by fortune than by reason; is to be regarded more as a dull pastime than as a serious occupation; and is more influenced by particular humour, than by general principles. Shall we engage ourselves in it with passion and anxiety? It is not worthy of so much concern. Shall we be indifferent about what happens? We lose all the pleasure of the game by our phlegm and carelessness. While we are reasoning concerning life, life is gone; and death, though *perhaps* they receive him differently, yet treats alike the fool and the philosopher. To reduce life to exact rule and method, is commonly a painful, oft a fruitless occupation: And is it not also a proof, that we overvalue the prize for which we contend? Even to reason so carefully concerning it, and to fix with accuracy its just idea, would be overvaluing it, were it not that, to some tempers, this occupation is one of the most amusing, in which life could possibly be employed.

ESSAY XIX.—*Of Polygamy and Divorces.*

As marriage is an engagement entered into by mutual consent, and has for its end the propagation of the species, it is evident, that it must be susceptible of all the variety of conditions, which consent establishes, provided they be not contrary to this end.

A man, in conjoining himself to a woman, is bound to her according to the terms of his engagement: In begetting children, he is bound, by all the ties of nature and humanity, to provide for their subsistence and education. When he has performed these two parts of duty, no one can reproach him with injustice or injury. And as the terms of his engagement, as well as the methods of subsisting his offspring, may be various, it is mere superstition to imagine, that marriage can be entirely uniform, and will admit only of one mode or form. Did not human laws restrain the natural liberty of men, every particular marriage would be as different as contracts or bargains of any other kind or species.

As circumstances vary, and the laws propose different advantages, we find, that, in different times and places, they impose different conditions on this important contract. In TONQUIN, it is usual for the sailors, when the ships come into harbour, to marry for the season; and notwithstanding this precarious engagement, they are assured, it is said, of the strictest fidelity to their bed, as well as in the whole management of their affairs, from those temporary spouses.

I cannot, at present, recollect my authorities; but I have somewhere read, that the republic of ATHENS, having lost many of its citizens by war and pestilence, allowed every man to marry two wives, in order the sooner to repair the waste which had been made by these calamities. The poet EURIPIDES happened to be coupled to two noisy Vixens who so plagued him with their jealousies and quarrels, that he became ever after a professed *woman-hater*; and is the only theatrical writer, perhaps the only poet, that ever entertained an aversion to the sex.

In that agreeable romance, called *the History of the* SEVARAMBIANS, where a great many men and a few women are supposed to be shipwrecked on a desert coast; the captain of the troop, in order to obviate those endless quarrels which arose, regulates their marriages after the following manner: He takes a handsome female to himself alone; assigns one to every couple of inferior officers; and to five of the lowest rank he gives one wife in common.[1]

The ancient BRITONS had a singular kind of marriage, to be met with among no other people. Any number of them, as ten or a dozen, joined in a society together, which was perhaps requisite for mutual defence in those barbarous times. In order to link this society the closer, they took an equal number of wives in common; and whatever children were

---

[1] [Editions C to P add the following: Could the greatest legislator, in such circumstances, have contrived matters with greater wisdom?]

born, were reputed to belong to all of them, and were accordingly provided for by the whole community.

Among the inferior creatures, nature herself, being the supreme legislator, prescribes all the laws which regulate their marriages, and varies those laws according to the different circumstances of the creature. Where she furnishes, with ease, food and defence to the newborn animal, the present embrace terminates the marriage; and the care of the offspring is committed entirely to the female. Where the food is of more difficult purchase, the marriage continues for one season, till the common progeny can provide for itself; and the union immediately dissolves, and leaves each of the parties free to enter into a new engagement at the ensuing season. But nature, having endowed man with reason, has not so exactly regulated every article of his marriage contract, but has left him to adjust them, by his own prudence, according to his particular circumstances and situation. Municipal laws are a supply to the wisdom of each individual; and, at the same time, by restraining the natural liberty of men, make private interest submit to the interest of the public. All regulations, therefore, on this head are equally lawful, and equally conformable to the principles of nature; though they are not all equally convenient, or equally useful to society. The laws may allow of polygamy, as among the *Eastern* nations; or of voluntary divorces, as among the GREEKS and ROMANS; or they may confine one man to one woman, during the whole course of their lives, as among the modern EUROPEANS. It may not be disagreeable to consider the advantages and disadvantages, which result from each of these institutions.

The advocates for polygamy may recommend it as the only effectual remedy for the disorders of love, and the only expedient for freeing men from that slavery to the females, which the natural violence of our passions has imposed upon us. By this means alone can we regain our right of sovereignty; and, sating our appetite, re-establish the authority of reason in our minds, and, of consequence, our own authority in our families. Man, like a weak sovereign, being unable to support himself against the wiles and intrigues of his subjects, must play one faction against another, and become absolute by the mutual jealousy of the females. *To divide and to govern* is an universal maxim; and by neglecting it, the Europeans undergo a more grievous and a more ignominious slavery than the Turks or Persians, who are subjected indeed to a sovereign, that lies at a distance from them, but in their domestic affairs rule with an uncontroulable sway.[1]

On the other hand, it may be urged with better reason, that this sovereignty of the male is a real usurpation, and destroys that nearness of rank, not to say equality, which nature has established between the sexes. We are, by nature, their lovers, their friends, their patrons: Would we willingly exchange such endearing appellations, for the barbarous title of master and tyrant?

In what capacity shall we gain by this inhuman proceeding? As lovers, or as husbands? The *lover*, is totally annihilated; and courtship, the most agreeable scene in life, can no longer have place, where women have not the free disposal of themselves, but are bought and sold, like the meanest animal. The *husband* is as little a gainer, having found the admirable secret of extinguishing every part of love, except its jealousy. No rose without its thorn; but he must be a foolish wretch indeed, that throws away the rose and preserves only the thorn.[2]

But the Asiatic manners are as destructive to friendship as to love. Jealousy excludes men from all intimacies and familiarities with each other. No one dares bring his friend to his house or table, lest he bring a lover to his numerous wives. Hence all over the east, each family is as much separate from another, as if they were so many distinct kingdoms. No wonder then, that Solomon, living like an eastern prince, with his seven hundred wives, and three hundred concubines, without one friend, could write so

---

[1] [Editions C to P add the following: An honest Turk, who should come from his seraglio, where every one trembles before him, would be surprized to see Sylvia in her drawing-room, adored by all the beaus and pretty fellows about town, and he would certainly take her for some mighty and despotic queen, surrounded by her guard of obsequious slaves and eunuchs.]

[2] [C to N add the following paragraph: I would not willingly insist upon it as an advantage in our European customs, what was observed by Mehemet Effendi the last Turkish ambassador in France. *We Turks, says he, are great simpletons in comparison of the Christians. We are at the expense and trouble of keeping a seraglio, each in his own house: But you ease yourselves of this burden, and have your seraglio in your friends' houses.* The known virtue of our British ladies frees them sufficiently from this imputation: And the Turk himself, had he travelled among us, must have owned, that our free commerce with the fair sex, more than any other invention, embellishes, enlivens, and polishes society.]

pathetically concerning the vanity of the world. Had he tried the secret of one wife or mistress, a few friends, and a great many companions, he might have found life somewhat more agreeable. Destroy love and friendship; what remains in the world worth accepting?

[1] The bad education of children, especially children of condition, is another unavoidable consequence of these eastern institutions. Those who pass the early part of life among slaves, are only qualified to be, themselves, slaves and tyrants; and in every future intercourse, either with their inferiors or superiors, are apt to forget the natural equality of mankind. What attention, too, can it be supposed a parent, whose seraglio affords him fifty sons, will give to instilling principles of morality or science into a progeny, with whom he himself is scarcely acquainted, and whom he loves with so divided an affection? Barbarism, therefore, appears, from reason as well as experience, to be the inseparable attendant of polygamy.

To render polygamy more odious, I need not recount the frightful effects of jealousy, and the constraint in which it holds the fair-sex all over the east. In those countries men are not allowed to have any commerce with the females, not even physicians, when sickness may be supposed to have extinguished all wanton passions in the bosoms of the fair, and, at the same time, has rendered them unfit objects of desire. TOURNEFORT tells us, that, when he was brought into the *grand signor's* seraglio as a physician, he was not a little surprized, in looking along a gallery, to see a great number of naked arms, standing out from the sides of the room. He could not imagine what this could mean; till he was told, that those arms belonged to bodies, which he must cure, without knowing any more about them, than what he could learn from the arms. He was not allowed to ask a question of the patient, or even of her attendants, lest he might find it necessary to enquire concerning circumstances, which the delicacy of the seraglio allows not to be revealed. Hence physicians in the east pretend to know all diseases from the pulse; as our quacks in EUROPE undertake to cure a person merely from seeing his water. I suppose, had *Monsieur* TOURNEFORT been of this latter kind, he would not, in CONSTANTINOPLE, have been allowed by the jealous TURKS

[1] [This paragraph does not occur in Editions C to K.]

to be furnished with materials requisite for exercising his art.

In another country, where polygamy is also allowed, they render their wives cripples, and make their feet of no use to them, in order to confine them to their own houses. But it will, perhaps, appear strange, that, in a EUROPEAN country, jealousy can yet be carried to such a height, that it is indecent so much as to suppose that a woman of rank can have feet or legs.[1] Witness the following story, which we have from very good authority.[2] When the mother of the late king of SPAIN was on her road towards MADRID, she passed through a little town in SPAIN, famous for its manufactory of gloves and stockings. The magistrates of the place thought they could not better express their joy for the reception of their new queen, than by presenting her with a sample of those commodities, for which alone their town was remarkable. The *major domo*, who conducted the princess, received the gloves very graciously: But when the stockings were presented, he flung them away with great indignation, and severely reprimanded the magistrates for this egregious piece of indecency. *Know*, says he, *that a queen of* SPAIN *has no legs*. The young queen, who, at that time, understood the language but imperfectly, and had often been frightened with stories of SPANISH jealousy, imagined that they were to cut off her legs. Upon which she fell a crying, and begged them to conduct her back to GERMANY; for that she never could endure the operation: And it was with some difficulty they could appease her. PHILIP IV. is said never in his life to have laughed heartily, but at the recital of this story.[3]

Having rejected polygamy, and matched one man with one woman, let us now consider what duration we shall assign to their union, and whether we shall admit of those voluntary

---

[1] [Editions C to P add the following: A SPANIARD is jealous of the very thoughts of those who approach his wife; and, if possible, will prevent his being dishonoured, even by the wantonness of imagination.]

[2] *Memoirs de la cour d'*ESPAGNE *par Madame d'*AUNOY.

[3] [Editions C to P add as follows: If a SPANISH lady must not be supposed to have legs, what must be supposed of a TURKISH lady? She must not be supposed to have a being at all. Accordingly, 'tis esteemed a piece of rudeness and indecency at CONSTANTINOPLE, ever to make mention of a man's wives before him.[1] In EUROPE, 'tis true, fine bred people make it also a rule never to talk of their wives. But the reason is not founded on our jealousy. I suppose it is because we should be apt, were it not for this rule, to become

[1] [*Memoires de Marquis d'Argens.*]

divorces, which were customary among the GREEKS and ROMANS. Those who would defend this practice may employ the following reasons.

How often does disgust and aversion arise after marriage, from the most trivial accidents, or from an incompatibility of humour; where time, instead of curing the wounds, proceeding from mutual injuries, festers them every day the more, by new quarrels and reproaches? Let us separate hearts, which were not made to associate together. Each of them may, perhaps, find another for which it is better fitted. At least, nothing can be more cruel than to preserve, by violence, an union, which, at first, was made by mutual love, and is now, in effect, dissolved by mutual hatred.

But the liberty of divorces is not only a cure to hatred and domestic quarrels: It is also an admirable preservative against them, and the only secret for keeping alive that love, which first united the married couple. The heart of man delights in liberty: The very image of constraint is grievous to it: When you would confine it by violence, to what would otherwise have been its choice, the inclination immediately changes, and desire is turned into aversion. If the public interest will not allow us to enjoy in polygamy that *variety*, which is so agreeable in love: at least, deprive us not of that liberty, which is so essentially requisite. In vain you tell me, that I had my choice of the person, with whom I would conjoin myself. I had my choice, it is true, of my prison; but this is but a small comfort, since it must still be a prison.

Such are the arguments which may be urged in favour of divorces: But there seem to be these three unanswerable objections against them. *First*, What must become of the children, upon the separation of the parents? Must they be committed to the care of a step-mother; and instead of the fond attention and concern of a parent, feel all the indifference or hatred of a stranger or an enemy? These inconveniences are sufficiently felt, where nature has made the divorce by the doom inevitable to all mortals: And shall we seek to multiply those inconveniences, by multiplying divorces,

troublesome to company, by talking too much of them.

The author of the PERSIAN letters has given a different reason for this polite maxim. *Men, says he, never care to mention their wives in company, lest they should talk of them before people, who are better acquainted with them than themselves.*]

and putting it in the power of parents, upon every caprice, to render their posterity miserable?

Secondly, If it be true, on the one hand, that the heart of man naturally delights in liberty, and hates every thing to which it is confined; it is also true, on the other, that the heart of man naturally submits to necessity, and soon loses an inclination, when there appears an absolute impossibility of gratifying it. These principles of human nature, you'll say, are contradictory: But what is man but a heap of contradictions! Though it is remarkable, that, where principles are, after this manner, contrary in their operation, they do not always destroy each other; but the one or the other may predominate on any particular occasion, according as circumstances are more or less favourable to it. For instance, love is a restless and impatient passion, full of caprices and variations: arising in a moment from a feature, from an air, from nothing, and suddenly extinguishing after the same manner. Such a passion requires liberty above all things; and therefore ELOISA had reason, when, in order to preserve this passion, she refused to marry her beloved ABELARD.

> *How oft, when prest to marriage, have I said,*
> *Curse on all laws but those which love has made;*
> *Love, free as air, at sight of human ties,*
> *Spreads his light wings, and in a moment flies.*

But *friendship* is a calm and sedate affection, conducted by reason and cemented by habit; springing from long acquaintance and mutual obligations; without jealousies or fears, and without those feverish fits of heat and cold, which cause such an agreeable torment in the amorous passion. So sober an affection, therefore, as friendship, rather thrives under constraint, and never rises to such a height, as when any strong interest or necessity binds two persons together, and gives them some common object of pursuit.[1] We need not, therefore, be afraid of drawing the marriage-knot, which chiefly subsists by friendship, the closest possible. The amity

---

[1] [Editions C to P add as follows: Let us consider then, whether love or friendship should most predominate in marriage; and we shall soon determine whether liberty or constraint be most favourable to it. The happiest marriages, to be sure, are found where love, by long acquaintance, is consolidated into friendship. Whoever dreams of raptures and extasies beyond the honey-month, is a fool. Even romances themselves, with all their liberty of fiction, are obliged to drop their lovers the very day of their marriage, and find it easier to support the passion for a dozen years under coldness, disdain and difficulties, than a week under possession and security.]

between the persons, where it is solid and sincere, will rather gain by it: And where it is wavering and uncertain, this is the best expedient for fixing it. How many frivolous quarrels and disgusts are there, which people of common prudence endeavour to forget, when they lie under a necessity of passing their lives together; but which would soon be inflamed into the most deadly hatred, were they pursued to the utmost, under the prospect of an easy separation?

In the *third* place, we must consider, that nothing is more dangerous than to unite two persons so closely in all their interests and concerns, as man and wife, without rendering the union entire and total. The least possibility of a separate interest must be the source of endless quarrels and suspicions. [1] The wife, not secure of her establishment, will still be driving some separate end or project; and the husband's selfishness, being accompanied with more power, may be still more dangerous.

Should these reasons against voluntary divorces be deemed insufficient, I hope no body will pretend to refuse the testimony of experience. At the time when divorces were most frequent among the ROMANS, marriages were most rare; and AUGUSTUS was obliged, by penal laws, to force men of fashion into the married state: A circumstance which is scarcely to be found in any other age or nation.[2] The more ancient laws of ROME, which prohibited divorces, are extremely praised by DIONYSIUS HALYCARNASSÆUS.[3] Wonderful was the harmony, says the historian, which this inseparable union of interests produced between married persons; while each of them considered the inevitable necessity by which they were linked together, and abandoned all prospect of any other choice or establishment.

The exclusion of polygamy and divorces sufficiently recommends our present EUROPEAN practice with regard to marriage.

---

[1] [In place of 'The wife, not secure of her establishment, will still be driving some separate end or project,' Editions P to C read: 'What Dr. PARNEL calls, The little pilf'ring temper of a wife, will be doubly ruinous.']

[2] [Editions C and D omit the remainder of the paragraph.]

[3] Lib. ii. 25.

ESSAY XX.—*Of Simplicity and Refinement in Writing.*

FINE writing, according to Mr. ADDISON, consists of sentiments, which are natural, without being obvious. There cannot be a juster, and more concise definition of fine writing

Sentiments, which are merely natural, affect not the mind with any pleasure, and seem not worthy of our attention. The pleasantries of a waterman, the observations of a peasant, the ribaldry of a porter or hackney coachman, all of these are natural, and disagreeable. What an insipid comedy should we make of the chit-chat of the tea-table, copied faithfully and at full length? Nothing can please persons of taste, but nature drawn with all her graces and ornaments, *la belle nature*; or if we copy low life, the strokes must be strong and remarkable, and must convey a lively image to the mind. The absurd naivety[1] of *Sancho Pancho* is represented in such inimitable colours by CERVANTES, that it entertains as much as the picture of the most magnanimous hero or softest lover.

The case is the same with orators, philosophers, critics, or any author who speaks in his own person, without introducing other speakers or actors. If his language be not elegant, his observations uncommon, his sense strong and masculine, he will in vain boast his nature and simplicity. He may be correct; but he never will be agreeable. It is the unhappiness of such authors, that they are never blamed or censured. The good fortune of a book, and that of a man, are not the same. The secret deceiving path of life, which HORACE talks of, *fallentis semita vitæ*, may be the happiest lot of the one; but is the greatest misfortune, which the other can possibly fall into.

On the other hand, productions, which are merely surprising, without being natural, can never give any lasting entertainment to the mind. To draw chimeras is not, properly speaking, to copy or imitate. The justness of the representation is lost, and the mind is displeased to find a picture, which bears no resemblance to any original. Nor are such excessive refinements more agreeable in the epistolary or philosophic style, than in the epic or tragic. Too much

---

[1] [Editions C to K: Naivety, a word which I have borrow'd from the *French*, and which is wanted in our language.]

ornament is a fault in every kind of production. Uncommon expressions, strong flashes of wit, pointed similes, and epigrammatic turns, especially when they recur too frequently, are a disfigurement, rather than any embellishment of discourse. As the eye, in surveying a GOTHIC building, is distracted by the multiplicity of ornaments, and loses the whole by its minute attention to the parts; so the mind, in perusing a work overstocked with wit, is fatigued and disgusted with the constant endeavour to shine and surprize. This is the case where a writer overabounds in wit, even though that wit, in itself, should be just and agreeable. But it commonly happens to such writers, that they seek for their favourite ornaments, even where the subject does not afford them; and by that means, have twenty insipid conceits for one thought which is really beautiful.

There is no subject in critical learning more copious, than this of the just mixture of simplicity and refinement in writing; and therefore, not to wander in too large a field, I shall confine myself to a few general observations on that head.

First, I observe, *That though excesses of both kinds are to be avoided, and though a proper medium ought to be studied in all productions; yet this medium lies not in a point, but admits of a considerable latitude.* Consider the wide distance, in this respect, between Mr. POPE and LUCRETIUS. These seem to lie in the two greatest extremes of refinement and simplicity, in which a poet can indulge himself, without being guilty of any blameable excess. All this interval may be filled with poets, who may differ from each other, but may be equally admirable, each in his peculiar stile and manner. CORNEILLE and CONGREVE, who carry their wit and refinement somewhat farther than Mr. POPE (if poets of so different a kind can be compared together), and SOPHOCLES and TERENCE, who are more simple than LUCRETIUS, seem to have gone out of that medium, in which the most perfect productions are found, and to be guilty of some excess in these opposite characters. Of all the great poets, VIRGIL and RACINE, in my opinion, lie nearest the center, and are the farthest removed from both the extremities.

My *second* observation on this head is, *That it is very difficult, if not impossible, to explain by words, where the just medium lies between the excesses of simplicity and refinement, or to give any rule by which we can know precisely the bounds between the fault and the beauty.* A critic may not only discourse very judiciously on this head, without instructing his readers, but even without understanding the matter perfectly himself. There is not a finer piece of criticism than *the dissertation on pastorals* by FONTENELLE; in which, by a number of reflections and philosophical reasonings, he endeavours to fix the just medium, which is suitable to that species of writing. But let any one read the pastorals of that author, and he will be convinced, that this judicious critic, notwithstanding his fine reasonings, had a false taste, and fixed the point of perfection much nearer the extreme of refinement than pastoral poetry will admit of. The sentiments of his shepherds are better suited to the toilettes of PARIS, than to the forests of ARCADIA. But this it is impossible to discover from his critical reasonings. He blames all excessive painting and ornament as much as VIRGIL could have done, had that great poet writ a dissertation on this species of poetry. However different the tastes of men, their general discourse on these subjects is commonly the same. No criticism can be instructive, which descends not to particulars, and is not full of examples and illustrations. It is allowed on all hands, that beauty, as well as virtue, always lies in a medium; but where this medium is placed, is the great question, and can never be sufficiently explained by general reasonings.

I shall deliver it as a *third* observation on this subject, *That we ought to be more on our guard against the excess of refinement than that of simplicity; and that because the former excess is both less* beautiful, *and more* dangerous *than the latter.*

It is a certain rule, that wit and passion are entirely incompatible. When the affections are moved, there is no place for the imagination. The mind of man being naturally limited, it is impossible that all its faculties can operate at once: And the more any one predominates, the less room is there for the others to exert their vigour. For this reason, a greater degree of simplicity is required in all compositions, where men, and actions, and passions are painted, than in such as consist of reflections and observations. And as the former species of writing is the more engaging and beautiful, one may safely, upon this account, give the preference to the extreme of simplicity above that of refinement.

We may also observe, that those compositions, which we

read the oftenest, and which every man of taste has got by heart, have the recommendation of simplicity, and have nothing surprising in the thought, when divested of that elegance of expression, and harmony of numbers, with which it is cloathed. If the merit of the composition lie in a point of wit; it may strike at first; but the mind anticipates the thought in the second perusal, and is not longer affected by it. When I read an epigram of MARTIAL, the first line recalls the whole; and I have no pleasure in repeating to myself what I know already. But each line, each word in CATULLUS, has its merit; and I am never tired with the perusal of him. It is sufficient to run over COWLEY once: But PARNEL, after the fiftieth reading, is as fresh as at the first. Besides, it is with books as with women, where a certain plainness of manner and of dress is more engaging than that glare of paint and airs and apparel, which may dazzle the eye, but reaches not the affections. TERENCE is a modest and bashful beauty, to whom we grant everything, because he assumes nothing, and whose purity and nature make a durable, though not a violent impression on us.

But refinement, as it is the less *beautiful*, so is it the more *dangerous* extreme, and what we are the aptest to fall into. Simplicity passes for dulness, when it is not accompanied with great elegance and propriety. On the contrary, there is something surprizing in a blaze of wit and conceit. Ordinary readers are mightily struck with it, and falsely imagine it to be the most difficult, as well as most excellent way of writing. SENECA abounds with agreeable faults, says QUINTILIAN, *abundat dulcibus vitiis*; and for that reason is the more dangerous, and the more apt to pervert the taste of the young and inconsiderate.

I shall add, that the excess of refinement is now more to be guarded against than ever; because it is the extreme, which men are the most apt to fall into, after learning has made some progress, and after eminent writers have appeared in every species of composition. The endeavour to please by novelty leads men wide of simplicity and nature, and fills their writings with affectation and conceit. [1] It was thus the ASIATIC eloquence degenerated so much from the ATTIC: It was thus the age of CLAUDIUS and NERO became so much inferior to that of AUGUSTUS in taste and

---

[1] [The first clause of this sentence was added in Edition K.]

genius: And perhaps there are, at present, some symptoms of a like degeneracy of taste, in FRANCE as well as in ENGLAND.

[1] Essay XXI.—*Of National Characters.*

THE vulgar are apt to carry all *national characters* to extremes; and having once established it as a principle, that any people are knavish, or cowardly, or ignorant, they will admit of no exception, but comprehend every individual under the same censure. Men of sense condemn these undistinguishing judgments: Though at the same time, they allow, that each nation has a peculiar set of manners, and that some particular qualities are more frequently to be met with among one people than among their neighbours. The common people in SWITZERLAND have probably more honesty than those of the same rank in IRELAND; and every prudent man will, from that circumstance alone, make a difference in the trust which he reposes in each. We have reason to expect greater wit and gaiety in a FRENCHMAN than in a SPANIARD; though CERVANTES was born in SPAIN. An ENGLISHMAN will naturally be supposed to have more knowledge than a DANE; though TYCHO BRAHE was a native of DENMARK.

Different reasons are assigned for these *national characters*; while some account for them from *moral*, others from *physical* causes. By *moral* causes, I mean all circumstances, which are fitted to work on the mind as motives or reasons, and which render a peculiar set of manners habitual to us. Of this kind are, the nature of the government, the revolutions of public affairs, the plenty or penury in which the people live, the situation of the nation with regard to its neighbours, and such like circumstances. By *physical* causes I mean those qualities of the air and climate, which are supposed to work insensibly on the temper, by altering the tone and habit of the body, and giving a particular complexion, which, though reflection and reason may sometimes overcome it, will yet prevail among the generality of mankind, and have an influence on their manners.

That the character of a nation will much depend on *moral* causes, must be evident to the most superficial observer; since a nation is nothing but a collection of individuals, and

[1] [This Essay was first published in Edition D.]

the manners of individuals are frequently determined by these causes. As poverty and hard labour debase the minds of the common people, and render them unfit for any science and ingenious profession; so where any government becomes very oppressive to all its subjects, it must have a proportional effect on their temper and genius, and must banish all the liberal arts from among them.[1]

The same principle of moral causes fixes the character of different professions, and alters even that disposition, which the particular members receive from the hand of nature. A *soldier* and a *priest* are different characters, in all nations, and all ages; and this difference is founded on circumstances, whose operation is eternal and unalterable.

The uncertainty of their life makes soldiers lavish and generous, as well as brave: Their idleness, together with the large societies, which they form in camps or garrisons, inclines them to pleasure and gallantry: By their frequent change of company, they acquire good breeding and an openness of behaviour: Being employed only against a public and an open enemy, they become candid, honest, and undesigning: And as they use more the labour of the body than that of the mind, they are commonly thoughtless and ignorant.[2]

It is a trite, but not altogether a false maxim, that *priests of all religions are the same*; and though the character of the profession will not, in every instance, prevail over the personal character, yet it is sure always to predominate with the greater number. For as chymists observe, that spirits, when raised to a certain height, are all the same, from whatever material they be extracted; so these men, being elevated above humanity, acquire a uniform character, which is entirely their own, and which, in my opinion, is, generally speaking, not the most amiable that is to be met with in human society. It is, in most points, opposite to that of a soldier; as is the way of life, from which it is derived.[3]

---

[1] [Editions D to P add: Instances of this nature are very frequent in the world.]

[2] It is a saying of MENANDER, Κομψὸς σρατιώτης, οὐδ' ἂν εἰ πλάττει θεὸς Οὐθεὶς γένοιτ' ἄν. MEN. apud STOBÆUM. *It is not in the power even of God to make a polite soldier.* The contrary observation with regard to the manners of soldiers takes place in our days. This seems to me a presumption, that the ancients owed all their refinement and civility to books and study; for which, indeed, a soldier's life is not so well calculated. Company and the world is their sphere. And if there be any politeness to be learned from company, they will certainly have a considerable share of it.

[3] Though all mankind have a strong

As to *physical causes*, I am inclined to doubt altogether of their operation in this particular; nor do I think, that men owe any thing of their temper or genius to the air, food, or climate. I confess, that the contrary opinion may justly, at propensity to religion at certain times and in certain dispositions; yet are there few or none, who have it to that degree, and with that constancy, which is requisite to support the character of this profession. It must, therefore, happen, that clergymen, being drawn from the common mass of mankind, as people are to other employments, by the views of profit, the greater part, though no atheists or free-thinkers, will find it necessary, on particular occasions, to feign more devotion than they are, at that time, possessed of, and to maintain the appearance of fervor and seriousness, even when jaded with the exercises of their religion, or when they have their minds engaged in the common occupations of life. They must not, like the rest of the world, give scope to their natural movements and sentiments: They must set a guard over their looks and words and actions: And in order to support the veneration paid them by the multitude, they must not only keep a remarkable reserve, but must promote the spirit of superstition, by a continued grimace and hypocrisy. This dissimulation often destroys the candor and ingenuity of their temper, and makes an irreparable breach in their character.

If by chance any of them be possessed of a temper more susceptible of devotion than usual, so that he has but little occasion for hypocrisy to support the character of his profession; it is so natural for him to over-rate this advantage, and to think that it atones for every violation of morality, that frequently he is not more virtuous than the hypocrite. And though few dare openly avow those exploded opinions, *that every thing is lawful to the saints,* and *that they alone have property in their goods;* yet may we observe, that these principles lurk in every bosom, and represent a zeal for religious observances as so great a merit, that it may compensate for many vices and enormities. This observation is so common, that all prudent men are on their guard, when they meet with any extraordinary appearance of religion; though at the same time, they confess, that there are many exceptions to this general rule, and that probity and superstition, or even probity and fanaticism, are not altogether and in every instance incompatible.

Most men are ambitious; but the ambition of other men may commonly be satisfied, by excelling in their particular profession, and thereby promoting the interests of society. The ambition of the clergy can often be satisfied only by promoting ignorance and superstition and implicit faith and pious frauds. And having got what ARCHIMEDES only wanted, (namely, another world, on which he could fix his engines) no wonder they move this world at their pleasure.

Most men have an overweening conceit of themselves; but *these* have a peculiar temptation to that vice, who are regarded with such veneration, and are even deemed sacred, by the ignorant multitude.

Most men are apt to bear a particular regard for members of their own profession; but as a lawyer, or physician, or merchant, does, each of them, follow out his business apart, the interests of men of these professions are not so closely united as the interests of clergymen of the same religion; where the whole body gains by the veneration, paid to their common tenets, and by the suppression of antagonists.

Few men can bear contradiction with patience; but the clergy too often proceed even to a degree of fury on this head: Because all their credit and livelihood depend upon the belief, which their opinions meet with; and they alone pretend to a divine and supernatural authority, or have any colour for representing their antagonists as impious and prophane. The *Odium Theologicum,* or Theological Hatred, is noted even to a proverb, and means that degree of rancour, which is the most furious and implacable.

Revenge is a natural passion to mankind; but seems to reign with the greatest force in priests and women: Because, being deprived of the immediate exertion of anger, in violence and combat, they are apt to fancy themselves despised on that account; and

first sight, seem probable; since we find, that these circumstances have an influence over every other animal, and that even those creatures, which are fitted to live in all climates, such as dogs, horses, &c. do not attain the same perfection in all. The courage of bull-dogs and gamecocks seems peculiar to ENGLAND. FLANDERS is remarkable for large and heavy horses: Spain for horses light, and of good mettle. And any breed of these creatures, transplanted from one country to another, will soon lose the qualities, which they derived from their native climate. It may be asked, why not the same with men?[1]

There are few questions more curious than this, or which will oftener occur in our enquiries concerning human

their pride supports their vindictive disposition. [This paragraph was added in Edition K.]

Thus many of the vices of human nature are, by fixed moral causes, inflamed in that possession; and though several individuals escape the contagion, yet all wise governments will be on their guard against the attempts of a society, who will for ever combine into one faction, and while it acts as a society, will for ever be actuated by ambition, pride, revenge, and a persecuting spirit.

The temper of religion is grave and serious; and this is the character required of priests, which confines them to strict rules of decency, and commonly prevents irregularity and intemperance amongst them. The gaiety, much less the excesses of pleasure, is not permitted in that body; and this virtue is, perhaps, the only one which they owe to their profession. In religions, indeed, founded on speculative principles, and where public discourses make a part of religious service, it may also be supposed that the clergy will have a considerable share in the learning of the times; though it is certain that their taste in eloquence will always be greater than their proficiency in reasoning and philosophy. But whoever possesses the other noble virtues of humanity, meekness, and moderation, as very many of them, no doubt, do, is beholden for them to nature or reflection, not to the genius of his calling.

It was no bad expedient in the old ROMANS, for preventing the strong effect of the priestly character, to make it a law that no one should be received into the sacerdotal office, till he was past fifty years of age, DION. *Hal.* lib. ii. 21. The living a layman till that age, it is presumed, would be able to fix the character. [This paragraph was added in Edition K.]

[1] CÆSAR (*de Bell.* GALLICO, lib. 4. 2.) says that the GALLIC horses were very good; the GERMAN very bad. We find in lib. 7. 65. that he was obliged to remount some GERMAN cavalry with GALLIC horses. At present, no part of EUROPE has so bad horses of all kinds as FRANCE: But GERMANY abounds with excellent war horses. This may beget a little suspicion, that even animals depend not on the climate; but on the different breeds, and on the skill and care in rearing them. The north of ENGLAND abounds in the best horses of all kinds which are in the world. In the neighbouring counties, north side the TWEED, no good horses of any kind are to be met with. STRABO, lib. 2. 103. rejects, in a great measure, the influence of climate upon men. All is custom and education, says he. It is not from nature, that the ATHENIANS are learned, the LACEDEMONIANS ignorant, and the THEBANS too, who are still nearer neighbours to the former. Even the difference of animals, he adds, depends not on climate. [This note is not in Edition D.]

---

[1] [This paragraph is not in Edition D.]

affairs; and therefore it may be proper to give it a full examination.

The human mind is of a very imitative nature; nor is it possible for any set of men to converse often together, without acquiring a similitude of manners, and communicating to each other their vices as well as virtues. The propensity to company and society is strong in all rational creatures; and the same disposition, which gives us this propensity, makes us enter deeply into each other's sentiments, and causes like passions and inclinations to run, as it were, by contagion, through the whole club or knot of companions. Where a number of men are united into one political body, the occasions of their intercourse must be so frequent, for defence, commerce, and government, that, together with the same speech or language, they must acquire a resemblance in their manners, and have a common or national character, as well as a personal one, peculiar to each individual. Now though nature produces all kinds of temper and understanding in great abundance, it does not follow, that she always produces them in like proportions, and that in every society the ingredients of industry and indolence, valour and cowardice, humanity and brutality, wisdom and folly, will be mixed after the same manner. In the infancy of society, if any of these dispositions be found in greater abundance than the rest, it will naturally prevail in the composition, and give a tincture to the national character. Or should it be asserted, that no species of temper can reasonably be presumed to predominate, even in those contracted societies, and that the same proportions will always be preserved in the mixture; yet surely the persons in credit and authority, being still a more contracted body, cannot always be presumed to be of the same character; and their influence on the manners of the people, must, at all times, be very considerable. If on the first establishment of a republic, a BRUTUS should be placed in authority, and be transported with such an enthusiasm for liberty and public good, as to overlook all the ties of nature, as well as private interest, such an illustrious example will naturally have an effect on the whole society, and kindle the same passion in every bosom. Whatever it be that forms the manners of one generation, the next must imbibe a deeper tincture of the same dye; men being more susceptible of all impressions during infancy, and retaining these impressions as long as they remain in the world. I assert, then, that all national characters, where they depend not on fixed *moral* causes, proceed from such accidents as these, and that physical causes have no discernible operation on the human mind. [1]It is a maxim in all philosophy, that causes which do not appear, are to be considered as not existing.

If we run over the globe, or revolve the annals of history, we shall discover every where signs of a sympathy or contagion of manners, none of the influence of air or climate.

First. We may observe, that, where a very extensive government has been established for many centuries, it spreads a national character over the whole empire, and communicates to every part a similarity of manners. Thus the CHINESE have the greatest uniformity of character imaginable: though the air and climate in different parts of those vast dominions, admit of very considerable variations.

Secondly. In small governments, which are contiguous, the people have notwithstanding a different character, and are often as distinguishable in their manners as the most distant nations. ATHENS and THEBES were but a short day's journey from each other; though the ATHENIANS were as remarkable for ingenuity, politeness, and gaiety, as the THEBANS for dulness, rusticity, and a phlegmatic temper. PLUTARCH, discoursing of the effects of air on the minds of men, observes, that the inhabitants of the PIRÆUM possessed very different tempers from those of the higher town in ATHENS, which was distant about four miles from the former: But I believe no one attributes the difference of manners in WAPPING and St. JAMES'S, to a difference of air or climate.

Thirdly. The same national character commonly follows the authority of government to a precise boundary; and upon crossing a river or passing a mountain, one finds a new set of manners, with a new government. The LANGUEDOCIANS and GASCONS are the gayest people in FRANCE; but whenever you pass the PYRENEES, you are among SPANIARDS. Is it conceivable, that the qualities of the air should change exactly with the limits of an empire, which depend so much on the accidents of battles, negociations, and marriages?

[1] [This sentence was added in Edition Q.]

Fourthly. Where any set of men, scattered over distant nations, maintain a close society or communication together, they acquire a similitude of manners, and have but little in common with the nations amongst whom they live. Thus the JEWS in EUROPE, and the ARMENIANS in the east, have a peculiar character; and the former are as much noted for fraud, as the latter for probity.[1] The *Jesuits*, in all *Roman-catholic* countries, are also observed to have a character peculiar to themselves.

Fifthly. Where any accident, as a difference in language or religion, keeps two nations inhabiting the same country, from mixing with each other, they will preserve, during several centuries, a distinct and even opposite set of manners. The integrity, gravity, and bravery of the TURKS, form an exact contrast to the deceit, levity, and cowardice of the modern GREEKS.

Sixthly. The same set of manners will follow a nation, and adhere to them over the whole globe, as well as the same laws and language. The SPANISH, ENGLISH, FRENCH and DUTCH colonies are all distinguishable even between the tropics.

Seventhly. The manners of a people change very considerably from one age to another, either by great alterations in their government, by the mixtures of new people, or by that inconstancy, to which all human affairs are subject. The ingenuity, industry, and activity of the ancient GREEKS have nothing in common with the stupidity and indolence of the present inhabitants of those regions. Candour, bravery, and love of liberty formed the character of the ancient ROMANS; as subtilty, cowardice, and a slavish disposition do that of the modern. The old SPANIARDS were restless, turbulent, and so addicted to war, that many of them killed themselves, when deprived of their arms by the ROMANS.[2] One would find an equal difficulty at present, (at least one would have found it fifty years ago) to rouze up the modern SPANIARDS to arms. The BATAVIANS were all soldiers of fortune, and

---

[1] A small sect or society amidst a greater are commonly most regular in their morals; because they are more remarked, and the faults of individuals draw dishonour on the whole. The only exception to this rule is, when the superstition and prejudices of the large society are so strong as to throw an infamy on the smaller society, independent of their morals. For in that case, having no character either to save or gain, they become careless of their behaviour, except among themselves. [This note was added in Edition K.]

[2] TIT. LIVII, lib. xxxiv. cap. 17.

hired themselves into the ROMAN armies. Their posterity make use of foreigners for the same purpose that the ROMANS did their ancestors. Though some few strokes of the FRENCH character be the same with that which CÆSAR has ascribed to the Gauls: yet what comparison between the civility, humanity, and knowledge of the modern inhabitants of that country, and the ignorance, barbarity, and grossness of the ancient? [1] Not to insist upon the great difference between the present possessors of BRITAIN, and those before the Roman conquest; we may observe that our ancestors, a few centuries ago, were sunk into the most abject superstition, last century they were inflamed with the most furious enthusiasm, and are now settled into the most cool indifference with regard to religious matters, that is to be found in any nation of the world.

Eighthly. Where several neighbouring nations have a very close communication together, either by policy, commerce, or travelling, they acquire a similitude of manners, proportioned to the communication. Thus all the Franks appear to have a uniform character to the eastern nations. The differences among them are like the peculiar accents of different provinces, which are not distinguishable, except by an ear accustomed to them, and which commonly escape a foreigner.

Ninthly. We may often remark a wonderful mixture of manners and characters in the same nation, speaking the same language, and subject to the same government: And in this particular the ENGLISH are the most remarkable of any people, that perhaps ever were in the world. Nor is this to be ascribed to the mutability and uncertainty of their climate, or to any other *physical* causes; since all these causes take place in the neighbouring country of SCOTLAND, without having the same effect. Where the government of a nation is altogether republican, it is apt to beget a peculiar set of manners. Where it is altogether monarchical, it is more apt to have the same effect; the imitation of superiors spreading the national manners faster among the people. If the governing part of a state consist altogether of merchants, as in HOLLAND, their uniform way of life will fix their character. If it consists chiefly of nobles and landed gentry, like GERMANY, FRANCE, and SPAIN, the same effect follows. The genius of a particular sect or religion is also apt to mould

[1] [This sentence was added in Edition K.]

the manners of a people. But the ENGLISH government is a mixture of monarchy, aristocracy, and democracy. The people in authority are composed of gentry and merchants. All sects of religion are to be found among them. And the great liberty and independency, which every man enjoys, allows him to display the manners peculiar to him. Hence the ENGLISH, of any people in the universe, have the least of a national character; unless this very singularity may pass for such.

If the characters of men depend on the air and climate, the degrees of heat and cold should naturally be expected to have a mighty influence; since nothing has a greater effect on all plants and irrational animals. And indeed there is some reason to think, that all the nations, which live beyond the polar circles or between the tropics, are inferior to the rest of the species, and are incapable of all the higher attainments of the human mind. The poverty and misery of the northern inhabitants of the globe, and the indolence of the southern, from their few necessities, may, perhaps, account for this remarkable difference, without our having recourse to *physical* causes. This however is certain, that the characters of nations are very promiscuous in the temperate climates, and that almost all the general observations, which have been formed of the more southern or more northern people in these climates, are found to be uncertain and fallacious.[1]

Shall we say, that the neighbourhood of the sun inflames the imagination of men, and gives it a peculiar spirit and vivacity. The FRENCH, GREEKS, EGYPTIANS, and PERSIANS are remarkable for gaiety. The SPANIARDS, TURKS, and

---

[1] I am apt to suspect the negroes, and in general all the other species of men (for there are four or five different kinds) to be naturally inferior to the whites. There never was a civilized nation of any other complexion than white, nor even any individual eminent either in action or speculation. No ingenious manufactures amongst them, no arts, no sciences. On the other hand, the most rude and barbarous of the whites, such as the ancient GERMANS, the present TARTARS, have still something eminent about them, in their valour, form of government, or some other particular. Such a uniform and constant difference could not happen, in so many countries and ages, if nature had not made an original distinction betwixt these breeds of men. Not to mention our colonies, there are NEGROE slaves dispersed all over EUROPE, of which none ever discovered any symptoms of ingenuity; tho' low people, without education, will start up amongst us, and distinguish themselves in every profession. In JAMAICA indeed they talk of one negroe as a man of parts and learning; but 'tis likely he is admired for very slender accomplishments, like a parrot, who speaks a few words plainly. [This note was added in Edition K.]

CHINESE are noted for gravity and a serious deportment, without any such difference of climate as to produce this difference of temper.

The GREEKS and ROMANS, who called all other nations barbarians, confined genius and a fine understanding to the more southern climates, and pronounced the northern nations incapable of all knowledge and civility. But our island has produced as great men, either for action or learning, as GREECE or ITALY has to boast of.

It is pretended, that the sentiments of men become more delicate as the country approaches nearer to the sun; and that the taste of beauty and elegance receives proportional improvements in every latitude; as we may particularly observe of the languages, of which the more southern are smooth and melodious, the northern harsh and untuneable. But this observation holds not universally. The ARABIC is uncouth and disagreeable: The MUSCOVITE soft and musical. Energy, strength, and harshness form the character of the LATIN tongue: The ITALIAN is the most liquid, smooth, and effeminate language that can possibly be imagined. Every language will depend somewhat on the manners of the people; but much more on that original stock of words and sounds, which they received from their ancestors, and which remain unchangeable, even while their manners admit of the greatest alterations. Who can doubt, but the English are at present a more polite and knowing people than the GREEKS were for several ages after the siege of Troy? Yet is there no comparison between the language of MILTON and that of HOMER. Nay, the greater are the alterations and improvements, which happen in the manners of a people, the less can be expected in their language. A few eminent and refined geniuses will communicate their taste and knowledge to a whole people, and produce the greatest improvements; but they fix the tongue by their writings, and prevent, in some degree, its farther changes.

Lord BACON has observed, that the inhabitants of the south are, in general, more ingenious than those of the north; but that, where the native of a cold climate has genius, he rises to a higher pitch than can be reached by the southern wits. This observation a late[1] writer confirms, by comparing the southern wits to cucumbers, which are commonly all good in

---

[1] Dr. Berkeley: Minute Philosopher.

their kind; but at best are an insipid fruit: While the northern geniuses are like melons, of which not one in fifty is good; but when it is so, it has an exquisite relish. I believe this remark may be allowed just, when confined to the EUROPEAN nations, and to the present age, or rather to the preceding one: But I think it may be accounted for from moral causes. All the sciences and liberal arts have been imported to us from the south; and it is easy to imagine, that, in the first order of application, when excited by emulation and by glory, the few, who were addicted to them, would carry them to the greatest height, and stretch every nerve, and every faculty, to reach the pinnacle of perfection. Such illustrious examples spread knowledge everywhere, and begot an universal esteem for the sciences: After which it is no wonder, that industry relaxes; while men meet not with suitable encouragement, nor arrive at such distinction by their attainments. The universal diffusion of learning among a people, and the entire banishment of gross ignorance and rusticity, is, therefore, seldom attended with any remarkable perfection in particular persons. [1] It seems to be taken for granted in the dialogue *de Oratoribus*, that knowledge was much more common in VESPASIAN'S age than in that of CICERO and AUGUSTUS. QUINTILIAN also complains of the profanation of learning, by its becoming too common. 'Formerly,' says JUVENAL, 'science was confined to GREECE and ITALY. Now the whole world emulates ATHENS and ROME. Eloquent GAUL has taught BRITAIN, knowing in the laws. Even THULE entertains thoughts of hiring rhetoricians for its instruction.'[2] This state of learning is remarkable; because JUVENAL is himself the last of the ROMAN writers, that possessed any degree of genius. Those, who succeeded, are valued for nothing but the matters of fact, of which they give us information. I hope the late conversion of MUSCOVY to the study of the sciences will not prove a like prognostic to the present period of learning.

Cardinal BENTIVOGLIO gives the preference to the northern nations above the southern with regard to candour and sin-

[1] [This sentence and the next were added in Edition K.]

[2] "Sed Cantaber unde Stoicus? antiqui præsertim ætate Metelli. Nunc totus GRAIAS, nostrasque habet orbis ATHENAS. GALLIA causidicos docuit facunda BRITANNOS: De conducendo loquitur jam rhetore THULE." Sat. 15. 108.

cerity; and mentions, on the one hand, the SPANIARDS and ITALIANS, and on the other, the FLEMINGS and GERMANS. But I am apt to think, that this has happened by accident. The ancient ROMANS seem to have been a candid sincere people, as are the modern TURKS. But if we must needs suppose, that this event has arisen from fixed causes, we may only conclude from it, that all extremes are apt to concur, and are commonly attended with the same consequences. Treachery is the usual concomitant of ignorance and barbarism; and if civilised nations ever embrace subtle and crooked politics, it is from an excess of refinement, which makes them disdain the plain direct path to power and glory.

Most conquests have gone from north to south; and it has hence been inferred, that the northern nations possess a superior degree of courage and ferocity. But it would have been juster to have said, that most conquests are made by poverty and want upon plenty and riches. The SARACENS, leaving the deserts of ARABIA, carried their conquests northwards upon all the fertile provinces of the ROMAN empire; and met the TURKS half way, who were coming southwards from the deserts of TARTARY.

An eminent writer [1] has remarked, that all courageous animals are also carnivorous, and that greater courage is to be expected in a people, such as the ENGLISH, whose food is strong and hearty, than in the half-starved commonalty of other countries. But the SWEDES, notwithstanding their disadvantages in this particular, are not inferior, in martial courage, to any nation that ever was in the world.

In general, we may observe, that courage, of all national qualities, is the most precarious; because it is exerted only at intervals, and by a few in every nation; whereas industry, knowledge, civility, may be of constant and universal use, and for several ages, may become habitual to the whole people. If courage be preserved, it must be by discipline, example, and opinion. The tenth legion of CÆSAR, and the regiment of PICARDY in FRANCE were formed promiscuously from among the citizens; but having once entertained a notion, that they were the best troops in the service, this very opinion really made them such.

As a proof how much courage depends on opinion, we may observe, that, of the two chief tribes of the GREEKS, the

[1] Sir WILLIAM TEMPLE's account of the Netherlands.

DORIANS, and IONIANS, the former were always esteemed, and always appeared more brave and manly than the latter; though the colonies of both the tribes were interspersed and intermingled throughout all the extent of GREECE, the Lesser ASIA, SICILY, ITALY, and the islands of the ÆGEAN sea. The ATHENIANS were the only IONIANS that ever had any reputation for valour or military achievements; though even these were deemed inferior to the LACEDEMONIANS, the bravest of the DORIANS.

The only observation, with regard to the difference of men in different climates, on which we can rest any weight, is the vulgar one, that people in the northern regions have a greater inclination to strong liquors, and those in the southern to love and women. One can assign a very probable *physical* cause for this difference. Wine and distilled waters warm the frozen blood in the colder climates, and fortify men against the injuries of the weather: As the genial heat of the sun, in the countries exposed to his beams, inflames the blood, and exalts the passion between the sexes.

Perhaps too, the matter may be accounted for by *moral* causes. All strong liquors are rarer in the north, and consequently are more coveted. DIODORUS SICULUS[1] tells us, that the GAULS in his time were great drunkards, and much addicted to wine; chiefly, I suppose, from its rarity and novelty. On the other hand, the heat in the southern climates, obliging men and women to go half naked, thereby renders their frequent commerce more dangerous, and inflames their mutual passion. This makes parents and husbands more jealous and reserved; which still further inflames the passion. Not to mention, that, as women ripen sooner in the southern regions, it is necessary to observe greater jealousy and care in their education; it being evident, that a girl of twelve cannot possess equal discretion to govern this passion, with one who feels not its violence till she be seventeen or eighteen. [2]Nothing so much encourages

---

[1] *Lib.* v. 26. The same author ascribes taciturnity to that people; a new proof that national characters may alter very much. ¹ Taciturnity, as a national character, implies unsociableness. ARISTOTLE in his Politics, book ii. cap. 9. says, that the GAULS are the only warlike nation, who are negligent of women.

[2] [This sentence was added in Edition R.]

---

[1] [This sentence was added in Edition K; and the next in Edition M.]

the passion of love as ease and leisure, or is more destructive to it than industry and hard labour; and as the necessities of men are evidently fewer in the warm climates than in the cold ones, this circumstance alone may make a considerable difference between them.

But perhaps the fact is doubtful, that nature has, either from moral or physical causes, distributed these respective inclinations to the different climates. The ancient GREEKS, though born in a warm climate, seem to have been much addicted to the bottle; nor were their parties of pleasure anything but matches of drinking among men, who passed their time altogether apart from the fair. Yet when ALEXANDER led the GREEKS into PERSIA, a still more southern climate, they multiplied their debauches of this kind, in imitation of the PERSIAN manners.[1] So honourable was the character of a drunkard among the PERSIANS, that CYRUS the younger, soliciting the sober LACEDEMONIANS for succour against his brother ARTAXERXES, claims it chiefly on account of his superior endowments, as more valorous, more bountiful, and a better drinker.[2] DARIUS HYSTASPES made it be inscribed on his tombstone, among his other virtues and princely qualities, that no one could bear a greater quantity of liquor. You may obtain any thing of the NEGROES by offering them strong drink; and may easily prevail with them to sell, not only their children, but their wives and mistresses, for a cask of brandy. In FRANCE and ITALY few drink pure wine, except in the greatest heats of summer; and indeed, it is then almost as necessary, in order to recruit the spirits, evaporated by heat, as it is in SWEDEN, during the winter, in order to warm the bodies congealed by the rigour of the season.

If jealousy be regarded as a proof of an amorous disposition, no people were more jealous than the MUSCOVITES, before their communication with EUROPE had somewhat altered their manners in this particular.

But supposing the fact true, that nature, by physical principles, has regularly distributed these two passions, the one to the northern, the other to the southern regions; we can only infer, that the climate may affect the grosser and more bodily organs of our frame; not that it can work upon those

[1] BABYLONII *maxime in vinum, & quæ ebrietatem sequuntur, effusi sunt.* QUINT. CUR lib. v. cap. i.
[2] PLUT. SYMP. lib. i. quæst. 4.

finer organs, on which the operations of the mind and understanding depend. And this is agreeable to the analogy of nature. The races of animals never degenerate when carefully tended; and horses, in particular, always show their blood in their shape, spirit, and swiftness: But a coxcomb may beget a philosopher; as a man of virtue may leave a worthless progeny.

I shall conclude this subject with observing, that though the passion for liquor be more brutal and debasing than love, which, when properly managed, is the source of all politeness and refinement; yet this gives not so great an advantage to the southern climates, as we may be apt, at first sight, to imagine. When love goes beyond a certain pitch, it renders men jealous, and cuts off the free intercourse between the sexes, on which the politeness of a nation will commonly much depend. And if we would subtilize and refine upon this point, we might observe, that the people, in very temperate climates, are the most likely to attain all sorts of improvement; their blood not being so inflamed as to render them jealous, and yet being warm enough to make them set a due value on the charms and endowments of the fair sex.

[1] Essay XXII.—*Of Tragedy.*

It seems an unaccountable pleasure, which the spectators of a well-written tragedy receive from sorrow, terror, anxiety, and other passions, that are in themselves disagreeable and uneasy. The more they are touched and affected, the more are they delighted with the spectacle; and as soon as the uneasy passions cease to operate, the piece is at an end. One scene of full joy and contentment and security is the utmost, that any composition of this kind can bear; and it is sure always to be the concluding one. If, in the texture of the piece, there be interwoven any scenes of satisfaction, they afford only faint gleams of pleasure, which are thrown in by way of variety, and in order to plunge the actors into deeper distress, by means of that contrast and disappointment. The whole heart of the poet is employed, in rouzing and supporting the compassion and indignation, the anxiety and resentment of his audience. They are pleased in proportion as they are afflicted, and never are so happy as when they employ tears, sobs, and cries to give vent to their sor-

[1] [This Essay was first published in Edition L.]

row, and relieve their heart, swoln with the tenderest sympathy and compassion.

The few critics who have had some tincture of philosophy, have remarked this singular phænomenon, and have endeavoured to account for it.

L'Abbe DUBOS, in his reflections on poetry and painting, asserts, that nothing is in general so disagreeable to the mind as the languid, listless state of indolence, into which it falls upon the removal of all passion and occupation. To get rid of this painful situation, it seeks every amusement and pursuit; business, gaming, shews, executions; whatever will rouze the passions, and take its attention from itself. No matter what the passion is: Let it be disagreeable, afflicting, melancholy, disordered; it is still better than that insipid languor, which arises from perfect tranquillity and repose.

It is impossible not to admit this account, as being, at least in part, satisfactory. You may observe, when there are several tables of gaming, that all the company run to those, where the deepest play is, even though they find not there the best players. The view, or, at least, imagination of high passions, arising from great loss or gain, affects the spectator by sympathy, gives him some touches of the same passions, and serves him for a momentary entertainment. It makes the time pass the easier with him, and is some relief to that oppression, under which men commonly labour, when left entirely to their own thoughts and meditations.

We find that common liars always magnify, in their narrations, all kinds of danger, pain, distress, sickness, deaths, murders, and cruelties; as well as joy, beauty, mirth, and magnificence. It is an absurd secret, which they have for pleasing their company, fixing their attention, and attaching them to such marvellous relations, by the passions and emotions, which they excite.

There is, however, a difficulty in applying to the present subject, in its full extent, this solution, however ingenious and satisfactory it may appear. It is certain, that the same object of distress, which pleases in a tragedy, were it really set before us, would give the most unfeigned uneasiness; though it be then the most effectual cure to languor and indolence. Monsieur FONTENELLE seems to have been sensible of this difficulty; and accordingly attempts another solution of the phænomenon; at least makes some addition to the theory above mentioned.[1]

'Pleasure and pain,' says he, 'which are two sentiments so different in themselves, differ not so much in their cause. From the instance of tickling, it appears, that the movement of pleasure, pushed a little too far, becomes pain; and that the movement of pain, a little moderated, becomes pleasure. Hence it proceeds, that there is such a thing as a sorrow, soft and agreeable: It is a pain weakened and diminished. The heart likes naturally to be moved and affected. Melancholy objects suit it, and even disastrous and sorrowful, provided they are softened by some circumstance. It is certain, that, on the theatre, the representation has almost the effect of reality; yet it has not altogether that effect. However we may be hurried away by the spectacle; whatever dominion the senses and imagination may usurp over the reason, there still lurks at the bottom a certain idea of falsehood in the whole of what we see. This idea, though weak and disguised, suffices to diminish the pain which we suffer from the misfortunes of those whom we love, and to reduce that affliction to such a pitch as converts it into a pleasure. We weep for the misfortune of a hero, to whom we are attached. In the same instant we comfort ourselves, by reflecting, that it is nothing but a fiction: And it is precisely that mixture of sentiments, which composes an agreeable sorrow, and tears that delight us. But as that affliction, which is caused by exterior and sensible objects, is stronger than the consolation which arises from an internal reflection, they are the effects and symptoms of sorrow, that ought to predominate in the composition.'

This solution seems just and convincing; but perhaps it wants still some new addition, in order to make it answer fully the phænomenon, which we here examine. All the passions, excited by eloquence, are agreeable in the highest degree, as well as those which are moved by painting and the theatre. The epilogues of CICERO are, on this account chiefly, the delight of every reader of taste; and it is difficult to read some of them without the deepest sympathy and sorrow. His merit as an orator, no doubt, depends much on his success in this particular. When he had raised tears in

[1] Reflexions sur la poetique, § 36.

his judges and all his audience, they were then the most highly delighted, and expressed the greatest satisfaction with the pleader. The pathetic description of the butchery, made by VERRES of the SICILIAN captains, is a masterpiece of this kind: But I believe none will affirm, that the being present at a melancholy scene of that nature would afford any entertainment. Neither is the sorrow here softened by fiction: For the audience were convinced of the reality of every circumstance. What is it then, which in this case raises a pleasure from the bosom of uneasiness, so to speak; and a pleasure, which still retains all the features and outward symptoms of distress and sorrow?

I answer: This extraordinary effect proceeds from that very eloquence, with which the melancholy scene is represented. The genius required to paint objects in a lively manner, the art employed in collecting all the pathetic circumstances, the judgment displayed in disposing them: the exercise, I say, of these noble talents, together with the force of expression, and beauty of oratorial numbers, diffuse the highest satisfaction on the audience, and excite the most delightful movements. By this means, the uneasiness of the melancholy passions is not only overpowered and effaced by something stronger of an opposite kind; but the whole impulse of those passions is converted into pleasure, and swells the delight which the eloquence raises in us. The same force of oratory, employed on an uninteresting subject, would not please half so much, or rather would appear altogether ridiculous; and the mind, being left in absolute calmness and indifference, would relish none of those beauties of imagination or expression, which, if joined to passion, give it such exquisite entertainment. The impulse or vehemence, arising from sorrow, compassion, indignation, receives a new direction from the sentiments of beauty. The latter, being the predominant emotion, seize the whole mind, and convert the former into themselves, at least tincture them so strongly as totally to alter their nature. And the soul, being, at the same time, rouzed by passion, and charmed by eloquence, feels on the whole a strong movement, which is altogether delightful.

The same principle takes place in tragedy; with this addition, that tragedy is an imitation; and imitation is always of itself agreeable. This circumstance serves still farther to smooth the motions of passion, and convert the whole feeling into one uniform and strong enjoyment. Objects of the greatest terror and distress please in painting, and please more than the most beautiful objects, that appear calm and indifferent.[1] The affection, rouzing the mind, excites a large stock of spirit and vehemence; which is all transformed into pleasure by the force of the prevailing movement. It is thus the fiction of tragedy softens the passion, by an infusion of a new feeling, not merely by weakening or diminishing the sorrow. You may by degrees weaken a real sorrow, till it totally disappears; yet in none of its graduations will it ever give pleasure; except, perhaps, by accident, to a man sunk under lethargic indolence, whom it rouzes from that languid state.

To confirm this theory, it will be sufficient to produce other instances, where the subordinate movement is converted into the predominant, and gives force to it, though of a different, and even sometimes though of a contrary nature.

Novelty naturally rouzes the mind, and attracts our attention; and the movements, which it causes, are always converted into any passion, belonging to the object, and join their force to it. Whether an event excite joy or sorrow, pride or shame, anger or good-will, it is sure to produce a stronger affection, when new or unusual. And though novelty of itself be agreeable, it fortifies the painful, as well as agreeable passions.

Had you any intention to move a person extremely by the narration of any event, the best method of encreasing its effect would be artfully to delay informing him of it, and first to excite his curiosity and impatience before you let him into the secret. This is the artifice practised by IAGO in the famous scene of SHAKESPEARE; and every spectator is sensible, that OTHELLO's jealousy acquires additional force from his preceding impatience, and that the subordinate passion is here readily transformed into the predominant one.

Difficulties encrease passions of every kind; and by rouz-

---

[1] Painters make no scruple of representing distress and sorrow as well as any other passion: But they seem not to dwell so much on these melancholy affections as the poets, who, tho' they copy every emotion of the human breast, yet pass very quickly over the agreeable sentiments. A painter represents only one instant; and if that be passionate enough, it is sure to affect and delight the spectator: But nothing can furnish to the poet a variety of scenes and incidents and sentiments, except distress, terror, or anxiety. Compleat joy and satisfaction is attended with security, and leaves no farther room for action.

ing our attention, and exciting our active powers, they produce an emotion, which nourishes the prevailing affection.

Parents commonly love that child most, whose sickly infirm frame of body has occasioned them the greatest pains, trouble, and anxiety in rearing him. The agreeable sentiment of affection here acquires force from sentiments of uneasiness.

Nothing endears so much a friend as sorrow for his death. The pleasure of his company has not so powerful an influence.

Jealousy is a painful passion; yet without some share of it, the agreeable affection of love has difficulty to subsist in its full force and violence. Absence is also a great source of complaint among lovers, and gives them the greatest uneasiness: Yet nothing is more favourable to their mutual passion than short intervals of that kind. And if long intervals often prove fatal, it is only because, through time, men are accustomed to them, and they cease to give uneasiness. Jealousy and absence in love compose the *dolce peccante* of the ITALIANS, which they suppose so essential to all pleasure.

There is a fine observation of the elder PLINY, which illustrates the principle here insisted on. *It is very remarkable, says he, that the last works of celebrated artists, which they left imperfect, are always the most prized, such as the* IRIS *of* ARISTIDES, *the* TYNDARIDES *of* NICOMACHUS, *the* MEDEA *of* TIMOMACHUS, *and the* VENUS *of* APELLES. *These are valued even above their finished productions: The broken lineaments of the piece, and the half-formed idea of the painter are carefully studied; and our very grief for that curious hand, which had been stopped by death, is an additional encrease to our pleasure.*[1]

These instances (and many more might be collected) are sufficient to afford us some insight into the analogy of nature, and to show us, that the pleasure, which poets, orators, and musicians give us, by exciting grief, sorrow, indignation, compassion, is not so extraordinary or paradoxical, as it may at first sight appear. The force of imagination, the energy

---

[1] Illud vero perquam rarum ac memoria dignum, etiam suprema opera artificum, imperfectasque tabulas, sicut, IRIN ARISTIDIS, TYNDARIDAS NICOMACHI, MEDEAM TIMOMACHI, & quam diximus VENEREM APELLIS, in majori admiratione esse quam perfecta. Quippe in iis lineamenta reliqua, ipsæque cogitationes artificum spectantur, atque in lenocinio commendationis dolor est manus, cum id ageret, extinctæ. Lib. xxxv. cap. 11.

of expression, the power of numbers, the charms of imitation; all these are naturally, of themselves, delightful to the mind: And when the object presented lays also hold of some affection, the pleasure still rises upon us, by the conversion of this subordinate movement into that which is predominant. The passion, though, perhaps, naturally, and when excited by the simple appearance of a real object, it may be painful; yet is so smoothed, and softened, and mollified, when raised by the finer arts, that it affords the highest entertainment.

To confirm this reasoning, we may observe, that if the movements of the imagination be not predominant above those of the passion, a contrary effect follows; and the former, being now subordinate, is converted into the latter and still farther encreases the pain and affliction of the sufferer.

Who could ever think of it as a good expedient for comforting an afflicted parent, to exaggerate, with all the force of elocution, the irreparable loss, which he has met with by the death of a favourite child? The more power of imagination and expression you here employ, the more you encrease his despair and affliction.

The shame, confusion, and terror of VERRES, no doubt, rose in proportion to the noble eloquence and vehemence of CICERO: So also did his pain and uneasiness. These former passions were too strong for the pleasure arising from the beauties of elocution; and operated, though from the same principle, yet in a contrary manner, to the sympathy, compassion, and indignation of the audience.

Lord CLARENDON, when he approaches towards the catastrophe of the royal party, supposes, that his narration must then become infinitely disagreeable; and he hurries over the king's death, without giving us one circumstance of it. He considers it as too horrid a scene to be contemplated with any satisfaction, or even without the utmost pain and aversion. He himself, as well as the readers of that age, were too deeply concerned in the events, and felt a pain from subjects, which an historian and a reader of another age would regard as the most pathetic and most interesting, and, by consequence, the most agreeable.

An action, represented in tragedy, may be too bloody and atrocious. It may excite such movements of horror as will not soften into pleasure; and the greatest energy of expression, bestowed on descriptions of that nature, serves only to augment our uneasiness. Such is that action represented in the *Ambitious Stepmother*, where a venerable old man, raised to the height of fury and despair, rushes against a pillar, and striking his head upon it, besmears it all over with mingled brains and gore. The ENGLISH theatre abounds too much with such shocking images.

Even the common sentiments of compassion require to be softened by some agreeable affection, in order to give a thorough satisfaction to the audience. The mere suffering of plaintive virtue, under the triumphant tyranny and oppression of vice, forms a disagreeable spectacle, and is carefully avoided by all masters of the drama. In order to dismiss the audience with entire satisfaction and contentment, the virtue must either convert itself into a noble courageous despair, or the vice receive its proper punishment.

Most painters appear in this light to have been very unhappy in their subjects. As they wrought much for churches and convents, they have chiefly represented such horrible subjects as crucifixions and martyrdoms, where nothing appears but tortures, wounds, executions, and passive suffering, without any action or affection. When they turned their pencil from this ghastly mythology, they had commonly recourse to OVID, whose fictions, though passionate and agreeable, are scarcely natural or probable enough for painting.

The same inversion of that principle, which is here insisted on, displays itself in common life, as in the effects of oratory and poetry. Raise so the subordinate passion that it becomes the predominant, it swallows up that affection which it before nourished and encreased. Too much jealousy extinguishes love: Too much difficulty renders us indifferent: Too much sickness and infirmity disgusts a selfish and unkind parent.

What so disagreeable as the dismal, gloomy, disastrous stories, with which melancholy people entertain their companions? The uneasy passion being there raised alone, unaccompanied with any spirit, genius, or eloquence, conveys a pure uneasiness, and is attended with nothing that can soften it into pleasure or satisfaction.

Essay XXIII.—*Of the Standard of Taste*.[1]

THE great variety of Taste, as well as of opinion, which prevails in the world, is too obvious not to have fallen under every one's observation. Men of the most confined knowledge are able to remark a difference of taste in the narrow circle of their acquaintance, even where the persons have been educated under the same government, and have early imbibed the same prejudices. But those, who can enlarge their view to contemplate distant nations and remote ages, are still more surprized at the great inconsistence and contrariety. We are apt to call *barbarous* whatever departs widely from our own taste and apprehension: But soon find the epithet of reproach retorted on us. And the highest arrogance and self-conceit is at last startled, on observing an equal assurance on all sides, and scruples, amidst such a contest of sentiment, to pronounce positively in its own favour.

As this variety of taste is obvious to the most careless enquirer; so will it be found, on examination, to be still greater in reality than in appearance. The sentiments of men often differ with regard to beauty and deformity of all kinds, even while their general discourse is the same. There are certain terms in every language, which import blame, and others praise; and all men, who use the same tongue, must agree in their application of them. Every voice is united in applauding elegance, propriety, simplicity, spirit in writing; and in blaming fustian, affectation, coldness, and a false brilliancy: But when critics come to particulars, this seeming unanimity vanishes; and it is found, that they had affixed a very different meaning to their expressions. In all matters of opinion and science, the case is opposite: The difference among men is there oftener found to lie in generals than in particulars; and to be less in reality than in appearance. An explanation of the terms commonly ends the controversy; and the disputants are surprized to find, that they had been quarrelling, while at bottom they agreed in their judgment.

Those who found morality on sentiment, more than on reason, are inclined to comprehend ethics under the former observation, and to maintain, that, in all questions, which regard conduct and manners, the difference among men is really greater than at first sight it appears. It is indeed

---

[1] [This Essay was first published in Edition L.]

obvious, that writers of all nations and all ages concur in applauding justice, humanity, magnanimity, prudence, veracity; and in blaming the opposite qualities. Even poets and other authors, whose compositions are chiefly calculated to please the imagination, are yet found, from HOMER down to FENELON, to inculcate the same moral precepts, and to bestow their applause and blame on the same virtues and vices. This great unanimity is usually ascribed to the influence of plain reason; which, in all these cases, maintains similar sentiments in all men, and prevents those controversies, to which the abstract sciences are so much exposed. So far as the unanimity is real, this account may be admitted as satisfactory: But we must also allow that some part of the seeming harmony in morals may be accounted for from the very nature of language. The word *virtue*, with its equivalent in every tongue, implies praise; as that of *vice* does blame: And no one, without the most obvious and grossest impropriety, could affix reproach to a term, which in general acceptation is understood in a good sense; or bestow applause, where the idiom requires disapprobation. HOMER's general precepts, where he delivers any such, will never be controverted; but it is obvious, that, when he draws particular pictures of manners, and represents heroism in ACHILLES and prudence in ULYSSES, he intermixes a much greater degree of ferocity in the former, and of cunning and fraud in the latter, than FENELON would admit of. The sage ULYSSES in the GREEK poet seems to delight in lies and fictions, and often employs them without any necessity or even advantage: But his more scrupulous son, in the FRENCH epic writer, exposes himself to the most imminent perils, rather than depart from the most exact line of truth and veracity.

The admirers and followers of the ALCORAN insist on the excellent moral precepts interspersed throughout that wild and absurd performance. But it is to be supposed, that the ARABIC words, which correspond to the ENGLISH, equity, justice, temperance, meekness, charity, were such as, from the constant use of that tongue, must always be taken in a good sense; and it would have argued the greatest ignorance, not of morals, but of language, to have mentioned them with any epithets, besides those of applause and approbation. But would we know, whether the pretended prophet had really attained a just sentiment of morals? Let us attend to his narration; and we shall soon find, that he bestows praise on such instances of treachery, inhumanity, cruelty, revenge, bigotry, as are utterly incompatible with civilized society. No steady rule of right seems there to be attended to; and every action is blamed or praised, so far only as it is beneficial or hurtful to the true believers.

The merit of delivering true general precepts in ethics is indeed very small. Whoever recommends any moral virtues, really does no more than is implied in the terms themselves. That people, who invented the word *charity*, and used it in a good sense, inculcated more clearly and much more efficaciously, the precept, *be charitable*, than any pretended legislator or prophet, who should insert such a *maxim* in his writings. Of all expressions, those, which, together with their other meaning, imply a degree either of blame or approbation, are the least liable to be perverted or mistaken.

It is natural for us to seek a *Standard of Taste*; a rule, by which the various sentiments of men may be reconciled; at least, a decision, afforded, confirming one sentiment, and condemning another.

There is a species of philosophy, which cuts off all hopes of success in such an attempt, and represents the impossibility of ever attaining any standard of taste. The difference, it is said, is very wide between judgment and sentiment. All sentiment is right; because sentiment has a reference to nothing beyond itself, and is always real, wherever a man is conscious of it. But all determinations of the understanding are not right; because they have a reference to something beyond themselves, to wit, real matter of fact; and are not always conformable to that standard. Among a thousand different opinions which different men may entertain of the same subject, there is one, and but one, that is just and true; and the only difficulty is to fix and ascertain it. On the contrary, a thousand different sentiments, excited by the same object, are all right: Because no sentiment represents what is really in the object. It only marks a certain conformity or relation between the object and the organs or faculties of the mind; and if that conformity did not really exist, the sentiment could never possibly have being. Beauty is no quality in things themselves: It exists merely in the mind which contemplates them; and each mind perceives a different beauty. One person may even perceive deformity, where another is sensible of beauty; and every individual ought to acquiesce in his own sentiment, without pretending to regulate those of others. To seek the real beauty, or real deformity, is as fruitless an enquiry, as to pretend to ascertain the real sweet or real bitter. According to the disposition of the organs, the same object may be both sweet and bitter; and the proverb has justly determined it to be fruitless to dispute concerning tastes. It is very natural, and even quite necessary, to extend this axiom to mental, as well as bodily taste; and thus common sense, which is so often at variance with philosophy, especially with the sceptical kind, is found, in one instance at least, to agree in pronouncing the same decision.

But though this axiom, by passing into a proverb, seems to have attained the sanction of common sense; there is certainly a species of common sense which opposes it, at least serves to modify and restrain it. Whoever would assert an equality of genius and elegance between OGILBY and MILTON, or BUNYAN and ADDISON, would be thought to defend no less an extravagance, than if he had maintained a mole-hill to be as high as TENERIFFE, or a pond as extensive as the ocean. Though there may be found persons, who give the preference to the former authors; no one pays attention to such a taste; and we pronounce without scruple the sentiment of these pretended critics to be absurd and ridiculous. The principle of the natural equality of tastes is then totally forgot, and while we admit it on some occasions, where the objects seem near an equality, it appears an extravagant paradox, or rather a palpable absurdity, where objects so disproportioned are compared together.

It is evident that none of the rules of composition are fixed by reasonings *a priori*, or can be esteemed abstract conclusions of the understanding, from comparing those habitudes and relations of ideas, which are eternal and immutable. Their foundation is the same with that of all the practical sciences, experience; nor are they any thing but general observations, concerning what has been universally found to please in all countries and in all ages. Many of the beauties of poetry and even of eloquence are founded on falsehood and fiction, on hyperboles, metaphors, and an abuse or perversion of terms from their natural meaning. To check the sallies of the imagination, and to reduce every expression to geometrical truth and exactness, would be the most contrary to the laws of criticism; because it would produce a work, which, by universal experience, has been found the most insipid and disagreeable. But though poetry can never submit to exact truth, it must be confined by rules of art, discovered to the author either by genius or observation. If some negligent or irregular writers have pleased, they have not pleased by their transgressions of rule or order, but in spite of these transgressions: They have possessed other beauties, which were conformable to just criticism; and the force of these beauties has been able to overpower censure, and give the mind a satisfaction superior to the disgust arising from the blemishes. ARIOSTO pleases; but not by his monstrous and improbable fictions, by his bizarre mixture of the serious and comic styles, by the want of coherence in his stories, or by the continual interruptions of his narration. He charms by the force and clearness of his expression, by the readiness and variety of his inventions, and by his natural pictures of the passions, especially those of the gay and amorous kind: And however his faults may diminish our satisfaction, they are not able entirely to destroy it. Did our pleasure really arise from those parts of his poem, which we denominate faults, this would be no objection to criticism in general: It would only be an objection to those particular rules of criticism, which would establish such circumstances to be faults, and would represent them as universally blameable. If they are found to please, they cannot be faults; let the pleasure, which they produce, be ever so unexpected and unaccountable.

But though all the general rules of art are founded only on experience and on the observation of the common sentiments of human nature, we must not imagine, that, on every occasion, the feelings of men will be conformable to these rules. Those finer emotions of the mind are of a very tender and delicate nature, and require the concurrence of many favourable circumstances to make them play with facility and exactness, according to their general and established principles. The least exterior hindrance to such small springs, or the least internal disorder, disturbs their motion, and confounds the operation of the whole machine. When we would make an experiment of this nature, and would try the force of any beauty or deformity, we must choose with care a proper time and place, and bring the fancy to a suitable situation and disposition. A perfect serenity of mind, a recollection of thought, a due attention to the object; if any of these circumstances be wanting, our experiment will be fallacious, and we shall be unable to judge of the catholic and universal beauty. The relation, which nature has placed between the form and the sentiment, will at least be more obscure; and it will require greater accuracy to trace and discern it. We shall be able to ascertain its influence not so much from the operation of each particular beauty, as from the durable admiration, which attends those works, that have survived all the caprices of mode and fashion, all the mistakes of ignorance and envy.

The same HOMER, who pleased at ATHENS and ROME two thousand years ago, is still admired at PARIS and at LONDON. All the changes of climate, government, religion, and language, have not been able to obscure his glory. Authority or prejudice may give a temporary vogue to a bad poet or orator; but his reputation will never be durable or general. When his compositions are examined by posterity or by foreigners, the enchantment is dissipated, and his faults appear in their true colours. On the contrary, a real genius, the longer his works endure, and the more wide they are spread, the more sincere is the admiration which he meets with. Envy and jealousy have too much place in a narrow circle; and even familiar acquaintance with his person may diminish the applause due to his performances: But when these obstructions are removed, the beauties, which are naturally fitted to excite agreeable sentiments, immediately display their energy; and while the world endures, they maintain their authority over the minds of men.

It appears then, that, amidst all the variety and caprice of taste, there are certain general principles of approbation or blame, whose influence a careful eye may trace in all operations of the mind. Some particular forms or qualities, from the original structure of the internal fabric, are calculated to please, and others to displease; and if they fail of their effect in any particular instance, it is from some apparent defect or imperfection in the organ. A man in a fever would not insist on his palate as able to decide concerning flavours; nor would one, affected with the jaundice, pretend to give a verdict with regard to colours. In each creature, there is a sound and a defective state; and the former alone can be supposed to afford us a true standard of taste and sentiment. If, in the sound state of the organ, there be an entire or a considerable uniformity of sentiment among men, we may thence derive an idea of the perfect beauty; in like manner as the appearance of objects in day-light, to the eye of a man in health, is denominated their true and real colour, even while colour is allowed to be merely a phantasm of the senses.

Many and frequent are the defects in the internal organs, which prevent or weaken the influence of those general principles, on which depends our sentiment of beauty or deformity. Though some objects, by the structure of the mind, be naturally calculated to give pleasure, it is not to be expected, that in every individual the pleasure will be equally felt. Particular incidents and situations occur, which either throw a false light on the objects, or hinder the true from conveying to the imagination the proper sentiment and perception.

One obvious cause, why many feel not the proper sentiment of beauty, is the want of that *delicacy* of imagination, which is requisite to convey a sensibility of those finer emotions. This delicacy every one pretends to: Every one talks of it; and would reduce every kind of taste or sentiment to its standard. But as our intention in this essay is to mingle some light of the understanding with the feelings of sentiment, it will be proper to give a more accurate definition of delicacy, than has hitherto been attempted. And not to draw our philosophy from too profound a source, we shall have recourse to a noted story in DON QUIXOTE.

It is with good reason, says SANCHO to the squire with the great nose, that I pretend to have a judgment in wine: This is a quality hereditary in our family. Two of my kinsmen were once called to give their opinion of a hogshead, which was supposed to be excellent, being old and of a good vintage. One of them tastes it; considers it; and after mature reflection pronounces the wine to be good, were it not for a small taste of leather, which he perceived in it. The other, after using the same precautions, gives also his verdict in favour of the wine; but with the reserve of a taste of iron, which he could easily distinguish. You cannot imagine how much they were both ridiculed for their judgment. But who laughed in the end? On emptying the hogshead, there was found at the bottom, an old key with a leathern thong tied to it.

The great resemblance between mental and bodily taste will easily teach us to apply this story. Though it be certain, that beauty and deformity, more than sweet and bitter, are not qualities in objects, but belong entirely to the sentiment, internal or external; it must be allowed, that there are certain qualities in objects, which are fitted by nature to produce those particular feelings. Now as these qualities may be found in a small degree, or may be mixed and confounded with each other, it often happens, that the taste is not affected with such minute qualities, or is not able to distinguish all the particular flavours, amidst the disorder, in which they are presented. Where the organs are so fine, as to allow nothing to escape them; and at the same time so exact as to perceive every ingredient in the composition: This we call delicacy of taste, whether we employ these terms in the literal or metaphorical sense. Here then the general rules of beauty are of use; being drawn from established models, and from the observation of what pleases or displeases, when presented singly and in a high degree: And if the same qualities, in a continued composition and in a smaller degree, affect not the organs with a sensible delight or uneasiness, we exclude the person from all pretensions to this delicacy. To produce these general rules or avowed patterns of composition is like finding the key with the leathern thong; which justified the verdict of Sancho's kinsmen, and confounded those pretended judges who had condemned them. Though the hogshead had never been emptied, the taste of the one was still equally delicate, and that of the other equally dull and languid: But it would have been more difficult to have proved the superiority of the former, to the conviction of every by-stander. In like manner, though the beauties of writing had never been methodized, or reduced to general principles; though no excellent models had ever been acknowledged; the different degrees of taste would still have subsisted, and the judgment of one man been preferable to that of another; but it would not have been so easy to silence the bad critic, who might always insist upon his particular sentiment, and refuse to submit to his antagonist. But when we show him an avowed principle of art; when we illustrate this principle by examples, whose operation, from his own particular taste, he acknowledges to be conformable to the principle; when we prove, that the same principle may be applied to the present case, where he did not perceive or feel its influence: He must conclude, upon the whole, that the fault lies in himself, and that he wants the delicacy, which is requisite to make him sensible of every beauty and every blemish, in any composition or discourse.

It is acknowledged to be the perfection of every sense or faculty, to perceive with exactness its most minute objects, and allow nothing to escape its notice and observation. The smaller the objects are, which become sensible to the eye, the finer is that organ, and the more elaborate its make and composition. A good palate is not tried by strong flavours; but by a mixture of small ingredients, where we are still sensible of each part, notwithstanding its minuteness and its confusion with the rest. In like manner, a quick and acute perception of beauty and deformity must be the perfection of our mental taste; nor can a man be satisfied with himself while he suspects, that any excellence or blemish in a discourse has passed him unobserved. In this case, the perfection of the man, and the perfection of the sense or feeling, are found to be united. A very delicate palate, on many occasions, may be a great inconvenience both to a man himself and to his friends: But a delicate taste of wit or beauty must always be a desirable quality; because it is the source of all the finest and most innocent enjoyments, of which human nature is susceptible. In this decision the sentiments of all mankind are agreed. Wherever you can ascertain a delicacy of taste, it is sure to meet with approbation; and the best way of ascertaining it is to appeal to those models and principles, which have been established by the uniform consent and experience of nations and ages.

But though there be naturally a wide difference in point of delicacy between one person and another, nothing tends further to encrease and improve this talent, than *practice* in a particular art, and the frequent survey or contemplation of a particular species of beauty. When objects of any kind are first presented to the eye or imagination, the sentiment, which attends them, is obscure and confused; and the mind is, in a great measure, incapable of pronouncing concerning their merits or defects. The taste cannot perceive the several excellences of the performance; much less distinguish the particular character of each excellency, and ascertain its quality and degree. If it pronounce the whole in general to be beautiful or deformed, it is the utmost that can be expected; and even this judgment, a person, so unpractised, will be apt to deliver with great hesitation and reserve But allow him to acquire experience in those objects, his feeling becomes more exact and nice: He not only perceives the beauties and defects of each part, but marks the distinguishing species of each quality, and assigns it suitable praise or blame. A clear and distinct sentiment attends him through the whole survey of the objects; and he discerns that very degree and kind of approbation or displeasure, which each part is naturally fitted to produce. The mist dissipates, which seemed formerly to hang over the object: The organ acquires greater perfection in its operations; and can pronounce, without danger of mistake, concerning the merits of every performance. In a word, the same address and dexterity, which practice gives to the execution of any work, is also acquired by the same means, in the judging of it.

So advantageous is practice to the discernment of beauty, that, before we can give judgment on any work of importance, it will even be requisite, that that very individual performance be more than once perused by us, and be surveyed in different lights with attention and deliberation. There is a flutter or hurry of thought which attends the first perusal of any piece, and which confounds the genuine sentiment of beauty. The relation of the parts is not discerned: The true characters of style are little distinguished: The several perfections and defects seem wrapped up in a species of confusion, and present themselves indistinctly to the imagination. Not to mention, that there is a species of beauty, which, as it is florid and superficial, pleases at first; but being found incompatible with a just expression either of reason or passion, soon palls upon the taste, and is then rejected with disdain, at least rated at a much lower value.

It is impossible to continue in the practice of contemplating any order of beauty, without being frequently obliged to form *comparisons* between the several species and degrees of excellence, and estimating their proportion to each other. A man, who has had no opportunity of comparing the different kinds of beauty, is indeed totally unqualified to pronounce an opinion with regard to any object presented to him. By comparison alone we fix the epithets of praise or blame, and learn how to assign the due degree of each. The coarsest daubing contains a certain lustre of colours and exactness of imitation, which are so far beauties, and would affect the mind of a peasant or Indian with the highest admiration. The most vulgar ballads are not entirely destitute of harmony or nature; and none but a person, familiarized to superior beauties, would pronounce their numbers harsh, or narration uninteresting. A great inferiority of beauty gives pain to a person conversant in the highest excellence of the kind, and is for that reason pronounced a deformity: As the most finished object, with which we are acquainted, is naturally supposed to have reached the pinnacle of perfection, and to be entitled to the highest applause. One accustomed to see, and examine, and weigh the several performances, admired in different ages and nations, can only rate the merits of a work exhibited to his view, and assign its proper rank among the productions of genius.

But to enable a critic the more fully to execute this undertaking, he must preserve his mind free from all *prejudice*, and allow nothing to enter into his consideration, but the very object which is submitted to his examination. We may observe, that every work of art, in order to produce its due effect on the mind, must be surveyed in a certain point of view, and cannot be fully relished by persons, whose situation, real or imaginary, is not conformable to that which is required by the performance. An orator addresses himself to a particular audience, and must have a regard to their particular genius, interests, opinions, passions, and prejudices; otherwise he hopes in vain to govern their resolutions, and inflame their affections. Should they even have entertained some prepossessions against him, however unreasonable, he must not overlook this disadvantage; but, before he enters upon the subject, must endeavour to conciliate their affection, and acquire their good graces. A critic of a different age or nation, who should peruse this discourse, must have all these circumstances in his eye, and must place himself in the same situation as the audience, in order to form a true judgment of the oration. In like manner, when any work is addressed to the public, though I should have a friendship or enmity with the author, I must depart from this situation; and considering myself as a man in general, forget, if possible, my individual being and my peculiar circumstances.

A person influenced by prejudice, complies not with this condition; but obstinately maintains his natural position, without placing himself in that point of view, which the performance supposes. If the work be addressed to persons of a different age or nation, he makes no allowance for their peculiar views and prejudices; but, full of the manners of his own age and country, rashly condemns what seemed admirable in the eyes of those for whom alone the discourse was calculated. If the work be executed for the public, he never sufficiently enlarges his comprehension, or forgets his interest as a friend or enemy, as a rival or commentator. By this means, his sentiments are perverted; nor have the same beauties and blemishes the same influence upon him, as if he had imposed a proper violence on his imagination, and had forgotten himself for a moment. So far his taste evidently departs from the true standard; and of consequence loses all credit and authority.

It is well known, that in all questions, submitted to the understanding, prejudice is destructive of sound judgment, and perverts all operations of the intellectual faculties: It is no less contrary to good taste; nor has it less influence to corrupt our sentiment of beauty. It belongs to *good sense* to check its influence in both cases; and in this respect, as well as in many others, reason, if not an essential part of taste, is at least requisite to the operations of this latter faculty. In all the nobler productions of genius, there is a mutual relation and correspondence of parts; nor can either the beauties or blemishes be perceived by him, whose thought is not capacious enough to comprehend all those parts, and compare them with each other, in order to perceive the consistence and uniformity of the whole. Every work of art has also a certain end or purpose, for which it is calculated; and is to be deemed more or less perfect, as it is more or less fitted to attain this end. The object of eloquence is to persuade, of history to instruct, of poetry to please by means of the passions and the imagination. These ends we must carry constantly in our view, when we peruse any performance; and we must be able to judge how far the means employed are adapted to their respective purposes. Besides, every kind of composition, even the most poetical, is nothing but a chain of propositions and reasonings; not always, indeed, the justest and most exact, but still plausible and specious, however disguised by the colouring of the imagination. The persons introduced in tragedy and epic poetry, must be represented as reasoning, and thinking, and concluding, and acting, suitably to their character and circumstances; and without judgment, as well as taste and invention, a poet can never hope to succeed in so delicate an undertaking. Not to mention, that the same excellence of faculties which contributes to the improvement of reason, the same clearness of conception, the same exactness of distinction, the same vivacity of apprehension, are essential to the operations of true taste, and are its infallible concomitants. It seldom, or never happens, that a man of sense, who has experience in any art, cannot judge of its beauty; and it is no less rare to meet with a man who has a just taste without a sound understanding.

Thus, though the principles of taste be universal, and, nearly, if not entirely the same in all men; yet few are qualified to give judgment on any work of art, or establish their own sentiment as the standard of beauty. The organs of internal sensation are seldom so perfect as to allow the general principles their full play, and produce a feeling correspondent to those principles. They either labour under some defect, or are vitiated by some disorder; and by that means, excite a sentiment, which may be pronounced erroneous. When the critic has no delicacy, he judges without any distinction, and is only affected by the grosser and more palpable qualities of the object: The finer touches pass unnoticed and disregarded. Where he is not aided by practice, his verdict is attended with confusion and hesitation. Where no comparison has been employed, the most frivolous beauties, such as rather merit the name of defects, are the object of his admiration. Where he lies under the influence of prejudice, all his natural sentiments are perverted. Where good sense is wanting, he is not qualified to discern the beauties of design and reasoning, which are the highest and most excellent. Under some or other of these imperfections, the generality of men labour; and hence a true judge in the finer arts is observed, even during the most polished ages, to be so rare a character: Strong sense, united to delicate sentiment, improved by practice, perfected by comparison, and cleared of all prejudice, can alone entitle critics to this valuable character; and the joint verdict of such, wherever they are to be found, is the true standard of taste and beauty.

But where are such critics to be found? By what marks are they to be known? How distinguish them from pretenders? These questions are embarrassing; and seem to throw us back into the same uncertainty, from which, during the course of this essay, we have endeavoured to extricate ourselves.

But if we consider the matter aright, these are questions of fact, not of sentiment. Whether any particular person be endowed with good sense and a delicate imagination, free from prejudice, may often be the subject of dispute, and be liable to great discussion and enquiry: But that such a character is valuable and estimable will be agreed in by all mankind. Where these doubts occur, men can do no more than in other disputable questions, which are submitted to the understanding: They must produce the best arguments, that their invention suggests to them; they must acknowledge a true and decisive standard to exist somewhere, to wit, real existence and matter of fact; and they must have indulgence to such as differ from them in their appeals to this standard. It is sufficient for our present purpose, if we have proved, that the taste of all individuals is not upon an equal footing, and that some men in general, however difficult to be particularly pitched upon, will be acknowledged by universal sentiment to have a preference above others.

But in reality the difficulty of finding, even in particulars, the standard of taste, is not so great as it is represented. Though in speculation, we may readily avow a certain criterion in science and deny it in sentiment, the matter is found in practice to be much more hard to ascertain in the former case than in the latter. Theories of abstract philosophy, systems of profound theology, have prevailed during one age: In a successive period, these have been universally exploded: Their absurdity has been detected: Other theories and systems have supplied their place, which again gave place to their successors: And nothing has been experienced more liable to the revolutions of chance and fashion than these pretended decisions of science. The case is not the same with the beauties of eloquence and poetry. Just expressions of passion and nature are sure, after a little time, to gain public applause, which they maintain for ever. ARISTOTLE, and PLATO, and EPICURUS, and DESCARTES, may successively yield to each other: But TERENCE and VIRGIL maintain an universal, undisputed empire over the minds of men. The abstract philosophy of CICERO has lost its credit: The vehemence of his oratory is still the object of our admiration.

Though men of delicate taste be rare, they are easily to be distinguished in society, by the soundness of their understanding and the superiority of their faculties above the rest of mankind. The ascendant, which they acquire, gives a prevalence to that lively approbation, with which they receive any productions of genius, and renders it generally predominant. Many men, when left to themselves, have but a faint and dubious perception of beauty, who yet are capable of relishing any fine stroke, which is pointed out to them. Every convert to the admiration of the real poet or orator is the cause of some new conversion. And though prejudices may prevail for a time, they never unite in celebrating any rival to the true genius, but yield at last to the force of nature and just sentiment. Thus, though a civilized nation may easily be mistaken in the choice of their admired philosopher, they never have been found long to err, in their affection for a favorite epic or tragic author.

But notwithstanding all our endeavours to fix a standard of taste, and reconcile the discordant apprehensions of men, there still remain two sources of variation, which are not sufficient indeed to confound all the boundaries of beauty and deformity, but will often serve to produce a difference in the degrees of our approbation or blame. The one is the different humours of particular men; the other, the particular manners and opinions of our age and country. The general principles of taste are uniform in human nature: Where men vary in their judgments, some defect or perversion in the faculties may commonly be remarked; proceeding either from prejudice, from want of practice, or want of delicacy; and there is just reason for approving one taste, and condemning another. But where there is such a diversity in the internal frame or external situation as is entirely blameless on both sides, and leaves no room to give one the preference above the other; in that case a certain degree of diversity in judgment is unavoidable, and we seek in vain for a standard, by which we can reconcile the contrary sentiments.

A young man, whose passions are warm, will be more sensibly touched with amorous and tender images, than a man more advanced in years, who takes pleasure in wise, philosophical reflections concerning the conduct of life and moderation of the passions. At twenty, OVID may be the favourite author; HORACE at forty; and perhaps TACITUS at fifty. Vainly would we, in such cases, endeavour to enter into the sentiments of others, and divest ourselves of those propensities, which are natural to us. We choose our favourite author as we do our friend, from a conformity of humour and disposition. Mirth or passion, sentiment or reflection; whichever of these most predominates in our temper, it gives us a peculiar sympathy with the writer who resembles us.

One person is more pleased with the sublime; another with the tender; a third with raillery. One has a strong sensibility to blemishes, and is extremely studious of correctness: Another has a more lively feeling of beauties, and pardons twenty absurdities and defects for one elevated or pathetic stroke. The ear of this man is entirely turned towards conciseness and energy; that man is delighted with a copious, rich, and harmonious expression. Simplicity is affected by one; ornament by another. Comedy, tragedy, satire, odes, have each its partizans, who prefer that particular species of writing to all others. It is plainly an error in a critic, to confine his approbation to one species or style of writing, and condemn all the rest. But it is almost impossible not to feel a predilection for that which suits our particular turn and disposition. Such preferences are innocent and unavoidable, and can never reasonably be the object of dispute, because there is no standard, by which they can be decided.

For a like reason, we are more pleased, in the course of our reading, with pictures and characters, that resemble objects which are found in our own age or country, than with those which describe a different set of customs. It is not without some effort, that we reconcile ourselves to the simplicity of ancient manners, and behold princesses carrying water from the spring, and kings and heroes dressing their own victuals. We may allow in general, that the representation of such manners is no fault in the author, nor deformity in the piece; but we are not so sensibly touched with them. For this reason, comedy is not easily transferred from one age or nation to another. A FRENCHMAN or ENGLISHMAN is not pleased with the ANDRIA of TERENCE, or CLITIA of MACHIAVEL; where the fine lady, upon whom all the play turns, never once appears to the spectators, but is always kept behind the scenes, suitably to the reserved humour of the ancient GREEKS and modern ITALIANS. A man of learning and reflection can make allowance for these peculiarities of manners; but a common audience can never divest themselves so far of their usual ideas and sentiments, as to relish pictures which in no wise resemble them.

But here there occurs a reflection, which may, perhaps, be useful in examining the celebrated controversy concerning ancient and modern learning; where we often find the one side excusing any seeming absurdity in the ancients from the manners of the age, and the other refusing to admit this excuse, or at least, admitting it only as an apology for the author, not for the performance. In my opinion, the proper boundaries in this subject have seldom been fixed between the contending parties. Where any innocent peculiarities of manners are represented, such as those above mentioned, they ought certainly to be admitted; and a man, who is shocked with them, gives an evident proof of false delicacy and refinement. The poet's *monument more durable than brass*, must fall to the ground like common brick or clay, were men to make no allowance for the continual revolutions of manners and customs, and would admit of nothing but what was suitable to the prevailing fashion. Must we throw aside the pictures of our ancestors, because of their ruffs and fardingales? But where the ideas of morality and decency alter from one age to another, and where vicious manners are described, without being marked with the proper characters of blame and disapprobation; this must be allowed to disfigure the poem, and to be a real deformity. I cannot, nor is it proper I should, enter into such sentiments; and however I may excuse the poet, on account of the manners of his age, I never can relish the composition. The want of humanity and of decency, so conspicuous in the characters drawn by several of the ancient poets, even sometimes by HOMER and the GREEK tragedians, diminishes considerably the merit of their noble performances, and gives modern authors an advantage over them. We are not interested in the fortunes and sentiments of such rough heroes: We are displeased to find the limits of vice and virtue so much confounded: And whatever indulgence we may give to the writer on account of his prejudices, we cannot prevail on ourselves to enter into his sentiments, or bear an affection to characters, which we plainly discover to be blameable.

The case is not the same with moral principles, as with speculative opinions of any kind. These are in continual flux and revolution. The son embraces a different system from the father. Nay, there scarcely is any man, who can boast of great constancy and uniformity in this particular. Whatever speculative errors may be found in the polite writings of any age or country, they detract but little from the value of those compositions. There needs but a certain turn of thought or imagination to make us enter into all the opinions, which then prevailed, and relish the sentiments or conclusions derived from them. But a very violent effort is requisite to change our judgment of manners, and excite sentiments of approbation or blame, love or hatred, different from those to which the mind from long custom has been familiarized. And where a man is confident of the rectitude of that moral standard, by which he judges, he is justly jealous of it, and will not pervert the sentiments of his heart for a moment, in complaisance to any writer whatsoever.

Of all speculative errors, those, which regard religion, are the most excusable in compositions of genius; nor is it ever permitted to judge of the civility or wisdom of any people, or even of single persons, by the grossness or refinement of their theological principles. The same good sense, that directs men in the ordinary occurrences of life, is not hearkened to in religious matters, which are supposed to be placed altogether above the cognizance of human reason. On this account, all the absurdities of the pagan system of theology must be overlooked by every critic, who would pretend to form a just notion of ancient poetry; and our posterity, in their turn, must have the same indulgence to their forefathers. No religious principles can ever be imputed as a fault to any poet, while they remain merely principles, and take not such strong possession of his heart, as to lay him under the imputation of *bigotry* or *superstition*. Where that happens, they confound the sentiments of morality, and alter the natural boundaries of vice and virtue. They are therefore eternal blemishes, according to the principle above mentioned; nor are the prejudices and false opinions of the age sufficient to justify them.

It is essential to the ROMAN catholic religion to inspire a violent hatred of every other worship, and to represent all pagans, mahometans, and heretics as the objects of divine wrath and vengeance. Such sentiments, though they are in reality very blameable, are considered as virtues by the zealots of that communion, and are represented in their tragedies and epic poems as a kind of divine heroism. This bigotry has disfigured two very fine tragedies of the FRENCH theatre, POLIEUCTE and ATHALIA; where an intemperate zeal for particular modes of worship is set off with all the pomp imaginable, and forms the predominant character of the heroes. 'What is this,' says the sublime JOAD to JOSABET, finding her in discourse with MATHAN, the priest of BAAL, 'Does the daughter of DAVID speak to this traitor? Are you not afraid, lest the earth should open and pour forth flames to devour you both? Or lest these holy walls should fall and crush you together? What is his purpose? Why comes that enemy of God hither to poison the air, which we breathe, with his horrid presence?' Such sentiments are received with great applause on the theatre of PARIS; but at LONDON the spectators would be full as much pleased to hear ACHILLES tell AGAMEMNON, that he was a dog in his forehead, and a deer in his heart, or JUPITER threaten JUNO with a sound drubbing, if she will not be quiet.

RELIGIOUS principles are also a blemish in any polite composition, when they rise up to superstition, and intrude themselves into every sentiment, however remote from any connection with religion. It is no excuse for the poet, that the customs of his country had burthened life with so many religious ceremonies and observances, that no part of it was exempt from that yoke. It must for ever be ridiculous in PETRARCH to compare his mistress LAURA, to JESUS CHRIST. Nor is it less ridiculous in that agreeable libertine, BOCCACE, very seriously to give thanks to GOD ALMIGHTY and the ladies, for their assistance in defending him against his enemies.

ESSAYS,

MORAL, POLITICAL,

AND

LITERARY.

PART II.*

* Published in 1752. [This Note was first given in Edition M.]

ESSAYS.

PART II.

Essay I.—*Of Commerce.*

The greater part of mankind may be divided into two classes; that of *shallow* thinkers, who fall short of the truth, and that of *abstruse* thinkers, who go beyond it. The latter class are by far the most rare; and I may add, by far the msot useful and valuable. They suggest hints, at least, and start difficulties, which they want, perhaps, skill to pursue; but which may produce fine discoveries, when handled by men who have a more just way of thinking. At worst, what they say is uncommon; and if it should cost some pains to comprehend it, one has, however, the pleasure of hearing something that is new. An author is little to be valued, who tells us nothing but what we can learn from every coffee-house conversation.

All people of *shallow* thought are apt to decry even those *of solid* understanding, as *abstruse* thinkers, and metaphysicians, and refiners; and never will allow any thing to be just which is beyond their own weak conceptions. There are some cases, I own, where an extraordinary refinement affords a strong presumption of falsehood, and where no reasoning is to be trusted but what is natural and easy. When a man deliberates concerning his conduct in any *particular* affair, and forms schemes in politics, trade, œconomy, or any business in life, he never ought to draw his arguments too fine, or connect too long a chain of consequences together. Something is sure to happen, that will disconcert his reasoning, and produce an event different from what he expected. But when we reason upon *general* subjects, one may justly affirm, that our speculations can scarcely ever be too fine, provided they be just; and that the difference between a common man and a man of genius is chiefly seen in the shallowness or depth of the principles upon which they proceed. General reasonings seem intricate, merely because they are general; nor is it easy for the bulk of mankind to distinguish, in a great number of particulars, that common circumstance in which they all agree, or to extract it, pure and unmixed, from the other superfluous circumstances. Every judgment or conclusion, with them, is particular. They cannot enlarge their view to those universal propositions, which comprehend under them an infinite number of individuals, and include a whole science in a single theorem. Their eye is confounded with such an extensive prospect; and the conclusions, derived from it, even though clearly expressed, seem intricate and obscure. But however intricate they may seem, it is certain, that general principles, if just and sound, must always prevail in the general course of things, though they may fail in particular cases; and it is the chief business of philosophers to regard the general course of things. I may add, that it is also the chief business of politicians; especially in the domestic government of the state, where the public good, which is, or ought to be their object, depends on the concurrence of a multitude of causes; not, as in foreign politics, on accidents and chances, and the caprices of a few persons. This therefore makes the difference between *particular* deliberations and *general* reasonings, and renders subtility and refinement much more suitable to the latter than to the former.

I thought this introduction necessary before the following discourses [1] on *commerce, money, interest, balance of trade,* &c. where, perhaps, there will occur some principles which are uncommon, and which may seem too refined and subtile for such vulgar subjects. If false, let them be rejected: But no one ought to entertain a prejudice against them, merely because they are out of the common road.

The greatness of a state, and the happiness of its subjects, how independent soever they may be supposed in some respects, are commonly allowed to be inseparable with regard to commerce; and as private men receive greater security, in the

---

[1] [On commerce, luxury, money, interest, &c. Editions H to M.]

possession of their trade and riches, from the power of the public, so the public becomes powerful in proportion to the opulence and extensive commerce of private men. This maxim is true in general; though I cannot forbear thinking, that it may possibly admit of exceptions, and that we often establish it with too little reserve and limitation. There may be some circumstances, where the commerce and riches and luxury of individuals, instead of adding strength to the public, will serve only to thin its armies, and diminish its authority among the neighbouring nations. Man is a very variable being, and susceptible of many different opinions, principles, and rules of conduct. What may be true, while he adheres to one way of thinking, will be found false, when he has embraced an opposite set of manners and opinions.

The bulk of every state may be divided into *husbandmen* and *manufacturers*. The former are employed in the culture of the land; the latter work up the materials furnished by the former, into all the commodities which are necessary or ornamental to human life. As soon as men quit their savage state, where they live chiefly by hunting and fishing, they must fall into these two classes; though the arts of agriculture employ *at first* the most numerous part of the society.[1] Time and experience improve so much these arts, that the land may easily maintain a much greater number of men, than those who are immediately employed in its culture, or who furnish the more necessary manufactures to such as are so employed.

If these superfluous hands apply themselves to the finer arts, which are commonly denominated the arts of *luxury*, they add to the happiness of the state; since they afford to many the opportunity of receiving enjoyments, with which they would otherwise have been unacquainted. But may not another scheme be proposed for the employment of these superfluous hands? May not the sovereign lay claim to them, and employ them in fleets and armies, to encrease the dominions of the state abroad, and spread its fame over distant nations? It is certain that the fewer desires and wants are

---

[1] Mons. MELON, in his political essay on commerce, asserts, that even at present, if you divide FRANCE into 20 parts, 16 are labourers or peasants; two only artizans; one belonging to the law, church, and military; and one merchants, financiers, and bourgeois. This calculation is certainly very erroneous. In FRANCE, ENGLAND, and indeed most parts of EUROPE, half of the inhabitants live in cities; and even of those who live in the country, a great number are artizans, perhaps above a third.

found in the proprietors and labourers of land, the fewer hands do they employ; and consequently the superfluities of the land, instead of maintaining tradesmen and manufacturers, may support fleets and armies to a much greater extent, than where a great many arts are required to minister to the luxury of particular persons. Here therefore seems to be a kind of opposition between the greatness of the state and the happiness of the subject. A state is never greater than when all its superfluous hands are employed in the service of the public. The ease and convenience of private persons require, that these hands should be employed in their service. The one can never be satisfied, but at the expence of the other. As the ambition of the sovereign must entrench on the luxury of individuals; so the luxury of individuals must diminish the force, and check the ambition of the sovereign.

Nor is this reasoning merely chimerical; but is founded on history and experience. The republic of SPARTA was certainly more powerful than any state now in the world, consisting of an equal number of people; and this was owing entirely to the want of commerce and luxury. The HELOTES were the labourers: The SPARTANS were the soldiers or gentlemen. It is evident, that the labour of the HELOTES could not have maintained so great a number of SPARTANS, had these latter lived in ease and delicacy, and given employment to a great variety of trades and manufactures. The like policy may be remarked in ROME. And indeed, throughout all ancient history, it is observable, that the smallest republics raised and maintained greater armies, than states consisting of triple the number of inhabitants, are able to support at present. It is computed, that, in all EUROPEAN nations, the proportion between soldiers and people does not exceed one to a hundred. But we read, that the city of ROME alone, with its small territory, raised and maintained, in early times, ten legions against the LATINS. ATHENS, the whole of whose dominions was not larger than YORKSHIRE, sent to the expedition against SICILY near forty thousand men.[1] DIONYSIUS the elder, it is said, maintained a standing army of a hundred thousand foot and ten thousand horse, besides a large fleet of four hundred sail;[2] though his territories extended no

---

[1] THUCYDIDES, lib. vii. 75.

[2] DIOD. SIC. lib. ii. 5. This account, I own, is somewhat suspicious, not to say worse; chiefly because this army was not composed of citizens, but of mercenary forces.

farther than the city of SYRACUSE, about a third of the island of SICILY, and some sea-port towns and garrisons on the coast of ITALY and ILLYRICUM. It is true, the ancient armies, in time of war, subsisted much upon plunder: But did not the enemy plunder in their turn? which was a more ruinous way of levying a tax, than any other that could be devised. In short, no probable reason can be assigned for the great power of the more ancient states above the modern, but their want of commerce and luxury. Few artizans were maintained by the labour of the farmers, and therefore more soldiers might live upon it. LIVY says, that ROME, in his time, would find it difficult to raise as large an army as that which, in her early days, she sent out against the GAULS and LATINS.[1] Instead of those soldiers who fought for liberty and empire in CAMILLUS's time, there were, in AUGUSTUS's days, musicians, painters, cooks, players, and tailors; and if the land was equally cultivated at both periods, it could certainly maintain equal numbers in the one profession as in the other. They added nothing to the mere necessaries of life, in the latter period more than in the former.

It is natural on this occasion to ask, whether sovereigns may not return to the maxims of ancient policy, and consult their own interest in this respect, more than the happiness of their subjects? I answer, that it appears to me, almost impossible; and that because ancient policy was violent, and contrary to the more natural and usual course of things. It is well known with what peculiar laws SPARTA was governed, and what a prodigy that republic is justly esteemed by every one, who has considered human nature as it has displayed itself in other nations, and other ages. Were the testimony of history less positive and circumstantial, such a government would appear a mere philosophical whim or fiction, and impossible ever to be reduced to practice. And though the ROMAN and other ancient republics were supported on principles somewhat more natural, yet was there an extraordinary concurrence of circumstances to make them submit to such grievous burthens. They were free states; they were small ones; and the age being martial, all their neighbours were continually in arms. Freedom naturally begets public spirit, especially in small states; and this public spirit, this *amor*

---

[1] TITI LIVII, lib. vii. cap. 25. 'Adeo in quæ laboramus,' says he, 'sola crevimus, divitias luxuriemque.'

patriæ, must encrease, when the public is almost in continual alarm, and men are obliged, every moment, to expose themselves to the greatest dangers for its defence. A continual succession of wars makes every citizen a soldier: He takes the field in his turn: And during his service he is chiefly maintained by himself. This service is indeed equivalent to a heavy tax; yet is it less felt by a people addicted to arms, who fight for honour and revenge more than pay, and are unacquainted with gain and industry as well as pleasure.[1] Not to mention the great equality of fortunes among the inhabitants of the ancient republics, where every field, belonging to a different proprietor, was able to maintain a family, and rendered the numbers of citizens very considerable, even without trade and manufactures.

But though the want of trade and manufactures, among a free and very martial people, may *sometimes* have no other effect than to render the public more powerful, it is certain, that, in the common course of human affairs, it will have a quite contrary tendency. Sovereigns must take mankind as they find them, and cannot pretend to introduce any violent change in their principles and ways of thinking. A long course of time, with a variety of accidents and circumstances, are requisite to produce those great revolutions, which so much diversify the face of human affairs. And the less natural any set of principles are, which support a particular society, the more difficulty will a legislator meet with in raising and cultivating them. It is his best policy to comply with the common bent of mankind, and give it all the improvements of which it is susceptible. Now, according to the most natural course of things, industry and arts and

---

[1] The more antient ROMANS lived in perpetual war with all their neighbours: and in old LATIN, the term, *hostis*, expressed both a stranger and an enemy. This is remarked by CICERO; but by him is ascribed to the humanity of his ancestors, who softened, as much as possible, the denomination of an enemy, by calling him by the same appellation which signified a stranger. *De Off.* lib. i. 12. 'Tis however much more probable, from the manners of the times, that the ferocity of those people was so great as to make them regard all strangers as enemies, and call them by the same name. It is not, besides, consistent with the most common maxims of policy or of nature, that any state should regard its public enemies with a friendly eye, or preserve any such sentiments for them as the ROMAN orator would ascribe to his ancestors. Not to mention, that the early ROMANS really exercised piracy, as we learn from their first treaties with CARTHAGE, preserved by POLYBIUS, lib. 3, and consequently like the SALLEE and ALGERINE rovers, were actually at war with most nations, and a stranger and an enemy were with them almost synonymous.

trade encrease the power of the sovereign as well as the happiness of the subjects; and that policy is violent, which aggrandises the public by the poverty of individuals. This will easily appear from a few considerations, which will present to us the consequences of sloth and barbarity.

Where manufactures and mechanic arts are not cultivated, the bulk of the people must apply themselves to agriculture; and if their skill and industry encrease, there must arise a great superfluity from their labour beyond what suffices to maintain them. They have no temptation, therefore, to encrease their skill and industry; since they cannot exchange that superfluity for any commodities, which may serve either to their pleasure or vanity. A habit of indolence naturally prevails. The greater part of the land lies uncultivated. What is cultivated, yields not its utmost for want of skill and assiduity in the farmers. If at any time the public exigencies require, that great numbers should be employed in the public service, the labour of the people furnishes now no superfluities, by which these numbers can be maintained. The labourers cannot encrease their skill and industry on a sudden. Lands uncultivated cannot be brought into tillage for some years. The armies, mean while, must either make sudden and violent conquests, or disband for want of subsistence. A regular attack or defence, therefore, is not to be expected from such a people, and their soldiers must be as ignorant and unskilful as their farmers and manufacturers.

Every thing in the world is purchased by labour; and our passions are the only causes of labour. When a nation abounds in manufactures and mechanic arts, the proprietors of land, as well as the farmers, study agriculture as a science, and redouble their industry and attention. The superfluity, which arises from their labour, is not lost; but is exchanged with manufactures for those commodities, which men's luxury now makes them covet. By this means, land furnishes a great deal more of the necessaries of life, than what suffices for those who cultivate it. In times of peace and tranquility, this superfluity goes to the maintenance of manufacturers, and the improvers of liberal arts. But it is easy for the public to convert many of these manufacturers into soldiers, and maintain them by that superfluity, which arises from the labour of the farmers. Accordingly we find, that this is the case in all civilized governments. When the sovereign raises an army, what is the consequence? He imposes a tax. This tax obliges all the people to retrench what is least necessary to their subsistence. Those, who labour in such commodities, must either enlist in the troops, or turn themselves to agriculture, and thereby oblige some labourers to enlist for want of business. And to consider the matter abstractedly, manufacturers encrease the power of the state only as they store up so much labour, and that of a kind to which the public may lay claim, without depriving any one of the necessaries of life. The more labour, therefore, is employed beyond mere necessaries, the more powerful is any state; since the persons engaged in that labour may easily be converted to the public service. In a state without manufacturers, there may be the same number of hands; but there is not the same quantity of labour, nor of the same kind. All the labour is there bestowed upon necessaries, which can admit of little or no abatement.

Thus the greatness of the sovereign and the happiness of the state are, in a great measure, united with regard to trade and manufactures. It is a violent method, and in most cases impracticable, to oblige the labourer to toil, in order to raise from the land more than what subsists himself and family. Furnish him with manufactures and commodities, and he will do it of himself. Afterwards you will find it easy to seize some part of his superfluous labour, and employ it in the public service, without giving him his wonted return. Being accustomed to industry, he will think this less grievous, than if, at once, you obliged him to an augmentation of labour without any reward. The case is the same with regard to the other members of the state. The greater is the stock of labour of all kinds, the greater quantity may be taken from the heap, without making any sensible alteration in it.

A public granary of corn, a storehouse of cloth, a magazine of arms; all these must be allowed real riches and strength in any state. Trade and industry are really nothing but a stock of labour, which, in times of peace and tranquillity, is employed for the ease and satisfaction of individuals; but in the exigencies of state, may, in part, be turned to public advantage. Could we convert a city into a kind of fortified camp, and infuse into each breast so martial a genius, and such a passion for public good, as to make every one willing to undergo the greatest hardships for the sake of the public; these affections might now, as in ancient times, prove alone a sufficient spur to industry, and support the community. It would then be advantageous, as in camps, to banish all arts and luxury; and, by restrictions on equipage and tables, make the provisions and forage last longer than if the army were loaded with a number of superfluous retainers. But as these principles are too disinterested and too difficult to support, it is requisite to govern men by other passions, and animate them with a spirit of avarice and industry, art and luxury. The camp is, in this case, loaded with a superfluous retinue; but the provisions flow in proportionably larger. The harmony of the whole is still supported; and the natural bent of the mind being more complied with, individuals, as well as the public, find their account in the observance of those maxims.

The same method of reasoning will let us see the advantage of *foreign* commerce, in augmenting the power of the state, as well as the riches and happiness of the subject. It encreases the stock of labour in the nation; and the sovereign may convert what share of it he finds necessary to the service of the public. Foreign trade, by its imports, furnishes materials for new manufactures; and by its exports, it produces labour in particular commodities, which could not be consumed at home. In short, a kingdom, that has a large import and export, must abound more with industry, and that employed upon delicacies and luxuries, than a kingdom which rests contented with its native commodities. It is, therefore, more powerful, as well as richer and happier. The individuals reap the benefit of these commodities, so far as they gratify the senses and appetites. And the public is also a gainer, while a greater stock of labour is, by this means, stored up against any public exigency; that is, a greater number of laborious men are maintained, who may be diverted to the public service, without robbing any one of the necessaries, or even the chief conveniencies of life.

If we consult history, we shall find, that, in most nations, foreign trade has preceded any refinement in home manufactures, and given birth to domestic luxury. The temptation is stronger to make use of foreign commodities, which are ready for use, and which are entirely new to us, than to make improvements on any domestic commodity, which always advance by slow degrees, and never affect us by their novelty. The profit is also very great, in exporting what is superfluous at home, and what bears no price, to foreign nations, whose soil or climate is not favourable to that commodity. Thus men become acquainted with the *pleasures* of luxury and the *profits* of commerce; and their *delicacy* and *industry*, being once awakened, carry them on to farther improvements, in every branch of domestic as well as foreign trade. And this perhaps is the chief advantage which arises from a commerce with strangers. It rouses men from their indolence; and presenting the gayer and more opulent part of the nation with objects of luxury, which they never before dreamed of, raises in them a desire of a more splendid way of life than what their ancestors enjoyed. And at the same time, the few merchants, who possess the secret of this importation and exportation, make great profits; and becoming rivals in wealth to the ancient nobility, tempt other adventurers to become their rivals in commerce. Imitation soon diffuses all those arts; while domestic manufactures emulate the foreign in their improvements, and work up every home commodity to the utmost perfection of which it is susceptible. Their own steel and iron, in such laborious hands, become equal to the gold and rubies of the INDIES.

When the affairs of the society are once brought to this situation, a nation may lose most of its foreign trade, and yet continue a great and powerful people. If strangers will not take any particular commodity of ours, we must cease to labour in it. The same hands will turn themselves towards some refinement in other commodities, which may be wanted at home. And there must always be materials for them to work upon; till every person in the state, who possesses riches, enjoys as great plenty of home commodities, and those in as great perfection, as he desires; which can never possibly happen. CHINA is represented as one of the most flourishing empires in the world; though it has very little commerce beyond its own territories.

It will not, I hope, be considered as a superfluous digression, if I here observe, that, as the multitude of mechanical arts is advantageous, so is the great number of persons to whose share the productions of these arts fall. A too great disproportion among the citizens weakens any state. Every person, if possible, ought to enjoy the fruits of his labour, in a full possession of all the necessaries, and many of the conveniencies of life. No one can doubt, but such an equality is most suitable to human nature, and diminishes much less from the *happiness* of the rich than it adds to that of the poor. It also augments the *power of the state*, and makes any extraordinary taxes or impositions be paid with more chearfulness. Where the riches are engrossed by a few, these must contribute very largely to the supplying of the public necessities. But when the riches are dispersed among multitudes, the burthen feels light on every shoulder, and the taxes make not a very sensible difference on any one's way of living.

Add to this, that, where the riches are in few hands, these must enjoy all the power, and will readily conspire to lay the whole burthen on the poor, and oppress them still farther, to the discouragement of all industry.

In this circumstance consists the great advantage of ENGLAND above any nation at present in the world, or that appears in the records of any story. It is true, the ENGLISH feel some disadvantages in foreign trade by the high price of labour, which is in part the effect of the riches of their artisans, as well as of the plenty of money: But as foreign trade is not the most material circumstance, it is not to be put in competition with the happiness of so many millions. And if there were no more to endear to them that free government under which they live, this alone were sufficient. The poverty of the common people is a natural, if not an infallible effect of absolute monarchy; though I doubt, whether it be always true, on the other hand, that their riches are an infallible result of liberty. Liberty must be attended with particular accidents, and a certain turn of thinking, in order to produce that effect. Lord BACON, accounting for the great advantages obtained by the ENGLISH in their wars with FRANCE, ascribes them chiefly to the superior ease and plenty of the common people amongst the former; yet the government of the two kingdoms was, at that time, pretty much alike. Where the labourers and artisans are accustomed to work for low wages, and to retain but a small part of the fruits of their labour, it is difficult for them, even in a free government, to better their condition, or conspire among themselves to heighten their wages. But even where they are accustomed to a more plentiful way of life, it is easy for the rich, in an arbitrary government, to conspire against *them*, and throw the whole burthen of the taxes on their shoulders.

It may seem an odd position, that the poverty of the common people in FRANCE, ITALY, and SPAIN, is, in some measure, owing to the superior riches of the soil and happiness of the climate; yet there want not reasons to justify this paradox. In such a fine mould or soil as that of those more southern regions, agriculture is an easy art; and one man, with a couple of sorry horses, will be able, in a season, to cultivate as much land as will pay a pretty considerable rent to the proprietor. All the art, which the farmer knows, is to leave his ground fallow for a year, as soon as it is exhausted; and the warmth of the sun alone and temperature of the climate enrich it, and restore its fertility. Such poor peasants, therefore, require only a simple maintenance for their labour. They have no stock or riches, which claim more; and at the same time they are for ever dependent on their landlord, who gives no leases, nor fears that his land will be spoiled by the ill methods of cultivation. In ENGLAND, the land is rich, but coarse; must be cultivated at a great expense; and produces slender crops, when not carefully managed, and by a method which gives not the full profit but in a course of several years. A farmer, therefore, in ENGLAND must have a considerable stock, and a long lease; which beget proportional profits. The fine vineyards of CHAMPAGNE and BURGUNDY, that often yield to the landlord about five pounds *per* acre, are cultivated by peasants who have scarcely bread: The reason is, that such peasants need no stock but their own limbs, with instruments of husbandry, which they can buy for twenty shillings. The farmers are commonly in some better circumstances in those countries. But the grasiers are most at their ease of all those who cultivate the land. The reason is still the same. Men must have profits proportionable to their expense and hazard. Where so considerable a number of the labouring poor as the peasants and farmers are in very low circumstances, all the rest must partake of their poverty, whether the government of that nation be monarchical or republican.

We may form a similar remark with regard to the general history of mankind. What is the reason, why no people, living between the tropics, could ever yet attain to any art or civility, or reach even any police in their government, and any military discipline; while few nations in the temperate climates have been altogether deprived of these advantages? It is probable that one cause of this phænomenon is the warmth and equality of weather in the torrid zone, which render clothes and houses less requisite for the inhabitants, and thereby remove, in part, that necessity, which is the great spur to industry and invention. *Curis acuens mortalia corda.* Not to mention, that the fewer goods or possessions of this kind any people enjoy, the fewer quarrels are likely to arise amongst them, and the less necessity will there be for a settled police or regular authority to protect and defend them from foreign enemies, or from each other.

Essay II.—*Of Refinement in the Arts.*[1]

LUXURY is a word of uncertain signification, and may be taken in a good as well as in a bad sense. In general, it means great refinement in the gratification of the senses; and any degree of it may be innocent or blameable, according to the age, or country, or condition of the person. The bounds between the virtue and the vice cannot here be exactly fixed, more than in other moral subjects. To imagine, that the gratifying of any sense, or the indulging of any delicacy in meat, drink, or apparel, is of itself a vice, can never enter into a head, that is not disordered by the frenzies of enthusiasm. I have, indeed, heard of a monk abroad, who, because the windows of his cell opened upon a noble prospect, made a *covenant with his eyes* never to turn that way, or receive so sensual a gratification. And such is the crime of drinking CHAMPAGNE or BURGUNDY, preferably to small beer or porter. These indulgences are only vices, when they are pursued at the expense of some virtue, as liberality or charity; in like manner as they are follies, when for them a man ruins his fortune, and reduces himself to want and beggary. Where they entrench upon no virtue, but leave ample subject whence to provide for friends, family, and every proper object of generosity or compassion, they are entirely innocent, and have in every age been acknowledged such by almost all moralists. To be entirely occupied with the luxury of the table, for instance, without any

---

[1] [In Editions H to M this Essay is headed: Of Luxury.]

relish for the pleasures of ambition, study, or conversation, is a mark of stupidity, and is incompatible with any vigour of temper or genius. To confine one's expense entirely to such a gratification, without regard to friends or family, is an indication of a heart destitute of humanity or benevolence. But if a man reserve time sufficient for all laudable pursuits, and money sufficient for all generous purposes, he is free from every shadow of blame or reproach.

Since luxury may be considered either as innocent or blameable, one may be surprized at those preposterous opinions, which have been entertained concerning it; while men of libertine principles bestow praises even on vicious luxury, and represent it as highly advantageous to society; and on the other hand, men of severe morals blame even the most innocent luxury, and represent it as the source of all the corruptions, disorders, and factions, incident to civil government. We shall here endeavour to correct both these extremes, by proving, *first*, that the ages of refinement are both the happiest and most virtuous: *secondly*, that wherever luxury ceases to be innocent, it also ceases to be beneficial; and when carried a degree too far, is a quality pernicious, though perhaps not the most pernicious, to political society.

To prove the first point, we need but consider the effects of refinement both on *private* and on *public* life. Human happiness, according to the most received notions, seems to consist in three ingredients; action, pleasure, and indolence: And though these ingredients ought to be mixed in different proportions, according to the particular disposition of the person; yet no one ingredient can be entirely wanting, without destroying, in some measure, the relish of the whole composition. Indolence or repose, indeed, seems not of itself to contribute much to our enjoyment; but, like sleep, is requisite as an indulgence to the weakness of human nature, which cannot support an uninterrupted course of business or pleasure. That quick march of the spirits, which takes a man from himself, and chiefly gives satisfaction, does in the end exhaust the mind, and requires some intervals of repose, which, though agreeable for a moment, yet, if prolonged, beget a languor and lethargy that destroys all enjoyment. Education, custom, and example, have a mighty influence in turning the mind to any of these pursuits; and it must be owned, that, where they promote a relish for action and pleasure, they are so far favourable to human happiness. In times when industry and the arts flourish, men are kept in perpetual occupation, and enjoy, as their reward, the occupation itself, as well as those pleasures which are the fruit of their labour. The mind acquires new vigour; enlarges its powers and faculties; and by an assiduity in honest industry, both satisfies its natural appetites, and prevents the growth of unnatural ones, which commonly spring up, when nourished by ease and idleness. Banish those arts from society, you deprive men both of action and of pleasure; and leaving nothing but indolence in their place, you even destroy the relish of indolence, which never is agreeable, but when it succeeds to labour, and recruits the spirits, exhausted by too much application and fatigue.

Another advantage of industry and of refinements in the mechanical arts, is, that they commonly produce some refinements in the liberal; nor can one be carried to perfection, without being accompanied, in some degree, with the other. The same age, which produces great philosophers and politicians, renowned generals and poets, usually abounds with skilful weavers, and ship-carpenters. We cannot reasonably expect, that a piece of woollen cloth will be brought to perfection in a nation, which is ignorant of astronomy, or where ethics are neglected. The spirit of the age affects all the arts; and the minds of men, being once roused from their lethargy, and put into a fermentation, turn themselves on all sides, and carry improvements into every art and science. Profound ignorance is totally banished, and men enjoy the privilege of rational creatures, to think as well as to act, to cultivate the pleasures of the mind as well as those of the body.

The more these refined arts advance, the more sociable men become: nor is it possible, that, when enriched with science, and possessed of a fund of conversation, they should be contented to remain in solitude, or live with their fellow-citizens in that distant manner, which is peculiar to ignorant and barbarous nations. They flock into cities; love to receive and communicate knowledge; to show their wit or their breeding; their taste in conversation or living, in clothes or furniture. Curiosity allures the wise; vanity the foolish; and pleasure both. Particular clubs and societies are everywhere formed: Both sexes meet in an easy and sociable manner: and the tempers of men, as well as their behaviour, refine apace. So that, beside the improvements which they receive from knowledge and the liberal arts, it is impossible but they must feel an encrease of humanity, from the very habit of conversing together, and contribute to each other's pleasure and entertainment. Thus *industry, knowledge,* and *humanity,* are linked together by an indissoluble chain, and are found, from experience as well as reason, to be peculiar to the more polished, and, what are commonly denominated, the more luxurious ages.

Nor are these advantages attended with disadvantages, that bear any proportion to them. The more men refine upon pleasure, the less they indulge in excess of any kind; because nothing is more destructive to true pleasure than such excesses. One may safely affirm, that the TARTARS are oftener guilty of beastly gluttony, when they feast on their dead horses, than EUROPEAN courtiers with all their refinements of cookery. And if libertine love, or even infidelity to the marriage-bed, be more frequent in polite ages, when it is often regarded only as a piece of gallantry; drunkenness, on the other hand, is much less common: A vice more odious, and more pernicious both to mind and body. And in this matter I would appeal, not only to an OVID or a PETRONIUS, but to a SENECA or a CATO. We know, that CÆSAR, during CATILINE'S conspiracy, being necessitated to put into CATO'S hands a *billet-doux,* which discovered an intrigue with SERVILIA, CATO'S own sister, that stern philosopher threw it back to him with indignation; and in the bitterness of his wrath, gave him the appellation of drunkard, as a term more opprobrious than that with which he could more justly have reproached him.

But industry, knowledge, and humanity, are not advantageous in private life alone: They diffuse their beneficial influence on the *public,* and render the government as great and flourishing as they make individuals happy and prosperous. The encrease and consumption of all the commodities, which serve to the ornament and pleasure of life, are advantageous to society; because, at the same time that they multiply those innocent gratifications to individuals, they are a kind of *storehouse* of labour, which, in the exigencies of state, may be turned to public service. In a nation, where there is no demand for such superfluities, men sink into indolence, lose all enjoyment of life, and are useless to the public, which cannot maintain or support its fleets and armies, from the industry of such slothful members.

The bounds of all the EUROPEAN kingdoms are, at present, nearly the same they were two hundred years ago: But what a difference is there in the power and grandeur of those kingdoms? Which can be ascribed to nothing but the encrease of art and industry. When CHARLES VIII. of FRANCE invaded ITALY, he carried with him about 20,000 men: Yet this armament so exhausted the nation, as we learn from GUICCIARDIN, that for some years it was not able to make so great an effort. The late king of FRANCE, in time of war, kept in pay above 400,000 men;[1] though from MAZARINE's death to his own, he was engaged in a course of wars that lasted near thirty years.

This industry is much promoted by the knowledge inseparable from ages of art and refinement; as, on the other hand, this knowledge enables the public to make the best advantage of the industry of its subjects. Laws, order, police, discipline; these can never be carried to any degree of perfection, before human reason has refined itself by exercise, and by an application to the more vulgar arts, at least, of commerce and manufacture. Can we expect, that a government will be well modelled by a people, who know not how to make a spinning-wheel, or to employ a loom to advantage? Not to mention, that all ignorant ages are infested with superstition, which throws the government off its bias, and disturbs men in the pursuit of their interest and happiness.

Knowledge in the arts of government naturally begets mildness and moderation, by instructing men in the advantages of humane maxims above rigour and severity, which drive subjects into rebellion, and make the return to submission impracticable, by cutting off all hopes of pardon. When the tempers of men are softened as well as their knowledge improved, this humanity appears still more conspicuous, and is the chief characteristic which distinguishes a civilized age from times of barbarity and ignorance. Factions are then less inveterate, revolutions less tragical, authority less severe, and seditions less frequent. Even foreign wars abate of their cruelty; and after the field of battle,

[1] The inscription on the PLACE-DE-VENDOME says 440,000.

where honour and interest steel men against compassion as well as fear, the combatants divest themselves of the brute, and resume the man.

Nor need we fear, that men, by losing their ferocity, will lose their martial spirit, or become less undaunted and vigorous in defence of their country or their liberty. The arts have no such effect in enervating either the mind or body. On the contrary, industry, their inseparable attendant, adds new force to both. And if anger, which is said to be the whetstone of courage, loses somewhat of its asperity, by politeness and refinement; a sense of honour, which is a stronger, more constant, and more governable principle, acquires fresh vigour by that elevation of genius which arises from knowledge and a good education. Add to this, that courage can neither have any duration, nor be of any use, when not accompanied with discipline and martial skill, which are seldom found among a barbarous people. The ancients remarked, that DATAMES was the only barbarian that ever knew the art of war. And PYRRHUS, seeing the ROMANS marshal their army with some art and skill, said with surprize, *These barbarians have nothing barbarous in their discipline!* It is observable, that, as the old ROMANS, by applying themselves solely to war, were almost the only uncivilized people that ever possessed military discipline; so the modern ITALIANS are the only civilized people, among EUROPEANS, that ever wanted courage and a martial spirit. Those who would ascribe this effeminacy of the ITALIANS to their luxury, or politeness, or application to the arts, need but consider the FRENCH and ENGLISH, whose bravery is as uncontestable, as their love for the arts, and their assiduity in commerce. The ITALIAN historians give us a more satisfactory reason for this degeneracy of their countrymen. They shew us how the sword was dropped at once by all the ITALIAN sovereigns; while the VENETIAN aristocracy was jealous of its subjects, the FLORENTINE democracy applied itself entirely to commerce; ROME was governed by priests, and NAPLES by women. War then became the business of soldiers of fortune, who spared one another, and to the astonishment of the world, could engage a whole day in what they called a battle, and return at night to their camp, without the least bloodshed.

What has chiefly induced severe moralists to declaim

against refinement in the arts, is the example of ancient ROME, which, joining, to its poverty and rusticity, virtue and public spirit, rose to such a surprising height of grandeur and liberty; but having learned from its conquered provinces [1]the ASIATIC luxury, fell into every kind of corruption; whence arose sedition and civil wars, attended at last with the total loss of liberty. All the LATIN classics, whom we peruse in our infancy, are full of these sentiments, and universally ascribe the ruin of their state to the arts and riches imported from the East: Insomuch that SALLUST represents a taste for painting as a vice, no less than lewdness and drinking. And so popular were these sentiments, during the later ages of the republic, that this author abounds in praises of the old rigid ROMAN virtue, though himself the most egregious instance of modern luxury and corruption; speaks contemptuously of the GRECIAN eloquence, though the most elegant writer in the world; nay, employs preposterous digressions and declamations to this purpose, though a model of taste and correctness.

But it would be easy to prove, that these writers mistook the cause of the disorders in the ROMAN state, and ascribed to luxury and the arts, what really proceeded from an ill modelled government, and the unlimited extent of conquests. [2]Refinement on the pleasures and conveniences of life has no natural tendency to beget venality and corruption. The value, which all men put upon any particular pleasure, depends on comparison and experience; nor is a porter less greedy of money, which he spends on bacon and brandy, than a courtier, who purchases champagne and ortolans. Riches are valuable at all times, and to all men; because they always purchase pleasures, such as men are accustomed to, and desire: Nor can anything restrain or regulate the love of money, but a sense of honour and virtue; which, if it be not nearly equal at all times, will naturally abound most in ages of knowledge and refinement.

Of all EUROPEAN kingdoms, POLAND seems the most defective in the arts of war as well as peace, mechanical as well as liberal; yet it is there that venality and corruption do most prevail. The nobles seem to have preserved their crown elective for no other purpose, than regularly to sell

---

[1] [The Grecian and Asiatic luxury: Editions H to K.]

[2] [Luxury or refinement on pleasure has, &c.: Editions H to M.]

it to the highest bidder. This is almost the only species of commerce, with which that people are acquainted.

The liberties of ENGLAND, so far from decaying since the improvements in the arts, have never flourished so much as during that period. And though corruption may seem to encrease of late years; this is chiefly to be ascribed to our established liberty, when our princes have found the impossibility of governing without parliaments, or of terrifying parliaments by the phantom of prerogative. Not to mention, that this corruption or venality prevails much more among the electors than the elected; and therefore cannot justly be ascribed to any refinements in luxury.

If we consider the matter in a proper light, we shall find, that a progress in the arts is rather favourable to liberty, and has a natural tendency to preserve, if not produce a free government. In rude unpolished nations, where the arts are neglected, all labour is bestowed on the cultivation of the ground; and the whole society is divided into two classes, proprietors of land, and their vassals or tenants. The latter are necessarily dependent, and fitted for slavery and subjection; especially where they possess no riches, and are not valued for their knowledge in agriculture; as must always be the case where the arts are neglected. The former naturally erect themselves into petty tyrants; and must either submit to an absolute master, for the sake of peace and order; or if they will preserve their independency, like the [1] ancient barons, they must fall into feuds and contests among themselves, and throw the whole society into such confusion, as is perhaps worse than the most despotic government. But where luxury nourishes commerce and industry, the peasants, by a proper cultivation of the land, become rich and independent; while the tradesmen and merchants acquire a share of the property, and draw authority and consideration to that middling rank of men, who are the best and firmest basis of public liberty. These submit not to slavery, like the peasants, from poverty and meanness of spirit; and having no hopes of tyrannizing over others, like the barons, they are not tempted, for the sake of that gratification, to submit to the tyranny of their sovereign. They covet equal laws, which may secure their property, and preserve them from monarchical, as well as aristocratical tyranny.

[1] [The Gothic barons: Editions H to N.]

The lower house is the support of our popular government; and all the world acknowledges, that it owed its chief influence and consideration to the encrease of commerce, which threw such a balance of property into the hands of the commons. How inconsistent then is it to blame so violently a refinement in the arts, and to represent it as the bane of liberty and public spirit!

To declaim against present times, and magnify the virtue of remote ancestors, is a propensity almost inherent in human nature: And as the sentiments and opinions of civilized ages alone are transmitted to posterity, hence it is that we meet with so many severe judgments pronounced against luxury, and even science; and hence it is that at present we give so ready an assent to them. But the fallacy is easily perceived, by comparing different nations that are contemporaries; where we both judge more impartially, and can better set in opposition those manners, with which we are sufficiently acquainted. Treachery and cruelty, the most pernicious and most odious of all vices, seem peculiar to uncivilised ages; and by the refined GREEKS and ROMANS were ascribed to all the barbarous nations, which surrounded them. They might justly, therefore, have presumed, that their own ancestors, so highly celebrated, possessed no greater virtue, and were as much inferior to their posterity in honour and humanity, as in taste and science. An ancient FRANK or SAXON may be highly extolled: But I believe every man would think his life or fortune much less secure in the hands of a MOOR or TARTAR, than in those of a FRENCH or ENGLISH gentleman, the rank of men the most civilized in the most civilized nations.

We come now to the *second* position which we propose to illustrate, to wit, that, as innocent luxury, or a refinement in the arts and conveniences of life, is advantageous to the public; so wherever luxury ceases to be innocent, it also ceases to be beneficial; and when carried a degree farther, begins to be a quality pernicious, though, perhaps, not the most pernicious, to political society.

Let us consider what we call vicious luxury. No gratification, however sensual, can of itself be esteemed vicious. A gratification is only vicious, when it engrosses all a man's expence, and leaves no ability for such acts of duty and generosity as are required by his situation and fortune.

Suppose, that he correct the vice, and employ part of his expence in the education of his children, in the support of his friends, and in relieving the poor: would any prejudice result to society? On the contrary, the same consumption would arise; and that labour, which, at present, is employed only in producing a slender gratification to one man, would relieve the necessitous, and bestow satisfaction on hundreds. The same care and toil that raise a dish of peas at CHRISTMAS, would give bread to a whole family during six months. To say, that, without a vicious luxury, the labour would not have been employed at all, is only to say, that there is some other defect in human nature, such as indolence, selfishness, inattention to others, for which luxury, in some measure, provides a remedy; as one poison may be an antidote to another. But virtue, like wholesome food, is better than poisons, however corrected.

Suppose the same number of men, that are present in GREAT BRITAIN, with the same soil and climate; I ask, is it not possible for them to be happier, by the most perfect way of life that can be imagined, and by the greatest reformation that Omnipotence itself could work in their temper and disposition? To assert, that they cannot, appears evidently ridiculous. As the land is able to maintain more than all its present inhabitants, they could never, in such a UTOPIAN state, feel any other ills than those which arise from bodily sickness; and these are not the half of human miseries. All other ills spring from some vice, either in ourselves or others; and even many of our diseases proceed from the same origin. Remove the vices, and the ills follow. You must only take care to remove all the vices. If you remove part, you may render the matter worse. By banishing *vicious* luxury, without curing sloth and an indifference to others, you only diminish industry in the state, and add nothing to men's charity or their generosity. Let us, therefore, rest contented with asserting, that two opposite vices in a state may be more advantageous than either of them alone; but let us never pronounce vice in itself advantageous. Is it not very inconsistent for an author to assert in one page, that moral distinctions are inventions of politicians for public interest; and in the next page maintain, that vice is advantageous to the public?[1] And indeed it seems upon any system of

[1] Fable of the Bees.

morality, little less than a contradiction in terms, to talk of a vice, which is in general beneficial to society.[1]

I thought this reasoning necessary, in order to give some light to a philosophical question, which has been much disputed in ENGLAND. I call it a *philosophical* question, not a *political* one. For whatever may be the consequence of such a miraculous transformation of mankind, as would endow them with every species of virtue, and free them from every species of vice; this concerns not the magistrate, who aims only at possibilities. He cannot cure every vice by substituting a virtue in its place. Very often he can only cure one vice by another; and in that case, he ought to prefer what is least pernicious to society. Luxury, when excessive, is the source of many ills; but is in general preferable to sloth and idleness, which would commonly succeed in its place, and are more hurtful both to private persons and to the public. When sloth reigns, a mean uncultivated way of life prevails amongst individuals, without society, without enjoyment. And if the sovereign, in such a situation, demands the service of his subjects, the labour of the state suffices only to furnish the necessaries of life to the labourers, and can afford nothing to those who are employed in the public service.

ESSAY III.—*Of Money.*

MONEY is not, properly speaking, one of the subjects of commerce; but only the instrument which men have agreed upon to facilitate the exchange of one commodity for another. It is none of the wheels of trade: It is the oil which renders the motion of the wheels more smooth and easy. If we consider any one kingdom by itself, it is evident, that the greater or less plenty of money is of no consequence; since the prices of commodities are always proportioned to the plenty of money, and a crown in HARRY VII.'s time served the same

---

[1] [Prodigality is not to be confounded with a refinement in the arts. It even appears, that that vice is much less frequent in the cultivated ages. Industry and gain beget this frugality, among the lower and middle ranks of men; and in all the busy professions. Men of high rank, indeed, it may be pretended, are more allured by the pleasures, which become more frequent. But idleness is the great source of prodigality at all times; and there are pleasures and vanities in every age, which allure men equally when they are unacquainted with better enjoyments. Not to mention, that the high interest, payed in rude times, quickly consumes the fortunes of the landed gentry, and multiplies their necessities.—Edition P in the text.]

purpose as a pound does at present. It is only the *publi*∗ which draws any advantage from the greater plenty of money; and that only in its wars and negociations with foreign states. And this is the reason, why all rich and trading countries from CARTHAGE to GREAT BRITAIN and HOLLAND, have employed mercenary troops, which they hired from their poorer neighbours. Were they to make use of their native subjects, they would find less advantage from their superior riches, and from their great plenty of gold and silver; since the pay of all their servants must rise in proportion to the public opulence. Our small army of 20,000 men is maintained at as great expence, as a FRENCH army [1] twice as numerous. The ENGLISH fleet, during the late war, required as much money to support it as all the ROMAN legions, which kept the whole world in subjection, during the time of the emperors.[2]

The greater number of people and their greater industry are serviceable in all cases; at home and abroad, in private and in public. But the greater plenty of money, is very limited in its use, and may even sometimes be a loss to a nation in its commerce with foreigners.

There seems to be a happy concurrence of causes in human affairs, which checks the growth of trade and riches, and hinders them from being confined entirely to one people; as might naturally at first be dreaded from the advantages of an established commerce. Where one nation has gotten the start of another in trade, it is very difficult for the latter to regain the ground it has lost; because of the superior in-

---

[1] [Thrice: Editions H to P.]

[2] A private soldier in the ROMAN infantry had a denarius a day, somewhat less than eightpence. The ROMAN emperors had commonly 25 legions in pay, which allowing 5000 men to a legion, makes 125,000. TACIT. *Ann.* lib. iv. 5. It is true, there were also auxiliaries to the legions; but their numbers are uncertain, as well as their pay. To consider only the legionaries, the pay of the private men could not exceed 1,600,000 pounds. Now, the parliament in the last war commonly allowed for the fleet 2,500,000. We have therefore 900,000 over for the officers and other expences of the ROMAN legions. There seem to have been but few officers in the ROMAN armies, in comparison of what are employed in all our modern troops, except some SWISS corps. And these officers had very small pay: A centurion, for instance, only double a common soldier. And as the soldiers from their pay (TACIT. *Ann.* lib. i. 17) bought their own cloaths, arms, tents, and baggage; this must also diminish considerably the other charges of the army. So little expensive was that mighty government, and so easy was its yoke over the world. And, indeed, this is the more natural conclusion from the foregoing calculations. For money, after the conquest of ÆGYPT, seems to have been nearly in as great plenty at ROME, as it is at present in the richest of the EUROPEAN kingdoms.

dustry and skill of the former, and the greater stocks, of which its merchants are possessed, and which enable them to trade on so much smaller profits. But these advantages are compensated, in some measure, by the low price of labour in every nation which has not an extensive commerce, and does not much abound in gold and silver. Manufactures, therefore gradually shift their places, leaving those countries and provinces which they have already enriched, and flying to others, whither they are allured by the cheapness of provisions and labour; till they have enriched these also, and are again banished by the same causes. And, in general, we may observe, that the dearness of every thing, from plenty of money, is a disadvantage, which attends an established commerce, and sets bounds to it in every country, by enabling the poorer states to undersel the richer in all foreign markets.

This has made me entertain a doubt concerning the benefit of *banks* and *paper-credit*, which are so generally esteemed advantageous to every nation. That provisions and labour should become dear by the encrease of trade and money, is in many respects, an inconvenience; but an inconvenience that is unavoidable, and the effect of that public wealth and prosperity which are the end of all our wishes. It is compensated by the advantages, which we reap from the possession of these precious metals, and the weight, which they give the nation in all foreign wars and negociations. But there appears no reason for encreasing that inconvenience by a counterfeit money, which foreigners will not accept of in any payment, and which any great disorder in the state will reduce to nothing. There are, it is true, many people in every rich state, who having large sums of money, would prefer paper with good security; as being of more easy transport and more safe custody. If the public provide not a bank, private bankers will take advantage of this circumstance; as the goldsmiths formerly did in LONDON, or as the bankers do at present in DUBLIN: And therefore it is better, it may be thought, that a public company should enjoy the benefit of that paper-credit, which always will have place in every opulent kingdom. But to endeavour artificially to encrease such a credit, can never be the interest of any trading nation; but must lay them under disadvantages, by encreasing money beyond its natural proportion to labour and commodities, and thereby heightening their price to the merchant and manufacturer. And in this view, it must be allowed, that no bank could be more advantageous, than such a one as locked up all the money it received,[1] and never augmented the circulating coin, as is usual, by returning part of its treasure into commerce. A public bank, by this expedient, might cut off much of the dealings of private bankers and money-jobbers; and though the state bore the charge of salaries to the directors and tellers of this bank (for, according to the preceding supposition, it would have no profit from its dealings), the national advantage, resulting from the low price of labour and the destruction of paper-credit, would be a sufficient compensation. Not to mention, that so large a sum, lying ready at command, would be a convenience in times of great public danger and distress; and what part of it was used might be replaced at leisure, when peace and tranquility was restored to the nation.

But of this subject of paper-credit we shall treat more largely hereafter. And I shall finish this essay on money, by proposing and explaining two observations, which may, perhaps, serve to employ the thoughts of our speculative politicians.[2]

It was a shrewd observation of ANACHARSIS[3] the SCYTHIAN, who had never seen money in his own country, that gold and silver seemed to him of no use to the GREEKS, but to assist them in numeration and arithmetic. It is indeed evident, that money is nothing but the representation of labour and commodities, and serves only as a method of rating or estimating them. Where coin is in greater plenty; as a greater quantity of it is required to represent the same quantity of goods; it can have no effect, either good or bad, taking a nation within itself; any more than it would make an alteration on a merchant's books, if, instead of the ARABIAN method of notation, which requires few characters, he should make use of the ROMAN, which requires a great many. Nay, the greater quantity of money, like the ROMAN characters, is rather inconvenient, and requires greater trouble both to keep

---

[1] This is the case with the bank of AMSTERDAM. [This note was added in Ed. K.]

[2] [Editions H to P add: For to these only I all along address myself. 'Tis enough that I submit to the ridicule sometimes, in this age, attached to the character of a philosopher, without adding to it that which belongs to a projector.]

[3] PLUT. *Quomodo quis suos profectus in virtute sentire possit.*

and transport it. But notwithstanding this conclusion, which must be allowed just, it is certain, that, since the discovery of the mines in AMERICA, industry has encreased in all the nations of EUROPE, except in the possessors of those mines; and this may justly be ascribed, amongst other reasons, to the encrease of gold and silver. Accordingly we find, that, in every kingdom, into which money begins to flow in greater abundance than formerly, every thing takes a new face: labour and industry gain life; the merchant becomes more enterprising, the manufacturer more diligent and skilful, and even the farmer follows his plough with greater alacrity and attention. This is not easily to be accounted for, if we consider only the influence which a greater abundance of coin has in the kingdom itself, by heightening the price of commodities, and obliging every one to pay a greater number of these little yellow or white pieces for every thing he purchases. And as to foreign trade, it appears, that great plenty of money is rather disadvantageous, by raising the price of every kind of labour.

To account, then, for this phenomenon, we must consider, that though the high price of commodities be a necessary consequence of the encrease of gold and silver, yet it follows not immediately upon that encrease; but some time is required before the money circulates through the whole state, and makes its effect be felt on all ranks of people. At first, no alteration is perceived; by degrees the price rises, first of one commodity, then of another; till the whole at last reaches a just proportion with the new quantity of specie which is in the kingdom. In my opinion, it is only in this interval or intermediate situation, between the acquisition of money and rise of prices, that the encreasing quantity of gold and silver is favourable to industry. When any quantity of money is imported into a nation, it is not at first dispersed into many hands; but is confined to the coffers of a few persons, who immediately seek to employ it to advantage. Here are a set of manufacturers or merchants, we shall suppose, who have received returns of gold and silver for goods which they sent to CADIZ. They are thereby enabled to employ more workmen than formerly, who never dream of demanding higher wages, but are glad of employment from such good paymasters. If workmen become scarce, the manufacturer gives higher wages, but at first requires an encrease of labour;

and this is willingly submitted to by the artisan, who can now eat and drink better, to compensate his additional toil and fatigue. He carries his money to market, where he finds every thing at the same price as formerly, but returns with greater quantity and of better kinds, for the use of his family. The farmer and gardener, finding, that all their commodities are taken off, apply themselves with alacrity to the raising more; and at the same time can afford to take better and more cloths from their tradesmen, whose price is the same as formerly, and their industry only whetted by so much new gain. It is easy to trace the money in its progress through the whole commonwealth; where we shall find, that it must first quicken the diligence of every individual, before it encrease the price of labour.

And that the specie may encrease to a considerable pitch, before it have this latter effect, appears, amongst other instances, from the frequent operations of the FRENCH king on the money; where it was always found, that the augmenting of the numerary value did not produce a proportional rise of the prices, at least for some time. In the last year of LOUIS XIV. money was raised three-sevenths, but prices augmented only one. Corn in FRANCE is now sold at the same price, or for the same number of livres, it was in 1683; though silver was then at 30 livres the mark, and is now at 50.[1] Not to mention the great addition of gold and silver, which may have come into that kingdom since the former period.

---

[1] These facts I give upon the authority of Mons. du Tot in his *Reflections politiques*, an author of reputation. Though I must confess, that the facts which he advances on other occasions, are often so suspicious, as to make his authority less in this matter. However, the general observation, that the augmenting of the money in FRANCE does not at first proportionably augment the prices, is certainly just.

By the by, this seems to be one of the best reasons which can be given, for a gradual and universal encrease of the denomination of money, though it has been entirely overlooked in all those volumes which have been written on that question by MELON, DU TOT, and PARIS de VERNEY. Were all our money, for instance, recoined, and a penny's worth of silver taken from every shilling, the new shilling would probably purchase every thing that could have been bought by the old; the prices of every thing would thereby be insensibly diminished; foreign trade enlivened; and domestic industry, by the circulation of a great number of pounds and shillings, would receive some encrease and encouragement. In executing such a project, it would be better to make the new shilling pass for 24 halfpence, in order to preserve the illusion, and make it be taken for the same. And as a recoinage of our silver begins to be requisite, by the continual wearing of our shillings and sixpences, it may be doubtful, whether we ought to imitate the example in KING WILLIAM's reign, when the clipt money was raised to the old standard.

[This last sentence is entered, to be added, in the list of errata in H: it was incorporated in the text of I.]

From the whole of this reasoning we may conclude, that it is of no manner of consequence, with regard to the domestic happiness of a state, whether money be in a greater or less quantity. The good policy of the magistrate consists only in keeping it, if possible, still encreasing; because, by that means, he keeps alive a spirit of industry in the nation, and encreases the stock of labour, in which consists all real power and riches. A nation, whose money decreases, is actually, at that time, weaker and more miserable than another nation, which possesses no more money, but is on the encreasing hand. This will be easily accounted for, if we consider, that the alterations in the quantity of money, either on one side or the other, are not immediately attended with proportionable alterations in the price of commodities. There is always an interval before matters be adjusted to their new situation; and this interval is as pernicious to industry, when gold and silver are diminishing, as it is advantageous when these metals are encreasing. The workman has not the same employment from the manufacturer and merchant; though he pays the same price for everything in the market. The farmer cannot dispose of his corn and cattle; though he must pay the same rent to his landlord. The poverty, and beggary, and sloth, which must ensue, are easily foreseen.

II. The second observation which I proposed to make with regard to money, may be explained after the following manner. There are some kingdoms, and many provinces in EUROPE, (and all of them were once in the same condition) where money is so scarce, that the landlord can get none at all from his tenants; but is obliged to take his rent in kind, and either to consume it himself, or transport it to places where he may find a market. In those countries, the prince can levy few or no taxes, but in the same manner: And as he will receive small benefit from impositions so paid, it is evident that such a kingdom has little force even at home; and cannot maintain fleets and armies to the same extent, as if every part of it abounded in gold and silver. There is surely a greater disproportion between the force of GERMANY, at present, and what it was three centuries ago,[1] than there is in its industry, people, and manufactures. The AUSTRIAN

---

[1] The ITALIANS gave to the Emperor MAXIMILIAN, the nickname of POCCI-DANARI. None of the enterprises of that prince ever succeeded, for want of money.

dominions in the empire are in general well peopled and well cultivated, and are of great extent; but have not a proportionable weight in the balance of EUROPE; proceeding, as is commonly supposed, from the scarcity of money. How do all these facts agree with that principle of reason, that the quantity of gold and silver is in itself altogether indifferent? According to that principle wherever a sovereign has numbers of subjects, and these have plenty of commodities, he should of course be great and powerful, and they rich and happy, independent of the greater or lesser abundance of the precious metals. These admit of divisions and subdivisions to a great extent; and where the pieces might become so small as to be in danger of being lost, it is easy to mix the gold or silver with a baser metal, as is practised in some countries of EUROPE; and by that means raise the pieces to a bulk more sensible and convenient. They still serve the same purposes of exchange, whatever their number may be, or whatever colour they may be supposed to have.

To these difficulties I answer, that the effect, here supposed to flow from scarcity of money, really arises from the manners and customs of the people; and that we mistake, as is too usual, a collateral effect for a cause. The contradiction is only apparent; but it requires some thought and reflection to discover the principles, by which we can reconcile *reason* to *experience*.

It seems a maxim almost self-evident, that the prices of every thing depend on the proportion between commodities and money, and that any considerable alteration on either has the same effect, either of heightening or lowering the price. Encrease the commodities, they become cheaper; encrease the money, they rise in their value. As, on the other hand, a diminution of the former, and that of the latter, have contrary tendencies.

It is also evident, that the prices do not so much depend on the absolute quantity of commodities and that of money, which are in a nation, as on that of the commodities, which come or may come to market, and of the money which circulates. If the coin be locked up in chests, it is the same thing with regard to prices, as if it were annihilated; if the commodities be hoarded in ¹ magazines and granaries, a like effect follows. As the money and commodities, in these

---

¹ [Magazines and : first added in Edition Q.]

cases, never meet, they cannot affect each other. Were we, at any time, to form conjectures concerning the price of provisions, the corn, which the farmer must reserve [1]for seed and for the maintenance of himself and family, ought never to enter into the estimation. It is only the overplus, compared to the demand, that determines the value.

To apply these principles, we must consider, that, in the first and more uncultivated ages of any state, ere fancy has confounded her wants with those of nature, men, content with the produce of their own fields, or with those rude improvements which they themselves can work upon them, have little occasion for exchange, at least for money, which, by agreement, is the common measure of exchange. The wool of the farmer's own flock, spun in his own family, and wrought by a neighbouring weaver, who receives his payment in corn or wool, suffices for furniture and cloathing. The carpenter, the smith, the mason, the tailor, are retained by wages of a like nature; and the landlord himself, dwelling in the neighbourhood, is content to receive his rent in the commodities raised by the farmer. The greater part of these he consumes at home, in rustic hospitality: The rest, perhaps, he disposes of for money to the neighbouring town, whence he draws the few materials of his expense and luxury.

But after men begin to refine on all these enjoyments, and live not always at home, nor are content with what can be raised in their neighbourhood, there is more exchange and commerce of all kinds, and more money enters into that exchange. The tradesmen will not be paid in corn; because they want something more than barely to eat. The farmer goes beyond his own parish for the commodities he purchases, and cannot always carry his commodities to the merchant who supplies him. The landlord lives in the capital, or in a foreign country; and demands his rent in gold and silver, which can easily be transported to him. Great undertakers, and manufacturers, and merchants, arise in every commodity; and these can conveniently deal in nothing but in specie. And consequently, in this situation of society, the coin enters into many more contracts, and by that means is much more employed than in the former.

The necessary effect is, that, provided the money encrease

[1] [For seed and: first added in Edition R.]

not in the nation, every thing must become much cheaper in times of industry and refinement, than in rude, uncultivated ages. It is the proportion between the circulating money, and the commodities in the market, which determines the prices. Goods, that are consumed at home, or exchanged with other goods in the neighbourhood, never come to market; they affect not in the least the current specie; with regard to it they are as if totally annihilated; and consequently this method of using them sinks the proportion on the side of the commodities, and encreases the prices. But after money enters into all contracts and sales, and is every where the measure of exchange, the same national cash has a much greater task to perform; all commodities are then in the market; the sphere of circulation is enlarged; it is the same case as if that individual sum were to serve a larger kingdom; and therefore, the proportion being here lessened on the side of the money, every thing must become cheaper, and the prices gradually fall.

By the most exact computations, that have been formed all over EUROPE, after making allowance for the alteration in the numerary value or the denomination, it is found, that the prices of all things have only risen three, or at most, four times, since the discovery of the WEST INDIES. But will any one assert, that there is not much more than four times the coin in EUROPE, that was in the fifteenth century, and the centuries preceding it? The SPANIARDS and PORTUGUESE from their mines, the ENGLISH, FRENCH, and DUTCH, by their AFRICAN trade, and by their interlopers in the WEST INDIES, bring home about [1]six millions a year, of which not above a third goes to the EAST INDIES. This sum alone, in ten years, would probably double the ancient stock of money in EUROPE. And no other satisfactory reason can be given, why all prices have not risen to a much more exorbitant height, except that which is derived from a change of customs and manners. Besides that more commodities are produced by additional industry, the same commodities come more to market, after men depart from their ancient simplicity of manners. And though this encrease has not been equal to that of money, it has, however, been considerable, and has preserved the proportion between coin and commodities nearer the ancient standard.

[1] [Editions H and I read: Seven millions . . . a tenth part.]

Were the question proposed, Which of these methods of living in the people, the simple or refined, is the most advantageous to the state or public? I should, without much scruple, prefer the latter, in a view to politics at least; and should produce this as an additional reason for the encouragement of trade and manufactures.

While men live in the ancient simple manner, and supply all their necessaries from domestic industry or from the neighbourhood, the sovereign can levy no taxes in money from a considerable part of his subjects; and if he will impose on them any burthens, he must take payment in commodities, with which alone they abound; a method attended with such great and obvious inconveniencies, that they need need not here be insisted on. All the money he can pretend to raise, must be from his principal cities, where alone it circulates; and these, it is evident, cannot afford him so much as the whole state could, did gold and silver circulate throughout the whole. But besides this obvious diminution of the revenue, there is another cause of the poverty of the public in such a situation. Not only the sovereign receives less money, but the same money goes not so far as in times of industry and general commerce. Every thing is dearer, where the gold and silver are supposed equal; and that because fewer commodities come to market, and the whole coin bears a higher proportion to what is to be purchased by it; whence alone the prices of every thing are fixed and determined.

Here then we may learn the fallacy of the remark, often to be met with in historians, and even in common conversation, that any particular state is weak, though fertile, populous, and well cultivated, merely because it wants money. It appears, that the want of money can never injure any state within itself: For men and commodities are the real strength of any community. It is the simple manner of living which here hurts the public, by confining the gold and silver to few hands, and preventing its universal diffusion and circulation. On the contrary, industry and refinements of all kinds incorporate it with the whole state, however small its quantity may be: They digest it into every vein, so to speak; and make it enter into every transaction and contract. No hand is entirely empty of it. And as the prices of every thing fall by that means, the sovereign has a double advantage: He may draw money by his taxes from every part of the state; and what he receives, goes farther in every purchase and payment.

We may infer, from a comparison of prices, that money is not more plentiful in CHINA, than it was in EUROPE three centuries ago: But what immense power is that empire possessed of, if we may judge by the civil and military establishment maintained by it? Polybius[1] tells us, that provisions were so cheap in ITALY during his time, that in some places the[2] stated price for a meal at the inns was a *semis* a head, little more than a farthing! Yet the ROMAN power had even then subdued the whole known world. About a century before that period, the CARTHAGINIAN ambassador said, by way of raillery, that no people lived more sociably amongst themselves than the ROMANS; for that, in every entertainment, which, as foreign ministers, they received, they still observed the same plate at every table.[3] The absolute quantity of the precious metals is a matter of great indifference. There are only two circumstances of any importance, namely, their gradual encrease, and their thorough concoction and circulation through the state; and the influence of both these circumstances has here been explained.

In the following Essay we shall see an instance of a like fallacy as that above mentioned; where a collateral effect is taken for a cause, and where a consequence is ascribed to the plenty of money; though it be really owing to a change in the manners and customs of the people.

ESSAY IV.—*Of Interest.*

NOTHING is esteemed a more certain sign of the flourishing condition of any nation than the lowness of interest: And with reason; though I believe the cause is somewhat different from what is commonly apprehended. Lowness of interest is generally ascribed to plenty of money. But money, however plentiful, has no other effect, *if fixed*, than to raise the price of labour. Silver is more common than gold; and therefore you receive a greater quantity of it for the same commodities. But do you pay less interest for it? Interest in BATAVIA and JAMAICA is at 10 *per cent.* in PORTUGAL at 6; though these

---

[1] Lib. ii. cap. 15.
[2] [Editions H to P read: The stated club at the inns.]
[3] PLIN. lib. xxxiii. cap. 11.

places, as we may learn from the prices of every thing, abound more in gold and silver than either LONDON or AMSTERDAM.

Were all the gold in ENGLAND annihilated at once, and one and twenty shillings substituted in the place of every guinea, would money be more plentiful or interest lower? No surely: We should only use silver instead of gold. Were gold rendered as common as silver, and silver as common as copper; would money be more plentiful or interest lower? We may assuredly give the same answer. Our shillings would then be yellow, and our halfpence white; and we should have no guineas. No other difference would ever be observed; no alteration on commerce, manufactures, navigation, or interest; unless we imagine, that the colour of the metal is of any consequence.

Now, what is so visible in these greater variations of scarcity or abundance in the precious metals, must hold in all inferior changes. If the multiplying of gold and silver fifteen times makes no difference, much less can the doubling or tripling them. All augmentation has no other effect than to heighten the price of labour and commodities; and even this variation is little more than that of a name. In the progress towards these changes, the augmentation may have some influence, by exciting industry; but after the prices are settled, suitably to the new abundance of gold and silver, it has no manner of influence.

An effect always holds proportion with its cause. Prices have risen near four times since the discovery of the INDIES; and it is probable gold and silver have multiplied much more: But interest has not fallen much above half. The rate of interest, therefore, is not derived from the quantity of the precious metals.

Money having chiefly a fictitious value,[1] the greater or less plenty of it is of no consequence, if we consider a nation within itself; and the quantity of specie, when once fixed, though ever so large, has no other effect, than to oblige every one to tell out a greater number of those shining bits of metal, for clothes, furniture or equipage, without encreasing any one convenience of life. If a man borrow money to build a house, he then carries home a greater load; because the stone, timber, lead, glass, &c. with the labour of the masons and

[1] [Value, arising from the agreement and convention of men: Editions H to P.]

carpenters, are represented by a greater quantity of gold and silver. But as these metals are considered chiefly as representations, there can no alteration arise, from their bulk or quantity, their weight or colour, either upon their real value or their interest. The same interest, in all cases, bears the same proportion to the sum. And if you lent me so much labour and so many commodities; by receiving five *per cent.* you always receive proportional labour and commodities, however represented, whether by yellow or white coin, whether by a pound or an ounce. It is in vain, therefore, to look for the cause of the fall or rise of interest in the greater or less quantity of gold and silver, which is fixed in any nation.

High interest arises from *three* circumstances: A great demand for borrowing; little riches to supply that demand; and great profits arising from commerce: And these circumstances are a clear proof of the small advance of commerce and industry, not of the scarcity of gold and silver. Low interest, on the other hand, proceeds from the three opposite circumstances: A small demand for borrowing; great riches to supply that demand; and small profits arising from commerce: And these circumstances are all connected together, and proceed from the encrease of industry and commerce, not of gold and silver. We shall endeavour to prove these points; and shall begin with the causes and the effects of a great or small demand for borrowing.

When a people have emerged ever so little from a savage state, and their numbers have encreased beyond the original multitude, there must immediately arise an inequality of property; and while some possess large tracts of land, others are confined within narrow limits, and some are entirely without any landed property. Those who possess more land than they can labour, employ those who possess none, and agree to receive a determinate part of the product. Thus the *landed* interest is immediately established; nor is there any settled government, however rude, in which affairs are not on this footing. Of these proprietors of land, some must presently discover themselves to be of different tempers from others; and while one would willingly store up the produce of his land for futurity, another desires to consume at present what should suffice for many years. But as the spending of a settled revenue is a way of life entirely without occupation; men have so much need of somewhat to fix and engage them, that pleasures, such as they are, will be the pursuit of the greater part of the landholders, and the prodigals among them will always be more numerous than the misers. In a state, therefore, where there is nothing but a landed interest, as there is little frugality, the borrowers must be very numerous, and the rate of interest must hold proportion to it. The difference depends not on the quantity of money, but on the habits and manners which prevail. By this alone the demand for borrowing is encreased or diminished. Were money so plentiful as to make an egg be sold for sixpence; so long as there are only landed gentry and peasants in the state, the borrowers must be numerous, and interest high. The rent for the same farm would be heavier and more bulky: But the same idleness of the landlord, with the higher price of commodities, would dissipate it in the same time, and produce the same necessity and demand for borrowing.[1]

Nor is the case different with regard to the *second* circumstance which we proposed to consider, namely, the great or little riches to supply the demand. This effect also depends on the habits and way of living of the people, not on the quantity of gold and silver. In order to have, in any state, a great number of lenders, it is not sufficient nor requisite, that there be great abundance of the precious metals. It is only requisite, that the property or command of that quantity, which is in the state, whether great or small, should be collected in particular hands, so as to form considerable sums, or compose a great monied interest. This begets a number of lenders, and sinks the rate of usury; and this I shall venture to affirm, depends not on the quantity of specie, but on particular manners and customs, which make the specie gather into separate sums or masses of considerable value.

For suppose, that, by miracle, every man in GREAT BRITAIN should have five pounds slipt into his pocket in one night;

---

[1] [Editions H to N add: I have been informed by a very eminent lawyer, and a man of great knowledge and observation, that it appears from antient papers and records, that, about four centuries ago, money in SCOTLAND, and probably in other parts of EUROPE, was only at five *per cent.* and afterwards rose to ten before the discovery of the WEST-INDIES. The fact is curious; but might easily be reconciled to the foregoing reasoning. Men, in that age, lived so much at home, and in so very simple and frugal a manner, that they had no occasion for money; and though the lenders were then few, the borrowers were still fewer. The high rate of interest among the early ROMANS is accounted for by historians from the frequent losses sustained by the inroads of the enemy.]

this would much more than double the whole money that is at present in the kingdom; yet there would not next day, nor for some time, be any more lenders, nor any variation in the interest. And were there nothing but landlords and peasants in the state, this money, however abundant, could never gather into sums; and would only serve to encrease the prices of every thing, without any farther consequence. The prodigal landlord dissipates it, as fast as he receives it; and the beggarly peasant has no means, nor view, nor ambition of obtaining above a bare livelihood. The overplus of borrowers above that of lenders continuing still the same, there will follow no reduction of interest. That depends upon another principle; and must proceed from an encrease of industry and frugality, of arts and commerce.

Every thing useful to the life of man arises from the ground; but few things arise in that condition which is requisite to render them useful. There must, therefore, beside the peasant and the proprietors of land, be another rank of men, who receiving from the former the rude materials, work them into their proper form, and retain part for their own use and subsistence. In the infancy of society, these contracts between the artisans and the peasants, and between one species of artisans and another are commonly entered into immediately by the persons themselves, who, being neighbours, are easily acquainted with each other's necessities, and can lend their mutual assistance to supply them. But when men's industry encreases, and their views enlarge, it is found, that the most remote parts of the state can assist each other as well as the more contiguous, and that this intercourse of good offices may be carried on to the greatest extent and intricacy. Hence the origin of *merchants*, one of the most useful races of men, who serve as agents between those parts of the state, that are wholly unacquainted, and are ignorant of each other's necessities. Here are in a city fifty workmen in silk and linen, and a thousand customers; and these two ranks of men, so necessary to each other, can never rightly meet, till one man erects a shop, to which all the workmen and all the customers repair. In this province, grass rises in abundance: The inhabitants abound in cheese, and butter, and cattle; but want bread and corn, which, in a neighbouring province, are in too great abundance for the use of the inhabitants. One man discovers this. He brings corn from the one province and returns with cattle; and supplying the wants of both, he is, so far, a common benefactor. As the people encrease in numbers and industry, the difficulty of their intercourse encreases: The business of the agency or merchandize becomes more intricate; and divides, subdivides, compounds, and mixes to a greater variety. In all these transactions, it is necessary, and reasonable, that a considerable part of the commodities and labour should belong to the merchant, to whom, in a great measure, they are owing. And these commodities he will sometimes preserve in kind, or more commonly convert into money, which is their common representation. If gold and silver have encreased in the state together with the industry, it will require a great quantity of these metals to represent a great quantity of commodities and labour. If industry alone has encreased, the prices of every thing must sink, and a small quantity of specie will serve as a representation.

There is no craving or demand of the human mind more constant and insatiable than that for exercise and employment; and this desire seems the foundation of most of our passions and pursuits. Deprive a man of all business and serious occupation, he runs restless from one amusement to another; and the weight and oppression, which he feels from idleness, is so great, that he forgets the ruin which must follow him from his immoderate expences. Give him a more harmless way of employing his mind or body, he is satisfied, and feels no longer that insatiable thirst after pleasure. But if the employment you give him be lucrative, especially if the profit be attached to every particular exertion of industry, he has gain so often in his eye, that he acquires, by degrees, a passion for it, and knows no such pleasure as that of seeing the daily encrease of his fortune. And this is the reason why trade encreases frugality, and why, among merchants, there is the same overplus of misers above prodigals, as, among the possessors of land, there is the contrary.

Commerce encreases industry, by conveying it readily from one member of the state to another, and allowing none of it to perish or become useless. It encreases frugality, by giving occupation to men, and employing them in the arts of gain, which soon engage their affection, and remove all relish for pleasure and expense. It is an infallible consequence of all industrious professions, to beget frugality, and make the love of gain prevail over the love of pleasure. Among lawyers and physicians who have any practice, there are many more who live within their income, than who exceed it, or even live up to it. But lawyers and physicians beget no industry; and it is even at the expence of others they acquire their riches; so that they are sure to diminish the possessions of some of their fellow-citizens, as fast as they encrease their own. Merchants, on the contrary, beget industry, by serving as canals to convey it through every corner of the state: And at the same time, by their frugality, they acquire great power over that industry, and collect a large property in the labour and commodities, which they are the chief instruments in producing. There is no other profession, therefore, except merchandize, which can make the monied interest considerable, or, in other words, can encrease industry, and, by also encreasing frugality, give a great command of that industry to particular members of the society. Without commerce, the state must consist chiefly of landed gentry, whose prodigality and expence make a continual demand for borrowing; and of peasants, who have no sums to supply that demand. The money never gathers into large stocks or sums, which can be lent at interest. It is dispersed into numberless hands, who either squander it in idle show and magnificence, or employ it in the purchase of the common necessaries of life. Commerce alone assembles it into considerable sums; and this effect it has merely from the industry which it begets, and the frugality which it inspires, independent of that particular quantity of precious metal which may circulate in the state.

Thus an encrease of commerce, by a necessary consequence, raises a great number of lenders, and by that means produces lowness of interest. We must now consider how far this encrease of commerce diminishes the profits arising from that profession, and gives rise to the *third* circumstance requisite to produce lowness of interest.

It may be proper to observe on this head, that low interest and low profits of merchandize are two events, that mutually forward each other, and are both originally derived from that extensive commerce, which produces opulent merchants, and renders the monied interest considerable. Where merchants possess great stocks, whether represented by few or many pieces of metal, it must frequently happen, that, when they either become tired of business, or leave heirs unwilling or unfit to engage in commerce, a great proportion of these riches naturally seeks an annual and secure revenue. The plenty diminishes the price, and makes the lenders accept of a low interest. This consideration obliges many to keep their stock employed in trade, and rather be content with low profits than dispose of their money at an under-value. On the other hand, when commerce has become extensive, and employs large stocks, there must arise rivalships among the merchants, which diminish the profits of trade, at the same time that they encrease the trade itself. The low profits of merchandize induce the merchants to accept more willingly of a low interest, when they leave off business, and begin to indulge themselves in ease and indolence. It is needless, therefore, to enquire which of these circumstances, to wit, *low interest or low profits,* is the cause, and which the effect? They both arise from an extensive commerce, and mutually forward each other. No man will accept of low profits, where he can have high interest; and no man will accept of low interest, where he can have high profits. An extensive commerce, by producing large stocks, diminishes both interest and profits; and is always assisted, in its diminution of the one, by the proportional sinking of the other. I may add, that, as low profits arise from the encrease of commerce and industry, they serve in their turn to its farther encrease, by rendering the commodities cheaper, encouraging the consumption, and heightening the industry. And thus, if we consider the whole connexion of causes and effects, interest is the barometer of the state, and its lowness is a sign almost infallible of the flourishing condition of a people. It proves the encrease of industry, and its prompt circulation through the whole state, little inferior to a demonstration. And though, perhaps, it may not be impossible but a sudden and a great check to commerce may have a momentary effect of the same kind, by throwing so many stocks out of trade; it must be attended with such misery and want of employment in the poor, that, besides its short duration, it will not be possible to mistake the one case for the other.

Those who have asserted, that the plenty of money was the cause of low interest, seem to have taken a collateral effect for a cause; since the same industry, which sinks the interest, commonly acquires great abundance of the precious metals. A variety of fine manufactures, with vigilant enterprising merchants, will soon draw money to a state, if it be any where to be found in the world. The same cause, by multiplying the conveniencies of life, and encreasing industry, collects great riches into the hands of persons, who are not proprietors of land, and produces, by that means, a lowness of interest. But though both these effects, plenty of money and low interest, naturally arise from commerce and industry, they are altogether independent of each other. For suppose a nation removed into the *Pacific* ocean, without any foreign commerce, or any knowledge of navigation: Suppose, that this nation possesses always the same stock of coin, but is continually encreasing in its numbers and industry: It is evident, that the price of every commodity must gradually diminish in that kingdom; since it is the proportion between money and any species of goods, which fixes their mutual value; and, upon the present supposition, the conveniencies of life become every day more abundant, without any alteration in the current specie. A less quantity of money, therefore, among this people, will make a rich man, during the times of industry, than would suffice to that purpose, in ignorant and slothful ages. Less money will build a house, portion a daughter, buy an estate, support a manufactory, or maintain a family and equipage. These are the uses for which men borrow money; and therefore, the greater or less quantity of it in a state has no influence on the interest. But it is evident, that the greater or less stock of labour and commodities must have a great influence; since we really and in effect borrow these, when we take money upon interest. It is true, when commerce is extended all over the globe, the most industrious nations always abound most with the precious metals: So that low interest and plenty of money are in fact almost inseparable. But still it is of consequence to know the principle whence any phenomenon arises, and to distinguish between a cause and a concomitant effect. Besides that the speculation is curious, it may frequently be of use in the conduct of public affairs. At least, it must be owned, that nothing can be of more use than to improve, by practice, the method of reasoning on these subjects, which of all others are the most important; though they are commonly treated in the loosest and most careless manner.

Another reason of this popular mistake with regard to the cause of low interest, seems to be the instance of some nations; where, after a sudden acquisition of money or of the precious metals, by means of foreign conquest, the interest has fallen, not only among them, but in all the neighbouring states, as soon as that money was dispersed, and had insinuated itself into every corner. Thus, interest in SPAIN fell near a half immediately after the discovery of the WEST INDIES, as we are informed by GARCILASSO DE LA VEGA: And it has been ever since gradually sinking in every kingdom of EUROPE. Interest in ROME, after the conquest of EGYPT, fell from 6 to 4 *per cent*. as we learn from DION.[1]

The causes of the sinking of interest, upon such an event, seem different in the conquering country and in the neighbouring states; but in neither of them can we justly ascribe that effect merely to the encrease of gold and silver.

In the conquering country, it is natural to imagine, that this new acquisition of money will fall into a few hands, and be gathered into large sums, which seek a secure revenue, either by the purchase of land or by interest; and consequently the same effect follows, for a little time, as if there had been a great accession of industry and commerce. The encrease of lenders above the borrowers sinks the interest; and so much the faster, if those, who have acquired those large sums, find no industry or commerce in the state, and no method of employing their money but by lending it at interest. But after this new mass of gold and silver has been digested, and has circulated through the whole state, affairs will soon return to their former situation; while the landlords and new money-holders, living idly, squander above their income; and the former daily contract debt, and the latter encroach on their stock till its final extinction. The whole money may still be in the state, and make itself felt by the encrease of prices: But not being now collected into any large masses or stocks, the disproportion between the borrowers and lenders is the same as formerly, and consequently the high interest returns.

Accordingly we find, in ROME, that, so early as TIBERIUS's time, interest had again mounted to 6 *per cent*.[2] though no accident had happened to drain the empire of money. In TRAJAN's time, money lent on mortgages in ITALY, bore

---

[1] Lib. 51, 21. [2] COLUMELLA, lib. iii. cap. 3.

6 *per cent.*[1]; on common securities in BITHYNIA, 12 [2]. And if interest in SPAIN has not risen to its old pitch; this can be ascribed to nothing but the continuance of the same cause that sunk it, to wit, the large fortunes continually made in the INDIES, which come over to SPAIN from time to time, and supply the demand of the borrowers. By this accidental and extraneous cause, more money is to be lent in SPAIN, that is, more money is collected into large sums than would otherwise be found in a state, where there are so little commerce and industry.

As to the reduction of interest, which has followed in ENGLAND, FRANCE, and other kingdoms of EUROPE, that have no mines, it has been gradual; and has not proceeded from the encrease of money, considered merely in itself; but from that of industry, which is the natural effect of the former encrease, in that interval, before it raises the price of labour and provisions. For to return to the foregoing supposition; if the industry of ENGLAND had risen as much from other causes, (and that rise might easily have happened, though the stock of money had remained the same) must not all the same consequences have followed, which we observe at present? The same people would, in that case, be found in the kingdom, the same commodities, the same industry, manufactures, and commerce; and consequently the same merchants, with the same stocks, that is, with the same command over labour and commodities, only represented by a smaller number of white or yellow pieces; which being a circumstance of no moment, would only affect the waggoner, porter, and trunk-maker. Luxury, therefore, manufactures, arts, industry, frugality, flourishing equally as at present, it is evident, that interest must also have been as low; since that is the necessary result of all these circumstances; so far as they determine the profits of commerce, and the proportion between the borrowers and lenders in any state.

ESSAY V.—*Of the Balance of Trade.*

IT is very usual, in nations ignorant of the nature of commerce, to prohibit the exportation of commodities, and to preserve among themselves whatever they think valuable and

---

[1] PLINII epist. lib. vii. ep. 18.   [2] Id. lib. x. ep. 62.

useful. They do not consider, that, in this prohibition, they act directly contrary to their intention; and that the more is exported of any commodity, the more will be raised at home, of which they themselves will always have the first offer.

It is well known to the learned, that the ancient laws of ATHENS rendered the exportation of figs criminal; that being supposed a species of fruit so excellent in ATTICA, that the ATHENIANS deemed it too delicious for the palate of any foreigner. And in this ridiculous prohibition they were so much in earnest, that informers were thence called *sycophants* among them, from two GREEK words, which signify *figs* and *discoverer*.[1] [2] There are proofs in many old acts of parliament of the same ignorance in the nature of commerce, particularly in the reign of EDWARD III. And to this day, in FRANCE, the exportation of corn is almost always prohibited; in order, as they say, to prevent famines; though it is evident, that nothing contributes more to the frequent famines, which so much distress that fertile country.

The same jealous fear, with regard to money, has also prevailed among several nations; and it required both reason and experience to convince any people, that these prohibitions serve to no other purpose than to raise the exchange against them, and produce a still greater exportation.

These errors, one may say, are gross and palpable: But there still prevails, even in nations well acquainted with commerce, a strong jealousy with regard to the balance of trade, and a fear, that all their gold and silver may be leaving them. This seems to me, almost in every case, a groundless apprehension; and I should as soon dread, that all our springs and rivers should be exhausted, as that money should abandon a kingdom where there are people and industry. Let us carefully preserve these latter advantages; and we need never be apprehensive of losing the former.

It is easy to observe, that all calculations concerning the balance of trade are founded on very uncertain facts and suppositions. The custom-house books are allowed to be an insufficient ground of reasoning; nor is the rate of exchange

---

[1] PLUT. *De Curiositate.*
[2] [For this sentence Editions H to M read: I have been told, that many old acts of parliament show the same ignorance in the nature of Commerce. And to this day, in a neighbouring kingdom, &c.
Edition N reads: There are proofs in many old acts of the SCOTCH parliament of the same ignorance in the nature of commerce. And to this day, in France, &c.]

much better; unless we consider it with all nations, and know also the proportions of the several sums remitted; which one may safely pronounce impossible. Every man, who has ever reasoned on this subject, has always proved his theory, whatever it was, by facts and calculations, and by an enumeration of all the commodities sent to all foreign kingdoms.

The writings of Mr. Gee struck the nation with an universal panic, when they saw it plainly demonstrated, by a detail of particulars, that the balance was against them for so considerable a sum as must leave them without a single shilling in five or six years. But luckily, twenty years have since elapsed, with an expensive foreign war; yet is it commonly supposed, that money is still more plentiful among us than in any former period.

Nothing can be more entertaining on this head than Dr. SWIFT; an author[1] so quick in discerning the mistakes and absurdities of others. He says, in his *short view of the state of* IRELAND, that the whole cash of that kingdom formerly amounted but to 500,000*l.*; that out of this the IRISH remitted every year a neat million to ENGLAND, and had scarcely any other source from which they could compensate themselves, and little other foreign trade than the importation of FRENCH wines, for which they paid ready money. The consequence of this situation, which must be owned to be disadvantageous, was, that, in a course of three years, the current money of IRELAND, from 500,000*l.* was reduced to less than two. And at present, I suppose, in a course of 30 years it is absolutely nothing. Yet I know not how, that opinion of the advance of riches in IRELAND, which gave the Doctor so much indignation, seems still to continue, and gain ground with every body.

In short, this apprehension of the wrong balance of trade, appears of such a nature, that it discovers itself, wherever one is out of humour with the ministry, or is in low spirits; and as it can never be refuted by a particular detail of all the exports, which counterbalance the imports, it may here be proper to form a general argument, that they may prove the impossibility of this event, as long as we preserve our people and our industry.

---

[1] [Editions H and I read: An author, who has more humour than knowledge, more taste than judgment, and more spleen, prejudice, and passion than any of these qualities.]

Suppose four-fifths of all the money in GREAT BRITAIN to be annihilated in one night, and the nation reduced to the same condition, with regard to specie, as in the reigns of the HARRYS and EDWARDS, what would be the consequence? Must not the price of all labour and commodities sink in proportion, and everything be sold as cheap as they were in those ages? What nation could then dispute with us in any foreign market, or pretend to navigate or to sell manufactures at the same price, which to us would afford sufficient profit? In how little time, therefore, must this bring back the money which we had lost, and raise us to the level of all the neighbouring nations? Where, after we have arrived, we immediately lose the advantage of the cheapness of labour and commodities; and the farther flowing in of money is stopped by our fulness and repletion.

Again, suppose, that all the money of GREAT BRITAIN were multiplied fivefold in a night, must not the contrary effect follow? Must not all labour and commodities rise to such an exorbitant height, that no neighbouring nations could afford to buy from us; while their commodities, on the other hand, became comparatively so cheap, that, in spite of all the laws which could be formed, they would be run in upon us, and our money flow out; till we fall to a level with foreigners, and lose that great superiority of riches, which had laid us under such disadvantages?

Now, it is evident, that the same causes, which would correct these exorbitant inequalities, were they to happen miraculously, must prevent their happening in the common course of nature, and must for ever, in all neighbouring nations, preserve money nearly proportionable to the art and industry of each nation. All water, wherever it communicates, remains always at a level. Ask naturalists the reason; they tell you, that, were it to be raised in any one place, the superior gravity of that part not being balanced, must depress it, till it meet a counterpoise; and that the same cause, which redresses the inequality when it happens, must for ever prevent it, without some violent external operation.[1]

---

[1] There is another cause, though more limited in its operation, which checks the wrong balance of trade, to every particular nation to which the kingdom trades. When we import more goods than we export, the exchange turns against us, and this becomes a new encouragement to export; as much as the charge of carriage and insurance of the money which becomes due would amount to. For the exchange can never rise but a little higher than that sum.

Can one imagine, that it had ever been possible, by any laws, or even by any art or industry, to have kept all the money in Spain, which the galleons have brought from the Indies? Or that all commodities could be sold in France for a tenth of the price which they would yield on the other side of the Pyrenees, without finding their way thither, and draining from that immense treasure? What other reason, indeed, is there, why all nations, at present, gain in their trade with Spain and Portugal; but because it is impossible to heap up money, more than any fluid, beyond its proper level? The sovereigns of these countries have shown, that they wanted not inclination to keep their gold and silver to themselves, had it been in any degree practicable.

But as any body of water may be raised above the level of the surrounding element, if the former has no communication with the latter; so in money, if the communication be cut off, by any material or physical impediment, (for all laws alone are ineffectual) there may, in such a case, be a very great inequality of money. Thus the immense distance of China, together with the monopolies of our India companies, obstructing the communication, preserve in Europe the gold and silver, especially the latter, in much greater plenty than they are found in that kingdom. But, notwithstanding this great obstruction, the force of the causes abovementioned is still evident. The skill and ingenuity of Europe in general surpasses perhaps that of China, with regard to manual arts and manufactures; yet are we never able to trade thither without great disadvantage. And were it not for the continual recruits, which we receive from America, money would soon sink in Europe, and rise in China, till it came nearly to a level in both places. Nor can any reasonable man doubt, but that industrious nation, were they as near us as Poland or Barbary, would drain us of the overplus of our specie, and draw to themselves a larger share of the West Indian treasures. We need not have recourse to a physical attraction, in order to explain the necessity of this operation. There is a moral attraction, arising from the interests and passions of men, which is full as potent and infallible.

How is the balance kept in the provinces of every kingdom among themselves, but by the force of this principle, which makes it impossible for money to lose its level, and either to rise or sink beyond the proportion of the labour and commodities which are in each province? Did not long experience make people easy on this head, what a fund of gloomy reflections might calculations afford to a melancholy YORKSHIREMAN, while he computed and magnified the sums drawn to LONDON by taxes, absentees, commodities, and found on comparison the opposite articles so much inferior? And no doubt, had the *Heptarchy* subsisted in ENGLAND, the legislature of each state had been continually alarmed by the fear of a wrong balance; and as it is probable that the mutual hatred of these states would have been extremely violent on account of their close neighbourhood, they would have loaded and oppressed all commerce, by a jealous and superfluous caution. Since the union has removed the barriers between SCOTLAND and ENGLAND, which of these nations gains from the other by this free commerce? Or if the former kingdom has received any encrease of riches, can it reasonably be accounted for by any thing but the encrease of its art and industry? It was a common apprehension in ENGLAND, before the union, as we learn from L'ABBE DU BOS,[1] that SCOTLAND would soon drain them of their treasure, were an open trade allowed; and on the other side the TWEED a contrary apprehension prevailed: With what justice in both, time has shown.

What happens in small portions of mankind, must take place in greater. The provinces of the ROMAN empire, no doubt, kept their balance with each other, and with ITALY, independent of the legislature; as much as the several counties of GREAT BRITAIN, or the several parishes of each county. And any man who travels over EUROPE at this day, may see, by the prices of commodities, that money, in spite of the absurd jealousy of princes and states, has brought itself nearly to a level; and that the difference between one kingdom and another is not greater in this respect, than it is often between different provinces of the same kingdom. Men naturally flock to capital cities, sea-ports, and navigable rivers. There we find more men, more industry, more commodities, and consequently more money; but still the latter difference holds proportion with the former, and the level is preserved[2].

[1] *Les interets d'* ANGLETERRE *malentendus*.

[2] It must carefully be remarked, that throughout this discourse, wherever I speak of the level of money, I mean always its proportional level to the commodities, labour, industry, and skill, which is in the several states. And I

Our jealousy and our hatred of FRANCE are without bounds; and the former sentiment, at least, must be acknowledged reasonable and well-grounded. These passions have occasioned innumerable barriers and obstructions upon commerce, where we are accused of being commonly the aggressors. But what have we gained by the bargain? We lost the FRENCH market for our woollen manufactures, and transferred the commerce of wine to SPAIN and PORTUGAL, where we buy worse liquor at a higher price. There are few ENGLISHMEN who would not think their country absolutely ruined, were FRENCH wines sold in ENGLAND so cheap and in such abundance as to supplant, in some measure, all ale, and home-brewed liquors: But would we lay aside prejudice, it would not be difficult to prove, that nothing could be more innocent, perhaps advantageous. Each new acre of vineyard planted in FRANCE, in order to supply ENGLAND with wine, would make it requisite for the FRENCH to take the produce of an ENGLISH acre, sown in wheat or barley, in order to subsist themselves; and it is evident, that we should thereby get command of the better commodity.

There are many edicts of the FRENCH king, prohibiting the planting of new vineyards, and ordering all those which are lately planted to be grubbed up: So sensible are they, in that country, of the superior value of corn, above every other product.

Mareschal VAUBAN complains often, and with reason, of the absurd duties which load the entry of those wines of LANGUEDOC, GUIENNE, and other southern provinces, that are imported into BRITANNY and NORMANDY. He entertained no doubt but these latter provinces could preserve their balance, notwithstanding the open commerce which he recommends. And it is evident, that a few leagues more navigation to ENGLAND would make no difference; or if it did, that it must operate alike on the commodities of both kingdoms.

assert, that where these advantages are double, triple, quadruple, to what they are in the neighbouring states, the money infallibly will also be double, triple, quadruple. The only circumstance that can obstruct the exactness of these proportions, is the expense of transporting the commodities from one place to another; and this expense is sometimes unequal. Thus the corn, cattle, cheese, butter, of DERBYSHIRE, cannot draw the money of LONDON, so much as the manufactures of LONDON draw the money of DERBYSHIRE. But this objection is only a seeming one: For so far as the transport of commodities is expensive, so far is the communication between the places obstructed and imperfect.

There is indeed one expedient by which it is possible to sink, and another by which we may raise money beyond its natural level in any kingdom; but these cases, when examined, will be found to resolve into our general theory, and to bring additional authority to it.

I scarcely know any method of sinking money below its level, but those institutions of banks, funds, and paper-credit,[1] which are so much practised in this kingdom. These render paper equivalent to money, circulate it throughout the whole state, make it supply the place of gold and silver, raise proportionably the price of labour and commodities, and by that means either banish a great part of those precious metals, or prevent their farther encrease. What can be more short-sighted than our reasonings on this head? We fancy, because an individual would be much richer, were his stock of money doubled, that the same good effect would follow were the money of every one encreased; not considering, that this would raise as much the price of every commodity, and reduce every man, in time, to the same condition as before. It is only in our public negociations and transactions with foreigners, that a greater stock of money is advantageous; and as our paper is there absolutely insignificant, we feel, by its means, all the ill effects arising from a great abundance of money, without reaping any of the advantages[2].

Suppose that there are 12 millions of paper, which circulate in the kingdom as money, (for we are not to imagine, that all our enormous funds are employed in that shape) and suppose the real cash of the kingdom to be 18 millions: Here is a state which is found by experience to be able to hold a stock of 30 millions. I say, if it be able to hold it, it must of necessity have acquired it in gold and silver, had we not obstructed the entrance of these metals by this new invention of paper. *Whence would it have acquired that sum?* From all the kingdoms of the world. *But why?* Because, if you remove these 12 millions, money in this state is below its level, compared with our neighbours; and we must im-

---

[1] [Editions H to N read: With which we are in this kingdom so much infatuated.]

[2] We observed in Essay III. that money, when encreasing, gives encouragement to industry, during the interval between the encrease of money and rise of the prices. A good effect of this nature may follow too from paper-credit; but it is dangerous to precipitate matters, at the risk of losing all by the failing of that credit, as must happen upon any violent shock in public affairs.

mediately draw from all of them, till we be full and saturate, so to speak, and can hold no more. By our present politics, we are as careful to stuff the nation with this fine commodity of bank-bills and chequer-notes, as if we were afraid of being overburthened with the precious metals.

It is not to be doubted, but the great plenty of bullion in FRANCE is, in a great measure, owing to the want of paper-credit. The FRENCH have no banks: Merchants bills do not there circulate as with us: Usury or lending on interest is not directly permitted; so that many have large sums in their coffers: Great quantities of plate are used in private houses; and all the churches are full of it. By this means, provisions and labour still remain cheaper among them, than in nations that are not half so rich in gold and silver. The advantages of this situation, in point of trade as well as in great public emergencies, are too evident to be disputed.

The same fashion a few years ago prevailed in GENOA, which still has place in ENGLAND and HOLLAND, of using services of CHINA-ware instead of plate; but the senate, foreseeing the consequence, prohibited the use of that brittle commodity beyond a certain extent; while the use of silver-plate was left unlimited. And I suppose, in their late distresses, they felt the good effect of this ordinance. Our tax on plate is, perhaps, in this view, somewhat impolitic.

Before the introduction of paper-money into our colonies, they had gold and silver sufficient for their circulation. Since the introduction of that commodity, the least inconveniency that has followed is the total banishment of the precious metals. And after the abolition of paper, can it be doubted but money will return, while these colonies possess manufactures and commodities, the only thing valuable in commerce, and for whose sake alone all men desire money.

What pity LYCURGUS did not think of paper-credit, when he wanted to banish gold and silver from SPARTA! It would have served his purpose better than the lumps of iron he made use of as money; and would also have prevented more effectually all commerce with strangers, as being of so much less real and intrinsic value.

[1] It must, however, be confessed, that, as all these questions of trade and money are extremely complicated, there are certain lights, in which this subject may be placed, so as

[1] [This paragraph does not occur in Editions H to N.]

represent the advantages of paper-credit and banks to be superior to their disadvantages. That they banish specie and bullion from a state is undoubtedly true; and whoever looks no farther than this circumstance does well to condemn them; but specie and bullion are not of so great consequence as not to admit of a compensation, and even an overbalance from the encrease of industry and of credit, which may be promoted by the right use of paper-money. It is well known of what advantage it is to a merchant to be able to discount his bills upon occasion; and every thing that facilitates this species of traffic is favourable to the general commerce of a state. But private bankers are enabled to give such credit by the credit they receive from the depositing of money in their shops; and the bank of ENGLAND in the same manner, from the liberty it has to issue its notes in all payments. There was an invention of this kind, which was fallen upon some years ago by the banks of EDINBURGH; and which, as it is one of the most ingenious ideas that has been executed in commerce, has also been thought advantageous to SCOTLAND. It is there called a BANK-CREDIT; and is of this nature. A man goes to the bank and finds surety to the amount, we shall suppose, of a thousand pounds. This money, or any part of it, he has the liberty of drawing out whenever he pleases, and he pays only the ordinary interest for it, while it is in his hands. He may, when he pleases, repay any sum so small as twenty pounds, and the interest is discounted from the very day of the repayment. The advantages, resulting from this contrivance, are manifold. As a man may find surety nearly to the amount of his substance, and his bank-credit is equivalent to ready money, a merchant does hereby in a manner coin his houses, his household furniture, the goods in his warehouse, the foreign debts due to him, his ships at sea; and can, upon occasion, employ them in all payments, as if they were the current money of the country. If a man borrow a thousand pounds from a private hand, besides that it is not always to be found when required, he pays interest for it, whether he be using it or not: His bank-credit costs him nothing except during the very moment in which it is of service to him: And this circumstance is of equal advantage as if he had borrowed money at much lower interest. Merchants, likewise from this invention, acquire a great facility in supporting each other's credit, which is a considerable security against bankruptcies. A man, when his own bank-credit is exhausted, goes to any of his neighbours who is not in the same condition; and he gets the money, which he replaces at his convenience.

[1] After this practice had taken place during some years at EDINBURGH, several companies of merchants at GLASGOW carried the matter farther. They associated themselves into different banks, and issued notes so low as ten shillings, which they used in all payments for goods, manufactures, tradesmen's labour of all kinds; and these notes, from the established credit of the companies, passed as money in all payments throughout the country. By this means, a stock of five thousand pounds was able to perform the same operations as if it were six or seven; and merchants were thereby enabled to trade to a greater extent, and to require less profit in all their transactions. But whatever other advantages result from these inventions, it must still be allowed that, besides giving too great facility to credit, which is dangerous, they banish the precious metals: and nothing can be a more evident proof of it, than a comparison of the past and present condition of SCOTLAND in that particular. It was found, upon the recoinage made after the union, that there was near a million of specie in that country: But notwithstanding the great encrease of riches, commerce and manufactures of all kinds, it is thought, that, even where there is no extraordinary drain made by ENGLAND, the current specie will not now amount to a third of that sum.

[2] But as our projects of paper-credit are almost the only expedient, by which we can sink money below its level; so, in my opinion, the only expedient, by which we can raise money above it, is a practice which we should all exclaim against as destructive, namely, the gathering of large sums into a public treasure, locking them up, and absolutely preventing their circulation. The fluid, not communicating with the neighbouring element, may, by such an artifice, be raised to what height we please. To prove this, we need only return to our first supposition, of annihilating the half or any part of our cash; where we

---

[1] [This paragraph does not occur in Editions H to N.]
[2] [Editions H to N resume: But as our darling projects of paper-credit are pernicious, being almost, &c.]

found, that the immediate consequence of such an event would be the attraction of an equal sum from all the neighbouring kingdoms. Nor does there seem to be any necessary bounds set, by the nature of things, to this practice of hoarding. A small city, like GENEVA, continuing this policy for ages, might engross nine tenths of the money of EUROPE. There seems, indeed, in the nature of man, an invincible obstacle to that immense growth of riches. A weak state, with an enormous treasure, will soon become a prey to some of its poorer, but more powerful neighbours. A great state would dissipate its wealth in dangerous and ill-concerted projects; and probably destroy, with it, what is much more valuable, the industry, morals, and numbers of its people. The fluid, in this case, raised to too great a height, bursts and destroys the vessel that contains it; and mixing itself with the surrounding element, soon falls to its proper level.

So little are we commonly acquainted with this principle, that, though all historians agree in relating uniformly so recent an event, as the immense treasure amassed by HARRY VII. (which they make amount to [1] 2,700,000 pounds,) we rather reject their concurring testimony, than admit of a fact, which agrees so ill with our inveterate prejudices. It is indeed probable, that this sum might be three-fourths of all the money in ENGLAND. But where is the difficulty in conceiving, that such a sum might be amassed in twenty years, by a cunning, rapacious, frugal, and almost absolute monarch? Nor is it probable, that the diminution of circulating money was ever sensibly felt by the people, or ever did them any prejudice. The sinking of the prices of all commodities would immediately replace it, by giving ENGLAND the advantage in its commerce with the neighbouring kingdoms.

Have we not an instance in the small republic of ATHENS with its allies, who, in about fifty years, between the MEDIAN and PELOPONNESIAN wars, amassed [2] a sum not much inferior to that of HARRY VII.? For all the GREEK historians[3] and orators[4] agree, that the ATHENIANS collected in the citadel

---

[1] [Editions H to P read: 1,700,000.]

[2] [Editions H to P read: A sum greater than that of Harry VII. (There were about eight ounces of silver in a pound *sterling* in Harry VII.'s time.]

[3] THUCYDIDES, lib. ii. 13 and DIOD. SIC. lib. xii. 40.

[4] *Vid.* ÆSCHINIS (p. 688) *et* DEMOSTHENIS *Epist.*

more than 10,000 talents, which they afterwards dissipated in their own ruin, in rash and imprudent enterprises. But when this money was set a running, and began to communicate with the surrounding fluid; what was the consequence? Did it remain in the state? No. For we find, by the memorable *census* mentioned by DEMOSTHENES[1] and POLYBIUS[2], that, in about fifty years afterwards, the whole value of the republic, comprehending lands, houses, commodities, slaves, and money, was less than 6,000 talents.

What an ambitious high-spirited people was this, to collect and keep in their treasury, with a view to conquests, a sum, which it was every day in the power of the citizens, by a single vote, to distribute among themselves, and which would have gone near to triple the riches of every individual! For we must observe, that the numbers and private riches of the ATHENIANS are said, by ancient writers, to have been no greater at the beginning of the PELOPONNESIAN war, than at the beginning of the MACEDONIAN.

Money was little more plentiful in GREECE during the age of PHILIP and PERSEUS, than in ENGLAND during that of HARRY VII.: Yet these two monarchs in thirty years[3] collected from the small kingdom of MACEDON, a larger treasure than that of the ENGLISH monarch. PAULUS ÆMILIUS brought to ROME about 1,700,000 pounds *Sterling*.[4] PLINY says, 2,400,000.[5] And that was but a part of the MACEDONIAN treasure. The rest was dissipated by the resistance and flight of PERSEUS.[6]

We may learn from STANIAN, that the canton of BERNE had 300,000 pounds lent at interest, and had above six times as much in their treasury. Here then is a sum hoarded of 1,800,000 pounds *Sterling*, which is at least quadruple what should naturally circulate in such a petty state; and yet no one, who travels in the PAIS DE VAUX, or any part of that canton, observes any want of money more than could be supposed in a country of that extent, soil, and situation. On the contrary, there are scarce any inland provinces in the continent of FRANCE or GERMANY, where the inhabitants are at this time so opulent, though that canton has vastly

---

[1] Περὶ Συμμορίας, 183.
[2] Lib. ii. cap. 62.
[3] TITI LIVII, lib. xlv. cap. 40.
[4] VEL. PATERC. lib. i. cap. 9.
[5] LIB. xxxiii. cap. 3.
[6] TITI LIVII, *ibid*.

encreased its treasure since 1714, the time when STANIAN wrote his judicious account of SWITZERLAND.[1]

The account given by APPIAN[2] of the treasure of the PTOLEMIES, is so prodigious, that one cannot admit of it; and so much the less, because the historian says, that the other successors of ALEXANDER were also frugal, and had many of them treasures not much inferior. For this saving humour of the neighbouring princes must necessarily have checked the frugality of the EGYPTIAN monarchs, according to the foregoing theory. The sum he mentions is 740,000 talents, or 191,166,666 pounds 13 shillings and 4 pence, according to Dr. ARBUTHNOT's computation. And yet APPIAN says, that he extracted his account from the public records; and he was himself a native of ALEXANDRIA.

From these principles we may learn what judgment we ought to form of those numberless bars, obstructions, and imposts, which all nations of Europe, and none more than ENGLAND, have put upon trade; from an exorbitant desire of amassing money, which never will heap up beyond its level, while it circulates; or from an ill-grounded apprehension of losing their specie, which never will sink below it. Could any thing scatter our riches, it would be such impolitic contrivances. But this general ill effect, however, results from them, that they deprive neighbouring nations of that free communication and exchange which the Author of the world has intended, by giving them soils, climates, and geniuses, so different from each other.

Our modern politics embrace the only method of banishing money, the using of paper-credit; they reject the only method of amassing it, the practice of hoarding; and they adopt a hundred contrivances, which serve to no purpose but to check industry, and rob ourselves and our neighbours of the common benefits of art and nature.

All taxes, however, upon foreign commodities, are not to be regarded as prejudicial or useless, but those only which are founded on the jealousy above-mentioned. A tax on German linen encourages home manufactures, and thereby

---

[1] The poverty which STANIAN speaks of is only to be seen in the most mountainous cantons, where there is no commodity to bring money. And even there the people are not poorer than in the diocese of SALTSBURGH on the one hand, or SAVOY on the other.

[2] *Proem.* 10.

multiplies our people and industry. A tax on brandy encreases the sale of rum, and supports our southern colonies. And as it is necessary, that imposts should be levied, for the support of government, it may be thought more convenient to lay them on foreign commodities, which can easily be intercepted at the port, and subjected to the impost. We ought, however, always to remember the maxim of Dr. SWIFT, That, in the arithmetic of the customs, two and two make not four, but often make only one. It can scarcely be doubted, but if the duties on wine were lowered to a third, they would yield much more to the government than at present: Our people might thereby afford to drink commonly a better and more wholesome liquor; and no prejudice would ensue to the balance of trade, of which we are so jealous. The manufacture of ale beyond the agriculture is but inconsiderable, and gives employment to few hands. The transport of wine and corn would not be much inferior.

But are there not frequent instances, you will say, of states and kingdoms, which were formerly rich and opulent, and are now poor and beggarly? Has not the money left them, with which they formerly abounded? I answer, If they lose their trade, industry, and people, they cannot expect to keep their gold and silver: For these precious metals will hold proportion to the former advantages. When LISBON and AMSTERDAM got the EAST-INDIA trade from VENICE and GENOA, they also got the profits and money which arose from it. Where the seat of government is transferred, where expensive armies are maintained at a distance, where great funds are possessed by foreigners; there naturally follows from these causes a diminution of the specie. But these, we may observe, are violent and forcible methods of carrying away money, and are in time commonly attended with the transport of people and industry. But where these remain, and the drain is not continued, the money always finds its way back again, by a hundred canals, of which we have no notion or suspicion. What immense treasures have been spent, by so many nations, in FLANDERS, since the revolution, in the course of three long wars! More money perhaps than the half of what is at present in EUROPE. But what has now become of it? Is it in the narrow compass of the AUSTRIAN provinces? No, surely: It has most of it returned to the several countries whence it came, and has followed

that art and industry, by which at first it was acquired.
[1] For above a thousand years, the money of EUROPE has been flowing to ROME, by an open and sensible current; but it has been emptied by many secret and insensible canals: And the want of industry and commerce renders at present the papal dominions the poorest territory in all ITALY.

In short, a government has great reason to preserve with care its people and its manufactures. Its money, it may safely trust to the course of human affairs, without fear or jealousy. Or if it ever give attention to this latter circumstance, it ought only to be so far as it affects the former.

[2] ESSAY VI.—*Of the Jealousy of Trade.*

Having endeavoured to remove one species of ill-founded jealousy, which is so prevalent among commercial nations, it may not be amiss to mention another, which seems equally groundless. Nothing is more usual, among states which have made some advances in commerce, than to look on the progress of their neighbours with a suspicious eye, to consider all trading states as their rivals, and to suppose that it is impossible for any of them to flourish, but at their expence. In opposition to this narrow and malignant opinion, I will venture to assert, that the encrease of riches and commerce in any one nation, instead of hurting, commonly promotes the riches and commerce of all its neighbours; and that a state can scarcely carry its trade and industry very far, where all the surrounding states are buried in ignorance, sloth, and barbarism.

It is obvious, that the domestic industry of a people cannot be hurt by the greatest prosperity of their neighbours; and as this branch of commerce is undoubtedly the most important in any extensive kingdom, we are so far removed from all reason of jealousy. But I go farther, and observe, that where an open communication is preserved among nations, it is impossible but the domestic industry of every one must receive an encrease from the improvements of the others. Compare the situation of GREAT BRITAIN at present, with what it was two centuries ago. All the arts both of agriculture and manufactures were then extremely rude and

---

[1] [This sentence is not in Editions H and I.]
[2] [This Essay first appeared in Edition M. See p. 72.]

imperfect. Every improvement, which we have since made, has arisen from our imitation of foreigners; and we ought so far to esteem it happy, that they had previously made advances in arts and ingenuity. But this intercourse is still upheld to our great advantage: Notwithstanding the advanced state of our manufactures, we daily adopt, in every art, the inventions and improvements of our neighbours. The commodity is first imported from abroad, to our great discontent, while we imagine that it drains us of our money: Afterwards, the art itself is gradually imported, to our visible advantage: Yet we continue still to repine, that our neighbours should possess any art, industry, and invention; forgetting that, had they not first instructed us, we should have been at present barbarians; and did they not still continue their instructions, the arts must fall into a state of languor, and lose that emulation and novelty, which contribute so much to their advancement.

The encrease of domestic industry lays the foundation of foreign commerce. Where a great number of commodities are raised and perfected for the home-market, there will always be found some which can be exported with advantage. But if our neighbours have no art or cultivation, they cannot take them; because they will have nothing to give in exchange. In this respect, states are in the same condition as individuals. A single man can scarcely be industrious, where all his fellow-citizens are idle. The riches of the several members of a community contribute to encrease my riches, whatever profession I may follow. They consume the produce of my industry, and afford me the produce of theirs in return.

Nor needs any state entertain apprehensions, that their neighbours will improve to such a degree in every art and manufacture, as to have no demand from them. Nature, by giving a diversity of geniuses, climates, and soils, to different nations, has secured their mutual intercourse and commerce, as long as they all remain industrious and civilized. Nay, the more the arts encrease in any state, the more will be its demands from its industrious neighbours. The inhabitants, having become opulent and skilful, desire to have every commodity in the utmost perfection; and as they have plenty of commodities to give in exchange, they make large importations from every foreign country. The industry of the nations, from whom they import, receives encouragement: Their own is also encreased, by the sale of the commodities which they give in exchange.

But what if a nation has any staple commodity, such as the woollen manufacture is in ENGLAND? Must not the interfering of our neighbours in that manufacture be a loss to us? I answer, that, when any commodity is denominated the staple of a kingdom, it is supposed that this kingdom has some peculiar and natural advantages for raising the commodity; and if, notwithstanding these advantages, they lose such a manufacture, they ought to blame their own idleness, or bad government, not the industry of their neighbours. It ought also to be considered, that, by the encrease of industry among the neighbouring nations, the consumption of every particular species of commodity is also encreased; and though foreign manufactures interfere with them in the market, the demand for their product may still continue, or even encrease. And should it diminish, ought the consequence to be esteemed so fatal? If the spirit of industry be preserved, it may easily be diverted from one branch to another; and the manufacturers of wool, for instance, be employed in linen, silk, iron, or any other commodities, for which there appears to be a demand. We need not apprehend, that all the objects of industry will be exhausted, or that our manufacturers, while they remain on an equal footing with those of our neighbours, will be in danger of wanting employment. The emulation among rival nations serves rather to keep industry alive in all of them: And any people is happier who possess a variety of manufactures, than if they enjoyed one single great manufacture, in which they are all employed. Their situation is less precarious; and they will feel less sensibly those revolutions and uncertainties, to which every particular branch of commerce will always be exposed.

The only commercial state, that ought to dread the improvements and industry of their neighbours, is such a one as the DUTCH, who enjoying no extent of land, nor possessing any number of native commodities, flourish only by their being the brokers, and factors, and carriers of others. Such a people may naturally apprehend, that, as soon as the neighbouring states come to know and pursue their interest, they will take into their own hands the management of their affairs, and deprive their brokers of that profit, which they formerly reaped from it. But though this consequence may naturally be dreaded, it is very long before it takes place; and by art and industry it may be warded off for many generations, if not wholly eluded. The advantage of superior stocks and correspondence is so great, that it is not easily overcome; and as all the transactions encrease by the encrease of industry in the neighbouring states, even a people whose commerce stands on this precarious basis, may at first reap a considerable profit from the flourishing condition of their neighbours. The DUTCH, having mortgaged all their revenues, make not such a figure in political transactions as formerly; but their commerce is surely equal to what it was in the middle of the last century, when they were reckoned among the great powers of EUROPE.

Were our narrow and malignant politics to meet with success, we should reduce all our neighbouring nations to the same state of sloth and ignorance that prevails in MOROCCO and the coast of BARBARY. But what would be the consequence? They could send us no commodities: They could take none from us: Our domestic commerce itself would languish for want of emulation, example and instruction: And we ourselves should soon fall into the same abject condition, to which we had reduced them. I shall therefore venture to acknowledge, that, not only as a man, but as a BRITISH subject, I pray for the flourishing commerce of GERMANY, SPAIN, ITALY, and even FRANCE itself. I am at least certain, that GREAT BRITAIN, and all those nations, would flourish more, did their sovereigns and ministers adopt such enlarged and benevolent sentiments towards each other.

ESSAY VII.—*Of the Balance of Power.*

IT is a question whether the *idea* of the balance of power be owing entirely to modern policy, or whether the *phrase* only has been invented in these later ages? It is certain, that XENOPHON,[1] in his Institution of CYRUS, represents the combination of the ASIATIC powers to have arisen from a jealousy of the encreasing force of the MEDES and PERSIANS; and though that elegant composition should be supposed

---

[1] Lib. i. 5, 3.

altogether a romance, this sentiment, ascribed by the author to the eastern princes, is at least a proof of the prevailing notion of ancient times.

In all the politics of GREECE, the anxiety, with regard to the balance of power, is apparent, and is expressly pointed out to us, even by the ancient historians. THUCYDIDES[1] represents the league, which was formed against ATHENS, and which produced the PELOPONNESIAN war, as entirely owing to this principle. And after the decline of ATHENS, when the THEBANS and LACEDEMONIANS disputed for sovereignty, we find, that the ATHENIANS (as well as many other republics) always threw themselves into the lighter scale, and endeavoured to preserve the balance. They supported THEBES against SPARTA, till the great victory gained by EPAMINONDAS at LEUCTRA; after which they immediately went over to the conquered, from generosity, as they pretended, but in reality from their jealousy of the conquerors.[2]

Whoever will read DEMOSTHENES's oration for the MEGALOPOLITANS, may see the utmost refinements on this principle, that ever entered into the head of a VENETIAN or ENGLISH speculatist. And upon the first rise of the MACEDONIAN power, this orator immediately discovered the danger, sounded the alarm throughout all GREECE, and at last assembled that confederacy under the banners of ATHENS, which fought the great and decisive battle of CHAERONEA.

It is true, the GRECIAN wars are regarded by historians as wars of emulation rather than of politics; and each state seems to have had more in view the honour of leading the rest, than any well-grounded hopes of authority and dominion. If we consider, indeed, the small number of inhabitants in any one republic, compared to the whole, the great difficulty of forming sieges in those times, and the extraordinary bravery and discipline of every freeman among that noble people; we shall conclude, that the balance of power was, of itself, sufficiently secured in GREECE, and needed not to have been guarded with that caution which may be requisite in other ages. But whether we ascribe the shifting of sides in all the GRECIAN republics to *jealous emulation* or *cautious politics*, the effects were alike, and every prevailing power was sure to meet with a confederacy against it, and that often composed of its former friends and allies.

[1] Lib. i. 23.   [2] XENOPH. Hist. GRAEC. lib. vi. and vii.

The same principle, call it envy or prudence, which produced the *Ostracism* of ATHENS, and *Petalism* of SYRACUSE, and expelled every citizen whose fame or power overtopped the rest; the same principle, I say, naturally discovered itself in foreign politics, and soon raised enemies to the leading state, however moderate in the exercise of its atthority.

The PERSIAN monarch was really, in his force, a petty prince, compared to the GRECIAN republics; and therefore it behoved him, from views of safety more than from emulation, to interest himself in their quarrels, and to support the weaker side in every contest. This was the advice given by ALCIBIADES to TISSAPHERNES,[1] and it prolonged near a century the date of the PERSIAN empire; till the neglect of it for a moment, after the first appearance of the aspiring genius of PHILIP, brought that lofty and frail edifice to the ground, with a rapidity of which there are few instances in the history of mankind.

The successors of ALEXANDER showed great jealousy of the balance of power; a jealousy founded on true politics and prudence, and which preserved distinct for several ages the partition made after the death of that famous conqueror. The fortune and ambition of ANTIGONUS[2] threatened them anew with a universal monarchy; but their combination and their victory at IPSUS saved them. And in subsequent times, we find, that, as the Eastern princes considered the GREEKS and MACEDONIANS as the only real military force, with whom they had any intercourse, they kept always a watchful eye over that part of the world. The PTOLEMIES, in particular, supported first ARATUS and the ACHAEANS, and then CLEOMENES king of SPARTA, from no other view than as a counterbalance to the MACEDONIAN monarchs. For this is the account which POLYBIUS gives of the EGYPTIAN politics.[3]

The reason, why it is supposed, that the ancients were entirely ignorant of the *balance of power*, seems to be drawn from the ROMAN history more than the GRECIAN; and as the transactions of the former are generally more familiar to us, we have thence formed all our conclusions. It must be owned, that the ROMANS never met with any such general combination or confederacy against them, as might naturally have been expected from the rapid conquests and

---

[1] THUCYD. lib. viii. 46.   [2] DION. SIC. lib. xx. 106.   [3] Lib. ii. cap. 51.

declared ambition; but were allowed peaceably to subdue their neighbours, one after another, till they extended their dominion over the whole known world. Not to mention the fabulous history of their [1] ITALIC wars; there was, upon HANNIBAL's invasion of the ROMAN state, a remarkable crisis, which ought to have called up the attention of all civilized nations. It appeared afterwards (nor was it difficult to be observed at the time) [2] that this was a contest for universal empire; yet no prince or state seems to have been the least alarmed about the event or issue of the quarrel. PHILIP of MACEDON remained neuter, till he saw the victories of HANNIBAL; and then most imprudently formed an alliance with the conqueror, upon terms still more imprudent. He stipulated, that he was to assist the CARTHAGINIAN state in their conquest of ITALY; after which they engaged to send over forces into GREECE, to assist him in subduing the GRECIAN commonwealths.[3]

The RHODIAN and ACHAEAN republics are much celebrated by ancient historians for their wisdom and sound policy; yet both of them assisted the ROMANS in their wars against PHILIP and ANTIOCHUS. And what may be esteemed still a

---

[1] [Editions H and L add as a note: There have strong suspicions, of late, arisen among critics, and, in my opinion, not without reason, concerning the first ages of the ROMAN history; as if they were almost entirely fabulous, 'till after the sacking of the city by the GAULS; and were even doubtful for some time afterwards, 'till the GREEKS began to give attention to ROMAN affairs, and commit them to writing. This scepticism, however, seems to me, scarcely defensible in its full extent, with regard to the domestic history of ROME, which has some air of truth and probability, and cou'd scarce be the invention of an historian, who had so little morals or judgment as to indulge himself in fiction and romance. The revolutions seem so well proportion'd to their causes: The progress of the factions is so conformable to political experience: The manners and maxims of the age are so uniform and natural, that scarce any real history affords more just reflection and improvement. Is not MACHIAVEL's comment on LIVY (a work surely of great judgment and genius) founded entirely on this period, which is represented as fabulous. I wou'd willingly, therefore, in my private sentiments, divide the matter with these critics; and allow, that the battles and victories and triumphs of those ages had been extremely falsify'd by family memoirs, as CICERO says they were: But as in the accounts of domestic factions, there were two opposite relations transmitted to posterity, this both serv'd as a check upon fiction, and enabled latter historians to gather some truth from comparison and reasoning. Half of the slaughter which LIVY commits on the Æqui and the VOLSCI, would depopulate FRANCE and GERMANY; and that historian, tho' perhaps he may be justly charged as superficial, is at last shock'd himself with the incredibility of his narration. The same love of exaggeration seems to have magnify'd the numbers of the ROMANS in their armies, and *census*.]

[2] It was observed by some, as appears by the speech of AGELAUS of NAUPACTUM, in the general congress of GREECE. See POLYB. lib. v. cap. 104.

[3] TITI LIVII. lib. xxiii. cap. 33.

stronger proof, that this maxim was not generally known in those ages; no ancient author has remarked the imprudence of these measures, nor has even blamed that absurd treaty above-mentioned, made by PHILIP with the CARTHAGINIANS. Princes and statesmen, in all ages, may, before-hand, be blinded in their reasonings with regard to events: But it is somewhat extraordinary, that historians, afterwards, should not form a sounder judgment of them.

MASSINISSA, ATTALUS, PRUSIAS, in gratifying their private passions, were, all of them, the instruments of the ROMAN greatness; and never seem to have suspected, that they were forging their own chains, while they advanced the conquests of their ally. A simple treaty and agreement between MASSINISSA and the CARTHAGINIANS, so much required by mutual interest, barred the ROMANS from all entrance into AFRICA, and preserved liberty to mankind.

The only prince we meet with in the ROMAN history, who seems to have understood the balance of power, is HIERO king of SYRACUSE. Though the ally of ROME, he sent assistance to the CARTHAGINIANS, during the war of the auxiliaries: 'Esteeming it requisite,' says POLYBIUS,[1] 'both in order to retain his dominions in SICILY, and to preserve the ROMAN friendship, that CARTHAGE should be safe; lest by its fall the remaining power should be able, without contrast or opposition, to execute every purpose and undertaking. And here he acted with great wisdom and prudence. For that is never, on any account, to be overlooked; nor ought such a force ever to be thrown into one hand, as to incapacitate the neighbouring states from defending their rights against it.' Here is the aim of modern politics pointed out in express terms.

In short, the maxim of preserving the balance of power is founded so much on common sense and obvious reasoning, that it is impossible it could altogether have escaped antiquity, where we find, in other particulars, so many marks of deep penetration and discernment. If it was not so generally known and acknowledged as at present, it had, at least, an influence on all the wiser and more experienced princes and politicians. And indeed, even at present, however generally known and acknowledged among speculative reasoners, it has

[1] Lib. i. cap. 83.

not, in practice, an authority much more extensive among those who govern the world.

After the fall of the ROMAN empire, the form of government, established by the northern conquerors, incapacitated them, in a great measure, for farther conquests, and long maintained each state in its proper boundaries. But when vassalage and the feudal militia were abolished, mankind were anew alarmed by the danger of universal monarchy, from the union of so many kingdoms and principalities in the person of the emperor CHARLES. But the power of the house of AUSTRIA, founded on extensive but divided dominions, and their riches, derived chiefly from mines of gold and silver, were more likely to decay, of themselves, from internal defects, than to overthrow all the bulwarks raised against them. In less than a century, the force of that violent and haughty race was shattered, their opulence dissipated, their splendor eclipsed. A new power succeeded, more formidable to the liberties of EUROPE, possessing all the advantages of the former, and labouring under none of its defects; except a share of that spirit of bigotry and persecution, with which the house of AUSTRIA was so long, and still is so much infatuated.

[1] In the general wars, maintained against this ambitious power, GREAT BRITAIN has stood foremost; and she still maintains her station. Beside her advantages of riches and situation, her people are animated with such a national spirit, and are so fully sensible of the blessings of their government, that we may hope their vigour never will languish in so necessary and so just a cause. On the contrary, if we

[1] [Editions H to P proceed as follows: Europe has now, for above a century, remained on the defensive against the greatest force that ever, perhaps, was formed by the civil or political combination of mankind. And such is the influence of the maxim here treated of, that tho' that ambitious nation, in the five last general wars, have been victorious in four,[1] and unsuccessful only in one,[2] they have not much enlarged their dominions, nor acquired a total ascendant over EUROPE. There remains rather room to hope, that, by maintaining the resistance for some time, the natural revolutions of human affairs, together with unforeseen events and accidents, may guard us against universal monarchy, and preserve the world from so great an evil.

In the three last of these general wars, BRITAIN has stood foremost in the glorious struggle; and she still maintains her station, as guardian of the general liberties of EUROPE, and patron of mankind.]

[1] Those concluded by the peace of the PYRENEES, NIMEGUEN, RYSWICK, and AIX-LA-CHAPELLE.

[2] That concluded by the peace of UTRECHT.

may judge by the past, their passionate ardour seems rather to require some moderation; and they have oftener erred from a laudable excess than from a blameable deficiency.

In the *first* place, we seem to have been more possessed with the ancient GREEK spirit of jealous emulation, than actuated by the prudent views of modern politics. Our wars with FRANCE have been begun with justice, and even, perhaps, from necessity; but have always been too far pushed from obstinacy and passion. The same peace, which was afterwards made at RYSWICK in 1697, was offered so early as the year ninety-two; that concluded at UTRECHT in 1712 might have been finished on as good conditions at GERTRUYTENBERG in the year eight; and we might have given at FRANKFORT, in 1743, the same terms, which we were glad to accept of at AIX-LA-CHAPELLE in the year forty-eight. Here then we see, that above half of our wars with FRANCE, and all our public debts, are owing more to our own imprudent vehemence, than to the ambition of our neighbours.

In the *second* place, we are so declared in our opposition to FRENCH power, and so alert in defence of our allies, that they always reckon upon our force as upon their own; and expecting to carry on war at our expence, refuse all reasonable terms of accommodation. *Habent subjectos, tanquam suos: viles, ut alienos.* All the world knows, that the factious vote of the House of Commons, in the beginning of the last parliament,[1] with the professed humour of the nation, made the queen of HUNGARY inflexible in her terms, and prevented that agreement with PRUSSIA, which would immediately have restored the general tranquillity of EUROPE.

In the *third* place, we are such true combatants, that, when once engaged, we lose all concern for ourselves and our posterity, and consider only how we may best annoy the enemy. To mortgage our revenues at so deep a rate, in wars, where we were only accessories, was surely the most fatal delusion, that a nation, which had any pretension to politics and prudence, has ever yet been guilty of. That remedy of funding, if it be a remedy, and not rather a poison, ought, in all reason, to be reserved to the last extremity; and no evil, but the greatest and most urgent, should ever induce us to embrace so dangerous an expedient.

These excesses, to which we have been carried, are preju-

[1] [At the close of the parliament of 1734-41. Ed.]

dicial; and may, perhaps, in time, become still more prejudicial another way, by begetting, as is usual, the opposite extreme, and rendering us totally careless and supine with regard to the fate of EUROPE. The ATHENIANS, from the most bustling, intriguing, warlike people of GREECE, finding their error in thrusting themselves into every quarrel, abandoned all attention to foreign affairs; and in no contest ever took part on either side, except by their flatteries and complaisance to the victor.

Enormous monarchies[1] are, probably, destructive to human nature; in their progress, in their continuance,[2] and even in their downfall, which never can be very distant from their establishment. The military genius, which aggrandized the monarchy, soon leaves the court, the capital, and the center of such a government; while the wars are carried on at a great distance, and interest so small a part of the state. The ancient nobility, whose affections attach them to their sovereign, live all at court; and never will accept of military employments, which would carry them to remote and barbarous frontiers, where they are distant both from their pleasures and their fortune. The arms of the state, must, therefore, be entrusted to mercenary strangers, without zeal, without attachment, without honour; ready on every occasion to turn them against the prince, and join each desperate malcontent, who offers pay and plunder. This is the necessary progress of human affairs: Thus human nature checks itself in its airy elevation: Thus ambition blindly labours for the destruction of the conqueror, of his family, and of every thing near and dear to him. The BOURBONS, trusting to the support of their brave, faithful, and affectionate nobility, would push their advantage, without reserve or limitation. These, while fired with glory and emulation, can bear the fatigues and dangers of war; but never would submit to languish in the garrisons of HUNGARY or LITHUANIA, forgot at court, and sacrificed to the intrigues of every minion or mistress, who approaches the prince. The troops are filled with CRAVATES and TARTARS, HUSSARS and COSSACS; intermingled, perhaps, with a few soldiers of fortune from the better provinces:

---

[1] [Editions H to O: Such as EUROPE is at present threatened with.]

[2] If the ROMAN empire was of advantage, it could only proceed from this, that mankind were generally in a very disorderly, uncivilized condition, before its establishment.

And the melancholy fate of the ROMAN emperors, from the same cause, is renewed over and over again, till the final dissolution of the monarchy.

Essay VIII.—*Of Taxes.*

THERE is a prevailing maxim,[1] among some reasoners, *that every new tax creates a new ability in the subject to bear it, and that each encrease of public burdens encreases proportionably the industry of the people.* This maxim is of such a nature as is most likely to be abused; and is so much the more dangerous, as its truth cannot be altogether denied: but it must be owned, when kept within certain bounds, to have some foundation in reason and experience.

When a tax is laid upon commodities, which are consumed by the common people, the necessary consequence may seem to be, either that the poor must retrench something from their way of living, or raise their wages, so as to make the burden of the tax fall entirely upon the rich. But there is a third consequence, which often follows upon taxes, namely, that the poor encrease their industry, perform more work, and live as well as before, without demanding more for their labour. Where taxes are moderate, are laid on gradually, and affect not the necessaries of life, this consequence naturally follows; and it is certain, that such difficulties often serve to excite the industry of a people, and render them more opulent and laborious, than others, who enjoy the greatest advantages. For we may observe, as a parallel instance, that the most commercial nations have not always possessed the greatest extent of fertile land; but, on the contrary, that they have laboured under many natural disadvantages. TYRE, ATHENS, CARTHAGE, RHODES, GENOA, VENICE, HOLLAND, are strong examples to this purpose. And in all history, we find only three instances of large and fertile countries, which have possessed much trade; the NETHERLANDS, ENGLAND, and FRANCE. The two former seem to have been allured by the advantages of their maritime situation, and the necessity they lay under of frequenting foreign ports, in order to procure what their own climate refused them. And as to FRANCE, trade has come late into that kingdom, and seems

---

[1] [Editions H to P read: Among those whom in this country we call *ways and means men*, and who are denominated *Financiers* and *Maltotiers* in FRANCE.]

to have been the effect of reflection and observation in an ingenious and enterprizing people, who remarked the riches acquired by such of the neighbouring nations as cultivated navigation and commerce.

The places mentioned by CICERO,[1] as possessed of the greatest commerce in his time, are ALEXANDRIA, COLCHUS, TYRE, SIDON, ANDROS, CYPRUS, PAMPHYLIA, LYCIA, RHODES, CHIOS, BYZANTIUM, LESBOS, SMYRNA, MILETUM, COOS. All these, except ALEXANDRIA, were either small islands, or narrow territories. And that city owed its trade entirely to the happiness of its situation.

Since therefore some natural necessities or disadvantages may be thought favourable to industry, why may not artificial burdens have the same effect? Sir WILLIAM TEMPLE,[2] we may observe, ascribes the industry of the DUTCH entirely to necessity, proceeding from their natural disadvantages; and illustrates his doctrine by a striking comparison with IRELAND; 'where,' says he, 'by the largeness and plenty of the soil, and scarcity of people, all things necessary to life are so cheap, that an industrious man, by two days' labour, may gain enough to feed him the rest of the week. Which I take to be a very plain ground of the laziness attributed to the people. For men naturally prefer ease before labour, and will not take pains if they can live idle; though when, by necessity, they have been inured to it, they cannot leave it, being grown a custom necessary to their health, and to their very entertainment. Nor perhaps is the change harder, from constant ease to labour, than from constant labour to ease.' After which the author proceeds to confirm his doctrine, by enumerating, as above, the places where trade has most flourished, in ancient and modern times; and which are commonly observed to be such narrow confined territories, as beget a necessity for industry.[3]

---

[1] Epist. ad ATT. lib. ix. ep. II.
[2] Account of the NETHERLANDS, chap. 6.
[3] [Editions H to P insert as follows: 'Tis always observed, in years of scarcity, if it be not extreme, that the poor labour more, and really live better, than in years of great plenty, when they indulge themselves in idleness and riot. I have been told, by a considerable manufacturer, that in the year 1740, when bread and provisions of all kinds were very dear, his workmen not only made a shift to live, but paid debts, which they had contracted in former years, that were much more favourable and abundant.'

This doctrine, therefore, with regard

---

[1] To this purpose see also Essay I. at the end.

The best taxes are such as are levied upon consumptions, especially those of luxury; because such taxes are least felt by the people. They seem, in some measure, voluntary; since a man may chuse how far he will use the commodity which is taxed: They are paid gradually, and insensibly:[1] They naturally produce sobriety and frugality, if judiciously imposed: And being confounded with the natural price of the commodity, they are scarcely perceived by the consumers. Their only disadvantage is, that they are expensive in the levying.

Taxes upon possessions are levied without expence; but have every other disadvantage. Most states, however, are obliged to have recourse to them, in order to supply the deficiencies of the other.

But the most pernicious of all taxes are the arbitrary. They are commonly converted, by their management, into punishments on industry; and also, by their unavoidable inequality, are more grievous, than by the real burden which they impose. It is surprising, therefore, to see them have place among any civilized people.

In general, all poll-taxes, even when not arbitrary, which they commonly are, may be esteemed dangerous: Because it is so easy for the sovereign to add a little more, and a little more, to the sum demanded, that these taxes are apt to become altogether oppressive and intolerable. On the other hand, a duty upon commodities checks itself; and a prince will soon find, that an encrease of the impost is no encrease of his revenue. It is not easy, therefore, for a people to be altogether ruined by such taxes.

Historians inform us, that one of the chief causes of the destruction of the ROMAN state, was the alteration, which CONSTANTINE introduced into the finances, by substituting an universal poll-tax, in lieu of almost all the tithes, customs, and excises, which formerly composed the revenue of the *empire*. The people, in all the provinces, were so grinded

to taxes, may be admitted in some degree: But beware of the abuse. Exorbitant taxes, like extreme necessity, destroy industry, by producing despair; and even before they reach this pitch, they raise the wages of the labourer and manufacturer, and heighten the price of all commodities. An attentive disinterested legislature, will observe the point when the emolument ceases, and the prejudice begins: But as the contrary character is much more common, 'tis to be feared that taxes, all over EUROPE, are multiplying to such a degree, as will intirely crush all art and industry; tho', perhaps, their first increase, together with other circumstances, might have contributed to the growth of these advantages.]

[1] [This clause was first added in Edition Q.]

and oppressed by the *publicans*, that they were glad to take refuge under the conquering arms of the barbarians; whose dominion, as they had fewer necessities and less art, was found preferable to the refined tyranny of the ROMANS.

[1] It is an opinion, zealously promoted by some political writers, that, since all taxes, as they pretend, fall ultimately upon land, it were better to lay them originally there, and abolish every duty upon consumptions. But it is denied, that all taxes fall ultimately upon land. If a duty be laid upon any commodity, consumed by an artisan, he has two obvious expedients for paying it; he may retrench somewhat of his expence, or he may encrease his labour. Both these resources are more easy and natural, than that of heightening his wages. We see, that, in years of scarcity, the weaver either consumes less or labours more, or employs both these expedients of frugality and industry, by which he is enabled to reach the end of the year. It is but just, that he should subject himself to the same hardships, if they deserve the name, for the sake of the publick, which gives him protection. By what contrivance can he raise the price of his labour? The manufacturer who employs him, will not give him more: Neither can he, because the merchant, who exports the cloth, cannot raise its price, being limited by the price which it yields in foreign markets. Every man, to be sure, is desirous of pushing off from himself the burden of any tax, which is imposed, and of laying it upon others: But as every man has the same inclination, and is upon the defensive; no set of men can be supposed to prevail altogether in this contest. And why the landed gentleman should be the victim of the whole, and should not be able to defend himself, as well as others are, I cannot readily imagine. All tradesmen, indeed, would willingly prey upon him, and divide him among them, if they could: But this inclination they always have, though no taxes were levied; and the same methods, by which he guards against the imposition of tradesmen before taxes, will serve him afterwards, and make them share the

[1] [Editions H to P omit the opening sentences as far as 'foreign markets,' and read instead of them: There is a prevailing opinion, that all taxes, however levied, fall upon the land at last. Such an opinion may be useful in BRITAIN, by checking the landed gentlemen, in whose hands our legislature is chiefly lodged, and making them preserve great regard for trade and industry. But I must confess, that this principle, tho' first advanced by a celebrated writer, has so little appearance of reason, that, were it not for his authority, it had never been received by any body.]

burden with him. [1] They must be very heavy taxes, indeed, and very injudiciously levied, which the artizan will not, of himself, be enabled to pay, by superior industry and frugality, without raising the price of his labour.

I shall conclude this subject with observing, that we have, with regard to taxes, an instance of what frequently happens in political institutions, that the consequences of things are diametrically opposite to what we should expect on the first appearance. It is regarded as a fundamental maxim of the TURKISH government, that the *Grand Signior*, though absolute master of the lives and fortunes of each individual, has no authority to impose a new tax; and every OTTOMAN prince, who has made such an attempt, either has been obliged to retract, or has found the fatal effects of his perseverance. One would imagine, that this prejudice or established opinion were the firmest barrier in the world against oppression; yet it is certain, that its effect is quite contrary. The emperor, having no regular method of encreasing his revenue, must allow all the bashaws and governors to oppress and abuse the subjects: And these he squeezes after their return from their government. Whereas, if he could impose a new tax, like our EUROPEAN princes, his interest would so far be united with that of his people, that he would immediately feel the bad effects of these disorderly levies of money, and would find, that a pound, raised by a general imposition, would have less pernicious effects, than a shilling taken in so unequal and arbitrary a manner.

ESSAY IX.—*Of Public Credit.*

IT appears to have been the common practice of antiquity, to make provision, during peace, for the necessities of war, and to hoard up treasures before-hand, as the instruments either of conquest or defence; without trusting to extraordinary impositions, much less to borrowing, in times of disorder and confusion. Besides the immense sums

---

[1] [The concluding sentence is not in Editions H to O.—Ed. P. reads in its place: No labour in any commodities, that are exported, can be very considerably raised in the price, without losing the foreign market; and as some part of almost every manufactory is exported, this circumstance keeps the price of most species of labour nearly the same after the imposition of taxes. I may add, that it has this effect upon the whole: For were any kind of labour paid beyond its proportion, all hands would flock to it, and would soon sink it to a level with the rest.]

above mentioned,[1] which were amassed by ATHENS, and by the PTOLEMIES, and other successors of ALEXANDER; we learn from PLATO,[2] that the frugal LACEDEMONIANS had also collected a great treasure; and ARRIAN[3] and PLUTARCH[4] take notice of the riches which ALEXANDER got possession of on the conquest of SUSA and ECBATANA, and which were reserved, some of them, from the time of CYRUS. If I remember right, the scripture also mentions the treasure of HEZEKIAH and the JEWISH princes; as profane history does that of PHILIP and PERSEUS, kings of MACEDON. The ancient republics of GAUL had commonly large sums in reserve.[5] Every one knows the treasure seized in ROME by JULIUS CÆSAR, during the civil wars: and we find afterwards, that the wiser emperors, AUGUSTUS, TIBERIUS, VESPASIAN, SEVERUS, &c. always discovered the prudent foresight, of saving great sums against any public exigency.

On the contrary, our modern expedient, which has become very general, is to mortgage the public revenues, and to trust that posterity will pay off the incumbrances contracted by their ancestors: And they, having before their eyes, so good an example of their wise fathers, have the same prudent reliance on *their* posterity; who, at last, from necessity more than choice, are obliged to place the same confidence in a new posterity. But not to waste time in declaiming against a practice which appears ruinous, [6] beyond all controversy; it seems pretty apparent, that the ancient maxims are, in this respect, more prudent than the modern; even though the latter had been confined within some reasonable bounds, and had ever, in any instance, been attended with such frugality, in time of peace, as to discharge the debts incurred by an expensive war. For why should the case be so different between the public and an individual, as to make us establish different maxims of conduct for each? If the funds of the former be greater, its necessary expences are proportionably larger; if its resources be more numerous, they are not infinite; and as its frame should be calculated for a much longer duration than the date of a single life, or

---

[1] Essay V.
[2] ALCIB. I. p. 123.
[3] Lib. iii. 16 and 19.
[4] PLUT *in vita* ALEX. 36, 37. He makes these treasures amount to 80,000 talents, or about 15 millions sterl. QUINTUS CURTIUS (lib. v. cap. 2) says, that ALEXANDER found in SUSA above 50,000 talents.
[5] STRABO, lib. iv. p. 188.
[6] [Editions H to P add: Beyond the evidence of a hundred demonstrations.]

even of a family, it should embrace maxims, large, durable, and generous, agreeably to the supposed extent of its existence. To trust to chances and temporary expedients, is, indeed, what the necessity of human affairs frequently renders unavoidable: but whoever voluntarily depend on such resources, have not necessity, but their own folly, to accuse for their misfortunes, when any such befal them.

If the abuses of treasures be dangerous, either by engaging the state in rash enterprizes, or making it neglect military discipline, in confidence of its riches; the abuses of mortgaging are more certain and inevitable; poverty, impotence, and subjection to foreign powers.

According to modern policy war is attended with every destructive circumstance; loss of men, encrease of taxes, decay of commerce, dissipation of money, devastation by sea and land. According to ancient maxims, the opening of the public treasure, as it produced an uncommon affluence of gold and silver, served as a temporary encouragement to industry, and atoned, in some degree, for the inevitable calamities of war.

[1] It is very tempting to a minister to employ such an expedient, as enables him to make a great figure during his administration, without overburthening the people with taxes, or exciting any immediate clamours against himself. The practice, therefore, of contracting debt will almost infallibly be abused, in every government. It would scarcely be more imprudent to give a prodigal son a credit in every banker's shop in London, than to impower a statesman to draw bills, in this manner, upon posterity.

What then shall we say to the new paradox, that public incumbrances are, of themselves, advantageous, independent of the necessity of contracting them; and that any state, even though it were not pressed by a foreign enemy, could not possibly have embraced a wiser expedient for promoting commerce and riches, than to create funds, and debts, and taxes, without limitation? Reasonings, such as these, might naturally have passed for trials of wit among rhetoricians, like the panegyrics on folly and a fever, on BUSIRIS and NERO, had we not seen such absurd maxims patronized by great ministers, and by a whole party among us.[2]

[1] [This paragraph was added in Ed. Q.]

[2] [Editions H to P add: And these puzzling arguments, (for they deserve

Let us examine the consequences of public debts, both in our domestic management, by their influence on commerce and industry; and in our foreign transactions, by their effect on wars and negociations.[1]

Public securities are with us become a kind of money, and pass as readily at the current price as gold or silver. Wherever any profitable undertaking offers itself, how expensive soever, there are never wanting hands enow to embrace it; nor need a trader, who has sums in the public stocks, fear to launch out into the most extensive trade; since he is possessed of funds, which will answer the most sudden demand that can be made upon him. No merchant thinks it necessary to keep by him any considerable cash. Bank-stock, or India-bonds, especially the latter, serve all the same purposes; because he can dispose of them, or pledge them to a banker, in a quarter of an hour; and at the same time they are not idle, even when in his scritoire, but bring him in a constant revenue. In short, our national debts furnish merchants with a species of money, that is continually multiplying in their hands, and produces sure gain, besides the

not the name of specious) though they could not be the foundation of LORD ORFORD's conduct, for he had more sense; served at least to keep his partizans in countenance, and perplex the understanding of the nation.]

[1] [Editions H to P add: There is a word, which is here in the mouth of every body, and which, I find, has also got abroad, and is much employed by foreign writers,[1] in imitation of the ENGLISH; and this is, CIRCULATION. This word serves as an account of every thing; and though I confess, that I have sought for its meaning in the present subject, ever since I was a school-boy, I have never yet been able to discover it. What possible advantage is there which the nation can reap by the easy transference of stock from hand to hand? Or is there any parallel to be drawn from the circulation of other commodities, to that of chequer-notes and INDIA bonds? Where a manufacturer has a quick sale of his goods to the merchant, the merchant to the shopkeeper, the shopkeeper to his customers; this enlivens industry, and gives new encouragement to the first dealer or the manufacturer and all his tradesmen, and makes them produce more and better commodities of the same species. A stagnation is here pernicious, wherever it happens; because it operates backwards, and stops or benumbs the industrious hand in its production of what is useful to human life. But what production we owe to CHANGE-ALLEY, or even what consumption, except that of coffee, and pen, ink, and paper, I have not yet learned; nor can one forsee the loss or decay of any one beneficial commerce or commodity, though that place and all its inhabitants were for ever buried in the ocean.

But though this term has never been explained by those who insist so much on the advantages that result from a circulation, there seems, however, to be some benefit of a similar kind, arising from our incumbrances: As indeed, what human evil is there, which is not attended with some advantage? This we shall endeavour to explain, that we may estimate the weight which we ought to allow it.]

---

[1] MELON, DU TOT, LAW, in the pamphlets published in FRANCE.

profits of their commerce. This must enable them to trade upon less profit. The small profit of the merchant renders the commodity cheaper, causes a greater consumption, quickens the labour of the common people, and helps to spread arts and industry throughout the whole society.

There are also, we may observe, in ENGLAND and in all states, which have both commerce and public debts, a set of men, who are half merchants, half stock-holders, and may be supposed willing to trade for small profits; because commerce is not their principal or sole support, and their revenues in the funds are a sure resource for themselves and their families. Were there no funds, great merchants would have no expedient for realizing or securing any part of their profit, but by making purchases of lands; and land has many disadvantages in comparison of funds. Requiring more care and inspection, it divides the time and attention of the merchant; upon any tempting offer or extraordinary accident in trade, it is not so easily converted into money; and as it attracts too much, both by the many natural pleasures it affords, and the authority it gives, it soon converts the citizen into the country gentleman. More men, therefore, with large stocks and incomes, may naturally be supposed to continue in trade, where there are public debts; and this, it must be owned, is of some advantage to commerce, by diminishing its profits, promoting circulation, and encouraging industry.[1]

But, in opposition to these two favourable circumstances, perhaps of no very great importance, weigh the many disadvantages which attend our public debts, in the whole *interior* œconomy of the state: You will find no comparison between the ill and the good which result from them.

First, It is certain, that national debts cause a mighty confluence of people and riches to the capital, by the great sums, levied in the provinces to pay the interest; and perhaps, too, by the advantages in trade above mentioned, which they give the merchants in the capital above the rest of the kingdom. The question is, whether, in our case, it be for the public

---

[1] [Editions H to O add as a note: On this head, I shall observe, without interrupting the thread of the argument, that the multiplicity of our public debts serves rather to sink the interest, and that the more the government borrows, the cheaper may they expect to borrow; contrary to first appearance, and contrary to common opinion. The profits of trade have an influence on interest. See Essay IV.]

interest, that so many privileges should be conferred on LONDON, which has already arrived at such an enormous size, and seems still encreasing? Some men are apprehensive of the consequences. For my own part, I cannot forbear thinking, that, though the head is undoubtedly too large for the body, yet that great city is so happily situated, that its excessive bulk causes less inconvenience than even a smaller capital to a greater kingdom. There is more difference between the prices of all provisions in PARIS and LANGUEDOC, than between those in LONDON and YORKSHIRE. [1] The immense greatness, indeed, of LONDON, under a government which admits not of discretionary power, renders the people factious, mutinous, seditious, and even perhaps rebellious. But to this evil the national debts themselves tend to provide a remedy. The first visible eruption, or even immediate danger, of public disorders must alarm all the stockholders, whose property is the most precarious of any; and will make them fly to the support of government, whether menaced by Jacobitish violence or democratical frenzy.

Secondly, Public stocks, being a kind of paper-credit, have all the disadvantages attending that species of money. They banish gold and silver from the most considerable commerce of the state, reduce them to common circulation, and by that means render all provisions and labour dearer than otherwise they would be.[2]

Thirdly, The taxes, which are levied to pay the interests of these debts,[3] are apt either to heighten the price of labour, or be an oppression on the poorer sort.

Fourthly, As foreigners possess a great share of our national funds, they render the public, in a manner, tributary to them, and may in time occasion the transport of our people and our industry.

Fifthly, The greater part of the public stock being always in the hands of idle people, who live on their revenue, our

---

[1] [The remainder of this paragraph was added in Ed. Q.]

[2] [Edition P adds: We may also remark, that this increase of prices, derived from paper-credit, has a more durable and a more dangerous influence than when it arises from a great increase of gold and silver: Where an accidental overflow of money raises the price of labor and commodities, the evil remedies itself in a little time: The money soon flows out into all the neighbouring nations: The prices fall to a level: And industry may be continued as before; a relief, which cannot be expected, where the circulating specie consists chiefly of paper, and has no intrinsic value.]

[3] [Editions H to N read: Are a check upon industry, heighten the price of labour, and are an oppr. &c.]

funds, in that view, give great encouragement to an useless and unactive life.

But though the injury, that arises to commerce and industry from our public funds, will appear, upon balancing the whole, not inconsiderable, it is trivial, in comparison of the prejudice that results to the state considered as a body politic, which must support itself in the society of nations, and have various transactions with other states in wars and negociations. The ill, there, is pure and unmixed, without any favourable circumstance to atone for it; and it is an ill too of a nature the highest and most important.

We have, indeed, been told, that the public is no weaker upon account of its debts; since they are mostly due among ourselves, and bring as much property to one as they take from another. It is like transferring money from the right hand to the left; which leaves the person neither richer nor poorer than before. Such loose reasonings and specious comparisons will always pass, where we judge not upon principles. I ask, Is it possible, in the nature of things, to overburthen a nation with taxes, even where the sovereign resides among them? The very doubt seems extravagant; since it is requisite, in every community, that there be a certain proportion observed between the laborious and the idle part of it. But if all our present taxes be mortgaged, must we not invent new ones? And may not this matter be carried to a length that is ruinous and destructive?

In every nation, there are always some methods of levying money more easy than others, agreeably to the way of living of the people, and the commodities they make use of. In GREAT BRITAIN, the excises upon malt and beer afford a large revenue; because the operations of malting and brewing are tedious, and are impossible to be concealed; and at the same time, these commodities are not so absolutely necessary to life, as that the raising of their price would very much affect the poorer sort. These taxes being all mortgaged, what difficulty to find new ones! what vexation and ruin of the poor!

Duties upon consumption are more equal and easy than those upon possessions. What a loss to the public, that the former are all exhausted, and that we must have recourse to the more grievous method of levying taxes!

Were all the proprietors of land only stewards to the public, must not necessity force them to practise all the arts of oppression used by stewards; where the absence or negligence of the proprietor render them secure against enquiry?

It will scarcely be asserted, that no bounds ought ever to be set to national debts; and that the public would be no weaker, were twelve or fifteen shillings in the pound, land-tax, mortgaged, with all the present customs and excises. There is something, therefore, in the case, beside the mere transferring of property from the one hand to another. In 500 years, the posterity of those now in the coaches, and of those upon the boxes, will probably have changed places, without affecting the public by these revolutions.

[1] Suppose the public once fairly brought to that condition, to which it is hastening with such amazing rapidity; suppose the land to be taxed eighteen or nineteen shillings in the pound; for it can never bear the whole twenty; suppose all the excises and customs to be screwed up to the utmost which the nation can bear, without entirely losing its commerce and industry; and suppose that all those funds are mortgaged to perpetuity, and that the invention and wit of all our projectors can find no new imposition, which may serve as the foundation of a new loan; and let us consider the necessary consequences of this situation. Though the imperfect state of our political knowledge, and the narrow capacities of men, make it difficult to fortel the effects which will result from any untried measure, the seeds of ruin are here scattered with such profusion as not to escape the eye of the most careless observer.

In this unnatural state of society, the only persons, who possess any revenue beyond the immediate effects of their industry, are the stock-holders, who draw almost all the rent of the land and houses, besides the produce of all the customs and excises. These are men, who have no connexions with the state, who can enjoy their revenue in any part of the globe in which they chuse to reside, who will naturally bury themselves in the capital or in great cities, and who will sink into the lethargy of a stupid and pampered luxury, without spirit, ambition, or enjoyment. Adieu to all ideas of nobility, gentry, and family. The stocks can be transferred in an instant, and being in such a fluctuating state, will seldom be transmitted during three generations from father to son. Or

[1] [The six following paragraphs were added in Ed. O.]

were they to remain ever so long in one family, they convey no hereditary authority or credit to the possessor; and by this means, the several ranks of men, which form a kind of independent magistracy in a state, instituted by the hand of nature, are entirely lost; and every man in authority derives his influence from the commission alone of the sovereign. No expedient remains for preventing or suppressing insurrections, but mercenary armies: No expedient at all remains for resisting tyranny: Elections are swayed by bribery and corruption alone: And the middle power between king and people being totally removed, a grievous despotism must infallibly prevail. The landholders, despised for their poverty, and hated for their oppressions, will be utterly unable to make any opposition to it.

Though a resolution should be formed by the legislature never to impose any tax which hurts commerce and discourages industry, it will be impossible for men, in subjects of such extreme delicacy, to reason so justly as never to be mistaken, or amidst difficulties so urgent, never to be seduced from their resolution. The continual fluctuations in commerce require continual alterations in the nature of the taxes; which exposes the legislature every moment to the danger both of wilful and involuntary error. And any great blow given to trade, whether by injudicious taxes or by other accidents, throws the whole system of government into confusion.

But what expedient can the public now employ, even supposing trade to continue in the most flourishing condition, in order to support its foreign wars and enterprizes, and to defend its own honour and interests, or those of its allies? I do not ask how the public is to exert such a prodigious power as it has maintained during our late wars; where we have so much exceeded, not only our own natural strength, but even that of the greatest empires. This extravagance is the abuse complained of, as the source of all the dangers, to which we are at present exposed. But since we must still suppose great commerce and opulence to remain, even after every fund is mortgaged; these riches must be defended by proportional power; and whence is the public to derive the revenue which supports it? It must plainly be from a continual taxation of their annuitants, or, which is the same thing, from mortgaging anew, on every exigency, a certain part of their annuities; and thus making them contribute to their own defence, and to that of the nation. But the difficulties, attending this system of policy, will easily appear, whether we suppose the king to have become absolute master, or to be still controuled by national councils, in which the annuitants themselves must necessarily bear the principal sway.

If the prince has become absolute, as may naturally be expected from this situation of affairs, it is so easy for him to encrease his exactions upon the annuitants, which amount only to the retaining money in his own hands, that this species of property would soon lose all its credit, and the whole income of every individual in the state must lie entirely at the mercy of the sovereign: A degree of despotism, which no oriental monarchy has ever yet attained. If, on the contrary, the consent of the annuitants be requisite for every taxation, they will never be persuaded to contribute sufficiently even to the support of government; as the diminution of their revenue must in that case be very sensible, would not be disguised under the appearance of a branch of excise or customs, and would not be shared by any other order of the state, who are already supposed to be taxed to the utmost. There are instances, in some republics, of a hundredth penny, and sometimes of the fiftieth, being given to the support of the state; but this is always an extraordinary exertion of power, and can never become the foundation of a constant national defence. We have always found, where a government has mortgaged all its revenues, that it necessarily sinks into a state of languor, inactivity, and impotence.

Such are the inconveniencies, which may reasonably be foreseen, of this situation, to which GREAT BRITAIN is visibly tending. Not to mention, the numberless inconveniencies, which cannot be foreseen, and which must result from so monstrous a situation as that of making the public the chief or sole proprietor of land, besides investing it with every branch of customs and excise, which the fertile imagination of ministers and projectors have been able to invent.

I must confess, that there is a strange supineness, from long custom, creeped into all ranks of men, with regard to public debts, not unlike what divines so vehemently complain of with regard to their religious doctrines. We all own, that the most sanguine imagination cannot hope, either that this or any future ministry will be possessed of such rigid and steady frugality, as to make a considerable progress in the payment of our debts; or that the situation of foreign affairs will, for any long time, allow them leisure and tranquillity for such an undertaking.[1] *What then is to become of us?* Were we ever so good Christians, and ever so resigned to Providence; this, methinks, were a curious question, even considered as a speculative one, and what it might not be altogether impossible to form some conjectural solution of. The events here will depend little upon the contingencies of battles, negociations, intrigues, and factions. There seems to be a natural progress of things, which may guide our reasoning. As it would have required but a moderate share of prudence, when we first began this practice of mortgaging, to have foretold, from the nature of men and of ministers, that things would necessarily be carried to the length we see; so now, that they have at last happily reached it, it may not be difficult to guess at the consequences. It must, indeed, be one of these two events; either the nation must destroy public credit, or public credit will destroy the nation. It is impossible that they can both subsist, after the manner they have been hitherto managed, in this, as well as in some other countries.

There was, indeed, a scheme for the payment of our debts, which was proposed by an excellent citizen, Mr. HUTCHINSON, above thirty years ago, and which was much approved of by some men of sense, but never was likely to take effect. He asserted, that there was a fallacy in imagining that the public owed this debt; for that really every individual owed a proportional share of it, and paid, in his taxes, a proportional share of the interest, beside the expence of levying these taxes. Had we not better, then, says he, make a distribution of the debt among ourselves, and each of us contribute a sum suitable to his property, and by that means

---

[1] [Editions H to P add the note: In times of peace and security, when alone it is possible to pay debt, the monied interest are averse to receive partial payments, which they know not how to dispose of to advantage; and the landed interest are averse to continue the taxes requisite for that purpose. Why therefore should a minister persevere in a measure so disagreeable to all parties? For the sake, I suppose, of a posterity, which he will never see, or of a few reasonable reflecting people, whose united interest, perhaps, will not be able to secure him the smallest burrough in ENGLAND. 'Tis not likely we shall ever find any minister so bad a politician. With regard to these narrow destructive maxims of politics, all ministers are expert enough.]

discharge at once all our funds and public mortgages? He seems not to have considered, that the laborious poor pay a considerable part of the taxes by their annual consumptions, though they could not advance, at once, a proportional part of the sum required. Not to mention, that property in money and stock in trade might easily be concealed or disguised; and that visible property in lands and houses would really at last answer for the whole: An inequality and oppression, which never would be submitted to. But though this project is not likely to take place; it is not altogether improbable, that, when the nation becomes heartily sick of their debts, and is cruelly oppressed by them, some daring projector may arise with visionary schemes for their discharge. And as public credit will begin, by that time, to be a little frail, the least touch will destroy it, as happened in FRANCE during the regency; and in this manner it will *die of the doctor*.[1]

But it is more probable, that the breach of national faith will be the necessary effect of wars, defeats, misfortunes, and public calamities, or even perhaps of victories and conquests. I must confess, when I see princes and states fighting and quarrelling, amidst their debts, funds, and public mortgages, it always brings to my mind a match of cudgel-playing fought in a *China* shop. How can it be expected, that sovereigns will spare a species of property, which is pernicious to themselves and to the public, when they have so little compassion on lives and properties, that are useful to both? Let the time come (and surely it will come) when the new funds, created for the exigencies of the year, are not subscribed to, and raise not the money projected. Suppose, either that the cash of the nation is exhausted; or that our faith, which has hitherto been so ample, begins to fail us. Suppose, that, in

---

[1] [Editions H to P add: Some neighbouring states practise an easy expedient, by which they lighten their public debts. The French have a custom (as the Romans formerly had) of augmenting their money; and this the nation has been so much familiarised to, that it hurts not public credit, though it be really cutting off at once, by an edict, so much of their debts. The Dutch diminish the interest without the consent of their creditors, or, which is the same thing, they arbitrarily tax the funds, as well as other property. Could we practise either of these methods, we need never be oppressed by the national debt; and it is not impossible but one of these, or some other method, may, at all adventures, be tried, on the augmentation of our incumbrances and difficulties. But people in this country are so good reasoners upon whatever regards their interests, that such a practice will deceive nobody; and public credit will probably tumble at once, by so dangerous a trial.]

this distress, the nation is threatened with an invasion; a rebellion is suspected or broken out at home; a squadron cannot be equipped for want of pay, victuals, or repairs; or even a foreign subsidy cannot be advanced. What must a prince or minister do in such an emergence? The right of self-preservation is unalienable in every individual, much more in every community. And the folly of our statesmen must then be greater than the folly of those who first contracted debt, or, what is more, than that of those who trusted or continue to trust this security, if these statesmen have the means of safety in their hands, and do not employ them. The funds, created and mortgaged, will, by that time, bring in a large yearly revenue, sufficient for the defence and security of the nation: Money is perhaps lying in the exchequer, ready for the discharge of the quarterly interest: Necessity calls, fear urges, reason exhorts, compassion alone exclaims: The money will immediately be seized for the current service, under the most solemn protestations, perhaps, of being immediately replaced. But no more is requisite. The whole fabric, already tottering, falls to the ground, and buries thousands in its ruins. And this, I think, may be called the *natural death* of public credit: For to this period it tends as naturally as an animal body to its dissolution and destruction.

[1]So great dupes are the generality of mankind, that, notwithstanding such a violent shock to public credit, as a voluntary bankruptcy in ENGLAND would occasion, it would not probably be long ere credit would again revive in as flourishing a condition as before. The present king of FRANCE, during the late war, borrowed money at lower interest than ever his grandfather did; and as low as the BRITISH parliament, comparing the natural rate of interest in both kingdoms. And though men are commonly more governed by what they have seen, than by what they foresee, with whatever certainty; yet promises, protestations, fair appearances, with the allurements of present interest, have such powerful influence as few are able to resist. Mankind are, in all ages, caught by the same baits: The same tricks, played over and over again, still trepan them. The heights of popularity and patriotism are still the beaten road to power and tyranny; flattery to treachery; standing armies

[1] [This paragraph appears in Editions H to P as a footnote.]

to arbitrary government; and the glory of God to the temporal interest of the clergy. The fear of an everlasting destruction of credit, allowing it to be an evil, is a needless bugbear. A prudent man, in reality, would rather lend to the public immediately after we had taken a spunge to our debts, than at present; as much as an opulent knave, even though one could not force him to pay, is a preferable debtor to an honest bankrupt: For the former, in order to carry on business, may find it his interest to discharge his debts where they are not exorbitant: The latter has it not in his power. The reasoning of TACITUS,[1] as it is eternally true, is very applicable to our present case. *Sed vulgus ad magnitudinem beneficiorum aderat: Stultissimus quisque pecuniis mercabatur: Apud sapientes cassa habebantur, quæ neque dari neque accipi, salva republica, poterant.* The public is a debtor, whom no man can oblige to pay. The only check which the creditors have upon her, is the interest of preserving credit; an interest, which may easily be overbalanced by a great debt, and by a difficult and extraordinary emergence, even supposing that credit irrecoverable. Not to mention, that a present necessity often forces states into measures, which are, strictly speaking, against their interest.

These two events, supposed above, are calamitous, but not the most calamitous. Thousands are thereby sacrificed to the safety of millions. But we are not without danger, that the contrary event may take place, and that millions may be sacrificed for ever to the temporary safety of thousands.[2] Our popular government, perhaps, will render it difficult or dangerous for a minister to venture on so desperate an expedient, as that of a voluntary bankruptcy. And though the house of Lords be altogether composed of proprietors of land, and the house of Commons chiefly; and consequently neither

---

[1] *Hist. lib.* iii. 55.

[2] I have heard it has been computed, that all the creditors of the public, natives and foreigners, amount only to 17,000. These make a figure at present on their income; but, in case of a public bankruptcy, would, in an instant, become the lowest, as well as the most wretched of the people. The dignity and authority of the landed gentry and nobility is much better rooted; and would render the contention very unequal, if ever we come to that extremity. One would incline to assign to this event a very near period, such as half a century, had not our fathers' prophecies of this kind been already found fallacious, by the duration of our public credit, so much beyond all reasonable expectation. When the astrologers in FRANCE were every year foretelling the death of HENRY IV. *These fellows*, says he, *must be right at last*. We shall, therefore, be more cautious than to assign any precise date; and shall content ourselves with pointing out the event in general.

of them can be supposed to have great property in the funds; yet the connections of the members may be so great with the proprietors, as to render them more tenacious of public faith, than prudence, policy, or even justice, strictly speaking, requires. And perhaps too, our foreign enemies [1] may be so politic as to discover, that our safety lies in despair, and may not, therefore, show the danger, open and barefaced, till it be inevitable. The balance of power in EUROPE, our grandfathers, our fathers, and we, have all deemed too unequal to be preserved without our attention and assistance. But our children, weary of the struggle, and fettered with incumbrances, may sit down secure, and see their neighbours oppressed and conquered; till, at last, they themselves and their creditors lie both at the mercy of the conqueror. And this may properly enough be denominated the *violent death* of our public credit.

These seem to be the events, which are not very remote, and which reason foresees as clearly almost as she can do any thing that lies in the womb of time. And though the ancients maintained, that in order to reach the gift of prophecy, a certain divine fury or madness was requisite, one may safely affirm, that, in order to deliver such prophecies as these, no more is necessary, than merely to be in one's senses, free from the influence of popular madness and delusion.

ESSAY X.—*Of some Remarkable Customs.*

I SHALL observe three remarkable customs in three celebrated governments; and shall conclude from the whole, that all general maxims in politics ought to be established with great caution; and that irregular and extraordinary appearances are frequently discovered in the moral, as well as in the physical world. The former, perhaps, we can better account for, after they happen, from springs and principles, of which every one has, within himself, or from observation, the strongest assurance and conviction: But it is often fully as impossible for human prudence, before-hand, to foresee and foretel them.

I. One would think it essential to every supreme council or assembly, which debates, that entire liberty of speech

---

[1] [Editions H to P: or rather enemy (for we have but one to dread.)]

should be granted to every member, and that all motions or reasonings should be received, which can any wise tend to illustrate the point under deliberation. One would conclude, with still greater assurance, that, after a motion was made, which was voted and approved by that assembly in which the legislative power is lodged, the member who made the motion must for ever be exempted from future trial or enquiry. But no political maxim can, at first sight, appear more undisputable, than that he must, at least, be secured from all inferior jurisdiction; and that nothing less than the same supreme legislative assembly, in their subsequent meetings, could make him accountable for those motions and harangues, to which they had before given their approbation. But these axioms, however irrefragable they may appear, have all failed in the ATHENIAN government, from causes and principles too, which appear almost inevitable.

By the γραφὴ παρανόμων, or *indictment of illegality*, (though it has not been remarked by antiquaries or commentators) any man was tried and punished in a common court of judicature, for any law which had passed upon his motion, in the assembly of the people, if that law appeared to the court unjust, or prejudicial to the public. Thus DEMOSTHENES, finding that ship-money was levied irregularly, and that the poor bore the same burden as the rich in equipping the gallies, corrected this inequality by a very useful law, which proportioned the expence to the revenue and income of each individual. He moved for this law in the assembly: he proved its advantages [1]; he convinced the people, the only legislature in ATHENS; the law passed, and was carried into execution: Yet was he tried in a criminal court for that law, upon the complaint of the rich, who resented the alteration that he had introduced into the finances.[2] He was indeed acquitted, upon proving anew the usefulness of his law.

CTESIPHON moved in the assembly of the people, that particular honours should be conferred on DEMOSTHENES, as on a citizen affectionate and useful to the commonwealth: The people, convinced of this truth, voted those honours: Yet was CTESIPHON tried by the γραφὴ παρανόμων. It was asserted, among other topics, that DEMOSTHENES was not a good citizen, nor affectionate to the commonwealth: And the orator was called upon to defend his friend, and consequently

---

[1] His harangue for it is still extant; περὶ Συμμορίας.   [2] Pro CTESIPHONTE.

himself; which he executed by that sublime piece of eloquence, that has ever since been the admiration of mankind.

After the battle of CHÆRONEA, a law was passed upon the motion of HYPERIDES, giving liberty to slaves, and inrolling them in the troops.[1] On account of this law, the orator was afterwards tried by the indictment above-mentioned, and defended himself, among other topics, by that stroke celebrated by PLUTARCH and LONGINUS. *It was not I, said he, that moved for this law: It was the necessities of war; it was the battle of* CHÆRONEA. The orations of DEMOSTHENES abound with many instances of trials of this nature, and prove clearly, that nothing was more commonly practised.

The ATHENIAN Democracy was such a tumultuous government as we can scarcely form a notion of in the present age of the world. The whole collective body of the people voted in every law, without any limitation of property, without any distinction of rank, without controul from any magistracy or senate[2]; and consequently without regard to order, justice, or prudence. The ATHENIANS soon became sensible of the mischiefs attending this constitution: But being averse to checking themselves by any rule or restriction, they resolved, at least, to check their demagogues or counsellors, by the fear of future punishment and enquiry. They accordingly instituted this remarkable law; a law esteemed so essential to their form of government, that ÆSCHINES insists on it as a known truth, that, were it abolished or neglected, it were impossible for the Democracy to subsist.[3]

The people feared not any ill consequence to liberty from the authority of the criminal courts; because these were nothing but very numerous juries, chosen by lot from among the people. And they justly considered themselves as in a state of perpetual pupillage; where they had an authority, after they came to the use of reason, not only to retract and con-

---

[1] PLUTARCHUS *in vita decem oratorum.* DEMOSTHENES gives a different account of this law. *Contra* ARISTOGITON. *orat.* II. 803-4. He says, that its purport was, to render the ἄτιμοι ἐπίτιμοι, or to restore the privilege of bearing offices to those who had been declared incapable. Perhaps these were both clauses of the same law.

[2] The senate of the Bean was only a less numerous mob, chosen by lot from among the people; and their authority was not great.

[3] *In* CTESIPHONTEM. It is remarkable, that the first step after the dissolution of the Democracy by CRITIAS and the Thirty, was to annul the γραφὴ παρανόμων, as we learn from DEMOSTHENES κατὰ Τιμοκ. The orator in this oration gives us the words of the law, establishing the γραφὴ παρανόμων, pag. 297. *ex edit.* ALDI. And he accounts for it, from the same principles we here reason upon.

troul whatever had been determined, but to punish any guardian for measures which they had embraced by his persuasion. The same law had place in THEBES;[1] and for the same reason.

It appears to have been a usual practice in ATHENS, on the establishment of any law esteemed very useful or popular, to prohibit for ever its abrogation and repeal. Thus the demagogue, who diverted all the public revenues to the support of shows and spectacles, made it criminal so much as to move for a repeal of this law.[2] Thus LEPTINES moved for a law, not only to recal all the immunities formerly granted, but to deprive the people for the future of the power of granting any more.[3] Thus all bills of attainder[4] were forbid, or laws that affected one ATHENIAN, without extending to the whole commonwealth. These absurd clauses, by which the legislature vainly attempted to bind itself for ever, proceeded from an universal sense in the people of their own levity and inconstancy.

II. A wheel within a wheel, such as we observe in the GERMAN empire, is considered by Lord SHAFTESBURY,[5] as an absurdity in politics: But what must we say to two equal wheels, which govern the same political machine, without any mutual check, controul, or subordination; and yet preserve the greatest harmony and concord? To establish two distinct legislatures, each of which possesses full and absolute authority within itself, and stands in no need of the other's assistance, in order to give validity to its acts; this may appear, before-hand, altogether impracticable, as long as men are actuated by the passions of ambition, emulation, and avarice, which have hitherto been their chief governing principles. And should I assert, that the state I have in my eye was divided into two distinct factions, each of which predominated in a distinct legislature, and yet produced no clashing in these independent powers; the supposition may appear incredible. And if, to augment the paradox, I should affirm, that this disjointed, irregular government, was the most active, triumphant, and illustrious commonwealth, that ever yet appeared; I should certainly be told, that such a political chimera was as absurd as any vision of priests or

---

[1] PLUT. *in vita* PELOP. c. 25.
[2] DEMOST. *Olynth.* 1. 2.
[3] DEMOST. *contra* LEPT. 457.
[4] DEMOST. *contra* ARISTOCRATEM, 649.
[5] Essay on the freedom of wit and humour, part 3. § 2.

poets. But there is no need for searching long, in order to prove the reality of the foregoing suppositions: For this was actually the case with the ROMAN republic.

The legislative power was there lodged in the *comitia centuriata* and *comitia tributa*. In the former, it is well known, the people voted according to their *census*; so that when the first class was unanimous, though it contained not, perhaps, the hundredth part of the commonwealth, it determined the whole; and, with the authority of the senate, established a law. In the latter, every vote was equal; and as the authority of the senate was not there requisite, the lower people entirely prevailed, and gave law to the whole state. In all party-divisions, at first between the PATRICIANS and PLEBEIANS, afterwards between the nobles and the people, the interest of the Aristocracy was predominant in the first legislature; that of the Democracy in the second: The one could always destroy what the other had established: Nay, the one, by a sudden and unforeseen motion, might take the start of the other, and totally annihilate its rival, by a vote, which, from the nature of the constitution, had the full authority of a law. But no such contest is observed in the history of ROME: No instance of a quarrel between these two legislatures; though many between the parties that governed in each. Whence arose this concord, which may seem so extraordinary?

The legislature established in ROME, by the authority of SERVIUS TULLIUS, was the *comitia centuriata*, which, after the expulsion of the kings, rendered the government, for some time, very aristocratical. But the people, having numbers and force on their side, and being elated with frequent conquests and victories in their foreign wars, always prevailed when pushed to extremity, and first extorted from the senate the magistracy of the tribunes, and next the legislative power of the *comitia tributa*. It then behoved the nobles to be more careful than ever not to provoke the people. For beside the force which the latter were always possessed of, they had now got possession of legal authority, and could instantly break in pieces any order or institution which directly opposed them. By intrigue, by influence, by money, by combination, and by the respect paid to their character, the nobles might often prevail, and direct the whole machine of government: But had they openly set their *comitia centuriata* in opposition to the *tributa*, they had soon lost the advantage of that institution, together with their consuls, prætors, ediles, and all the magistrates elected by it. But the *comitia tributa*, not having the same reason for respecting the *centuriata*, frequently repealed laws favourable to the Aristocracy: They limited the authority of the nobles, protected the people from oppression, and controuled the actions of the senate and magistracy. The *centuriata* found it convenient always to submit; and though equal in authority, yet being inferior in power, durst never directly give any shock to the other legislature, either by repealing its laws, or establishing laws, which, it foresaw, would soon be repealed by it.

No instance is found of any opposition or struggle between these *comitia;* except one slight attempt of this kind, mentioned by APPIAN in the third book of his civil wars. MARK ANTHONY, resolving to deprive DECIMUS BRUTUS of the government of CISALPINE GAUL, railed in the *Forum*, and called one of the *comitia*, in order to prevent the meeting of the other, which had been ordered by the senate. But affairs were then fallen into such confusion, and the Roman constitution was so near its final dissolution, that no inference can be drawn from such an expedient. This contest, besides, was founded more on form than party. It was the senate who ordered the *comitia tributa*, that they might obstruct the meeting of the *centuriata*, which, by the constitution, or at least forms of the government, could alone dispose of provinces.

CICERO was recalled by the *comitia centuriata*, though banished by the *tributa*, that is, by a *plebiscitum*. But his banishment, we may observe, never was considered as a legal deed, arising from the free choice and inclination of the people. It was always ascribed to the violence alone of CLODIUS, and to the disorders introduced by him into the government.

III. The *third* custom, which we purpose to remark, regards ENGLAND; and though it be not so important as those which we have pointed out in ATHENS and ROME, is no less singular and unexpected. It is a maxim in politics, which we readily admit as undisputed and universal, that a power, however great, when granted by law to an eminent magistrate, is not so dangerous to liberty, as an authority, however inconsiderable, which he acquires from violence and usurpation. For, besides that the law always limits every power which it bestows, the very receiving it as a concession establishes the authority whence it is derived, and preserves the harmony of the constitution. By the same right that one prerogative is assumed without law, another may also be claimed, and another, with still greater facility, while the first usurpations both serve as precedents to the following, and give force to maintain them. Hence the heroism of HAMPDEN's conduct, who sustained the whole violence of royal prosecution, rather than pay a tax of twenty shillings, not imposed by parliament; hence the care of all ENGLISH patriots to guard against the first encroachments of the crown; and hence alone the existence, at this day, of ENGLISH liberty.

There is, however, one occasion, where the parliament has departed from this maxim; and that is, in the *pressing of seamen*. The exercise of an irregular power is here tacitly permitted in the crown; and though it has frequently been under deliberation, how that power might be rendered legal, and granted, under proper restrictions, to the sovereign, no safe expedient could ever be proposed for that purpose; and the danger to liberty always appeared greater from law than from usurpation. While this power is exercised to no other end than to man the navy, men willingly submit to it, from a sense of its use and necessity; and the sailors, who are alone affected by it, find no body to support them, in claiming the rights and privileges, which the law grants, without distinction, to all ENGLISH subjects. But were this power, on any occasion, made an instrument of faction or ministerial tyranny, the opposite faction, and indeed all lovers of their country, would immediately take the alarm, and support the injured party; the liberty of ENGLISHMEN would be asserted; juries would be implacable; and the tools of tyranny, acting both against law and equity, would meet with the severest vengeance. On the other hand, were the parliament to grant such an authority, they would probably fall into one of these two inconveniencies: They would either bestow it under so many restrictions as would make it lose its effect, by cramping the authority of the crown; or they would render it so large and comprehensive, as might give occasion to great abuses, for which we could, in that case, have no remedy. The very irregularity of the practice, at present, prevents its abuses, by affording so easy a remedy against them.

I pretend not, by this reasoning, to exclude all possibility of contriving a register for seamen, which might man the navy, without being dangerous to liberty. I only observe, that no satisfactory scheme of that nature has yet been proposed. Rather than adopt any project hitherto invented, we continue a practice seemingly the most absurd and unaccountable. Authority, in times of full internal peace and concord, is armed against law. A continued violence is permitted in the crown, amidst the greatest jealousy and watchfulness in the people; nay proceeding from those very principles: Liberty, in a country of the highest liberty, is left entirely to its own defence, without any countenance or protection: The wild state of nature is renewed, in one of the most civilised societies of mankind: And great violence and disorder[1] are committed with impunity; while the one party pleads obedience to the supreme magistrate, the other the sanction of fundamental laws.

Essay XI.—*Of the Populousness of Ancient Nations.*[2]

THERE is very little ground, either from reason or observation, to conclude the world eternal or incorruptible. The continual and rapid motion of matter, the violent revolutions with which every part is agitated, the changes remarked in the heavens, the plain traces as well as tradition of an universal deluge, or general convulsion of the elements; all these prove strongly the mortality of this fabric of the world, and its passage, by corruption or dissolution, from one state or order to another. It must therefore, as well as each individual form which it contains, have its infancy, youth, manhood, and old age; and it is probable, that, in all these variations, man, equally with every animal and vegetable, will partake. In the flourishing age of the world, it may be expected, that the human species should possess greater vigour both of mind and body, more prosperous health, higher spirits, longer

---

[1] [Editions H to P: Among the people, the most humane and the best natured.]

[2] [For the history of this Essay see p. 56.]

life, and a stronger inclination and power of generation. But if the general system of things, and human society of course, have any such gradual revolutions, they are too slow to be discernible in that short period which is comprehended by history and tradition. Stature and force of body, length of life, even courage and extent of genius, seem hitherto to have been naturally, in all ages, pretty much the same. The arts and sciences, indeed, have flourished in one period, and have decayed in another: But we may observe, that, at the time when they rose to greatest perfection among one people, they were perhaps totally unknown to all the neighbouring nations; and though they universally decayed in one age, yet in a succeeding generation they again revived, and diffused themselves over the world. As far, therefore, as observation reaches, there is no universal difference discernible in the human species; and though it were allowed, that the universe, like an animal body, had a natural progress from infancy to old age; yet as it must still be uncertain, whether, at present, it be advancing to its point of perfection, or declining from it, we cannot thence presuppose any decay in human nature.[1] To prove, therefore, or account for that superior populousness of antiquity, which is commonly supposed, by the imaginary youth or vigour of the world, will scarcely be admitted by any just reasoner. These *general physical* causes ought entirely to be excluded from this question.

There are indeed some more *particular physical* causes of importance. Diseases are mentioned in antiquity, which are almost unknown to modern medicine; and new diseases have arisen and propagated themselves, of which there are no traces in ancient history. In this particular we may observe, upon comparison, that the disadvantage is much on the side of the moderns. Not to mention some others of less moment; the small-pox commits such ravages, as would almost alone account for the great superiority ascribed to ancient times. The tenth or the twelfth part of mankind, destroyed every

---

[1] Columella says, lib. iii. cap. 8., that in Egypt and Africa the bearing of twins was frequent, and even customary; *gemini partus familiares, ac pœne solennes sunt.* If this was true, there is a physical difference both in countries and ages. For travellers make no such remarks on these countries at present. On the contrary, we are apt to suppose the northern nations more prolific. As those two countries were provinces of the Roman empire, it is difficult, though not altogether absurd, to suppose that such a man as Columella might be mistaken with regard to them.

generation, should make a vast difference, it may be thought, in the numbers of the people; and when joined to venereal distempers, a new plague diffused every where, this disease is perhaps equivalent, by its constant operation, to the three great scourges of mankind, war, pestilence, and famine. Were it certain, therefore, that ancient times were more populous than the present, and could no moral causes be assigned for so great a change; these physical causes alone, in the opinion of many, would be sufficient to give us satisfaction on that head.

But is it certain, that antiquity was so much more populous, as is pretended? The extravagancies of VOSSIUS, with regard to this subject, are well known. But an author of much greater genius and discernment has ventured to affirm, that, according to the best computations which these subjects will admit of, there are not now, on the face of the earth, the fiftieth part of mankind, which existed in the time of JULIUS CÆSAR.[1] It may easily be observed, that the comparison, in this case, must be imperfect, even though we confine ourselves to the scene of ancient history; EUROPE, and the nations round the MEDITERRANEAN. We know not exactly the numbers of any EUROPEAN kingdom, or even city, at present: How can we pretend to calculate those of ancient cities and states, where historians have left us such imperfect traces? For my part, the matter appears to me so uncertain, that, as I intend to throw together some reflections on that head, I shall intermingle the enquiry concerning *causes* with that concerning *facts*; which ought never to be admitted, where the facts can be ascertained with any tolerable assurance. We shall, *first*, consider whether it be probable, from what we know of the situation of society in both periods, that antiquity must have been more populous; *secondly*, whether in reality it was so. If I can make it appear, that the conclusion is not so certain as is pretended, in favour of antiquity, it is all I aspire to.

In general, we may observe, that the question, with regard to the comparative populousness of ages or kingdoms, implies important consequences, and commonly determines concerning the preference of their whole police, their manners, and the constitution of their government. For as there is in all men, both male and female, a desire and power of generation,

Lettres PERSANES. See also *L'Esprit de Loix*, liv. xxiii. cap. 17, 18, 19.

more active than is ever universally exerted, the restraints, which they lie under, must proceed from some difficulties in their situation, which it belongs to a wise legislature carefully to observe and remove. Almost every man who thinks he can maintain a family will have one; and the human species, at this rate of propagation, would more than double every generation.[1] How fast do mankind multiply in every colony or new settlement; where it is an easy matter to provide for a family; and where men are nowise straitened or confined, as in long established governments? History tells us frequently of plagues, which have swept away the third or fourth part of a people: Yet in a generation or two, the destruction was not perceived; and the society had again acquired their former number. The lands which were cultivated, the houses built, the commodities raised, the riches acquired, enabled the people, who escaped, immediately to marry, and to rear families, which supplied the place of those who had perished.[2] And for a like reason, every wise, just, and mild government, by rendering the condition of its subjects easy and secure, will always abound most in people, as well as in commodities and riches.[3] A country, indeed, whose climate and soil are fitted for vines, will naturally be more populous than one which produces corn only, and that more populous than one which is only fitted for pasturage. In general, warm climates, as the necessities of the inhabitants are there fewer, and vegetation more powerful, are likely to be most populous: But if everything else be equal, it seems natural to expect, that, wherever there are most happiness and virtue, and the wisest institutions, there will also be most people.

The question, therefore, concerning the populousness of ancient and modern times, being allowed of great importance, it will be requisite, if we would bring it to some determination, to compare both the *domestic* and *political* situation of these two periods, in order to judge of the facts

---

[1] [Editions H to W add: Were every one coupled as soon as he comes to the age of puberty.]

[2] This too is a good reason why the small-pox does not depopulate countries so much as may at first sight be imagined. Where there is room for more people, they will always arise, even without the assistance of naturalization bills. It is remarked by Don Geronimo de Ustariz, that the provinces of Spain, which send most people to the Indies, are most populous; which proceeds from their superior riches.

[3] [A country ... to ... pasturage, was added in Edition H, and In general ... to ... populous, in Edition Q.]

by their moral causes; which is the *first* view in which we proposed to consider them.

The chief difference between the *domestic* œconomy of the ancients and that of the moderns consists in the practice of slavery, which prevailed among the former, and which has been abolished for some centuries throughout the greater part of EUROPE. Some passionate admirers of the ancients, and zealous partizans of civil liberty, (for these sentiments, as they are, both of them, in the main, extremely just, are found to be almost inseparable) cannot forbear regretting the loss of this institution; and whilst they brand all submission to the government of a single person with the harsh denomination of slavery, they would gladly reduce the greater part of mankind to real slavery and subjection. But to one who considers coolly on the subject it will appear, that human nature, in general, really enjoys more liberty at present, in the most arbitrary government of EUROPE, than it ever did during the most flourishing period of ancient times. As much as submission to a petty prince, whose dominions extend not beyond a single city, is more grievous than obedience to a great monarch; so much is domestic slavery more cruel and oppressive than any civil subjection whatsoever. The more the master is removed from us in place and rank, the greater liberty we enjoy; the less are our actions inspected and controled; and the fainter that cruel comparison becomes between our own subjection, and the freedom, and even dominion of another. The remains which are found of domestic slavery, in the AMERICAN colonies, and among some EUROPEAN nations, would never surely create a desire of rendering it more universal. The little humanity, commonly observed in persons, accustomed, from their infancy, to exercise so great authority over their fellow-creatures, and to trample upon human nature, were sufficient alone to disgust us with that unbounded dominion. Nor can a more probable reason be assigned for the severe, I might say, barbarous manners of ancient times, than the practice of domestic slavery; by which every man of rank was rendered a petty tyrant, and educated amidst the flattery, submission, and low debasement of his slaves.

According to ancient practice, all checks were on the inferior, to restrain him to the duty of submission; none on the superior, to engage him to the reciprocal duties of gentleness and humanity. In modern times, a bad servant finds not easily a good master, nor a bad master a good servant; and the checks are mutual, suitably to the inviolable and eternal laws of reason and equity.

The custom of exposing old, useless, or sick slaves in an island of the TYBER, there to starve, seems to have been pretty common in ROME; and whoever recovered, after having been so exposed, had his liberty given him, by an edict of the emperor. CLAUDIUS; in which it was likewise forbidden to kill any slave merely for old age or sickness.[1] But supposing that this edict was strictly obeyed, would it better the domestic treatment of slaves, or render their lives much more comfortable? We may imagine what others would practise, when it was the professed maxim of the elder CATO, to sell his superannuated slaves for any price, rather than maintain what he esteemed a useless burden.[2]

The *ergastula*, or dungeons, where slaves in chains were forced to work, were very common all over ITALY. COLUMELLA[3] advises, that they be always built under ground; and recommends[4] it as the duty of a careful overseer, to call over every day the names of these slaves, like the mustering of a regiment or ship's company, in order to know presently when any of them had deserted. A proof of the frequency of these *ergastula*, and of the great number of slaves usually confined in them.[5]

A chained slave for a porter, was usual in ROME, as appears from OVID,[6] and other authors.[7] Had not these people shaken off all sense of compassion towards that unhappy part of their species, would they have presented their friends, at the first entrance, with such an image of the severity of the master, and misery of the slave?

Nothing so common in all trials, even of civil causes, as to call for the evidence of slaves; which was always extorted by the most exquisite torments. DEMOSTHENES says,[8] that, where it was possible to produce, for the same fact, either freemen or slaves, as witnesses, the judges always preferred the torturing of slaves, as a more certain evidence.[9]

---

[1] SUETONIUS in vita CLAUDII, 25.
[2] PLUT. in vita CATONIS, 4.
[3] Lib. i. cap. 6.
[4] Id. lib. xi. cap. 1.
[5] [Editions H and I added the misquotation: Partem Italiæ ergastula a solitudine vindicant.]
[6] Amor. lib. i. eleg. 6.
[7] SUETON, *de claris rhetor*, 3. So also the ancient poet, *Janitoris tintinnire impedimenta audio*. [Nigid. ap Non. Ed.]
[8] In *Onetor. orat.* 1. 874.
[9] The same practice was very common in ROME; but CICERO seems not to think

SENECA draws a picture of that disorderly luxury, which changes day into night, and night into day, and inverts every stated hour of every office in life. Among other circumstances, such as displacing the meals and times of bathing, he mentions, that, regularly about the third hour of the night, the neighbours of one, who indulges this false refinement, hear the noise of whips and lashes; and, upon enquiry, find that he is then taking an account of the conduct of his servants, and giving them due correction and discipline. This is not remarked as an instance of cruelty, but only of disorder, which even in actions the most usual and methodical, changes the fixed hours that an established custom had assigned for them.[1]

But our present business is only to consider the influence of slavery on the populousness of a state. It is pretended, that, in this particular, the ancient practice had infinitely the advantage, and was the chief cause of that extreme populousness, which is supposed in those times. At present, all masters discourage the marrying of their male servants, and admit not by any means the marriage of the female, who are then supposed altogether incapacitated for their service. But where the property of the servants is lodged in the master, their marriage forms his riches, and brings him a succession of slaves that supply the place of those whom age and infirmity have disabled. He encourages, therefore, their propagation as much as that of his cattle; rears the young with the same care; and educates them to some art or calling, which may render them more useful or valuable to him. The opulent are, by this policy, interested in the being at least, though not in the well-being of the poor; and enrich themselves, by encreasing the number and industry

---

this evidence so certain as the testimony of free-citizens. *Pro Cælio*, 28.

[1] *Epist.* 122. The inhuman sports exhibited at ROME, may justly be considered too as an effect of the people's contempt for slaves, and was also a great cause of the general inhumanity of their princes and rulers. Who can read the accounts of the amphitheatrical entertainments without horror? Or who is surprized, that the emperors should treat that people in the same way the people treated their inferiors? One's humanity, on that occasion, is apt to renew the barbarous wish of CALIGULA, that the people had but one neck. A man could almost be pleased, by a single blow, to put an end to such a race of monsters. You may thank GOD, says the author above cited, (*epist.* 7) addressing himself to the ROMAN people, that you have a master, (*viz.* the mild and merciful NERO) who is incapable of learning cruelty from your example. This was spoke in the beginning of his reign: But he fitted them very well afterwards; and no doubt was considerably improved by the sight of the barbarous objects, to which he had, from his infancy, been accustomed.

of those who are subjected to them. Each man, being a sovereign in his own family, has the same interest with regard to it, as the prince with regard to the state; and has not, like the prince, any opposite motives of ambition or vainglory, which may lead him to depopulate his little sovereignty. All of it is, at all times, under his eye; and he has leisure to inspect the most minute detail of the marriage and education of his subjects.[1]

Such are the consequences of domestic slavery, according to the first aspect and appearance of things: But if we enter more deeply into the subject, we shall perhaps find reason to retract our hasty determinations. The comparison is shocking between the management of human creatures and that of cattle; but being extremely just, when applied to the present subject, it may be proper to trace the consequences of it. At the capital, near all great cities, in all populous, rich, industrious provinces, few cattle are bred. Provisions, lodging, attendance, labour are there dear; and men find their account better in buying the cattle, after they come to a certain age, from the remoter and cheaper countries. These are consequently the only breeding countries for cattle; and by a parity of reason, for men too, when the latter are put on the same footing with the former. To rear a child in LONDON, till he could be serviceable, would cost much dearer, than to buy one of the same age from SCOTLAND or IRELAND; where he had been bred in a cottage, covered with rags, and fed on oatmeal or potatoes. Those who had slaves, therefore, in all the richer and more populous countries, would discourage the pregnancy of the females, and either prevent or destroy the birth. The human species would perish in those places where it ought to encrease the fastest; and a perpetual recruit be wanted from the poorer and more desert provinces. Such a continued drain would tend mightily to depopulate the state, and render great cities ten times more destructive than with us; where every man is master of himself, and provides for his children from the powerful instinct of nature, not the

[1] We may here observe, that if domestic slavery really encreased populousness, it would be an exception to the general rule, that the happiness of any society and its populousness are necessary attendants. A master, from humour or interest, may make his slaves very unhappy, yet be careful, from interest, to increase their number. Their marriage is not a matter of choice with them, more than any other action of their life.

calculations of sordid interest. If LONDON, at present, without much encreasing, needs a yearly recruit from tne country, of 5000 people, as is usually computed, what must it require, if the greater part of the tradesmen and common people were slaves, and were hindered from breeding by their avaricious masters?

All ancient authors tell us, that there was a perpetual flux of slaves to ITALY from the remoter provinces, particularly SYRIA, CILICIA,[1] CAPPADOCIA, and the Lesser ASIA, THRACE, and ÆGYPT: Yet the number of people did not encrease in ITALY; and writers complain of the continual decay of industry and agriculture.[2] Where then is that extreme fertility of the ROMAN slaves, which is commonly supposed? So far from multiplying, they could not, it seems, so much as keep up the stock, without immense recruits. And though great numbers were continually manumitted and converted into ROMAN citizens, the numbers even of these did not encrease,[3] till the freedom of the city was communicated to foreign provinces.

The term for a slave, born and bred in the family, was *verna*[4]; and these slaves seem to have been entitled by custom

---

[1] Ten thousand slaves in a day have often been sold for the use of the ROMANS, at DELUS in CILICIA. STRABO, lib. xiv., 668.

[2] COLUMELLA, lib. i. *proœm.* et cap. 2, et. 7. VARRO, lib. iii. cap. 1. HORAT, lib. ii. od. 15. TACIT. *annal.* lib. iii. cap. 54. SUETON. *in vita* AUG. cap. xlii. PLIN. lib. xviii, cap. 13.

[3] *Minore indies plebe ingenua*, says TACITUS, *ann.* lib. iv. cap. 27.

[4] As *servus* was the name of the genus, and *verna* of the species, without any correlative, this forms a strong presumption, that the latter were by far the least numerous. It is an universal observation which we may form upon language, that where two related parts of a whole bear any proportion to each other, in numbers, rank or consideration, there are always correlative terms invented, which answer to both the parts, and express their mutual relation. If they bear no proportion to each other, the term is only invented for the less, and marks its distinction from the whole. Thus *man* and *woman*, *master* and *servant*, *father* and *son*, *prince* and *subject*, *stranger* and *citizen*, are correlative terms. But the words, *seaman, carpenter, smith, tailor,* &c. have no correspondent terms, which express those who are no seamen, or carpenters, &c. Languages differ very much with regard to the particular words where this distinction obtains; and may thence afford very strong inferences, concerning the manners and customs of different nations. The military government of the ROMAN emperors had exalted the soldiery so high, that they balanced all the other orders of the state: Hence *miles* and *paganus* became relative terms; a thing, till then, unknown to ancient, and still so to modern languages. Modern superstition exalted the clergy so high, that they overbalanced the whole state: Hence *clergy* and *laity* are terms opposed in all modern languages; and in these alone. And from the same principles I infer, that if the number of slaves bought by the ROMANS from foreign countries, had not extremely exceeded those which were bred at home, *verna* would have had a correlative, which would have expressed the former species of slaves. But these, it would seem, composed the main body of the ancient slaves, and the latter were but a few exceptions.

to privileges and indulgences beyond others; a sufficient reason why the masters would not be fond of rearing many of that kind.¹ Whoever is acquainted with the maxims of our planters, will acknowledge the justness of this observation.²

ATTICUS is much praised by his historian for the care, which he took in recruiting his family from the slaves born in it³: May we not thence infer, that this practice was not then very common?

The names of slaves in the GREEK comedies, SYRUS, MYSUS, GETA, THRAX, DAVUS, LYDUS, PHRYX, &c. afford a presumption, that, at ATHENS at least, most of the slaves were imported from foreign countries. The ATHENIANS, says STRABO,⁴ gave to their slaves, either the names of the nations whence they were bought, as LYDUS, SYRUS; or the names that were most common among those nations, as MANES or MIDAS to a PHRYGIAN, TIBIAS to a PAPHLAGONIAN.

DEMOSTHENES, having mentioned a law which forbad any man to strike the slave of another, praises the humanity of this law; and adds, that, if the barbarians from whom the slaves were bought, had information, that their countrymen met with such gentle treatment, they would entertain a great esteem for the ATHENIANS.⁵ ISOCRATES⁶ too insinuates, that the slaves of the GREEKS were generally or very commonly barbarians.⁷ ARISTOTLE in his Politics⁸ plainly supposes, that a

---

¹ *Verna* is used by ROMAN writers as a word equivalent to *scurra*, on account of the petulance and impudence of those slaves. MART. lib. i. ep. 42. HORACE also mentions the *vernæ procaces*; and PETRONIUS, cap. 24. *vernula urbanitas*. SENECA, *de provid.* cap. 1. *vernularum licentia.*

² It is computed in the WEST INDIES, that a stock of slaves grow worse five *per cent.* every year, unless new slaves be bought to recruit them. They are not able to keep up their number, even in those warm countries, where cloaths and provisions are so easily got. How much more must this happen in EUROPEAN countries, and in or near great cities?¹ I shall add, that, from the experience of our planters, slavery is as little advantageous to the master as to the slave, wherever hired servants can be procured. A man is obliged to cloath and feed his slave; and he does no more for his servant: The price of the first purchase is, therefore, so much loss to him: not to mention, that the fear of punishment will never draw so much labour from a slave, as the dread of being turned off and not getting another service, will from a freeman.

³ CORN. NEPOS in vita ATTICI. We may remark, that ATTICUS's estate lay chiefly in EPIRUS, which, being a remote, desolate place, would render it profitable for him to rear slaves there.

⁴ Lib. vii., 304.

⁵ In MIDIAM, p. 221, ex edit. ALDI.

⁶ Panegyr. [See p. 59.]

⁷ [The remainder of this paragraph was added in Edition M.]

⁸ Lib. vii. cap. 10, sub fin.

---

¹ [The remainder of this note was added in Ed. R.]

slave is always a foreigner. The ancient comic writers represented the slaves as speaking a barbarous language.[1] This was an imitation of nature.

It is well known that DEMOSTHENES, in his nonage, had been defrauded of a large fortune by his tutors, and that afterwards he recovered, by a prosecution at law, the value of his patrimony. His orations, on that occasion, still remain, and contain an exact detail of the whole substance left by his father,[2] in money, merchandise, houses, and slaves, together with the value of each particular. Among the rest were 52 slaves, handicraftsmen, namely, 32 sword-cutlers, and 20 cabinet-makers[3]; all males; not a word of any wives, children or family, which they certainly would have had, had it been a common practice at ATHENS to breed from the slaves: And the value of the whole must have much depended on that circumstance. No female slaves are even so much as mentioned, except some house-maids, who belonged to his mother. This argument has great force, if it be not altogether conclusive.

Consider this passage of PLUTARCH,[4] speaking of the Elder CATO. 'He had a great number of slaves, whom he took 'care to buy at the sales of prisoners of war; and he chose 'them young, that they might easily be accustomed to any 'diet or manner of life, and be instructed in any business or 'labour, as men teach any thing to young dogs or horses.—— 'And esteeming love the chief source of all disorders, he 'allowed the male slaves to have a commerce with the female 'in his family, upon paying a certain sum for this privilege: 'But he strictly prohibited all intrigues out of his family.' Are there any symptoms in this narration of that care which is supposed in the ancients, of the marriage and propagation of their slaves? If that was a common practice, founded on general interest, it would surely have been embraced by Cato, who was a great œconomist, and lived in times when the ancient frugality and simplicity of manners were still in credit and reputation.

It is expressly remarked by the writers of the ROMAN law, that scarcely any ever purchase slaves with a view of breeding from them.[5]

[1] ARISTOPH. Equites. l. 17. The ancient scholiast remarks on this passage βαρβαρίζει ὡς δοῦλος.
[2] In *Aphobum orat.* 1. 816.
[3] κλινοποιοί, makers of those beds which the ancients lay upon at meals.
[4] In vita CATONIS, 21.
[5] 'Non temere ancillæ ejus rei causa

Our lackeys and house-maids, I own, do not serve much to multiply their species: But the ancients, besides those who attended on their person, had almost all their labour performed, [1] and even manufactures executed, by slaves, who lived, many of them, in their family; and some great men possessed to the number of 10,000. If there be any suspicion, therefore, that this institution was unfavourable to propagation, (and the same reason, at least in part, holds with regard to ancient slaves as modern servants) how destructive must slavery have proved?

History mentions a ROMAN nobleman, who had 400 slaves under the same roof with him: And having been assassinated at home by the furious revenge of one of them, the law was executed with rigour, and all without exception were put to death.[2] Many other ROMAN noblemen had families equally, or more numerous; and I believe every one will allow, that this would scarcely be practicable, were we to suppose all the slaves married, and the females to be breeders.[3]

So early as the poet HESIOD,[4] married slaves, whether male or female, were esteemed inconvenient. How much more, where families had encreased to such an enormous size as in ROME, and where the ancient simplicity of manners was banished from all ranks of people?

XENOPHON in his Oeconomics, where he gives directions

---

comparantur ut pariant.' *Digest.* lib. 5. tit. 3. *de hæred. petit. lex* 27. The following texts are to the same purpose. 'Spadonem morbosum non esse, neque vitiosum, verius mihi videtur; sed sanum esse, sicuti illum qui unum testiculum habet, qui etiam generare potest.' *Digest.* lib. 2. tit. 1. *de ædilitio edicto, lex,* 6. § 2. 'Sin autem quis ita spado sit, ut tam necessaria pars corporis penitus absit, morbosus est.' *Id. lex* 7. His impotence, it seems, was only regarded so far as his health or life might be affected by it. In other respects, he was full as valuable. The same reasoning is employed with regard to female slaves. 'Quæritur de ea muliere quæ semper mortuos parit, an morbosa sit? et ait Sabinus, si vulvæ vitio hoc contingit, morbosam esse.' *Id lex* 14. It has even been doubted, whether a woman pregnant was morbid or vitiated; and it is determined, that she is sound, not on account of the value of her offspring, but because it is the natural part or office of women to bear children. 'Si mulier prægnans venerit, inter omnes convenit sanam eam esse. Maximum enim ac præcipuum munus fœminarum accipere ac tueri conceptum. Puerperam quoque sanam esse; si modo nihil extrinsecus accedit, quod corpus ejus in aliquam valetudinem immitteret. De sterili Cœlius distinguere Trebatium dicit, ut si natura sterilis sit, sana sit; si vitio corporis, contra.' *Id.*

[1] [And even manufactures executed; added in Edition Q.]

[2] TACIT. *ann.* lib. xiv. cap. 43.

[3] The slaves in the great houses had little rooms assigned to them, called *cellæ.* Whence the name of cell was transferred to the monk's room in a convent. See farther on this head, JUST. LIPSIUS, Saturn. i. cap. 14. These form strong presumptions against the marriage and propagation of the family slaves.

[4] Opera et Dies, 405, also 602.

for the management of a farm, recommends a strict care and attention of laying the male and the female slaves at a distance from each other. He seems not to suppose that they are ever married. The only slaves among the GREEKS that appear to have continued their own race, were the HELOTES, who had houses apart, and were more the slaves of the public than of individuals.[1]

[2] The same author[3] tells us that NICIAS's overseer, by agreement with his master, was obliged to pay him an obolus a day for each slave; besides maintaining them, and keeping up the number. Had the ancient slaves been all breeders, this last circumstance of the contract had been superfluous.

The ancients talk so frequently of a fixed, stated portion of provisions assigned to each slave,[4] that we are naturally led to conclude, that slaves lived almost all single, and received that portion as a kind of board-wages.

The practice, indeed, of marrying slaves seems not to have been very common, even among the country-labourers, where it is more naturally to be expected. CATO,[5] enumerating the slaves requisite to labour a vineyard of a hundred acres, makes them amount to 15; the overseer and his wife, *villicus* and *villica*, and 13 male slaves; for an olive plantation of 240 acres, the overseer and his wife, and 11 male slaves; and so in proportion to a greater or less plantation or vineyard.

VARRO,[6] quoting this passage of CATO, allows his computation to be just in every respect, except the last. For as it is requisite, says he, to have an overseer and his wife, whether the vineyard or plantation be great or small, this must alter the exactness of the proportion. Had CATO's computation been erroneous in any other respect, it had certainly been corrected by VARRO, who seems fond of discovering so trivial an error.

The same author,[7] as well as COLUMELLA,[8] recommends it as requisite to give a wife to the overseer, in order to attach him the more strongly to his master's service. This

---

[1] STRABO, lib. viii. 365.
[2] [This paragraph was added in Edition K.]
[3] De ratione reditunm, 4,14.
[4] See CATO de re rustica, cap. 56. Donatus in Phormion, l. 1, 9. SENECAE epist. 80.
[5] De re rust. cap. 10, 11.
[6] Lib. i. cap. 18.
[7] Lib. i. cap. 17.
[8] Lib. i. cap 18.

was therefore a peculiar indulgence granted to a slave, in whom so great confidence was reposed.

In the same place, VARRO mentions it as an useful precaution, not to buy too many slaves from the same nation, lest they beget factions and seditions in the family: A presumption, that in ITALY, the greater part, even of the country labouring slaves, (for he speaks of no other) were bought from the remoter provinces. All the world knows, that the family slaves in ROME, who were instruments of show and luxury, were commonly imported from the east. *Hoc profecere*, says PLINY, speaking of the jealous care of masters, *mancipiorum legiones, et in domo turba externa, ac servorum quoque causa nomenclator adhibendus.*[1]

It is indeed recommended by VARRO,[2] to propagate young shepherds in the family from the old ones. For as grasing farms were commonly in remote and cheap places, and each shepherd lived in a cottage apart, his marriage and encrease were not liable to the same inconveniencies as in dearer places, and where many servants lived in the family; which was universally the case in such of the ROMAN farms as produced wine or corn. If we consider this exception with regard to shepherds, and weigh the reasons of it, it will serve for a strong confirmation of all our foregoing suspicions.[3]

COLUMELLA,[4] I own, advises the master to give a reward, and even liberty to a female slave, that had reared him above three children: A proof that sometimes the ancients propagated from their slaves; which, indeed, cannot be denied. Were it otherwise, the practice of slavery, being so common in antiquity, must have been destructive to a degree which no expedient could repair. All I pretend to infer from these reasonings is, that slavery is in general disadvantageous both to the happiness and populousness of mankind, and that its place is much better supplied by the practice of hired servants.

The laws, or, as some writers call them, the seditions of the GRACCHI, were occasioned by their observing the encrease of slaves all over ITALY, and the diminution of free citizens. APPIAN[5] ascribes this encrease to the propagation of the

---

[1] Lib. xxxiii. cap. 1. So likewise TACITUS, *annal.* lib. xiv. cap. 44. [This reference to TACITUS was added in Edition K.]

[2] Lib. ii. cap. 10.

[3] *Pastoris duri est hic filius, ille bubulci.* JUVEN, sat. 11, 151.

[4] Lib. i. cap. 8.

[5] De bel. civ. lib. i. 7.

slaves: PLUTARCH[1] to the purchasing of barbarians, who were chained and imprisoned, βαρβαρικα δεσμωτηρια.[2] It is to be presumed that both causes concurred.

SICILY, says FLORUS,[3] was full of *ergastula*, and was cultivated by labourers in chains. EUNUS and ATHENIO excited the servile war, by breaking up these monstrous prisons, and giving liberty to 60,000 slaves. The younger POMPEY augmented his army in SPAIN by the same expedient.[4] If the country labourers, throughout the ROMAN empire, were so generally in this situation, and if it was difficult or impossible to find separate lodgings for the families of the city servants, how unfavourable to propagation, as well as to humanity, must the institution of domestic slavery be esteemed?

CONSTANTINOPLE, at present, requires the same recruits of slaves from all the provinces, that ROME did of old; and these provinces are of consequence far from being populous.

EGYPT, according to Mons. MAILLET, sends continual colonies of black slaves to the other parts of the TURKISH empire; and receives annually an equal return of white: The one brought from the inland parts of AFRICA; the other from MINGRELIA, CIRCASSIA, and TARTARY.

Our modern convents are, no doubt, bad institutions: But there is reason to suspect, that anciently every great family in Italy, and probably in other parts of the world, was a species of convent. And though we have reason to condemn all those popish institutions, as nurseries[5] of superstition, burthensome to the public, and oppressive to the poor prisoners, male as well as female; yet may it be questioned whether they be so destructive to the populousness of a state, as is commonly imagined. Were the land, which belongs to a convent, bestowed on a nobleman, he would spend its

---

[1] In vita TIB. & C. GRACCHI.
[2] To the same purpose is that passage of the elder SENECA, ex controversia 5, lib. v. 'Arata quondam populis rura, singulorum ergastulorum sunt; latiusque nunc villici, quam olim reges, imperant. At nunc eadem,' says PLINY, 'vincti pedes, damnatae manus, inscripti vultus exercent.' Lib. xviii. cap. 3. So also MARTIAL.
'Et sonet innumera compede Thuscus ager.' Lib. ix. ep. 23.
And LUCAN. 'Tum longos jungere fines

Agrorum, et quondam duro sulcata Camilli
Vomere, et antiquas Curiorum passa ligones
Longa sub ignotis extendere rura colonis.' Lbi. i. 167.

'Vincto fossore coluntur
Hesperiae segetes.——' Lib. vii. 402.

[3] Lib. iii. cap. 19.
[4] Id. lib. iv. cap. 8.
[5] [Of the most abject superstition: Editions H to P.]

revenue on dogs, horses, grooms, footmen, cooks, and housemaids; and his family would not furnish many more citizens than the convent.

The common reason, why any parent thrusts his daughters into nunneries, is, that he may not be overburthened with too numerous a family; but the ancients had a method almost as innocent, and more effectual to that purpose, to wit, exposing their children in early infancy. This practice was very common; and is not spoken of by any author of those times with the horror it deserves, or scarcely[1] even with disapprobation. PLUTARCH, the humane, good-natured PLUTARCH,[2] mentions it as a merit in ATTALUS, king of PERGAMUS, that he murdered, or, if you will, exposed all his own children, in order to leave his crown to the son of his brother, EUMENES; signalizing in this manner his gratitude and affection to EUMENES, who had left him his heir preferably to that son. It was SOLON, the most celebrated of the sages of GREECE, that gave parents permission by law to kill their children.[3]

Shall we then allow these two circumstances to compensate each other, to wit, monastic vows, and the exposing of children, and to be unfavourable, in equal degrees, to the propagation of mankind? I doubt the advantage is here on the side of antiquity. Perhaps, by an odd connexion of causes, the barbarous practice of the ancients might rather render those times more populous. By removing the terrors of too numerous a family it would engage many people in marriage; and such is the force of natural affection, that very few, in comparison, would have resolution enough, when it came to the push, to carry into execution their former intentions.

CHINA, the only country where this practice of exposing children prevails at present, is the most populous country we know off; and every man is married before he is twenty. Such early marriages could scarcely be general, had not men the prospect of so easy a method of getting rid of their children. I own that [4] PLUTARCH speaks of it as a very general maxim of the poor to expose their children; and

---

[1] TACITUS blames it. De morib. Germ. 19.

[2] De fraterno amore. SENECA also approves of the exposing of sickly infirm children. De ira, lib. i. cap. 15.

[3] SEXT. EMP. lib. iii. cap. 24.

[4] De amore prolis.

as the rich were then averse to marriage, on account of the courtship they met with from those who expected legacies from them, the public must have been in a bad situation between them.[1]

Of all sciences there is none, where first appearances are more deceitful than in politics. Hospitals for foundlings seem favourable to the encrease of numbers; and perhaps, may be so, when kept under proper restrictions. But when they open the door to every one, without distinction, they have probably a contrary effect, and are pernicious to the state. It is computed, that every ninth child born at PARIS, is sent to the hospital; though it seems certain, according to the common course of human affairs, that it is not a hundredth child whose parents are altogether incapacitated to rear and educate him. The [2] great difference, for health, industry, and morals, between an education in an hospital and that in a private family, should induce us not to make the entrance into the former too easy and engaging. To kill one's own child is shocking to nature, and must therefore be somewhat unusual; but to turn over the care of him upon others, is very tempting to the natural indolence of mankind.

Having considered the domestic life and manners of the ancients, compared to those of the moderns; where, in the main, we seem rather superior, so far as the present question is concerned; we shall now examine the *political* customs and institutions of both ages, and weigh their influence in retarding or forwarding the propagation of mankind.

Before the encrease of the ROMAN power, or rather till its full establishment, almost all the nations, which are the scene of ancient history, were divided into small territories or petty commonwealths, where of course a great equality of

---

[1] The practice of leaving great sums of money to friends, tho' one had near relations, was common in GREECE as well as ROME; as we may gather from LUCIAN. This practice prevails much less in modern times; and BEN. JOHNSON'S VOLPONE is therefore almost entirely extracted from antient authors, and suits better the manners of those times.

It may justly be thought, that the liberty of divorces in Rome was another discouragement to marriage. Such a practice prevents not quarrels from *humour*, but rather increases them; and occasions also those from *interest*, which are much more dangerous and destructive. See farther on this head, Essays moral, political, and literary, Part I. essay XIX. Perhaps too the unnatural lusts of the antients ought to be taken into consideration, as of some moment.

[2] [Infinite: Editions H to P.]

fortune prevailed, and the center of the government was always very near its frontiers.

This was the situation of affairs not only in GREECE and ITALY, but also in SPAIN, GAUL, GERMANY, AFRIC, and a great part of the Lesser ASIA: And it must be owned, that no institution could be more favourable to the propagation of mankind. For, though a man of an overgrown fortune, not being able to consume more than another, must share it with those who serve and attend him; yet their possession being precarious, they have not the same encouragement to marry, as if each had a small fortune, secure and independent. Enormous cities are, besides, destructive to society, beget vice and disorder of all kinds, starve the remoter provinces, and even starve themselves, by the prices to which they raise all provisions. Where each man had his little house and field to himself, and each county had its capital, free and independent; what a happy situation of mankind! How favourable to industry and agriculture; to marriage and propagation! The prolific virtue of men, were it to act in its full extent, without that restraint which poverty and necessity imposes on it, would double the number every generation: And nothing surely can give it more liberty, than such small commonwealths, and such an equality of fortune among the citizens. All small states naturally produce equality of fortune, because they afford no opportunities of great encrease; but small commonwealths much more, by that division of power and authority which is essential to them.

When XENOPHON[1] returned after the famous expedition with CYRUS, he hired himself and 6000 of the GREEKS into the service of SEUTHES, a prince of THRACE; and the articles of his agreement were, that each soldier should receive a *daric* a month, each captain two *darics*, and he himself, as general, four: A regulation of pay which would not a little surprise our modern officers.

DEMOSTHENES and ÆSCHINES, with eight more, were sent ambassadors to PHILIP of MACEDON, and their appointments for above four months were a thousand *drachmas*, which is less than a *drachma* a day for each ambassador.[2] But a *drachma* a day, nay sometimes two,[3] was the pay of a common foot-soldier.

---

[1] *De exp.* CYR. lib. vii. 6.
[2] DEMOST. *de falsa leg.* 390. He calls it a considerable sum.
[3] THUCYD. lib. iii. 17.

A centurion among the ROMANS had only double pay to a private man, in POLYBIUS'S time,[1] and we accordingly find the gratuities after a triumph regulated by that proportion.[2] But MARK ANTHONY and the triumvirate gave the centurions five times the reward of the other.[3] So much had the encrease of the commonwealth encreased the inequality among the citizens.[4]

It must be owned, that the situation of affairs in modern times, with regard to civil liberty, as well as equality of fortune, is not near so favourable, either to the propagation or happiness of mankind. EUROPE is shared out mostly into great monarchies; and such parts of it as are divided into small territories, are commonly governed by absolute princes, who ruin their people by a mimicry of the greater monarchs, in the splendor of their court and number of their forces. SWISSERLAND alone and HOLLAND resemble the ancient republics; and though the former is far from possessing any advantage either of soil, climate, or commerce, yet the numbers of people, with which it abounds, notwithstanding their enlisting themselves into every service in Europe, prove sufficiently the advantages of their political institutions.

The ancient republics derived their chief or only security from the numbers of their citizens. The TRACHINIANS having lost great numbers of their people, the remainder, instead of enriching themselves by the inheritance of their fellow-citizens, applied to SPARTA, their metropolis, for a new stock of inhabitants. The SPARTANS immediately collected ten thousand men; among whom the old citizens divided the lands of which the former proprietors had perished.[5]

After TIMOLEON had banished DIONYSIUS from SYRACUSE, and had settled the affairs of SICILY, finding the cities of SYRACUSE and SELLINUNTIUM extremely depopulated by tyranny, war, and faction, he invited over from GREECE some new inhabitants to repeople them.[6] Immediately forty thousand men (PLUTARCH[7] says sixty thousand) offered themselves; and he distributed so many

[1] Lib. vi. cap. 37.
[2] TIT. LIV. lib. xli. cap. 7, 13 & alibi passim.
[3] APPIAN. De bell. civ. lib. iv., 20.
[4] CÆSAR gave the centurions ten times the gratuity of the common soldiers, De bello Gallico, lib. viii. 4. In the RHODIAN cartel, mentioned afterwards, no distinction in the ransom was made on account of ranks in the army.
[5] DIOD. SIC. lib. xii. 59. THUCYD. lib. iii. 92.
[6] DIOD. SIC. lib. xvi. 82.
[7] In vita TIMOL. 23.

lots of land among them, to the great satisfaction of the ancient inhabitants: A proof at once of the maxims of ancient policy, which affected populousness more than riches; and of the good effects of these maxims, in the extreme populousness of that small country, GREECE, which could at once supply so great a colony. The case was not much different with the ROMANS in early times. He is a pernicious citizen, said M. CURIUS, who cannot be content with seven acres.[1] Such ideas of equality could not fail of producing great numbers of people.

We must now consider what disadvantages the ancients lay under with regard to populousness, and what checks they received from their political maxims and institutions. There are commonly compensations in every human condition: and though these compensations be not always perfectly equal, yet they serve, at least, to restrain the prevailing principle. To compare them and estimate their influence, is indeed difficult, even where they take place in the same age, and in neighbouring countries: But where several ages have intervened, and only scattered lights are afforded us by ancient authors; what can we do but amuse ourselves by talking *pro* and *con*, on an interesting subject, and thereby correcting all hasty and violent determinations?

First, We may observe, that the ancient republics were almost in perpetual war, a natural effect of their martial spirit, their love of liberty, their mutual emulation, and that hatred which generally prevails among nations that live in close neighbourhood. Now, war in a small state is much more destructive than in a great one; both because all the inhabitants, in the former case, must serve in the armies; and because the whole state is frontier, and is all exposed to the inroads of the enemy.

The maxims of ancient war were much more destructive than those of modern; chiefly by that distribution of plunder, in which the soldiers were indulged. The private men in our armies are such a low set of people,

---

[1] PLIN. lib. 18. cap. 3. The same author, in cap. 6, says, *Verumque fatentibus latifundia perdidere* ITALIAM; *jam vero et provincias. Sex domi semissem* AFRICÆ *possidebant, cum interfecit eos* NERO *princeps.* In this view, the barbarous butchery committed by the first ROMAN emperors, was not, perhaps, so destructive to the public as we may imagine. These never ceased till they had extinguished all the illustrious families, which had enjoyed the plunder of the world, during the latter ages of the republic. The new nobles who rose in their place, were less splendid, as we learn from TACIT. *ann.* lib. 3. cap. 55.

that we find any abundance, beyond their simple pay, breeds confusion and disorder among them, and a total dissolution of discipline. The very wretchedness and meanness of those, who fill the modern armies, render them less destructive to the countries which they invade: One instance, among many, of the deceitfulness of first appearances in all political reasonings.[1]

Ancient battles were much more bloody, by the very nature of the weapons employed in them. The ancients drew up their men 16 or 20, sometimes 50 men deep, which made a narrow front; and it was not difficult to find a field, in which both armies might be marshalled, and might engage with each other. Even where any body of the troops was kept off by hedges, hillocks, woods, or hollow ways, the battle was not so soon decided between the contending parties, but that the others had time to overcome the difficulties which opposed them, and take part in the engagement. And as the whole army was thus engaged, and each man closely buckled to his antagonist, the battles were commonly very bloody, and great slaughter was made on both sides, especially on the vanquished. The long thin lines, required by fire-arms, and the quick decision of the fray, render our modern engagements but partial rencounters, and enable the general, who is foiled in the beginning of the day, to draw off the greater part of his army, sound and entire.[2]

The battles of antiquity, both by their duration, and their resemblance to single combats, were wrought up to a degree of fury quite unknown to later ages. Nothing could then engage the combatants to give quarter, but the hopes of profit, by making slaves of their prisoners. In civil wars, as we learn from TACITUS,[3] the battles were the most bloody, because the prisoners were not slaves.

---

[1] The ancient soldiers, being free citizens, above the lowest rank, were all married. Our modern soldiers are either forced to live unmarried, or their marriages turn to small account towards the encrease of mankind. A circumstance which ought, perhaps, to be taken into consideration, as of some consequence in favour of the ancients.

[2] [Editions H to P add: Could FOLARD's project of the column take place (which seems impracticable[1]) it would render modern battles as destructive as the antient.]

[3] Hist. lib. ii. cap. 44.

---

[1] What is the advantage of the column after it has broke the enemy's line? only, that it then takes them in flank, and dissipates whatever stands near it by a fire from all sides. But till it has broke them, does it not present a flank to the enemy, and that exposed to their musquetry, and, what is much worse, to their cannon?

What a stout resistance must be made, where the vanquished expected so hard a fate! How inveterate the rage, where the maxims of war were, in every respect, so bloody and severe!

Instances are frequent, in ancient history, of cities besieged, whose inhabitants, rather than open their gates, murdered their wives and children, and rushed themselves on a voluntary death, sweetened perhaps by a little prospect of revenge upon the enemy. GREEKS,[1] as well as BARBARIANS, have often been wrought up to this degree of fury. And the same determined spirit and cruelty must, in other instances less remarkable, have been destructive to human society, in those petty commonwealths, which lived in close neighbourhood, and were engaged in perpetual wars and contentions.

Sometimes the wars in GREECE, says PLUTARCH,[2] were carried on entirely by inroads, and robberies, and piracies. Such a method of war must be more destructive in small states, than the bloodiest battles and sieges.

By the laws of the twelve tables, possession during two years formed a prescription for land; one year for moveables[3]: An indication, that there was not in ITALY, at that time, much more order, tranquillity, and settled police, than there is at present among the TARTARS.

The only cartel I remember in ancient history, is that between DEMETRIUS POLIORCETES and the RHODIANS; when it was agreed, that a free citizen should be restored for 1000 *drachmas*, a slave bearing arms for 500.[4]

But, *secondly*, it appears that ancient manners were more unfavourable than the modern, not only in times of war, but also in those of peace; and that too in every respect, except the love of civil liberty and of equality, which is, I own, of considerable importance. To exclude faction from a free government, is very difficult, if not altogether impracticable; but such inveterate rage between the factions, and such bloody maxims, are found, in modern times amongst religious

---

[1] As ABYDUS, mentioned by LIVY, lib. xxxi. cap. 17, 18, and POLYB. lib. xvi. 34. As also the XANTHIANS, APPIAN. *de bell. civil.* lib. iv. 80.

[2] *In vita* ARATI. 6.
[3] INST. lib. ii. cap. 6.[1]
[4] DIOD. SICUL. lib. xx. 84.

[1] [Editions H to P add: 'Tis true the same law seems to have continued till the time of JUSTINIAN. But abuses introduced by barbarism are not always corrected by civility.]

parties alone.¹ In ancient history, we may always observe, where one party prevailed, whether the nobles or people (for I can observe no difference in this respect²) that they immediately butchered all of the opposite party who fell into their hands, and banished such as had been so fortunate as to escape their fury. No form of process, no law, no trial, no pardon. A fourth, a third, perhaps near half of the city was slaughtered, or expelled, every revolution; and the exiles always joined foreign enemies, and did all the mischief possible to their fellow-citizens; till fortune put it in their power to take full revenge by a new revolution. And as these were frequent in such violent governments, the disorder, diffidence, jealousy, enmity, which must prevail, are not easy for us to imagine in this age of the world.

There are only two revolutions I can recollect in ancient history, which passed without great severity, and great effusion of blood in massacres and assassinations, namely, the restoration of the ATHENIAN Democracy by THRASYBULUS, and the subduing of the ROMAN republic by CÆSAR. We learn from ancient history, that THRASYBULUS passed a general amnesty for all past offences; and first introduced that word, as well as practice, into GREECE.³ It appears, however, from many orations of LYSIAS,⁴ that the chief, and even some of the subaltern offenders, in the preceding tyranny, were tried and capitally punished.⁵ And as to CÆSAR's clemency, though much celebrated, it would not gain great applause in the present age. He butchered, for instance, all CATO's senate, when he became master of UTICA⁶; and these, we may readily believe, were not the most worthless of the party. All those who had borne arms against that usurper, were attainted; and, by HIRTIUS's law, declared incapable of all public offices.

These people were extremely fond of liberty; but seem not to have understood it very well. When the thirty tyrants first established their dominion at ATHENS, they began with

---

¹ [Editions H to P add: Where bigotted priests are the accusers, judges, and executioners.]

² LYSIAS, who was himself of the popular faction, and very narrowly escaped from the thirty tyrants, says, that the Democracy was as violent a government as the Oligarchy. *Orat.* 25, *de statu popul.*

³ CICERO, PHILIP. 1, 1.

⁴ As *orat.* 12. *contra* ERATOST. *orat.* 13. *contra.* AGORAT. *orat.* 16, pro MANTITH.

⁵ [Editions H to Q add: This is a difficulty not cleared up, and even not observed by antiquarians and historians.]

⁶ APPIAN, *de bell. civ.* lib. ii. 100.

seizing all the sycophants and informers, who had been so troublesome during the Democracy, and putting them to death by an arbitrary sentence and execution. *Every man,* says SALLUST[1] and LYSIAS,[2] *was rejoiced at these punishments;* not considering, that liberty was from that moment annihilated.

The utmost energy of the nervous style of THUCYDIDES, and the copiousness and expression of the GREEK language, seem to sink under that historian, when he attempts to describe the disorders, which arose from faction throughout all the GRECIAN commonwealths. You would imagine, that he still labours with a thought greater than he can find words to communicate. And he concludes his pathetic description with an observation, which is at once refined and solid. 'In these contests,' says he, 'those who were the dullest, and most stupid, and had the least foresight, commonly prevailed. For being conscious of this weakness, and dreading to be over-reached by those of greater penetration, they went to work hastily, without premeditation, by the sword and poinard, and thereby got the start of their antagonists, who were forming fine schemes and projects for their destruction.'[3]

Not to mention DIONYSIUS[4] the elder, who is computed to have butchered in cool blood above 10,000 of his fellow-citizens; or AGATHOCLES,[5] NABIS,[6] and others, still more bloody than he; the transactions, even in free governments, were extremely violent and destructive. At ATHENS, the thirty tyrants and the nobles, in a twelvemonth, murdered, without trial, about 1200 of the people, and banished above the half of the citizens that remained.[7] In ARGOS, near the

---

[1] See CÆSAR's speech *de bell. Catil.* c. 51.

[2] *Orat.* 25, 173. And in *orat.* 30, 184, he mentions the factious spirit of the popular assemblies as the only cause why these illegal punishments should displease.

[3] Lib. iii. [The country in EUROPE in which I have observed the factions to be most violent, and party-hatred the strongest, is IRELAND. This goes so far as to cut off even the most common intercourse of civilities between the Protestants and Catholics. Their cruel insurrections and the severe revenges which they have taken of each other, are the causes of this mutual ill will, which is the chief source of the disorder, poverty, and depopulation of that country. The GREEK factions I imagine to have been inflamed still to a higher degree of rage: the revolutions being commonly more frequent, and the maxims of assassination much more avowed and acknowledged. Editions H to P.]

[4] PLUT. *de virt. & fort.* ALEX.

[5] DIOD. SIC. lib. xviii, xix.

[6] TIT. LIV. xxxi. xxxiii. xxxiv.

[7] DIOD. SIC. lib. xiv. 5. ISOCRATES says there were only 5000 banished. He makes the number of those killed amount to 1500. AREOP. 153. ÆSCHINES *contra.* CTESIPH. 455 assigns precisely the same number. SENECA (*de tranq. anim.* cap. 5.) says 1300.

same time, the people killed 1200 of the nobles; and afterwards their own demagogues, because they had refused to carry their prosecutions farther.[1] The people also in CORCYRA killed 1500 of the nobles, and banished a thousand.[2] These numbers will appear the more surprising, if we consider the extreme smallness of these states. But all ancient history is full of such instances.[3]

When ALEXANDER ordered all the exiles to be restored throughout all the cities; it was found, that the whole amounted to 20,000 men[4]; the remains probably of still greater slaughters and massacres. What an astonishing multitude in so narrow a country as ancient GREECE! And what domestic confusion, jealousy, partiality, revenge, heartburnings, must tear those cities, where factions were wrought up to such a degree of fury and despair.

It would be easier, says ISOCRATES to PHILIP, to raise an army in GREECE at present from the vagabonds than from the cities.

---

[1] DIOD. SIC. lib. xv. c. 58.
[2] DIOD. SIC. lib. xiii. c. 48.
[3] We shall mention from DIODORUS SICULUS alone a few massacres, which passed in the course of sixty years, during the most shining age of GREECE. There were banished from SYBARIS 500 of the nobles and their partizans; lib. xii. p. 77, *ex edit.* RHODOMANNI. Of CHIANS, 600 citizens banished; lib. xiii. p. 189. At EPHESUS, 340 killed, 1000 banished; lib. xiii. p. 223. Of CYRENIANS, 500 nobles killed, all the rest banished; lib. xiv. p. 263. The CORINTHIANS killed 120, banished 500; lib. xiv. p. 304. PHŒBIDAS the SPARTAN banished 300 BŒOTIANS; lib. xv. p. 342. Upon the fall of the LACEDÆMONIANS, Democracies were restored in many cities, and severe vengeance taken of the nobles, after the GREEK manner. But matters did not end there. For the banished nobles, returning in many places, butchered their adversaries at PHIALÆ, in CORINTH, in MEGARA, in PHLIASIA. In this last place they killed 300 of the people; but these again revolting, killed above 600 of the nobles, and banished the rest; lib. xv. p. 357. In ARCADIA 1400 banished, besides many killed. The banished retired to SPARTA and to PALLANTIUM: The latter were delivered up to their countrymen, and all killed; lib. xv. p. 373. Of the banished from ARGOS and THEBES, there were 509 in the SPARTAN army; *id.* p. 374. Here is a detail of the most remarkable of AGATHOCLES's cruelties from the same author. The people before his usurpation had banished 600 nobles; lib. xix. p. 655. Afterwards that tyrant, in concurrence with the people, killed 4000 nobles, and banished 6000; *id.* p. 647. He killed 4000 people at GELA; *id.* p. 741. By AGATHOCLES's brother 8000 banished from SYRACUSE; lib. xx. p. 757. The inhabitants of ÆGESTA, to the number of 40,000, were killed, man, woman, and child; and with tortures, for the sake of their money; *id.* p. 802. All the relations, to wit, father, brother, children, grandfather, of his LIBYAN army, killed; *id.* p. 803. He killed 7000 exiles after capitulation; *id.* p. 816. It is to be remarked, that AGATHOCLES was a man of great sense and courage,[1] and is not to be suspected of wanton cruelty, contrary to the maxims of his age.
[4] DIOD. SIC. lib. xviii. c. 8.

[1] [The remainder is not in Editions H to O. P has instead of it: His violent tyranny, therefore, is a stronger proof of the measures of the age.]

Even when affairs came not to such extremities (which they failed not to do almost in every city twice or thrice every century) property was rendered very precarious by the maxims of ancient government. XENOPHON, in the Banquet of SOCRATES, gives us a natural unaffected description of the tyranny of the ATHENIAN people. 'In my poverty,' says CHARMIDES, 'I am much more happy than I ever was while possessed of riches: as much as it is happier to be in security than in terrors, free than a slave, to receive than to pay court, to be trusted than suspected. Formerly I was obliged to caress every informer; some imposition was continually laid upon me; and it was never allowed me to travel, or be absent from the city. At present, when I am poor I look big, and threaten others. The rich are afraid of me, and show me every kind of civility and respect; and I am become a kind of tyrant in the city.'[1]

In one of the pleadings of LYSIAS,[2] the orator very coolly speaks of it, by the by, as a maxim of the ATHENIAN people, that, whenever they wanted money, they put to death some of the rich citizens as well as strangers, for the sake of the forfeiture. In mentioning this, he seems not to have any intention of blaming them; still less of provoking them, who were his audience and judges.

Whether a man was a citizen or a stranger among that people, it seems indeed requisite, either that he should impoverish himself, or that the people would impoverish him, and perhaps kill him into the bargain. The orator last mentioned gives a pleasant account of an estate laid out in the public service[3]; that is, above the third of it in raree-shows and figured dances.

---

[1] Pag. 885. *ex edit.* LEUNCLAV.

[2] *Orat.* 29. *in* NICOM. 185.

[3] In order to recommend his client to the favour of the people, he enumerates all the sums he had expended. When χορηγὸς, 30 minas: Upon a chorus of men 20 minas; εἰς πυρριχιστὰς, 8 minas; ἀνδράσι χορηγῶν, 50 minas; κυκλικῷ χορῷ, 3 minas; Seven times trierarch, where he spent 6 talents: Taxes, once 30 minas, another time 40; γυμνασιαρχῶν, 12 minas; χορηγὸς παιδικῷ χορῷ, 15 minas; κωμῳδοῖς χορηγῶν, 18 minas; πυρριχισταῖς ἀγενείοις, 7 minas; τριήρει ἀμιλλώμενος, 15 minas; ἀρχιθέωρος, 30 minas: In the whole ten talents 38 minas. An immense sum for an ATHENIAN fortune, and what alone would be esteemed great riches, *Orat.* 21, 161. 'Tis true, he says, the law did not oblige him absolutely to be at so much expence, not above a fourth. But without the favour of the people, no body was so much as safe; and this was the only way to gain it. See farther, *orat.* 25. *de pop. statu.* In another place, he introduces a speaker, who says that he had spent his whole fortune, and an immense one, eighty talents, for the people. *Orat.* 26 *de prob.* EVANDRI. The μέτοικοι, or strangers, find, says he, if they do not contribute largely enough to the people's fancy, that they have reason to repent. *Orat.* 31 *contra* PHIL. You may see with what

I need not insist on the GREEK tyrannies, which were altogether horrible. Even the mixed monarchies, by which most of the ancient states of GREECE were governed, before the introduction of republics, were very unsettled. Scarcely any city, but ATHENS, says ISOCRATES, could show a succession of kings for four or five generations.[1]

Besides many other obvious reasons for the instability of ancient monarchies, the equal division of property among the brothers in private families, must, by a necessary consequence, contribute to unsettle and disturb the state. The universal preference given to the elder by modern laws, though it encreases the inequality of fortunes, has, however, this good effect, that it accustoms men to the same idea in public succession, and cuts off all claim and pretension of the younger.

The new settled colony of HERACLEA, falling immediately into faction, applied to SPARTA, who sent HERIPIDAS with full authority to quiet their dissentions. This man, not provoked by any opposition, not inflamed by party rage, knew no better expedient than immediately putting to death about 500 of the citizens.[2] A strong proof how deeply rooted these violent maxims of government were throughout all GREECE.

If such was the disposition of men's minds among that refined people, what may be expected in the commonwealths of ITALY, AFRIC, SPAIN, and GAUL, which were denominated barbarous? Why otherwise did the GREEKS so much value themselves on their humanity, gentleness, and moderation, above all other nations? This reasoning seems very natural. But unluckily the history of the ROMAN commonwealth, in its earlier times, if we give credit to the received accounts, presents an opposite conclusion. No blood was ever shed in any sedition at ROME, till the murder of the GRACCHI. DIONYSIUS HALICARNASSÆUS,[3] observing the singular humanity of the ROMAN people in this particular, makes use of it as an argument that they were orginally of GRECIAN extraction: Whence we may conclude, that the factions and revolutions in the barbarous republics were usually more violent than even those of GREECE above-mentioned.

care DEMOSTHENES displays his expences of this nature, when he pleads for himself *de corona*; and how he exaggerates MIDIAS's stinginess in this particular, in his accusation of that criminal. All this, by the by, is a mark of a very iniquitous judicature: And yet the ATHENIANS valued themselves on having the most legal and regular administration of any people in GREECE.

[1] Panath. 258.
[2] DIOD. SIC. lib. xiv. 38.
[3] Lib. i. 89.

If the ROMANS were so late in coming to blows, they made ample compensation, after they had once entered upon the bloody scene; and APPIAN's history of their civil wars contains the most frightful picture of massacres, proscriptions, and forfeitures, that ever was presented to the world. What pleases most, in that historian, is that he seems to feel a proper resentment of these barbarous proceedings; and talks not with that provoking coolness and indifference, which custom had produced in many of the GREEK historians.[1]

The maxims of ancient politics contain, in general, so little humanity and moderation, that it seems superfluous to give any particular reason for the acts of violence committed at any particular period. Yet I cannot forbear observing, that the laws, in the later period of the ROMAN commonwealth, were so absurdly contrived, that they obliged the heads of parties to have recourse to these extremities. All capital punishments were abolished: However criminal, or, what is more, however dangerous any citizen might be, he could not regularly be punished otherwise than by banishment: And it became necessary, in the revolutions of party, to draw the sword of private vengeance; nor was it easy, when laws were once violated, to set bounds to these sanguinary proceedings. Had BRUTUS himself prevailed over the *triumvirate*, could he, in common prudence have allowed OCTAVIUS and ANTHONY, to live, and have contented himself with banishing them to RHODES or MARSEILLES, where they might still have plotted new commotions and rebellions? His executing C. ANTONIUS, brother to the *triumvir*, shows evidently his sense of the matter. Did not CICERO,

[1] The authorities cited above, are all historians, orators, and philosophers, whose testimony is unquestioned. 'Tis dangerous to rely upon writers who deal in ridicule and satyr. What will posterity, for instance, infer from this passage of Dr. SWIFT? 'I told him, that in the kingdom of TRIBNIA (BRITAIN) by the natives called LANGDON (LONDON) where I had sojourned some time in my travels. the bulk of the people consist, in a manner, wholly of discoverers, witnesses, informers, accusers, prosecutors, evidences, swearers, together with their several subservient and subaltern instruments, all under the colours, the conduct, and pay of ministers of state and their deputies. The plots in that kingdom are usually the workmanship of those persons,' &c. GULLIVER's *travels*. Such a representation might suit the government of ATHENS; but not that of ENGLAND, which is a prodigy even in modern times, for humanity, justice, and liberty. Yet the Doctor's satyr, tho' carried to extremes, as is usual with him, even beyond other satyrical writers, did not altogether want an object. The Bishop of ROCHESTER, who was his friend, and of the same party, had been banished a little before by a bill of attainder, with great justice, but without such a proof as was legal, or according to the strict forms of common law.

with the approbation of all the wise and virtuous of ROME, arbitrarily put to death CATILINE's accomplices, contrary to law, and without any trial or form of process? And if he moderated his executions, did it not proceed, either from the clemency of his temper, or the conjunctures of the times? A wretched security in a government which pretends to laws and liberty!

Thus, one extreme produces another. In the same manner as excessive severity in the laws is apt to beget great relaxation in their execution; so their excessive lenity naturally produces cruelty and barbarity. It is dangerous to force us, in any case, to pass their sacred boundaries.

One general cause of the disorders, so frequent in all ancient governments, seems to have consisted in the great difficulty of establishing any Aristocracy in those ages, and the perpetual discontents and seditions of the people, whenever even the meanest and most beggarly were excluded from the legislature and from public offices. The very quality of *freemen* gave such a rank, being opposed to that of slave, that it seemed to entitle the possessor to every power and privilege of the commonwealth. SOLON's[1] laws excluded no freeman from votes or elections, but confined some magistracies to a particular *census*; yet were the people never satisfied till those laws were repealed. By the treaty with ANTIPATER,[2] no ATHENIAN was allowed a vote whose *census* was less than 2000 *drachmas* (about 60*l.* *Sterling*). And though such a government would to us appear sufficiently democratical, it was so disagreeable to that people, that above two-thirds of them immediately left their country.[3] CASSANDER reduced that *census* to the half;[4] yet still the government was considered as an oligarchical tyranny, and the effect of foreign violence.

SERVIUS TULLIUS's[5] laws seem equal and reasonable, by fixing the power in proportion to the property: Yet the ROMAN people could never be brought quietly to submit to them.

In those days there was no medium between a severe, jealous Aristocracy, ruling over discontented subjects; and a turbulent, factious, tyrannical Democracy.[6] At present,

[1] PLUTARCHUS *in vita* SOLON, 18.
[2] DIOD. SIC. lib. xviii. 18.
[3] Id. ibid.
[4] Id. ibid. 74.
[5] TIT. LIV. lib. i. cap. 43.
[6] [The remainder of this paragraph was added in Edition R.]

there is not one republic in EUROPE, from one extremity of it to the other, that is not remarkable for justice, lenity, and stability, equal to, or even beyond MARSEILLES, RHODES, or the most celebrated in antiquity. Almost all of them are well-tempered Aristocracies.

But *thirdly*, there are many other circumstances, in which ancient nations seem inferior to the modern, both for the happiness and encrease of mankind. Trade, manufactures, industry, were no where, in former ages, so flourishing as they are at present in EUROPE. The only garb of the ancients, both for males and females, seems to have been a kind of flannel, which they wore commonly white or grey, and which they scoured as often as it became dirty. TYRE, which carried on, after CARTHAGE, the greatest commerce of any city in the MEDITERRANEAN, before it was destroyed by ALEXANDER, was no mighty city, if we credit ARRIAN's account of its inhabitants.[1] ATHENS is commonly supposed to have been a trading city: But it was as populous before the MEDIAN war as at any time after it, according to HERODOTUS;[2] yet its commerce, at that time, was so inconsiderable, that, as the same historian observes,[3] even the neighbouring coasts of ASIA were as little frequented by the GREEK as the pillars of HERCULES: For beyond these he conceived nothing.

Great interest of money, and great profits of trade, are an infallible indication, that industry and commerce are but in their infancy. We read in LYSIAS[4] of 100 *per cent.* profit made on a cargo of two talents, sent to no greater distance than from ATHENS to the ADRIATIC: Nor is this mentioned as an instance of extraordinary profit. ANTIDORUS, says DEMOSTHENES,[5] paid three talents and a half for a house which he let at a talent a year: And the orator blames his own tutors for not employing his money to like advantage. My fortune, says he, in eleven years minority, ought to have been tripled. The value of 20 of the slaves left by his father, he computes at 40 minas, and the yearly profit of their labour at 12.[6] The most moderate interest at ATHENS, (for there

---

[1] Lib. ii. 24. There were 8,000 killed during the siege; and the captives amounted to 30,000. DIODORUS SICULUS, lib. xvii. 46, says only 13,000: But he accounts for this small number, by saying that the TYRIANS had sent away before-hand part of their wives and children to CARTHAGE.

[2] Lib. v. 97, he makes the number of the citizens amount to 30,000.

[3] Ib. viii. 132.

[4] *Orat.* 32, 908 *advers.* DIOGIT.

[5] *Contra* APHOB. p. 25. *ex edit.* ALDI.

[6] Id. p. 19.

was higher[1] often paid) was 12 *per cent.*,[2] and that paid monthly. Not to insist upon the high interest, to which the vast sums distributed in elections had raised money[3] at ROME, we find, that VERRES, before that factious period, stated 24 *per cent.* for money which he left in the hands of the publicans: And though CICERO exclaims against this article, it is not on account of the extravagant usury; but because it had never been customary to state any interest on such occasions.[4] Interest, indeed, sunk at Rome, after the settlement of the empire: But it never remained any considerable time so low, as in the commercial states of modern times.[5]

Among the other inconveniencies, which the ATHENIANS felt from the fortifying of DECELIA by the LACEDEMONIANS, it is represented by THUCYDIDES,[6] as one of the most considerable, that they could not bring over their corn from EUBEA by land, passing by OROPUS; but were obliged to embark it, and to sail round the promontory of SUNIUM. A surprising instance of the imperfection of ancient navigation! For the water-carriage is not here above double the land.

I do not remember a passage in any ancient author, where the growth of a city is ascribed to the establishment of a manufacture. The commerce, which is said to flourish, is chiefly the exchange of those commodities, for which different soils and climates were suited. The sale of wine and oil into AFRICA, acccording to DIODORUS SICULUS,[7] was the foundation of the riches of AGRIGENTUM. The situation of the city of SYBARIS, according to the same author,[8] was the cause of its immense populousness; being built near the two rivers CRATHYS and SYBARIS. But these two rivers, we may observe, are not navigable; and could only produce some fertile vallies, for agriculture and tillage; an advantage so inconsiderable, that a modern writer would scarcely have taken notice of it.

The barbarity of the ancient tyrants, together with the extreme love of liberty, which animated those ages, must have banished every merchant and manufacturer, and have

[1] Id. ibid.
[2] Id. ibid. and ÆSCHINES *contra* CTESIPH. 104.
[3] *Epist. ad* ATTIC. lib. iv. epist. 15.
[4] *Contra* VERR. *orat.* 3, 71.
[5] See Essay IV.
[6] Lib. vii. 28.
[7] Lib. xiii. 81.
[8] Lib. xii. 9.

quite depopulated the state, had it subsisted upon industry and commerce. While the cruel and suspicious DIONYSIUS was carrying on his butcheries, who, that was not detained by his landed property, and could have carried with him any art or skill to procure a subsistence in other countries, would have remained exposed to such implacable barbarity? The persecutions of PHILIP II. and LEWIS XIV. filled all EUROPE with the manufacturers of FLANDERS and of FRRACE.

I grant, that agriculture is the species of industry chiefly requisite to the subsistence of multitudes; and it is possible, that this industry may flourish, even where manufactures and other arts are unknown and neglected. SWISSERLAND is at present a remarkable instance where, we find, at once, the most skilful husbandmen, and the most bungling tradesmen, that are to be met with in EUROPE. That agriculture flourished in GREECE and ITALY, at least in some parts of them, and at some periods, we have reason to presume; And whether the mechanical arts had reached the same degree of perfection, may not be esteemed so material; especially, if we consider the great equality of riches in the ancient republics, where each family was obliged to cultivate, with the greatest care and industry, its own little field, in order to its subsistence.

But is it just reasoning, because agriculture may, in some instances, flourish without trade or manufactures, to conclude, that, in any great extent of country, and for any great tract of time, it would subsist alone? The most natural way, surely, of encouraging husbandry, is, first, to excite other kinds of industry, and thereby afford the labourer a ready market for his commodities, and a return of such goods as may contribute to his pleasure and enjoyment. This method is infallible and universal; and, as it prevails more in modern government than in the ancient, it affords a presumption of the superior populousness of the former.

Every man, says XENOPHON,[1] may be a farmer: No art or skill is requisite: All consists in industry, and in attention to the execution. A strong proof, as COLUMELLA hints, that agriculture was but little known in the age of XENOPHON.

All our later improvements and refinements, have they done nothing towards the easy subsistence of men, and

[1] Oecon.15, 10.

consequently towards their propagation and encrease? Our superior skill in mechanics; the discovery of new worlds, by which commerce has been so much enlarged; the establishment of posts; and the use of bills of exchange: These seem all extremely useful to the encouragement of art, industry, and populousness. Were we to strike off these, what a check should we give to every kind of business and labour, and what multitudes of families would immediately perish from want and hunger? And it seems not probable, that we could supply the place of these new inventions by any other regulation or institution.

Have we reason to think, that the police of ancient states was any wise comparable to that of modern, or that men had then equal security, either at home, or in their journies by land or water? I question not, but every impartial examiner would give us the preference in this particular.[1]

Thus, upon comparing the whole, it seems impossible to assign any just reason, why the world should have been more populous in ancient than in modern times. The equality of property among the ancients, liberty, and the small divisions of their states, were indeed circumstances favourable to the propagation of mankind: But their wars were more bloody and destructive, their governments more factious and unsettled, commerce and manufactures more feeble and languishing, and the general police more loose and irregular. These latter disadvantages seem to form a sufficient counterbalance to the former advantages; and rather favour the opposite opinion to that which commonly prevails with regard to this subject.

But there is no reasoning, it may be said, against matter of fact. If it appear that the world was then more populous than at present, we may be assured that our conjectures are false, and that we have overlooked some material circumstance in the comparison. This I readily own: All our preceding reasonings, I acknowledge to be mere trifling, or, at least, small skirmishes and frivolous rencounters, which decide nothing. But unluckily the main combat, where we compare facts, cannot be rendered much more decisive. The facts, delivered by ancient authors, are either so uncertain or so imperfect as to afford us nothing positive in this matter. How indeed could it be otherwise? The very facts, which

[1] See Part I. Essay XI.

we must oppose to them, in computing the populousness of modern states, are far from being either certain or complete. Many grounds of calculation proceeded on by celebrated writers, are little better than those of the Emperor HELIOGABALUS, who formed an estimate of the immense greatness of ROME, from ten thousand pound weight of cobwebs which had been found in that city.[1]

It is to be remarked, that all kinds of numbers are uncertain in ancient manuscripts, and have been subject to much greater corruptions than any other part of the text; and that for an obvious reason. Any alteration, in other places, commonly affects the sense or grammar, and is more readily perceived by the reader and transcriber.

Few enumerations of inhabitants have been made of any tract of country by any ancient author of good authority, so as to afford us a large enough view for comparison.

It is probable, that there was formerly a good foundation for the number of citizens assigned to any free city; because they entered for a share in the government, and there were exact registers kept of them. But as the number of slaves is seldom mentioned, this leaves us in as great uncertainty as ever, with regard to the populousness even of single cities.

The first page of THUCYDIDES is, in my opinion, the commencement of real history. All preceding narrations are so intermixed with fable, that philosophers ought to abandon them, in a great measure, to the embellishment of poets and orators.[2]

With regard to remote times, the numbers of people assigned are often ridiculous, and lose all credit and authority. The free citizens of SYBARIS, able to bear arms, and actually drawn out in battle, were 300,000. They encountered at SIAGRA with 100,000 citizens of CROTONA, another GREEK city contiguous to them; and were defeated. This

---

[1] ÆLII LAMPRID. *in vita* HELIOGAB. cap. 26.

[2] In general, there is more candour and sincerity in ancient historians, but less exactness and care, than in the moderns. Our speculative factions, especially those of religion, throw such an illusion over our minds, that men seem to regard impartiality to their adversaries and to heretics, as a vice or weakness: But the commonness of books, by means of printing, has obliged modern historians to be more careful in avoiding contradictions and incongruities. DIODORUS SICULUS is a good writer, but it is with pain I see his narration contradict, in so many particulars, the two most authentic pieces of all GREEK history, to wit, XENOPHON's expedition, and DEMOSTHENES's orations. PLUTARCH and APPIAN seem scarce ever to have read CICERO's epistles.

is Diodorus Siculus's [1] account; and is very seriously insisted on by that historian.[2] Strabo also mentions the same number of Sybarites.

Diodorus Siculus,[3] enumerating the inhabitants of Agrigentum, when it was destroyed by the Carthaginians, says, that they amounted to 20,000 citizens, 200,000 strangers, besides slaves, who, in so opulent a city as he represents it, would probably be, at least, as numerous. We must remark, that the women and the children are not included; and that, therefore, upon the whole, this city must have contained near two millions of inhabitants.[4] And what was the reason of so immense an encrease! They were industrious in cultivating the neighbouring fields, not exceeding a small English county; and they traded with their wine and oil to Africa, which, at that time, produced none of these commodities.

Ptolemy, says Theocritus,[5] commands 33,339 cities. I suppose the singularity of the number was the reason of assigning it. Diodorus Siculus [6] assigns three millions of inhabitants to Ægypt, a small number: But then he makes the number of cities amount to 18,000: An evident contradiction.

He says,[7] the people were formerly seven millions. Thus remote times are always most envied and admired.

That Xerxes's army was extremely numerous, I can readily believe; both from the great extent of his empire, and from the practice among the eastern nations, of encumbering their camp with a superfluous multitude: But will any rational man cite Herodotus's wonderful narrations as an authority? There is something very rational, I own, in Lysias's [8] argument upon this subject. Had not Xerxes's army been incredibly numerous, says he, he had never made a bridge over the Hellespont: It had been much easier to have transported his men over so short a passage, with the numerous shipping of which he was master.

Polybius [9] says, that the Romans, between the first and second Punic wars, being threatened with an invasion from

---

[1] Lib. xii. 9.
[2] Lib. vi. 26.
[3] Lib. xiii. 90.
[4] Diogenes Laertius (*in vita* Empedoclis) says, that Agrigentum contained only 800,000 inhabitants.
[5] Idyll. 17.
[6] Lib. i. 18.
[7] Id. ibid.
[8] *Orat. funebris*, 193.
[9] Lib. ii. 24.

the GAULS, mustered all their own forces, and those of their allies, and found them amount to seven hundred thousand men able to bear arms: A great number surely, and which, when joined to the slaves, is probably [1] not less, if not rather more, than that extent of country affords at present.[2] The enumeration too seems to have been made with some exactness; and POLYBIUS gives us the detail of the particulars. But might not the number be magnified, in order to encourage the people?

DIODORUS SICULUS[3] makes the same enumeration amount to near a million. These variations are suspicious. He plainly too supposes, that ITALY in his time was not so populous: Another suspicious circumstance. For who can believe, that the inhabitants of that country diminished from the time of the first PUNIC war to that of the *triumvirates?*

JULIUS CÆSAR, according to APPIAN,[4] encountered four millions of GAULS, killed one million, and made another million prisoners.[5] Supposing the number of the enemy's army and that of the slain could be exactly assigned, which never is possible; how could it be known how often the same man returned into the armies, or how distinguish the new from the old levied soldiers? No attention ought ever to be given to such loose, exaggerated calculations; especially where the author does not tell us the mediums, upon which the calculations were founded.

PATERCULUS[6] makes the number of GAULS killed by CÆSAR amount only to 400,000: A more probable account, and more easily reconciled to the history of these wars given by that conqueror himself in his Commentaries.[7] [8]The most bloody of his battles were fought against the HELVETII and the GERMANS.

[1] [Not less, if not rather — added in Edition M.]

[2] The country that supplied this number, was not above a third of ITALY, *viz.* the Pope's dominions, TUSCANY, and a part of the kingdom of NAPLES: But perhaps in those early times there were very few slaves, except in ROME, or the great cities. [The last clause was added in Edition K.]

[3] Lib. ii. 5.

[4] CELTICA, c. 2.

[5] PLUTARCH (*in vita* CÆS. 15) makes the number that CÆSAR fought with amount to three millions; JULIAN (*in Aesaribus*) to two.

[6] Lib. ii. cap. 47.

[7] PLINY, lib. vii. cap. 25, says, that CÆSAR used to boast, that there had fallen in battle against him one million one hundred and ninety-two thousand men, besides those who perished in the civil wars. It is not probable, that that conqueror could ever pretend to be so exact in his computation. But allowing the fact, it is likely, that the HELVETII, GERMANS, and BRITONS, whom he slaughtered, would amount to near a half of the number. [This note was added in Edition R.]

[8] [This sentence was added in Edition R.]

One would imagine, that every circumstance of the life and actions of DIONYSIUS the elder might be regarded as authentic, and free from all fabulous exaggeration; both because he lived at a time when letters flourished most in GREECE, and because his chief historian was PHILISTUS, a man allowed to be of great genius, and who was a courtier and minister of that prince. But can we admit, that he had a standing army of 100,000 foot, 10,000 horse, and a fleet of 400 gallies?[1] These, we may observe, were mercenary forces, and subsisted upon pay, like our armies in EUROPE. For the citizens were all disarmed; and when DION afterwards invaded SICILY, and called on his countrymen to vindicate their liberty, he was obliged to bring arms along with him, which he distributed among those who joined him.[2] In a state where agriculture alone flourishes, there may be many inhabitants; and if these be all armed and disciplined, a great force may be called out upon occasion: But great bodies of mercenary troops can never be maintained, without either great trade and numerous manufactures, or extensive dominions. The United Provinces never were masters of such a force by sea and land, as that which is said to belong to DIONYSIUS; yet they possess as large a territory, perfectly well cultivated, and have much more resources from their commerce and industry. DIODORUS SICULUS allows, that, even in his time, the army of DIONYSIUS appeared incredible; that is, as I interpret it, was entirely a fiction, and the opinion arose from the exaggerated flattery of the courtiers, and perhaps from the vanity and policy of the tyrant himself.[3]

---

[1] DIOD. SIC. lib. ii. 5.
[2] PLUTARCH *in vita* DIONYS, 25.
[3] [Editions H to M proceed as follows: The critical art may very justly be suspected of temerity, when it pretends to correct or dispute the plain testimony of ancient historians by any probable or analogical reasonings: Yet the licence of authors upon all subjects, particularly with regard to numbers, is so great, that we ought still to retain a kind of doubt or reserve, whenever the facts advanced depart in the least from the common bounds of nature and experience. I shall give an instance with regard to modern history. Sir William Temple tells us, in his memoirs, that having a free conversation with Charles the II., he took the opportunity of representing to that monarch the impossibility of introducing into this island the religion and government of France, chiefly on account of the great force requisite to subdue the spirit and liberty of so brave a people. 'The Romans,' says he, 'were forced to keep up twelve legions for that purpose' (a great absurdity),[1] ' and Cromwell left an army

[1] Strabo, lib. iv. 200, says, that one legion would be sufficient, with a few cavalry; but the Romans commonly kept up somewhat a greater force in this island, which they never took the pains entirely to subdue.

It is a usual fallacy, to consider all the ages of antiquity as one period, and to compute the numbers contained in the great cities mentioned by ancient authors, as if these cities had been all cotemporary. The GREEK colonies flourished extremely in SICILY during the age of ALEXANDER: But in AUGUSTUS's time they were so decayed, that almost all the produce of that fertile island was consumed in ITALY.[1]

Let us now examine the numbers of inhabitants assigned to particular cities in antiquity; and omitting the numbers of NINEVEH, BABYLON, and the EGYPTIAN THEBES, let us confine ourselves to the sphere of real history, to the GRECIAN and ROMAN states. I must own, the more I consider this subject, the more am I inclined to scepticism, with regard to the great populousness ascribed to ancient times.

ATHENS is said by PLATO[2] to be a very great city; and it was surely the greatest of all the GREEK[3] cities, except SYRACUSE, which was nearly about the same size in THUCYDIDES'S[4] time, and afterwards encreased beyond it. For CICERO[5] mentions it as the greatest of all the GREEK cities in his time; not comprehending, I suppose, either ANTIOCH or ALEXANDRIA under that denomination. ATHENÆUS[6] says,

---

of near eighty thousand men.' Must not this last be regarded as unquestioned by future critics, when they find it asserted by a wise and learned minister of state cotemporary to the fact, and who addressed his discourse, upon an ungrateful subject, to a great monarch who was also cotemporary, and who himself broke those very forces about fourteen years before? Yet, by the most undoubted authority, we may insist, that Cromwell's army, when he died, did not amount to half the number here mentioned.']

[1] STRABO, lib. vi. 273.

[2] *Apolog.* SOCR. 29 D.

[3] ARGOS seems also to have been a great city; for LYCIAS contents himself with saying that it did not exceed ATHENS. Orat. 34, 922.

[4] Lib. vi. See also PLUTARCH *in vita* NICIÆ, 17.

[5] *Orat. contra* VERREM, lib. iv. cap. 52. STRABO, lib. vi. 270, says, it was twenty-two miles in compass. But then we are to consider, that it contained two harbours within it; one of which was a very large one, and might be regarded as a kind of bay.

[6] Lib. vi. cap. 20.

---

[1] It appears that Cromwell's parliament, in 1656, settled but 1,300,000 pounds a year on him for the constant charges of government in all the three kingdoms. See Scobel, chap. 31. This was to supply the fleet, army, and civil list. It appears from Whitelocke, that in the year 1649, the sum of 80,000 pounds a month was the estimate for 40,000 men. We must conclude, therefore, that Cromwell had much less than that number upon pay in 1656. In the very instrument of government, 20,000 foot and 10,000 horse are fixed by Cromwell himself, and afterwards confirmed by the parliament, as the regular standing army of the commonwealth. That number, indeed, seems not to have been much exceeded during the whole time of the protectorship. See farther Thurlo, Vol. II. pp. 413, 499, 568. We may there see, that though the Protector had more considerable armies in Ireland and Scotland, he had not sometimes more than 4,000 or 5,000 men in England.

that, by the enumeration of DEMETRIUS PHALEREUS, there were in ATHENS 21,000 citizens, 10,000 strangers, and 400,000 slaves. This number is much insisted on by those whose opinion I call in question, and is esteemed a fundamental fact to their purpose: But, in my opinion, there is no point of criticism more certain, than that ATHENÆUS and CTESICLES, whom he quotes, are here mistaken, and that the number of slaves is, at least, augmented by a whole cypher, and ought not to be regarded as more than 40,000.

First, When the number of citizens is said to be 21,000 by ATHENÆUS,[1] men of full age are only understood. For, (1.) HERODOTUS says,[2] that ARISTAGORAS, ambassador from the IONIANS, found it harder to deceive one SPARTAN than 30,000 ATHENIANS; meaning, in a loose way, the whole state, supposed to be met in one popular assembly, excluding the women and children. (2.) THUCYDIDES[3] says, that, making allowance for all the absentees in the fleet, army, garrisons, and for people employed in their private affairs, the ATHENIAN assembly never rose to five thousand. (3.) The forces, enumerated by the same historian,[4] being all citizens, and amounting to 13,000 heavy-armed infantry, prove the same method of calculation; as also the whole tenor of the GREEK historians, who always understand men of full age when they assign the number of citizens in any republic. Now, these being but the fourth of the inhabitants, the free ATHENIANS were by this account 84,000; the strangers 40,000; and the slaves, calculating by the smaller number, and allowing that they married and propagated at the same rate with freemen, were 160,000; and the whole of the inhabitants 284,000: A number surely large enough. The other number, 1,720,000, makes ATHENS larger than LONDON and PARIS united.

Secondly, There were but 10,000 houses in ATHENS.[5]

Thirdly, Though the extent of the walls, as given us by THUCYDIDES,[6] be great, (to wit, eighteen miles, beside the sea-coast): Yet XENOPHON[7] says, there was much waste ground within the walls. They seem indeed to have joined four distinct and separate cities.[8]

---

[1] DEMOSTHENES assigns 20,000; contra ARISTOG, 785.
[2] Lib. v. 99.
[3] Lib. viii. 72.
[4] Lib. ii. 13. DIODORUS SICULUS's account perfectly agrees, lib. xii. 40.
[5] XENOPHON. *Mem*. lib. iii. 6, 14.
[6] Lib. ii. 13.
[7] *De ratione red*. 2, 6.
[8] We are to observe, that when

Fourthly, No insurrection of the slaves, or suspicion of insurrection, is ever mentioned by historians; except one commotion of the miners.[1]

Fifthly, The treatment of slaves by the ATHENIANS is said by XENOPHON,[2] and DEMOSTHENES,[3] and PLAUTUS,[4] to have been extremely gentle and indulgent: Which could never have been the case, had the disproportion been twenty to one. The disproportion is not so great in any of our colonies; yet are we obliged to exercise a rigorous military government over the negroes.

Sixthly, No man is ever esteemed rich for possessing what may be reckoned an equal distribution of property in any country, or even triple or quadruple that wealth. Thus every person in England is computed by some to spend sixpence a day: Yet is he esteemed but poor who has five times that sum. Now TIMARCHUS is said by ÆSCHINES[5] to have been left in easy circumstances; but he was master only of ten slaves employed in manufactures. LYSIAS and his brother, two strangers, were proscribed by the thirty for their great riches; though they had but sixty a-piece.[6] DEMOSTHENES was left very rich by his father; yet he had no more than fifty-two slaves.[7] His work-house, of twenty cabinet-makers, is said to be a very considerable manufactory.[8]

Seventhly, During the DECELIAN war, as the GREEK historians call it, 20,000 slaves deserted, and brought the ATHENIANS to great distress, as we learn from THUCYDIDES.[9] This could not have happened, had they been only the twentieth part. The best slaves would not desert.

Eighthly, XENOPHON[10] proposes a scheme for maintaining by the public 10,000 slaves: And that so great a number may possibly be supported, any one will be convinced, says

---

DIONYSIUS HALYCARNASSÆUS says, that if we regard the ancient walls of ROME, the extent of that city will not appear greater than that of ATHENS; he must mean the ACROPOLIS and high town only. No ancient author ever speaks of the PYRÆUM, PHALERUS, and MUNYCHIA, as the same with ATHENS. Much less can it be supposed, that DIONYSIUS would consider the matter in that light, after the walls of CIMON and PERICLES were destroyed, and ATHENS was entirely separated from these other towns. This observation destroys all VOSSIUS's reasonings, and introduces common sense into these calculations.

[1] ATHEN. lib. vi. 104.
[2] *De rep.* ATHEN, 1.
[3] PHILIP. 3, 31.
[4] STICHO. 3. 1, 39.
[5] *Contra* TIMARCH. 42.
[6] *Orat.* xii.
[7] *Contra* APHOB. 816.
[8] Ibid.
[9] Lib. vii. 27.
[10] *De rat. red.* 4, 25.

POPULOUSNESS OF ANCIENT NATIONS.

he, who considers the numbers we possessed before the DECELIAN war. A way of speaking altogether incompatible with the larger number of ATHENÆUS.

Ninthly, The whole *census* of the state of ATHENS was less than 6000 talents. And though numbers in ancient manuscripts be often suspected by critics, yet this is unexceptionable; both because DEMOSTHENES,[1] who gives it, gives also the detail, which checks him; and because POLYBIUS[2] assigns the same number, and reasons upon it. Now, the most vulgar slave could yield by his labour an *obolus* a day, over and above his maintenance, as we learn from XENOPHON,[3] who says, that NICIAS's overseer paid his master so much for slaves, whom he employed in[4] mines. If you will take the pains to estimate an *obolus* a day, and the slaves at 400,000, computing only at four years purchase, you will find the sum above 12,000 talents; even though allowance be made for the great number of holidays in ATHENS. Besides, many of the slaves would have a much greater value from their art. The lowest that DEMOSTHENES estimates any of his[5] father's slaves is two minas a head. And upon this supposition, it is a little difficult, I confess, to reconcile even the number of 40,000 slaves with the *census* of 6000 talents.

Tenthly, CHIOS is said by THUCYDIDES,[6] to contain more slaves than any GREEK city, except SPARTA. SPARTA then had more than ATHENS, in proportion to the number of citizens. The SPARTANS were 9000 in the town, 30,000 in the country.[7] The male slaves, therefore, of full age, must have been more than 780,000; the whole more than 3,120,000. A number impossible to be maintained in a narrow barren country, such as LACONIA, which has no trade. Had the HELOTES been so very numerous, the murder of 2000 mentioned by THUCYDIDES,[8] would have irritated them, without weakening them.

Besides, we are to consider, that the number assigned by ATHENÆUS,[9] whatever it is, comprehends all the inhabitants

---

[1] *De classibus*, 183.
[2] Lib. ii. cap. 62.
[3] *De rat. red.* 4, 14.
[4] [In digging of mines, and also kept up the number of slaves: Editions H I. In digging of mines: K to Q.]
[5] *Contra* APHOBUM, 816.
[6] Lib. viii. 40.
[7] PLUTARCH, *in vita* LYCURG, 8.
[8] Lib. iv. 80.
[9] The same author affirms, that CORINTH had once 460,000 slaves, ÆGINA 470,000. But the foregoing arguments hold stronger against these facts, which are indeed entirely absurd and impossible. It is however remarkable, that

of ATTICA, as well as those of ATHENS. The ATHENIANS affected much a country life, as we learn from THUCYDIDES;[1] and when they were all chased into town, by the invasion of their territory during the PELOPONNESIAN war, the city was not able to contain them; and they were obliged to lie in the porticoes, temples, and even streets, for want of lodging.[2]

The same remark is to be extended to all the other GREEK cities; and when the number of citizens is assigned, we must always understand it to comprehend the inhabitants of the neighbouring country, as well as of the city. Yet, even with this allowance, it must be confessed, that GREECE was a populous country, and exceeded what we could imagine concerning so narrow a territory, naturally not very fertile, and which drew no supplies of corn from other places. For, excepting ATHENS, which traded to PONTUS for that commodity, the other cities seem to have subsisted chiefly from their neighbouring territory.[3]

RHODES is well known to have been a city of extensive commerce, and of great fame and splendor; yet it contained only 6,000 citizens able to bear arms, when it was besieged by DEMETRIUS.[4]

THEBES was always one of the capital cities of GREECE:[5] But the number of its citizens exceeded not those of RHODES.[6]

ATHENÆUS cites so great an authority, as ARISTOTLE for this last fact: And the scholiast on PINDAR mentions the same number of slaves in Ægina.

[1] Liv. ii. 14.
[2] Id. lib. ii. 17.
[3] DEMOST. contra LEPT. 466. The Athenians brought yearly from Pontus 400,000 medimni or bushels of corn, as appeared from the custom-house books. And this was the greater part of their importation of corn. This, by the by, is a strong proof that there is some great mistake in the foregoing passage of Athenæus. For Attica itself was so barren of corn, that it produced not enough even to maintain the peasants. Tit. Liv. lib. xliii. cap. 6. 'And 400,000 medimni would scarcely feed 100,000 men during a twelvemonth. Lucian, in his *navigium sive vota*, says, that a ship, which, by the dimensions he gives, seems to have been about the size of our third rates, carried as much corn as would maintain Attica for a twelvemonth. But perhaps Athens was decayed at that time; and, besides, it is not safe to trust to such loose rhetorical calculations.

[4] DIOD. SIC. lib. xx. 84.
[5] ISOCR. *paneg.*
[6] DIOD. SIC. lib. xvii. 14.[2] When Alexander attacked Thebes, we may safely conclude that almost all the inhabitants were present. Whoever is acquainted with the spirit of the Greeks, especially of the Thebans, will never suspect that any of them would desert their country when it was reduced to such extreme peril and distress. As Alexander took the town by storm, all those who bore arms were put to the sword without mercy, and they amounted only to 6,000 men. Among these were some strangers

---

[1] [This sentence was added in Edition Q.]

[2] [DIOD. SIC. lib. 15 and 17: Editions H and I, and omit the rest of this note.]

PHLIASIA is said to be a small city by XENOPHON,[1] yet we find that it contained 6,000 citizens.[2] I pretend not to reconcile these two facts.[3] Perhaps, XENOPHON calls PHLIASIA a small town, because it made but a small figure in GREECE, and maintained only a subordinate alliance with SPARTA; or perhaps the country, belonging to it, was extensive, and most of the citizens were employed in the cultivation of it, and dwelt in the neighbouring villages.

MANTINEA was equal to any city in ARCADIA:[4] Consequently it was equal to MEGALOPOLIS, which was fifty stadia, or six miles and a quarter in circumference.[5] But MANTINEA had only 3,000 citizens.[6] The GREEK cities, therefore, contained often fields and gardens, together with the houses; and we cannot judge of them by the extent of their walls. ATHENS contained no more than 10,000 houses; yet its walls, with the sea-coast, were above twenty miles in extent. SYRACUSE was twenty-two miles in circumference; yet was scarcely ever spoken of by the ancients as more populous than ATHENS. BABYLON was a square of fifteen miles, or sixty miles in circuit; but it contained large cultivated fields and inclosures, as we learn from PLINY. Though AURELIAN's wall was fifty miles in circumference;[7] the circuit of all the thirteen divisions of ROME, taken apart, according to PUBLIUS VICTOR, was only about forty-three miles. When an enemy invaded the country, all the inhabitants retired within the walls of the ancient cities, with their cattle and furniture, and instruments of husbandry: and the great height, to which the walls were raised, enabled a small number to defend them with facility.

SPARTA, says XENOPHON,[8] is one of the cities of GREECE

and manumitted slaves. The captives, consisting of old men, women, children, and slaves, were sold, and they amounted to 30,000. We may therefore conclude, that the free citizens in Thebes, of both sexes and all ages, were near 24,000, the strangers and slaves about 12,000. These last, we may observe, were somewhat fewer in proportion than at Athens, as is reasonable to imagine from this circumstance, that Athens was a town of more trade to support slaves, and of more entertainment to allure strangers. It is also to be remarked, that 36,000 was the whole number of people, both in the city of Thebes and the neighbouring territory.

A very moderate number, it must be confessed; and this computation, being founded on facts which appear indisputable, must have great weight in the present controversy. The above-mentioned number of Rhodians, too, were all the inhabitants of the island who were free, and able to bear arms.

[1] Hist. GRÆC. lib. vii. 2, 1.
[2] Id. lib. vii.
[3] [The remainder of the paragraph was added in Edition K.]
[4] POLYB. lib. ii. 56.
[5] POLYC. lib. ix. cap. 20.
[6] LYSIAS, orat. 34, 92..
[7] VOPISCUS *in vita* AURĒL, 222 B.
[8] *De rep.* LACED. 1, 1. This passage is

that has the fewest inhabitants. Yet POLYBIUS[1] says that it was forty-eight stadia in circumference, and was round.

All the ÆTOLIANS able to bear arms in ANTIPATER'S time, [2]deducting some few garrisons, were but ten thousand men.[3]

POLYBIUS[4] tells us, that the ACHÆAN league might, without any inconvenience, march 30 or 40,000 men: And this account seems probable: For that league comprehended the greater part of PELOPONNESUS. Yet PAUSANIAS,[5] speaking of the same period, says, that all the ACHÆANS able to bear arms, even when several manumitted slaves were joined to them, did not amount to fifteen thousand.

The THESSALIANS, till their final conquest by the ROMANS, were, in all ages, turbulent, factious, seditious, disorderly.[6] It is not therefore natural to suppose, that this part of GREECE abounded much in people.

[7]We are told by THUCYDIDES,[8] that the part of PELOPONNESUS, adjoining to PYLOS, was desart and uncultivated. HERODOTUS says,[9] that MACEDONIA was full of lions and wild bulls; animals which can only inhabit vast unpeopled forests. These were the two extremities of GREECE.

All the inhabitants of EPIRUS, of all ages, sexes, and conditions, who were sold by PAULUS ÆMILIUS, amounted only to 150,000.[10] Yet EPIRUS might be double the extent of YORKSHIRE.[11]

---

not easily reconciled with that of PLUTARCH above, who says, that SPARTA had 9000 citizens.

[1] POLYB. lib. ix. cap. 20.

[2] [Deducting some few garrisons: not in F G.]

[3] DIOD. SIC. lib. xviii. 24.

[4] LEGAT.

[5] In ACHAICIS, 7. 15, 7.

[6] TIT. LIV lib. xxxiv. cap. 51. PLATO in CRITONE, 53 D.

[7] [This paragraph was added in Edition K.]

[8] Lib. iv. 3.

[9] Lib. vii. 126.

[10] TIT. LIV. lib. xlv. cap. 34.

[11] [Editions H and I add the following note, in place of the following paragraph: A late *French* writer, in his *observations on the Greeks*, has remark'd, that *Philip of Macedon*, being declar'd captain-general of the GREEKS, wou'd have been back'd by the force of 230,000 of that nation in his intended expedition against *Persia*. This number comprehends, I suppose, all the free citizens, throughout all the cities; but the authority, on which that compilation is founded, has, I own, escap'd either my memory or reading; and that writer, tho' otherwise very ingenious, has given into a bad practice, of delivering a great deal of erudition, without one citation. But supposing, that that enumeration cou'd be justify'd by good authority from antiquity, we may establish the following computation. The free *Greeks* of all ages and sexes were 920,000. The slaves, computing them by the number of *Athenian* slaves as above, who seldom marry'd or had families, were double the male citizens of full age, viz. 460,000. And the whole inhabitants of antient *Greece* about one million, three hundred and eighty thousand. No mighty number nor much exceeding what may be found at present in Scotland, a country of nearly the same extent, and which is very indifferently peopl'd.]

[1] JUSTIN[2] tells us, that, when PHILIP of MACEDON was declared head of the GREEK confederacy, he called a congress of all the states, except the LACEDEMONIANS, who refused to concur; and he found the force of the whole, upon computation, to amount to 200,000 infantry, and 15,000 cavalry. This must be understood to be all the citizens capable of bearing arms. For as the GREEK republics maintained no mercenary forces, and had no militia distinct from the whole body of the citizens, it is not conceivable what other medium there could be of computation. That such an army could ever, by GREECE, be brought into the field, and be maintained there, is contrary to all history. Upon this supposition, therefore, we may thus reason. The free GREEKS of all ages and sexes were 860,000. The slaves, estimating them by the number of ATHENIAN slaves as above, who seldom married or had families, were double the male citizens of full age, to wit, 430,000. And all the inhabitants of ancient GREECE, excepting LACONIA, were about one million two hundred and ninety thousand: No mighty number, nor exceeding what may be found at present in SCOTLAND, a country of not much greater extent, and very indifferently peopled.

We may now consider the numbers of people in ROME and ITALY, and collect all the lights afforded us by scattered passages in ancient authors. We shall find, upon the whole, a great difficulty in fixing any opinion on that head; and no reason to support those exaggerated calculations, so much insisted on by modern writers.

DIONYSIUS HALICARNASSÆUS[3] says, that the ancient walls of ROME were nearly of the same compass with those of ATHENS, but that the suburbs ran out to a great extent; and it was difficult to tell, where the town ended or the country began. In some places of ROME, it appears, from the same author,[4] from JUVENAL,[5] and from other ancient writers,[6] that the houses were high, and families lived in

---

[1] [This paragraph was added in Edition K.]
[2] Lib. ix. cap. 5.
[3] Lib. iv. 13.
[4] Lib. x. 32.
[5] Satyr. iii. l. 269. 270.
[6] STRABO, liv. v. says, that the emperor AUGUSTUS prohibited the raising houses higher than seventy feet. In another passage, lib. xvi. he speaks of the houses of ROME as remarkably high. See also to the same purpose VITRUVIUS, lib. ii. cap. 8. ARISTIDES the sophist, in his oration εἰς Ῥώμην, says, that ROME consisted of cities on the top of cities; and that if one were to spread it out, and unfold it, it would cover the whole surface of ITALY. Where an author indulges himself in such extravagant declamations, and gives so much into the hyperbolical style, one knows not how far he must be reduced.

separate storeys, one above another: But it is probable, that these were only the poorer citizens, and only in some few streets. If we may judge from the younger PLINY's[1] account of his own house, and from BARTOLI's plans of ancient buildings, the men of quality had very spacious palaces; and their buildings were like the CHINESE houses at this day, where each apartment is separated from the rest, and rises no higher than a single storey.[2] To which if we add, that the ROMAN nobility much affected extensive porticoes, and even woods[3] in town; we may perhaps allow VOSSIUS (though there is no manner of reason for it) to read the famous passage of the elder PLINY[4] his own way, with-

---

But this reasoning seems natural: If ROME was built in so scattered a manner as DIONYSIUS says, and ran so much into the country, there must have been very few streets where the houses were raised so high. It is only for want of room, that any body builds in that inconvenient manner.

[1] LIB. ii. epist. 16. lib. v. epist. 6. It is true, PLINY there describes a country-house: But since that was the idea which the ancients formed of a magnificent and convenient building, the great men would certainly build the same way in town. 'In laxitatem ruris excurrunt,' says SENECA of the rich and voluptuous, epist. 114. VALERIUS MAXIMUS, lib. iv. cap. 4. speaking of CINCINNATUS's field of four acres, says, 'Anguste se habitare nunc putat, cujus domus tantum patet quantum CINCINNATI rura patuerant.' To the same purpose see lib. xxxvi. cap. 15. also lib. xviii. cap. 2.

[2] [For the history of this sentence see p. 57.]

[3] VITRUV. lib. v. cap. 11. TACIT. annal. lib. xi. cap. 3. SUETON. in vita OCTAV. cap. 72, &c.

[4] 'MOENIA ejus (ROMÆ) collegere ambitu imperatoribus, censoribusque VESPASIANIS, A. U. C. 828. pass. xiii. MCC. complexa montes septem, ipsa dividitur in regiones quatuordecim, compita earum 265. Ejusdem spatii mensura, currente a milliario in capite ROM. Fori statuto, ad singulas portas, quæ sunt hodie numero 37, ita ut duodecim portæ semel numerentur. prætereanturque ex veteribus septem, quæ esse desierunt, efficit passuum per directum 30,775. Ad extrema vero tectorum cum castris prætoriis ab eodem Milliario, per vicos omnium viarum, mensura collegit paulo amplius septuaginta millia passuum. Quo si quis altitudinem tectorum addat, dignam profecto, æstimationem concipiat, fateaturque nullius urbis magnitudinem in toto orbe potuisse ei comparari.' PLIN. lib. iii. cap. 5.

All the best manuscripts of PLINY read the passage as here cited, and fix the compass of the walls of ROME to be thirteen miles. The question is, What PLINY means by 30,775 paces, and how that number was formed? The manner in which I conceive it, is this. ROME was a semicircular area of thirteen miles circumference. The Forum, and consequently the Milliarium, we know, was situated on the banks of the TYBER, and near the center of the circle, or upon the diameter of the semicircular area. Though there were thirty-seven gates to ROME, yet only twelve of them had straight streets, leading from them to the Milliarium. PLINY, therefore, having assigned the circumference of ROME, and knowing that that alone was not sufficient to give us a just notion of its surface, uses this farther method. He supposes all the streets, leading from the Milliarium to the twelve gates, to be laid together into one straight line, and supposes we run along that line, so as to count each gate once: In which case, he says, that the whole line is 30,775 paces. Or, in other words, that each street or radius of the semicircular area is upon an average two miles and a half; and the whole length of ROME is five miles, and its breadth about half as much, besides the scattered suburbs.

PERE HARDOUIN understands this

out admitting the extravagant consequences which he draws from it.

The number of citizens who received corn by the public distribution in the time of AUGUSTUS, were two hundred thousand.[1] This one would esteem a pretty certain ground of calculation: Yet is it attended with such circumstances as throw us back into doubt and uncertainty.

passage in the same manner; with regard to the laying together the several streets of ROME into one line, in order to compose 30,775 paces: But then he supposes, that streets led from the Milliarium to every gate, and that no street exceeded 800 paces in length. But (1.) a semicircular area, whose radius was only 800 paces, could never have a circumference near thirteen miles, the compass of ROME as assigned by PLINY. A radius of two miles and a half forms very nearly that circumference. (2.) There is an absurdity in supposing a city so built as to have streets running to its center from every gate in its circumference. These streets must interfere as they approach. (3.) This diminishes too much from the greatness of ancient ROME, and reduces that city below even BRISTOL or ROTTERDAM.

The sense which VOSSIUS in his *Observationes variæ* puts on this passage of PLINY, errs widely in the other extreme. One manuscript of no authority, instead of thirteen miles, has assigned thirty miles for the compass of the walls of ROME. And VOSSIUS understands this only of the curvilinear part of the circumference; supposing, that as the TYBER formed the diameter, there were no walls built on that side. But (1.) this reading is allowed to be contrary to almost all the manuscripts. (2.) Why should PLINY, a concise writer, repeat the compass of the walls of ROME in two successive sentences? (3.) Why repeat it with so sensible a variation? (4.) What is the meaning of PLINY's mentioning twice the MILLIARIUM, if a line was measured that had no dependence on the MILLIARIUM? (5.) AURELIAN's wall is said by VOPISCUS to have been drawn *laxiore ambitu*, and to have comprehended all the buildings and suburbs on the north side of the TYBER; yet its compass was only fifty miles; and even here critics suspect some mistake or corruption in the text; since the walls, which remain, and which are supposed to be the same with Aurelian's, exceed not twelve miles. It is not probable, that ROME would diminish from AUGUSTUS to AURELIAN. It remained still the capital of the same empire; and none of the civil wars in that long period, except the tumults on the death of MAXIMUS and BALBINUS, ever affected the city. CARACALLA is said by AURELIUS VICTOR to have encreased ROME. (6.) There are no remains of ancient buildings, which mark any such greatness of ROME. VOSSIUS's reply to this objection seems absurd. That the rubbish would sink sixty or seventy feet under ground. It appears from SPARTIAN (*in vita Severi*) that the five-mile stone *in via Lavicana* was out of the city. (7.) OLYMPIODORUS and PUBLIUS VICTOR fix the number of houses in ROME to be betwixt forty and fifty thousand. (8.) The very extravagance of the consequences drawn by this critic, as well as LIPSIUS, if they be necessary, destroys the foundation on which they are grounded: That ROME contained fourteen millions of inhabitants; while the whole kingdom of FRANCE contains only five, according to his computation, &c.

The only objection to the sense which we have affixed above to the passage of PLINY, seems to lie in this, That PLINY, after mentioning the thirty-seven gates of ROME, assigns only a reason for suppressing the seven old ones, and says nothing of the eighteen gates, the streets leading from which terminated, according to my opinion, before they reached the Forum. But as PLINY was writing to the ROMANS, who perfectly knew the disposition of the streets, it is not strange he should take a circumstance for granted, which was so familiar to every body. Perhaps too, many of these gates led to wharfs upon the river.

[1] *Ex monument. Ancyr.*

Did the poorer citizens only receive the distribution? It was calculated, to be sure, chiefly for their benefit. But it appears from a passage in CICERO[1] that the rich might also take their portion, and that it was esteemed no reproach in them to apply for it.

To whom was the corn given; whether only to heads of families, or to every man, woman, and child? The portion every month was five *modii* to each[2] (about ⅚ of a bushel). This was too little for a family, and too much for an individual. A very accurate antiquary,[3] therefore, infers, that it was given to every man of full age: But he allows the matter to be uncertain.

Was it strictly enquired, whether the claimant lived within the precincts of Rome; or was it sufficient, that he presented himself at the monthly distribution? This last seems more probable.[4]

Were there no false claimants? We are told,[5] that CÆSAR struck off at once 170,000, who had creeped in without a just title; and it is very little probable, that he remedied all abuses.

But, lastly, what proportion of slaves must we assign to these citizens? This is the most material question; and the most uncertain. It is very doubtful, whether ATHENS can be established as a rule for ROME. Perhaps the ATHENIANS had more slaves, because they employed them in manufactures, for which a capital city, like ROME, seems not so proper. Perhaps, on the other hand, the ROMANS had more slaves, on account of their superior luxury and riches.

There were exact bills of mortality kept at ROME; but no ancient author has given us the number of burials, except SUETONIUS,[6] who tells us, that in one season, there were 30,000 names carried to the temple of LIBITINA: But this was during a plague; which can afford no certain foundation for any inference.

The public corn, though distributed only to 20,000 citizens,

---

[1] *Tusc. Quæst.* lib. iii. cap. 48.
[2] *Licinius apud Sallust. hist. frag.* lib. iii.
[3] *Nicolaus Hortensius de re frumentaria Roman.*
[4] Not to take the people too much from their business, AUGUSTUS ordained the distribution of corn to be made only thrice a-year: But the people finding the monthly distributions more convenient, (as preserving, I suppose, a more regular œconomy in their family) desired to have them restored, SUETON. AUGUST, cap. 40. Had not some of the people come from some distance for their corn, AUGUSTUS's precaution seems superfluous.
[5] *Sueton. in Jul.* cap. 41.
[6] *In vita Neronis.* 39.

affected very considerably the whole agriculture of ITALY:[1] a fact no wise reconcileable to some modern exaggerations with regard to the inhabitants of that country.

The best ground of conjecture I can find concerning the greatness of ancient Rome is this: We are told by HERODIAN,[2] that ANTIOCH and ALEXANDRIA were very little inferior to ROME. It appears from DIODORUS SICULUS,[3] that one straight street of ALEXANDRIA reaching from gate to gate, was five miles long; and as ALEXANDRIA was much more extended in length than breadth, it seems to have been a city nearly of the bulk of PARIS;[4] and ROME might be about the size of LONDON.

There lived in ALEXANDRIA, in DIODORUS SICULUS's time,[5] 300,000 free people, comprehending, I suppose, women and children.[6] But what number of slaves? Had we any just ground to fix these at an equal number with the free inhabitants, it would favour the foregoing computation.

There is a passage in HERODIAN, which is a little surprising. He says positively, that the palace of the Emperor was as large as all the rest of the city.[7] This was NERO's golden house, which is indeed represented by SUETONIUS[8] and PLINY

---

[1] *Sueton. Aug.* cap. 42.

[2] Lib. iv. cap. 5.

[3] Lib. xvii. 52.

[4] Quintus Curtius says, its walls were ten miles in circumference, when founded by Alexander, lib. iv. cap. 8. Strabo, who had travelled to Alexandria as well as Diodorus Siculus, says it was scarce four miles long, and in most places about a mile broad, lib. xvii. Pliny says it resembled a Macedonian cassock, stretching out in the corners, lib. v. cap. 10. Notwithstanding this bulk of Alexandria, which seems but moderate, Diodorus Siculus, speaking of its circuit as drawn by Alexander (which it never exceeded, as we learn from Ammianus Marcellinus, lib. xxii. cap. 16,) says it was μεγέθει διαφέροντα, *extremely great*, ibid. The reason which he assigns for its surpassing all cities in the world (for he excepts not Rome) is, that it contained 300,000 free inhabitants. He also mentions the revenues of the kings, to wit, 6,000 talents, as another circumstance to the same purpose; no such mighty sum in our eyes, even though we make allowance for the different value of money. What Strabo says of the neighbouring country, means only that it was peopled, οἰκούμενα καλῶς. Might not one affirm, without any great hyperbole, that the whole banks of the river, from Gravesend to Windsor, are one city? This is even more than Strabo says of the banks of the lake Mareotis, and of the canal to Canopus. It is a vulgar saying in Italy, that the king of Sardinia has but one town in Piedmont, for it is all a town. Agrippa, *in Josephus de bello Judaic.* lib. ii. cap. 16, to make his audience comprehend the excessive greatness of Alexandria, which he endeavours to magnify, describes only the compass of the city as drawn by Alexander; a clear proof that the bulk of the inhabitants were lodged there, and that the neighbouring country was no more than what might be expected about all great towns, very well cultivated, and well peopled.

[5] Lib. xvii. 52.

[6] He says ἐλεύθεροι, not πολῖται, which last expression must have been understood of citizens alone, and grown men.

[7] Lib. iv. cap. 1. πάσης πόλεως. POLITIAN interprets it 'aedibus majoribus etiam reliqua urbe.'

[8] He says (in NERONE cap. 30.) that a portico or piazza of it was 3000

as of an enormous extent;[1] but no power of imagination can make us conceive it to bear any proportion to such a city as LONDON.

We may observe, had the historian been relating NERO's extravagance, and had he made use of such an expression, it would have had much less weight; these rhetorical exaggerations being so apt to creep into an author's style, even when the most chaste and correct. But it is mentioned by HERODIAN only by the by, in relating the quarrels between GETA and CARACALLA.

It appears from the same historian,[2] that there was then much land uncultivated, and put to no manner of use; and he ascribes it as a great praise to PERTINAX, that he allowed every one to take such land either in ITALY or elsewhere, and cultivate it as he pleased, without paying any taxes. *Lands uncultivated, and put to no manner of use!* This is not heard of in any part of CHRISTENDOM; except in some remote parts of HUNGARY; as I have been informed. And it surely corresponds very ill with that idea of the extreme populousness of antiquity, so much insisted on.

We learn from VOPISCUS,[3] that there was even in ETRURIA much fertile land uncultivated, which the Emperor AURELIAN intended to convert into vineyards, in order to furnish the ROMAN people with a gratuitous distribution of wine; a very proper expedient for depopulating still farther that capital and all the neighbouring territories.

It may not be amiss to take notice of the account which POLYBIUS[4] gives of the great herds of swine to be met with in TUSCANY and LOMBARDY, as well as in GREECE, and of the method of feeding them which was then practised. 'There are great herds of swine,' says he, 'throughout all 'ITALY, particularly in former times, through ETRURIA and 'CISALPINE GAUL. And a herd frequently consists of a

feet long; 'tanta laxitas ut porticus triplices milliarias haberet.' He cannot mean three miles. For the whole extent of the house from the PALATINE to the ESQUILINE was not near so great. So when VOPISC. in AURELIANO mentions a portico in SALLUST's gardens, which he calls *porticus milliarensis*, it must be understood of a thousand feet. So also HORACE;

'Nulla decempedis
Metata privatis opacam
Porticus excipiebat Arcton.' Lib. 2. ode 15.

So also in lib. 1. satyr. 8.

'Mille pedes in fronte, trecentos
cippus in agrum
Hic dabat.'

[1] PLINIUS, lib. xxxvi. cap. 15. 'Bis vidimus urbem totam cingi domibus principum, CAII ac NERONIS.'
[2] Lib. ii. cap. 15.
[3] In AURELIAN. cap. 48.
[4] Lib. xii. cap. 2.

'thousand or more swine. When one of these herds in
'feeding meets with another, they mix together; and the
'swine-herds have no other expedient for separating them
'than to go to different quarters, where they sound their horn;
'and these animals, being accustomed to that signal, run
'immediately each to the horn of his own keeper. Whereas
'in GREECE, if the herds of swine happen to mix in the
'forests, he who has the greater flock, takes cunningly the
'opportunity of driving all away. And thieves are very apt
'to purloin the straggling hogs, which have wandered to a
'great distance from their keeper in search of food.'

May we not infer from this account, that the north of ITALY, as well as GREECE, was then much less peopled, and worse cultivated, than at present? How could these vast herds be fed in a country so full of inclosures, so improved by agriculture, so divided by farms, so planted with vines and corn intermingled together? I must confess, that POLYBIUS's relation has more the air of that œconomy which is to be met with in our AMERICAN colonies, than the management of a EUROPEAN country.

We meet with a reflection in ARISTOTLE's[1] Ethics, which seems unaccountable on any supposition, and by proving too much in favour of our present reasoning, may be thought really to prove nothing. That philosopher, treating of friendship, and observing, that this relation ought neither to be contracted to a very few, nor extended over a great multitude, illustrates his opinion by the following argument. 'In like 'manner,' says he, 'as a city cannot subsist, if it either have 'so few inhabitants as ten, or so many as a hundred thousand; 'so is there a mediocrity required in the number of friends; 'and you destroy the essence of friendship by running into 'either extreme.' What! impossible that a city can contain a hundred thousand inhabitants! Had ARISTOTLE never seen nor heard of a city so populous? This, I must own, passes my comprehension.

PLINY[2] tells us that SELEUCIA, the seat of the GREEK empire in the East, was reported to contain 600,000 people. CARTHAGE is said by STRABO[3] to have contained 700,000. The inhabitants of PEKIN are not much more numerous.

---

[1] Lib. ix. cap. 10. His expression is ἄνθρωπος, not πολίτης; inhabitant, not citizen.

[2] Lib. vi. cap. 28.
[3] Lib. xvii. 833.

London, Paris, and Constantinople, may admit of nearly the same computation; at least, the two latter cities do not exceed it. Rome, Alexandria, Antioch, we have already spoken of. From the experience of past and present ages, one might conjecture that there is a kind of impossibility, that any city could ever rise much beyond this proportion. Whether the grandeur of a city be founded on commerce or on empire, there seem to be invincible obstacles, which prevent its farther progress. The seats of vast monarchies, by introducing extravagant luxury, irregular expence, idleness, dependence, and false ideas of rank and superiority, are improper for commerce. Extensive commerce checks itself, by raising the price of all labour and commodities. When a great court engages the attendance of a numerous nobility, possessed of overgrown fortunes, the middling gentry remain in their provincial towns, where they can make a figure on a moderate income. And if the dominions of a state arrive at an enormous size, there necessarily arise many capitals, in the remoter provinces, whither all the inhabitants, except a few courtiers, repair for education, fortune, and amusement.[1] London, by uniting extensive commerce and middling empire, has, perhaps, arrived at a greatness, which no city will ever be able to exceed.

Chuse Dover or Calais for a center: Draw a circle of two hundred miles radius: You comprehend London, Paris, the Netherlands, the United Provinces, and some of the best cultivated parts of France and England. It may safely, I think, be affirmed, that no spot of ground can be found, in antiquity, of equal extent, which contained near so many great and populous cities, and was so stocked with riches and inhabitants. To balance, in both periods, the states, which possessed most art, knowledge, civility, and the best police, seems the truest method of comparison.

It is an observation of L'Abbe du Bos,[2] that Italy is warmer at present than it was in ancient times. 'The annals 'of Rome tell us,' says he, 'that in the year 480 *ab U.C.* the 'winter was so severe that it destroyed the trees. The 'Tyber froze in Rome, and the ground was covered with

---

[1] Such were Alexandria, Antioch, Carthage, Ephesus, Lyons, &c. in the Roman empire. Such are even Bourdeaux, Tholouse, Dijon, Rennes, Rouen, Aix, &c. in France; Dublin, Edinburgh, York, in the British dominions.

[2] Vol. 2. Sect. 16.

'snow for forty days. When JUVENAL[1] describes a super-
'stitious woman, he represents her as breaking the ice of the
'TYBER, that she might perform her ablutions:

> '*Hybernum fracta glacie descendet in amnem,*
> '*Ter matutino Tyberi mergetur.*

'He speaks of that river's freezing as a common event.
'Many passages of HORACE suppose the streets of ROME full
'of snow and ice. We should have more certainty with
'regard to this point, had the ancients known the use of
'thermometers: But their writers, without intending it, give
'us information, sufficient to convince us, that the winters
'are now much more temperate at ROME than formerly. At
'present the TYBER no more freezes at ROME than the
'NILE at CAIRO. The ROMANS esteem the winters very
'rigorous, if the snow lie two days, and if one see for eight
'and forty hours a few icicles hang from a fountain that has
'a north exposure.'

The observation of this ingenious critic may be extended to other EUROPEAN climates. Who could discover the mild climate of FRANCE in DIODORUS SICULUS'S[2] description of that of GAUL? 'As it is a northern climate,' says he, 'it is
'infested with cold to an extreme degree. In cloudy weather,
'instead of rain there fall great snows; and in clear weather
'it there freezes so excessive hard, that the rivers acquire
'bridges of their own substance, over which, not only
'single travellers may pass, but large armies, accompanied
'with all their baggage and loaded waggons. And there
'being many rivers in GAUL, the RHONE, the RHINE, &c.,
'almost all of them are frozen over; and it is usual, in order
'to prevent falling, to cover the ice with chaff and straw at
'the places where the road passes.' [3]*Colder than a* GALLIC *Winter*, is used by PETRONIUS as a proverbial expression. ARISTOTLE says, that GAUL is so cold a climate that an ass could not live in it.[4]

North of the CEVENNES, says STRABO,[5] GAUL produces not figs and olives: And the vines, which have been planted, bear not grapes, that will ripen.

OVID positively maintains, with all the serious affirmation

---

[1] Sat. 6. 522.
[2] Lib. iv. 25.
[3] [The next two sentences are not in Editions H to K: and the latter was added in Edition R.]
[4] De generat. anim. lib. ii. 8, 14.
[5] Lib. iv. 178.

of prose, that the EUXINE sea was frozen over every winter in his time; and he appeals to ROMAN governours, whom he names, for the truth of his assertion.[1] This seldom or never happens at present in the latitude of TOMI, whither OVID was banished. All the complaints of the same poet seem to mark a rigour of the seasons, which is scarcely experienced at present in PETERSBURGH or STOCKHOLM.

TOURNEFORT, a *Provençal*, who had travelled into the same country, observes that there is not a finer climate in the world: And he asserts that nothing but OVID's melancholy could have given him such dismal ideas of it. But the facts, mentioned by that poet, are too circumstantial to bear any such interpretation.

POLYBIUS [2] says that the climate in ARCADIA was very cold, and the air moist.

'ITALY,' says VARRO,[3] 'is the most temperate climate in EUROPE. The inland parts' (GAUL, GERMANY, and PANNONIA, no doubt) 'have almost perpetual winter.'

The northern parts of SPAIN, according to STRABO,[4] are but ill inhabited, because of the great cold.

Allowing, therefore, this remark to be just, that EUROPE is become warmer than formerly; how can we account for it? Plainly, by no other method, than by supposing that the land is at present much better cultivated, and that the woods are cleared, which formerly threw a shade upon the earth, and kept the rays of the sun from penetrating to it. Our northern colonies in AMERICA become more temperate, in proportion as the woods are felled;[5] but in general, every one may remark that cold is still much more severely felt, both in North and South AMERICA, than in places under the same latitude in EUROPE.

SASERNA, quoted by COLUMELLA,[6] affirmed that the disposition of the heavens was altered before his time, and that the air had become much milder and warmer; as appears hence, says he, that many places now abound with vineyards and olive plantations, which formerly, by reason of the rigour

---

[1] *Trist.* lib. iii. eleg. 10. *De Ponto*, lib. iv. eleg. 7, 9, 10.

[2] Lib. iv. cap. 21.

[3] Lib. i. cap. 2.

[4] Lib. iii. 137.

[5] The warm southern colonies also become more healthful: And it is remarkable, that in the SPANISH histories of the first discovery and conquest of these countries, they appear to have been very healthful; being then well peopled and cultivated. No account of the sickness or decay of CORTES's or PIZARRO's small armies.

[6] Lib. i. cap. 1.

of the climate, could raise none of these productions. Such a change, if real, will be allowed an evident sign of the better cultivation and peopling of countries before the age of SASERNA;[1] and if it be continued to the present times, is a proof, that these advantages have been continually encreasing throughout this part of the world.

Let us now cast our eye over all the countries which are the scene of ancient and modern history, and compare their past and present situation: We shall not, perhaps, find such foundation for the complaint of the present emptiness and desolation of the world. ÆGYPT is represented by MAILLET, to whom we owe the best account of it, as extremely populous; though he esteems the number of its inhabitants to be diminished. SYRIA, and the Lesser ASIA, as well as the coast of BARBARY, I can readily own, to be desart in comparison of their ancient condition. The depopulation of GREECE is also obvious. But whether the country now called TURKEY in EUROPE may not, in general, contain more inhabitants than during the flourishing period of GREECE, may be a little doubtful. The THRACIANS seem then to have lived like the TARTARS at present, by pasturage and plunder:[2] The GETES were still more uncivilized:[3] And the ILLYRIANS were no better.[4] These occupy nine-tenths of that country: And though the government of the TURKS be not very favourable to industry and propagation; yet it preserves at least peace and order among the inhabitants; and is preferable to that barbarous, unsettled condition, in which they anciently lived.

POLAND and MUSCOVY in EUROPE are not populous; but are certainly much more so than the ancient SARMATIA and SCYTHIA; where no husbandry or tillage was ever heard of, and pasturage was the sole art by which the people were maintained. The like observation may be extended to DENMARK and SWEDEN. No one ought to esteem the immense swarms of people, which formerly came from the North, and over-ran all EUROPE, to be any objection to this opinion. Where a whole nation, or even half of it remove their seat, it is easy to imagine, what a prodigious multitude they must form; with what desperate valour they must

[1] He seems to have lived about the time of the younger AFRICANUS; lib. i. cap. 1.
[2] *Xenoph. Exp.* lib. vii. *Polyb.* lib. iv. cap. 45.
[3] *Ovid. passim, &c. Strabo,* lib. vii.
[4] *Polyb.* lib. ii. cap. 12.

make their attacks; and how the terror they strike into the invaded nations will make these magnify, in their imagination, both the courage and multitude of the invaders. SCOTLAND is neither extensive nor populous; but were the half of its inhabitants to seek new seats, they would form a colony as numerous as the TEUTONS and CIMBRI; and would shake all EUROPE, supposing it in no better condition for defence than formerly.

GERMANY has surely at present twenty times more inhabitants than in ancient times, when they cultivated no ground, and each tribe valued itself on the extensive desolation which it spread around; as we learn from CÆSAR,[1] and TACITUS,[2] and STRABO.[3] A proof, that the division into small republics will not alone render a nation populous, unless attended with the spirit of peace, order, and industry.

The barbarous condition of BRITAIN in former times is well known, and the thinness of its inhabitants may easily be conjectured, both from their barbarity, and from a circumstance mentioned by HERODIAN,[4] that all BRITAIN was marshy, even in SEVERUS's time, after the ROMANS had been fully settled in it above a century.

It is not easily imagined, that the GAULS were anciently much more advanced in the arts of life than their northern neighbours; since they travelled to this island for their education in the mysteries of the religion and philosophy of the DRUIDS.[5] I cannot, therefore, think, that GAUL was then near so populous as FRANCE is at present.

Were we to believe, indeed, and join together the testimony of APPIAN, and that of DIODORUS SICULUS, we must admit of an incredible populousness in GAUL. The former historian[6] says, that there were 400 nations in that country; the latter[7] affirms, that the largest of the GALLIC nations consisted of 200,000 men, besides women and children, and the least of 50,000. Calculating, therefore, at a medium, we must admit of near 200 millions of people, in a country, which we esteem populous at present, though supposed to contain little more than twenty.[8] Such calculations, there-

---

[1] *De Bello Gallico*, lib. vi. 23.
[2] *De Moribus Germ.*
[3] Lib. vii.
[4] Lib. iii. cap. 47.
[5] CÆSAR *de Bello Gallico*, lib. vi. 13. STRABO, lib. vii. 200 says, the GAULS were not much more improved than the GERMANS.
[6] Celt. pars 1. lib. iv. 2.
[7] Lib. v. 25.
[8] Ancient GAUL was more extensive than modern FRANCE.

fore, by their extravagance, lose all manner of authority. We may observe, that the equality of property, to which the populousness of antiquity may be ascribed, had no place among the GAULS.¹ Their intestine wars also, before CÆSAR's time, were almost perpetual.² And STRABO³ observes, that, though all GAUL was cultivated, yet was it not cultivated with any skill or care; the genius of the inhabitants leading them less to arts than arms, till their slavery under ROME produced peace among themselves.

CÆSAR⁴ enumerates very particularly the great forces which were levied in BELGIUM to oppose his conquest, and makes them amount to 208,000. These were not the whole people able to bear arms: For the same historian tells us, that the BELLOVACI could have brought a hundred thousand men into the field, though they engaged only for sixty. Taking the whole, therefore, in this proportion of ten to six, ⁵ the sum of fighting men in all the states of BELGIUM was about 350,000; all the inhabitants a million and a half. And BELGIUM being about a fourth of GAUL, that country might contain six millions, which is not⁶ near the third of its present inhabitants.⁷ ⁸ We are informed by CÆSAR, that the GAULS had no fixed property in land; but that the chieftains, when any death happened in a family, made a new division of all the lands among the several members of the family. This is the custom of *Tanistry*, which so long prevailed in IRELAND, and which retained that country in a state of misery, barbarism and desolation.

¹ CÆSAR *de Bello Gallico*, lib. vi. 13.
² *Id. ibid.* 15.
³ Lib. iv. 178.
⁴ *De Bello Gallico*, lib. ii. 4.
⁵ [Editions H and I read as follows: The sum of fighting men in all the States of BELGIUM was above half a million; the whole inhabitants two millions. And BELGIUM being about the fourth of GAUL, that country might contain eight millions, which is scarce above the third of its present inhabitants.]
⁶ ['Near' was added in Edition R.]
⁷ It appears from CÆSAR's account, that the GAULS had no domestic slaves,¹ (who formed a different order from the *Plebes*.) The whole common people were indeed a kind of slaves to the nobility, as the people of POLAND are at this day: And a nobleman of GAUL had sometimes ten thousand dependants of this kind. Nor can we doubt, that the armies were composed of the people as well as of the nobility: An army of 100,000 noblemen from a very small state is incredible. The fighting men amongst the HELVETII were the fourth part of the whole inhabitants; a clear proof that all the males of military age bore arms. See CÆSAR *de bello Gall.* lib. 1.

We may remark, that the numbers in CÆSAR's commentaries can be more depended on than those of any other antient author, because of the GREEK translation, which still remains, and which checks the LATIN original.

⁸ [The remainder of the paragraph was added in Edition N]

¹ ['who—Plebes' not in Editions H and I.]

The ancient HELVETIA was 250 miles in length, and 180 in breadth, according to the same author;[1] yet contained only 360,000 inhabitants. The canton of BERNE alone has, at present, as many people.

After this computation of APPIAN and DIODORUS SICULUS, I know not, whether I dare affirm, that the modern DUTCH are more numerous than the ancient BATAVI.

SPAIN is, perhaps, decayed from what it was three centuries ago; but if we step backward two thousand years, and consider the restless, turbulent, unsettled condition of its inhabitants, we may probably be inclined to think that it is now much more populous. Many SPANIARDS killed themselves, when deprived of their arms by the ROMANS.[2] It appears from PLUTARCH[3], that robbery and plunder were esteemed honourable among the SPANIARDS. HIRTIUS[4] represents in the same light the situation of that country in CÆSAR's time; and he says, that every man was obliged to live in castles and walled towns for his security. It was not till its final conquest under AUGUSTUS, that these disorders were repressed.[5] The account which STRABO[6] and JUSTIN[7] give of SPAIN, corresponds exactly with those above mentioned. How much, therefore, must it diminish from our idea of the populousness of antiquity, when we find that TULLY, comparing ITALY, AFRIC, GAUL, GREECE, and SPAIN, mentions the great number of inhabitants, as the peculiar circumstance, which rendered this latter country formidable?[8]

ITALY, however, it is probable, has decayed: But how many great cities does it still contain? VENICE, GENOA, PAVIA, TURIN, MILAN, NAPLES, FLORENCE, LEGHORN, which either subsisted not in ancient times, or were then very inconsiderable? If we reflect on this, we shall not be apt to carry matters to so great an extreme as is usual, with regard to this subject.

When the ROMAN authors complain, that ITALY, which

---

[1] *De Bello Gallico*, lib. i. 2.
[2] *Titi Livii*, lib. xxxiv. cap. 17.
[3] *In vita Marii.* 6.
[4] *De Bello Hisp.* 8.
[5] *Vell. Paterc.* lib. ii. § 90.
[6] Lib. iii.
[7] Lib. xliv.
[8] 'Nec numero Hispanos, nec robore Gallos, nec calliditate Pœnos, nec artibus Græcos, nec denique hoc ipso hujus gentis, ac terræ domestico nativoque sensu, Italos ipsos ac Latinos—superavimus.' *De harusp. resp.* cap. 9. The disorders of SPAIN seem to have been almost proverbial: 'Nec impacatos a tergo horrebis Iberos.' *Virg. Georg.* lib. iii. 408. The IBERI are here plainly taken, by a poetical figure, for robbers in general.

formerly exported corn, became dependent on all the provinces for its daily bread, they never ascribe this alteration to the encrease of its inhabitants, but to the neglect of tillage and agriculture.[1] A natural effect of that pernicious practice of importing corn, in order to distribute it *gratis* among the ROMAN citizens, and a very bad means of multiplying the inhabitants of any country.[2] The *sportula*, so much talked of by MARTIAL and JUVENAL, being presents regularly made by the great lords to their smaller clients, must have had a like tendency to produce idleness, debauchery, and a continual decay among the people. The parish-rates have at present the same bad consequences in ENGLAND.

Were I to assign a period, when I imagine this part of the world might possibly contain more inhabitants than at present, I should pitch upon the age of TRAJAN and the ANTONINES; the great extent of the ROMAN empire being then civilized and cultivated, settled almost in a profound peace both foreign and domestic, and living under the same regular police and government.[3] But we are told that all extensive governments, especially absolute monarchies, are pernicious to population, and contain a secret vice and poison, which

---

[1] VARRO *de re rustica*, lib. ii. præf. COLUMELLA præf. SUETON. AUGUST. cap. 42.

[2] Though the observations of L'Abbé du Bos should be admitted, that ITALY is now warmer than in former times, the consequence may not be necessary, that it is more populous or better cultivated. If the other countries of EUROPE were more savage and woody, the cold winds that blew from them, might affect the climate of Italy.

[3] The inhabitants of MARSEILLES lost not their superiority over the GAULS in commerce and the mechanic arts, till the ROMAN dominion turned the latter from arms to agriculture and civil life. See STRABO, lib. iv. 180-1. That author, in several places, repeats the observation concerning the improvement arising from the ROMAN arts and civility: And he lived at the time when the change was new, and would be more sensible. So also PLINY: 'Quis enim non, communicato orbe terrarum, majestate ROMANI imperii, profecisse vitam putet, commercio rerum ac societate festæ pacis, omniaque etiam, quæ occulta antea fuerant, in promiscuo usu facta. Lib. xiv. proœm. Numine deûm electa (speaking of ITALY) quæ cœlum ipsum clarius faceret, sparsa congregaret imperia, ritusque molliret, & tot populorum discordes, ferasque linguas sermonis commercio contraheret ad colloquia, & humanitatem homini daret; breviterque, una cunctarum gentium in toto orbe patria fieret;' lib. ii. cap. 5. Nothing can be stronger to this purpose than the following passage from TERTULLIAN, who lived about the age of SEVERUS. 'Certe quidem ipse orbis in promptu est, cultior de die & instructior pristino. Omnia jam pervia, omnia nota, omnia negotiosa. Solitudines famosas retro fundi amœnissimi obliteraverunt, silvas arva domuerunt, feras pecora fugaverunt; arenæ seruntur, saxa panguntur, paludes eliquantur, tantæ urbes, quantæ non casæ quondam. Jam nec insulæ horrent, nec scopuli terrent; ubique domus, ubique populus, ubique respublica, ubique vita. Summum testimonium frequentiæ humanæ, onerosi sumus mundo, vix nobis elementa sufficiunt; & necessitates arctiores, et querelæ apud omnes, dum jam nos natura non sustinet.' De anima, cap. 30. The air of rhetoric and declamation which appears in this passage,

destroy the effect of all these promising appearances.¹ To confirm this, there is a passage cited from PLUTARCH,² which being somewhat singular, we shall here examine it.

That author, endeavouring to account for the silence of many of the oracles, says, that it may be ascribed to the present desolation of the world, proceeding from former wars and factions; which common calamity, he adds, has fallen heavier upon GREECE than on any other country; insomuch, that the whole could scarcely at present furnish three thousand warriors; a number which, in the time of the MEDIAN war, were supplied by the single city of MEGARA. The gods, therefore, who affect works of dignity and importance, have suppressed many of their oracles, and deign not to use so many interpreters of their will to so diminutive a people.

I must confess, that this passage contains so many difficulties, that I know not what to make of it. You may observe,

---

diminishes somewhat from its authority, but does not entirely destroy it.¹ The same remark may be extended to the following passage of ARISTIDES the sophist, who lived in the age of ADRIAN. 'The whole world,' says he, addressing himself to the ROMANS, 'seems to keep one holiday; and mankind, laying aside the sword which they formerly wore, now betake themselves to feasting and to joy. The cities, forgetting their ancient animosities, preserve only one emulation, which shall embellish itself most by every art and ornament; Theatres every where arise, amphitheatres, porticoes, aqueducts, temples, schools, academies; and one may safely pronounce, that the sinking world has been again raised by your auspicious empire. Nor have cities alone received an encrease of ornament and beauty; but the whole earth, like a garden or paradise, is cultivated and adorned: Insomuch, that such of mankind as are placed out of the limits of your empire (who are but few) seem to merit our sympathy and compassion.'

It is remarkable, that though DIODORUS SICULUS makes the inhabitants of ÆGYPT, when conquered by the ROMANS, amount only to three millions; yet JOSEPH. *de bello Jud.* lib. ii. cap. 16. says, that its inhabitants, excluding those of ALEXANDRIA, were seven millions and a half, in the reign of NERO: And he expressly says, that he drew this account from the books of the ROMAN publicans, who levied the poll-tax. STRABO, lib. xvii. 797, praises the superior police of the ROMANS with regard to the finances of ÆGYPT, above that of its former monarchs: And no part of administration is more essential to the happiness of a people. Yet we read in ATHENÆUS, (lib. i. cap. 25.) who flourished during the reign of the ANTONINES, that the town MAREIA, near ALEXANDRIA, which was formerly a large city, had dwindled into a village. This is not, properly speaking, a contradiction. SUIDAS (AUGUST.) says, that the Emperor AUGUSTUS, having numbered the whole ROMAN empire, found it contained only 4,101,017 men (ἄνδρες). There is here surely some great mistake, either in the author or transcriber. But this authority, feeble as it is, may be sufficient to counterbalance the exaggerated accounts of HERODOTUS and DIODORUS SICULUS with regard to more early times.

¹ *L'Esprit de Loix*, liv. xxiii. chap. 19.
² *De Orac. Defectu.*

---

¹ [Editions H and I add: A man of violent imagination, such as TERTULLIAN, augments everything equally; and for that reason his comparative judgments are the most to be depended on.]

that Plutarch assigns, for a cause of the decay of mankind, not the extensive dominion of the Romans, but the former wars and factions of the several states; all which were quieted by the Roman arms. Plutarch's reasoning, therefore, is directly contrary to the inference, which is drawn from the fact he advances.

Polybius supposes, that Greece had become more prosperous and flourishing after the establishment of the Roman yoke[1]; and though that historian wrote before these conquerors had degenerated, from being the patrons, to be the plunderers of mankind; yet, as we find from Tacitus,[2] that the severity of the emperors afterwards corrected the licence of the governors, we have no reason to think that extensive monarchy so destructive as it is often represented.

We learn from Strabo,[3] that the Romans, from their regard to the Greeks, maintained, to his time, most of the privileges and liberties of that celebrated nation; and Nero afterwards rather encreased them.[4] How therefore can we imagine, that the Roman yoke was so burdensome over that part of the world? The oppression of the proconsuls was checked; and the magistracies in Greece being all bestowed, in the several cities, by the free votes of the people, there was no necessity for the competitors to attend the emperor's court. If great numbers went to seek their fortunes in Rome, and advance themselves by learning or eloquence, the commodities of their native country, many of them would return with the fortunes which they had acquired, and thereby enrich the Grecian commonwealths.

But Plutarch says, that the general depopulation had been more sensibly felt in Greece than in any other country. How is this reconcileable to its superior privileges and advantages?

Besides, this passage, by proving too much, really proves nothing. *Only three thousand men able to bear arms in all* Greece! Who can admit so strange a proposition, espe-

---

[1] Lib. ii. cap. 62. It may perhaps be imagined, that Polybius, being dependent on Rome, would naturally extol the Roman dominion. But, in the *first* place, Polybius, though one sees sometimes instances of his caution, discovers no symptoms of flattery. *Secondly*, This opinion is only delivered in a single stroke, by the by, while he is intent upon another subject; and it is allowed, if there be any suspicion of an author's insincerity, that these oblique propositions discover his real opinion better than his more formal and direct assertions.

[2] *Annal.* lib. i. cap. 2.

[3] Lib. viii. and ix.

[4] Plutarch. *De his qui sero a Numine puniuntur.*

cially if we consider the great number of GREEK cities, whose names still remain in history, and which are mentioned by writers long after the age of PLUTARCH? There are there surely ten times more people at present, when there scarcely remains a city in all the bounds of ancient GREECE. That country is still tolerably cultivated, and furnishes a sure supply of corn, in case of any scarcity in SPAIN, ITALY, or the south of FRANCE.

We may observe, that the ancient frugality of the GREEKS, and their equality of property, still subsisted during the age of PLUTARCH; as appears from LUCIAN.[1] Nor is there any ground to imagine, that that country was possessed by a few masters, and a great number of slaves.

It is probable, indeed, that military discipline, being entirely useless, was extremely neglected in GREECE after the establishment of the ROMAN empire; and if these commonwealths, formerly so warlike and ambitious, maintained each of them a small city-guard, to prevent mobbish disorders, it is all they had occasion for: And these, perhaps, did not amount to 3,000 men, throughout all GREECE. I own, that, if PLUTARCH had this fact in his eye, he is here guilty of a gross paralogism, and assigns causes no wise proportioned to the effects. But is it so great a prodigy, that an author should fall into a mistake of this nature?[2]

---

[1] *De mercede conductis.*

[2] I must confess that that discourse of PLUTARCH, concerning the silence of the oracles, is in general of so odd a texture, and so unlike his other productions, that one is at a loss what judgment to form of it. 'Tis wrote in dialogue, which is a method of composition that PLUTARCH commonly little affects. The personages he introduces advance very wild, absurd, and contradictory opinions, more like the visionary systems or ravings of PLATO than the solid sense of PLUTARCH. There runs also thro' the whole an air of superstition and credulity, which resembles very little the spirit that appears in other philosophical compositions of that author. For 'tis remarkable, that tho' PLUTARCH be an historian as superstitious as HERODOTUS or LIVY, yet there is scarcely, in all antiquity, a philosopher less superstitious, excepting CICERO and LUCIAN. I must therefore confess, that a passage of PLUTARCH, cited from this discourse, has much less authority with me, than if it had been found in most of his other compositions.

There is only one other discourse of PLUTARCH liable to like objections, *viz.* that *concerning those whose punishment is delayed by the Deity.* It is also wrote in dialogue, contains like superstitious, wild visions, and seems to have been chiefly composed in rivalship to PLATO, particularly his last book *de republica.*

And here I cannot but observe, that Mons. FONTENELLE, a writer eminent for candor, seems to have departed a little from his usual character, when he endeavours to throw a ridicule upon PLUTARCH on account of passages to be met with in this dialogue concerning oracles. The absurdities here put into the mouths of the several personages are not to be ascribed to PLUTARCH. He makes them refute each other; and, in general, he seems to intend the ridiculing of those very opinions, which FONTENELLE would ridicule him for maintaining. See *Histoire des oracles.*

But whatever force may remain in this passage of Plutarch, we shall endeavour to counterbalance it by as remarkable a passage in Diodorus Siculus, where the historian, after mentioning Ninus's army of 1,700,000 foot and 200,000 horse, endeavours to support the credibility of this account by some posterior facts; and adds, that we must not form a notion of the ancient populousness of mankind from the present emptiness and depopulation which is spread over the world.[1] Thus an author, who lived at that very period of antiquity which is represented as most populous,[2] complains of the desolation which then prevailed, gives the preference to former times, and has recourse to ancient fables as a foundation for his opinion. The humour of blaming the present, and admiring the past, is strongly rooted in human nature, and has an influence even on persons endued with the profoundest judgment and most extensive learning.[3]

Essay XII.—*Of the Original Contract.*

As no party, in the present age, can well support itself, without a philosophical or speculative system of principles, annexed to its political or practical one; we accordingly find, that each of the factions, into which this nation is divided, has reared up a fabric of the former kind, in order to protect and cover that scheme of actions, which it pursues. The people being commonly very rude builders, especially in this speculative way, and more especially still, when actuated by party-zeal; it is natural to imagine, that their workmanship must be a little unshapely, and discover evident marks of that violence and hurry, in which it was raised. The one party, by tracing up Government to the Deity, endeavour to render it so sacred and inviolate, that it must be little less than sacrilege, however tyrannical it may become, to touch or invade it, in the smallest article. The other party, by founding government altogether on the consent of the People, suppose that there is a kind of *original contract*, by which the subjects have tacitly reserved the power of resisting their sovereign, whenever they find themselves aggrieved by that authority, with which they have, for certain purposes, voluntarily entrusted him. These are the speculative prin-

---

[1] Lib. ii. 5.
[2] He was cotemporary with Cæsar and Augustus.
[3] [Most of the references throughout these two volumes have been verified; and in very many cases the page, chapter, or line has been added.—Ed.]

ciples of the two parties; and these too are the practical consequences deduced from them.

I shall venture to affirm, *That both these systems of speculative principles are just; though not in the sense, intended by the parties:* And, *That both the schemes of practical consequences are prudent; though not in the extremes, to which each party, in opposition to the other, has commonly endeavoured to carry them.*

That the DEITY is the ultimate author of all government, will never be denied by any, who admit a general providence, and allow, that all events in the universe are conducted by an uniform plan, and directed to wise purposes. As it is impossible for the human race to subsist, at least in any comfortable or secure state, without the protection of government; this institution must certainly have been intended by that beneficent Being, who means the good of all his creatures: And as it has universally, in fact, taken place, in all countries, and all ages; we may conclude, with still greater certainty, that it was intended by that omniscient Being, who can never be deceived by any event or operation. But since he gave rise to it, not by any particular or miraculous interposition, but by his concealed and universal efficacy; a sovereign cannot, properly speaking, be called his vice-gerent, in any other sense than every power or force, being derived from him, may be said to act by his commission. Whatever actually happens is comprehended in the general plan or intention of providence; nor has the greatest and most lawful prince any more reason, upon that account, to plead a peculiar sacredness or inviolable authority, than an inferior magistrate, or even an usurper, or even a robber and a pyrate. The same divine superintendant, who, for wise purposes, invested [1] a TITUS or a TRAJAN with authority, did also, for purposes, no doubt, equally wise, though unknown, bestow power on a BORGIA or an ANGRIA. The same causes, which gave rise to the sovereign power in every state, established likewise every petty jurisdiction in it, and every limited authority. A constable, therefore, no less than a king, acts by a divine commission, and possesses an indefeasible right.

When we consider how nearly equal all men are in their bodily force, and even in their mental powers and faculties, till cultivated by education; we must necessarily allow, that

[1] [An Elizabeth or a Henry the 4th of France: Editions D to P.]

nothing but their own consent could, at first, associate them together, and subject them to any authority. The people, if we trace government to its first origin in the woods and desarts, are the source of all power and jurisdiction, and voluntarily, for the sake of peace and order, abandoned their native liberty, and received laws from their equal and companion. The conditions, upon which they were willing to submit, were either expressed, or were so clear and obvious, that it might well be esteemed superfluous to express them. If this, then, be meant by the *original contract*, it cannot be denied, that all government is, at first, founded on a contract, and that the most ancient rude combinations of mankind were formed chiefly by that principle. In vain, are we asked in what records this charter of our liberties is registered. It was not written on parchment, nor yet on leaves or barks of trees. It preceded the use of writing and all the other civilized arts of life. But we trace it plainly in the nature of man, and in the equality, [1] or something approaching equality, which we find in all the individuals of that species. The force, which now prevails, and which is founded on fleets and armies, is plainly political, and derived from authority, the effect of established government. A man's natural force consists only in the vigour of his limbs, and the firmness of his courage; which could never subject multitudes to the command of one. Nothing but their own consent, and their sense of the advantages resulting from peace and order, could have had that influence.

[2] Yet even this consent was long very imperfect, and could not be the basis of a regular administration. The chieftain, who had probably acquired his influence during the continuance of war, ruled more by persuasion than command; and till he could employ force to reduce the refractory and disobedient, the society could scarcely be said to have attained a state of civil government. No compact or agreement, it is evident, was expressly formed for general submission; an idea far beyond the comprehension of savages: Each exertion of authority in the chieftain must have been particular, and called forth by the present exigencies of the case: The sensible utility, resulting from his interposition, made these exertions become daily more frequent; and their frequency

---

[1] [Or—equality: added in Editions Q.]

[2] [This paragraph was added in Edtion R.]

gradually produced an habitual, and, if you please to call it so, a voluntary, and therefore precarious, acquiescence in the people.

But philosophers, who have embraced a party (if that be not a contradiction in terms) are not contented with these concessions. They assert, not only that government in its earliest infancy arose from consent or rather the voluntary acquiescence of the people; but also, that, even at present, when it has attained its full maturity, it rests on no other foundation. They affirm, that all men are still born equal, and owe allegiance to no prince or government, unless bound by the obligation and sanction of a *promise*. And as no man, without some equivalent, would forego the advantages of his native liberty, and subject himself to the will of another; this promise is always understood to be conditional, and imposes on him no obligation, unless he meet with justice and protection from his sovereign. These advantages the sovereign promises him in return; and if he fail in the execution, he has broken, on his part, the articles of engagement, and has thereby freed his subject from all obligations to allegiance. Such, according to these philosophers, is the foundation of authority in every government; and such the right of resistance, possessed by every subject.

But would these reasoners look abroad into the world, they would meet with nothing that, in the least, corresponds to their ideas, or can warrant so refined and philosophical a system. On the contrary, we find, every where, princes, who claim their subjects as their property, and assert their independent right of sovereignty, from conquest or succession. We find also, every where, subjects, who acknowledge this right in their prince, and suppose themselves born under obligations of obedience to a certain sovereign, as much as under the ties of reverence and duty to certain parents. These connexions are always conceived to be equally independent of our consent, in PERSIA and CHINA; in FRANCE and SPAIN; and even in HOLLAND and ENGLAND, wherever the doctrines above-mentioned have not been carefully inculcated. Obedience or subjection becomes so familiar, that most men never make any enquiry about its origin or cause, more than about the principle of gravity, resistance, or the most universal laws of nature. Or if curiosity ever move them; as soon as they learn, that they themselves and their ancestors have, for several ages, or from time immemorial, been subject to such a form of government or such a family; they immediately acquiesce, and acknowledge their obligation to allegiance. Were you to preach, in most parts of the world, that political connexions are founded altogether on voluntary consent or a mutual promise, the magistrate would soon imprison you, as seditious, for loosening the ties of obedience; if your friends did not before shut you up as delirious, for advancing such absurdities. It is strange, that an act of the mind, which every individual is supposed to have formed, and after he came to the use of reason too, otherwise it could have no authority; that this act, I say, should be so much unknown to all of them, that, over the face of the whole earth, there scarcely remain any traces or memory of it.

But the contract, on which government is founded, is said to be the *original contract*; and consequently may be supposed too old to fall under the knowledge of the present generation. If the agreement, by which savage men first associated and conjoined their force, be here meant, this is acknowledged to be real; but being so ancient, and being obliterated by a thousand changes of government and princes, it cannot now be supposed to retain any authority. If we would say any thing to the purpose, we must assert, that every particular government, which is lawful, and which imposes any duty of allegiance on the subject, was, at first, founded on consent and a voluntary compact. But besides that this supposes the consent of the fathers to bind the children, even to the most remote generations, (which republican writers will never allow) besides this, I say, it is not justified by history or experience, in any age or country of the world.

Almost all the governments, which exist at present, or of which there remains any record in story, have been founded originally, either on usurpation or conquest, or both, without any pretence of a fair consent, or voluntary subjection of the people. When an artful and bold man is placed at the head of an army or faction, it is often easy for him, by employing, sometimes violence, sometimes false pretences, to establish his dominion over a people a hundred times more numerous than his partizans. He allows no such open communication, that his enemies can know, with certainty, their number or force. He gives them no leisure to assemble together in a body to oppose him. Even all those, who are the instruments of his usurpation, may wish his fall; but their ignorance of each other's intention keeps them in awe, and is the sole cause of his security. By such arts as these, many governments have been established; and this is all the *original contract*, which they have to boast of.

The face of the earth is continually changing, by the encrease of small kingdoms into great empires, by the dissolution of great empires into smaller kingdoms, by the planting of colonies, by the migration of tribes. Is there any thing discoverable in all these events, but force and violence? Where is the mutual agreement or voluntary association so much talked of?

Even the smoothest way, by which a nation may receive a foreign master, by marriage or a will, is not extremely honourable for the people; but supposes them to be disposed of, like a dowry or a legacy, according to the pleasure or interest of their rulers.

But where no force interposes, and election takes place; what is this election so highly vaunted? It is either the combination of a few great men, who decide for the whole, and will allow of no opposition: Or it is the fury of a multitude, that follow a seditious ringleader, who is not known, perhaps, to a dozen among them, and who owes his advancement merely to his own impudence, or to the momentary caprice of his fellows.

Are these disorderly elections, which are rare too, of such mighty authority, as to be the only lawful foundation of all government and allegiance?

In reality, there is not a more terrible event, than a total dissolution of government, which gives liberty to the multitude, and makes the determination or choice of a new establishment depend upon a number, which nearly approaches to that of the body of the people: For it never comes entirely to the whole body of them. Every wise man, then, wishes to see, at the head of a powerful and obedient army, a general, who may speedily seize the prize, and give to the people a master, which they are so unfit to chuse for themselves. So little correspondent is fact and reality to those philosophical notions.

Let not the establishment at the *Revolution* deceive us, or make us so much in love with a philosophical origin to government, as to imagine all others monstrous and irregular. Even that event was far from corresponding to these refined ideas. It was only the succession, and that only in the regal part of the government, which was then changed: And it was only the majority of seven hundred, who determined that change for near ten millions. I doubt not, indeed, but the bulk of those ten millions acquiesced willingly in the determination: But was the matter left, in the least, to their choice? Was it not justly supposed to be, from that moment, decided, and every man punished, who refused to submit to the new sovereign? How otherwise could the matter have ever been brought to any issue or conclusion?

The republic of ATHENS was, I believe, the most extensive democracy, that we read of in history: Yet if we make the requisite allowances for the women, the slaves, and the strangers, we shall find, that that establishment was not, at first, made, nor any law ever voted, by a tenth part of those who were bound to pay obedience to it: Not to mention the islands and foreign dominions, which the ATHENIANS claimed as theirs by right of conquest. And as it is well known, that popular assemblies in that city were always full of licence and disorder, notwithstanding the institutions and laws by which they were checked: How much more disorderly must they prove, where they form not the established constitution, but meet tumultuously on the dissolution of the ancient government, in order to give rise to a new one? How chimerical must it be to talk of a choice in such circumstances?

[1] The ACHÆANS enjoyed the freest and most perfect democracy of all antiquity; yet they employed force to oblige some cities to enter into their league, as we learn from POLYBIUS.[2]

HARRY the IVth and HARRY the VIIth of ENGLAND, had really no title to the throne but a parliamentary election; yet they never would acknowledge it, lest they should thereby weaken their authority. Strange, if the only real foundation of all authority be consent and promise!

It is in vain to say, that all governments are or should be, at first, founded on popular consent, as much as the necessity of human affairs will admit. This favours entirely my

[1] [The two following paragraphs were added in Edition K.]
[2] Lib. ii. cap. 38.

pretension. I maintain, that human affairs will never admit of this consent; seldom of the appearance of it. But that conquest or usurpation, that is, in plain terms, force, by dissolving the ancient governments, is the origin of almost all the new ones, which were ever established in the world. And that in the few cases, where consent may seem to have taken place, it was commonly so irregular, so confined, or so much intermixed either with fraud or violence, that it cannot have any great authority.

[1] My intention here is not to exclude the consent of the people from being one just foundation of government where it has place. It is surely the best and most sacred of any. I only pretend, that it has very seldom had place in any degree, and never almost in its full extent. And that therefore some other foundation of government must also be admitted.

Were all men possessed of so inflexible a regard to justice, that, of themselves, they would totally abstain from the properties of others; they had for ever remained in a state of absolute liberty, without subjection to any magistrate or political society : But this is a state of perfection, of which human nature is justly deemed incapable. Again; were all men possessed of so perfect an understanding, as always to know their own interests, no form of government had ever been submitted to, but what was established on consent, and was fully canvassed by every member of the society : But this state of perfection is likewise much superior to human nature. Reason, history, and experience shew us, that all political societies have had an origin much less accurate and regular; and were one to choose a period of time, when the people's consent was the least regarded in public transactions, it would be precisely on the establishment of a new government. In a settled constitution, their inclinations are often consulted; but during the fury of revolutions, conquests, and public convulsions, military force or political craft usually decides the controversy.

When a new government is established, by whatever means, the people are commonly dissatisfied with it, and pay obedience more from fear and necessity, than from any idea of allegiance or of moral obligation. The prince is watchful and jealous, and must carefully guard against every beginning or appearance of insurrection. Time, by degrees,

[1] [This paragraph and the next were added in Edition K.]

removes all these difficulties, and accustoms the nation to regard, as their lawful or native princes, that family, which, at first, they considered as usurpers or foreign conquerors. In order to found this opinion, they have no recourse to any notion of voluntary consent or promise, which, they know, never was, in this case, either expected or demanded. The original establishment was formed by violence, and submitted to from necessity. The subsequent administration is also supported by power, and acquiesced in by the people, not as a matter of choice, but of obligation. They imagine not that their consent gives their prince a title: But they willingly consent, because they think, that, from long possession, he has acquired a title, independent of their choice or inclination.

Should it be said, that, by living under the dominion of a prince, which one might leave, every individual has given a *tacit* consent to his authority, and promised him obedience; it may be answered, that such an implied consent can only have place, where a man imagines, that the matter depends on his choice. But where he thinks (as all mankind do who are born under established governments) that by his birth he owes allegiance to a certain prince or certain form of government; it would be absurd to infer a consent or choice, which he expressly, in this case, renounces and disclaims.

Can we seriously say, that a poor peasant or artizan has a free choice to leave his country, when he knows no foreign language or manners, and lives from day to day, by the small wages which he acquires? We may as well assert, that a man, by remaining in a vessel, freely consents to the dominion of the master; though he was carried on board while asleep, and must leap into the ocean, and perish, the moment he leaves her.

What if the prince forbid his subjects to quit his dominions; as in TIBERIUS's time, it was regarded as a crime in a ROMAN knight that he had attempted to fly to the PARTHIANS, in order to escape the tyranny of that emperor?[1] Or as the ancient MUSCOVITES prohibited all travelling under pain of death? And did a prince observe, that many of his subjects were seized with the frenzy of migrating to foreign countries, he would doubtless, with great reason and justice, restrain them, in order to prevent the depopulation of his own kingdom. Would he forfeit the allegiance of all his subjects, by

[1] TACIT. Ann. vi. cap. 14.

so wise and reasonable a law? Yet the freedom of their choice is surely, in that case, ravished from them.

A company of men, who should leave their native country, in order to people some uninhabited region, might dream of recovering their native freedom; but they would soon find, that their prince still laid claim to them, and called them his subjects, even in their new settlement. And in this he would but act conformably to the common ideas of mankind.

The truest *tacit* consent of this kind, that is ever observed, is when a foreigner settles in any country, and is beforehand acquainted with the prince, and government, and laws, to which he must submit: Yet is his allegiance, though more voluntary, much less expected or depended on, than that of a natural born subject. On the contrary, his native prince still asserts a claim to him. And if he punish not the renegade, when he seizes him in war with his new prince's commission; this clemency is not founded on the municipal law, which in all countries condemns the prisoner; but on the consent of princes, who have agreed to this indulgence, in order to prevent reprisals.

[1] Did one generation of men go off the stage at once, and another succeed, as is the case with silk-worms and butterflies, the new race, if they had sense enough to choose their government, which surely is never the case with men, might voluntarily, and by general consent, establish their own form of civil polity, without any regard to the laws or precedents, which prevailed among their ancestors. But as human society is in perpetual flux, one man every hour going out of the world, another coming into it, it is necessary, in order to preserve stability in government, that the new brood should conform themselves to the established constitution, and nearly follow the path which their fathers, treading in the footsteps of theirs, had marked out to them. Some innovations must necessarily have place in every human institution, and it is happy where the enlightened genius of the age gives these a direction to the side of reason, liberty, and justice: but violent innovations no individual is entitled to make: they are even dangerous to be attempted by the legislature: more ill than good is ever to be expected from them: and if history affords examples to the contrary, they are not to be drawn into precedent, and are only to be regarded as proofs, that the science of politics affords few rules, which will not admit of

[1] [This paragraph was added in Edition R.]

some exception, and which may not sometimes be controuled by fortune and accident. The violent innovations in the reign of HENRY VIII. proceeded from an imperious monarch, seconded by the appearance of legislative authority : Those in the reign of CHARLES I. were derived from faction and fanaticism, and both of them have proved happy in the issue : But even the former were long the source of many disorders, and still more dangers; and if the measures of allegiance were to be taken from the latter, a total anarchy must have place in human society, and a final period at once be put to every government.

Suppose, that an usurper, after having banished his lawful prince and royal family, should establish his dominion for ten or a dozen years in any country, and should preserve so exact a discipline in his troops, and so regular a disposition in his garrisons, that no insurrection had ever been raised, or even murmur heard, against his administration: Can it be asserted, that the people, who in their hearts abhor his treason, have tacitly consented to his authority, and promised him allegiance, merely because, from necessity, they live under his dominion? Suppose again their native prince restored, by means of an army, which he levies in foreign countries : They receive him with joy and exultation, and shew plainly with what reluctance they had submitted to any other yoke. I may now ask, upon what foundation the prince's title stands? Not on popular consent surely : For though the people willingly acquiesce in his authority, they never imagine, that their consent made him sovereign. They consent; because they apprehend him to be already, by birth, their lawful sovereign. And as to that tacit consent, which may now be inferred from their living under his dominion, this is no more than what they formerly gave to the tyrant and usurper.

When we assert, that all lawful government arises from the consent of the people, we certainly do them a great deal more honour than they deserve, or even expect and desire from us. After the ROMAN dominions became too unwieldly for the republic to govern them, the people, over the whole known world, were extremely grateful to AUGUSTUS for that authority, which, by violence, he had established over them; and they showed an equal disposition to submit to the successor, whom he left them, by his last will and testament. It was afterwards their misfortune, that there never was, in one family, any long regular succession; but that their line of princes was continually broken, either by private assassinations or public rebellions. The *prætorian* bands, on the failure of every family, set up one emperor; the legions in the East a second; those in GERMANY, perhaps, a third: And the sword alone could decide the controversy. The condition of the people, in that mighty monarchy, was to be lamented, not because the choice of the emperor was never left to them; for that was impracticable: But because they never fell under any succession of masters, who might regularly follow each other. As to the violence and wars and bloodshed, occasioned by every new settlement; these were not blameable, because they were inevitable.

The house of LANCASTER ruled in this island about sixty years;[1] yet the partizans of the white rose seemed daily to multiply in ENGLAND. The present establishment has taken place during a still longer period. Have all views of right in another family been utterly extinguished; even though scarce any man now alive had arrived at years of discretion, when it was expelled, or could have consented to its dominion, or have promised it allegiance? A sufficient indication surely of the general sentiment of mankind on this head. For we blame not the partizans of the abdicated family, merely on account of the long time, during which they have preserved their imaginary loyalty. We blame them for adhering to a family, which, we affirm, has been justly expelled, and which, from the moment the new settlement took place, had forfeited all title to authority.

But would we have a more regular, at least a more philosophical, refutation of this principle of an original contract or popular consent; perhaps, the following observations may suffice.

All *moral* duties may be divided into two kinds. The *first* are those, to which men are impelled by a natural instinct or immediate propensity, which operates on them, independent of all ideas of obligation, and of all views, either to public or private utility. Of this nature are, love of children, gratitude to benefactors, pity to the unfortunate. When we reflect on the advantage, which results to society from such humane instincts, we pay them the just tribute of moral approba-

---

[1] [The latter half of this sentence was added in Edition K.]

tion and esteem: But the person, actuated by them, feels their power and influence, antecedent to any such reflection.

The *second* kind of moral duties are such as are not supported by any original instinct of nature, but are performed entirely from a sense of obligation, when we consider the necessities of human society, and the impossibility of supporting it, if these duties were neglected. It is thus *justice* or a regard to the property of others, *fidelity* or the observance of promises, become obligatory, and acquire an authority over mankind. For as it is evident, that every man loves himself better than any other person, he is naturally impelled to extend his acquisitions as much as possible; and nothing can restrain him in this propensity, but reflection and experience, by which he learns the pernicious effects of that licence, and the total dissolution of society which must ensue from it. His original inclination, therefore, or instinct, is here checked and restrained by a subsequent judgment or observation.

The case is precisely the same with the political or civil duty of *allegiance*, as with the natural duties of justice and fidelity. Our primary instincts lead us, either to indulge ourselves in unlimited freedom, or to seek dominion over others: And it is reflection only, which engages us to sacrifice such strong passions to the interests of peace and public order. A small degree of experience and observation suffices to teach us, that society cannot possibly be maintained without the authority of magistrates, and that this authority must soon fall into contempt, where exact obedience is not paid to it. The observation of these general and obvious interests is the source of all allegiance, and of that moral obligation, which we attribute to it.

What necessity, therefore, is there to found the duty of *allegiance* or obedience to magistrates on that of *fidelity* or a regard to promises, and to suppose, that it is the consent of each individual, which subjects him to government; when it appears, that both allegiance and fidelity stand precisely on the same foundation, and are both submitted to by mankind, on account of the apparent interests and necessities of human society? We are bound to obey our sovereign, it is said; because we have given a tacit promise to that purpose. But why are we bound to observe our promise? It must here be asserted, that the commerce and intercourse of mankind, which are of such mighty advantage, can have no security where men pay no regard to their engagements. In like manner, may it be said, that men could not live at all in society, at least in a civilized society, without laws and magistrates and judges, to prevent the encroachments of the strong upon the weak, of the violent upon the just and equitable. The obligation to allegiance being of like force and authority with the obligation to fidelity, we gain nothing by resolving the one into the other. The general interests or necessities of society are sufficient to establish both.

If the reason be asked of that obedience, which we are bound to pay to government, I readily answer, *because society could not otherwise subsist*: And this answer is clear and intelligible to all mankind. Your answer is, *because we should keep our word*. But besides, that no body, till trained in a philosophical system, can either comprehend or relish this answer: Besides this, I say, you find yourself embarrassed, when it is asked, *why we are bound to keep our word?* Nor can you give any answer, but what would, immediately, without any circuit, have accounted for our obligation to allegiance.

But *to whom is allegiance due? And who is our lawful sovereign?* This question is often the most difficult of any, and liable to infinite discussions. When people are so happy, that they can answer, *Our present sovereign, who inherits, in a direct line, from ancestors, that have governed us for many ages;* this answer admits of no reply; even though historians, in tracing up to the remotest antiquity, the origin of that royal family, may find, as commonly happens, that its first authority was derived from usurpation and violence. It is confessed, that private justice, or the abstinence from the properties of others, is a most cardinal virtue: Yet reason tells us, that there is no property in durable objects, such as lands or houses, when carefully examined in passing from hand to hand, but must, in some period, have been founded on fraud and injustice. The necessities of human society, neither in private nor public life, will allow of such an accurate enquiry: And there is no virtue or moral duty, but what may, with facility, be refined away, if we indulge a false philosophy, in sifting and scrutinizing it, by every captious rule of logic, in every light or position, in which it may be placed.

The questions with regard to private property have filled

infinite volumes of law and philosophy, if in both we add the commentators to the original text; and in the end, we may safely pronounce, that many of the rules, there established, are uncertain, ambiguous, and arbitrary. The like opinion may be formed with regard to the succession and rights of princes and forms of government.[1] Several cases, no doubt, occur, especially in the infancy of any constitution, which admit of no determination from the laws of justice and equity: And our historian RAPIN [2]pretends, that the controversy between EDWARD the THIRD and PHILIP DE VALOIS was of this nature, and could be decided only by an appeal to heaven, that is, by war and violence.

Who shall tell me, whether GERMANICUS or DRUSUS ought to have succeeded to TIBERIUS, had he died, while they were both alive, without naming any of them for his successor? Ought the right of adoption to be received as equivalent to that of blood, in a nation, where it had the same effect in private families, and had already, in two instances, taken place in the public? Ought GERMANICUS to be esteemed the elder son because he was born before DRUSUS; or the younger, because he was adopted after the birth of his brother? Ought the right of the elder to be regarded in a nation, where he had no advantage in the succession of private families? Ought the ROMAN empire at that time to be deemed hereditary, because of two examples; or ought it, even so early, to be regarded as belonging to the stronger or to the present possessor, as being founded on so recent an usurpation?

COMMODUS mounted the throne after a pretty long succession of excellent emperors, who had acquired their title, not by birth, or public election, but by the fictitious rite of adoption. That bloody debauchee being murdered by a conspiracy suddenly formed between his wench and her gallant, who happened at that time to be *Prætorian Præfect*; these immediately deliberated about choosing a master to human kind, to speak in the style of those ages; and they cast their

---

[1] [Edition D omits from this sentence down to 'monarchies' on page 459: and substitutes as follows—The Discussion of these Matters would lead us entirely beyond the Compass of these Essays. 'Tis sufficient for our present Purpose, if we have been able to determine, in general, the Foundation of that Allegiance, which is due to the established Government, in every Kingdom and Commonwealth. When there is no legal Prince, who has a Title to a Throne, I believe it may safely be determined to belong to the first Occupier. This was frequently the Case with the ROMAN Empire.]

Allows: Editions K to P.]

eyes on PERTINAX. Before the tyrant's death was known, the *Præfect* went secretly to that senator, who, on the appearance of the soldiers, imagined that his execution had been ordered by COMMODUS. He was immediately saluted emperor by the officer and his attendants; chearfully proclaimed by the populace; unwillingly submitted to by the guards; formally recognized by the senate; and passively received by the provinces and armies of the empire.

The discontent of the *Prætorian* bands broke out in a sudden sedition, which occasioned the murder of that excellent prince: And the world being now without a master and without government, the guards thought proper to set the empire formally to sale. JULIAN, the purchaser, was proclaimed by the soldiers, recognized by the senate, and submitted to by the people; and must also have been submitted to by the provinces, had not the envy of the legions begotten opposition and resistance. PESCENNIUS NIGER in SYRIA elected himself emperor, gained the tumultuary consent of his army, and was attended with the secret good-will of the senate and people of ROME. ALBINUS in BRITAIN found an equal right to set up his claim; but SEVERUS, who governed PANNONIA, prevailed in the end above both of them. That able politician and warrior, finding his own birth and dignity too much inferior to the imperial crown, professed, at first, an intention only of revenging the death of PERTINAX. He marched as general into ITALY; defeated JULIAN; and without our being able to fix any precise commencement even of the soldiers' consent, he was from necessity acknowledged emperor by the senate and people; and fully established in his violent authority by subduing NIGER and ALBINUS.[1]

Inter hæc Gordianus CÆSAR (says CAPITOLINUS, speaking of another period) *sublatus a militibus,* Imperator *est appellatus, quia non erat alius in præsenti,* It is to be remarked, that GORDIAN was a boy of fourteen years of age.

Frequent instances of a like nature occur in the history of the emperors; in that of ALEXANDER's successors; and of many other countries: Nor can anything be more unhappy than a despotic government of this kind; where the succession is disjoined and irregular, and must be determined, on every vacancy, by force or election. In a free government, the matter is often unavoidable, and is also much less dan-

[1] HERODIAN, lib. ii.

gerous. The interests of liberty may there frequently lead the people, in their own defence, to alter the succession of the crown. And the constitution, being compounded of parts, may still maintain a sufficient stability, by resting on the aristocratical or democratical members, though the monarchical be altered, from time to time, in order to accommodate it to the former.

In an absolute government, when there is no legal prince, who has a title to the throne, it may safely be determined to belong to the first occupant. Instances of this kind are but too frequent, especially in the eastern monarchies. [1] When any race of princes expires, the will or destination of the last sovereign will be regarded as a title. Thus the edict of LEWIS the XIVth, who called the bastard princes to the succession in case of the failure of all the legitimate princes, would, in such an event, have some authority.[2] [3] Thus the will of CHARLES the Second disposed of the whole SPANISH monarchy. The cession of the ancient proprietor, especially when joined to conquest, is likewise deemed a good title. The general obligation, which binds us to government, is the interest and necessities of society; and this obligation is very strong. The determination of it to this or that particular prince or form of government is frequently more uncertain and dubious. Present possession has considerable authority in these cases, and greater than in private property; because of the disorders which attend all revolutions and changes of government.[4]

---

[1] [In Edition D the remainder of this paragraph is given in continuation of the following note.]

[2] It is remarkable, that, in the remonstrance of the duke of BOURBON and the legitimate princes, against this destination of LOUIS the XIVth, the doctrine of the *original contract* is insisted on, even in that absolute government. The FRENCH nation, say they, chusing HUGH CAPET and his posterity to rule over them and their posterity, where the former line fails, there is a tacit right reserved to choose a new royal family; and this right is invaded by calling the bastard princes to the throne, without the consent of the nation. But the Comte de BOULAINVILLIERS, who wrote in defence of the bastard princes, ridicules this notion of an original contract, especially when applied to HUGH CAPET; who mounted the throne, says he, by the same arts, which have ever been employed by all conquerors and usurpers. He got his title, indeed, recognized by the states after he had put himself in possession: But is this a choice or a contract? The Comte de BOULAINVILLIERS, we may observe, was a noted republican; but being a man of learning, and very conversant in history, he knew that the people were never almost consulted in these revolutions and new establishments, and that time alone bestowed right and authority on what was commonly at first founded on force and violence. See *Etat de la France*, Vol. III.

[3] [This sentence was added in Edition M.]

[4] [Here Editions K to P subjoin in a note what is now the concluding paragraph of the Essay.]

We shall only observe, before we conclude, that, though an appeal to general opinion may justly, in the speculative sciences of metaphysics, natural philosophy, or astronomy, be deemed unfair and inconclusive, yet in all questions with regard to morals, as well as criticism, there is really no other standard, by which any controversy can ever be decided. And nothing is a clearer proof, that a theory of this kind is erroneous, than to find, that it leads to paradoxes, repugnant to the common sentiments of mankind, and to the practice and opinion of all nations and all ages. The doctrine, which founds all lawful government on an *original contract*, or consent of the people, is plainly of this kind; nor has the most noted of its partizans, in prosecution of it, scrupled to affirm, *that absolute monarchy is inconsistent with civil society, and so can be no form of civil government at all;*[1] and *that the supreme power in a state cannot take from any man, by taxes and impositions, any part of his property, without his own consent or that of his representatives.*[2] What authority any moral reasoning can have, which leads into opinions so wide of the general practice of mankind, in every place but this single kingdom, it is easy to determine.[3]

The only passage I meet with in antiquity, where the obligation of obedience to government is ascribed to a promise, is in Plato's *Crito* : where Socrates refuses to escape from prison, because he had tacitly promised to obey the laws. Thus he builds a *tory* consequence of passive obedience, on a *whig* foundation of the original contract.

New discoveries are not to be expected in these matters. If scarce any man, till very lately, ever imagined that government was founded on compact, it is certain that it cannot, in general, have any such foundation.

The crime of rebellion among the ancients was commonly expressed by the terms νεωτερίζειν, *novas res moliri*.

Essay XIII.—*Of Passive Obedience.*

In the former essay, we endeavoured to refute the *speculative* systems of politics advanced in this nation; as well the

---

[1] See Locke on Government, chap. vii. § 90.
[2] Id. chap. xi. § 138, 139, 140.
[3] [At this point editions D to P stop. Editions K to P give the two next paragraphs as a note; they have already given the concluding one as a note on page 492.]

religious system of the one party, as the philosophical of the other. We come now to examine the *practical* consequences, deduced by each party, with regard to the measures of submission due to sovereigns.

As the obligation to justice is founded entirely on the interests of society, which require mutual abstinence from property, in order to preserve peace among mankind; it is evident, that, when the execution of justice would be attended with very pernicious consequences, that virtue must be suspended, and give place to public utility, in such extraordinary and such pressing emergencies. The maxim, *fiat Justitia et ruat Cœlum*, let justice be performed, though the universe be destroyed, is apparently false, and by sacrificing the end to the means, shews a preposterous idea of the subordination of duties. What governor of a town makes any scruple of burning the suburbs, when they facilitate the approaches of the enemy? Or what general abstains from plundering a neutral country, when the necessities of war require it, and he cannot otherwise subsist his army? The case is the same with the duty of allegiance; and common sense teaches us, that, as government binds us to obedience only on account of its tendency to public utility, that duty must always, in extraordinary cases, when public ruin would evidently attend obedience, yield to the primary and original obligation. *Salus populi suprema Lex*, the safety of the people is the supreme law. This maxim is agreeable to the sentiments of mankind in all ages: Nor is any one, when he reads of the insurrections against NERO[1] or PHILIP the Second, so infatuated with party-systems, as not to wish success to the enterprize, and praise the undertakers. Even our high monarchical party, in spite of their sublime theory, are forced, in such cases, to judge, and feel, and approve, in conformity to the rest of mankind.

Resistance, therefore, being admitted in extraordinary emergencies, the question can only be among good reasoners, with regard to the degree of necessity, which can justify resistance, and render it lawful or commendable. And here I must confess, that I shall always incline to their side, who draw the bond of allegiance very close, and consider an infringement of it, as the last refuge in desperate cases, when the public is in the highest danger, from violence and

[1] [Or a Caracalla: Edition D; or a Philip: Editions K to P.]

tyranny. For besides the mischiefs of a civil war, which commonly attends insurrection, it is certain, that, where a disposition to rebellion appears among any people, it is one chief cause of tyranny in the rulers, and forces them into many violent measures which they never would have embraced, had every one been inclined to submission and obedience. Thus the *tyrannicide* or assassination, approved of by ancient maxims, instead of keeping tyrants and usurpers in awe, made them ten times more fierce and unrelenting; and is now justly, upon that account, abolished by the laws of nations, and universally condemned as a base and treacherous method of bringing to justice these disturbers of society.

Besides we must consider, that, as obedience is our duty in the common course of things, it ought chiefly to be inculcated; nor can any thing be more preposterous than an anxious care and solicitude in stating all the cases, in which resistance may be allowed. In like manner, though a philosopher reasonably acknowledges, in the course of an argument, that the rules of justice may be dispensed with in cases of urgent necessity; what should we think of a preacher or casuist who should make it his chief study to find out such cases, and enforce them with all the vehemence of argument and eloquence? Would he not be better employed in inculcating the general doctrine, than in displaying the particular exceptions, which we are, perhaps, but too much inclined, of ourselves, to embrace and to extend?

There are, however, two reasons, which may be pleaded in defence of that party among us, who have, with so much industry, propagated the maxims of resistance; maxims, which, it must be confessed, are, in general, so pernicious, and so destructive of civil society. The *first* is, that their antagonists carrying the doctrine of obedience to such an extravagant height, as not only never to mention the exceptions in extraordinary cases (which might, perhaps, be excusable), but even positively to exclude them; it became necessary to insist on these exceptions, and defend the rights of injured truth and liberty. The *second*, and, perhaps, better reason, is founded on the nature of the BRITISH constitution and form of government.

It is almost peculiar to our constitution to establish a first magistrate with such high pre-eminence and dignity, that, though limited by the laws, he is, in a manner, so far as regards his own person, above the laws, and can neither be questioned nor punished for any injury or wrong, which may be committed by him. His ministers alone, or those who act by his commission, are obnoxious to justice; and while the prince is thus allured, by the prospect of personal safety, to give the laws their free course, an equal security is, in effect, obtained by the punishment of lesser offenders, and at the same time a civil war is avoided, which would be the infallible consequence, were an attack, at every turn, made directly upon the sovereign. But though the constitution pays this salutary compliment to the prince, it can never reasonably be understood, by that maxim, to have determined its own destruction, or to have established a tame submission, where he protects his ministers, perseveres in injustice, and usurps the whole power of the commonwealth. This case, indeed, is never expressly put by the laws; because it is impossible for them, in their ordinary course, to provide a remedy for it, or establish any magistrate, with superior authority, to chastise the exorbitancies of the prince. But as a right without a remedy would be an absurdity; the remedy, in this case, is the extraordinary one of resistance, when affairs come to that extremity, that the constitution can be defended by it alone. Resistance therefore must, of course, become more frequent in the BRITISH government, than in others, which are simpler, and consist of fewer parts and movements. Where the king is an absolute sovereign, he has little temptation to commit such enormous tyranny as may justly provoke rebellion: But where he is limited, his imprudent ambition, without any great vices, may run him into that perilous situation. This is frequently supposed to have been the case with CHARLES the First; and if we may now speak truth, after animosities are ceased, this was also the case with JAMES the Second. These were harmless, if not, in their private character, good men; but mistaking the nature of our constitution, and engrossing the whole legislative power, it became necessary to oppose them with some vehemence; and even to deprive the latter formally of that authority, which he had used with such imprudence and indiscretion.

ESSAY XIV.—*Of the Coalition of Parties.*[1]

To abolish all distinctions of party may not be practicable, perhaps not desirable, in a free government. The only dangerous parties are such as entertain opposite views with regard to the essentials of government, the succession of the crown, or the more considerable privileges belonging to the several members of the constitution; where there is no room for any compromise or accommodation, and where the controversy may appear so momentous as to justify even an opposition by arms to the pretensions of antagonists. Of this nature was the animosity, continued for above a century past, between the parties in ENGLAND; an animosity which broke out sometimes into civil war, which occasioned violent revolutions, and which continually endangered the peace and tranquillity of the nation. But as there have appeared of late the strongest symptoms of an universal desire to abolish these party distinctions; this tendency to a coalition affords the most agreeable prospect of future happiness, and ought to be carefully cherished and promoted by every lover of his country.

There is not a more effectual method of promoting so good an end, than to prevent all unreasonable insult and triumph of the one party over the other, to encourage moderate opinions, to find the proper medium in all disputes, to persuade each that its antagonist may possibly be sometimes in the right, and to keep a balance in the praise and blame, which we bestow on either side. The two former Essays, concerning the *original contract* and *passive obedience*, are calculated for this purpose with regard to the *philosophical*[2] and *practical* controversies between the parties, and tend to show that neither side are in these respects so fully supported by reason as they endeavour to flatter themselves. We shall proceed to exercise the same moderation with regard to the *historical* disputes between the parties, by proving that each of them was justified by plausible topics; that there were on both sides wise men, who meant well to their country; and that the past animosity between the factions had no

---

[1] [This Essay first appeared in Edition M.]

[2] [And practical: added in Edition R.]

better foundation than narrow prejudice or interested passion.

The popular party, who afterwards acquired the name of whigs, might justify, by very specious arguments, that opposition to the crown, from which our present free constitution is derived. Though obliged to acknowledge, that precedents in favour of prerogative had uniformly taken place during many reigns before CHARLES the First, they thought, that there was no reason for submitting any longer to so dangerous an authority. Such might have been their reasoning: As the rights of mankind are for ever to be deemed sacred, no prescription of tyranny or arbitrary power can have authority sufficient to abolish them. Liberty is a blessing so inestimable, that, wherever there appears any probability of recovering it, a nation may willingly run many hazards, and ought not even to repine at the greatest effusion of blood or dissipation of treasure. All human institutions, and none more than government, are in continual fluctuation. Kings are sure to embrace every opportunity of extending their prerogatives: And if favourable incidents be not also laid hold of for extending and securing the privileges of the people, an universal despotism must for ever prevail amongst mankind. The example of all the neighbouring nations proves, that it is no longer safe to entrust with the crown the same high prerogatives, which had formerly been exercised during the rude and simple ages. And though the example of many late reigns may be pleaded in favour of a power in the prince somewhat arbitrary, more remote reigns afford instances of stricter limitations imposed on the crown; and those pretensions of the parliament, now branded with the title of innovations, are only a recovery of the just rights of the people.

These views, far from being odious, are surely large, and generous, and noble: To their prevalence and success the kingdom owes its liberty; perhaps its learning, its industry, commerce, and naval power: By them chiefly the ENGLISH name is distinguished among the society of nations, and aspires to a rivalship with that of the freest and most illustrious commonwealths of antiquity. But as all these mighty consequences could not reasonably be foreseen at the time when the contest began, the royalists of that age wanted not specious arguments on their side, by which they could justify their defence of the then established prerogatives of the prince. We shall state the question, as it might have appeared to them at the assembling of that parliament, which, by its violent encroachments on the crown, began the civil wars.

The only rule of government, they might have said, known and acknowledged among men, is use and practice: Reason is so uncertain a guide that it will always be exposed to doubt and controversy: Could it ever render itself prevalent over the people, men had always retained it as their sole rule of conduct: They had still continued in the primitive, unconnected, state of nature, without submitting to political government, whose sole basis is, not pure reason, but authority and precedent. Dissolve these ties, you break all the bonds of civil society, and leave every man at liberty to consult his private interest, by those expedients, which his appetite, disguised under the appearance of reason, shall dictate to him. The spirit of innovation is in itself pernicious, however favourable its particular object may sometimes appear: A truth so obvious, that the popular party themselves are sensible of it; and therefore cover their encroachments on the crown by the plausible pretence of their recovering the ancient liberties of the people.

But the present prerogatives of the crown, allowing all the suppositions of that party, have been incontestably established ever since the accession of the House of TUDOR; a period, which, as it now comprehends a hundred and sixty years, may be allowed sufficient to give stability to any constitution. Would it not have appeared ridiculous, in the reign of the Emperor ADRIAN, to have talked of the republican constitution as the rule of government; or to have supposed, that the former rights of the senate, and consuls, and tribunes were still subsisting?

But the present claims of the ENGLISH monarchs are much more favourable than those of the ROMAN emperors during that age. The authority of AUGUSTUS was a plain usurpation, grounded only on military violence, and forms such an epoch in the ROMAN history, as is obvious to every reader. But if HENRY VII. really, as some pretend, enlarged the power of the crown, it was only by insensible acquisitions, which escaped the apprehension of the people, and have scarcely been remarked even by historians and politicians.

The new government, if it deserve the epithet, is an imperceptible transition from the former; is entirely engrafted on it; derives its title fully from that root; and is to be considered only as one of those gradual revolutions, to which human affairs, in every nation, will be for ever subject.

The House of TUDOR, and after them that of STUART, exercised no prerogatives, but what had been claimed and exercised by the PLANTAGENETS. Not a single branch of their authority can be said to be an innovation. The only difference is, that, perhaps, former kings exerted these powers only by intervals, and were not able, by reason of the opposition of their barons, to render them so steady a rule of administration.[1] But the sole inference from this fact is, that those ancient times were more turbulent and seditious; and that royal authority, the constitution, and the laws have happily of late gained the ascendant.

Under what pretence can the popular party now speak of recovering the ancient constitution? The former controul over the kings was not placed in the commons, but in the barons: The people had no authority, and even little or no liberty; till the crown, by suppressing these factious tyrants, enforced the execution of the laws, and obliged all the subjects equally to respect each others rights, privileges, and properties. If we must return to the ancient barbarous and [2] feudal constitution; let those gentlemen, who now behave themselves with so much insolence to their sovereign, set the first example. Let them make court to be admitted as retainers to a neighbouring baron; and by submitting to slavery under him, acquire some protection to themselves: together with the power of exercising rapine and oppression over their inferior slaves and villains. This was the condition of the commons among their remote ancestors.

But how far back must we go, in having recourse to ancient constitutions and governments? There was a constitution still more ancient than that to which these innovators affect so much to appeal. During that period there was no *magna*

---

[1] [Editions M to Q append the note: The author believes that he was the first writer who advanced that the family of TUDOR possessed in general more authority than their immediate predecessors: An opinion, which, he hopes, will be supported by history, but which he proposes with some diffidence. There are strong symptoms of arbitrary power in some former reigns, even after signing of the charters. The power of the crown in that age depended less on the constitution than on the capacity and vigour of the prince who wore it.

[2] [GOTHIC: Editions M to Q.]

charta: The barons themselves possessed few regular, stated privileges: And the house of commons probably had not an existence.

It is ridiculous to hear the commons, while they are assuming, by usurpation, the whole power of government, talk of reviving ancient institutions. Is it not known, that, though representatives received wages from their constituents; to be a member of the lower house was always considered as a burden, and an exemption from it as a privilege? Will they persuade us, that power, which, of all human acquisitions, is the most coveted, and in comparison of which even reputation and pleasure and riches are slighted, could ever be regarded as a burden by any man?

The property, acquired of late by the commons, it is said, entitles them to more power than their ancestors enjoyed. But to what is this encrease of their property owing, but to an encrease of their liberty and their security? Let them therefore acknowledge, that their ancestors, while the crown was restrained by the seditious barons, really enjoyed less liberty than they themselves have attained, after the sovereign acquired the ascendant: And let them enjoy that liberty with moderation; and not forfeit it by new exorbitant claims, and by rendering it a pretence for endless innovations.

The true rule of government is the present established practice of the age. That has most authority, because it is recent: It is also best known, for the same reason. Who has assured those tribunes, that the PLANTAGENETS did not exercise as high acts of authority as the TUDORS? Historians, they say, do not mention them. But historians are also silent with regard to the chief exertions of prerogative by the TUDORS. Where any power or prerogative is fully and undoubtedly established, the exercise of it passes for a thing of course, and readily escapes the notice of history and annals. Had we no other monuments of ELIZABETH's reign, than what are preserved even by CAMDEN, the most copious, judicious, and exact of our historians, we should be entirely ignorant of the most important maxims of her government.

Was not the present monarchical government, in its full extent, authorized by lawyers, recommended by divines, acknowledged by politicians, acquiesced in, nay passionately cherished, by the people in general; and all this during a period of at least a hundred and sixty years, and till of late, without the smallest murmur or controversy? This general consent surely, during so long a time, must be sufficient to render a constitution legal and valid. If the origin of all power be derived, as is pretended, from the people; here is their consent in the fullest and most ample terms that can be desired or imagin'd.

But the people must not pretend, because they can, by their consent, lay the foundations of government, that therefore they are to be permitted, at their pleasure, to overthrow and subvert them. There is no end of these seditious and arrogant claims. The power of the crown is now openly struck at: The nobility are also in visible peril: The gentry will soon follow: The popular leaders, who will then assume the name of gentry, will next be exposed to danger: And the people themselves, having become incapable of civil government, and lying under the restraint of no authority, must, for the sake of peace, admit, instead of their legal and mild monarchs, a succession of military and despotic tyrants.

These consequences are the more to be dreaded, as the present fury of the people, though glossed over by pretensions to civil liberty, is in reality incited by the fanaticism of religion; a principle the most blind, headstrong, and ungovernable, by which human nature can possibly be actuated. Popular rage is dreadful, from whatever motive derived: But must be attended with the most pernicious consequences, when it arises from a principle, which disclaims all controul by human law, reason, or authority.

These are the arguments, which each party may make use of to justify the conduct of their predecessors, during that great crisis. The event, if that can be admitted as a reason, has shown, that the arguments of the popular party were better founded; but perhaps, according to the established maxims of lawyers and politicians, the views of the royalists ought, before-hand, to have appeared more solid, more safe, and more legal. But this is certain, that the greater moderation we now employ in representing past events; the nearer shall we be to produce a full coalition of the parties, and an entire acquiescence in our present establishment. Moderation is of advantage to every establishment: Nothing but zeal can overturn a settled power: And an over-active zeal in friends is apt to beget a like spirit in antagonists. The transition from a moderate opposition against an es tablishment, to an entire acquiescence in it, is easy and insensible.

There are many invincible arguments, which should induce the malcontent party to acquiesce entirely in the present settlement of the constitution. They now find, that the spirit of civil liberty, though at first connected with religious fanaticism, could purge itself from that pollution, and appear under a more genuine and engaging aspect; a friend to toleration, and an encourager of all the enlarged and generous sentiments that do honour to human nature. They may observe, that the popular claims could stop at a proper period; and after retrenching the high claims of prerogative, could still maintain a due respect to monarchy, to nobility, and to all ancient institutions. Above all, they must be sensible, that the very principle, which made the strength of their party, and from which it derived its chief authority, has now deserted them, and gone over to their antagonists. The plan of liberty is settled; its happy effects are proved by experience; a long tract of time has given it stability; and whoever would attempt to overturn it, and to recall the past government or abdicated family, would, besides other more criminal imputations, be exposed, in their turn, to the reproach of faction and innovation. While they peruse the history of past events, they ought to reflect, both that those rights of the crown are long since annihilated, and that the tyranny, and violence, and oppression, to which they often gave rise, are ills, from which the established liberty of the constitution has now at last happily protected the people. These reflections will prove a better security to our freedom and privileges, than to deny, contrary to the clearest evidence of facts, that such regal powers ever had an existence. There is not a more effectual method of betraying a cause, than to lay the stress of the argument on a wrong place, and by disputing an untenable post, enure the adversaries to success and victory.

[1] Essay XV.—*Of the Protestant Succession.*

I suppose, that a member of parliament, in the reign of King William or Queen Anne, while the establishment of the *Protestant Succession* was yet uncertain, were deliberating

[1] [For the history of the publication of this Essay, see p. 48.]

concerning the party he would chuse in that important question, and weighing, with impartiality, the advantages and disadvantages on each side. I believe the following particulars would have entered into his consideration.

He would easily perceive the great advantage resulting from the restoration of the STUART family; by which we should preserve the succession clear and undisputed, free from a pretender, with such a specious title as that of blood, which, with the multitude, is always the claim, the strongest and most easily comprehended. It is in vain to say, as many have done, that the question with regard to *governors*, independent of *government*, is frivolous, and little worth disputing, much less fighting about. The generality of mankind never will enter into these sentiments; and it is much happier, I believe, for society, that they do not, but rather continue in their natural prepossessions. How could stability be preserved in any monarchical government, (which, though, perhaps, not the best, is, and always has been, the most common of any) unless men had so passionate a regard for the true heir of their royal family; and even though he be weak in understanding, or infirm in years, gave him so sensible a preference above persons the most accomplished in shining talents, or celebrated for great atchievements? Would not every popular leader put in his claim at every vacancy, or even without any vacancy; and the kingdom become the theatre of perpetual wars and convulsions? The condition of the ROMAN empire, surely, was not, in this respect, much to be envied; nor is that of the *Eastern* nations, who pay little regard to the titles of their sovereign, but sacrifice them, every day, to the caprice or momentary humour of the populace or soldiery. It is but a foolish wisdom, which is so carefully displayed, in undervaluing princes, and placing them on a level with the meanest of mankind. To be sure, an anatomist finds no more in the greatest monarch than in the lowest peasant or day-labourer; and a moralist may, perhaps, frequently find less. But what do all these reflections tend to? We, all of us, still retain these prejudices in favour of birth and family; and neither in our serious occupations, nor most careless amusements, can we ever get entirely rid of them. A tragedy, that should represent the adventures of sailors, or porters, or even of private gentlemen, would presently disgust us; but one that introduces kings and princes, acquires in our eyes an air of importance and dignity. Or should a man be able, by his superior wisdom, to get entirely above such prepossessions, he would soon, by means of the same wisdom, again bring himself down to them, for the sake of society, whose welfare he would perceive to be intimately connected with them. Far from endeavouring to undeceive the people in this particular, he would cherish such sentiments of reverence to their princes; as requisite to preserve a due subordination in society. And though the lives of twenty thousand men be often sacrificed to maintain a king in possession of his throne, or preserve the right of succession undisturbed, he entertains no indignation at the loss, on pretence that every individual of these was, perhaps, in himself, as valuable as the prince he served. He considers the consequences of violating the hereditary right of kings: Consequences, which may be felt for many centuries; while the loss of several thousand men brings so little prejudice to a large kingdom, that it may not be perceived a few years after.

The advantages of the HANOVER succession are of an opposite nature, and arise from this very circumstance, that it violates hereditary right; and places on the throne a prince, to whom birth gave no title to that dignity. It is evident, from the history of this island, that the privileges of the people have, during near two centuries, been continually upon the encrease, by the division of the church-lands, by the alienations of the barons' estates, by the progress of trade, and above all, by the happiness of our situation, which, for a long time, gave us sufficient security, without any standing army or military establishment. On the contrary, public liberty has, almost in every other nation of EUROPE, been, during the same period, extremely upon the decline; while the people were disgusted at the hardships of the old [1] feudal militia, and rather chose to entrust their prince with mercenary armies, which he easily turned against themselves. It was nothing extraordinary, therefore, that some of our BRITISH sovereigns mistook the nature of the constitution, at least, the genius of the people; and as they embraced all the favourable precedents left them by their ancestors, they overlooked all those which were contrary, and which supposed a limitation in our government. They were encouraged in this mistake, by the example of all the neighbouring princes,

[1] [GOTHIC: Editions H to N.]

OF THE PROTESTANT SUCCESSION.

who bearing the same title or appellation, and being adorned with the same ensigns of authority, naturally led them to claim the same powers and prerogatives. [1]It appears from the speeches, and proclamations of JAMES I. and the whole train of that prince's actions, as well as his son's, that he regarded the ENGLISH government as a simple monarchy, and never imagined that any considerable part of his subjects entertained a contrary idea. This opinion made those monarchs discover their pretensions, without preparing any force to support them; and even without reserve or disguise, which are always employed by those, who enter upon any new project, or endeavour to innovate in any government. The flattery of courtiers farther [2]confirmed their prejudices; and above all, that of the clergy, who from several passages of

---

[1] [For this sentence and the next, Editions H to P read as follows; K to P, in a note: It appears from the speeches, and proclamations, and whole train of King JAMES I.'s actions, as well as his son's, that they considered the ENGLISH government as a simple monarchy, and never imagined that any considerable part of their subjects entertained a contrary idea. This made them discover their pretensions, without preparing any force to support them; and even without reserve or disguise, which are always employed by those, who enter upon any new project, or endeavour to innovate in any government. King JAMES told his parliament plainly, when they meddled in state affairs, *Ne sutor ultra crepidam.* He used also, at his table, in promiscuous companies, to advance his notions, in a manner still more undisguised: As we may learn from a story told in the life of Mr. WALLER, and which that poet used frequently to repeat. When Mr. WALLER was young, he had the curiosity to go to court; and he stood in the circle, and saw King JAMES dine, where, amongst other company, there sat at table two bishops. The King, openly and aloud, proposed this question, *Whether he might not take his subjects money, when he had occasion for it, without all this formality of parliament?* The one bishop readily replied, *God forbid you should not: For you are the breath of our nostrils.* The other bishop declined answering, and said he was not skilled in parliamentary cases: But upon the King's urging him, and saying he would admit of no evasion, his lordship replied very pleasantly, *Why, then, I think your majesty may lawfully take my brother's money: For he offers it.* In Sir WALTER RALEIGH's preface to the History of the World, there is this remarkable passage. PHILIP II. *by strong hand and main force, attempted to make himself not only an* absolute monarch *over the* Netherlands, *like unto the kings and sovereigns of* England *and* France; *but* Turk-like, *to tread under his feet all their natural and fundamental laws, privileges, and antient rights.* SPENSER, speaking of some grants of the ENGLISH kings to the IRISH corporations, says, 'All which, tho', at the time of their first grant, they were tolerable, and perhaps reasonable, yet now are most unreasonable and inconvenient. But all these will easily be cut off with the superior power of her majesty's prerogative, against which her own grants are not to be pleaded or inforced.' *State of* IRELAND, p. 1537. Edit. 1706.

As these were very common, if not, perhaps, the universal notions of the times, the two first princes of the house of STUART were the more excusable for their mistake. And RAPIN,[1] suitable to his usual malignity and partiality, seems to treat them with too much severity, upon account of it.

[2] [Blinded them: Editions H to N.]

---

[1] [Editions H and I read: The most judicious of historians.]

scripture, and these wrested too, had erected a regular and avowed system of arbitrary power. The only method of destroying, at once, all these high claims and pretensions, was to depart from the true hereditary line, and choose a prince, who, being plainly a creature of the public, and receiving the crown on conditions, expressed and avowed, found his authority established on the same bottom with the privileges of the people. By electing him in the royal line, we cut off all hopes of ambitious subjects, who might, in future emergencies, disturb the government by their cabals and pretensions: By rendering the crown hereditary in his family, we avoided all the inconveniencies of elective monarchy: And by excluding the lineal heir, we secured all our constitutional limitations, and rendered our government uniform and of a piece. The people cherish monarchy, because protected by it: The monarch favours liberty, because created by it. And thus every advantage is obtained by the new establishment, as far as human skill and wisdom can extend itself.

These are the separate advantages of fixing the succession, either in the house of STUART, or in that of HANOVER. There are also disadvantages in each establishment, which an impartial patriot would ponder and examine, in order to form a just judgment upon the whole.

The disadvantages of the protestant succession consist in the foreign dominions, which are possessed by the princes of the HANOVER line, and which, it might be supposed, would engage us in the intrigues and wars of the continent, and lose us, in some measure, the inestimable advantage we possess, of being surrounded and guarded by the sea, which we command. The disadvantages of recalling the abdicated family consist chiefly in their religion, which is more prejudicial to society than that established amongst us, is contrary to it, and affords no toleration, or peace, or security to any other communion.

It appears to me, that these advantages and disadvantages are allowed on both sides; at least, by every one who is at all susceptible of argument or reasoning. No subject, however loyal, pretends to deny, that the disputed title and foreign dominions of the present royal family are a loss. Nor is there any partizan of the STUARTS, but will confess, that the claim of hereditary, indefeasible right, and the Roman Catholic religion, are also disadvantages in that family. It belongs, therefore, to a philosopher alone, who is of neither party, to put all the circumstances in the scale, and assign to each of them its proper poise and influence. Such a one will readily, at first, acknowledge that all political questions are infinitely complicated, and that there scarcely ever occurs, in any deliberation, a choice, which is either purely good, or purely ill. Consequences, mixed and varied, may be foreseen to flow from every measure: And many consequences, unforseen, do always, in fact, result from every one. Hesitation, and reserve, and suspense, are, therefore, the only sentiments he brings to this essay or trial. Or if he indulges any passion, it is that of derision against the ignorant multitude, who are always clamorous and dogmatical, even in the nicest questions, of which, from want of temper, perhaps still more than of understanding, they are altogether unfit judges.

But to say something more determinate on this head, the following reflections will, I hope, show the temper, if not the understanding of a philosopher.

Were we to judge merely by first appearances, and by past experience, we must allow that the advantages of a parliamentary title in the house of HANOVER are greater than those of an undisputed hereditary title in the house of STUART; and that our fathers acted wisely in preferring the former to the latter. So long as the house of STUART ruled in GREAT BRITAIN, which, with some interruption, was above eighty years, the government was kept in a continual fever, by the contention between the privileges of the people and the prerogatives of the crown. If arms were dropped, the noise of disputes continued: Or if these were silenced, jealousy still corroded the heart, and threw the nation into an unnatural ferment and disorder. And while we were thus occupied in domestic disputes, a foreign power, dangerous to public liberty, erected itself in Europe, without any opposition from us, and even sometimes with our assistance.

But during these last sixty years, when a parliamentary establishment has taken place; whatever factions may have prevailed either among the people or in public assemblies, the whole force of our constitution has always fallen to one side, and an uninterrupted harmony has been preserved between our princes and our parliaments. Public liberty, with internal peace and order, has flourished almost without interruption: Trade and manufactures, and agriculture, have encreased: The arts, and sciences, and philosophy, **have been** cultivated. Even religious parties have been **necessitated to** lay aside their mutual rancour: And the glory of **the nation** has spread itself all over EUROPE;[1] derived equally from our progress in the arts of peace, and from valour and success in war. So long and so glorious a period no nation almost can boast of: Nor is there another instance in the whole history of mankind, that so many millions of people have, during such a space of time, been held together, in a manner so free, so rational, and so suitable to the dignity of human nature.

But though this recent experience seems clearly to decide in favour of the present establishment, there are some circumstances to be thrown into the other scale; and it is dangerous to regulate our judgment by one event or example.

We have had two rebellions during the flourishing period above mentioned, besides plots and conspiracies without number. And if none of these have produced any very fatal event, we may ascribe our escape chiefly to the narrow genius of those princes who disputed our establishment; and we may esteem ourselves so far fortunate. But the claims of the banished family, I fear, are not yet antiquated; and who can foretel, that their future attempts will produce no greater disorder?

The disputes between privilege and prerogative may easily be composed by laws, and votes, and conferences, and concessions; where there is tolerable temper or prudence on both sides, or on either side. Among contending titles, the question can only be determined by the sword, and by devastation, and by civil war.

A prince, who fills the throne with a disputed title, dares not arm his subjects: the only method of securing a people fully, both against domestic oppression and foreign conquest.

Notwithstanding our riches and renown, what a critical escape did we make, by the late peace, from dangers, which were owing not so much to bad conduct and ill success in war, as to the pernicious practice of mortgaging our finances, and the still more pernicious maxim of never paying off our incumbrances? Such fatal measures would not probably

---

[1] [For the remainder of this sentence, Editions H to P substitute: While we stand the bulwark against oppression, and the great antagonist of that power which threatens every people with conquest and subjection.]

have been embraced, had it not been to secure a precarious establishment.[1]

But to convince us, that an hereditary title is to be embraced rather than a parliamentary one, which is not supported by any other views or motives; a man needs only transport himself back to the æra of the restoration, and suppose, that he had had a seat in that parliament which recalled the royal family, and put a period to the greatest disorders that ever arose from the opposite pretensions of prince and people. What would have been thought of one, that had proposed, at that time, to set aside CHARLES II. and settle the crown on the Duke of YORK or GLOUCESTER, merely in order to exclude all high claims, like those of their father and grandfather? Would not such a one have been regarded as an extravagant projector, who loved dangerous remedies, and could tamper and play with a government and national constitution, like a quack with a sickly patient?[2]

In reality, the reason assigned by the nation for excluding the race of STUART, and so many other branches of the royal family, is not on account of their hereditary title (a reason, which would, to vulgar apprehensions, have appeared altogether absurd), but on account of their religion. Which leads us to compare the disadvantages above mentioned in each established.

I confess, that, considering the matter in general, it were much to be wished, that our prince had no foreign dominions, and could confine all his attention to the government of this island. For not to mention some real inconveniencies that may result from territories on the continent, they afford such a handle for calumny and defamation, as is greedily seized by the people, always disposed to think ill of their superiors. It must, however, be acknowledged, that HANOVER, is, per-

---

[1] [Editions H to P add the note: Those who consider how universal this pernicious practice of lending has become all over EUROPE, may perhaps dispute this last opinion. But we lay under less necessity than other states.]

[2] [Editions H to P add the following paragraph: The advantages which result from a parliamentary title, preferably to an hereditary one, tho' they are great, are too refined ever to enter into the conception of the vulgar. The bulk of mankind would never allow them to be sufficient for committing what would be regarded as an injustice to the prince. They must be supported by some gross, popular, and familiar topics; and wise men, though convinced of their force, would reject them, in compliance with the weakness and prejudices of the people. An incroaching tyrant or deluded bigot alone, by his misconduct, is able to enrage the nation, and render practicable what was always perhaps desirable.]

haps, the spot of ground in EUROPE the least inconvenient for a King of ENGLAND. It lies in the heart of GERMANY, at a distance from the great powers, which are our natural rivals: It is protected by the laws of the empire, as well as by the arms of its own sovereign: And it serves only to connect us more closely with the house of AUSTRIA, our natural ally.[1]

The religious persuasion of the house of STUART is an inconvenience of a much deeper dye, and would threaten us with much more dismal consequences. The Roman Catholic religion, with its train of priests and friers, is more expensive than ours: Even though unaccompanied with its natural attendants of inquisitors, and stakes, and gibbets, it is less tolerating: And not content with dividing the sacerdotal from the regal office (which must be prejudicial to any state), it bestows the former on a foreigner, who has always a separate interest from that of the public, and may often have an opposite one.

But were this religion ever so advantageous to society, it is contrary to that which is established among us, and which is likely to keep possession, for a long time, of the minds of the people. And though it is much to be hoped, that the progress of reason will, by degrees, abate the [2] acrimony of opposite religions all over EUROPE; yet the spirit of moderation has, as yet, made too slow advances to be entirely trusted.[3]

Thus, upon the whole, the advantages of the settlement in

---

[1] [Editions H to P insert the following paragraph: In the last war, it has been of service to us, by furnishing us with a considerable body of auxiliary troops, the bravest and most faithful in the world. The Elector of HANOVER is the only considerable prince in the empire, who has pursued no separate end, and has raised up no stale pretensions, during the late commotions of EUROPE; but has acted, all along, with the dignity of a King of BRITAIN. And ever since the accession of that family, it would be difficult to show any harm we have ever received from the electoral dominions, except that short disgust in 1718, with CHARLES XII., who, regulating himself by maxims very different from those of other princes; made a personal quarrel of every public injury.][1]

[2] [The virulent acrimony: Editions H to N.]

[3] [Editions H to P add: The conduct of the SAXON family, where the same person can be a Catholic King and Protestant Elector, is, perhaps, the first instance, in modern times, of so reasonable and prudent a behaviour. And the gradual progress of the Catholic superstition does, even there, prognosticate a speedy alteration: After which, 'tis justly to be apprehended, that persecutions will put a speedy period to the Protestant religion in the place of its nativity.]

---

[1] [Editions O and P append the note: This was published in 1752.]

the family of STUART, which frees us from a disputed title, seem to bear some proportion with those of the settlement in the family of HANOVER, which frees us from the claims of prerogative: But at the same time, its disadvantages, by placing on the throne a Roman Catholic, are greater than those of the other establishment, in settling the crown on a foreign prince. What party an impartial patriot, in the reign of K. WILLIAM or Q. ANNE, would have chosen amidst these opposite views, may, perhaps, to some appear hard to determine.[1]

But the settlement in the House of HANOVER has actually taken place. The princes of that family, without intrigue, without cabal, without solicitation on their part, have been called to mount our throne, by the united voice of the whole legislative body. They have, since their accession, displayed, in all their actions, the utmost mildness, equity, and regard to the laws and constitutions. Our own ministers, our own parliaments, ourselves have governed us; and if aught ill has befallen us, we can only blame fortune or ourselves. What a reproach must we become among nations, if, disgusted with a settlement so deliberately made, and whose conditions have been so religiously observed, we should throw every thing again into confusion; and by our levity and rebellious disposition, prove ourselves totally unfit for any state but that of absolute slavery and subjection?

The greatest inconvenience, attending a disputed title, is, that it brings us in danger of civil wars and rebellions. What wise man, to avoid this inconvenience, would run directly into a civil war and rebellion? Not to mention, that so long possession, secured by so many laws, must, ere this time, in the apprehension of a great part of the nation, have begotten a title in the house of HANOVER, independent of their present possession: So that now we should not, even by a revolution, obtain the end of avoiding a disputed title.

No revolution made by national forces, will ever be able, without some other great necessity, to abolish our debts and incumbrances, in which the interest of so many persons is concerned. And a revolution made by foreign forces, is a conquest: A calamity, with which the precarious balance of

---

[1] [Editions H to P add: For my part, I esteem liberty so invaluable a blessing in society, that whatever favours its progress and security, can scarce be too fondly cherished by every one who is a lover of human kind.]

power threatens us, and which our civil dissentions are likely, above all other circumstances, to bring upon us.

Essay XVI.—*Idea of a perfect Commonwealth.*

[1] It is not with forms of government, as with other artificial contrivances; where an old engine may be rejected, if we can discover another more accurate and commodious, or where trials may safely be made, even though the success be doubtful. An established government has an infinite advantage, by that very circumstance of its being established; the bulk of mankind being governed by authority, not reason, and never attributing authority to any thing that has not the recommendation of antiquity. To tamper, therefore, in this affair, or try experiments merely upon the credit of supposed argument and philosophy, can never be the part of a wise magistrate, who will bear a reverence to what carries the marks of age; and though he may attempt some improvements for the public good, yet will he adjust his innovations, as much as possible, to the ancient fabric, and preserve entire the chief pillars and supports of the constitution.

The mathematicians in Europe have been much divided concerning that figure of a ship, which is the most commodious for sailing; and Huygens, who at last determined the controversy, is justly thought to have obliged the learned, as well as commercial world; though Columbus had sailed to America, and Sir Francis Drake made the tour of the world, without any such discovery. As one form of government must be allowed more perfect than another, independent of the manners and humours of particular men; why may we not enquire what is the most perfect of all, though the common botched and inaccurate governments seem to serve the purposes of society, and though it be not so easy to establish a new system of government, as to build a vessel upon a new construction? The subject is surely the most worthy curiosity of any the wit of man can possibly devise. And who knows, if this controversy were fixed by the

---

[1] [Editions H to P begin as follows: Of all mankind there are none so pernicious as political projectors, if they have power; nor so ridiculous, if they want it: As on the other hand, a wise politician is the most beneficial character in nature, if accompanied with authority; and the most innocent, and not altogether useless, even if deprived of it.]

universal consent of the wise and learned, but, in some future age, an opportunity might be afforded of reducing the theory to practice, either by a dissolution of some old government, or by the combination of men to form a new one, in some distant part of the world? In all cases, it must be advantageous to know what is most perfect in the kind, that we may be able to bring any real constitution or form of government as near it as possible, by such gentle alterations and innovations as may not give too great disturbance to society.

All I pretend to in the present essay is to revive this subject of speculation; and therefore I shall deliver my sentiments in as few words as possible. A long dissertation on that head would not, I apprehend, be very acceptable to the public, who will be apt to regard such disquisitions both as useless and chimerical.

All plans of government, which suppose great reformation in the manners of mankind, are plainly imaginary. Of this nature, are the *Republic* of PLATO, and the *Utopia* of Sir THOMAS MORE. The OCEANA is the only valuable model of a commonwealth, that has yet been offered to the public.

The chief defects of the OCEANA seem to be these. *First*, Its rotation is inconvenient, by throwing men, of whatever abilities, by intervals, out of public employments. *Secondly*, Its *Agrarian* is impracticable. Men will soon learn the art, which was practised in ancient ROME, of concealing their possessions under other people's name; till at last, the abuse will become so common, that they will throw off even the appearance of restraint. *Thirdly*, The OCEANA provides not a sufficient security for liberty, or the redress of grievances. The senate must propose, and the people consent; by which means, the senate have not only a negative upon the people, but, what is of much greater consequence, their negative goes before the votes of the people. Were the King's negative of the same nature in the ENGLISH constitution, and could he prevent any bill from coming into parliament, he would be an absolute monarch. As his negative follows the votes of the houses, it is of little consequence: Such a difference is there in the manner of placing the same thing. When a popular bill has been debated in parliament, is brought to maturity, all its conveniencies and inconveniences, weighed and balanced; if afterwards it be presented for the royal assent, few princes will venture to reject the unanimous desire of the people. But could the King crush a disagreeable bill in embryo (as was the case, for some time, in the SCOTTISH parliament, by means of the lords of the articles), the BRITISH government would have no balance, nor would grievances ever be redressed: And it is certain, that exorbitant power proceeds not, in any government, from new laws, so much as from neglecting to remedy the abuses, which frequently rise from the old ones. A government, says MACHIAVEL, must often be brought back to its original principles. It appears then, that, in the OCEANA, the whole legislature may be said to rest in the senate; which HARRINGTON would own to be an inconvenient form of government, especially after the *Agrarian* is abolished.

Here is a form of government, to which I cannot, in theory, discover any considerable objection.

Let GREAT BRITAIN and IRELAND, or any territory of equal extent, be divided into 100 counties, and each county into 100 parishes, making in all 10,000. If the country, proposed to be erected into a commonwealth, be of more narrow extent, we may diminish the number of counties; but never bring them below thirty. If it be of greater extent, it were better to enlarge the parishes, or throw more parishes into a county, than encrease the number of counties.

[1] Let all the freeholders of twenty pounds a-year in the county, and all the householders worth 500 pounds in the town parishes, meet annually in the parish church, and chuse, by ballot, some freeholder of the county for their member, whom we shall call the county *representative*.

Let the 100 county representatives, two days after their election, meet in the county town, and chuse by ballot, from their own body, ten county *magistrates*, and one *senator*. There are, therefore, in the whole commonwealth, 100 senators, 1100 county magistrates, and 10,000 county representatives. For we shall bestow on all senators the authority of county magistrates, and on all county magistrates the authority of county representatives.

Let the senators meet in the capital, and be endowed with the whole executive power of the commonwealth; the power

---

[1] [Editions H and I read: Let all the freeholders in the country parishes, and those who pay scot and lot in the town parishes, &c. K to P, read: Let all the freeholders of ten pounds a year in the country, and all the householders worth 200 pounds in the town-parishes, &c.]

of peace and war, of giving orders to generals, admirals, and ambassadors, and, in short, all the prerogatives of a BRITISH King, except his negative.

Let the county representatives meet in their particular counties, and possess the whole legislative power of the commonwealth; the greater number of counties deciding the question; and where these are equal, let the senate have the casting vote.

Every new law must first be debated in the senate; and though rejected by it, if ten senators insist and protest, it must be sent down to the counties. The senate, if they please, may join to the copy of the law their reasons for receiving or rejecting it.

Because it would be troublesome to assemble all the county representatives for every trivial law, that may be requisite, the senate have their choice of sending down the law either to the county magistrates or county representatives.

The magistrates, though the law be referred to them, may, if they please, call the representatives, and submit the affair to their determination.

Whether the law be referred by the senate to the county magistrates or representatives, a copy of it, and of the senate's reasons, must be sent to every representative eight days before the day appointed for the assembling, in order to deliberate concerning it. And though the determination be, by the senate, referred to the magistrates, if five representatives of the county order the magistrates to assemble the whole court of representatives, and submit the affair to their determination, they must obey.

Either the county magistrates or representatives may give, to the senator of the county, the copy of a law to be proposed to the senate; and if five counties concur in the same order, the law, though refused by the senate, must come either to the county magistrates or representatives, as is contained in the order of the five counties.

Any twenty counties, by a vote either of their magistrates or representatives, may throw any man out of all public offices for a year. Thirty counties for three years.

The senate has a power of throwing out any member or number of members of its own body, not to be re-elected for that year. The senate cannot throw out twice in a year the senator of the same county.

The power of the old senate continues for three weeks after the annual election of the county representatives. Then all the new senators are shut up in a conclave, like the cardinals; and by an intricate ballot, such as that of VENICE or MALTA, they chuse the following magistrates; a protector, who represents the dignity of the commonwealth, and presides in the senate; two secretaries of state; these six councils, a council of state, a council of religion and learning, a council of trade, a council of laws, a council of war, a council of the admiralty, each council consisting of five persons; together with six commissioners of the treasury and a first commissioner. All these must be senators. The senate also names all the ambassadors to foreign courts, who may either be senators or not.

The senate may continue any or all of these, but must re-elect them every year.

The protector and two secretaries have session and suffrage in the council of state. The business of that council is all foreign politics. The council of state has session and suffrage in all the other councils.

The council of religion and learning inspects the universities and clergy. That of trade inspects every thing that may affect commerce. That of laws inspects all the abuses of law by the inferior magistrates, and examines what improvements may be made of the municipal law. That of war inspects the militia and its discipline, magazines, stores, &c., and when the republic is in war, examines into the proper orders for generals. The council of admiralty has the same power with regard to the navy, together with the nomination of the captains and all inferior officers.

None of these councils can give orders themselves, except where they receive such powers from the senate. In other cases, they must communicate every thing to the senate.

When the senate is under adjournment, any of the councils may assemble it before the day appointed for its meeting.

Besides these councils or courts, there is another called the court of *competitors*; which is thus constituted. If any candidates for the office of senator have more votes than a third of the representatives, that candidate, who has most votes, next to the senator elected, becomes incapable for one year of all public offices, even of being a magistrate or representative: But he takes his seat in the court of competitors. Here then is a court which may sometimes consist of a hundred members, sometimes have no members at all; and by that means, be for a year abolished.

The court of competitors has no power in the commonwealth. It has only the inspection of public accounts, and the accusing of any man before the senate. If the senate acquit him, the court of competitors may, if they please, appeal to the people, either magistrates or representatives. Upon that appeal, the magistrates or representatives meet on the day appointed by the court of competitors, and chuse in each county three persons, from which number every senator is excluded. These, to the number of 300, meet in the capital, and bring the person accused to a new trial.

The court of competitors may propose any law to the senate; and if refused, may appeal to the people, that is, to the magistrates or representatives, who examine it in their counties. Every senator, who is thrown out of the senate by a vote of the court, takes his seat in the court of competitors.

The senate possesses all the judicative authority of the house of Lords, that is, all the appeals from the inferior courts. It likewise appoints the Lord Chancellor, and all the officers of the law.

Every county is a kind of republic within itself, and the representatives may make bye-laws, which have no authority 'till three months after they are voted. A copy of the law is sent to the senate, and to every other county. The senate, or any single county, may, at any time, annul any bye-law of another county.

The representatives have all the authority of the BRITISH justices of peace in trials, commitments, &c.

The magistrates have the appointment of all the officers of the revenue in each county. All causes with regard to the revenue are carried ultimately by appeal before the magistrates. They pass the accompts of all the officers; but must have their own accompts examined and passed at the end of the year by the representatives.

The magistrates name rectors or ministers to all the parishes.

The Presbyterian government is established; and the highest ecclesiastical court is an assembly or synod of all the presbyters of the county. The magistrates may take any cause from this court, and determine it themselves.

The magistrates may try, and depose or suspend any presbyter.

The militia is established in imitation of that of SWISSERLAND, which being well known, we shall not insist upon it. It will only be proper to make this addition, that an army of 20,000 men be annually drawn out by rotation, paid and encamped during six weeks in summer; that the duty of a camp may not be altogether unknown.

The magistrates appoint all the colonels and downwards. The senate all upwards. During war, the general appoints the colonel and downwards, and his commission is good for a twelvemonth. But after that, it must be confirmed by the magistrates of the county, to which the regiment belongs. The magistrates may break any officer in the county regiment. And the senate may do the same to any officer in the service. If the magistrates do not think proper to confirm the general's choice, they may appoint another officer in the place of him they reject.

All crimes are tried within the county by the magistrates and a jury. But the senate can stop any trial, and bring it before themselves.

Any county may indict any man before the senate for any crime.

The protector, the two secretaries, the council of state, with any five or more that the senate appoints, are possessed, on extraordinary emergencies, of *dictatorial* power for six months.

The protector may pardon any person condemned by the inferior courts.

In time of war, no officer of the army that is in the field can have any civil office in the commonwealth.

The capital, which we shall call LONDON, may be allowed four members in the senate. It may therefore be divided into four counties. The representatives of each of these chuse one senator, and ten magistrates. There are therefore in the city four senators, forty-four magistrates, and four hundred representatives. The magistrates have the same authority as in the counties. The representatives also have the same authority; but they never meet in one general court: They give their votes in their particular county, or division of hundreds.

When they enact any bye-law, the greater number of counties or divisions determines the matter. And where these are equal, the magistrates have the casting vote.

The magistrates chuse the mayor, sheriff, recorder, and other officers of the city.

In the commonwealth, no representative, magistrate, or senator, as such, has any salary. The protector, secretaries, councils, and ambassadors, have salaries.

The first year in every century is set apart for correcting all inequalities, which time may have produced in the representative. This must be done by the legislature.

The following political aphorisms may explain the reason of these orders.

The lower sort of people and small proprietors are good judges enough of one not very distant from them in rank or habitation; and therefore, in their parochial meetings, will probably chuse the best, or nearly the best representative: But they are wholly unfit for county-meetings, and for electing into the higher offices of the republic. Their ignorance gives the grandees an opportunity of deceiving them.

Ten thousand, even though they were not annually elected, are a basis large enough for any free government. It is true, the nobles in POLAND are more than 10,000, and yet these oppress the people. But as power always continues there in the same persons and families, this makes them, in a manner, a different nation from the people. Besides the nobles are there united under a few heads of families.

All free governments must consist of two councils, a lesser and greater; or, in other words, of a senate and people. The people, as HARRINGTON observes, would want wisdom, without the senate: The senate, without the people, would want honesty.

A large assembly of 1,000, for instance, to represent the people, if allowed to debate, would fall into disorder. If not allowed to debate, the senate has a negative upon them, and the worst kind of negative, that before resolution.

Here therefore is an inconvenience, which no government has yet fully remedied, but which is the easiest to be remedied in the world. If the people debate, all is confusion: If they do not debate, they can only resolve; and then the senate carves for them. Divide the people into many separate bodies; and then they may debate with safety, and every inconvenience seems to be prevented.

Cardinal de RETZ says, that all numerous assemblies, however composed, are mere mob, and swayed in their debates by the least motive This we find confirmed by daily experience. When an absurdity strikes a member, he conveys it to his neighbour, and so on, till the whole be infected. Separate this great body; and though every member be only of middling sense, it is not probable, that any thing but reason can prevail over the whole. Influence and example being removed, good sense will always get the better of bad among a number of people.[1]

There are two things to be guarded against in every *senate* : Its combination, and its division. Its combination is most dangerous. And against this inconvenience we have provided the following remedies. 1. The great dependence of the senators on the people by annual elections; and that not by an undistinguishing rabble, like the ENGLISH electors, but by men of fortune and education. 2. The small power they are allowed. They have few offices to dispose of. Almost all are given by the magistrates in the counties. 3. The court of competitors, which being composed of men that are their rivals, next to them in interest, and uneasy in their present situation, will be sure to take all advantages against them.

The division of the senate is prevented, 1. By the smallness of their number. 2. As faction supposes a combination in a separate interest, it is prevented by their dependence on the people. 3. They have a power of expelling any factious member. It is true, when another member of the same spirit comes from the county, they have no power of expelling him: Nor is it fit they should; for that shows the humour to be in the people, and may possible arise from some ill conduct in public affairs. 4. Almost any man, in a senate so regularly chosen by the people, may be supposed fit for any civil office. It would be proper, therefore, for the senate to form some *general* resolutions with regard to the disposing of offices among the members: Which resolutions would not confine them in critical times, when extraordinary

---

[1] [Editions H to P add: Good sense is one thing: But follies are numberless; and every man has a different one. The only way of making a people wise, is to keep them from uniting into large assemblies.]

parts on the one hand, or extraordinary stupidity on the other, appears in any senator; but they would be sufficient to prevent[1] intrigue and faction, by making the disposal of the offices a thing of course. For instance, let it be a resolution, that no man shall enjoy any office, till he has sat four years in the senate: That, except ambassadors, no man shall be in office two years following: That no man shall attain the higher offices but through the lower: That no man shall be protector twice, &c. The senate of VENICE govern themselves by such resolutions.

In foreign politics the interest of the senate can scarcely ever be divided from that of the people; and therefore it is fit to make the senate absolute with regard to them; otherwise there could be no secrecy or refined policy. Besides, without money no alliance can be executed; and the senate is still sufficiently dependant. Not to mention that the legislative power being always superior to the executive, the magistrates or representatives may interpose whenever they think proper.

The chief support of the BRITISH government is the opposition of interests; but that, though in the main serviceable, breeds endless factions. In the foregoing plan, it does all the good without any of the harm. The *competitors* have no power of controlling the senate: they have only the power of accusing, and appealing to the people.

It is necessary, likewise, to prevent both combination and division in the thousand magistrates. This is done sufficiently by the separation of places and interest.

But lest that should not be sufficient, their dependence on the 10,000 for their elections, serves to the same purpose.

Nor is that all: For the 10,000 may resume the power whenever they please; and not only when they all please, but when any five of a hundred please, which will happen upon the very first suspicion of a separate interest.

The 10,000 are too large a body either to unite or divide, except when they meet in one place, and fall under the guidance of ambitious leaders. Not to mention their annual election,[2] by the whole body of the people, that are of any consideration.

A small commonwealth is the happiest government in the

[1] [Brigue: Editions H to P.]
[2] [By almost the whole body of the people: so editions H to M end the paragraph.]

world within itself, because every thing lies under the eye of the rulers: But it may be subdued by great force from without. This scheme seems to have all the advantages both of a great and a little commonwealth.

Every county-law may be annulled either by the senate or another county; because that shows an opposition of interest: In which case no part ought to decide for itself. The matter must be referred to the whole, which will best determine what agrees with general interest.

As to the clergy and militia, the reasons of these orders are obvious. Without the dependence of the clergy on the civil magistrates, and without a militia, it is in vain to think that any free government will ever have security or stability.

In many governments, the inferior magistrates have no rewards but what arise from their ambition, vanity, or public spirit. The salaries of the FRENCH judges amount not to the interest of the sums they pay for their offices. The DUTCH burgo-masters have little more immediate profit than the ENGLISH justices of peace, or the members of the house of commons formerly. But lest any should suspect, that this would beget negligence in the administration (which is little to be feared, considering the natural ambition of mankind), let the magistrates have competent salaries. The senators have access to so many honourable and lucrative offices, that their attendance needs not be bought. There is little attendance required of the representatives.

That the foregoing plan of government is practicable, no one can doubt, who considers the resemblance that it bears to the commonwealth of the United Provinces,[1] a wise and renowned government. The alterations in the present scheme seem all evidently for the better. 1. The representation is more equal. 2. The unlimited power of the burgo-masters in the towns, which forms a perfect aristocracy in the DUTCH commonwealth, is corrected by a well-tempered democracy, in giving to the people the annual election of the county representatives. 3. The negative, which every province and town has upon the whole body of the DUTCH republic, with regard to alliances, peace and war, and the imposition of taxes, is here removed. 4. The counties, in the present plan, are not so independent of each other, nor do they form

[1] [Formerly one of the wisest and most renowned governments in the world: Editions H to P.

separate bodies so much as the seven provinces; where the jealousy and envy of the smaller provinces and towns against the greater, particularly HOLLAND and AMSTERDAM, have frequently disturbed the government. 5. Larger powers, though of the safest kind, are intrusted to the senate than the States-General possess; by which means, the former may become more expeditious, and secret in their resolutions, than it is possible for the latter.

The chief alterations that could be made on the BRITISH government, in order to bring it to the most perfect model of limited monarchy, seem to be the following. *First*, The plan of [1] CROMWELL's parliament ought to be restored, by making the representation equal, and by allowing none to vote in the county elections who possess not [2] a property of 200 pounds value. *Secondly*, As such a house of Commons would be too weighty for a frail house of Lords, like the present, the Bishops and SCOTCH Peers ought to be removed:[3] The number of the upper house ought to be raised to three or four hundred: Their seats not hereditary, but during life: They ought to have the election of their own members; and no commoner should be allowed to refuse a seat that was offered him. By this means the house of Lords would consist entirely of the men of chief credit, abilities, and interest in the nation; and every turbulent leader in the house of Commons might be taken off, and connected by interest with the house of Peers. Such an aristocracy would be an excellent barrier both to the monarchy and against it. At present, the balance of our government depends in some measure on the abilities and behaviour of the sovereign; which are variable and uncertain circumstances.

This plan of limited monarchy, however corrected, seems still liable to three great inconveniences. *First*, It removes not entirely, though it may soften, the parties of *court* and *country*. *Secondly*, The king's personal character must still have great influence on the government. *Thirdly*, The sword is in the hands of a single person, who will always neglect to discipline the militia, in order to have a pretence for keeping up a standing army.[4]

[1] [Of the republican parliament: Editions H to P.]

[2] [A hundred a year: Editions H and I.]

[3] [Whose behaviour, *in former par-liaments*, destroyed entirely the authority of that house: Editions H to P.]

[4] [Editions H to P add: It is evident, that this is a mortal distemper in the BRITISH government, of which it

We shall conclude this subject, with observing the falsehood of the common opinion, that no large state, such as FRANCE or GREAT BRITAIN, could ever be modelled into a commonwealth, but that such a form of government can only take place in a city or small territory. The contrary seems probable. Though it is more difficult to form a republican government in an extensive country than in a city; there is more facility, when once it is formed, of preserving it steady and uniform, without tumult and faction. It is not easy, for the distant parts of a large state to combine in any plan of free government; but they easily conspire in the esteem and reverence for a single person, who, by means of this popular favour, may seize the power, and forcing the more obstinate to submit, may establish a monarchical government. On the other hand, a city readily concurs in the same notions of government, the natural equality of property favours liberty, and the nearness of habitation enables the citizens mutually to assist each other. Even under absolute princes, the subordinate government of cities is commonly republican; while that of counties and provinces is monarchical. But these same circumstances, which facilitate the erection of commonwealths in cities, render their constitution more frail and uncertain. Democracies are turbulent. For however the people may be separated or divided into small parties, either in their votes or elections; their near habitation in a city will always make the force of popular tides and currents very sensible. Aristocracies are better adapted for peace and order, and accordingly were most admired by ancient writers; but they are jealous and oppressive. In a large government, which is modelled with masterly skill, there is compass and room enough to refine the democracy, from the lower people, who may be admitted into the first elections or first concoction of the commonwealth, to the higher magistrates, who direct all the movements. At the same time, the parts are so distant and remote, that it is very difficult, either by intrigue, prejudice, or passion, to hurry them into any measures against the public interest.

It is needless to enquire, whether such a government would be immortal. I allow the justness of the poet's exclamation

must at last inevitably perish. I must, however, confess, that SWEDEN seems, in some measure, to have remedied this inconvenience, and to have a militia, with its limited monarchy, as well as a standing army, which is less dangerous than the BRITISH.]

on the endless projects of human race, *Man and for ever!* The world itself probably is not immortal. Such consuming plagues may arise as would leave even a perfect government a weak prey to its neighbours. We know not to what length enthusiasm, or other extraordinary movements of the human mind, may transport men, to the neglect of all order and public good. Where difference of interest is removed, whimsical and unaccountable factions often arise, from personal favour or enmity. Perhaps, rust may grow to the springs of the most accurate political machine, and disorder its motions. Lastly, extensive conquests, when pursued, must be the ruin of every free government; and of the more perfect governments sooner than of the imperfect; because of the very advantages which the former possess above the latter. And though such a state ought to establish a fundamental law against conquests; yet republics have ambition as well as individuals, and present interest makes men forgetful of their posterity. It is a sufficient incitement to human endeavours, that such a government would flourish for many ages; without pretending to bestow, on any work of man, that immortality, which the Almighty seems to have refused to his own productions.

INDEX

TO

THE THIRD VOLUME.

f. means 'and following pages.'

ADD

Addison, 195
Ægina, slaves in, 421
Æschines, 376, 398, 404, 411
Agathocles, cruelties of, 405
Agriculture, in Greece and Italy, 412
Alexander VI., character of, by Guicciardin, 29
Alexander the Great, 103; his successors jealous of balance of power, 350; treasures amassed by his successors, 361
Alexandria, ancient, greatness of, 429
America, discovery of mines a stimulant to industry, 313
Ammianus Marcellinus, 429
Anacharsis the Scythian, remark of, 312
Ancients, instance of their outspokenness, 189; war caused by their want of politeness, 191; rude custom, of, 193; slavery among, 387, f; pay of their public servants, 388; supposed to be ignorant of balance of power, 350; infanticide among, 396; their soldiers all married, 401; their battles more destructive than modern battles, 401; cold-blooded butcheries of, 404, 405; insecurity of property among, 406; cause of their political disorders, 409; inferior to the moderns, 410; their populousness, 414, f.—See *Greece, Rome*
Annandale, Hume tutor to Marquis of, 47
Antigonus, anecdote of, 181
Antipater, repartee of, 226
Appian, his account of the treasures of the Ptolemies, 343; quoted, 394, 399, 402, 416, 436, 438

ATH

Ariosto, 192; as a poet, 270
Aristides the Sophist, 440
Aristocracy, power of in a state, 100; Venetian and Polish, *ib.*; best form of, 101
Aristophanes, 391
Aristotle, 431, 433
Armies, ancient, 290, f.; employment of mercenaries, 310; cost of Roman, *ib.*; cost, &c. of Cromwell's army, 418; Philip of Macedon's, 424, 425; a model army, 486
Arrian, his vanity, 188; cited, 104, 361, 410
Arts and Sciences: cultivation of the liberal arts, 93; the product of free nations, 157; decline of in Greece, 158; progress of in Rome and Florence, *ib.*; in France, 159; in England, *ib.*; rise and advancement of, 174, f.: causes, *ib.*; caution needed in tracing history of, 176; impossible, except under free government, 177, 179; discouraging causes, 180; conditions favourable to, 181; influence of monarchy and republic on, 185; depend on refined taste, *ib.*; commencement of their decline, 195; emulation in, 196; French literature a hindrance to German, *ib.*; influence on temper, 223; refinements in, 299, f., 305; increase power of nations, 303; flourishing state of in England, 306; favourable to liberty, *ib.*; innocent luxury beneficial, 307
Astronomy, discouraging to ambition, 227
Athenæus, 418, 419, 421, 422, 440

ATH

Athenians, pay enormous interest on loans, 163; their taste formed by orators, 169; tyranny of, 406
Athens, plague of, 228; prohibition to export figs, 331; money amassed by, 341, 361; singular customs, 375, f.; slavery at, 390; the Thirty Tyrants, 404; greatness of, 418; population and extent, 419; census of, 421
Attalus of Pergamus, praised for infanticide, 396
Atticus, makes a poor figure in Cicero, 189
Austria, empire of, 353
Authors, ancient, their licentiousness, 188
Autobiography, Hume's, Adam Smith's share in it, 80; hostile criticism, 81

Bacon, Lord, 253, 297
Balance of Power, 348, f.; anxiety as to in Greece, 349; founded on common sense, 352
Banks, doubt as to benefit of, 311; effect of, 339; in Scotland, 340
Batavians, the ancient, 250
Belgium, ancient, population of, 437
Bentivoglio, Cardinal, 255
Berkeley, Dr., 35, 253
Berne, money lent by, 342
Boccaccio, 228
Bolingbroke, Lord, Hume's opinion of, 74; his eloquence, 173
Boswell, passages cited from, 83
Britain, ancient, marriage in, 232; barbarous condition of, 436
British Constitution.—See *Constitution*
Burgoyne, Géométrie du Duc de, 40
Burton, Mr., mistake in his Life of Hume, 38; cited, 47; his account of Hume's Dialogues on Natural Religion, 77
Butler, Dr., 24

Cæsar, Julius, his good sense, 169; cited, 247, 399, 404, 436; hands Cato a billet-doux, 302; his subjugation of the Republic, 403
Capitolinus, 458
Carthaginians, oppression of, 103
Cato, 189; his indignation with Cæsar, 302; his slaves, 391, 393
Catullus, 243
Cervantes, his Sancho Panza, 240
Character.—See *National*
Charles II., 137

CRO

Charles VIII. of France, his invasion of Italy, 303
China, progress of Confucianism in, 183; commerce of, 296; infanticide in, 396
Chios, number of slaves in, 421
Christian Religion, 131, f.; a system of speculative opinions, 132; priesthood promotes hatred and discord, 132, 133
Christians, Early, charged with bigotry and imprudence, 132
Cicero, 29, 161, 254, 357, 386, 411, 418, 428; proscribed by Mark Antony, 102; a party man, 134; dissatisfied with his own eloquence, 164; with that of Demosthenes, 165; a rhetorical flight, 166; the finest gentleman of his age, 188; his scepticism and vanity, 189; *De Oratore*, *ib.*; his solace for deafness, 226; his epilogues, 260; as an orator, 261
Civil Liberty, 156; England an example of, 97; involved in liberty of press, 98
Clarendon, Lord, 264
Clephane, Dr., Hume's letter to, 56
Clergy.—See *Priest*, *Priesthood*, *Christian Religion*
Climate, alterations in, 433, f.
Columella, 382, 389, 393, 394, 412, 434
Commerce, 287.—See *Trade* and *Manufactures*
Commodus, Emperor, 457
Commonwealth, idea of a perfect, 480, 482, f.; false opinion as to, 492; probable duration of it, 493
Condé, Prince of, 181
Congreve, 241
Confucius, resemblance of the Quakers to his followers, 149; progress of his doctrines, 183
Constitution, British, 120, f.; power of King, Lords, and Commons, *ib.*; influence of the Crown, 121; Hume's remarks on, 126
Contract, Original, 443; meaning of, 445; debated in France, 459
Convents, nurseries of superstition, 395; reason why women become nuns, 396
Conway, General, 6
Corinth, great number of slaves in, 421
Corneille, 106, 241
Crassus, wealth of, 123
Credit, public, 360, f.
Cromwell, number and cost of his army, 418; plan of his parliament, 491
Crown, British, revenues of, 123; power of on the increase, 125; prerogative of, 465, f.; of Tudors and Stuarts, 467; privileges usurped by Commons 468

CUS

Customs, some remarkable, 374, f.; at Athens, 375, f.; ancient and modern, 385, f.; destructive of population, 402
Cyrus, the Younger, a toper, 257

Datames, remark of the ancients concerning, 304
D'Aunoy, Madame, 236
Decelean war, desertion of slaves during, 420
Delicacy of passion. hurtful, 91; cure for, 92
—— —— of taste, desirable, 92; favourable to love and friendship, 93; exclusiveness of, 94
— French, 190
Democracy, effects of, 100; best form of, 101; the Athenian, 376; restoration of, 403
Demosthenes pleading, 165; his daring apostrophe, 166; his slaves, 391; quoted, 342, 349, 375, 376, 377, 386, 390, 391, 398, 407, 410, 419, 420, 422
De Retz, Cardinal, 124, 171, 488
Dialogues concerning Natural Religion, account of, 77; letters to Adam Smith, 78; A. Smith's objections to publishing, 79; Hume's dispositions regarding, ib.; published by his nephew, 80
Diodorus Siculus, 104, 169, 256, 290, 399, 404, 405, 409, 411, 415, 416, 417, 422, 424, 429, 433, 436, 438, 440, 443
Diogenes Laertius, 415
Dionysius Halicarnassus, 230, 425
—— —— the Elder, 290, 417; butcheries of, 404
Dissenters, the country party, 135
Dissertations, Hume's four, 60, 67; mutilation of, 68, f.; Dr. Horne's remarks, ib.
Divorce, voluntary, 233, 237; reasons against, 238, 239; ancient laws of Rome, ib.
Douglas, Home's, 64; Hume's remarks on, 64, 66
Du Bos, l'Abbé, 259, 335, 432, 439
Duelling, character of men of honour, 194
Dutch, the, first introduced the practice of borrowing, 163; commerce of, 348; cause of their industry, 357
Du Tot, 314

Eclectics, the Roman, 184
Editions of Hume's Works, list of, 85
Egypt, population when conquered by Romans, 440

FRA

Elliot, Gilbert, Hume's letter to, 52; Elliot's reply, ib
Eloisa and Abelard, 239
Eloquence, ancient, 164; English, 165, 166 decline of, 167; difference of ancient and modern, ib.; discouragements of modern, 168; Roman and Greek, ib.; causes of its decline, ib.; conditions favouring it in ancient times, 170; want of genius in modern, ib.; of French sermons, superior to English, 171; French lawyers, ib.; English temper disadvantageous to, ib.; false taste in, 172; common opinion of, ib.; Attic, 173; Lysias and Calvus compared with Demosthenes and Cicero, ib.; Lord Bolingbroke, ib.
England, government of, a compromise, 96; liberty in, ib.; parties in, 107, f., 117, 133, 136, 139; increase of venality, 306; cost of her army and fleet, 310; guardian of liberties of Europe, 353; wars with France, 354; her revenues, 366; her creditors, 373; singular custom, 379; innovations of Henry VIII. and Charles I., 453
Enthusiasm, true sources of, 145; its consequences to society, 146; opposed to priestly power, ib; religions arising from, 148; its fury soon spent, ib.
Epicurean, the, 197, f.
Epirus, inhabitants sold by P. Æmilius, 424
Erskine, Sir H., 3
Essays, Moral and Political, Hume's, 40; their success, 41; preface to, ib.; list of, 42; classification of, 43, f.
Ethics.—See *Morals*.
Euxine, climate described by Ovid, 434; by Tournefort, ib.
Euripides, the two wives of, 232

Factions, political and religious, 129, f.; in ancient Greece, 404; in Ireland, ib.
Fanaticism, 148
Flamininus, Titus, his conference with Philip of Macedon, 189
Fléchier, his funeral sermon on Marshal Turenne, 171
Florus, 395
Fontenelle, 94, 227, 242, 260, 442
Fowler, Professor, on quoting Hume's Treatise, 39
France, form of government, 95; under Henri III. and IV., 98; disputes of Molinists and Jansenists in, 150; progress of the arts and sciences in, 159; of drama, ib.; of trade, 160, 336; abuses in government of, 162;

GAL

poverty of peasantry, 298; abundance of bullion in, 338

Gallantry, the passion of, 192, f.
Gaul, character and condition of people, 256, 437; climate of, 433; population of, 436
Gee, Mr., his writings on Trade, 322
Genoa, anarchy in, 105; bank of St. George, 106
Gentleman's Magazine, notices of Hume's Dissertations in, 68, f.
Germany, scarcity of money in, 316; inhabitants, 436
Gorgias Leontinus, 169
Government, absolute, inconveniences of, 99; free and republican, depending upon checks, *ib.*; anarchy in Roman, 100; Venetian and Polish, *ib.*; Eastern mode of, 105; stability of the Venetian, *ib.*; first principles of, 100; founded on opinion, 110; origin and object of, 113; consolidation of, 115; origin of kingly, *ib.*; struggle between authority and liberty, 116; system of mixed, 119; modern monarchical, great improvements in, 161; abuses in the French, 162; sources of abuse in free governments, *ib.*, the Chinese, 183; monarchical, owes its perfection to the republican, 186; difference between monarchies and republics, 187; ill manners of European republics, 188; knowledge in the arts of, 303; different theories of in England, 443; Deity, ultimate author of, 444; the people the pretended source of power, 445; original foundation of, 446; revolution, 448; Athenian democracy, 449; force the origin of most governments, 450; allegiance to, 455; succession of Roman Emperors, 458; title, 459; passive obedience to, 460; when resistance to, lawful, 461; true rule of, 468; English, as regarded by James I., 473; under the Stuarts, 474; plan of, 482; chief support of British, 469
Gracchi, sedition of, 394
Grant, General, 3
Greece, ancient, decline of arts in, 158; small states favourable to the arts. 182; anxiety as to the balance of power, 349; cold-blooded butcheries in, 404, f.; unsettled state, 407; size and population of cities, 418, f., 422; neglect of military discipline, 442

HUM

Greeks, ancient, fond of the bottle, 257; their privileges observed by Romans, 441
Guelfs and Ghibellines, factions of, 129
Guicciardin, 29, 303
Gustavus Vasa, 135

Hannibal, his victories in Italy, 351
Happiness, attainment of, 205, 220; Spartan idea, 226; no perfect distribution of, 230
Hardouin, Père, 426
Harrington, J., his 'Oceana' the only valuable model of a commonwealth, 481; prediction of, 122
Helvetia, inhabitants, 438
Henriade, 96
Henri IV., remark of, about astrologers, 373
Henry VII., treasure amassed by, 341
Herodian, 429, 436
Herodotus, 104, 410, 419, 424
Hertford, Earl of, 6
Hiero of Syracuse, understood the balance of power, 352
Hirtius, 438
History of House of Tudor, Hume's, 6
Holland, form of government of, 95; Presbyterian and Arminian factions in, 136
Home, J., author of *Douglas*, 9, 64, 65
Homer, moral characters of his heroes, 267
Horace, 159, 177, 190, 194, 390
Horne, Dr., remarks on Hume's Dissertations, 68; attacks Hume and Adam Smith, 80, f.
Hortensius, Nicolaus, 428
House of Commons, British, 112; support of popular government, 307
Human Life, more governed by fortune than reason, 231
Human Nature, dignity and meanness of, 150, f.; estimate of, 152; comparison of men and animals, *ib.*; its passions, 154, f.; ills of, 226, f.
Human Understanding, Hume's Enquiry concerning, 3
Hume, his birth and family, 1; residence in France, 2, 3; rising reputation, 4; plan of history, *ib.*; success of his works, 6; attached to embassy to Paris, *ib.*; illness, 7; his character drawn by himself, *ib.*; his death, 13; his passion for literature, 15; letter to M. Ramsay, *ib.*; his mode of life, 18, f.; letters to Prof. Hutcheson, 27, f., 33; his Collection of Scotticisms, 35; dissatisfied with his own style, 36; desire of applause, *ib.*; criticism of his own works, 36, f.; Johnson's observations, 40, 83; his *Sceptic*, 46;

HUM

Stoic, ib.; tendency to materialism, *ib.*; residence in Edinburgh, 47; appointed Judge-Advocate of expedition against Port l'Orient, *ib.*; Philosophical Essays concerning the Human Understanding, 49; sale of his works, 50; Warburton's attack, *ib.*; his Essay on Miracles, 50; Conversation with a Jesuit, 51; his Enquiry concerning the Principles of Morals, 52; his letters to Gilbert Elliot, 51, 54, f.; his Dialogues concerning Natural Religion, 54, 77; literary activity, 55; political discourses, 56; becomes known abroad, *ib.*; letter to Dr. Clephane, *ib.*; appointed keeper of Advocates' library, 59; his History of Great Britain, *ib.*; letters to Adam Smith, 59, 78; translates Plutarch's Lives, *ib.*; declines editing a newspaper, 60; his Four Dissertations, 60, 67; his remarks on Dr. Warburton, 64; dedication of his Dissertations, 65; letters to Andrew Millar, 60, 65; Essays on Suicide and Immortality of the Soul, 69, f.,—surreptitiously published, *ib.*; his care in preparing his works for the press, 73; his changes of opinion, 73, 74; remarks on Bolingbroke and Swift, *ib.*; neglects philosophy, 75, f.; appoints W. Strahan his literary executor, 79; publication of his Autobiography, 80; hostile criticism, 81; Wesley's sermon on, 82; his deathbed, 83; supplement to the Life of, 84; watching his grave, *ib.*; list of editions of his works, 85; his remarks on English parties, 107, f., 117, f.; on the British constitution, 126; charges early Christians with 'imprudence and bigotry,' 132; his definition of 'Priests,' 147; on Judaism and Popery, 148; on Church of England, *ib.*; on English sects, *ib.*; his objection to mixed companies, 194; his ideas of happiness, 198, 220; on the value of money, 314; his plan of a commonwealth, 482, f.

Hunt, Mr., on Hume's Treatise of Human Nature, 39; on Hume's scepticism, 75

Hurd, Dr., his pamphlet against Hume, 5; a pious fraud, 62

Hutcheson, Professor, 27, f.

Hutchinson, Mr., his scheme for payment of National Debt, 370

Independents, character of, 148; political union with Deists, 150

MAN

Interest, low, a sign of prosperity, 320.—See *Money*

Ireland, Swift on financial condition of, 332; factions in, 404

Isocrates, 404, 405

Italy, factions, 129; poverty of peasantry, 298; want of martial spirit in modern Italians, 304; cheap prices in ancient, 320; population, 425, f.; uncultivated land, 430; herds of swine, *ib.*

Jacobites, the, 144

James I., anecdote by Waller, 473

Jansenists, enthusiasm of, 150

Jealousy, in Asia, 235; in Spain, 236

Jesuits, tyrants of the people, 150

Johnson, remark on Hume's Collection of Scotticisms, 35; his strictures on Hume, 40, 83

Johnson, Ben, Volpone of, 397

Josephus, 429, 440

Justin, 438

Juvenal, 188, 193, 254, 433

Kames, Lord, Hume's letters to, 23, 48

Koran, moral precepts of, 267

La Flèche, Hume's residence at, 22, 23, 40; conversation with a Jesuit at, 51

Language, dependent on manners, 253

Le Blanc, l'Abbé, translates Hume's Political Discourses, 56

Liberty.—See *Civil Liberty*

Literature, simplicity and refinement in writing, 240, 243; sensational, *ib.*; style, 241; great authors compared, *ib.*; taste in, 266, f.

Livy, 106, 129, 291, 342, 399, 404, 409, 424, 438

Locke, 35, 460

Longinus, 159

Longman, T., publishes 3rd vol. of Treatise of Human Nature, 30, 32

Lucan, 395

Lucian, 442

Lucretius, 188, 199, 241

Luxury, indulgences in, 299; different estimates of, 300; refined arts, 301, f.; vicious, 307, f.

Lysias, 406, 410, 422

Machiavel, 103; his defective reasonings, 156; his character of a weak prince, 157; cited, 351

Mallet, his account of Egypt, 435

Manufactures, absence of supplied by

MAR

agriculture, 293; contribute to the power of a state, 294
Marriage, contract of, 231; an extra wife allowed by Athenians, 232; among the ancient Britons, *ib.*; polygamy, 233; duration of, 237 f.
Martial, 390, 395
Mauvillon, Eléazar publishes translation of Hume's Political Discourses in France, 56
Medici, their wealth makes them masters of Florence, 123
Mehemet Effendi, saying of, 234
Melon, M., 289
Menander, 245
Miller, A., Hume's letters to, 60, 65; letter to Hume, 68
Miracles, Hume's Essay on, 50; its style, 51
Molinists, friends to superstition, 150
Monarchy, absolute, points of resemblance to a republic, 95; inconvenience of an elective, 101; the best form of, *ib.*; improved character of modern monarchs, 161; absolute, repugnant to law, 180; the Chinese, 183; enormous monarchies destructive to human nature, 355; plan of limited, 482 f.
Money, not one of the subjects of commerce, 309; representative of labour, 312; causes high prices, 313; value of in France, 314; its quantity of little consequence to a State, 315 f.; scarcity in some parts of Europe, *ib.*; rise of prices after discovery of West Indies, 318; in China, 320; has a fictitious value, 321; causes of high interest, 322; rise of interest in Scotland, 323; causes of low interest, 326; interest the barometer of the State, 327; proportion between, and goods, 328; interest in Roman Spain, 329; reduction of interest in England and France, 330; methods of sinking and raising its value, 337; treasures amassed by Henry VII., 341; by Philip of Macedon and Perseus, 342
Montesquieu, 440
Morals, Hume's Inquiry concerning the Principles of, 52; a delicate sense of, 151; harmony of authors as to, 267
More, Sir T., Utopia of, 481
Morocco, wars of colour in, 129, 130
Muscovites, ancient, 193

National Character, Hume's Essay on, 49; influence of physical causes,

PHI

244, 246 f.; of example, 248; of government, 249; similarity of Jews and Armenians, 250; ancient Greek and Roman, *ib.*; French and British, 251; negroes inferior to whites, 252; pretended influence of climate, 253; language dependent on, *ib.*; of Northern and Southern countries, 253 f. 256; Turks and ancient Romans, 255; moral causes of, 256; addiction to strong drinks, 257; amorousness, 258
National Debt, a *modern* expedient, 361 f.; consequences of, 363, 368 f.; scheme for payment of, 370
Nepos, Cornelius, Life of Atticus, 390
Newton, 183
Nicole, his Perpétuité de la Foi, 54
Ninus, immense army of, 443
Noone, John, 25

Obedience, a duty in a State, 114
Oceana, Harrington's, its defects, 481. See *Harrington*
Opinion, of two kinds, 110; its defenders and assailants, 118; changes in, 125; influence in formation of character, 255 f.
Optimates and *Populares*, Roman parties, 134
Orators, ancient and modern, 164 f.; Roman and Greek, 169; scurrility of ancient, 188. See *Eloquence*
Ovid, 177, 386, 433, 435

Parties, in general, 127, 131, 133; in Greek empire, 128; in Rome, 129, 134; in Italy, *ib.*; in Morocco, *ib.*; in England, 133, 134; ecclesiastical, court, and country, 135; origin— Whig and Tory, 136 f.; coalition of, 464 f.
Passive obedience, 460
Paten, pleadings of, 171
Paterculus, 416
Persecution, religious, among the ancients, 132
Persian empire, cause of its overthrow, 350
Persian Letters, 237
Persians, ancient, Machiavel on their subjugation by the Greeks, 103 f.; drunkenness in repute among, 257
Personal Identity, 33
Petronius, 390
Phædrus, 190
Philip of Macedon, his rejoinder to a candid Roman, 189; treasure amassed

by, 342; his army as Captain-General of Greece, 424 f.
Philosophy, attention paid to in England, 33; in the early Christian period, 132; excellence of the English in, 159; Peripatetic introduced in the schools, 182; Cartesian, 183; the Eclectics, 184; the Epicurean, 197 f.; Stoic, 203 f.; Platonist, 210 f.; Sceptic, 213 f.; devotion to, 220; considerations on, 224 f.
Plato, 361, 418, 420, 424, 481
Platonist, the, 210
Plautus, 420
Pleasure, Hume on, 198 f.
Pliny, 193, 263, 342, 389, 394, 400, 416, 426, 429, 439
Plutarch, 190, 191, 226, 227, 249, 257, 361, 331, 376, 386, 391, 395, 396, 404, 409, 416, 438, 440, 441, 442
Poetry, pretended inspiration, 177; taste and genius in, 270 f.
Poisoning, among the Romans, prevalence of, 106
Poland, deficient in the arts, 305
Politeness, ancient, 188 f.; modern, 190 f.
Politian, 429
Politics, science of, 98; 'every man a knave,' 118
Polybius, 103, 104, 121, 189, 292, 320, 342, 399, 402, 415, 416, 423, 424, 434, 435, 436, 441
Polygamy, reasons for and against, 233, 234, 235
Pope, 226
Population, of ancient nations, 381, 383; effect of slavery on, 387; of monasticism and infanticide, 396; disadvantages of the ancients as regards, 400; ancient and modern compared, 413, 432, 435; of Greek and Roman cities, 418 f.; of Roman Empire under Augustus and Trajan, 439, 440
Presbyterians, character of, 148
Press, liberty of, 94; peculiar to Great Britain, 95; accounted for in England, 96; advantages of, 97
Priests, enemies of liberty, 135; definition of, 147; a superstitious invention, *ib.*; of all religions the same, 245; their hypocrisy, 246; their self-deception, ambition and fury, *ib.*; among the Romans, 247
Protestant Succession, Hume's Essay on, 48; its advantages and disadvantages considered, 471 f., 475; reasons for excluding the Stuarts, 477 f.

Ptolemies, their treasures, 343
Pyrrhus, on Roman discipline, 304

Quakers, resemble Confucians, 148 f.
Quintilian, 254
Quintus Curtius, 257, 429
Quixote, Don, 272

Raleigh, 473
Ramsay, M., Hume's letters to, 15, 26
Rapin, 74, 457
Religion, truth in, 54; ancient, 131; Christian, *ib.*; above human cognizance, 283
Republics, oppressions of, 101; great armies of ancient, 290. See *Government*
Rheims, Hume's residence at, 2, 23
Rhodes, 422
Right, origin of, 110
Rochester, Lord, licentiousness of, 188
Rome, buildings of ancient, 56, 57; government under Emperors, 96; Roman tyranny, 102; most illustrious period of its history, 106; parties in, 129, 134; progress of arts in, 158; arbitrary decisions of consuls, 179; Roman rudeness, 191; Romans a candid race, 255; always at war, 292; corrupted by luxury, 305; armies of, 310; doubts as to Roman history, 351; cause of the destruction of the empire, 358; public spectacles, 387; influx of slaves, 389, 391; Civil Law, 391; pay of troops, 399; Roman humanity, 407; massacres during civil wars, 408; extent of, 423, 426, 427; how built, 425; population of, 425, 427; bills of mortality, 428; streets full of snow and ice, 433; largest population of empire, 450; how the emperors succeeded each other, 458
Romish Church, acquisition of power by, 149; a hindrance to learning, 183; inspires hatred of other religions, 284
Rousseau, 187

Sallust, 161, 188, 305, 428
Saserna, 434, 435
Saxony, Catholic King and Protestant Elector of, 478
Sceptic, the, 213
Sciences. See *Arts*
Senate, an ideal, 488
Seneca, 387, 390, 393, 395, 396, 404

Severambians, history of the, 232
Shaftesbury, Lord, 117, 154, 191, 377
Shakespeare, 262
Slavery, Roman, 385 f.; influence on population, 387 f.; privileges of, 390; at Athens, 390, 420; in West Indies, 390; at Rome, 391 f.; in Sicily, 395; in Turkey and Egypt, 395; in Sparta, 421; in Corinth and Ægina, ib.
Smith, Adam, letter to W. Strahan, Esq., 9; correspondence with Hume, 77 f.; assailed for his share in Hume's Autobiography, 80 f.
Solomon, his polygamy, 234
Solon, legalizes infanticide, 396
Sophocles, 211
Spain, poverty of peasantry, 298; condition of ancient, 438
Sparta, absence of commerce, 290
Spenser, 473
Spinoza, 40
St. Clair, General, 3; Hume appointed secretary to, 47
Stage, English, licentiousness of, 183; the French, 284
Stanian, 342, 343
State, chief magistrate in a, 100; inconvenience of an elective monarchy, 101; necessity for wise laws, 105; ascendancy of one man, 115; authority and liberty in, 116; possessors of wealth in, 123; trade not regarded as an affair of, 157; internal police, 161; small states favourable to the arts, 182; divisions of the, 289; agricultural, 293; causes of its greatness, 294 f.; quantity of money of little consequence to, 315; refined life beneficial to, 319
Stoic, the, 203 f.
Strabo, 247, 389, 393, 417, 425, 433, 436, 438, 440, 441
Strahan, letter to, from Adam Smith, 9; appointed Hume's literary executor, 79; declines, 80
Suetonius, 103, 386, 389, 426, 428
Suicide and the Immortality of the Soul, Hume's Essays on, 69 f.; note by Allan Ramsay (?) 71
Suidas, 410
Superstition, 144; true sources of, 145; favourable to priestly power, 146; its insidiousness, 149; an enemy to civil liberty, ib.
Sweden, military force of, 492
Swift, Dr., 74, 332, 408
Sybaris, cause of its populousness, 411
Syracuse, greatness of, 418

Tacitus, 96, 103, 135, 310, 373, 389, 392, 394, 396, 401, 426, 436, 441
Talon, 171
Tasso, 201
Taste, standard of, 266, 279; varieties, 269, f.; want of imaginative delicacy, 272; right criticism, 275, 278; its principles, 276; influenced by manners, 280; by religious principles 283
Taxes, dangerous maxim as to, 356; best kind of, 358; on land, 359
Temple, Sir W., 357
Terence, 241
Tertullian, 439, 440
Thebes, conquest by Alexander, 422
Theocritus, 415
Thought, liberty of in ancient times, 66
Thucydides, 104, 228, 290, 399, 404, 411, 414, 419, 421, 422, 424
Tiber, frozen, 432
Timoleon, 399
Toleration, religious, 97
Tories, character and conduct of, 139, f.; none in Scotland, 143; union of High Church with Roman Catholics, 150
Tournefort, his visit to the Grand Turk's seraglio, 235; cited, 434
Trachinians, their application to Sparta, 399
Trade, not regarded as an affair of state, 157; needs a free government. 159; ancient marts, 160, 357; progress in France, 160; decay under absolute government, ib.; contributes to greatness of state, 289, 294; banks and paper currency, 311, 365; increases industry, 325; ignorance, 330, f.; restrictions in France, 336; obstructions to, 343; taxes on foreign commodities, ib.; domestic industry basis of foreign commerce, 346, f.; nations pre-eminent in, 356
Tragedy, power of, 258, f.; cause of pleasure produced by, 261, f.; tragic scenes in painting and poetry, 262; action of, 265
Treatise on Human Nature, Hume's, 2, 25, 32, 33, 36, 37, 40, 49
Turkey, taxes in, 360; slave trade in, 395
Tyre, destruction of, 410

United provinces, government of, 490
Upper House, plan for an, 491
Ustariz, Geronimo di, 384

Valerius Maximus, 426
Varro, 389, 393, 394, 434

VAU

Vauban, Marshal, 336
Velleius Paterculus, 342, 438
Venetian Government, stability of, 105
Venice, factions in, 129; not eminent in the arts, 158
Verres, cruelties of, 102; proscribed, *ib.*
Virgil, 190
Vitruvius, 426
Voltaire, 96
Vopiscus, 423, 430

Wallace, Dr., his Dissertation on Populousness of Ancient and Modern Times, 58
Waller, 170, 197
Walpole, Sir R., his character by Hume, 45

ZEA

Warburton, attacks Hume, 50, 61, 62
Wars, religious, 129, 132
Wesley, J., sermon on Hume, 82
West Indies, slavery in, 390
Whigs, character and conduct of, 139, f.; definition of, 139; their leaders Deists, 150.—See *Tories*
Wilkes, J., 67
Wolsey, Card. 191
Works of the Learned, review in, 33

Xenophon, 104, 163, 348, 393, 398, 406, 412, 419, 420, 421, 423, 435
Xerxes, in want of a new pleasure, 198

Zeal, public 106; needs moderating, 108

THE

PHILOSOPHICAL WORKS

OF

DAVID HUME

VOL. III.

THE
PHILOSOPHICAL WORKS
OF
DAVID HUME

EDITED BY

T. H. GREEN AND T. H. GROSE
LATE FELLOW AND TUTOR OF BALLIOL COLLEGE, OXFORD
FELLOW AND TUTOR OF QUEEN'S COLLEGE, OXFORD

IN FOUR VOLUMES
VOL. III.

NEW IMPRESSION

LONGMANS, GREEN, AND CO.
39 PATERNOSTER ROW, LONDON
NEW YORK AND BOMBAY
1898

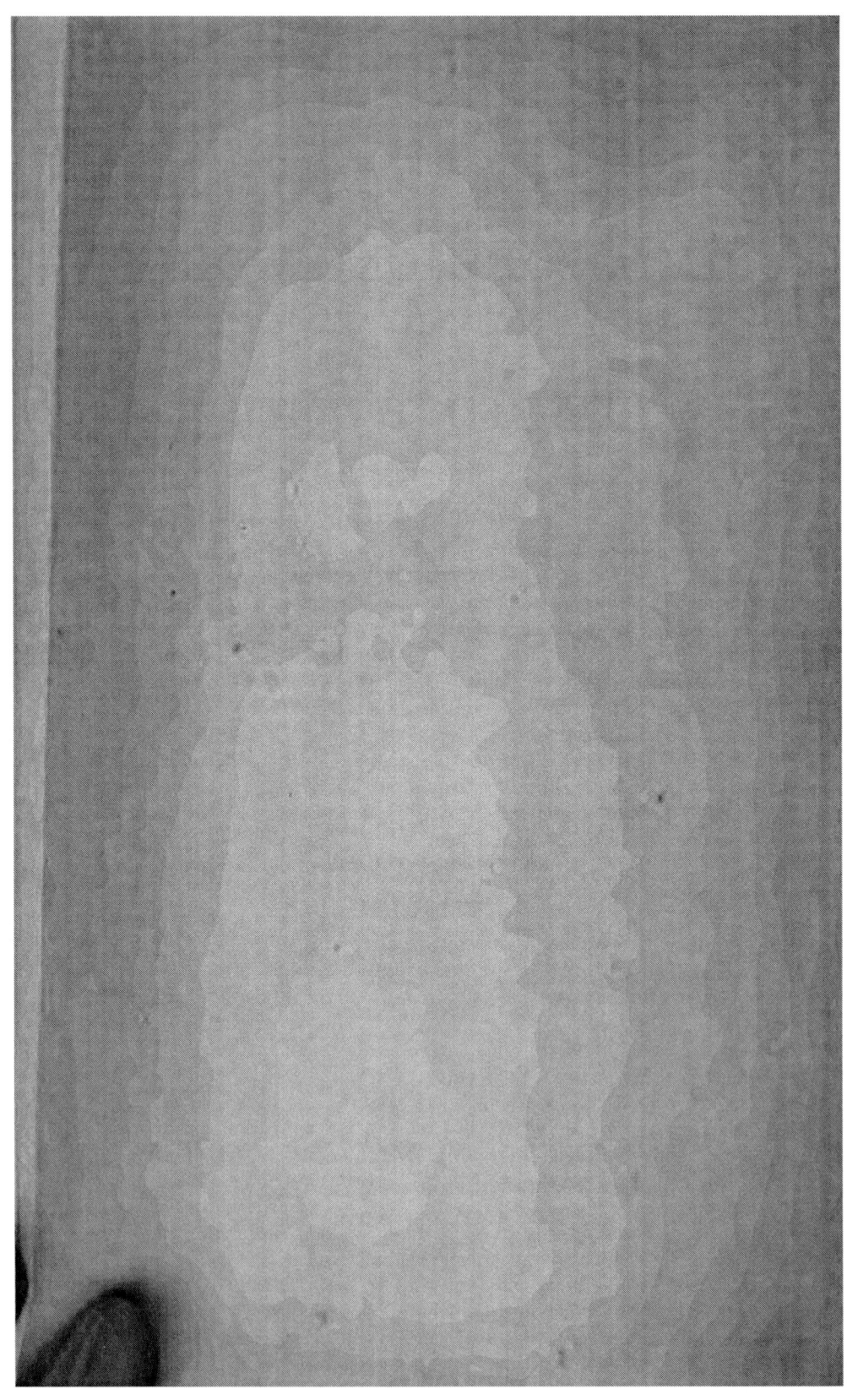

LaVergne, TN USA
09 September 2010
196482LV00003B/19/P